PENGUIN BOOKS

The Complete Poems

Beryl Graves, the poet's widow, met Robert Graves in London in 1937 and returned with him at the end of the Second World War to Mallorca, where she still lives at Canelluñ, the house he built in 1931–2 in Deyá. She assisted Graves with many of his late works.

Dunstan Ward teaches English in Paris at the University of London's British Institute. President of the Robert Graves Society, he co-edited with Beryl Graves the three-volume annotated *Complete Poems* from which the texts in this edition have been reproduced.

T0322106

Robert Graves

THE COMPLETE POEMS
IN ONE VOLUME

Edited by Beryl Graves and
Dunstan Ward

PENGUIN BOOKS

PENGUIN BOOKS

Published by the Penguin Group
Penguin Books Ltd, 80 Strand, London wc2r 0rl, England
Penguin Putnam Inc., 375 Hudson Street, New York, New York 10014, USA
Penguin Books Australia Ltd, 250 Camberwell Road, Camberwell, Victoria 3124, Australia
Penguin Books Canada Ltd, 10 Alcorn Avenue, Toronto, Ontario, Canada m4v 3b2
Penguin Books India (P) Ltd, 11 Community Centre, Panchsheel Park, New Delhi – 110 017, India
Penguin Books (NZ) Ltd, Cnr Rosedale and Airborne Roads, Albany, Auckland, New Zealand
Penguin Books (South Africa) (Pty) Ltd, 24 Sturdee Avenue, Rosebank 2196, South Africa

Penguin Books Ltd, Registered Offices: 80 Strand, London wc2r 0rl, England

www.penguin.com

First published in one volume in the UK by Carcanet Press Limited 2000
First published in Penguin Classics 2003

022

ISBN-13: 978-0-14-118206-3

www.greenpenguin.co.uk

CONTENTS

Acknowledgements   xxxvii
Introduction   xxxix

I

OVER THE BRAZIER (1916)
The Poet in the Nursery   3
PART I. – POEMS MOSTLY WRITTEN AT CHARTERHOUSE – 1910-1914
Star-Talk   4
The Dying Knight and the Fauns   5
Willaree   6
The Face of the Heavens   6
Jolly Yellow Moon   7
Youth and Folly   7
Ghost Music   8
In Spite [Free Verse]   9
In the Wilderness   10
Oh, and Oh!   11
Cherry-Time   11
PART II. – POEMS WRITTEN BEFORE LA BASSÉE – 1915
On Finding Myself a Soldier   12
The Shadow of Death   13
A Renascence   13
The Morning Before the Battle   14
Limbo   14
The Trenches   15
Nursery Memories:
    I   The First Funeral   15
    II   The Adventure   16
    III I Hate the Moon   17
Big Words   17
The Dead Fox Hunter   18
It's a Queer Time   19
1915   20
Over the Brazier   20

GOLIATH AND DAVID (1916)

The Bough of Nonsense   22
Goliath and David   23
A Pinch of Salt   24
Babylon   25
Careers   26
The Lady Visitor in the Pauper Ward   26
The Last Post   27
A Dead Boche   27
Escape   27
Not Dead   28

From FAIRIES AND FUSILIERS (1917)

To an Ungentle Critic   29
The Legion   30
To Lucasta on Going to the Wars – for the Fourth Time   30
Two Fusiliers   31
To R.N.   [To Robert Nichols]   32
Dead Cow Farm   32
Mr. Philosopher   33
The Cruel Moon   34
Finland   34
The Caterpillar   34
Sorley's Weather   35
The Cottage   36
When I'm Killed   37
Familiar Letter to Siegfried Sassoon   [Letter to S.S. from
     Mametz Wood]   37
Faun   40
The Spoilsport   40
The Shivering Beggar   41
Jonah   42
John Skelton   43
I Wonder What It Feels Like to be Drowned?   44
Double Red Daisies   45
I'd Love to Be a Fairy's Child   46
The Next War   46
Strong Beer   47
Marigolds   48
Love and Black Magic   49
Smoke-Rings   50
A Child's Nightmare   50
A Boy in Church   52
Corporal Stare   53

Contents

'The Assault Heroic'   54

From TREASURE BOX   (1919)
Song: A Phoenix Flame   [Morning Phoenix]   56
Catherine Drury   56
The Treasure Box   57
The Kiss   58
Lost Love   59
Fox's Dingle   60
Mirror, Mirror!   60

COUNTRY SENTIMENT   (1920)
A Frosty Night   61
A Song for Two Children   62
Dicky   62
The Three Drinkers   64
The Boy out of Church   64
After the Play   [The Forbidden Play]   65
One Hard Look   67
True Johnny   67
The Voice of Beauty Drowned   68
The God Called Poetry   69
Rocky Acres   71
Advice to Lovers   72
Nebuchadnezzar's Fall   72
Give Us Rain   73
Allie   73
Loving Henry   74
Brittle Bones   75
Apples and Water   76
Manticor in Arabia   77
Outlaws   78
Baloo Loo for Jenny   79
Hawk and Buckle   80
The *Alice Jean*   80
The Cupboard   82
The Beacon   82
Pot and Kettle   83
The Haunted House   [Ghost Raddled]   84
Neglectful Edward   84
The Well-Dressed Children   85
Thunder at Night   86
Wild Strawberries   [To E.M. – A Ballad of Nursery Rhyme]   86
Jane   87

Vain and Careless 88
Nine o' Clock 89
The Picture Book 89
The Promised Lullaby 91
RETROSPECT
Haunted 92
Retrospect: The Jests of the Clock 92
Here They Lie 93
Tom Taylor 93
Country at War 94
Sospan Fach 95
The Leveller 96
Hate Not, Fear Not 97
A Rhyme of Friends 97
A First Review 99

From THE PIER-GLASS (1921)
The Stake 101
The Troll's Nosegay 102
The Pier-Glass 102
The Finding of Love 103
Reproach 104
The Magical Picture 104
Distant Smoke 106
Raising the Stone 108
The Gnat 108
The Patchwork Bonnet 110
Kit Logan and Lady Helen 111
Down 112
Saul of Tarsus 113
Storm: At the Farm Window 113
Black Horse Lane 114
Return 115
Incubus 116
The Hills of May 117
The Coronation Murder 117

WHIPPERGINNY (1923)
Whipperginny 119
The Bedpost 120
A Lover Since Childhood 121
Song of Contrariety 122
Love in Barrenness [The Ridge-Top] 122
Song in Winter 123

Unicorn and the White Doe 123
Song: Sullen Moods 124
Angry Samson [A False Report] 125
Children of Darkness 125
Richard Roe and John Doe 126
The Dialecticians [The Philosophers] 127
The Land of Whipperginny 127
'The General Eliott' 128
A Fight to the Death 129
Mermaid, Dragon, Fiend [Old Wives' Tales] 129
Christmas Eve 130
The Snake and the Bull 131
The Red Ribbon Dream 133
In Procession 134
Henry and Mary 136
An English Wood 137
What Did I Dream? [The Dream] 137
Interlude: On Preserving a Poetical Formula 138
Epitaph on an Unfortunate Artist 139
A History of Peace 139
The Rock Below 139
An Idyll of Old Age 140
The Lord Chamberlain Tells of a Famous Meeting 142
The Sewing Basket 145
Against Clock and Compasses 148
The Avengers 148
The Poet's Birth 149
The Technique of Perfection 150
The Sibyl 151
A Crusader 152
A New Portrait of Judith of Bethulia 152
A Reversal 153
The Martyred Decadents: A Sympathetic Satire 153
Epigrams:
   On Christopher Marlowe 154
   A Village Feud [A Village Conflict] 154
   Dedicatory 155
   To R. Graves, Senior 155
   'A Vehicle, to Wit, A Bicycle' 155
   Motto to a Book of Emblems 156
The Bowl and Rim 156
A Forced Music 157
The Turn of a Page 158
The Manifestation in the Temple 158

To Any Saint   160
A Dewdrop   161
A Valentine   161

THE FEATHER BED   (1923)
The Witches' Cauldron   [Prologue]   162
The Feather Bed   163
I Am the Star of Morning   [Epilogue]   173

MOCK BEGGAR HALL   (1924)
Diplomatic Relations   [George II and the Chinese Emperor]   174
Hemlock   176
Full Moon   178
Myrrhina   179
Twin Souls   180
The North Window   181
Attercop: The All-Wise Spider   182
Antinomies   183
Northward from Oxford   187
Witches   188
Antigonus: An Eclogue   190
Essay on Continuity   197
Knowledge of God   200
Mock Beggar Hall: A Progression   201
The Rainbow and the Sceptic   214

WELCHMAN'S HOSE   (1925)
Alice   217
Burrs and Brambles   218
From Our Ghostly Enemy   219
Death of the Farmer   [The Figure-Head]   221
Ovid in Defeat   222
Diversions:
    To an Editor   224
    The Kingfisher's Return   227
    Love Without Hope   227
    Traveller's Curse After Misdirection   228
    Tilly Kettle   228
The College Debate   229
Sergeant-Major Money   232
A Letter from Wales   232
The Presence   237
The Clipped Stater   237
The Poetic State   240

Vanity [Essay on Knowledge]   241
At the Games   242

THE MARMOSITE'S MISCELLANY (1925)
To M. in India   251
The Marmosite's Miscellany   252
The Moment of Weakness   265

From POEMS (1914-26) (1927)
The Country Dance   267
The Rose and the Lily   267
An Occasion   268
A Dedication of Three Hats   268
Ancestors   269
The Corner Knot   270
Virgil the Sorcerer   270
RECENT POEMS: 1925-26
Pygmalion to Galatea   272
In Committee   273
A Letter to a Friend   275
In Single Syllables [This Is Noon]   276
The Time of Day   276
Blonde or Dark?   277
Boots and Bed   278
The Taint   278
Dumplings' Address to Gourmets   279
Sorrow   280
The Nape of the Neck   280
A Visit to Stratford   281
Pure Death   282
The Cool Web   283

II

From POEMS (1914-27) (1927)
The Progress   287
Hell   287
The Furious Voyage [The Dead Ship; Ship Master]   288
O Jorrocks, I Have Promised   288
Lost Acres   290
Gardener [The Awkward Gardener]   291
To a Charge of Didacticism   291
The Philatelist-Royal   292
Song: To Be Less Philosophical   293

POEMS 1929 (1929)

Sick Love [Between Dark and Dark; O Love in Me]   295
In No Direction   295
In Broken Images   296
Thief [To the Galleys]   297
Warning to Children   297
Dismissal   298
Guessing Black or White   299
Hector   300
Against Kind   300
Midway   302
Cabbage Patch [Green Cabbage Wit]   302
The Castle   303
Welsh Incident [Railway Carriage]   303
Back Door   305
Front Door Soliloquy [Front Door]   306
Anagrammagic [The Tow-Path]   306
Vision in the Repair-Shop [Repair Shop]   307
Nature's Lineaments [Landscape]   308
Sea Side [Sandhills]   308
Wm. Brazier [Pavement]   309
A Former Attachment [Quayside]   310
Return Fare   310
Single Fare   311
It Was All Very Tidy   311
A Sheet of Paper   312

TEN POEMS MORE (1930)

The Reader Over My Shoulder   314
History of the Word   314
Interruption   315
Survival of Love   316
New Legends [The Age of Certainty]   316
Saint [The Beast]   317
Tap Room [Cracking the Nut Against the Hammer]   318
The Terraced Valley   319
Oak, Poplar, Pine   320
Act V, Scene 5   321
Song: Lift-Boy [Tail Piece: A Song to Make You and Me Laugh]   321

From POEMS 1926-1930 (1931)

Brother   323
Bay of Naples   323
Flying Crooked   323

Reassurance to the Satyr   324
Synthetic Such   324
Dragons   325
The Next Time   325

TO WHOM ELSE? (1931)   327
Largesse to the Poor   328
The Felloe'd Year   328
Time   329
On Rising Early   329
On Dwelling   330
On Necessity   330
The Foolish Senses   331
Devilishly Provoked [Devilishly Disturbed] 331
The Legs   332
Ogres and Pygmies   333
To Whom Else?   334
As It Were Poems, i, ii, iii   336
On Portents

From POEMS 1930-1933 (1933)   337
The Bards [Lust in Song]   337
Ulysses   338
Down, Wanton, Down!   339
The Philosopher [The Cell]   340
The Succubus   340
Nobody   341
Danegeld   342
Trudge, Body!   342
Music at Night   343
Without Pause   344
The Clock Man [The Clock Men]   344
The Commons of Sleep   345
What Times Are These?

From COLLECTED POEMS (1938)
The Christmas Robin [Wanderings of Christmas] 347
Certain Mercies   347
The Cuirassiers of the Frontier   348
Callow Captain   349
The Stranger   350
The Smoky House   350
Variables of Green [Green Loving] 351
The Goblet   351

Fiend, Dragon, Mermaid   352
Fragment of a Lost Poem   353
Galatea and Pygmalion   353
The Devil's Advice to Story-Tellers   354
Lunch-Hour Blues   354
Hotel Bed at Lugano   [Hotel Bed]   355
Progressive Housing   356
Leda   356
The Florist Rose   357
Being Tall   357
At First Sight   358
Recalling War   358
X   359
Parent to Children   360
To Challenge Delight   361
To Walk on Hills   361
To Bring the Dead to Life   363
To Evoke Posterity   363
Any Honest Housewife   [The Poets]   364
Defeat of the Rebels   365
The Grudge   365
Never Such Love   366
The Halfpenny   366
The Fallen Signpost   367
The China Plate   368
Idle Hands   369
The Laureate   369
A Jealous Man   370
The Cloak   371
The Halls of Bedlam   372
Or to Perish Before Day   373
A Country Mansion   374
The Eremites   376
Advocates   377
Self-Praise   377
The Challenge   378
To the Sovereign Muse   380
The Ages of Oath   381
Like Snow   381
The Climate of Thought   382
End of Play   382
The Fallen Tower of Siloam   383
The Great-Grandmother   384
No More Ghosts   385

Leaving the Rest Unsaid   386

From NO MORE GHOSTS (1940)
The Glutton   [The Beast]   387
A Love Story   387
The Thieves   388
To Sleep   389

From WORK IN HAND (1942)
Dawn Bombardment   390
The Worms of History   390
A Withering Herb   391
The Shot   392
Dream of a Climber   392
Lollocks   393
Despite and Still   394
The Suicide in the Copse   395
Frightened Men   395
A Stranger at the Party   396
The Oath   396
Language of the Seasons   397
Mid-Winter Waking   398
The Rock at the Corner   398

From POEMS 1938-1945 (1945)
The Beach   399
The Villagers and Death   399
The Door   400
Under the Pot   400
Through Nightmare   400
To Lucia at Birth   401
Death by Drums   401
She Tells Her Love While Half Asleep   402
Instructions to the Orphic Adept   402
Theseus and Ariadne   404
Lament for Pasiphaë   404
The Twelve Days of Christmas   405
Cold Weather Proverb   405
To Juan at the Winter Solstice   405
SATIRES AND GROTESQUES
The Persian Version   407
The Weather of Olympus   407
Apollo of the Physiologists   408
The Oldest Soldier   408

Grotesques, i, ii, iii, iv, v, vi
The Eugenist   409
1805   411
At the Savoy Chapel   412
                                                              413

From COLLECTED POEMS (1914-1947) (1948)
To Poets Under Pisces
June   414
The Last Day of Leave   414
To Be Called a Bear   [To Be Named a Bear]   414
A Civil Servant   416
Gulls and Men   416
MAGICAL POEMS   417
The Allansford Pursuit
Amergin's Charm   [The Alphabet Calendar of Amergin]   418
The Sirens' Welcome to Cronos   419
Dichetal do Chennaib   420
The Battle of the Trees   421
The Song of Blodeuwedd   422
Intercession in Late October   425
The Tetragrammaton   425
Nuns and Fish   426
The Destroyer   426
Return of the Goddess   426
                                                              427

From POEMS AND SATIRES 1951 (1951)
The White Goddess
The Chink   428
Counting the Beats   428
The Jackals' Address to Isis   429
The Death Room   430
The Young Cordwainer   430
Your Private Way   431
My Name and I   432
Conversation Piece   432
The Ghost and the Clock   434
Advice on May Day   434
For the Rain It Raineth Every Day   435
Questions in a Wood   436
The Portrait   436
Darien   437
The Survivor   438
Prometheus   439
                                                              440

SATIRES
Queen-Mother to New Queen   440
Secession of the Drones   441
Damocles   441
Homage to Texas   442
The Dilemma   442
General Bloodstock's Lament for England   443
'¡Wellcome, to the Caves of Artá!'   443
To a Poet in Trouble   444

From POEMS 1953 (1953)
To Calliope   445
The Straw   445
The Foreboding   446
Cry Faugh!   447
Hercules at Nemea   447
Dialogue on the Headland   448
Lovers in Winter   449
Esau and Judith   449
The Mark   450
With the Gift of a Ring   450
Liadan and Curithir   451
The Sea Horse   452
The Devil at Berry Pomeroy   452
Reproach to Julia   453
Dethronement   453
Cat-Goddesses   454
The Blue-Fly   454
Rhea   455
The Hero   456
Marginal Warning   456
The Encounter   457
I'm Through with You For Ever   457
With Her Lips Only   458
The Blotted Copy-Book   459
The Sacred Mission   459
From the Embassy   460
Sirocco at Deyá   460

From COLLECTED POEMS 1955 (1955)
Penthesileia   461
Poets' Corner   461
Coronation Address   462
Beauty in Trouble   463

A Lost Jewel   464
The Window Sill   464
Spoils   465

From THE CROWNING PRIVILEGE (1955)
The Clearing   466
The Three Pebbles   466
Possibly [The Question]   467
End of the World   467
To a Pebble in My Shoe   468
The Tenants   468
My Moral Forces   469
Interview   469

From 5 PENS IN HAND (1958)
The Face in the Mirror   470
Forbidden Words   470
Song for New Year's Eve   471
Alexander and Queen Janet [A Ballad of Alexander and
    Queen Janet]   471
The Coral Pool   473
Gratitude for a Nightmare   474
Friday Night   474
The Naked and the Nude   475
Woman and Tree   476
Destruction of Evidence   476
The Second-Fated   476
A Slice of Wedding Cake [Bitter Thoughts on Receiving a
    Slice of Cordelia's Wedding Cake]   477
A Plea to Boys and Girls   478
A Bouquet from a Fellow Roseman   478
Yes   479
The Outsider   479

From STEPS (1958)
The Enlisted Man   480
Mike and Mandy [Caroline and Charles]   480
Nothing   481
Call It a Good Marriage   482
Read Me, Please!   482
The Twin of Sleep   483
Around the Mountain   484

III

From FOOD FOR CENTAURS (1960)
Twice of the Same Fever 487
Established Lovers 487
The Quiet Glades of Eden 488
Heroes in Their Prime 489
Catkind 490
Two Children [The Young Goddess] 490
Here Live Your Life Out! 490
Joan and Darby 491
Superman on the Riviera 492
The Picture Nail 492
Old World Dialogue 492
The Were-Man 493
The Person from Porlock 493

From THE PENNY FIDDLE (1960)
The Penny Fiddle 494
Robinson Crusoe 494
The Six Badgers 495
Jock o' Binnorie 495

From MORE POEMS (1961)
Lyceia 496
Symptoms of Love 497
The Sharp Ridge 497
Under the Olives 498
The Visitation 498
Fragment 499
Apple Island 499
The Falcon Woman 499
Troughs of Sea 500
The Laugh 501
The Death Grapple 501
The Starred Coverlet 501
The Intrusion 502
Patience 502
The Cure 503
Hag-Ridden 503
Turn of the Moon 503
The Secret Land 504
Seldom Yet Now 505
To Myrto of Myrtles 505

Anchises to Aphrodite   506
A Lost World   506
The Dangerous Gift   507
Surgical Ward: Men   507
Nightfall at Twenty Thousand Feet   508
The Simpleton   508
Two Rhymes About Fate and Money   509
The Two Witches   509
Burn It!   510
Song: Come, Enjoy Your Sunday!   511

From COLLECTED POEMS 1961 (1961)
Ruby and Amethyst   512

From THE MORE DESERVING CASES (1962)
The Miller's Man   513
July 24th   513
Safe Receipt of a Censored Letter   514

From NEW POEMS 1962 (1962)
Recognition   515
The Watch   515
Name Day   516
Uncalendared Love   516
The Meeting   516
Lack   517
Not at Home   518
Horizon   519
Golden Anchor   519
Lion Lover   520
Ibycus in Samos   520
Possessed   521
The Winged Heart   522
In Trance at a Distance   523
The Wreath   523
In Her Praise   524
The Alabaster Throne   524
A Restless Ghost   525
Between Moon and Moon   525
Beware, Madam!   525
The Cliff Edge   526
Acrobats   526
Ouzo Unclouded   527
The Broken Girth   527

Inkidoo and the Queen of Babel 528
Three Songs for the Lute:
   I   Truth Is Poor Physic 529
   II In Her Only Way 529
   III Hedges Freaked with Snow 529
The Ambrosia of Dionysus and Semele 530
The Unnamed Spell 531

From MAN DOES, WOMAN IS (1964)
A Time of Waiting 532
Expect Nothing 532
No Letter 533
The Why of the Weather 533
In Time 533
Fire Walker 533
Deed of Gift 534
At Best, Poets 534
She Is No Liar 534
A Last Poem 535
The Pearl 535
The Leap 535
Bank Account 536
Judgement of Paris 536
Man Does, Woman Is 536
The Ample Garden 537
To Myrto About Herself 537
The Three-Faced 538
Dazzle of Darkness 538
Myrrhina 538
Food of the Dead 539
Eurydice 539
To Beguile and Betray 540
I Will Write 540
Bird of Paradise 540
The Metaphor 541
Secrecy 541
Joseph and Mary 542
An East Wind 542
Dance of Words 542
A Blind Arrow 543
The Oleaster 543
The Septuagenarian 544
Non Cogunt Astra 544
Song: Sword and Rose 545

Endless Pavement   545
In Disguise   545
A Measure of Casualness   546
In Time of Absence   546
The Green Castle   546
Not to Sleep   547
The Hearth   548
That Other World   548
The Beds of Grainne and Diarmuid   549
Rain of Brimstone   549
Consortium of Stones   550
The Black Goddess   550
Broken Neck   551
O   551
Woman of Greece   551
The Colours of Night   552
Between Trains   552
To the Teumessian Vixen   552
The Hung Wu Vase   553
La Mejicana   553
Lamia In Love   553
After the Flood   554
A Late Arrival   555
Song: With No Return   556
All I Tell You From My Heart   556
The Undead   557

From ANN AT HIGHWOOD HALL (1964)
Ann at Highwood Hall   559
St Valentine's Day   560
I Have a Little Cough, Sir   561
Joseph and Jesus   561

LOVE RESPELT (1965)
The Red Shower   562
Above the Edge of Doom   562
Wild Cyclamen   562
Gift of Sight   563
Batxóca   563
The Snap-Comb Wilderness   564
Change   564
A Court of Love   565
Black   565
Between Hyssop and Axe   565

Gold and Malachite 566
Ambience 566
The Vow 566
The Frog and the Golden Ball 567
Those Who Came Short 568
Whole Love 568
This Holy Month 569
The Blow 569
The Impossible 570
The Fetter 570
Iron Palace 571
True Joy 571
Tomorrow's Envy of Today 572
The Hidden Garden 572
The Wedding 573
What Will Be, Is 573
Son Altesse 574
Everywhere Is Here 575
Song: The Far Side of Your Moon 575
Deliverance 576
Conjunction 576
Nothing Now Astonishes 577
I'd Die for You   [Postscript] 577

From COLLECTED POEMS 1965 (1965)
Grace Notes 578
Good Night to the Old Gods 578
The Sweet-Shop Round the Corner 579
Double Bass 579
Descent into Hell 579
The Pardon 580
Point of No Return 580
A Shift of Scene 580

From SEVENTEEN POEMS MISSING FROM 'LOVE RESPELT' (1966)
Cock in Pullet's Feathers 581
Dead Hand 581
Arrears of Moonlight 581
What Did You Say? 582
Lure of Murder 582
The Gorge 583
Ecstasy of Chaos 583
Stolen Jewel 583
The Eagre 584

The Snapped Thread   [The Tangled Thread]   584
Fortunate Child   584
Loving True, Flying Blind   585
The Near Eclipse   585
Dancing Flame   585
Birth of Angels   586
On Giving   586

From COLOPHON TO 'LOVE RESPELT' (1967)
The P'eng that was a K'un   587
Like Owls   587
In Perspective   588
The Utter Rim   588
Bower-Bird   588
Mist   589
The Word   589
Perfectionists   590
Prison Walls   590
A Dream of Hell   591
Our Self   592
Bites and Kisses   592
Sun-Face and Moon-Face   593
Freehold   593
The Necklace   593
A Bracelet   594
Blackening Sky   594
Blessed Sun   594
Lion-Gentle   595
Song: The Palm Tree   595
Spite of Mirrors   596
Pride of Love   596
Hooded Flame   597
Injuries   597
Her Brief Withdrawal   597
The Crane   598
Strangeness   598

From THE POOR BOY WHO FOLLOWED HIS STAR (1968)
Hide and Seek   599
The Hero   599
At Seventy-Two   600

From POEMS 1965-1968 (1968)
Song: How Can I Care?   601

Song: Though Once True Lovers   601
Song: Cherries or Lilies   602
Song: Crown of Stars   602
Song: Fig Tree in Leaf   603
Song: Dew-drop and Diamond   603
Song: Just Friends   603
Song: Of Course   604
Song: Three Rings for Her   604
Sincèrement   605
Dans un Seul Lit   605
Is Now the Time?   605
Twins   605
Sail and Oar   606
Gooseflesh Abbey   606
The Home-Coming   606
With the Gift of a Lion's Claw   607
Wigs and Beards   607
Personal Packaging, Inc.   608
Work Room   608
The Ark   608
All Except Hannibal   609
The Beggar Maid and King Cophetua   609
For Ever   610
Jugum Improbum   610
De Arte Poetica   610
Sit Mihi Terra Levis   610
Astymelusa   611
Tousled Pillow   611
To Be In Love   612
Fact of the Act   612
To Ogmian Hercules   613
Arrow Shots   613
She to Him   614
Within Reason   614
The Yet Unsayable   615
None the Wiser   615
The Narrow Sea   616
The Olive-Yard   616

BEYOND GIVING   (1969)
PART I
Song: To a Rose   617
Song: Dream Warning   617
Song: Beyond Giving   618

Trial of Innocence   618
Poisoned Day   618
Superstition   [Leave-Taking]   618
In the Name of Virtue   619
What We Did Next   620
Compact   620
Song: New Year Kisses   621
Song: The Clocks of Time   621
Gold Cloud   622
Song: Basket of Blossom   622
Song: Wherever We May Be   623
What Is Love?   623
Song: The Promise   624
Song: Yesterday Only   624
PART II
Semi-Detached   625
Iago   626
Against Witchcraft   626
Troublesome Fame   626
Tolling Bell   627
Blanket Charge   628
The Strayed Message   629
Song: The Sundial's Lament   629
Poem: A Reminder   630
Antorcha y Corona, 1968; Torch and Crown, 1968   631
Armistice Day, 1918   633
The Motes   634

From POEMS ABOUT LOVE   (1969)
If and When   635

From POEMS 1968-1970   (1970)
Song: The Sigil   636
Song: Twinned Heart   636
Song: Olive Tree   637
Song: Once More   637
Song: Victims of Calumny   638
Love Gifts   638
Mankind and Ocean   639
Virgin Mirror   639
Secret Theatre   640
How It Started   640
Brief Reunion   641
The Judges   641

Love and Night 642
Child with Veteran 643
Purification 643
Powers Unconfessed 644
Pandora 645
Solomon's Seal 645
To Put It Simply 646
To Tell and Be Told 646
The Theme of Death 647
At the Well 647
Logic 648
Robbers' Den 648
The Accomplice 649
First Love 649
Through a Dark Wood 650
In the Vestry 650
When Love Is Not 650
The Reiteration 651
Man of Evil 651
The Raft 652
The Uncut Diamond 653
My Ghost   [The Co-Walker] 653
The Risk 654
Something to Say 654
OCCASIONALIA
Research and Development: Classified 655
The Imminent Seventies 656
Carol of Patience 656
H 658
Invitation to Bristol 658
The Primrose Bed 658
The Strangling in Merrion Square 659
The Awakening 659

From THE GREEN-SAILED VESSEL (1971)
The Hoopoe Tells Us How   [Dedicatory] 660
PART I: LOVE POEMS
The Wand 660
Five; *Quinque* 661
Arrow on the Vane 661
Gorgon Mask 661
To Be Poets 662
With a Gift of Rings 662
Casse-Noisette 663

The Garden   663
The Green-Sailed Vessel   664
Dreaming Children   664
The Prohibition   665
Serpent's Tail   665
Until We Both …   665
The Miracle   666
The Rose   666
Testament   667
The Crab-Tree   667
Three Locked Hoops   668
Cliff and Wave   668
PART II: MAINLY SATIRES
Those Blind from Birth   668
Fools   669
The Gateway   669
Advice from a Mother   669
A Reduced Sentence   670
The Gentleman   671
Complaint and Reply   671
Song: Reconciliation   672
Knobs and Levers   672
The Virus   673
Druid Love   673
Problems of Gender   674
Confess, Marpessa   674
Jus Primae Noctis   675
Work Drafts   675

From POEMS 1970-1972 (1972)
Her Beauty   676
Always   676
Desert Fringe   677
The Title of Poet   677
Depth of Love   678
Breakfast Table   678
The Half-Finished Letter   678
The Hazel Grove   679
Pity   679
Silent Visit   679
Coronet of Moonlight   680
Song: To Become Each Other   681
Heaven   681
Growing Pains   682

Friday Night   682
The Pact   683
Poor Others   683
A Toast to Death   684
The Young Sibyl   684
Records   685
The Flowering Aloe   685
Circus Ring   685
Ageless Reason   686
As When the Mystic   686
Unposted Letter (1963)   686
Birth of a Goddess   687
Beatrice and Dante   687
The Dilemma   687
The Wall   688
Women and Masks (translation)   688
Tilth   689
The Last Fistful   690
The Traditionalist   690
The Prepared Statement   690
St Antony of Padua   691
Broken Compact   691
A Dream of Frances Speedwell   692
The Encounter   692
Age Gap   692
Nightmare of Senility   693
Absent Crusader   693
Dream Recalled on Waking   694
Colophon   694

From TIMELESS MEETING (1973)

The Promised Ballad   695
The Impossible Day   695
The Poet's Curse   696
Seven Years   [Where Is the Truth?]   696
Love as Lovelessness   697
The Scared Child   697
As All Must End   698
Touch My Shut Lips   698
The Moon's Last Quarter   699
True Evil   699
When and Why   700
The Window Pane   700
Pride of Progeny   700

That Was the Night   700
Song: The Queen of Time   701
Should I Care?   701
Timeless Meeting   701
Envoi   702

AT THE GATE (1974)
Ours Is No Wedlock   703
The Discarded Love Poem   703
Earlier Lovers   704
Fast Bound Together   704
£. s. d.   704
Three Words Only   705
True Magic   706
The Tower of Love   706
The Love Letter   707
Song: Seven Fresh Years   707
As a Less Than Robber   708
Singleness in Love   708
Love Charms   709
At the Gate   709
The Moon's Tear   709
Song: From Otherwhere or Nowhere   710
Name   711
Two Disciplines   711
The Ugly Secret   712
Three Years Waiting   712

From COLLECTED POEMS 1975 (1975)
The Crystal   713
A Charm for Sound Sleeping   713
The New Eternity   714
History of the Fall   714
Elsewhere   714
What Can We Not Ask?   715
Two Crucial Generations   715
To Come of Age   716
September Landscape   716
Crucibles of Love   716
Woman Poet and Man Poet   717
The Field-Postcard   717
If No Cuckoo Sings   718
Mountain Lovers   719
Three Times In Love   719

The Sentence 719
Spring 1974 720
Advent of Summer 720
The Unpenned Poem 721
The Green Woods of Unrest 722

UNCOLLECTED POEMS
JUVENILIA: 1910-1914
A Pot of White Heather 723
The Mountain Side at Evening 723
The Will o' the Wisp 724
The King's Son 724
The Miser of Shenham Heath 725
Rondeau 726
'Am and Advance: A Cockney Study 727
Peeping Tom 727
The Ballad of the White Monster 728
The Future 729
Alcaics Addressed to My Study Fauna 730
The Cyclone 731
The Ape God 731
Lament in December 732
Merlin and the Child 732
A Day in February 733
The Wasp 733
Five Rhymes:
    My Hazel-Twig 734
    After the Rain 734
    Envy 735
    The King's Highway 735
    The Glorious Harshness of the Parrot's Voice 735
Two Moods 736
The Briar Burners 736
The Tyranny of Books 737
The Exhaust-Pipe 738
The Organ Grinder 739
1918-1927
The Two Brothers 739
Peace 740
Bazentin, 1916 741
The Dancing Green 743
The Personal Touch 744
Song: The Ring and Chain 744
The Oxford English School 745

The Stepmother and the Princess   746
Cynics and Romantics   747
Records for Wonder   748
Old Lob-Lie-by-the-Fire   750
Misgivings, on Reading a Popular 'Outline of Science'   750
The Toads   751
A History   752
Four Children   753
The Bargain   754
In the Beginning Was a Word   754
The Bait   755
An Independent   755
[The Untidy Man]   756
1934-1939
Midsummer Duet   756
Majorcan Letter, 1935   760
Assumption Day   767
The Moon Ends in Nightmare   768
1952-1959
The Housing Project   768
Advice to Colonel Valentine   769
Hippopotamus's Address to the Freudians   770
Twin to Twin   770
Considine   771
The Juggler   771
The Young Witch   772
Birth of a Great Man   772
To Magdalena Mulet, Margita Mora & Lucia Graves   773
The Pumpkin   774
Max Beerbohm at Rapallo   774
The Grandfather's Complaint   775
Song: A Beach in Spain   776
Bathunts at Bathurst   777
To a Caricaturist, Who Got Me Wrong   777
In Jorrocks's Warehouse   778
A Fever   779
Augeias and I   780
Is It Peace?   780
Fingers in the Nesting Box   781
Barabbas's Summer List   782
Stable Door   782
Flight Report   783
School Hymn for St Trinian's   784

1960-1974
A Piebald's Tail   784
The Intruders   785
Teiresias   785
Song: The Smile of Eve   787
[Verse Composed over the Telephone]   787
[Fir and Yew]   787
Song: Gardens Close at Dusk   788
[Privacy]   788
Matador Gored   · 788
Confiteor Ut Fas   788
New Moon Through Glass   789
Dynamite Barbee   789
When a Necklace Breaks   790
A Queen   790
If Love Becomes a Game   791
Queen Silver and King Gold   791
Learn That By Heart   791
Song: One in Many   792
A Late Daffodil for the Prince of Gwynedd   792
1999   793
Angry Gardener   793
Song: Weather   793
Fiery Orchard   793
Defeat of Time   794
Six Blankets   794
The Note   794
The Hedgepig   795
When He Sat Writing   795
Four Poems from *DEYÁ: A PORTFOLIO* (1972):
    [Ours has no bearing on quotidian love]   796
    [Love makes poor sense in either speech or letters]   796
    [Is there another man?]   797
    [Confess, sweetheart, confess]   797
The Noose   798
The Moral Law   798
Bodies Entranced   799
Who Must It Be?   799
This Is the Season   800
Unco   800

UNPUBLISHED AND POSTHUMOUSLY PUBLISHED POEMS
JUVENILIA: 1910-1914
The First Poem   801

Nightmare   801
The Dragon-Fly   802
Boy-Morality   802
The Coracle   803
1915-1919
The Last Drop   804
Trench Life   804
Through the Periscope   805
Machine Gun Fire: Cambrin   806
The Fusilier   806
O   807
To My Unborn Son   807
Return   808
The Savage Story of Cardonette   808
Died of Wounds   809
Six Poems from 'The Patchwork Flag' (1918):
      Foreword   809
      Letter to S.S. from Bryn-y-pin   810
      Night March   811
      Poetic Injustice   814
      The Survivor Comes Home   814
      The Pudding   815
Mother's Song in Winter   816
To Jean and John   816
1920s-1930s
From an Upper Window   816
Drink and Fever   817
Vestry   818
The End   819
The Sand Glass   820
This What-I-Mean   820
The Fingerhold   821
Then What?   822
Historical Particulars   822
Address to Self   823
Prosperity of Poets   824
1940s-1950s
Diotima Dead   824
The Hearth   825
In the Lion House   825
An Appeal   826
A Ghost from Arakan   826
1960s-1970s
Robin and Marian   826

Never Yet 827
Tanka 827
House on Fire 827
The Lilac Frock 828
Departure 828
North Side 829
A 829
Song: John Truelove 830
Requirements for a Poem 830
The Atom 830
The Cupid 830
Olives of March 831
The Undying Worm 831
Song: Though Time Conceals Much 832
Always and For Ever 832
ACROSS THE GULF (1992)
   The Snapped Rope 833
   The Goldsmiths 833
   Adam in Hell 833
   The Cards Are Wild 834
   Unless 834
   The Poised Pen 835
   [Fragment] 835
   [How Is It a Man Dies?] 835
   Green Flash 836
   Peisinoë 836
   Across the Gulf 836
   To His Temperate Mistress 836
   Foot-Holder-Royal 837
   The Pressure Gauge 837

Index of Titles 839
Index of First Lines 869

ACKNOWLEDGEMENTS

The editors wish to thank the following individuals and institutions for enabling us to examine materials, and for permission to quote from them: the Beinecke Rare Book and Manuscript Library, Yale University; the Henry W. and Albert A. Berg Collection, New York Public Library, Astor, Lennox and Tilden Foundations; the Bodleian Library, Oxford; the Poetry/Rare Books Collection, University Libraries, State University of New York at Buffalo; Ms Lorna Knight, Curator of Manuscripts, and the Carl A. Kroch Library, Cornell University; Mr George Newkey-Burden, and the staff of the *Daily Telegraph* Library; Mr Michael Meredith, Curator, and the College Library, Eton College; the Harry Ransom Humanities Research Center, University of Texas at Austin; Ms Lori N. Curtis, Associate Curator of Special Collections, and the McFarlin Library, University of Tulsa, Oklahoma; Ms Shelley Cox, Rare Books Librarian, and the Morris Library, Southern Illinois University at Carbondale; Mr D.M. Bownes, Assistant Curator, Royal Welch Fusiliers Regimental Museum, Caernarvon; the St John's College Robert Graves Trust, Oxford; the National Library of Scotland, Edinburgh; Mr Christopher G. Petter, Special Collections Librarian, and the University Library, University of Victoria, British Columbia, Canada; Mr William S. Reese, and Mr Terry Halliday, Literary Manager, William Reese Company, New Haven, Connecticut. Special thanks are due to the Curator of the Poetry/Rare Books Collection, SUNY at Buffalo, Professor Robert J. Bertholf, for his aid and encouragement, and to Dr Michael Basinski, Assistant Curator.

We are grateful to the Board of Literary Management of the late Laura (Riding) Jackson for permission to reprint 'Midsummer Duet', from Laura Riding's *Collected Poems* (London: Cassell, 1938; and Manchester: Carcanet, and New York: Persea Books, 1980), copyright © 1938, 1980; and 'Majorcan Letter, 1935', from *Focus*, 4 (Dec. 1935). The Board, 'in conformity with her wish', asks us 'to record that, in 1941, Laura (Riding) Jackson renounced, on grounds of linguistic principle, the writing of poetry: she had come to hold that "poetry obstructs general attainment to something better in our linguistic way-of-life than we have"'.

We should like to thank again the many others whose help is acknowledged in the three-volume annotated *Complete Poems*, from which the texts for this edition have been reproduced.

Dunstan Ward gratefully acknowledges a grant from the British Academy to visit libraries and collections in the United States, and the support of the University of London's British Institute in Paris.

Finally, we wish to thank our editor, Ms Sarah Rigby, for her care and patience.

INTRODUCTION

Fierce poems of our past –
How can they ever die,
Condemned by love to last
Word for word and exactly
Under a wide and changeful sky?

('If No Cuckoo Sings')

There were two dramatic turning-points in the life of Robert Graves (1895–1985). One was his 'death' from wounds in the Battle of the Somme in 1916, just before his twenty-first birthday (it was even reported in *The Times*). The other was in 1929, when he said 'Good-bye to all that' (the title of his classic autobiography) and, accompanied only by the American poet Laura Riding, left England for a remote mountain village in Mallorca.

If his extraordinary survival seemed to confirm his poetic destiny, his departure was no less symbolic. It affirmed Graves's absolute commitment to his vocation, which shaped both his artistic and his personal life: 'Since the age of fifteen poetry has been my ruling passion and I have never intentionally undertaken any task or formed any relationship that seemed inconsistent with poetic principles'.[1]

Graves's poetry falls into three main periods, 1910–1926, 1927–1959 and 1960–1975, delimited by the publication of major collections, and bearing the impress of the relationships that inspired many of the poems they contain.

Intimations of his dedication to poetry can already be found in 'The First Poem', written in January 1910 during his unhappy schooldays at Charterhouse, and in 'The Poet in the Nursery', which opens his first book, *Over the Brazier* (1916), published while he was on service in France (he joined the Royal Welch Fusiliers a week after Britain declared war).

The personal background to the poetry of this period includes his romantic attachment to a younger schoolmate, and his friendships with Edward Marsh, editor of the influential *Georgian Poetry* anthologies, and with the poet and fellow-Fusilier Siegfried Sassoon; his traumatic experiences as a young officer in the trenches; the aftermath of shell-shock and religious crisis; his marriage in 1918 to Nancy Nicholson (daughter of the

painter William Nicholson), and the birth of their four children; studies at
Oxford; his intense if short-lived involvements in psychology and philos-
ophy, through two mentors, the psychologist W.H.R. Rivers and the
Bengali philosopher Basanta Mallik; the beginning of his relationship with
Laura Riding (they met on 2 January 1926); and his sole spell of conven-
tional employment – six months as Professor of English at the University
of Cairo.

By December 1926, when Graves was thirty-one, he had published
nineteen books, of which eleven were verse. He had acquired a reputa-
tion as a poet during the war, but his post-war poetry attracted little
attention from the critics or the public.

Poems (1914–26) marks the end of this period. His first 'collected'
volume, it was, however, 'selective rather than collective, intended as a
disavowal of over half the poetry that I had so far printed';[2] from more
than 280 poems he chose only 134.

This drastic thinning-out continued through the six volumes of *Collected
Poems* (two of them American) that appeared in 1938, 1948, 1955, 1959,
1961 and 1965, with the result that the greater proportion of the poetry
written before 1960, among it some of Graves's finest work, was elimi-
nated from the canon.

The second period, 1927–1959, divides into two. The first is defined by
Graves's association with Laura Riding, whom he came to identify with
the 'Sovereign Muse'. After the break with her in 1939, his relationship
with Beryl Hodge, whom he had met in London in June 1937, establishes
the other period, during which the White Goddess becomes the central
presence.

If, as he afterwards stated, Graves was 'learning all the time' while he
was with Riding,[3] these were also years of drama and upheaval: the end
of his first marriage; Riding's attempted suicide; their departure abroad,
and the sensation created by *Good-bye to All That*; seven years in Mallorca
where, for all that is positive in his diary, their life together 'grew more
and more painful';[4] then, uprooted by the Spanish Civil War, exile in
England, Switzerland, France and America; finally, the 'horror' of their
parting, evoked in 'The Moon Ends in Nightmare'.

In contrast, the following two decades – despite World War II, in which
his eldest son, David, was killed – brought Graves stability, with his
marriage to Beryl Hodge, another family of four children, and his return
in 1946, after six years in Devon, to his Mallorcan home in Deyá.

During the period with Laura Riding his poetry did not reach a large
readership. Besides being geographically isolated, he had virtually ceased
contributing to periodicals and anthologies, and of the six books up to
1938, four were limited editions amounting to just 740 copies.

The publication in November 1938 of Graves's second *Collected Poems* was the culmination of his literary collaboration with Riding. For more than a decade he had submitted every poem to her as it was written. Most had to be further revised before she eventually 'passed' them; some were destroyed. Then, in preparing his new collection, he went over all his work again with her, rewriting and deleting. *Collected Poems* (1938) is consequently 'selective rather than collective', like *Poems (1914–26)*, from which only forty-one poems are preserved. The 'Foreword' offers an explanation: 'I have suppressed whatever I felt misrepresented my poetic seriousness at the time when it was written.'[5] But it was Riding, in fact, who formulated this, and Graves's own attitude is better conveyed in his foreword to *Poems and Satires 1951*: 'A volume of collected poems should form a sequence of the intenser moments of the poet's spiritual autobiography'; in suppressing (and occasionally restoring) his poems, and reordering them in their sections – from 1938 designated simply by a roman numeral (like the chapters in *Good-bye to All That*) – he was reshaping, with the canon, his life 'story'.[6]

In the 1940s came his most creative phase, in prose and verse alike, with eleven prose books as well as three volumes of poetry and two selections. 'These last years [...] with Beryl', he wrote, 'have been the happiest of my life and I have done my best work in them.'[7] The rigour he had achieved in his poetry was now combined with a renewed lyricism, as revealed in *Work in Hand* (1942) and *Poems 1938–1945*, and epitomized by 'Mid-Winter Waking'; in such poems as 'Despite and Still' and 'She Tells Her Love While Half Asleep', gentler personal emotions have recovered the right to be expressed openly.

From 'a sudden overwhelming obsession'[8] in 1944 emerged *The White Goddess*, eventually published (through the perceptiveness of T.S. Eliot) in 1948 – a whole system of thought and belief within which lifelong poetic preoccupations could find their place.

The Goddess – 'the ancient power of love and terror'[9] – pervades Graves's poetry. Anticipated in the early work ('The God Called Poetry', 'Love in Barrenness', 'The Red Ribbon Dream', for example, and in those poems that feature moon imagery), she is prefigured while he is in the service of an exacting muse (in 'On Portents', or 'As It Were Poems', iii, where she is actually named), then celebrated by the poet as her mythologist and, increasingly, her devotee (in such numinous poems as 'To Juan at the Winter Solstice', 'The White Goddess', 'Rhea'). In his mid-fifties he experienced again – through his encounter with a girl of seventeen – her inspiration and apparent betrayal, a pattern that was to continue and dominate the future.

The favourable critical reception of *Poems 1938–1945* marked a watershed in Graves's reputation. In the 1950s the number of poems he published in periodicals climbed back to the level of the early 1920s; paperback editions in 1957 and 1958 made his poetry widely available; lecture

tours in America and television appearances swelled his audience. By the
end of the decade he had become a celebrity, receiving – or refusing –
awards and honours. Yet the newer verse caused him some misgivings;
when he wrote the last addition to *Collected Poems 1959*, 'Around the
Mountain', he was wondering whether he had reached his 'menopause'.[10]
But if his major poetic achievement was behind him, his most prolific years
still lay ahead.

Nearly half the 1202 poems in this book were written in the fifteen years
from 1960 to 1975 – an astonishing late outpouring.

'Love is the main theme and origin of true poems', Graves declared in
1965.[11] Most of the poems of the last period are, indeed, love poems (or,
to use his own distinction, poems about love); their focus is 'the personal
Muse', an incarnation (as he now believed) of the Goddess. The period
can thus be divided into three phases: 1960–1963, 1963–1966 and
1966–1975, corresponding to Graves's relationships with his so-called
'muses', though the continuities are perhaps more significant than the
contrasts. During the first phase, Graves sought to 'dramatize, truthfully
and factually, the vicissitudes of a poet's dealings with the White Goddess,
the Muse, the perpetual Other Woman'. His quest then turned to the
White Goddess's 'mysterious sister', the Black Goddess of Wisdom, who
'represents a miraculous certitude in love'.[12]

The 'muses' were a source not only of inspiration but also of frequent
disquiet. In the later work there are still, however, a number of witty, light-
hearted or ironic poems. It was this ability to distance himself that to a
large extent helped him through some difficult emotional situations. (For
example, he wrote 'Ann at Highwood Hall' in a few days at a particularly
distressing time in his personal life.)[13]

The twenty-three books of verse that Graves published during this
period include three *Collected Poems*. In the 1965 volume he suppressed
almost a quarter of the contents of *Collected Poems 1959*, mainly on the
grounds of suspected 'lovelessness';[14] but he reprinted the mass of recent
love poetry, as he did again in his last volume, published in 1975 when he
was eighty: the final version of his 'spiritual autobiography' was designed
to tell 'one story only' ...

Graves's fame attained its height in the 1960s. Each new book of poetry
received virtually unanimous praise from the reviewers (until the
predictable reaction). The 1961 paperback edition of *The White Goddess*
even made him 'something of a cult-figure'.[15] His lectures as Professor of
Poetry at Oxford from 1961 to 1965 drew exceptional audiences, and their
publication, among half a dozen books of essays, ensured a wider circu-
lation for his views. He gave numerous talks and readings; besides his
frequent visits to America, he travelled to Greece, Hungary, Poland,
Russia, Mexico and Australia. He was awarded a gold medal at the 1968

Mexican 'Cultural Olympics', and, later that year, the Queen's Gold Medal for Poetry. But he was never part of the literary establishment, remaining obstinately removed.

In his last years Graves suffered increasingly from ill health and loss of memory, yet to the end of this third period he worked as he had always done, producing draft upon draft in his life-long 'obsession about getting poems *right*'.[16] Among the latest poems are some of his most poignant: 'Unless', 'The Moon's Last Quarter', 'The Unpenned Poem', 'The Green Woods of Unrest'; he left another fifty completed poems in manuscript. Until he could no longer write, he continued to 'treat poetry with a single-minded devotion which may be called religious'.[17]

'I can promise that no silver spoons have been thrown out with the refuse, and that I have been fair to my younger, middle and elder selves', wrote Graves in *Collected Poems 1959*, which contained considerably less than half his output to date. If both those claims might have been questioned in 1959, it is evident that the 1975 *Collected Poems* favoured the elder self at the expense of the middle and younger: of the 632 poems, more than two-thirds were from the last fifteen years. The canon was left unbalanced.

The present edition shows the full range of Graves's poetic work. It brings together all the 1133 poems that he published, with sixty-nine chosen from his unpublished and posthumously published poetry. The three-volume annotated edition of the *Complete Poems* (Manchester: Carcanet, 1995, 1997, 1999) records his changes to the canon, summarizing the publication history of the individual poems, and listing the contents of the successive volumes of *Collected Poems*.

All the known uncollected poems (printed only in periodicals and the press) have been included, several of them not previously recorded; any further poems traced will be added in the future.

In making what is inevitably a personal selection from over two hundred unpublished and posthumously published poems, the editors have given priority to poems whose publication was approved by Graves, but was prevented by some external factor (as was the case, for example, with 'Diotima Dead', removed from *Work in Hand* when the printers requested cuts). Apart from these, they have chosen poems that were treated by Graves as 'finished' (or that reached a comparably 'finished' state), and which are, in their judgement, of literary, historical or biographical interest, and representative of Graves's poetry at the time.

The arrangement of the poems from Graves's books of verse corresponds to the first editions, and follows the order within them. 'From' before the title of a book (e.g. 'From *Fairies and Fusiliers*') indicates the omission of a poem or poems already included in an earlier book (or incorporated into a later poem); the full contents of each book are listed in the three-volume edition.

The uncollected poems are in order of first publication (for publication details, see the annotated *Complete Poems*, Volume III). The unpublished and posthumously published poems are in order of composition, to the extent that it has been possible to determine this.

In accordance with Graves's practice, this edition prints the latest texts of the poems, reproducing them from the annotated *Complete Poems*. The poems from Graves's books and the uncollected poems appear in the last version that he published, with further revisions (e.g. in his own copies of his books) incorporated, and the unpublished and posthumously published poems in the version of the latest manuscript/typescript. Anomalies and misprints have been corrected in the light of manuscripts and previous printings (as reported in the three-volume *Complete Poems* notes); when an earlier printed variant in wording or punctuation has been adopted, it has been checked wherever possible against manuscripts and proofs, as have the texts of the uncollected poems.

Revision, for Graves, was not just a question of craftsmanship, consummate craftsman though he was. It was an integral part of the actual process of composition, which he described as 'a painful process of continual corrections and corrections on top of corrections and persistent dissatisfaction'.[18] 'Getting poems *right*' often meant continuing to revise them over a period of years or even decades, making cuts if he felt this would improve them. Thus it was eighteen years before he found the seemingly inevitable concluding line in 'Vanity'; and even more protracted 'secondary elaboration'[19] was required for one of his best-known poems, 'The Cool Web', to reach its ultimate precision and expressiveness. A case of Graves's radical surgery was 'The Pier-Glass', whose excised twenty-four-line fourth section had attempted to force a resolution. Some poems ('The Finding of Love', for instance) were originally more than twice as long.

Where Graves republished a poem with substantive revisions, the principal differences between the version in the first edition of the book of verse concerned (or, for uncollected poems, the version first published) and the last version are recorded in the notes to the three-volume *Complete Poems*. The notes also give background information on the poems, with quotations from and/or references to other poems, letters, diaries and prose works. There are notes on all the uncollected poems and the unpublished and posthumously published poems.

Titles provided editorially in the present edition are in square brackets. Some details of punctuation – ellipses, the use of single quotation marks (double for quotations within them), punctuation relative to quotation marks and italics – have been normalized in line with Graves's later practice; and some inconsistent spelling has been altered (though the earlier use of the hyphenated form of certain words – 'to-day', 'to-morrow' – has been respected, as in the *Collected Poems*). American spelling in uncollected poems has been Anglicized. Where Graves used an ampersand (&) in the manuscript of an unpublished poem it has been spelt out ('and'). Inconsistencies in the capitalization of titles in upper-and-lower-case in contents lists have been removed.

In the last section, a dagger (†) after the title of a poem indicates that it was posthumously published.

1. *The White Goddess: A Historical Grammar of Poetic Myth*, fourth edition, edited by Grevel Lindop (Manchester: Carcanet, 1997; London: Faber Paperback, 1999), p.13.
2. *Good-bye to All That: An Autobiography* (London: Cape, 1929), p.439.
3. Graves to Gertrude Stein, n.d. [February(?) 1946]; *In Broken Images: Selected Letters of Robert Graves 1914–1946*, edited by Paul O'Prey (London: Hutchinson, 1982), p.341.
4. Graves to Gertrude Stein, 28 January 1946; *In Broken Images*, p.337.
5. *Collected Poems* (London: Cassell, 1938), p.xiv.
6. *Poems and Satires 1951* (London: Cassell, 1951), 'Foreword', pp.viii, ix.
7. See note 3, above.
8. *The White Goddess*, p.479.
9. 'The Personal Muse', *Oxford Addresses on Poetry* (London: Cassell, 1962), p.61, and *Collected Writings on Poetry*, edited by Paul O'Prey (Manchester: Carcanet, 1995), p.339 ('fright and lust', *The White Goddess*, p.20).
10. Graves to James Reeves, 4 December 1957; *Between Moon and Moon: Selected Letters of Robert Graves 1946–1972*, edited by Paul O'Prey (London: Hutchinson, 1984), p.172.
11. 'Lecture One, 1965', *Poetic Craft and Principle* (London: Cassell, 1967), p.116, republished as 'The Duende', *Collected Writings on Poetry*, p.473.
12. 'Intimations of the Black Goddess', *Mammon and the Black Goddess* (London: Cassell, 1965), pp.151, 162, and *Collected Writings on Poetry*, pp.390, 397.
13. Graves's 1956–66 diary (Canelluñ), 25–27 February, 1963.
14. 'Foreword', *Collected Poems 1965* (London: Cassell, 1965).
15. *The White Goddess*, Introduction, p.xvii.
16. Graves to James Reeves, 3 June 1954; *Between Moon and Moon*, p.136.
17. 'The Poet and his Public', *The Crowning Privilege* (London: Cassell, 1955), p.187, and *Collected Writings on Poetry*, p.242.
18. *Good-bye to All That*, pp.388–89.
19. Graves employs this term from Freudian psychology in *Poetic Unreason and Other Studies* (London: Cecil Palmer, 1925), Chapter V.

I

OVER THE BRAZIER

(1916)

THE POET IN THE NURSERY

The youngest poet down the shelves was fumbling
    In a dim library, just behind the chair
From which the ancient poet was mum-mumbling
    A song about some lovers at a Fair,
Pulling his long white beard and gently grumbling
    That rhymes were troublesome things and never there.

And as I groped, the whole time I was thinking
    About the tragic poem I'd been writing,…
An old man's life of beer and whisky drinking,
    His years of kidnapping and wicked fighting;
And how at last, into a fever sinking,
    Remorsefully he died, his bedclothes biting.

But suddenly I saw the bright green cover
    Of a thin pretty book right down below;
I snatched it up and turned the pages over,
    To find it full of poetry, and so
Put it down my neck with quick hands like a lover,
    And turned to watch if the old man saw it go.

The book was full of funny muddling mazes,
    Each rounded off into a lovely song,
And most extraordinary and monstrous phrases
    Knotted with rhymes like a slave-driver's thong,
And metre twisting like a chain of daisies
    With great big splendid words a sentence long.

I took the book to bed with me and gloated,
    Learning the lines that seemed to sound most grand;
So soon the lively emerald green was coated
    With intimate dark stains from my hot hand,
While round the nursery for long months there floated
    Wonderful words no one could understand.

PART I. – Poems Mostly Written at Charterhouse – 1910-1914

STAR-TALK

'Are you awake, Gemelli,
    This frosty night?'
'We'll be awake till reveillé,
Which is Sunrise,' say the Gemelli,
'It's no good trying to go to sleep:
If there's wine to be got we'll drink it deep,
    But sleep is gone for to-night,
    But sleep is gone for to-night.'

'Are you cold too, poor Pleiads,
    This frosty night?'
'Yes, and so are the Hyads:
See us cuddle and hug,' say the Pleiads,
'All six in a ring: it keeps us warm:
We huddle together like birds in a storm:
    It's bitter weather to-night,
    It's bitter weather to-night.'

'What do you hunt, Orion,
    This starry night?'
'The Ram, the Bull and the Lion,
And the Great Bear,' says Orion,
'With my starry quiver and beautiful belt
I am trying to find a good thick pelt
    To warm my shoulders to-night,
    To warm my shoulders to-night.'

'Did you hear that, Great She-bear,
    This frosty night?'
'Yes, he's talking of stripping *me* bare
Of my own big fur,' says the She-bear,
'I'm afraid of the man and his terrible arrow:
The thought of it chills my bones to the marrow,
    And the frost so cruel to-night!
    And the frost so cruel to-night!'

'How is your trade, Aquarius,
     This frosty night?'
'Complaints is many and various
And my feet are cold,' says Aquarius,
'There's Venus objects to Dolphin-scales,
And Mars to Crab-spawn found in my pails,
     And the pump has frozen to-night,
     And the pump has frozen to-night.'

THE DYING KNIGHT AND THE FAUNS

Through the dreams of yesternight
My blood brother great in fight
I saw lying, slowly dying
Where the weary woods were sighing
With the rustle of the birches,
With the quiver of the larches...
Woodland fauns with hairy haunches
Grin in wonder through the branches,
Woodland fauns who know not fear:
Wondering they wander near,
Munching mushrooms red as coral,
Bunches, too, of rue and sorrel,
With uncouth and bestial sounds,
Knowing naught of war and wounds.
But the crimson life-blood oozes
And makes roses of the daisies,
Persian carpets of the mosses –
Softly now his spirit passes
As the bee forsakes the lily,
As the berry leaves the holly;
But the fauns still think him living,
And with bay leaves they are weaving
Crowns to deck him. Well they may!
He was worthy of the Bay.

WILLAREE

On the rough mountain wind
    That blows so free
Rides a little storm-sprite
    Whose name is Willaree.

The fleecy cloudlets are not his,
    No shepherd is he,
For he drives the shaggy thunderclouds
    Over land and sea.

His home is on the mountain-top
    Where I love to be,
Amid grey rocks and brambles
    And the red rowan-tree.

He whistles down the chimney,
    He whistles to me,
And I send greeting back to him
    Whistling cheerily.

The great elms are battling,
    Waves are on the sea,
Loud roars the mountain-wind –
    God rest you, Willaree!

THE FACE OF THE HEAVENS

Little winds in a hurry,
    Great winds over the sky,
Clouds sleek or furry,
    Storms that rage and die,

The whole cycle of weather
    From calm to hurricane
Of four gales wroth together,
    Thunder, lightning, rain,

The burning sun, snowing,
    Hailstones pattering down,
Blue skies and red skies showing,
    Skies with a black frown,

By these signs and wonders
  You may tell God's mood:
He shines, rains, thunders,
  But all His works are good.

JOLLY YELLOW MOON

Oh, now has faded from the West
  A sunset red as wine,
And beast and bird are hushed to rest
  When the jolly yellow moon doth shine.

Come comrades, roam we round the mead
  Where couch the sleeping kine;
The breath of night blows soft indeed,
  And the jolly yellow moon doth shine.

And step we slowly, friend with friend,
  Let arm with arm entwine,
And voice with voice together blend,
  For the jolly yellow moon doth shine.

Whether we loudly sing or soft,
  The tune goes wondrous fine;
Our chorus sure will float aloft
  Where the jolly yellow moon doth shine.

YOUTH AND FOLLY

*('Life is a very awful thing! You young fellows are
too busy being jolly to realize the folly of your lives.'
                          – A Charterhouse Sermon)*

In Chapel often when I bawl
The hymns, to show I'm musical,
With bright eye and cheery voice
Bidding Christian folk rejoice,
Shame be it said, I've not a thought
Of the One Being whom I ought
To worship: with unwitting roar

Other godheads I adore.
I celebrate the Gods of Mirth
And Love and Youth and Springing Earth,
Bacchus, beautiful, divine,
Gulping down his heady wine,
Dear Pan piping in his hollow,
Fiery-headed King Apollo
And rugged Atlas all aloof
Holding up the purple roof.
I have often felt and sung,
'It's a good thing to be young:
Though the preacher says it's folly,
Is it foolish to be jolly?'
I have often prayed in fear,
'Let me never grow austere;
Let me never think, I pray,
Too much about Judgement Day;
Never, never feel in Spring,
"Life's a very awful thing!"'
Then I realize and start
And curse my arrogant young heart,
Bind it over to confess
Its horrible ungodliness,
Set myself penances, and sigh
That I was born in sin, and try
To find the whole world vanity.

GHOST MUSIC

Gloomy and bare the organ-loft,
Bent-backed and blind the organist.
From rafters looming shadowy,
From the pipes' tuneful company,
Drifted together drowsily,
Innumerable, formless, dim,
The ghosts of long-dead melodies,
Of anthems, stately, thunderous,
Of Kyries shrill and tremulous:
In melancholy drowsy-sweet
They huddled there in harmony,
Like bats at noontide rafter-hung.

IN SPITE

I now delight,
In spite
Of the might
And the right
Of classic tradition,
In writing
And reciting
Straight ahead,
Without let or omission,
Just any little rhyme
In any little time
That runs in my head;
Because, I've said,
My rhymes no longer shall stand arrayed
Like Prussian soldiers on parade
That march,
Stiff as starch,
Foot to foot,
Boot to boot,
Blade to blade,
Button to button,
Cheeks and chops and chins like mutton.
No! No!
My rhymes must go
Turn 'ee, twist 'ee,
Twinkling, frosty,
Will-o'-the-wisp-like, misty;
Rhymes I will make
Like Keats and Blake
And Christina Rossetti,
With run and ripple and shake.
How petty
To take
A merry little rhyme
In a jolly little time
And poke it,
And choke it,
Change it, arrange it,
Straight-lace it, deface it,
Pleat it with pleats,
Sheet it with sheets
Of empty conceits,

And chop and chew,
And hack and hew,
And weld it into a uniform stanza,
And evolve a neat,
Complacent, complete,
Academic extravaganza!

IN THE WILDERNESS

He, of his gentleness,
Thirsting and hungering
Walked in the wilderness;
Soft words of grace he spoke
Unto lost desert-folk
That listened wondering.
He heard the bittern call
From ruined palace-wall,
Answered him brotherly;
He held communion
With the she-pelican
Of lonely piety.
Basilisk, cockatrice,
Flocked to his homilies,
With mail of dread device,
With monstrous barbèd stings,
With eager dragon-eyes;
Great bats on leathern wings
And old, blind, broken things
Mean in their miseries.
Then ever with him went,
Of all his wanderings
Comrade, with ragged coat,
Gaunt ribs – poor innocent –
Bleeding foot, burning throat,
The guileless young scapegoat:
For forty nights and days
Followed in Jesus' ways,
Sure guard behind him kept,
Tears like a lover wept.

OH, AND OH!

Oh, and oh!
The world's a muddle,
The clouds are untidy,
Moon lopsidey,
Shining in a puddle.
Down dirty streets in stench and smoke
The pale townsfolk
Crawl and kiss and cuddle,
In doorways hug and huddle;
Loutish he
And sluttish she
In loathsome love together press
And unbelievable ugliness.
These spiders spin a loathly woof!
I walk aloof,
Head burning and heart snarling,
Tread feverish quick;
My love is sick;
Far away lives my darling.

CHERRY-TIME

Cherries of the night are riper
    Than the cherries pluckt at noon:
Gather to your fairy piper
    When he pipes his magic tune:
            Merry, merry,
            Take a cherry;
            Mine are sounder,
            Mine are rounder,
            Mine are sweeter
            For the eater
            Under the moon.
And you'll be fairies soon.

In the cherry pluckt at night,
    With the dew of summer swelling,
There's a juice of pure delight,
    Cool, dark, sweet, divinely smelling.
            Merry, merry,

Take a cherry;
Mine are sounder,
Mine are rounder,
Mine are sweeter
For the eater
In the moonlight.
And you'll be fairies quite.

When I sound the fairy call,
Gather here in silent meeting,
Chin to knee on the orchard wall,
Cooled with dew and cherries eating.
Merry, merry,
Take a cherry;
Mine are sounder,
Mine are rounder,
Mine are sweeter
For the eater,
When the dews fall.
And you'll be fairies all.

PART II. – *Poems Written Before La Bassée – 1915*

ON FINDING MYSELF A SOLDIER

My bud was backward to unclose,
    A pretty baby-queen,
Furled petal-tips of creamy rose
    Caught in a clasp of green.

Somehow, I never thought to doubt
    That when her heart should show
She would be coloured in as out,
    Like the flush of dawn on snow:

But yesterday aghast I found,
    Where last I'd left the bud,
Twelve flamy petals ringed around
    A heart more red than blood.

THE SHADOW OF DEATH

Here's an end to my art!
   I must die and I know it,
With battle murder at my heart –
   Sad death for a poet!

Oh my songs never sung,
   And my plays to darkness blown!
I am still so young, so young,
   And life was my own.

Some bad fairy stole
   The baby I nursed:
Was this my pretty little soul,
   This changeling accursed?

To fight and kill is wrong –
   To stay at home wronger:
Oh soul, little play and song,
   I may father no longer!

Here's an end to my art!
   I must die and I know it,
With battle murder at my heart –
   Sad death for a poet!

A RENASCENCE

White flabbiness goes brown and lean,
   Dumpling arms are now brass bars,
They've learnt to suffer and live clean,
   And to think below the stars.

They've steeled a tender, girlish heart,
   Tempered it with a man's pride,
Learning to play the butcher's part
   Though the woman screams inside –

Learning to leap the parapet,
   Face the open rush, and then
To stab with the stark bayonet,
   Side by side with fighting men.

On Achi Baba's rock their bones
    Whiten, and on Flanders' plain,
But of their travailings and groans
    Poetry is born again.

THE MORNING BEFORE THE BATTLE

To-day, the fight: my end is very soon,
    And sealed the warrant limiting my hours:
I knew it walking yesterday at noon
    Down a deserted garden full of flowers.
…Carelessly sang, pinned roses on my breast,
    Reached for a cherry-bunch – and then, then, Death
Blew through the garden from the North and East
    And blighted every beauty with chill breath.

I looked, and ah, my wraith before me stood,
    His head all battered in by violent blows:
The fruit between my lips to clotted blood
    Was transubstantiate, and the pale rose
Smelt sickly, till it seemed through a swift tear-flood
    That dead men blossomed in the garden-close.

LIMBO

After a week spent under raining skies,
    In horror, mud and sleeplessness, a week
Of bursting shells, of blood and hideous cries
    And the ever-watchful sniper: where the reek
Of death offends the living…but poor dead
    Can't sleep, must lie awake with the horrid sound
That roars and whirs and rattles overhead
    All day, all night, and jars and tears the ground;
When rats run, big as kittens: to and fro
    They dart, and scuffle with their horrid fare,
And then one night relief comes, and we go
    Miles back into the sunny cornland where
Babies like tickling, and where tall white horses
Draw the plough leisurely in quiet courses.

THE TRENCHES

(Heard in the Ranks)

Scratches in the dirt?
No, that sounds much too nice.
Oh, far too nice.
Seams, rather, of a Greyback Shirt,
And we're the little lice
Wriggling about in them a week or two,
Till one day, suddenly, from the blue
Something bloody and big will come
Like – watch this fingernail and thumb! –
Squash! and he needs no twice.

NURSERY MEMORIES

I. – THE FIRST FUNERAL

*(The first corpse I saw was on the
German wires, and couldn't be buried)*

The whole field was so smelly;
    We smelt the poor dog first:
His horrid swollen belly
    Looked just like going burst.

His fur was most untidy;
    He hadn't any eyes.
It happened on Good Friday
    And there was lots of flies.

And then I felt the coldest
    I'd ever felt, and sick,
But Rose, 'cause she's the oldest,
    Dared poke him with her stick.

He felt quite soft and horrid:
    The flies buzzed round his head
And settled on his forehead:
    Rose whispered: 'That dog's dead.

'You bury all dead people,
    When they're quite really dead,
Round churches with a steeple:
    Let's bury this,' Rose said.

'And let's put mint all round it
    To hide the nasty smell.'
I went to look and found it –
    Lots, growing near the well.

We poked him through the clover
    Into a hole, and then
We threw brown earth right over
    And said: 'Poor dog, Amen!'

II. – THE ADVENTURE

*(Suggested by the claim of a machine-gun team to have
annihilated an enemy wire party: no bodies were found however)*

To-day I killed a tiger near my shack
Among the trees: at least, it must have been,
Because his hide was yellow, striped with black,
            And his eyes were green.

I crept up close and slung a pointed stone
With all my might: I must have hit his head,
For there he died without a twitch or groan,
            And he lay there dead.

I expect that he'd escaped from a Wild Beast Show
By pulling down his cage with an angry tear;
He'd killed and wounded all the people – so
            He was hiding there.

I brought my brother up as quick's I could
But there was nothing left when he did come:
The tiger's mate was watching in the wood
            And she'd dragged him home.

But, anyhow, I killed him by the shack,
'Cause – listen! – when we hunted in the wood
My brother found my pointed stone all black
    With the clotted blood.

III. – I HATE THE MOON

(After a moonlight patrol near the Brickstacks)

I hate the Moon, though it makes most people glad,
    And they giggle and talk of silvery beams – you know!
But *she* says the look of the Moon drives people mad,
    And that's the thing that always frightens me so.

I hate it worst when it's cruel and round and bright,
    And you can't make out the marks on its stupid face,
Except when you shut your eyelashes, and all night
    The sky looks green, and the world's a horrible place.

I like the stars, and especially the Big Bear
    And the W star, and one like a diamond ring,
But I *hate* the Moon and its horrible stony stare,
    And I know one day it'll do me some dreadful thing.

BIG WORDS

'I've whined of coming death, but now, no more!
It's weak and most ungracious. For, say I,
Though still a boy if years are counted, why!
I've lived those years from roof to cellar-floor,
And feel, like grey-beards touching their fourscore,
Ready, so soon as the need comes, to die:
    And I'm satisfied.
For winning confidence in those quiet days
Of peace, poised sickly on the precipice side
Of Lliwedd crag by Snowdon, and in war
Finding it firmlier with me than before;
Winning a faith in the wisdom of God's ways
That once I lost, finding it justified
Even in this chaos; winning love that stays

And warms the heart like wine at Easter-tide;
    Having earlier tried
False loves in plenty; oh! my cup of praise
Brims over, and I know I'll feel small sorrow,
Confess no sins and make no weak delays
If death ends all and I must die to-morrow.'

But on the firestep, waiting to attack,
He cursed, prayed, sweated, wished the proud words back.

THE DEAD FOX HUNTER

*(In memory of Captain A. L. Samson, 2nd Battalion Royal
Welch Fusiliers, killed near Cuinchy, Sept. 25th, 1915)*

We found the little captain at the head;
    His men lay well aligned.
We touched his hand – stone cold – and he was dead,
    And they, all dead behind,
Had never reached their goal, but they died well;
They charged in line, and in the same line fell.

The well-known rosy colours of his face
    Were almost lost in grey.
We saw that, dying and in hopeless case,
    For others' sake that day
He'd smothered all rebellious groans: in death
His fingers were tight clenched between his teeth.

For those who live uprightly and die true
    Heaven has no bars or locks,
And serves all taste...or what's for him to do
    Up there, but hunt the fox?
Angelic choirs? No, Justice must provide
For one who rode straight and in hunting died.

So if Heaven had no Hunt before he came,
    Why, it must find one now:
If any shirk and doubt they know the game,
    There's one to teach them how:
And the whole host of Seraphim complete
Must jog in scarlet to his opening Meet.

IT'S A QUEER TIME

It's hard to know if you're alive or dead
When steel and fire go roaring through your head.

One moment you'll be crouching at your gun
Traversing, mowing heaps down half in fun:
The next, you choke and clutch at your right breast –
No time to think – leave all – and off you go...
To Treasure Island where the Spice winds blow,
To lovely groves of mango, quince and lime –
Breathe no goodbye, but ho, for the Red West!
          It's a queer time.

You're charging madly at them yelling 'Fag!'
When somehow something gives and your feet drag.
You fall and strike your head; yet feel no pain
And find... you're digging tunnels through the hay
In the Big Barn, 'cause it's a rainy day.
Oh springy hay, and lovely beams to climb!
You're back in the old sailor suit again.
          It's a queer time.

Or you'll be dozing safe in your dug-out –
A great roar – the trench shakes and falls about –
You're struggling, gasping, struggling, then... hullo!
Elsie comes tripping gaily down the trench,
Hanky to nose – that lyddite makes a stench –
Getting her pinafore all over grime.
Funny! because she died ten years ago!
          It's a queer time.

The trouble is, things happen much too quick;
Up jump the Bosches, rifles thump and click,
You stagger, and the whole scene fades away:
Even good Christians don't like passing straight
From Tipperary or their Hymn of Hate
To Alleluiah-chanting, and the chime
Of golden harps ... and... I'm not well to-day...
          It's a queer time.

1915

I've watched the Seasons passing slow, so slow,
In the fields between La Bassée and Béthune;
Primroses and the first warm day of Spring,
Red poppy floods of June,
August, and yellowing Autumn, so
To Winter nights knee-deep in mud or snow,
And you've been everything,

Dear, you've been everything that I most lack
In these soul-deadening trenches – pictures, books,
Music, the quiet of an English wood,
Beautiful comrade-looks,
The narrow, bouldered mountain-track,
The broad, full-bosomed ocean, green and black,
And Peace, and all that's good.

OVER THE BRAZIER

What life to lead and where to go
    After the War, after the War?
    We'd often talked this way before.
But I still see the brazier glow
That April night, still feel the smoke
And stifling pungency of burning coke.

I'd thought: 'A cottage in the hills,
    North Wales, a cottage full of books,
    Pictures and brass and cosy nooks
And comfortable broad window-sills,
Flowers in the garden, walls all white.
I'd live there peacefully and dream and write.'

But Willie said: 'No, Home's no good:
    Old England's quite a hopeless place,
    I've lost all feeling for my race:
But France has given my heart and blood
Enough to last me all my life,
I'm off to Canada with my wee wife.

'Come with us, Mac, old thing,' but Mac
    Drawled: 'No, a Coral Isle for me,
    A warm green jewel in the South Sea.
There's merit in a lumber shack,
And labour is a grand thing...but –
Give me my hot beach and my cocoanut.'

So then we built and stocked for Willie
    His log-hut, and for Mac a calm
    Rock-a-bye cradle on a palm –
Idyllic dwellings – but this silly
Mad War has now wrecked both, and what
Better hopes has my little cottage got?

GOLIATH AND DAVID

(1916)

THE BOUGH OF NONSENSE

(An Idyll)

    Back from the Somme two Fusiliers
    Limped painfully home; the elder said,
S. 'Robert, I've lived three thousand years
    This Summer, and I'm nine parts dead.'
R. 'But if that's truly so,' I cried, 'quick, now,
    Through these great oaks and see the famous bough

    'Where once a nonsense built her nest
    With skulls and flowers and all things queer,
    In an old boot, with patient breast
    Hatching three eggs; and the next year… '
S. 'Foaled thirteen squamous young beneath, and rid
    Wales of drink, melancholy and psalms, she did.'

    Said he, 'Before this quaint mood fails,
    We'll sit and weave a nonsense hymn,'
R. 'Hanging it up with monkey tails
    In a deep grove all hushed and dim…'
S. 'To glorious yellow-bunched banana-trees,'
R. 'Planted in dreams by pious Portuguese,'

S. 'Which men are wise beyond their time,
    And worship nonsense, no one more.'
R. 'Hard by, among old quince and lime,
    They've built a temple with no floor,'
S. 'And whosoever worships in that place
    He disappears from sight and leaves no trace.'

R. 'Once the Galatians built a fane
    To Sense: what duller God than that?'
S. 'But the first day of autumn rain
    The roof fell in and crushed them flat.'
R. 'Ay, for a roof of subtlest logic falls
    When nonsense is foundation for the walls.'

I tell him old Galatian tales;
He caps them in quick Portuguese,
While phantom creatures with green scales
Scramble and roll among the trees.
The hymn swells; on a bough above us sings
A row of bright pink birds, flapping their wings.

GOLIATH AND DAVID

*(For Lieut. David Thomas, 1st Batt. Royal Welch
Fusiliers, killed at Fricourt, March, 1916)*

'If I am Jesse's son,' said he,
'Where must that tall Goliath be?'
For once an earlier David took
Smooth pebbles from the brook:
Out between the lines he went
To that one-sided tournament,
A shepherd boy who stood out fine
And young to fight a Philistine
Clad all in brazen mail. He swears
That he's killed lions, he's killed bears,
And those that scorn the God of Zion
Shall perish so like bear or lion.
But ... the historian of that fight
Had not the heart to tell it right.

Striding within javelin range,
Goliath marvels at this strange
Goodly-faced boy so proud of strength.
David's clear eye measures the length;
With hand thrust back, he cramps one knee,
Poises a moment thoughtfully,
And hurls with a long vengeful swing.
The pebble, humming from the sling
Like a wild bee, flies a sure line
For the forehead of the Philistine;
Then...but there comes a brazen clink,
And quicker than a man can think
Goliath's shield parries each cast,
Clang! clang! And clang! was David's last.

Scorn blazes in the Giant's eye,
Towering unhurt six cubits high.
Says foolish David, 'Curse your shield!
And curse my sling! but I'll not yield.'
He takes his staff of Mamre oak,
A knotted shepherd-staff that's broke
The skull of many a wolf and fox
Come filching lambs from Jesse's flocks.
Loud laughs Goliath, and that laugh
Can scatter chariots like blown chaff
To rout; but David, calm and brave,
Holds his ground, for God will save.
Steel crosses wood, a flash, and oh!
Shame for beauty's overthrow!
(God's eyes are dim, His ears are shut),
One cruel backhand sabre-cut –
'I'm hit! I'm killed!' young David cries,
Throws blindly forward, chokes…and dies.
Steel-helmeted and grey and grim
Goliath straddles over him.

A PINCH OF SALT

When a dream is born in you
    With a sudden clamorous pain,
When you know the dream is true
    And lovely, with no flaw nor stain,
O then, be careful, or with sudden clutch
You'll hurt the delicate thing you prize so much.

Dreams are like a bird that mocks,
    Flirting the feathers of his tail.
When you seize at the salt-box
    Over the hedge you'll see him sail.
Old birds are neither caught with salt nor chaff:
They watch you from the apple bough and laugh.

Poet, never chase the dream.
    Laugh yourself and turn away.
Mask your hunger, let it seem
    Small matter if he come or stay;
But when he nestles in your hand at last,
Close up your fingers tight and hold him fast.

BABYLON

The child alone a poet is:
Spring and Fairyland are his.
Truth and Reason show but dim,
And all's poetry with him.
Rhyme and music flow in plenty
For the lad of one-and-twenty,
But Spring for him is no more now
Than daisies to a munching cow;
Just a cheery pleasant season,
Daisy buds to live at ease on.
He's forgotten how he smiled
And shrieked at snowdrops when a child,
Or wept one evening secretly
For April's glorious misery.
Wisdom made him old and wary
Banishing the Lords of Faery.
Wisdom made a breach and battered
Babylon to bits: she scattered
To the hedges and the ditches
All our nursery gnomes and witches.
Lob and Puck, poor frantic elves,
Drag their treasures from the shelves.
Jack the Giant-killer's gone,
Mother Goose and Oberon,
Bluebeard and King Solomon.
Robin, and Red Riding Hood
Take together to the wood,
And Sir Galahad lies hid
In a cave with Captain Kidd.
None of all the magic hosts,
None remain but a few ghosts
Of timorous heart, to linger on
Weeping for lost Babylon.

CAREERS

Father is quite the greatest poet
    That ever lived anywhere.
You say you're going to write great music –
    I chose that first: it's unfair.
Besides, now I can't be the greatest painter and do
        Christ and angels, or lovely pears and apples
        and grapes on a green dish, or storms at sea,
        or anything lovely,
Because that's been taken by Claire.

It's stupid to be an engine-driver,
    And soldiers are horrible men.
I won't be a tailor, I won't be a sailor,
    And gardener's taken by Ben.
It's unfair if you say that you'll write great music,
        you horrid, you unkind (I simply loathe you,
        though you are my sister), you beast, cad,
        coward, cheat, bully, liar!
Well? Say what's left for me then!

But we won't go to your ugly music.
    (Listen!) Ben will garden and dig,
And Claire will finish her wondrous pictures
    All flaming and splendid and big.
And I'll be a perfectly marvellous carpenter, and I'll
        make cupboards and benches and tables
        and…and baths, and nice wooden boxes
        for studs and money,
And you'll be jealous, you pig!

THE LADY VISITOR IN THE PAUPER WARD

Why do you break upon this old, cool peace,
This painted peace of ours,
With harsh dress hissing like a flock of geese,
With garish flowers?

Why do you churn smooth waters rough again,
Selfish old Skin-and-bone?
Leave us to quiet dreaming and slow pain,
Leave us alone.

THE LAST POST

(On Sick Leave)

The bugler sent a call of high romance –
'Lights out! Lights out!' to the deserted square.
On the thin brazen notes he threw a prayer,
'God, if it's *this* for me next time in France...
O spare the phantom bugle as I lie
Dead in the gas and smoke and roar of guns,
Dead in a row with the other broken ones
Lying so stiff and still under the sky,
Jolly young Fusiliers too good to die.'

A DEAD BOCHE

To you who'd read my songs of War
    And only hear of blood and fame,
I'll say (you've heard it said before)
    'War's Hell!' and if you doubt the same,
To-day I found in Mametz Wood
A certain cure for lust of blood:

Where, propped against a shattered trunk,
    In a great mess of things unclean,
Sat a dead Boche; he scowled and stunk
    With clothes and face a sodden green,
Big-bellied, spectacled, crop-haired,
Dribbling black blood from nose and beard.

ESCAPE

*(August 6th, 1916. – Officer previously reported died of wounds, now
reported wounded. Graves, Captain R., Royal Welch Fusiliers.)*

...But I *was* dead, an hour or more.
I woke when I'd already passed the door
That Cerberus guards, half-way along the road
To Lethe, as an old Greek signpost showed.
Above me, on my stretcher swinging by,
I saw new stars in the subterrene sky:
A Key, a Rose in bloom, a Cage with bars,

And a barbed Arrow feathered in fine stars.
I felt the vapours of forgetfulness
Float in my nostrils. Oh, may Heaven bless
Dear Lady Proserpine, who saw me wake
And, stooping over me, for Henna's sake
Cleared my poor buzzing head and sent me back
Breathless, with leaping heart along the track.
After me roared and clattered angry hosts
Of demons, heroes, and policeman-ghosts.
'Life! life! I can't be dead! I won't be dead!
Damned if I'll die for anyone!' I said....
Cerberus stands and grins above me now,
Wearing three heads – lion, and lynx, and sow.
Quick, a revolver! But my Webley's gone,
Stolen...No bombs...no knife...The crowd swarms on,
Bellows, hurls stones....Not even a honeyed sop...
Nothing....Good Cerberus!...Good dog!...but stop!
Stay!...A great luminous thought...I do believe
There's still some morphia that I bought on leave.
Then swiftly Cerberus' wide mouths I cram
With army biscuit smeared with ration jam;
And sleep lurks in the luscious plum and apple.
He crunches, swallows, stiffens, seems to grapple
With the all-powerful poppy...then a snore,
A crash; the beast blocks up the corridor
With monstrous hairy carcase, red and dun –
Too late! for I've sped through.
                                    O Life! O Sun!

NOT DEAD

Walking through trees to cool my heat and pain,
I know that David's with me here again.
All that is simple, happy, strong, he is.
Caressingly I stroke
Rough bark of the friendly oak.
A brook goes bubbling by: the voice is his.
Turf burns with pleasant smoke;
I laugh at chaffinch and at primroses.
All that is simple, happy, strong, he is.
Over the whole wood in a little while
Breaks his slow smile.

From *FAIRIES AND FUSILIERS*

(1917)

TO AN UNGENTLE CRITIC

The great sun sinks behind the town
Through a red mist of Volnay wine....
But what's the use of setting down
That glorious blaze behind the town?
You'll only skip the page, you'll look
For newer pictures in this book;
You've read of sunsets rich as mine.

A fresh wind fills the evening air
With horrid crying of night birds....
But what reads new or curious there
When cold winds fly across the air?
You'll only frown; you'll turn the page,
But find no glimpse of your 'New Age
Of Poetry' in my worn-out words.

Must winds that cut like blades of steel
And sunsets swimming in Volnay,
The holiest, cruellest pains I feel,
Die stillborn, because old men squeal
For something new: 'Write something new:
We've read this poem – that one too,
And twelve more like 'em yesterday'?

No, no! my chicken, I shall scrawl
Just what I fancy as I strike it,
Fairies and Fusiliers, and all.
Old broken knock-kneed thought will crawl
Across my verse in the classic way.
And, sir, be careful what you say;
There are old-fashioned folk still like it.

THE LEGION

'Is that the Three-and-Twentieth, Strabo mine,
Marching below, and we still gulping wine?'
From the sad magic of his fragrant cup
The red-faced old centurion started up,
Cursed, battered on the table. 'No,' he said,
'Not that! The Three-and-Twentieth Legion's dead,
Dead in the first year of this damned campaign –
The Legion's dead, dead, and won't rise again.
Pity? Rome pities her brave lads that die,
But we need pity also, you and I,
Whom Gallic spear and Belgian arrow miss,
Who live to see the Legion come to this:
Unsoldierlike, slovenly, bent on loot,
Grumblers, diseased, unskilled to thrust or shoot.
O brown cheek, muscled shoulder, sturdy thigh!
Where are they now? God! watch it straggle by,
The sullen pack of ragged, ugly swine!
Is that the Legion, Gracchus? Quick, the wine!'
'Strabo,' said Gracchus, 'you are strange to-night.
The Legion is the Legion, it's all right.
If these new men are slovenly, in your thinking,
Hell take it! you'll not better them by drinking.
They all try, Strabo; trust their hearts and hands.
The Legion is the Legion while Rome stands,
And these same men before the autumn's fall
Shall bang old Vercingetorix out of Gaul.'

TO LUCASTA ON GOING TO THE WARS
– FOR THE FOURTH TIME

It doesn't matter what's the cause,
    What wrong they say we're righting,
A curse for treaties, bonds and laws,
    When we're to do the fighting!
And since we lads are proud and true,
    What else remains to do?
Lucasta, when to France your man
Returns his fourth time, hating war,
Yet laughs as calmly as he can
    And flings an oath, but says no more,

That is not courage, that's not fear –
Lucasta he's a Fusilier,
   And his pride sends him here.

Let statesmen bluster, bark and bray
   And so decide who started
This bloody war, and who's to pay
   But he must be stout-hearted,
Must sit and stake with quiet breath,
   Playing at cards with Death.
Don't plume yourself he fights for you;
It is no courage, love, or hate
That lets us do the things we do;
   It's pride that makes the heart so great;
It is not anger, no, nor fear –
Lucasta he's a Fusilier,
   And his pride keeps him here.

TWO FUSILIERS

And have we done with War at last?
Well, we've been lucky devils both,
And there's no need of pledge or oath
To bind our lovely friendship fast,
By firmer stuff
Close bound enough.

By wire and wood and stake we're bound,
By Fricourt and by Festubert,
By whipping rain, by the sun's glare,
By all the misery and loud sound,
By a Spring day,
By Picard clay.

Show me the two so closely bound
As we, by the wet bond of blood,
By friendship blossoming from mud,
By Death: we faced him, and we found
Beauty in Death,
In dead men, breath.

TO R.N.

(From Frise on the Somme in February 1917, in answer to a letter, saying: 'I am just finishing my "Faun" poem: I wish you were here to feed him with cherries.')

Here by a snow-bound river
In scrapen holes we shiver,
And like old bitterns we
Boom to you plaintively.
Robert, how can I rhyme
Verses at your desire –
Sleek fauns and cherry-time,
Vague music and green trees,
Hot sun and gentle breeze,
England in June attire,
And life born young again,
For your gay goatish brute
Drunk with warm melody
Singing on beds of thyme
With red and rolling eye,
Waking with wanton lute
All the Devonian plain,
Lips dark with juicy stain,
Ears hung with bobbing fruit?
Why should I keep him time?
Why in this cold and rime
Where even to think is pain?
No, Robert, there's no reason;
Cherries are out of season,
Ice grips at branch and root,
And singing birds are mute.

DEAD COW FARM

An ancient saga tells us how
In the beginning the First Cow
(For nothing living yet had birth
But elemental Cow on Earth)
Began to lick cold stones and mud:
Under her warm tongue flesh and blood
Blossomed, a miracle to believe;

And so was Adam born, and Eve.
Here now is chaos once again,
Primaeval mud, cold stones and rain.
Here flesh decays and blood drips red
And the Cow's dead, the old Cow's dead.

MR. PHILOSOPHER

Old Mr. Philosopher
 Comes for Ben and Claire,
An ugly man, a tall man,
 With bright-red hair.

The books that he's written
 No one can read.
'In fifty years they'll understand:
 Now there's no need.

'All that matters now
 Is getting the fun.
Come along, Ben and Claire;
 Plenty to be done.'

Then old Philosopher,
 Wisest man alive,
Plays at Lions and Tigers
 Down along the drive –

Gambolling fiercely
 Through bushes and grass,
Making monstrous mouths,
 Braying like an ass,

Twisting buttercups
 In his orange hair,
Hopping like a kangaroo,
 Growling like a bear.

Right up to tea-time
 They frolic there.
'My legs *are* wingle,'
 Says Ben to Claire.

THE CRUEL MOON

The cruel Moon hangs out of reach
Up above the shadowy beech.
Her face is stupid, but her eye
Is small and sharp and very sly.
Nurse says the Moon can drive you mad?
No, that's a silly story, lad!
Though she be angry, though she would
Destroy all England if she could,
Yet think, what damage can she do
Hanging there so far from you?
Don't heed what frightened nurses say:
Moons hang much too far away.

FINLAND

Feet and faces tingle
    In that frore land:
Legs wobble and go wingle,
    You scarce can stand.

The skies are jewelled all around,
The ploughshare snaps in the iron ground,
The Finn with face like paper
And eyes like a lighted taper
Hurls his rough rune
At the wintry moon
And stamps to mark the tune.

THE CATERPILLAR

Under this loop of honeysuckle,
A creeping, coloured caterpillar,
I gnaw the fresh green hawthorn spray,
I nibble it leaf by leaf away.

Down beneath grow dandelions,
Daisies, old-man's-looking-glasses;
Rooks flap croaking across the lane.
I eat and swallow and eat again.

Here come raindrops helter-skelter;
I munch and nibble unregarding:
Hawthorn leaves are juicy and firm.
I'll mind my business: I'm a good worm.

When I'm old, tired, melancholy,
I'll build a leaf-green mausoleum
Close by, here on this lovely spray,
And die and dream the ages away.

Some say worms win resurrection,
With white wings beating flitter-flutter,
But wings or a sound sleep, why should I care?
Either way I'll not miss my share.

Under this loop of honeysuckle,
A hungry, hairy caterpillar,
I crawl on my high and swinging seat,
And eat, eat, eat – as one ought to eat.

SORLEY'S WEATHER

When outside the icy rain
    Comes leaping helter-skelter,
Shall I tie my restive brain
    Snugly under shelter?

Shall I make a gentle song
    Here in my firelit study,
When outside the winds blow strong
    And the lanes are muddy?

With old wine and drowsy meats
    Am I to fill my belly?
Shall I glutton here with Keats?
    Shall I drink with Shelley?

Tobacco's pleasant, firelight's good:
    Poetry makes both better.
Clay is wet and so is mud,
    Winter rains are wetter.

Yet rest there, Shelley, on the sill,
    For though the winds come frorely
I'm away to the rain-blown hill
    And the ghost of Sorley.

THE COTTAGE

Here in turn succeed and rule
Carter, smith, and village fool,
Then again the place is known
As tavern, shop, and Sunday-school;
Now somehow it's come to me
To light the fire and hold the key,
Here in Heaven to reign alone.

All the walls are white with lime,
Big blue periwinkles climb
And kiss the crumbling window-sill;
Snug inside I sit and rhyme,
Planning poem, book, or fable,
At my darling beech-wood table
Fresh with bluebells from the hill.

Through the window I can see
Rooks above the cherry-tree,
Sparrows in the violet bed,
Bramble-bush and bumble-bee,
And old red bracken smoulders still
Among boulders on the hill,
Far too bright to seem quite dead.

But old Death, who can't forget,
Waits his time and watches yet,
Waits and watches by the door.
Look, he's got a great new net,
And when my fighting starts afresh
Stouter cord and smaller mesh
Won't be cheated as before.

Nor can kindliness of Spring,
Flowers that smile nor birds that sing,
Bumble-bee nor butterfly,
Nor grassy hill nor anything
Of magic keep me safe to rhyme
In this Heaven beyond my time.
No! for Death is waiting by.

WHEN I'M KILLED

When I'm killed, don't think of me
Buried there in Cambrin Wood,
Nor as in Zion think of me
With the Intolerable Good.
And there's one thing that I know well,
I'm damned if I'll be damned to Hell!

So when I'm killed, don't wait for me,
Walking the dim corridor;
In Heaven or Hell, don't wait for me,
Or you must wait for evermore.
You'll find me buried, living-dead
In these verses that you've read.

So when I'm killed, don't mourn for me,
Shot, poor lad, so bold and young,
Killed and gone – don't mourn for me.
On your lips my life is hung:
O friends and lovers, you can save
Your playfellow from the grave.

FAMILIAR LETTER TO SIEGFRIED SASSOON

(From Bivouacs at Mametz Wood, July 13th, 1916)

I never dreamed we'd meet that day
In our old haunts down Fricourt way,
Plotting such marvellous journeys there
For golden-houred 'Après-la-guerre.'

Well, when it's over, first we'll meet
At Gweithdy Bach, my country seat
In Wales, a curious little shop
With two rooms and a roof on top,
A sort of Morlancourt-ish billet
That never needs a crowd to fill it.
But oh, the country round about!
The sort of view that makes you shout
For want of any better way
Of praising God: there's a blue bay
Shining in front, and on the right
Snowdon and Hebog capped with white,
And lots of other mountain peaks
That you could wonder at for weeks,
With jag and spur and hump and cleft.
There's a grey castle on the left,
And back in the high hinterland
You'll see the grave of Shawn Knarlbrand
Who slew the savage Buffaloon
By the Nant-col one night in June,
And won his surname from the horn
Of this prodigious unicorn.
Beyond, where the two Rhinogs tower,
Rhinog Fach and Rhinog Fawr,
Close there after a four years' chase
From Thessaly and the woods of Thrace,
The beaten Dog-cat stood at bay
And growled and fought and passed away.
You'll see where mountain conies grapple
With prayer and creed in their rock chapel
Which three young children once built for them;
They call it Söar Bethlehem.
You'll see where in old Roman days,
Before Revivals changed our ways,
The Virgin 'scaped the Devil's grab,
Printing her foot on a stone slab
With five clear toe-marks; and you'll find
The fiendish thumb-print close behind.
You'll see where Math, Mathonwy's son,
Spoke with the wizard Gwydion
And bade him for South Wales set out
To steal that creature with the snout,
That new-discovered grunting beast
Divinely flavoured for the feast.

No traveller yet has hit upon
A wilder land than Meirion,
For desolate hills and tumbling stones,
Bogland and melody and old bones.
Fairies and ghosts are here galore,
And poetry most splendid, more
Than can be written with the pen
Or understood by common men.

In Gweithdy Bach we'll rest a while,
We'll dress our wounds and learn to smile
With easier lips; we'll stretch our legs,
And live on bilberry tart and eggs,
And store up solar energy,
Basking in sunshine by the sea,
Until we feel a match once more
For *anything* but another war.
So then we'll kiss our families,
And sail away across the seas
(The God of Song protecting us)
To the great hills of Caucasus.
Robert will learn the local *bat*
For billeting and things like that,
If Siegfried learns the piccolo
To charm the people as we go.
The simple peasants clad in furs
Will greet the foreign officers
With open arms, and ere they pass
Will make them tuneful with Kavasse.
In old Bagdad we'll call a halt
At the Sashuns' ancestral vault;
We'll catch the Persian rose-flowers' scent,
And understand what Omar meant.
Bitlis and Mush will know our faces,
Tiflis and Tomsk, and all such places.
Perhaps eventually we'll get
Among the Tartars of Thibet,
Hobnobbing with the Chungs and Mings,
And doing wild, tremendous things
In free adventure, quest and fight,
And God! what poetry we'll write!

FAUN

Here down this very way,
Here only yesterday
    King Faun went leaping.
He sang, with careless shout
Hurling his name about;
He sang, with oaken stock
His steps from rock to rock
    In safety keeping,
        'Here Faun is free,
        Here Faun is free!'

To-day against yon pine,
Forlorn yet still divine,
    King Faun leant weeping.
'They drank my holy brook,
My strawberries they took,
My private path they trod.'
Loud wept the desolate God,
    Scorn on scorn heaping,
        'Faun, what is he,
        Faun, what is he?'

THE SPOILSPORT

My familiar ghost again
    Comes to see what he can see,
Critic, son of Conscious Brain,
    Spying on our privacy.

Slam the window, bolt the door,
    Yet he'll enter in and stay;
In to-morrow's book he'll score
    Indiscretions of to-day.

Whispered love and muttered fears,
    How their echoes fly about!
None escape his watchful ears,
    Every sigh might be a shout.

No kind words nor angry cries
    Turn away this grim spoilsport;
No fine lady's pleading eyes,
    Neither love, nor hate, nor...port.

Critic wears no smile of fun,
    Speaks no word of blame nor praise,
Counts our kisses one by one,
    Notes each gesture, every phrase.

My familiar ghost again
    Stands or squats where suits him best;
Critic, son of Conscious Brain,
    Listens, watches, takes no rest.

THE SHIVERING BEGGAR

Near Clapham village, where fields began,
Saint Edward met a beggar man.
It was Christmas morning, the church bells tolled,
The old man trembled for the fierce cold.

Saint Edward cried, 'It is monstrous sin
A beggar to lie in rags so thin!
An old grey-beard and the frost so keen:
I shall give him my fur-lined gaberdine.'

He stripped off his gaberdine of scarlet
And wrapped it round the aged varlet,
Who clutched at the folds with a muttered curse,
Quaking and chattering seven times worse.

Said Edward, 'Sir, it would seem you freeze
Most bitter at your extremities.
Here are gloves and shoes and stockings also,
That warm upon your way you may go.'

The man took stocking and shoe and glove,
Blaspheming Christ our Saviour's love,
Yet seemed to find but little relief,
Shaking and shivering like a leaf.

Said the saint again, 'I have no great riches,
Yet take this tunic, take these breeches,
My shirt and my vest, take everything,
And give due thanks to Jesus the King.'

The saint stood naked upon the snow
Long miles from where he was lodged at Bowe,
Praying, 'O God! my faith, it grows faint!
This would try the temper of any saint.

'Make clean my heart, Almighty, I pray,
And drive these sinful thoughts away.
Make clean my heart if it be Thy will,
This damned old rascal's shivering still!'

He stooped, he touched the beggar man's shoulder;
He asked him did the frost nip colder?
'Frost!' said the beggar, 'no, stupid lad!
'Tis the palsy makes me shiver so bad.'

JONAH

A purple whale
Proudly sweeps his tail
Towards Nineveh;
Glassy green
Surges between
A mile of roaring sea.

'O town of gold,
Of splendour multifold,
Lucre and lust,
Leviathan's eye
Can surely spy
Thy doom of death and dust.'

On curving sands
Vengeful Jonah stands.
'Yet forty days,
Then down, down,
Tumbles the town
In flaming ruin ablaze.'

With swift lament
Those Ninevites repent.
They cry in tears,
'Our hearts fail!
The whale, the whale!
Our sins prick us like spears.'

Jonah is vexed;
He cries, 'What next? what next?'
And shakes his fist.
'Stupid city,
The shame, the pity,
The glorious crash I've missed.'

Away goes Jonah grumbling,
Murmuring and mumbling;
Off ploughs the purple whale,
With disappointed tail.

JOHN SKELTON

What could be dafter
Than John Skelton's laughter?
What sound more tenderly
Than his pretty poetry?
So where to rank old Skelton?
He was no monstrous Milton,
Nor wrote no *Paradise Lost*,
So wondered at by most,
Phrased so disdainfully,
Composed so painfully.
He struck what Milton missed,
Milling an English grist
With homely turn and twist.
He was English through and through,
Not Greek, nor French, nor Jew,
Though well their tongues he knew,
The living and the dead:
Learned Erasmus said,
Hic, unum Britannicarum
Lumen et decus literarum.
But oh, Colin Clout!

How his pen flies about,
Twiddling and turning,
Scorching and burning,
Thrusting and thrumming!
How it hurries with humming,
Leaping and running,
At the tipsy-topsy Tunning
Of Mistress Eleanor Rumming!
How for poor Philip Sparrow
Was murdered at Carow,
How our hearts he does harrow!
Jest and grief mingle
In this jangle-jingle,
For he will not stop
To sweep nor mop,
To prune nor prop,
To cut each phrase up
Like beef when we sup,
Nor sip at each line
As at brandy-wine,
Or port when we dine.
But angrily, wittily,
Tenderly, prettily,
Laughingly, learnedly,
Sadly, madly,
Helter-skelter John
Rhymes serenely on,
As English poets should.
Old John, you do me good!

I WONDER WHAT IT FEELS LIKE TO BE DROWNED?

Look at my knees,
That island rising from the steamy seas!
The candle's a tall lightship; my two hands
Are boats and barges anchored to the sands,
With mighty cliffs all round;
They're full of wine and riches from far lands....
I wonder what it feels like to be drowned?

I can make caves,
By lifting up the island and huge waves
And storms, and then with head and ears well under
Blow bubbles with a monstrous roar like thunder,
A bull-of-Bashan sound.
The seas run high and the boats split asunder....
I wonder what it feels like to be drowned?

The thin soap slips
And slithers like a shark under the ships.
My toes are on the soap-dish – that's the effect
Of my huge storms; an iron steamer's wrecked.
The soap slides round and round;
He's biting the old sailors, I expect....
I wonder what it feels like to be drowned?

DOUBLE RED DAISIES

Double red daisies, they're my flowers,
    Which nobody else may grow.
In a big quarrelsome house like ours
    They try it sometimes – but no,
I root them up because they're my flowers,
    Which nobody else may grow.

Claire has a tea-rose, but she didn't plant it;
Ben has an iris, but I don't want it.
Daisies, double red daisies for me,
The beautifulest flowers in the garden.

Double red daisy, that's my mark:
    I paint it in all my books!
It's carved high up on the beech-tree bark,
    How neat and lovely it looks!
So don't forget that it's my trade mark;
    Don't copy it in your books.

Claire has a tea-rose, but she didn't plant it;
Ben has an iris, but I don't want it.
Daisies, double red daisies for me,
The beautifulest flowers in the garden.

I'D LOVE TO BE A FAIRY'S CHILD

Children born of fairy stock
Never need for shirt or frock,
Never want for food or fire,
Always get their heart's desire:
Jingle pockets full of gold,
Marry when they're seven years old.
Every fairy child may keep
Two strong ponies and ten sheep;
All have houses, each his own,
Built of brick or granite stone;
They live on cherries, they run wild –
I'd love to be a fairy's child.

THE NEXT WAR

You young friskies who to-day
Jump and fight in Father's hay
With bows and arrows and wooden spears,
Playing at Royal Welch Fusiliers,
Happy though these hours you spend,
Have they warned you how games end?
Boys, from the first time you prod
And thrust with spears of curtain-rod,
From the first time you tear and slash
Your long-bows from the garden ash,
Or fit your shaft with a blue jay feather,
Binding the split tops together,
From that same hour by fate you're bound
As champions of this stony ground,
Loyal and true in everything,
To serve your Army and your King,
Prepared to starve and sweat and die
Under some fierce foreign sky,
If only to keep safe those joys
That belong to British boys,
To keep young Prussians from the soft
Scented hay of Father's loft,
And stop young Slavs from cutting bows
And bendy spears from Welsh hedgerows.
    Another War soon gets begun,
A dirtier, a more glorious one;

Then, boys, you'll have to play, all in;
It's the cruellest team will win.
So hold your nose against the stink
And never stop too long to think.
Wars don't change except in name;
The next one must go just the same,
And new foul tricks unguessed before
Will win and justify this War.
Kaisers and Czars will strut the stage
Once more with pomp and greed and rage;
Courtly ministers will stop
At home and fight to the last drop;
By the million men will die
In some new horrible agony;
And children here will thrust and poke,
Shoot and die, and laugh at the joke,
With bows and arrows and wooden spears,
Playing at Royal Welch Fusiliers.

STRONG BEER

'What do you think
The bravest drink
Under the sky?'
'Strong beer,' said I.

'There's a place for everything,
Everything, anything,
There's a place for everything
Where it ought to be:
For a chicken, the hen's wing;
For poison, the bee's sting;
For almond-blossom, Spring;
A beerhouse for me.

'There's a prize for everyone,
Everyone, anyone,
There's a prize for everyone,
Whoever he may be:
Crags for the mountaineer,
Flags for the Fusilier,
For all good fellows, beer!
Strong beer for me!'

'Tell us, now, how and when
We may find the bravest men?'
'A sure test, an easy test:
Those that drink beer are the best,
Brown beer strongly brewed,
Plain man's drink, plain man's food.'

Oh, never choose as Gideon chose
By the cold well, but rather those
Who look on beer when it is brown,
Smack their lips and gulp it down.
Leave the lads who tamely drink
With Gideon by the water brink,
But search the benches of the Plough,
The Tun, the Sun, the Spotted Cow,
For jolly rascal lads who pray,
Pewter in hand, at close of day,
'Teach me to live that I may fear
The grave as little as my beer.'

MARIGOLDS

With a fork drive Nature out,
    She will ever yet return;
Hedge the flower bed all about,
    Pull or stab or cut or burn,
    She will ever yet return.

Look: the constant marigold
    Springs again from hidden roots.
Baffled gardener, you behold
    New beginnings and new shoots
    Spring again from hidden roots.
    Pull or stab or cut or burn,
    They will ever yet return.

Gardener, cursing at the weed,
    Ere you curse it further, say:
Who but you planted the seed
    In my fertile heart, one day?
    Ere you curse me further, say!
    New beginnings and new shoots

Spring again from hidden roots.
Pull or stab or cut or burn,
Love must ever yet return.

LOVE AND BLACK MAGIC

To the woods, to the woods is the wizard gone;
In his grotto the maiden sits alone.
She gazes up with a weary smile
At the rafter-hanging crocodile,
The slowly swinging crocodile.
Scorn has she of her master's gear,
Cauldron, alembic, crystal sphere,
Phial, philtre – 'Fiddlededee
For all such trumpery trash!' quo' she.
'A soldier is the lad for me;
Hey and hither, my lad!

'Oh, here have I ever lain forlorn:
My father died ere I was born,
Mother was by a wizard wed,
And oft I wish I had died instead –
Often I wish I were long time dead.
But, delving deep in my master's lore,
I have won of magic power such store
I can turn a skull – oh, fiddlededee
For all this curious craft!' quo' she.
'A soldier is the lad for me;
Hey and hither, my lad!

'To bring my brave boy unto my arms,
What need have I of magic charms –
"Abracadabra!" and "Prestopuff"?
I have but to wish, and that is enough.
The charms are vain, one wish is enough.
My master pledged my hand to a wizard;
Transformed would I be to toad or lizard
If e'er he guessed – but fiddlededee
For a black-browed sorcerer, now,' quo' she.
'Let Cupid smile and the fiend must flee;
Hey and hither, my lad.'

SMOKE-RINGS

Boy: Most venerable and learned sir,
                Tall and true Philosopher,
                These rings of smoke you blow all day
                With such deep thought, what sense have they?

Philosopher: Small friend, with prayer and meditation
                I make an image of Creation.
                And if your mind is working nimble
                Straightway you'll recognize a symbol
                Of the endless and eternal ring
                Of God, who girdles everything –
                God, who in His own form and plan
                Moulds the fugitive life of man.
                These vaporous toys you watch me make,
                That shoot ahead, pause, turn and break –
                Some glide far out like sailing ships,
                Some weak ones fail me at my lips.
                He who ringed His awe in smoke,
                When He led forth His captive folk,
                In like manner, East, West, North, and South,
                Blows us ring-wise from His mouth.

A CHILD'S NIGHTMARE

Through long nursery nights he stood
By my bed unwearying,
Loomed gigantic, formless, queer,
Purring in my haunted ear
That same hideous nightmare thing,
Talking, as he lapped my blood,
In a voice cruel and flat,
Saying for ever, 'Cat!…Cat!…Cat!…'

That one word was all he said,
That one word through all my sleep,
In monotonous mock despair.
Nonsense may be light as air,
But there's Nonsense that can keep
Horror bristling round the head,
When a voice cruel and flat
Says for ever, 'Cat!…Cat!…Cat!…'

He had faded, he was gone
Years ago with Nursery Land,
When he leapt on me again
From the clank of a night train,
Overpowered me foot and hand,
Lapped my blood, while on and on
The old voice cruel and flat
Purred for ever, 'Cat!…Cat!…Cat!…'

Morphia drowsed, again I lay
In a crater by High Wood:
He was there with straddling legs,
Staring eyes as big as eggs,
Purring as he lapped my blood,
His black bulk darkening the day,
With a voice cruel and flat,
'Cat!…Cat!…Cat!…' he said,
          'Cat!…Cat!…'

When I'm shot through heart and head,
And there's no choice but to die,
The last word I'll hear, no doubt,
Won't be 'Charge!' or 'Bomb them out!'
Nor the stretcher-bearer's cry,
'Let that body be, he's dead!'
But a voice cruel and flat
Saying for ever, 'Cat!…Cat!…Cat!'

A BOY IN CHURCH

'Gabble-gabble,...brethren,...gabble-gabble!'
  My window frames forest and heather.
I hardly hear the tuneful babble,
  Not knowing nor much caring whether
The text is praise or exhortation,
Prayer or thanksgiving, or damnation.

Outside it blows wetter and wetter,
  The tossing trees never stay still.
I shift my elbows to catch better
  The full round sweep of heathered hill.
The tortured copse bends to and fro
In silence like a shadow-show.

The parson's voice runs like a river
  Over smooth rocks. I like this church:
The pews are staid, they never shiver,
  They never bend or sway or lurch.
'Prayer,' says the kind voice, 'is a chain
That draws down Grace from Heaven again.'

I add the hymns up, over and over,
  Until there's not the least mistake.
Seven-seventy-one. (Look! there's a plover!
  It's gone!) Who's that Saint by the lake?
The red light from his mantle passes
Across the broad memorial brasses.

It's pleasant here for dreams and thinking,
  Lolling and letting reason nod,
With ugly serious people linking
  Sad prayers to a forgiving God....
But a dumb blast sets the trees swaying
With furious zeal like madmen praying.

CORPORAL STARE

Back from the Line one night in June
I gave a dinner at Béthune:
Seven courses, the most gorgeous meal
Money could buy or batman steal.
Five hungry lads welcomed the fish
With shouts that nearly cracked the dish;
Asparagus came with tender tops,
Strawberries in cream, and mutton chops.
Said Jenkins, as my hand he shook,
'They'll put this in the history book.'
We bawled Church anthems *in choro*
Of Bethlehem and Hermon snow,
And drinking songs, a mighty sound
To help the good red Pommard round.
Stories and laughter interspersed,
We drowned a long La Bassée thirst –
Trenches in June make throats damned dry.
Then through the window suddenly,
Badge, stripes and medals all complete,
We saw him swagger up the street,
Just like a live man – Corporal Stare!

Stare! Killed last month at Festubert,
Caught on patrol near the Boche wire,
Torn horribly by machine-gun fire!
He paused, saluted smartly, grinned,
Then passed away like a puff of wind,
Leaving us blank astonishment.
The song broke, up we started, leant
Out of the window – nothing there,
Not the least shadow of Corporal Stare,
Only a quiver of smoke that showed
A fag-end dropped on the silent road.

'THE ASSAULT HEROIC'

Down in the mud I lay,
Tired out by my long day
Of five damned days and nights,
Five sleepless days and nights,...
Dream snatched, and set me where
The dungeon of Despair
Looms over Desolate Sea,
Frowning and threatening me
With aspect high and steep –
A most malignant keep.
My foes that lay within
Shouted and made a din,
Hooted and grinned and cried:
'To-day we've killed your pride;
To-day your ardour ends.
We've murdered all your friends;
We've undermined by stealth
Your happiness and your health.
We've taken away your hope;
Now you may droop and mope
To misery and to death.'
But with my spear of faith,
Stout as an oaken rafter,
With my round shield of laughter,
With my sharp, tongue-like sword
That speaks a bitter word,
I stood beneath the wall
And there defied them all.
The stones they cast I caught
And alchemized with thought
Into such lumps of gold
As dreaming misers hold.
The boiling oil they threw
Fell in a shower of dew,
Refreshing me; the spears
Flew harmless by my ears,
Struck quivering in the sod;
There, like the prophet's rod,
Put leaves out, took firm root,
And bore me instant fruit.
My foes were all astounded,
Dumbstricken and confounded,

Gaping in a long row;
They dared not thrust nor throw.
Thus, then, I climbed a steep
Buttress and won the keep,
And laughed and proudly blew
My horn, *'Stand to! Stand to!*
Wake up, sir! Here's a new
Attack! Stand to! Stand to!'

From *TREASURE BOX*

(1919)

SONG: A PHOENIX FLAME

In my heart a phoenix flame
    Darts and scorches me all day –
Should a fierce sun do the same,
    I die away.

O for pools with sunken rocks,
    Minnow-haunted mountain brooks,
Blustering gales of Equinox,
    Cold, green nooks.

Who could boast a careless wit,
    Doubly roasted, heart and hide,
Turning on the Sun's red spit,
    Consumed inside?

CATHERINE DRURY

Mother: Edward will not taste his food,
        Nor touch his drink,
    Flings me answers gruff and rude:
        Why, I dare not think.

Sister: Mother, do not try to know
    All that moves in Edward's heart,
    The fiery gloom he will not show;
    You and he who lay so near
        Fall wide apart.
    Watch your rival, mother dear:
    Catherine Drury does not guess
    His dark love or your envious fear,
        Her own loveliness.
    She will laugh, she will play,

Never know the hurt she does:
Edward's heart will melt away,
　　His head go buzz,
And if he thinks you read his mind,
Better you had been struck stone blind.

THE TREASURE BOX

Ann in chill moonlight unlocks
Her polished brassbound treasure-box,
Draws a soft breath, prepares to spread
The toys around her on the bed.
She dips for luck: by luck pulls out
A silver pig with ring in snout,
The sort that Christmas puddings yield;
Next comes a painted nursery shield
Boy-carved; and then two yellow gloves,
A Limerick wonder that Ann loves,
Leather so thin and sewn so well
The pair fold in a walnut shell;
Here's patchwork that her sister made
With antique silk and flower brocade,
Small faded scraps in memory rich
Joined each to each with feather-stitch;
Here's cherry and forget-me-not
Ribbon bunched in a great knot;
A satin purse with pansies on it;
A Tudor baby's christening bonnet;
Old Mechlin lace minutely knit
(Some woman's eyes went blind for it);
And Spanish broideries that pinch
Three blossomed rosetrees to one inch;
Here are Ann's brooches, simple pins,
A Comet brooch, two Harlequins,
A Posy; here's a great resplendent
Dove-in-bush Italian pendant;
A Chelsea gift-bird; a toy whistle;
A halfpenny stamped with the Scots thistle;
A Breguet watch; a coral string;
Her mother's thin-worn wedding ring;
A straw box full of hard smooth sweets;
A book, the *Poems of John Keats*;

A chessman; a pink paper rose;
A diary dwindling to its close
Nine months ago; a worsted ball;
A patchbox; a stray match – that's all,
All but a few small treasured scraps
Of paper; things forbid perhaps –
See how slowly Ann unties
The packet where her heartache lies;
Watch her lips move; she slants a letter
Up towards the moon to read it better,
(The moon may master what he can).
R stands for Richard, A for Ann
And L… at this the old moon blinks
And softly from the window shrinks.

THE KISS

Are you shaken, are you stirred
    By a whisper of love,
Spellbound to a word
    Does Time cease to move,
Till her calm grey eye
    Expands to a sky
And the clouds of her hair
    Like storms go by?

Then the lips that you have kissed
    Turn to frost and fire,
And a white-steaming mist
    Obscures desire:
So back to their birth
    Fade water, air, earth,
And the First Power moves
    Over void and dearth.

Is that Love? no, but Death,
   A passion, a shout,
The deep in-breath,
   The breath roaring out,
And once that is flown,
   You must lie alone,
Without hope, without life,
   Poor flesh, sad bone.

LOST LOVE

His eyes are quickened so with grief,
He can watch a grass or leaf
Every instant grow; he can
Clearly through a flint wall see,
Or watch the startled spirit flee
From the throat of a dead man.
   Across two counties he can hear
And catch your words before you speak.
The woodlouse or the maggot's weak
Clamour rings in his sad ear,
And noise so slight it would surpass
Credence – drinking sound of grass,
Worm talk, clashing jaws of moth
Chumbling holes in cloth;
The groan of ants who undertake
Gigantic loads for honour's sake
(Their sinews creak, their breath comes thin);
Whir of spiders when they spin,
And minute whispering, mumbling, sighs
Of idle grubs and flies.
   This man is quickened so with grief,
He wanders god-like or like thief
Inside and out, below, above,
Without relief seeking lost love.

FOX'S DINGLE

Take now a country mood,
    Resolve, distil it: –
Nine Acre swaying alive,
    June flowers that fill it,

Spicy sweet-briar bush,
    The uneasy wren
Fluttering from ash to birch
    And back again,

Milkwort on its low stem,
    Spread hawthorn tree,
Sunlight patching the wood,
    A hive-bound bee....

Girls riding nim-nim-nim,
    Ladies, trot-trot,
Gentlemen hard at gallop,
    Shouting, steam-hot.

Now over the rough turf
    Bridles go jingle,
And there's a well loved pool,
    By Fox's Dingle,

Where Sweetheart, my brown mare,
    Old Glory's daughter,
May loll her leathern tongue
    In snow-cool water.

MIRROR, MIRROR!

Mirror, Mirror, tell me,
    Am I pretty or plain?
Or am I downright ugly
    And ugly to remain?

Shall I marry a gentleman?
    Shall I marry a clown?
Or shall I marry old Knives-and-Scissors
    Shouting through the town?

COUNTRY SENTIMENT

(1920)

A FROSTY NIGHT

'Alice, dear, what ails you,
　　Dazed and lost and shaken?
Has the chill night numbed you?
　　Is it fright you have taken?'

'Mother, I am very well,
　　I was never better.
Mother, do not hold me so,
　　Let me write my letter.'

'Sweet, my dear, what ails you?'
　　'No, but I am well.
The night was cold and frosty –
　　There's no more to tell.'

'Ay, the night was frosty,
　　Coldly gaped the moon,
Yet the birds seemed twittering
　　Through green boughs of June.

'Soft and thick the snow lay,
　　Stars danced in the sky –
Not all the lambs of May-day
　　Skip so bold and high.

'Your feet were dancing, Alice,
　　Seemed to dance on air,
You looked a ghost or angel
　　In the star-light there.

'Your eyes were frosted star-light;
　　Your heart, fire and snow.
Who was it said, "I love you"?'
　　'Mother, let me go!'

A SONG FOR TWO CHILDREN

'Make a song, father, make a new song,
    All for Jenny and Davey.'
Balow lalow or *Hey derry down*,
    Or *The Dog that Licked the Gravy*?

Is there any song sweet enough
    For Davey and for Jenny?
Said Simple Simon to the pieman,
    'Indeed I know not any.

'I've counted the miles to Babylon,
    I've flown the earth like a bird,
I've ridden cock-horse to Banbury Cross,
    But no such song have I heard.'

Some speak of Alexander,
    And some of Hercules,
But where are there any like Davey and Jenny,
    Where are there any like these?

DICKY

Mother: Oh, what a heavy sigh!
                Dicky, are you ailing?
Dicky: Even by this fireside, mother,
                My heart is failing.

            To-night, across the down,
                Whistling and jolly,
            I sauntered out from town
                With my stick of holly.

            Bounteous and cool from sea
                The wind was blowing,
            Cloud shadows under the moon
                Coming and going.

I sang old roaring songs,
    Ran and leaped quick,
And turned home by St. Swithin's
    Twirling my stick.

And there as I was passing
    The churchyard gate,
An old man stopped me, 'Dicky,
    You're walking late.'

I did not know the man,
    I grew afeared
At his lean, lolling jaw,
    His spreading beard,

His garments old and musty,
    Of antique cut,
His body very lean and bony,
    His eyes tight shut.

Oh, even to tell it now
    My courage ebbs...
His face was clay, mother,
    His beard, cobwebs.

In that long horrid pause
    'Good-night,' he said,
Entered and clicked the gate,
    'Each to his bed.'

Mother: Do not sigh or fear, Dicky.
    How is it right
To grudge the dead their ghostly dark
    And wan moonlight?

We have the glorious sun,
    Lamp and fireside.
Grudge not the dead their moon-beams
    When abroad they ride.

THE THREE DRINKERS

Blacksmith Green had three strong sons,
    With bread and beef did fill 'em,
Now John and Ned are perished and dead,
    But plenty remains of William.

John Green was a whiskey drinker,
    The Land of Cakes supplied him,
Till at last his soul flew out by the hole
    That the fierce drink burned inside him.

Ned Green was a water drinker,
    And, Lord, how Ned would fuddle!
He rotted away his mortal clay
    Like an old boot thrown in a puddle.

Will Green was a wise young drinker,
    Shrank from whiskey or water,
But he made good cheer with headstrong beer,
    And married an alderman's daughter.

THE BOY OUT OF CHURCH

As Jesus and his followers
    Upon a Sabbath morn
Were walking by a wheat field
    They plucked the ears of corn.

They plucked it, they rubbed it,
    They blew the husks away,
Which grieved the pious Pharisees
    Upon the Sabbath day.

And Jesus said, 'A riddle
    Answer if you can,
Was man made for the Sabbath
    Or Sabbath made for man?'

I do not love the Sabbath,
    The soapsuds and the starch,
The troops of solemn people
    Who to Salvation march.

I take my book, I take my stick
  On the Sabbath day,
In woody nooks and valleys
  I hide myself away,

To ponder there in quiet
  God's Universal Plan,
Resolved that church and Sabbath
  Were never made for man.

AFTER THE PLAY

Father: Have you spent the money I gave you to-day?
John: Ay, father I have.
         A fourpence on cakes, two pennies that away
             To a beggar I gave.

Father: The lake of yellow brimstone boil for you in Hell,
             Such lies that you spin.
         Tell the truth now, John, ere the falsehood swell,
             Say, where have you been?

John: I'll lie no more to you, father, what is the need?
             To the Play I went,
         With sixpence for a near seat, money's worth indeed,
             The best ever spent.

       Grief to you, shame or grief, here is the story –
             My splendid night!
       It was colour, scents, music, a tragic glory,
             Fear with delight.

       Hamlet, Prince of Denmark, title of the tale:
             He of that name,
       A tall, glum fellow, velvet cloaked, with a shirt of mail,
             Two eyes like flame.

       All the furies of fate circled round the man,
             Maddening his heart,
       There was old murder done before play began,
             Ay, the ghost took part.

There were grave-diggers delving, they brought up bones,
        And with rage and grief
All the players shouted in full, kingly tones,
        Grand, passing belief.

Oh, there were ladies there radiant like day,
        And changing scenes:
Great sounding words were tossed about like hay
        By kings and queens.

How the plot turned about I watched in vain,
        Though for grief I cried,
As one and all they faded, poisoned or slain,
        In great agony died.

Father, you'll drive me forth never to return,
        Doubting me your son –
Father: So I shall, John.
John: – but that glory for which I burn
        Shall be soon begun.

I shall wear great boots, shall strut and shout,
        Keep my locks curled.
The fame of my name shall go ringing about
        Over half the world.

Father: Horror that your Prince found, John, may you find,
        Ever and again
Dying before the house in such torture of mind
        As you need not feign.

While they clap and stamp at your nightly fate,
        They shall never know
The curse that drags at you, until Hell's gate.
        You have heard me. Go!

ONE HARD LOOK

Small gnats that fly
In hot July
And lodge in sleeping ears,
Can rouse therein
A trumpet's din
With Day of Judgement fears.

Small mice at night
Can wake more fright
Than lions at midday;
A straw will crack
The camel's back –
There is no easier way.

One smile relieves
A heart that grieves
Though deadly sad it be,
And one hard look
Can close the book
That lovers love to see.

TRUE JOHNNY

Johnny, sweetheart, can you be true
To all those famous vows you've made?
Will you love me as I love you
Until we both in earth are laid?
Or shall the old wives nod and say
'His love was only for a day:
    The mood goes by,
    His fancies fly,
And Mary's left to sigh'?

Mary, alas, you've hit the truth,
And I with grief can but admit
Hot-blooded haste controls my youth,
My idle fancies veer and flit
From flower to flower, from tree to tree,
And when the moment catches me,
   Oh, love goes by
   Away I fly
And leave my girl to sigh.

Could you but now foretell the day,
Johnny, when this sad thing must be,
When light and gay you'll turn away
And laugh and break the heart in me?
For like a nut for true love's sake
My empty heart shall crack and break,
   When fancies fly
   And love goes by
And Mary's left to die.

When the sun turns against the clock,
When Avon waters upward flow,
When eggs are laid by barn-door cock,
When dusty hens do strut and crow,
When up is down, when left is right,
Oh, then I'll break the troth I plight,
   With careless eye
   Away I'll fly
And Mary here shall die.

THE VOICE OF BEAUTY DROWNED

Cry from the thicket my heart's bird!
The other birds woke all around,
Rising with toot and howl they stirred
Their plumage, broke the trembling sound,
They craned their necks, they fluttered wings,
'While we are silent no one sings,
And while we sing you hush your throat,
Or tune your melody to our note.'

Cry from the thicket my heart's bird!
The screams and hootings rose again:
They gaped with raucous beaks, they whirred
Their noisy plumage; small but plain
The lonely hidden singer made
A well of grief within the glade.
'Whist, silly fool, be off,' they shout,
'Or we'll come pluck your feathers out.'

Cry from the thicket my heart's bird!
Slight and small the lovely cry
Came trickling down, but no one heard.
Parrot and cuckoo, crow, magpie
Jarred horrid notes, the jangling jay
Ripped the fine threads of song away,
For why should peeping chick aspire
To challenge their loud woodland choir?

Cried it so sweet that unseen bird?
Lovelier could no music be,
Clearer than water, soft as curd,
Fresh as the blossomed cherry tree.
How sang the others all around?
Piercing and harsh, a maddening sound,
With *Pretty Poll, tuwit-tu-woo,*
Peewit, caw caw, cuckoo-cuckoo.

THE GOD CALLED POETRY

Now I begin to know at last,
These nights when I sit down to rhyme,
The form and measure of that vast
God we call Poetry, he who stoops
And leaps me through his paper hoops
A little higher every time.

Tempts me to think I'll grow a proper
Singing cricket or grass-hopper
Making prodigious jumps in air
While shaken crowds about me stare
Aghast, and I sing, growing bolder
To fly up on my master's shoulder
Rustling the thick strands of his hair.

He is older than the seas,
Older than the plains and hills,
And older than the light that spills
From the sun's hot wheel on these.
He wakes the gale that tears your trees,
He sings to you from window sills.

At you he roars, or he will coo,
He shouts and screams when hell is hot,
Riding on the shell and shot.
He smites you down, he succours you,
And where you seek him, he is not.

To-day I see he has two heads
Like Janus – calm, benignant, this;
That, grim and scowling: his beard spreads
From chin to chin: this god has power
Immeasurable at every hour:
He first taught lovers how to kiss,
He brings down sunshine after shower,
Thunder and hate are his also,
He is YES and he is NO.

The black beard spoke and said to me,
'Human frailty though you be,
Yet shout and crack your whip, be harsh!
They'll obey you in the end:
Hill and field, river and marsh
Shall obey you, hop and skip
At the terrour of your whip,
To your gales of anger bend.'

The pale beard spoke and said in turn
'True: a prize goes to the stern,
But sing and laugh and easily run
Through the wide airs of my plain,
Bathe in my waters, drink my sun,
And draw my creatures with soft song;
They shall follow you along
Graciously with no doubt or pain.'

Then speaking from his double head
The glorious fearful monster said
'I am YES and I am NO,
Black as pitch and white as snow,
Love me, hate me, reconcile
Hate with love, perfect with vile,
So equal justice shall be done
And life shared between moon and sun.
Nature for you shall curse or smile:
A poet you shall be, my son.'

ROCKY ACRES

This is a wild land, country of my choice,
With harsh craggy mountain, moor ample and bare.
Seldom in these acres is heard any voice
But voice of cold water that runs here and there
Through rocks and lank heather growing without care.
No mice in the heath run, no song-birds fly
For fear of the buzzard that floats in the sky.

He soars and he hovers, rocking on his wings,
He scans his wide parish with a sharp eye,
He catches the trembling of small hidden things,
He tears them in pieces, dropping them from the sky;
Tenderness and pity the heart will deny,
Where life is but nourished by water and rock –
A hardy adventure, full of fear and shock.

Time has never journeyed to this lost land,
Crakeberry and heather bloom out of date,
The rocks jut, the streams flow singing on either hand,
Careless if the season be early or late,
The skies wander overhead, now blue, now slate;
Winter would be known by his cutting snow
If June did not borrow his armour also.

Yet this is my country, beloved by me best,
The first land that rose from Chaos and the Flood,
Nursing no valleys for comfort or rest,
Trampled by no shod hooves, bought with no blood.
Sempiternal country whose barrows have stood
Stronghold for demigods when on earth they go,
Terror for fat burghers on far plains below.

ADVICE TO LOVERS

I knew an old man at a Fair
Who made it his twice-yearly task
To clamber on a cider cask
And cry to all the yokels there: –

> *'Lovers assembled here today*
> *Give due attention when I say:*
> *Love is not kindly nor yet grim*
> *But does to you as you to him.*

> *'Whistle, and Love will come to you,*
> *Hiss, and he fades without a word,*
> *Do wrong, and he great wrong will do,*
> *Speak, he retells what he has heard.*

> *'Then all you lovers have good heed,*
> *Vex not young Love in word or deed:*
> *Love never leaves an unpaid debt,*
> *He will not pardon nor forget.'*

The old man's voice was sweet yet loud
And this shows what a man was he,
He'd scatter apples to the crowd
And give great draughts of cider, free.

NEBUCHADNEZZAR'S FALL

Frowning over the riddle that Daniel told,
Down through the mist-hung garden, below a feeble sun,
The King of Persia walked: oh, the chilling cold!
His mind was webbed with a grey shroud vapour-spun.

Here for the pride of his soaring eagle heart,
Here for his great hand searching the skies for food,
Here for his courtship of Heaven's high stars he shall smart,
Nebuchadnezzar shall fall, crawl, be subdued.

Hot sun struck through the vapour, leaf-strewn mould
Breathed sweet decay: old Earth called for her child.
Mist drew off from his mind, Sun scattered gold,
Warmth came and earthy motives fresh and wild.

Down on his knees he sinks, the stiff-necked King,
Stoops and kneels and grovels, chin to the mud.
Out from his changed heart flutter on startled wing
The fancy birds of his Pride, Honour, Kinglihood.

He crawls, he grunts, he is beast-like, frogs and snails
His diet, and grass, and water with hand for cup.
He herds with brutes that have hooves and horns and tails,
He roars in his anger, he scratches, he looks not up.

GIVE US RAIN

'Give us Rain, Rain,' said the bean and the pea,
      'Not so much Sun,
      Not so much Sun.'
But the Sun smiles bravely and encouragingly,
And no rain falls and no waters run.

'Give us Peace, Peace,' said the peoples oppressed,
      'Not so many Flags,
      Not so many Flags.'
But the Flags fly and the Drums beat, denying rest,
And the children starve, they shiver in rags.

ALLIE

Allie, call the birds in,
    The birds from the sky!
Allie calls, Allie sings,
    Down they all fly:
First there came
Two white doves,
    Then a sparrow from his nest,
Then a clucking bantam hen,
    Then a robin red-breast.

Allie, call the beasts in,
   The beasts, every one!
Allie calls, Allie sings,
   In they all run:
First there came
Two black lambs,
   Then a grunting Berkshire sow,
Then a dog without a tail,
   Then red and white cow.

Allie, call the fish up,
   The fish from the stream!
Allie calls, Allie sings,
   Up they all swim:
First there came
Two gold fish,
   A minnow and a miller's thumb,
Then a school of little trout,
   Then the twisting eels come.

Allie, call the children,
   Call them from the green!
Allie calls, Allie sings,
   Soon they run in:
First there came
Tom and Madge,
   Kate and I who'll not forget
How we played by the water's edge
   Till the April sun set.

LOVING HENRY

Henry, Henry, do you love me?
Do I love you, Mary?
Oh can you mean to liken me
To the aspen tree
Whose leaves do shake and vary
From white to green
And back again,
Shifting and contrary?

Henry, Henry, do you love me,
Do you love me truly?
Oh, Mary, must I say again
My love's a pain,
A torment most unruly?
It tosses me
Like a ship at sea
When the storm rages fully.

Henry, Henry, why do you love me?
Mary, dear, have pity!
I swear, of all the girls there are
Both near and far,
In country or in city,
There's none like you,
So kind, so true,
So wise, so brave, so pretty.

BRITTLE BONES

Though I am an old man
    With my bones very brittle,
Though I am a poor old man
    Worth very little,
Yet I suck at my long pipe
    At peace in the sun,
I do not fret nor much regret
    That my work is done.

If I were a young man
    With my bones full of marrow,
Oh, if I were a bold young man
    Straight as an arrow,
And if I had the same years
    To live once again,
I would not change their simple range
    Of laughter and pain.

If I were a young man
    And young was my Lily,
A smart girl, a bold young man,
    Both of us silly,
And though from time before I knew
    She'd stab me with pain,
Though well I knew she'd not be true,
    I'd love her again.

If I were a young man
    With a brisk, healthy body,
Oh, if I were a bold young man
    With love of rum toddy,
Though I knew that I was spiting
    My old age with pain,
My happy lip would touch and sip
    Again and again.

If I were a young man
    With my bones full of marrow,
Oh, if I were a bold young man
    Straight as an arrow,
I'd store up no virtue
    For Heaven's distant plain,
I'd live at ease as I did please
    And sin once again.

APPLES AND WATER

Dust in a cloud, blinding weather,
    Drums that rattle and roar!
A mother and daughter stood together
    By their cottage door.

'Mother, the heavens are bright like brass,
    The dust is shaken high,
With labouring breath the soldiers pass,
    Their lips are cracked and dry.

'Mother, I'll throw them apples down,
    I'll fetch them cups of water.'
The mother turned with an angry frown,
    Holding back her daughter.

'But, mother, see, they faint with thirst,
    They march away to war.'
'Ay, daughter, these are not the first
    And there will come yet more.

'There is no water can supply them
    In western streams that flow;
There is no fruit can satisfy them
    On orchard-trees that grow.

'Once in my youth I gave, poor fool,
    A soldier apples and water;
And may I die before you cool
    Such drouth as his, my daughter.'

MANTICOR IN ARABIA

(The manticors of the montaines
Mighte feed them on thy braines. – *Skelton.*)

Thick and scented daisies spread
Where with surface dull like lead
Arabian pools of slime invite
Manticors down from neighbouring height
To dip heads, to cool fiery blood
In oozy depths of sucking mud.
Sing then of ringstraked manticor,
Man-visaged tiger who of yore
Held whole Arabian waste in fee
With raging pride from sea to sea,
That every lesser tribe would fly
Those armèd feet, that hooded eye;
Till preying on himself at last
Manticor dwindled, sank, was passed
By gryphon flocks he did disdain.
Ay, wyverns and rude dragons reign
In ancient keep of manticor
Agreed old foe can rise no more.
Only here from lakes of slime
Drinks manticor and bides due time:
Six times Fowl Phoenix in yon tree
Must mount his pyre and burn and be

Renewed again, till in such hour
As seventh Phoenix flames to power
And lifts young feathers, overnice
From scented pool of steamy spice
Shall manticor his sway restore
And rule Arabian plains once more.

OUTLAWS

Owls – they whinny down the night;
   Bats go zigzag by.
Ambushed in shadow beyond sight
   The outlaws lie.

Old gods, tamed to silence, there
   In the wet woods they lurk,
Greedy of human stuff to snare
   In nets of murk.

Look up, else your eye will drown
   In a moving sea of black;
Between the tree-tops, upside down,
   Goes the sky-track.

Look up, else your feet will stray
   Into that ambuscade
Where spider-like they trap their prey
   With webs of shade.

For though creeds whirl away in dust,
   Faith dies and men forget,
These agèd gods of power and lust
   Cling to life yet –

Old gods almost dead, malign,
   Starving for unpaid dues:
Incense and fire, salt, blood and wine
   And a drumming muse,

Banished to woods and a sickly moon,
   Shrunk to mere bogey things,
Who spoke with thunder once at noon
   To prostrate kings:

With thunder from an open sky
    To warrior, virgin, priest,
Bowing in fear with a dazzled eye
    Toward the dread East –

Proud gods, humbled, sunk so low,
    Living with ghosts and ghouls,
And ghosts of ghosts and last year's snow
    And dead toadstools.

BALOO LOO FOR JENNY

Sing baloo loo for Jenny
    And where is she gone?
Away to spy her mother's land,
    Riding all alone.

To the rich towns of Scotland,
    The woods and the streams,
High upon a Spanish horse
    Saddled for her dreams.

By Oxford and by Chester,
    To Berwick-on-the-Tweed,
Then once across the borderland
    She shall find no need.

A loaf for her at Stirling,
    A scone at Carlisle,
Honeyed cakes at Edinbro' –
    That shall make her smile.

At Aberdeen clear cider,
    Mead for her at Nairn,
A cup of wine at John o' Groat's –
    That shall please my bairn.

Sing baloo loo for Jenny,
    Mother will be fain
To see her little truant child
    Riding home again.

HAWK AND BUCKLE

Where is the landlord of old Hawk and Buckle,
And what of Master Straddler this hot summer weather?
He's along in the tap-room with broad cheeks a-chuckle,
And ten bold companions all drinking together.

Where is the daughter of old Hawk and Buckle,
And what of Mistress Jenny this hot summer weather?
She sits in the parlour with smell of honeysuckle,
Trimming her bonnet with red ostrich feather.

Where is the ostler of old Hawk and Buckle,
And what of Willy Jakeman this hot summer weather?
He is rubbing his eyes with a slow and lazy knuckle
As he wakes from his nap on a bank of fresh heather.

Where is the page boy of old Hawk and Buckle,
And what of our young Charlie this hot summer weather?
He is bobbing for tiddlers in a little trickle-truckle,
With his line and his hook and his breeches of leather.

Where is the grey goat of old Hawk and Buckle,
And what of pretty Nanny this hot summer weather?
She stays not contented with little or with muckle,
Straining for daisies at the end of her tether.

For this is our motto at old Hawk and Buckle,
We cling to it close and we sing all together,
'Every man for himself at our old Hawk and Buckle,
And devil take the hindmost this hot summer weather.'

THE *ALICE JEAN*

One moonlit night a ship drove in,
  A ghost ship from the west,
Drifting with bare mast and lone tiller,
  Like a mermaid drest
In long green weed and barnacles:
  She beached and came to rest.

All the watchers of the coast
  Flocked to view the sight,
Men and women streaming down
  Through the summer night,
Found her standing tall and ragged
  Beached in the moonlight.

Then one old woman looked and wept:
  'The *Alice Jean*? But no!
The ship that took my Dick from me
  Sixty years ago
Drifted back from the utmost west
  With the ocean's flow?

'Caught and caged in the weedy pool
  Beyond the western brink,
Where crewless vessels lie and rot
  In waters black as ink,
Torn out again by a sudden storm –
  Is it the *Jean*, you think?'

A hundred women stared agape,
  The menfolk nudged and laughed,
But none could find a likelier story
  For the strange craft
With fear and death and desolation
  Rigged fore and aft.

The blind ship came forgotten home
  To all but one of these
Of whom none dared to climb aboard her:
  And by and by the breeze
Sprang to a storm and the *Alice Jean*
  Foundered in frothy seas.

THE CUPBOARD

Mother: What's in that cupboard, Mary?
Mary: Which cupboard, mother, dear?
Mother: The cupboard of red mahogany
               With handles shining clear.

Mary: That cupboard, dearest mother,
                With shining crystal handles?
             There's naught inside but rags and jags
                And yellow tallow candles.

Mother: What's in that cupboard, Mary?
Mary: Which cupboard, mother mine?
Mother: That cupboard stands in your sunny chamber,
               The silver corners shine.

Mary: There's nothing there inside, mother,
                But wool and thread and flax,
             And bits of faded silk and velvet,
                And candles of white wax.

Mother: What's in that cupboard, Mary?
               And this time tell me true.
Mary: White clothes for an unborn baby, mother,
               But what's the truth to you?

THE BEACON

The silent shepherdess,
    She of my vows,
Here with me exchanging love
    Under dim boughs.

Shines on our mysteries
    A sudden spark.
'Dout the candle, glow-worm,
    Let all be dark.

'The birds have sung their last notes,
    The Sun's to bed.
Glow-worm, dout your candle.'
    The glow-worm said:

'I also am a lover;
    The lamp I display
Is beacon for my true love
    Wandering astray.

'Through the thick bushes
    And the grass comes he
With a heart load of longing
    And love for me.

'Sir, enjoy your fancy
    But spare me harm.
A lover is a lover,
    Though but a worm.'

POT AND KETTLE

Come close to me, dear Annie, while I tie a lover's knot,
To tell of burning love between a kettle and a pot:
The pot was stalwart iron and the kettle trusty tin,
And though their sides were black with smoke they bubbled love within.

Forget that kettle, Jamie, and that pot of boiling broth.
I know a dismal story of a candle and a moth:
For while your pot is boiling and while your kettle sings
My moth makes love to candle flame and burns away his wings.

Your moth I envy, Annie, that died by candle flame,
But here are two more lovers, unto no damage came.
There was a cuckoo loved a clock and found her always true.
For every hour they told their hearts, 'Ring! ting! Cuckoo! Cuckoo!'

As the pot boiled for the kettle, as the kettle for the pot,
So boils my love within me till my breast is glowing hot.
As the moth died for the candle, so could I die for you,
And my fond heart beats time with yours and cries, 'Cuckoo! Cuckoo!'

THE HAUNTED HOUSE

'Come, surly fellow, come: a song!'
    What, fools? Sing to you?
Choose from the clouded tales of wrong
    And terror I bring to you:

Of a night so torn with cries,
    Honest men sleeping
Start awake with rabid eyes,
    Bone-chilled, flesh creeping,

Of spirits in the web-hung room
    Up above the stable,
Groans, knockings in the gloom,
    The dancing table,

Of demons in the dry well
    That cheep and mutter,
Clanging of an unseen bell,
    Blood choking the gutter,

Of lust frightful, past belief,
    Lurking unforgotten,
Unrestrainable endless grief
    In breasts long rotten.

A song? What laughter or what song
    Can this house remember?
Do flowers and butterflies belong
    To a blind December?

NEGLECTFUL EDWARD

Nancy: 'Edward back from the Indian Sea,
             What have you brought for Nancy?'

Edward: 'A rope of pearls and a gold earring,
             And a bird of the East that will not sing,
             A carven tooth, a box with a key –'

Nancy:	'God be praised you are back,' says she,
	'Have you nothing more for your Nancy?'

Edward:	'Long as I sailed the Indian Sea
	I gathered all for your fancy;
	Toys and silk and jewels I bring,
	And a bird of the East that will not sing:
	What more can you want, dear girl, from me?'

Nancy:	'God be praised you are back,' said she,
	'Have you nothing better for Nancy?'

Edward:	'Safe and home from the Indian Sea,
	And nothing to take your fancy?'

Nancy:	'You can keep your pearls and your gold earring,
	And your bird of the East that will not sing,
	But, Ned, have you *nothing* more for me
	Than heathenish gew-gaw toys?' says she,
	'Have you nothing better for Nancy?'

THE WELL-DRESSED CHILDREN

Here's flowery taffeta for Mary's new gown:
   Here's black velvet, all the rage, for Dick's birthday coat.
Pearly buttons for you, Mary, all the way down,
   Lace ruffles, Dick, for you; you'll be a man of note.

Mary, here I've bought you a green gingham shade
   And a silk purse brocaded with roses gold and blue,
You'll learn to hold them proudly like colours on parade.
   No banker's wife in all the town half so grand as you.

I've bought for young Diccon a long walking-stick,
   Yellow gloves, well tanned, at Woodstock village made.
I'll teach you to flourish 'em and show your name is DICK,
   Strutting by your sister's side with the same parade.

On Sunday to church you go, each with a book of prayer:
   Then up the street and down the aisles, everywhere you'll see
Of all the honours paid around, how small is Virtue's share,
   How large the share of Vulgar Pride in peacock finery.

THUNDER AT NIGHT

Restless and hot two children lay
    Plagued with uneasy dreams,
Each wandered lonely through false day,
    A twilight torn with screams.

True to the bed-time story, Ben
    Pursued his wounded bear,
Ann dreamed of chattering monkey men,
    Of snakes twined in her hair....

Now high aloft above the town
    The thick clouds gather and break,
A flash, a roar, and rain drives down:
    Aghast the young things wake,

Trembling for what their terror was,
    Surprised by instant doom,
With lightning in the looking-glass,
    Thunder that rocks the room.

The monkeys' paws patter again,
    Snakes hiss and flash their eyes:
The bear roars out in hideous pain:
    Ann prays: her brother cries.

They cannot guess, could not be told
    How soon comes careless day,
With birds and dandelion gold,
    Wet grass, cool scents of May.

WILD STRAWBERRIES

Strawberries that in gardens grow
    Are plump and juicy fine,
But sweeter far, as wise men know,
    Spring from the woodland vine.

No need for bowl or silver spoon,
    Sugar or spice or cream,
Has the wild berry plucked in June
    Beside the trickling stream.

One such, to melt at the tongue's root
    Confounding taste with scent,
Beats a full peck of garden fruit:
    Which points my argument: –

May sudden justice overtake
    And snap the froward pen,
That old and palsied poets shake
    Against the minds of men;

Blasphemers trusting to hold caught
    In far-flung webs of ink
The utmost ends of human thought
    Till nothing's left to think.

But may the gift of heavenly peace
    And glory for all time
Keep the boy Tom who tending geese
    First made the nursery rhyme.

JANE

As Jane walked out below the hill,
She saw an old man standing still,
His eyes in trancèd sorrow bound
On the broad stretch of barren ground.

His limbs were knarled like aged trees,
His thin beard wrapt about his knees,
His visage broad and parchment white,
Aglint with pale reflected light.

He seemed a creature fall'n afar
From some dim planet or faint star.
Jane scanned him very close, and soon
Cried, ''Tis the old man from the moon.'

He raised his voice, a grating creak,
But only to himself would speak,
Groaning with tears in piteous pain,
'O! O! would I were home again.'

Then Jane ran off, quick as she could,
To cheer his heart with drink and food.
But ah, too late came ale and bread,
She found the poor soul stretched stone-dead.
And a new moon rode overhead.

VAIN AND CARELESS

Lady, lovely lady,
    Careless and gay!
Once, when a beggar called,
    She gave her child away.

The beggar took the baby,
    Wrapped it in a shawl –
'Bring him back,' the lady said,
    'Next time you call.'

Hard by lived a vain man,
    So vain and so proud
He would walk on stilts
    To be seen by the crowd,

Up above the chimney pots,
    Tall as a mast –
And all the people ran about
    Shouting till he passed.

'A splendid match surely,'
    Neighbours saw it plain,
'Although she is so careless,
    Although he is so vain.'

But the lady played bobcherry,
    Did not see or care,
As the vain man went by her,
    Aloft in the air.

This gentle-born couple
    Lived and died apart –
Water will not mix with oil,
    Nor vain with careless heart.

NINE O'CLOCK

I

Nine of the clock, oh!
    Wake my lazy head!
Your shoes of red morocco,
    Your silk bed-gown:
Rouse, rouse, speck-eyed Mary
    In your high bed!
A yawn, a smile, sleepy-starey,
    Mary climbs down.
'Good-morning to my brothers,
    Good-day to the Sun,
Halloo, halloo to the lily-white sheep
    That up the mountain run.'

II

Good-night to the meadow, farewell to the nine o'clock Sun,
'He loves me not, loves me, he loves me not' (O jealous one!)
'He loves me, he loves me not, loves me' – O soft nights of June,
A bird sang for love on the cherry-bough: up swam the Moon.

THE PICTURE BOOK

When I was not quite five years old
    I first saw the blue picture book,
And Fräulein Spitzenburger told
Stories that sent me hot and cold;
    I loathed it, yet I had to look:
    It was a German book.

I smiled at first, for she'd begun
    With a back-garden broad and green,
And rabbits nibbling there: page one
Turned; and the gardener fired his gun
    From the low hedge: he lay unseen
    Behind: oh, it was mean!

They're hurt, they can't escape, and so
   He stuffs them head-down in a sack,
Not quite dead, wriggling in a row,
And Fräulein laughed, 'Ho, ho! Ho, ho!'
   And gave my middle a hard smack.
   I wish that I'd hit back.

Then when I cried she laughed again;
   On the next page was a dead boy
Murdered by robbers in a lane;
His clothes were red with a big stain
   Of blood, he held a broken toy,
   The poor, poor little boy!

I had to look: there was a town
   Burning where every one got caught,
Then a fish pulled a nigger down
Into the lake and made him drown,
   And a man killed his friend; they fought
   For money, Fräulein thought.

Old Fräulein laughed, a horrid noise.
   'Ho, ho!' Then she explained it all.
How robbers kill the little boys
And torture them and break their toys.
   Robbers are always big and tall:
   I cried: I was so small.

How a man often kills his wife,
   How every one dies in the end
By fire, or water or a knife.
If you're not careful in this life,
   Even if you can trust your friend,
   You won't have long to spend.

I hated it – old Fräulein picked
   Her teeth, slowly explaining it.
I had to listen, Fräulein licked
Her fingers several times and flicked
   The pages over; in a fit
   Of rage I spat at it...

And lying in my bed that night
  Hungry, tired out with sobs, I found
A stretch of barren years in sight,
Where right is wrong, but strength is right,
  Where weak things must creep underground,
And I could not sleep sound.

THE PROMISED LULLABY

Can I find True-Love a gift
  In this dark hour to restore her,
When body's vessel breaks adrift,
  When hope and beauty fade before her?
But in this plight I cannot think
  Of song or music, that would grieve her,
Or toys or meat or snow-cooled drink;
  Not this way can her sadness leave her.
  She lies and frets in childish fever,
All I can do is but to cry
  'Sleep, sleep, True-Love and lullaby!'

Lullaby, and sleep again.
  Two bright eyes through the window stare,
A nose is flattened on the pane
  And infant fingers fumble there.
'Not yet, not yet, you lovely thing,
  But count and come nine weeks from now,
When winter's tail has lost the sting,
  When buds come striking through the bough,
  Then here's True-Love will show you how
Her name she won, will hush your cry
  With "Sleep, my baby! Lullaby!"'

RETROSPECT

HAUNTED

Gulp down your wine, old friends of mine,
Roar through the darkness, stamp and sing
And lay ghost hands on everything,
But leave the noonday's warm sunshine
To living lads for mirth and wine.

I meet you suddenly down the street,
Strangers assume your phantom faces,
You grin at me from daylight places,
Dead, long dead, I'm ashamed to greet
Dead men down the morning street.

RETROSPECT: THE JESTS OF THE CLOCK

He had met hours of the clock he never guessed before –
Dumb, dragging, mirthless hours confused with dreams and fear,
Bone-chilling, hungry hours when the gods sleep and snore,
Bequeathing earth and heaven to ghosts, and will not hear,
And will not hear man groan chained to the sodden ground,
Rotting alive; in feather beds they slumber sound.

When noisome smells of day were sicklied by cold night,
When sentries froze and muttered; when beyond the wire
Blank shadows crawled and tumbled, shaking, tricking the sight,
When impotent hatred of Life stifled desire,
Then soared the sudden rocket, broke in blanching showers.
O lagging watch! O dawn! O hope-forsaken hours!

How often with numbed heart, stale lips, venting his rage
He swore he'd be a dolt, a traitor, a damned fool,
If, when the guns stopped, ever again from youth to age
He broke the early-rising, early-sleeping rule.
No, though more bestial enemies roused a fouler war
Never again would he bear this, no never more!

'Rise with the cheerful sun, go to bed with the same,
Work in your field or kailyard all the shining day,
But,' he said, 'never more in quest of wealth, honour, fame,
Search the small hours of night before the East goes grey.
A healthy mind, an honest heart, a wise man leaves
Those ugly impious times to ghosts, devils, soldiers, thieves.'

Poor fool, knowing too well deep in his heart
That he'll be ready again if urgent orders come,
To quit his rye and cabbages, kiss his wife and part
At the first sullen rapping of the awakened drum,
Ready once more to sweat with fear and brace for the shock,
To greet beneath a falling flare the jests of the clock.

HERE THEY LIE

Here they lie who once learned here
   All that is taught of hurt or fear;
Dead, but by free will they died:
   They were true men, they had pride.

TOM TAYLOR

On pay-day nights, neck-full with beer,
Old soldiers stumbling homeward here,
Homeward (still dazzled by the spark
Love kindled in some alley dark)
Young soldiers mooning in slow thought,
Start suddenly, turn about, are caught
By a dancing sound, merry as a grig,
Tom Taylor's piccolo playing jig.
Never was blown from human cheeks
Music like this, that calls and speaks
Till sots and lovers from one string
Dangle and dance in the same ring.
Tom, of your piping I've heard said
And seen – that you can rouse the dead,
Dead-drunken men awash who lie
In stinking gutters hear your cry,
I've seen them twitch, draw breath, grope, sigh,
Heave up, sway, stand; grotesquely then

You set them dancing, these dead men.
They stamp and prance with sobbing breath,
Victims of wine or love or death,
In ragged time they jump, they shake
Their heads, sweating to overtake
The impetuous tune flying ahead.
They flounder after, with legs of lead.
Now, suddenly as it started, play
Stops, the short echo dies away,
The corpses drop, a senseless heap,
The drunk men gaze about like sheep
Grinning; the lovers sigh and stare
Up at the broad moon hanging there,
While Tom, five fingers to his nose,
Skips off... And the last bugle blows.

COUNTRY AT WAR

And what of home – how goes it, boys,
While we die here in stench and noise?
'The hill stands up and hedges wind
Over the crest and drop behind;
Here swallows dip and wild things go
On peaceful errands to and fro
Across the sloping meadow floor,
And make no guess at blasting war.
In woods that fledge the round hill-shoulder
Leaves shoot and open, fall and moulder,
And shoot again. Meadows yet show
Alternate white of drifted snow
And daisies. Children play at shop,
Warm days, on the flat boulder-top,
With wildflower coinage, and the wares
Are bits of glass and unripe pears.
Crows perch upon the backs of sheep,
The wheat goes yellow: women reap,
Autumn winds ruffle brook and pond,
Flutter the hedge and fly beyond.
So the first things of nature run,
And stand not still for any one,
Contemptuous of the distant cry
Wherewith you harrow earth and sky

And high French clouds, praying to be
Back, back in peace beyond the sea,
Where nature with accustomed round
Sweeps and garnishes the ground
With kindly beauty, warm or cold –
Alternate seasons never old:
Heathen, how furiously you rage,
Cursing this blood and brimstone age,
How furiously against your will
You kill and kill again, and kill:
All thought of peace behind you cast,
Till like small boys with fear aghast,
Each cries for God to understand,
"I could not help it, it was my hand."'

SOSPAN FACH

(The Little Saucepan)

Four collier lads from Ebbw Vale
Took shelter from a shower of hail,
And there beneath a spreading tree
Attuned their mouths to harmony.

With smiling joy on every face
Two warbled tenor, two sang bass,
And while the leaves above them hissed with
Rough hail, they started 'Aberystwyth'.

Old Parry's hymn, triumphant, rich,
They chanted through with even pitch,
Till at the end of their grand noise
I called: 'Give us the "Sospan" boys!'

Who knows a tune so soft, so strong,
So pitiful as that 'Saucepan' song
For exiled hope, despaired desire
Of lost souls for their cottage fire?

Then low at first with gathering sound
Rose their four voices, smooth and round,
Till back went Time: once more I stood
With Fusiliers in Mametz Wood.

Fierce burned the sun, yet cheeks were pale,
For ice hail they had leaden hail;
In that fine forest, green and big,
There stayed unbroken not one twig.

They sang, they swore, they plunged in haste,
Stumbling and shouting through the waste;
The little 'Saucepan' flamed on high,
Emblem of hope and ease gone by.

Rough pit-boys from the coaly South,
They sang, even in the cannon's mouth;
Like Sunday's chapel, Monday's inn,
The death-trap sounded with their din.

*   *   *   *   *

The storm blows over, Sun comes out,
The choir breaks up with jest and shout,
With what relief I watch them part –
Another note would break my heart!

THE LEVELLER

Near Martinpuisch that night of hell
Two men were struck by the same shell,
Together tumbling in one heap
Senseless and limp like slaughtered sheep.

One was a pale eighteen-year-old,
Blue-eyed and thin and not too bold,
Pressed for the war ten years too soon,
The shame and pity of his platoon.

The other came from far-off lands
With bristling chin and whiskered hands,
He had known death and hell before
In Mexico and Ecuador.

Yet in his death this cut-throat wild
Groaned 'Mother! Mother!' like a child,
While that poor innocent in man's clothes
Died cursing God with brutal oaths.

Old Sergeant Smith, kindest of men,
Wrote out two copies there and then
Of his accustomed funeral speech
To cheer the womenfolk of each: –

'He died a hero's death: and we
His comrades of "A" Company
Deeply regret his death; we shall .
All deeply miss so true a pal.'

HATE NOT, FEAR NOT

Kill if you must, but never hate:
    Man is but grass and hate is blight,
The sun will scorch you soon or late,
    Die wholesome then, since you must fight.

Hate is a fear, and fear is rot
    That cankers root and fruit alike,
Fight cleanly then, hate not, fear not,
    Strike with no madness when you strike.

Fever and fear distract the world,
    But calm be you though madmen shout,
Through blazing fires of battle hurled,
    Hate not, strike, fear not, stare Death out!

A RHYME OF FRIENDS

(In a Style Skeltonical)

Listen now this time
Shortly to my rhyme
That herewith starts
About certain kind hearts
In those stricken parts
That lie behind Calais,
Old crones and aged men
And young childrén.
About the Picardais,
Who earned my thousand thanks,

Dwellers by the banks
Of the mournful Somme
(God keep me therefrom
Until War ends) –
These, then, are my friends:
Madame Averlant Lune,
From the town of Béthune;
Good Professeur la Brune
From that town also.
He played the piccolo,
And left his locks to grow.
Dear Madame Hojdés,
Sempstress of Saint Fé.
With Jules and Suzette
And Antoinette,
Her children, my sweethearts,
For whom I made darts
Of paper to throw
In their mimic show,
'La guerre aux tranchées'.
That was a pretty play.

There was old Jacques Caron,
Of the hamlet Mailleton.
He let me look
At his household book,
'Comment vivre cent ans'.
What cares I took
To obey this wise book,
I, who feared each hour
Lest Death's cruel power
On the poppied plain
Might make cares vain!

By Nœux-les-Mines
Lived old Adelphine,
Withered and clean,
She nodded and smiled,
And used me like a child.
How that old trot beguiled
My leisure with her chatter,
Gave me a china platter
Painted with Cherubim
And mottoes on the rim.

But when instead of thanks
I gave her francs
How her pride was hurt!
She counted francs as dirt,
(God knows, she was not rich)
She called the Kaiser bitch,
She spat on the floor,
Cursing this Prussian war,
That she had known before
Forty years past and more.

There was also 'Tomi',
With looks sweet and free,
Who called me *cher ami*.
This orphan's age was nine,
His folk were in their graves,
Else they were slaves
Behind the German line
To terror and rapine –
O, little friends of mine
How kind and brave you were,
You smoothed away care
When life was hard to bear.
And you, old women and men,
Who gave me billets then,
How patient and great-hearted!
Strangers though we started,
Yet friends we ever parted.
God bless you all: now ends
This homage to my friends.

A FIRST REVIEW

Love, Fear and Hate and Childish Toys
  Are here discreetly blent;
Admire, you ladies, read, you boys,
  My Country Sentiment.

But Kate says, 'Cut that anger and fear,
  True love's the stuff we need!
With laughing children and the running deer
  That makes a book indeed.'

Then Tom, a hard and bloody chap,
    Though much beloved by me,
'Robert, have done with nursery pap,
    Write like a man,' says he.

Hate and Fear are not wanted here,
    Nor Toys nor Country Lovers,
Everything they took from my new poem book
    But the flyleaf and the covers.

From *THE PIER-GLASS*

(1921)

THE STAKE

Naseboro' held him guilty,
  Crowther took his part,
Who lies at the cross-roads,
  A stake through his heart.

Spring calls, and the stake answers,
  Throwing out shoots;
The towns debate what life is this
  Sprung from such roots.

Naseboro' says 'A Upas Tree';
  'A Rose,' says Crowther;
But April's here to declare it
  Neither one nor other,

Neither ill nor very fair,
  Rose nor Upas,
But an honest oak-tree,
  As its parent was,

A green-tufted oak-tree
  On the green wold,
Careless as the dead heart
  That the roots enfold.

THE TROLL'S NOSEGAY

A simple nosegay! was that much to ask?
(Winter still nagged, with scarce a bud yet showing.)
He loved her ill, if he resigned the task.
'Somewhere,' she cried, 'there must be blossom blowing.'
It seems my lady wept and the troll swore
By Heaven he hated tears: he'd cure her spleen –
Where she had begged one flower he'd shower fourscore,
A bunch fit to amaze a China Queen.

Cold fog-drawn Lily, pale mist-magic Rose
He conjured, and in a glassy cauldron set
With elvish unsubstantial Mignonette
And such vague bloom as wandering dreams enclose.
But she?
              Awed,
                        Charmed to tears,
                                        Distracted,
                                                        Yet –
Even yet, perhaps, a trifle piqued – who knows?

THE PIER-GLASS

Lost manor where I walk continually
A ghost, though yet in woman's flesh and blood.
Up your broad stairs mounting with outspread fingers
And gliding steadfast down your corridors
I come by nightly custom to this room,
And even on sultry afternoons I come
Drawn by a thread of time-sunk memory.

Empty, unless for a huge bed of state
Shrouded with rusty curtains drooped awry
(A puppet theatre where malignant fancy
Peoples the wings with fear). At my right hand
A ravelled bell-pull hangs in readiness
To summon me from attic glooms above
Service of elder ghosts; here, at my left,
A sullen pier-glass, cracked from side to side,
Scorns to present the face (as do new mirrors)
With a lying flush, but shows it melancholy
And pale, as faces grow that look in mirrors.

Is there no life, nothing but the thin shadow
And blank foreboding, never a wainscot rat
Rasping a crust? Or at the window-pane
No fly, no bluebottle, no starveling spider?
The windows frame a prospect of cold skies
Half-merged with sea, as at the first creation –
Abstract, confusing welter. Face about,
Peer rather in the glass once more, take note
Of self, the grey lips and long hair dishevelled,
Sleep-staring eyes. Ah, mirror, for Christ's love
Give me one token that there still abides
Remote – beyond this island mystery,
So be it only this side Hope, somewhere,
In streams, on sun-warm mountain pasturage –
True life, natural breath; not this phantasma.

THE FINDING OF LOVE

Pale at first and cold,
Like wizard's lily-bloom
Conjured from the gloom,
Like torch of glow-worm seen
Through grasses shining green
By children half in fright,
Or Christmas candlelight
Flung on the outer snow,
Or tinsel stars that show
Their evening glory
With sheen of fairy story –

Now with his blaze
Love dries the cobweb maze
Dew-sagged upon the corn,
He brings the flowering thorn,
Mayfly and butterfly,
And pigeons in the sky,
Robin and thrush,
And the long bulrush,
Bird-cherry under the leaf,
Earth in a silken dress,
With end to grief,
With joy in steadfastness.

REPROACH

Your grieving moonlight face looks down
    Through the forest of my fears,
Crowned with a spiny bramble-crown,
    Bedewed with evening tears.

Why do you say 'untrue, unkind',
    Reproachful eyes that vex my sleep?
Straining in memory, I can find
    No cause why you should weep.

Untrue? But when, what broken oath?
    Unkind? I know not even your name.
Unkind, untrue, you brand me both,
    Scalding my heart with shame.

The black trees shudder, dropping snow,
    The stars tumble and spin.
Speak, speak, or how may a child know
    His ancestral sin?

THE MAGICAL PICTURE

Glinting on the roadway
A broken mirror lay:
Then what did the child say
    Who found it there?
He cried there was a goblin
Looking out as he looked in –
Wild eyes and speckled skin,
    Black, bristling hair!

He brought it to his father
Who being a simple sailor
Swore, 'This is a true wonder,
    Deny it who can!
Plain enough to me, for one,
It's a portrait aptly done
Of Admiral, the great Lord Nelson
    When a young man.'

The sailor's wife perceiving
Her husband had some pretty thing
At which he was peering,
    Seized it from his hand.
Then tears started and ran free,
'Jack, you have deceived me,
I love you no more,' said she,
    'So understand!'

'But, Mary,' says the sailor,
'This is a famous treasure,
Admiral Nelson's picture
    Taken in youth.'
'Viper and fox,' she cries,
'To trick me with such lies,
Who is this wench with the bold eyes?
    Tell me the truth!'

Up rides the parish priest
Mounted on a fat beast.
Grief and anger have not ceased
    Between those two;
Little Tom still weeps for fear;
He has seen Hobgoblin, near,
Great white teeth and foul leer
    That pierced him through.

Now the old priest lifts his glove
Bidding all for God's love
To stand and not to move,
    Lest blood be shed.
'O, O!' cries the urchin,
'I saw the devil grin,
He glared out, as I looked in;
    A true death's head!'

Mary weeps, 'Ah, Father,
My Jack loves another!
On some voyage he courted her
    In a land afar.'
This, with cursing, Jack denies: –
'Father, use your own eyes:
It is Lord Nelson in disguise
    As a young tar.'

When the priest took the glass,
Fresh marvels came to pass:
'A saint of glory, by the Mass!
    Where got you this?'
He signed him with the good Sign,
Be sure the relic was divine,
He would fix it in a shrine
    For pilgrims to kiss.

There the chapel folk who come
(Honest, some, and lewd, some),
See the saint's eyes and are dumb,
    Kneeling on the flags.
Some see the Doubter Thomas,
And some Nathaniel in the glass,
And others whom but old Saint Judas
    With his money bags?

DISTANT SMOKE

Seth and the sons of Seth who followed him
Halted in silence: labour, then, was vain.
Fast at the zenith, blazoned in his splendour,
Hung the fierce Sun, wherefore these travelling folk
Stood centred each in his own disc of shade.
The term proposed was ended; now to enjoy
The moment's melancholy; their tears fell shining.

Yesterday early at the dreadful hour,
When life ebbs lowest, when the strand of being
Is slowly bared until discovered show
Weed-mantelled hulks that foundered years ago
At autumn anchorage, then father Adam
Summoned in haste his elder generations
To his death-tent, and gasping spoke to them,
Forthwith defining an immediate journey
Beyond the eastern ridge, in quest for one
Whom he named Cain, brother to Seth, true uncle
To these young spearmen; they should lead him here
For a last benediction at his hands.

First-born yet outlawed! Scarcely they believed
In this strange word of 'Cain', in this new man,
Man, yet outside the tents; but Adam swore
And gave them a fair sign of recognition.
There was a brand, he said, a firm red pillar
Parting Cain's brows, and Cain had mighty hands,
Sprouting luxurious hair, red, like his beard.
Moreover Adam said that by huge strength
Himself could stay this ebb of early morning,
Yet three days longer, three days, though no more –
This for the stern desire and long disquietude
That was his love for Cain; whom God had cursed.
Then would he kiss all fatherly and so die –
Kneeling, with eyes abased, they made him promise,
Swore, at the midpoint of their second day,
If unsped in the search of whom he named,
They would come hasting home to Adam's tent.
They touched his bony fingers; forth they went.

Now Seth, shielding his eyes, sees mistily
Breaking the horizon thirty miles away
(A full day's journey) what but a wisp, a feather,
A thin line, half a nothing – distant smoke!
Blown smoke, a signal from that utmost ridge
Of desolation – the camp fire of Cain.
He to restrain his twelve impetuous sons
(He knows the razor-edge of their young spirit)
Dissembles seeing, turns his steps about,
Bids them come follow, but they little heeding,
Scarce noting his commands, fasten their eyes
On smoke, so forfeit Adam's benediction,
Striding forward into the wilderness
With eager thighs, forgetful of their oath,
Adventurous for this monster, a new man,
Their own kin – how accursed? – they haste for wonder.

RAISING THE STONE

A shaft of moon from the cloud-hurried sky
    Has coursed the wide dark heath, but nowhere found
One paler patch to illumine – oats nor rye,
    Chalk-pit nor waterpool nor sandy ground –
Till, checked by our thronged faces on the mound
    (A wedge of whiteness) universally
Strained backward from the task that holds us bound,
    It beams on set jaw and hate-maddened eye.

The vast stone lifts, turns, topples, in its fall
    Spreads death: but we who live raise a shrill chant
Of joy for sacrifice cleansing us all.
    Once more we heave. Erect in earth we plant
The interpreter of our dumb furious call,
    Outraging Heaven, pointing
                                                    'I want, I want.'

THE GNAT

The shepherd Watkin heard an inner voice
Calling 'My creature, ho! be warned, be ready!'
Calling, 'The moment comes, therefore be ready!'
And a third time calling, 'Creature, be ready!'

This old poor man mistook the call, which sounded
Not for himself, but for his pensioner.
Now (truth or phantasy) the shepherd nourished
Fast in his brain, due earnings of transgression,
A creature like to that avenging fly
Once crept unseen in at the ear of Titus,
Tunnelling gradually inwards, upwards,
Heading for flowery pastures of the brain,
And battened on such grand, presumptuous fare
As grew him brazen claws and brazen hair
And wings of iron mail. Old Watkin felt
A like intruder channelling to and fro.
He cursed his day and sin done in past years,
Repentance choked, pride that outlawed his heart,
So that at night often in thunderous weather
Racked with the pain he'd start

From sleep, incontinently howling, leaping,
Striking his hoar head on the cottage walls,
Stamping his feet, dragging his hair by the roots.
He'd rouse the Gnat to anger, send it buzzing
Like a huge mill, scraping with metal claws
At his midpoint of being; forthwith tumble
With a great cry for Death to stoop and end him.

Now Watkin hears the voice and weeps for bliss,
The voice that warned 'Creature, the time is come.'
Merciful Death, was it Death, all his desire?
Promised of Heaven, and speedy? O Death, come!

Only for one thought must he make provision,
For honest Prinny, for old bob-tail Prinny.
Another master? Where? These hillside crofters
Were spiteful to their beasts and mercenary.
Prinny to such? No, Prinny too must die.
By his own hand, then? Murder! By what other?
No human hand should touch the sacrifice,
No human hand;
God's hand then, through his temporal minister.

Three times has Watkin in the morning early
When not a soul was rising, left his flock,
Come to the Minister's house through the cold mist,
Clicked at the latch and slowly moved the gate,
Faltered, held back and dared not enter in.
'Not this time, Prinny, we'll not rouse them yet,
To-morrow, surely, for our death is tokened,
My death and your death with small interval.
We meet in fields beyond; be sure of it, Prinny!'

On the next night
The busy Gnat, swollen to giant size,
Pent-up within the skull, knew certainly,
As a bird knows in the egg, his hour was come…
The thrice-repeated call had given him summons…
He must out, crack the shell, out, out!
He strains, claps his wings, arches his back,
Drives in his talons, out! out!

In the white anguish of this travail, Watkin
Hurls off his blankets, tears an axe from the nail,
Batters the bed, hews table, splits the floor,
Hears Prinny whine at his feet, leaps, strikes again,
Strikes, yammering.

                  At that instant with a clatter,
Noise of a bursting dam, a toppling wall,
Out flies the new-born creature from his mouth
And humming fearsomely like a huge engine,
Rackets about the room, smites the unseen
Glass of half-open windows, reels, recovers,
Soars out into the meadows, and is gone.

Silence prolonged to an age. Watkin still lives?
The hour of travail by the voice foretold
Brought no last throbbings of the dying Body
In child-birth of the Soul. Watkin still lives.
Labourer Watkin delves in the wet fields.
Did an old shepherd die that night with Prinny,
Die weeping with his head on the outraged corpse?
Oh, he's forgotten. A dead dream, a cloud.
Labourer Watkin delves drowsily, numbly,
His harsh spade grates among the buried stones.

THE PATCHWORK BONNET

Across the room my silent love I throw,
    Where you sit sewing in bed by candlelight,
        Your young stern profile and industrious fingers
Displayed against the blind in a shadow show,
    To Dinda's grave delight.

The needle dips and pokes, the cheerful thread
    Runs after, follow-my-leader down the seam:
        The patchwork pieces cry for joy together,
O soon to sit as a crown on Dinda's head,
    Fulfilment of their dream.

Snippets and odd ends folded by, forgotten,
    With camphor on the top shelf, hard to find,
        Now wake to this most happy resurrection,
To Dinda playing toss with a reel of cotton
    And staring at the blind.

Dinda in sing-song stretching out one hand
    Calls for the playthings; mother does not hear:
      Her mind sails far away on a patchwork Ocean,
And all the world must wait till she touches land,
    So Dinda cries in fear,

Then Mother turns, laughing like a young fairy,
    And Dinda smiles to see her look so kind,
      Calls out again for playthings, playthings, playthings,
And now the shadows make an Umbrian '*Mary
    Adoring*', on the blind.

KIT LOGAN AND LADY HELEN

Here is Kit Logan with her love-child come
    To Lady Helen's gate:
Then down sweeps Helen from the Italian room,
    She, with her child of hate.

Kit's boy was born of violent hot desire,
    Helen's of hate and dread:
Poor girl, betrayed to union with the Squire,
    Loathing her marriage bed.

Kit Logan, who is father to your boy?
    But Helen knows, too well:
Listen what biting taunts they both employ,
    Watch their red anger swell.

Yet each would give her undying soul to be
    Changed to the other's place.
Kit from the wet road's tasking cruelty
    Looks up to silk and lace,

Helen looks down at rags, her fluttering pride
    Caught in this cage of glass,
Eager to trudge, thieve, beg by the road-side,
    Or starving to eat grass…

Silence. Wrath dies. For Woman's old good name
    Each swears a sister's oath;
Weeping, they kiss; to the Squire's lasting shame,
    Who broke the heart in both.

DOWN

Downstairs a clock had chimed, two o'clock only.
Then outside from the hen-roost crowing came.
Why should the shift-wing call against the clock,
Three hours from dawn? Now shutters click and knock,
And he remembers a sad superstition
Unfitting for the sick-bed....Turn aside,
Distract, divide, ponder the simple tales
That puzzled childhood; riddles, turn them over –
Half-riddles, answerless, the more intense.
Lost bars of music tinkling with no sense
Recur, drowning uneasy superstition.

Mouth open he was lying, this sick man,
And sinking all the while; how had he come
To sink? On better nights his dream went flying,
Dipping, sailing the pasture of his sleep,
But now (since clock and cock) had sunk him down
Through mattress, bed, floor, floors beneath, stairs, cellars,
Through deep foundations of the manse; still sinking
Through unturned earth. How had he magicked space
With inadvertent motion or word uttered
Of too-close-packed intelligence (such there are),
That he should penetrate with sliding ease
Dense earth, compound of ages, granite ribs
And groins? Consider: there was some word uttered,
Some abracadabra – then, like a stage-ghost,
Funereally with weeping, down, drowned, lost!

Oh, to be a child once more, sprawling at ease
On smooth turf of a ruined castle court!
Once he had dropped a stone between the slabs
That masked an ancient well, mysteriously
Plunging his mind down with it. Hear it go
Rattling and rocketing into secret void!
Count slowly: one, two, three! and echoes come
Fainter and fainter, merged in the general hum
Of bees and flies; only a thin draught rises
To chill the drowsy air. There he had lain
As if unborn, until life floated back
From the deep waters.

                                Oh, to renew now
That bliss of repossession, kindly sun
Forfeit for ever, and the towering sky!

Falling, falling! Day closed up behind him.
Now stunned by the violent subterrene flow
Of rivers, whirling down to hiss below
On the flame-axis of this terrible earth;
Toppling upon their waterfall, O spirit....

SAUL OF TARSUS

'Share and share alike
    In the nest' was the rule,
But Paul had a wide throat,
    He loved his belly-full.

Over the edge went Peter,
    After him went John,
True-blooded young nestlings
    Thrown out, one by one.

If Mother Church was proud
    Of her great cuckoo son,
He bit off her simple head
    Before he had done.

STORM: AT THE FARM WINDOW

The unruly member (for relief
    Of aching head) clacks without care;
Pastures lie sullen; hung with grief
    The steading: thunder binds the air.

Gulls on the blue sea-surface rock:
    The cows move lowing to scant shade;
Jess lays aside the half-worked smock,
    Dan, in his ditch, lets fall the spade.

*   *   *   *   *

Now swoops the outrageous hurricane
    With lightning in steep pitchfork jags;
The blanched hill leaps in sheeted rain,
    Sea masses white to assault the crags.

Such menace tottering overhead,
    Old Jess for ague scolds no more;
She sees grey bobtail flung down dead
    Lightning-blazed by the barn door –

Wonder and panic chase our grief,
    Purge our thick distempered blood;
Man, cattle, harvest shock and sheaf,
    Stagger below the sluicing flood....

BLACK HORSE LANE

Dame Jane the music mistress,
        the music mistress;
Sharkie the baker of Black Horse Lane,
    At sound of a fiddle
    Caught her up by the middle –
And away like swallows from the lane,
    Flying out together –
    From the crooked lane.

What words said Sharkie to her,
        said Sharkie to her?
How did she look in the lane?
    No neighbour heard
    One sigh or one word,
Not a sound but the fiddling in Black Horse Lane,
    The happy noise of music –
    Again and again.

Where now be those two old 'uns,
        be those two old 'uns?
Sharkie the baker run off with Jane?
    Hark ye up to Flint Street,
    Halloo to Pepper-Mint Street,
Follow by the fells to the great North Plain,
    By the fells and the river –
    To the cold North Plain.

How came this passion to them,
        this passion to them,
Love in a freshet on Black Horse Lane?
    It came without warning

One blue windy morning
So they scarcely might know was it joy or pain,
    With scarce breath to wonder –
    Was it joy or pain.

Took they no fardels with them,
        no fardels with them,
Out and alone on the ice-bound plain?
    Sharkie he had rockets
    And crackers in his pockets,
Aye, and she had a plaid shawl to keep off the rain,
    An old Highland plaid shawl –
    To keep off the rain.

RETURN

The seven years' curse is ended now
That drove me forth from this kind land,
From mulberry-bough and apple-bough
And gummy twigs the west wind shakes,
To drink the brine from crusted lakes
And grit my teeth on sand.

Now for your cold, malicious brain
And most uncharitable, cold heart,
You, too, shall clank the seven years' chain
On sterile ground for all time cursed
With famine's itch and flames of thirst,
The blank sky's counterpart.

The load that from my shoulder slips
Straightway upon your own is tied:
You, too, shall scorch your finger-tips
With scrabbling on the desert's face
Such thoughts I had of this green place,
Sent scapegoat for your pride.

Here, Robin on a tussock sits,
And Cuckoo with his call of hope
Cuckoos awhile, then off he flits,
While peals of dingle-dongle keep
Troop-discipline among the sheep
That graze across the slope.

A brook from fields of gentle sun
Through the glade its water heaves,
The falling cone would well-nigh stun
That Squirrel wantonly lets drop
When up he scampers to tree-top
And dives among the green.

But no, I ask a surer peace
Than vengeance on you could provide.
So fear no ill from my release:
Be off, elude the curse, disgrace
Some other green and happy place –
This world of fools is wide.

INCUBUS

Asleep, amazed, with lolling head,
Arms in supplication spread,
Body shudders, dumb with fear;
There lifts the Moon, but who am I,
Cloaked in shadow wavering by,
Stooping, muttering at his ear?
Bound is Body, foot and hand,
Bound to lie at my command,
Horror bolted to lie still
While I sap what sense I will.

Through the darkness here come I,
Softly fold about the prey;
Body moaning must obey,
Must not question who or why,
Must accept me, come what may,
Dumbly must obey.

When owls and cocks dispute the dawn,
Through the window I am drawn
Streaming out, a foggy breath.
…Body waking with a sigh
From the spell that was half Death,
Smiles for freedom, blinks an eye
At the sun-commanded sky,
'O morning scent and tree-top song,
Slow-rising smoke and nothing wrong!'

THE HILLS OF MAY

Walking with a virgin heart
   The green hills of May,
Me, the Wind, she took as lover
   By her side to play,

Let me toss her untied hair,
   Let me shake her gown,
Careless though the daisies redden,
   Though the sun frown,

Scorning in her gay habit
   Lesser love than this,
My cool spiritual embracing,
   My secret kiss.

So she walked, the proud lady,
   So danced or ran,
So she loved with a whole heart,
   Neglecting man....

Fade, fail, innocent stars
   On the green of May:
She has left our bournes for ever,
   Too fine to stay.

THE CORONATION MURDER

Old Becker crawling in the night
   From his grave at the stair-foot,
Labours up the long flight,
   Feeble, dribbling, black as soot,
Quakes at his own ghostly fright.

A cat goes past with lantern eyes,
   Shooting splendour through the dark.
'Murder! Help!' a voice cries
   In nightmare; the son dreams that stark
In lead his vanished father lies.

A stair-top glimmer points the goal.
    Becker goes wavering up, tongue-tied,
Stoops, with eye to keyhole....
    There, a tall candle by her side,
Delilah sits, serene and whole.

Her fingers turn the prayer-book leaves
    And, free from spiritual strife,
Soft and calm her breast heaves:
    Thus calmly with his cobbling knife
She stabbed him through; now never grieves.

Baffled, aghast with hate, mouse-poor,
    He glares and clatters the brass knob.
Through his heart it slid sure:
    He bowed, he fell with never a sob.
Again she stabbed, now sits secure,

Praying (as she has always prayed)
    For great Victoria's Majesty,
Droning prayer for God's aid
    To succour long dead Royalty,
The Consort Prince, Queen Adelaide....

She falls asleep, the clocks chime two;
    Old Becker sinks to unquiet rest.
Loud and sad the cats mew.
    Lead weighs cruelly on his breast,
His bones are tufted with mildew.

WHIPPERGINNY

(1923)

WHIPPERGINNY

('A card game, obsolete.' – *Standard Dictionary*.)

To cards we have recourse
 When Time with cruelty runs,
To courtly Bridge for stress of love,
 To Nap for noise of guns.

On fairy earth we tread,
 No present problems vex
Where man's four humours fade to suits,
 With red and black for sex.

Where phantom gains accrue
 By tricks instead of cash,
Where pasteboard federacies of Powers
 In battles-royal clash.

Then read the antique word
 That hangs above this page
As type of mirth-abstracted joy,
 Calm terror, noiseless rage,

A realm of ideal thought,
 Obscured by veils of Time,
Cipher remote enough to stand
 As namesake for my rhyme,

A game to play apart
 When all but crushed with care;
Let right and left, your jealous hands,
 The lists of love prepare.

THE BEDPOST

Sleepy Betsy from her pillow
   Sees the post and ball
Of her sister's wooden bedstead
   Shadowed on the wall.

Now this grave young warrior standing
   With uncovered head
Tells her stories of old battle
   As she lies in bed:

How the Emperor and the Farmer,
   Fighting knee to knee,
Broke their swords but whirled their scabbards
   Till they gained the sea.

How the ruler of that shore
   Foully broke his oath,
Gave them beds in his sea cave,
   Then stabbed them both.

How the daughters of the Emperor,
   Diving boldly through,
Caught and killed their father's murderer
   Old Cro-bar-cru.

How the Farmer's sturdy sons
   Fought the Giant Gog,
Threw him into Stony Cataract
   In the land of Og.

Will and Abel were their names,
   Though they went by others:
He could tell ten thousand stories
   Of these lusty brothers.

How the Emperor's elder daughter
   Fell in love with Will
And went with him to the Court of Venus
   Over Hoo Hill;

How Gog's wife encountered Abel
  Whom she hated most,
Stole away his arms and helmet,
  Turned him to a post.

As a post he shall stay rooted
  For yet many years,
Until a maiden shall release him
  With pitying tears.

But Betsy likes the bloodier stories,
  Clang and clash of fight,
And Abel wanes with the spent candle –
  'Sweetheart, good-night!'

A LOVER SINCE CHILDHOOD

Tangled in thought am I,
Stumble in speech do I?
Do I blunder and blush for the reason why?
Wander aloof do I,
Lean over gates and sigh,
Making friends with the bee and the butterfly?

If thus and thus I do,
Dazed by the thought of you,
Walking my sorrowful way in the early dew,
My heart cut through and through
In this despair for you,
Starved for a word or look will my hope renew;

Give then a thought for me
Walking so miserably,
Wanting relief in the friendship of flower or tree;
Do but remember, we
Once could in love agree,
Swallow your pride, let us be as we used to be.

SONG OF CONTRARIETY

Far away is close at hand,
Close joined is far away,
Love shall come at your command
Yet will not stay.

At summons of your dream-despair
She might not disobey,
But slid close down beside you there,
And complaisant lay.

Yet now her flesh and blood consent
In the hours of day,
Joy and passion both are spent,
Twining clean away.

Is the person empty air,
Is the spectre clay,
That love, lent substance by despair,
Wanes and leaves you lonely there
On the bridal day?

LOVE IN BARRENNESS

Below the ridge a raven flew
And we heard the lost curlew
Mourning out of sight below.
Mountain tops were touched with snow;
Even the long dividing plain
Showed no wealth of sheep or grain,
But fields of boulders lay like corn
And raven's croak was shepherd's horn
Where slow cloud-shadow strayed across
A pasture of thin heath and moss.

The North Wind rose: I saw him press
With lusty force against your dress,
Moulding your body's inward grace
And streaming off from your set face;
So now no longer flesh and blood
But poised in marble flight you stood.
O wingless Victory, loved of men,
Who could withstand your beauty then?

SONG IN WINTER

The broken spray left hanging
Can hold his dead leaf longer
Into your glum November
Than this live twig tossed shivering
By your East Wind anger.

Unrepentant, hoping Spring,
Flowery hoods of glory hoping,
Carelessly I sing,
With envy none for the broken spray
When the Spring comes, fallen away.

UNICORN AND THE WHITE DOE

Unicorn with burning heart
Breath of love has drawn
On his desolate peak apart
At rumour of dawn,

Has trumpeted his pride
These long years mute,
Tossed his horn from side to side,
Lunged with his foot.

Like a storm of sand has run
Breaking his own boundaries,
Gone in hiding from the sun
Under camphor trees.

Straight was the course he took
Across the plain, but here with briar
And mire the tangled alleys crook,
Baulking desire.

A shoulder glistened white –
The bough still shakes –
A white doe darted out of sight
Through the forest brakes.

Tall and close the camphors grow
The grass grows thick –
Where you are I do not know,
You fly so quick.

Where have you fled from me?
I pursue, you fade,
I hunt, you hide from me
In the chequered glade.

Often from my hot lair
I would watch you drink,
A mirage of tremulous air,
At the pool's brink.

Vultures, rocking high in air
By the western gate,
Warned me with discordant cry
You are even such as I:
You have no mate.

SONG: SULLEN MOODS

Love, never count your labour lost
    Though I turn sullen or retired
Even at your side; my thought is crossed
    With fancies by no evil fired.

And when I answer you, some days,
    Vaguely and wildly, never fear
That my love walks forbidden ways,
    Snapping the ties that hold it here.

If I speak gruffly, this mood is
    Mere indignation at my own
Shortcomings, plagues, uncertainties:
    I forget the gentler tone.

You, now that you have come to be
    My one beginning, prime and end,
I count at last as wholly me,
    Lover no longer nor yet friend.

Help me to see you as before
    When overwhelmed and dead, almost,
I stumbled on that secret door
    Which saves the live man from the ghost.

Be once again the distant light,
    Promise of glory, not yet known
In full perfection – wasted quite
    When on my imperfection thrown.

ANGRY SAMSON

Are they blind, the lords of Gaza
    In their strong towers,
Who declare Samson pillow-smothered
    And stripped of his powers?

O stolid Philistines,
    Stare now in amaze
At my foxes running in your cornfields
    With their tails ablaze,

At swung jaw-bone, at bees swarming
    In the stark lion's hide,
At these, the gates of well-walled Gaza
    A-clank to my stride.

CHILDREN OF DARKNESS

We spurred our parents to the kiss,
Though doubtfully they shrank from this –
Day had no courage to pursue
What lusty dark alone might do:
Then were we joined from their caress
In heat of midnight, one from two.

This night-seed knew no discontent:
In certitude our changings went.
Though there were veils about his face,
With forethought, even in that pent place,
Down toward the light his way we bent
To kingdoms of more ample space.

Is Day prime error, that regret
For Darkness roars unstifled yet?
That in this freedom, by faith won,
Only acts of doubt are done?
That unveiled eyes with tears are wet:
We loathe to gaze upon the sun?

RICHARD ROE AND JOHN DOE

Richard Roe wished himself Solomon,
Made cuckold, you should know, by one John Doe:
Solomon's neck was firm enough to bear
Some score of antlers more than Roe could wear.

Richard Roe wished himself Alexander,
Being robbed of house and land by the same hand:
Ten thousand acres or a principal town
Would have cost Alexander scarce a frown.

Richard Roe wished himself Job the prophet,
Sunk past reclaim in stinking rags and shame –
However ill Job's plight, his own was worse:
He knew no God to call on or to curse.

He wished himself Job, Solomon, Alexander,
For patience, wisdom, power to overthrow
Misfortune; but with spirit so unmanned
That most of all he wished himself John Doe.

THE DIALECTICIANS

I heard two poets
    Down by the sea,
Discussing a burdensome
    Relativity.

Thought has a bias,
    Direction a bend,
Space its inhibitions,
    Time a dead end.

Is whiteness white?
    O then, call it black:
Farthest from the truth
    Is yet half-way back.

Effect ordains cause,
    Head swallowing the tail;
Does whale engulf sprat,
    Or sprat assume whale?

Contentions weary,
    It giddies to think;
Then swim, poet, swim!
    Or drink, poet, drink!

THE LAND OF WHIPPERGINNY

Come closer yet, my honeysuckle, my sweetheart Jinny:
    A low sun is gilding the bloom of the wood –
Is it Heaven, or Hell, or the Land of Whipperginny
    That holds this fairy lustre, not understood?

For stern proud psalms from the chapel on the moors
    Waver in the night wind, their firm rhythm broken,
Lugubriously twisted to a howling of whores
    Or lent an airy glory too strange to be spoken.

Soon the risen Moon will peer down with pity,
    Drawing us in secret by an ivory gate
To the fruit-plats and fountains of her silver city
    Where lovers need not argue the tokens of fate.

'THE GENERAL ELIOTT'

He fell in victory's fierce pursuit,
    Holed through and through with shot;
A sabre sweep had hacked him deep
    'Twixt neck and shoulder-knot.

The potman cannot well recall,
    The ostler never knew,
Whether that day was Malplaquet,
    The Boyne, or Waterloo.

But there he hangs, a tavern sign,
    With foolish bold regard
For cock and hen and loitering men
    And wagons down the yard.

Raised high above the hayseed world
    He smokes his china pipe;
And now surveys the orchard ways,
    The damsons clustering ripe –

Stares at the churchyard slabs beyond,
    Where country neighbours lie:
Their brief renown set lowly down,
    But his invades the sky.

He grips a tankard of brown ale
    That spills a generous foam:
Often he drinks, they say, and winks
    At drunk men lurching home.

No upstart hero may usurp
    That honoured swinging seat;
His seasons pass with pipe and glass
    Until the tale's complete –

And paint shall keep his buttons bright
    Though all the world's forgot
Whether he died for England's pride
    By battle or by pot.

A FIGHT TO THE DEATH

Two blind old men in a blind corridor
    Fought to the death, by sense of sound or touch.
Doom flailed unseen, an iron hook-hand tore
    Flesh from the enemy's ribs who swung the crutch.
One gasped, 'She looked on me and smiled, I say',
    So life was battered out, for yea or nay.

MERMAID, DRAGON, FIEND

In my childhood rumours ran
    Of a world beyond our door –
Terrors to the life of man
    That the highroad held in store.

Of the mermaids' doleful game
    In deep water I heard tell,
Of lofty dragons belching flame,
    Of the hornèd fiend of Hell.

Tales like these were too absurd
    For my laughter-loving ear:
Soon I mocked at all I heard,
    Though with cause indeed for fear.

Now I know the mermaid kin
    I find them bound by natural laws:
They have neither tail nor fin,
    But are deadlier for that cause.

Dragons have no darting tongues,
    Teeth saw-edged, nor rattling scales;
No fire issues from their lungs,
    No black poison from their tails:

For they are creatures of dark air,
    Unsubstantial tossing forms,
Thunderclaps of man's despair
    In mid-whirl of mental storms.

And there's a true and only fiend
    Worse than prophets prophesy,
Whose full powers to hurt are screened
    Lest the race of man should die.

Ever in vain will courage plot
    The dragon's death, in coat of proof;
Or love abjure the mermaid grot;
    Or faith denounce the cloven hoof.

Mermaids will not be denied
    The last bubbles of our shame,
The dragon flaunts an unpierced hide,
    The true fiend governs in God's name.

CHRISTMAS EVE

On Christmas Eve the brute Creation
    Lift up their heads and speak with human voices;
The Ox roars out his song of jubilation
    And the Ass rejoices.

They dance for mirth in simple credence
    That man from devildom this day was savèd,
That of his froward spirit he has found riddance:
    They hymn the Son of David.

Ox and Ass cloistered in stable,
    Break bounds to-night and see what shall astound you,
A second Fall, a second death of Abel,
    Wars renewed around you.

Cabals of great men against small men,
    Mobs, murders, informations, the packed jury,
While Ignorance, the lubber prince of all men,
    Glowers with old-time fury.

Excellent beasts, resign your speaking,
    Tempted in man's own choleric tongue to name him,
Hoof-and-horn vengeance have no thought of wreaking,
    Let your dumb grief shame him.

THE SNAKE AND THE BULL

Snake Bull, my namesake, man of wrath,
By no expense of knives or cloth,
Only by work of muttered charms
Could draw all woman to his arms;
None whom he summoned might resist
Nor none recall whom once he kissed
And loosed them from his kiss, by whom
This mother-shame had come.

The power of his compelling flame
Was bound in virtue of our name,
But when in secret he taught me
Like him a thief of love to be,
For half his secret I had found
And half explored the wizard ground
Of words, and when giving consent
Out at his heels I went,

Then Fessé, jungle-god, whose shape
Is one part man and three parts ape,
Avenger of misuse by man
Of lust that by his art began,
And master of all mimicries,
Made tittering laughter in the trees.
With girlish whispers, sighs and giggling
Set the Bull prancing, the Snake wriggling;
Where leaves were broadest and light dim,
Fessé ambushed him.

Up through the air I saw him swung
To bridal bowers with red flowers hung:
He choked for mercy like a maid
By his own violent whim betrayed;
Blood broke in fountains from his neck,
I heard his hugged ribs creak and break,
But what the tree-top rites might be
How should I stay to see?

In terror of the Ape God's power
I changed my person in that hour,
Cast off the livery of my clan,
Over unlawful hills I ran,

I soiled me with forbidden earth.
In nakedness of second birth
I scorched away the Snake's red eyes
Tattooed for name about my thighs,
And slew the Sacred Bull oppressed
With passion on my breast.

The girls of my new tribe are cold,
Amazon, scarred, not soft to hold.
They seek not men, nor are they sought,
Whose children are not theirs, but bought
From outlaw tribes who dwell in trees –
Tamed apes suckle these.

Young men of the tribe are such
That knife or bow they dare not touch,
But in close watching of the skies
And reckoning counts they dim their eyes.
Closed, each by each, in thoughtful bars
They plot the circuits of the stars,
And frozen music dulls their need
Of drink and man-flesh greed.

They hold that virtue from them slips
When eye greets eye or lips touch lips;
Down to the knee their broad beards fall
And hardly are they men at all.
Possessions they have none, nor schools
For tribal duties, nor close rules,
No gods, no rites, no totem beasts,
No friendships, no love feasts.

Now quit, as they, of gong-roused lust,
The leap of breasts, the scattering dust,
In hermit splendour at my glass
I watch the skies' procession pass,
Tracing my figures on the floor
Of planets' paths and comets' lore;
In calm amaze I cloak my will,
I gaze, I count, until

Harsh from his House the Bull roars out,
Forked lightning leaps his points about,
Tattoos his shape upon the sky;
Night anger fills the Serpent's eye

With desolating fire for one
Who thought the Serpent's days were done,
And girlish titterings from the trees
Loosen my firm knees.

THE RED RIBBON DREAM

As I stood by the stair-head in the upper hall
      The rooms to left and right were locked as before.
      It was senseless to hammer at an unreal door
Painted on the plaster of a ten-foot wall.

There was half-light here, piled darkness beyond
      Rising up sheer as the mountain of Time,
      The blank rock-face that no thought can climb,
Girdled around with the Slough of Despond.

I stood quite dumb, sunk fast in the mire,
      Lonely as the first man, or the last man,
      Chilled to despair since evening began,
Dazed for the memory of a lost desire.

But a voice said 'Easily', and a voice said 'Come!'
      Easily I followed with no thought of doubt,
      Turned to the right hand, and the way stretched out;
The ground held firmly; I was no more dumb.

For that was the place where I longed to be,
      And past all hope there the kind lamp shone,
      The carpet was holy that my feet were on,
And logs on the fire lay hissing for me.

The cushions were friendship and the chairs were love,
      Shaggy with love was the great wolf skin,
      The clock ticked 'Easily' as I entered in,
'Come,' called the bullfinch from his cage above.

Love went before me; it was shining now
      From the eyes of a girl by the window wall,
      Whose beauty I knew to be fate and all
By the thin red ribbon on her calm brow.

Then I was a hero and a bold boy
    Kissing the hand I had never yet kissed;
    I felt red ribbon like a snake twist
In my own thick hair, so I laughed for joy.

      *   *   *   *   *

I stand by the stair-head in the upper hall;
    The rooms to the left and right are locked as before.
    Once I found entrance, but now never more,
And Time leans forward with his glassy wall.

IN PROCESSION

Often, half-way to sleep,
Not yet sunken deep –
The sudden moment on me comes
From a mountain shagged and steep,
With terrible roll of dream drums,
Reverberations, cymbals, horns replying,
When with standards flying,
Horsemen in clouds behind,
The coloured pomps unwind
Carnival wagons
With their saints and their dragons
On the scroll of my teeming mind:
The Creation and Flood
With our Saviour's Blood
And fat Silenus' flagons,
And every rare beast
From the South and East,
Both greatest and least,
On and on,
In endless, variant procession.
I stand at the top rungs
Of a ladder reared in the air,
And I rail in strange tongues,
So the crowds murmur and stare;
Then volleys again the blare
Of horns, and summer flowers
Fly scattering in showers,
And the sun leaps in the sky,
While the drums thumping by
Proclaim me....

Oh, then, when I wake,
Could I courage take
To renew my speech,
Could I stretch and reach
The flowers and the ripe fruit
Laid out at the ladder's foot,
Could I rip a silken shred
From the banner tossed ahead,
Could I call a double-flam
From the drums, could the goat
Horned with gold, could the ram
With a flank like a barn-door,
The dwarf, the blackamoor,
Could Jonah and the Whale
And the Holy Grail,
The Ape with his platter
Going clitter-clatter,
The Nymphs and the Satyr,
And every marvellous matter
Come before me here,
Standing near and clear –
Could I make it so that you
Might wonder at them too!
– Glories of land and sea,
Of Heaven glittering free,
Castles hugely built in Spain,
Glories of Cockaigne,
Of that spicy kingdom, Cand,
Of the Delectable Land,
Of the Land of Crooked Stiles,
Of the Fortunate Isles,
Of the more than three-score miles
That to Babylon lead
(A pretty city indeed
Built on a four-square plan),
Of the Land of the Gold Man
Whose eager horses whinny
In their cribs of gold,
Of the Land of Whipperginny,
Of the land where none grows old....

But cowardly I tell,
Rather, of the Town of Hell –
A huddle of dirty woes

And houses in fading rows
Straggled through space:
Hell has no market-place,
Nor point where four ways meet,
Nor principal street,
Nor barracks, nor Town Hall,
Nor shops at all,
Nor rest for weary feet,
Nor theatre, square, or park,
Nor lights after dark,
Nor churches, nor inns,
Nor convenience for sins –
Neither ends nor begins,
Rambling, limitless, hated well,
This Town of Hell
Where between sleep and sleep I dwell.

HENRY AND MARY

Henry was a young king,
    Mary was his queen;
He gave her a snowdrop
    On a stalk of green.

Then all for his kindness
    And all for his care
She gave him a new-laid egg
    In the garden there.

'Love, can you sing?'
                        'I cannot sing.'
    'Or tell a tale?'
                        'Not one I know.'
'Then let us play at queen and king
    As down the garden walks we go.'

AN ENGLISH WOOD

This valley wood is pledged
To the set shape of things,
And reasonably hedged:
Here are no harpies fledged,
No rocs may clap their wings,
Nor gryphons wave their stings.
Here, poised in quietude,
Calm elementals brood
On the set shape of things:
They fend away alarms
From this green wood.
Here nothing is that harms –
No bulls with lungs of brass,
No toothed or spiny grass,
No tree whose clutching arms
Drink blood when travellers pass,
No mount of glass;
No bardic tongues unfold
Satires or charms.
Only, the lawns are soft,
The tree-stems, grave and old;
Slow branches sway aloft,
The evening air comes cold,
The sunset scatters gold.
Small grasses toss and bend,
Small pathways idly tend
Towards no fearful end.

WHAT DID I DREAM?

What did I dream? I do not know –
    The fragments fly like chaff.
Yet, strange, my mind was tickled so
    I cannot help but laugh.

Pull the curtains close again,
    Tuck me grandly in;
Must a world of humour wane
    Because birds begin

Complaining in a fretful tone,
    Rousing me from sleep –
The finest entertainment known,
    And given rag-cheap?

INTERLUDE: ON PRESERVING A POETICAL FORMULA

I

'There's less and less cohesion
In each collection
Of my published poetries?'
You are taking me to task?
And 'What were my last Royalties?
Reckoned in pounds, were they, or shillings,
Or even perhaps in pence?'
                                    No, do not ask!
I'm lost, in buyings and sellings.
But please permit only once more for luck
Irreconcilabilities in my book....

For these are all the same stuff really,
The obverse and reverse, if you look closely,
Of busy Imagination's new-coined money;
And if you watch the blind
Phototropisms of my fluttering mind,
Whether, growing strong, I wrestle Jacob-wise
With fiendish darkness blinking threatfully
Its bale-fire eyes,
Or whether childishly

I dart to Mother-skirts of love and peace
To play with toys until those horrors leave me –
Yet note, whichever way I find release,
By fight or flight,
By being harsh or tame,
The SPIRIT's the same, the Pen-and-Ink's the same.

II

EPITAPH ON AN UNFORTUNATE ARTIST

He found a formula for drawing comic rabbits:
    This formula for drawing comic rabbits paid,
So in the end he could not change the tragic habits
    This formula for drawing comic rabbits made.

A HISTORY OF PEACE

(Solitudinem faciunt, pacem appellant)

Here rest in peace the bones of Henry Reece,
Dead through his bitter championship of Peace
Against all eagle-nosed and cynic lords
Who keep the Pax Romana with their swords.

Henry was only son of Thomas Reece,
Banker and sometime Justice of the Peace,
And of Jane Reece whom Thomas kept in dread
By Pax Romana of his board and bed.

THE ROCK BELOW

Comes a muttering from the earth
    Where speedwell grows and daisies grow,
'Pluck these weeds up, root and all,
    Search what hides below.'

Root and all I pluck them out;
    There, close under, I have found
Stumps of thorn with ancient crooks
    Grappled in the ground.

I wrench the thorn-stocks from their hold
    To set a rose-bush in that place;
Love has pleasure in my roses
    For a summer space.

Yet the bush cries out in grief:
    'Our lowest rootlets turn on rock,
We live in terror of the drought
    Withering crown and stock.'

I grow angry with my creature,
    Tear it out and see it die;
Far beneath I strike the stone,
    Jarring hatefully.

Impotently must I mourn
    Roses never to flower again?
Are heart and back too slightly built
    For a heaving strain?

Heave shall break my proud back never,
    Strain shall never burst my heart:
Steely fingers hook in the crack,
    Up the rock shall start.

Now from the deep and frightful pit
    Shoots forth the spiring phoenix-tree
Long despaired in this bleak land,
Holds the air with boughs, with bland
    Fragrance welcome to the bee,
    With fruits of immortality.

AN IDYLL OF OLD AGE

Two gods once visited a hermit couple,
Philemon and his Baucis, old books tell;
They sampled elder-wine and called it nectar,
Though nectar is the tastier drink by far.
They made ambrosia of pot-herb and lentil,
They ate pease-porridge even, with a will.
Why, and so forth....
    But that night in the spare bedroom
Where they lay shivering in the musty gloom,
Hermes and Zeus overheard conversation
Behind the intervening wall drag on
In thoughtful snatches through the night. They idly
Listened, and first they heard Philemon sigh: –

Phi.:   'Since two souls meet and merge at time of marriage,
Conforming to one stature and one age,
An honest token each with each exchanging
Of Only Love unbroken as a ring –
What signified my boyhood's ideal friendship
That stared its ecstasy at eye and lip,
But dared not touch because love seemed too holy
For flesh with flesh in real embrace to lie?'

Bau.:   Then Baucis sighed in answer to Philemon,
'Many's the young man that my eye rests on
(Our younger guest to-night provides the instance)
Whose body brings my heart hotter romance
Than your dear face could ever spark within me;
Often I wish my heart from yours set free.'

Phi.:   'In this wild medley round us of Bought Love,
Free Love and Forced Love and pretentious No-Love,
Let us walk upright, yet with care consider
Whether, in living thus, we do not err.
Why might we not approve adulterous licence
Increasing pleasurable experience?
What could the soul lose through the body's rapture
With a body not its mate, where thought is pure?'

Bau.:   'Are children bonds of love? But even children
Grow up too soon as women and as men,
And in the growing find their own love private,
Meet parent-love with new suspicious hate.
Our favourites run the surest to the Devil
In spite of early cares and all good will.'

Phi.:   'Sweetheart, you know that you have my permission
To go your own way and to take love on
Wherever love may signal.'
                        She replying

Bau.:   Said, 'I allow you, dearest, the same thing.'

    Zeus was struck dumb at this unholy compact,
But Hermes knew the shadow from the fact
And took an oath that for whole chests of money
Neither would faithless to the other be,
Would not and could not, being twined together

In such close love that he for want of her
Removed one night-time from his side would perish,
And she was magnet-drawn by his least wish.

Eternal Gods deny the sense of humour
That well might prejudice their infallible power,
So Hermes and King Zeus not once considered,
In treating of this idyll overheard,
That love rehearses after life's defeat
Remembered conflicts of an earlier heat.
Baucis, kind soul, was palsied, withered and bent,
Philemon, too, was ten years impotent.

THE LORD CHAMBERLAIN TELLS OF A FAMOUS MEETING

Unknown to each other in a hostile camp,
Spies of two empire nations unallied,
These heroes met, princes of East and West,
Over a ragged pack of cards, by chance.
Never believe what credulous annalists
Record you in good faith of that encounter.
I was there myself, East's man, and witnessed all.
In the main camp of the Middle Kingdom's army
At a soldier's mess, shortly before Retreat,
East, a pretended trooper, stepping in,
Glanced round the room, shortly discerning West,
Who sat dejected at a corner table.
East moved by curiosity or compassion
Pulled out his cards, offering West the cut,
And West, disguised as a travelling ballad-man,
Took and cut; they played together then
For half an hour or more; then went their ways.

Never believe such credulous annalists
As tell you, West for sign of recognition,
Greatness to greatness, wit to dexterous wit,
With sleight of magic most extraordinary
Alters the Duty of his Ace of Spades,
Making three-pence, three-halfpence; East, it's said,
For a fantastic sly acknowledgement,
While his grave eyes betoken no surprise,
Makes magic too; presto, the Knave of Hearts

Nims the Queen's rose and cocks it in his cap
Furtively, so that only West remarks it.
But such was not the fact; contrariwise,
When Proteus meets with Proteus, each annuls
The variability of the other's mind;
Single they stand, casting their mutable cloaks.
So for this present chance, I take my oath
That leaning across and watching the cards close
I caught no hint of prestidigitation.

Never believe approved biographers
Who'll show a sequence of the games then played,
Explaining that the minds of these two princes
Were of such subtlety and such nimbleness
That Whipperginny on the fall of a card
Changed to Bézique or Cribbage or Piquet,
Euchre or Écarté, then back once more,
Each comprehending with no signal shown
The opposing fancies of the other's mind.
It's said, spectators of this play grew dazed,
They turned away, thinking the gamesters drunk,
But I, who sat there watching, keeping score,
Say they observed the rules of but one game
The whole bout, playing neither well nor ill
But slowly, with their thoughts in other channels,
Serene and passionless like wooden men.

Neither believe those elegant essayists
Who reconstruct the princes' conversation
From grotesque fabrics of their own vain brains.
I only know that East gave West a nod,
Asking him careless questions about trade;
West gave the latest rumours from the front,
Raising of sieges, plots and pillages.
He told a camp-fire yarn to amuse the soldiers,
Whereat they all laughed emptily (East laughed too).
He sang a few staves of the latest catch,
And pulling out his roll of rhymes, unfurled it –
Ballads and songs, measured by the yard-rule.
But do not trust the elegant essayists
Who'd have you swallow all they care to tell
Of the riddling speech in painful *double entendre*
That West and East juggled across the cards,
So intricate, so exquisitely resolved

In polished antithetical periods
That by comparison, as you must believe,
Solomon himself faced with the Queen of Sheba,
And Bishop Such preaching before the King,
Joined in one person would have seemed mere trash.
I give my testimony beyond refutal,
Nailing the lie for all who ask the facts.

Pay no heed to those vagabond dramatists
Who, to present this meeting on the stage,
Would make my Prince, stealthily drawing out
A golden quill and stabbing his arm for blood,
Scratch on a vellum slip some hasty sentence
And pass it under the table; which West signs
With his blood, so the treaty's made between them
All unobserved and two far nations wedded
While enemy soldiers loll, yawning, around.
I was there myself, I say, seeing everything.
Truly, this is what passed, that East regarding
West with a steady look and knowing him well,
For an instant let the heavy soldier-mask,
His best protection, a dull cast of face,
Light up with joy, and his eyes shoot out mirth.
West then knew East, checked, and misdealt the cards.
Nothing at all was said, on went the game.
But East bought from West's bag of ballads, after,
Two sombre histories, and some songs for dancing.

Also distrust those allegorical
Painters who treating of this famous scene
Are used to splash the skies with lurching Cupids,
Goddesses with loose hair, and broad-cheeked Zephyrs;
They burnish up the soldiers' breastplate steel,
Rusted with languor of their long campaign,
To twinkling high-lights of unmixed white paint,
Giving them buskins and tall plumes to wear,
While hard by, in a wanton imagery,
Aquatic Triton thunders on his conch
And Satyrs gape from behind neighbouring trees.
I who was there, sweating in my shirt-sleeves,
Felt no divinity brooding in that mess,
For human splendour gave the gods rebuff.

Do not believe them, seem they never so wise,
Credibly posted with all new research,
Those elegant essayists, vagabond dramatists,
Authentic and approved biographers,
Solemn annalists, allegorical
Painters, each one misleading or misled.
One thing is true, that of all sights I have seen
In any quarter of this world of men,
By night, by day, in court, field, tavern, or barn,
That was the noblest, East encountering West,
Their silent understanding and restraint,
Meeting and parting like the Kings they were
With plain indifference to all circumstance;
Saying no good-bye, no handclasp and no tears,
But letting speech between them fade away,
In casual murmurs and half compliments,
East sauntering out for fresh intelligence,
And West shuffling away, not looking back;
Though each knew well that this chance meeting stood
For turning movement of world history.
And I? I trembled, knowing these things must be.

THE SEWING BASKET

*(Accompanying a wedding present from
Jenny Nicholson to Winifred Roberts)*

To Winifred
The day she's wed
(Having no gold) I send instead
This sewing basket,
And lovingly
Demand that she,
If ever wanting help from me,
Will surely ask it.

Which being gravely said,
Now to go straight ahead
With a cutting of string,
An unwrapping of paper,
With a haberdasher's flourish,
The airs of a draper,
To review
And search this basket through.

Here's one place full
Of coloured wool,
And various yarn
With which to darn;
A sampler, too,
I've worked for you,
Lettered from A to Z,
The text of which
In small cross-stitch
Is 'Love to Winifred'.

Here's a rag-doll wherein
To thrust the casual pin.
His name in Benjamin
For his ingenuous face;
Be sure I've not forgotten
Black thread or crochet cotton;
While Brussels lace
Has found a place
Behind the needle-case.
(But the case for the scissors?
Empty, as you see;
Love must never be sundered
Between you and me.)

Winifred Roberts,
Think of me, do,
When the friends I am sending
Are working for you.
The song of the thimble
Is, 'Oh, forget her not.'
Says the tape-measure,
'Absent but never forgot.'

Benjamin's song
He sings all day long
Though his voice is not strong:
He hoarsely holloas
   More or less as follows: –

'Button boxes
Never have locks-es,
For the keys would soon disappear.
But here's a linen button

   With a smut on,
  And a big bone button
   With a cut on,
  A pearly and a fancy
  Of small significancy,
  And the badges of a Fireman and a Fusilier.'

  Which song he'll alternate
  With sounds like a Turkish hubble-bubble
  Smoked at a furious rate,
  The words are scarcely intelligible: –

  (Prestissimo)
  'Needles and ribbons and packets of pins,
  Prints and chintz and odd bod-a-kins,
   They'd never mind whether
   You laid 'em together
  Or one from the other in pockets and tins.

  'For packets of pins and ribbons and needles
  Or odd bod-a-kins and chintz and prints,
   Being birds of a feather,
   Would huddle together
  Like minnows on billows or pennies in mints.'

  He'll learn to sing more prettily
  When you take him out to Italy
  On your honeymoon,
  (Oh come back soon!)
  To Florence or to Rome,
  The prima donnas' home,
  To Padua or to Genoa
  Where tenors all sing tra-la-la....

  Good-bye, Winifred,
  Bless your heart, Ben.
  Come back happy
  And safe agen.

AGAINST CLOCK AND COMPASSES

'Beauty dwindles into shadow,
*   Beauty dies, preferred by Fate,*
Past the rescue of bold thought.
*   Sentries drowsed,'* they say, *'at Beauty's gate.'*

'Time duteous to his hour-glass,
*   Time with unerring sickle,*
Garners to a land remote
*   Where your vows of true love are proved fickle.'*

'Love chill upon her forehead,
*   Love fading from her cheek,*
Love dulled in either eye,
*   With voice of love,'* they say, *'no more to speak.'*

I deny to Time his terror;
    Come-and-go prevails not here;
Spring is constant, loveless winter
    Looms, but elsewhere, for he comes not near.

I deny to Space the sorrow;
    No leagues measure love from me;
Turning boldly from her arms,
    Into her arms I shall come certainly.

Time and Space, folly's wonder,
    Three-card shufflers, magic-men!
True love is, that none shall say
    It ever was, or ever flowers again.

THE AVENGERS

Who grafted quince on Western may?
    Sharon's mild rose on Northern briar?
In loathing since that Gospel day
    The two saps flame, the tree's on fire.

The briar-rose weeps for injured right,
    May sprouts up red to choke the quince.
With angry throb of equal spite
    Our wood leaps maddened ever since.

Then mistletoe, of gods not least,
   Kindler of warfare since the Flood,
Against green things of South and East
   Voices the vengeance of our blood.

Crusading ivy Southward breaks
   And sucks your lordly palms upon,
Our island oak the water takes
   To war with cedared Lebanon.

Our slender ash-twigs feathered fly
   Against your vines; bold buttercup
Pours down his legions; malt of rye
   Inflames and burns your lentils up....

For bloom of quince yet caps the may,
   The briar is held by Sharon's rose,
Monsters of thought through earth we stray,
   And how remission comes, God knows.

THE POET'S BIRTH

A page, a huntsman, and a priest of God,
   Her lovers, met in jealous contrariety,
Equally claiming the sole parenthood
   Of him the perfect crown of their variety.
Then, whom to admit, herself she could not tell;
That always was her fate, she loved too well.

'But, many-fathered little one,' she said,
   'Whether of high or low, of smooth or rough,
Here is your mother whom you brought to bed.
   Acknowledge only me, be this enough,
For such as worship after shall be told
A white dove sired you or a rain of gold.'

THE TECHNIQUE OF PERFECTION

Said hermit monk to hermit monk,
    'Friend, in this island anchorage
Our life has tranquilly been sunk
    From pious youth to pious age,

'In such clear waves of quietness,
    Such peace from argument or brawl
That one prime virtue I confess
    Has never touched our hearts at all.

'Forgiveness, friend! who can forgive
    But after anger or dissent?
This never-pardoning life we live
    May earn God's blackest punishment.'

His friend, resolved to find a ground
    For rough dispute between the two
That mutual pardons might abound,
    With cunning from his wallet drew

A curious pebble of the beach
    And scowled, 'This treasure is my own':
He hoped for sharp unfriendly speech
    Or angry snatching at the stone.

But honeyed words his friend outpours,
    'Keep it, dear heart, you surely know
Even were it mine it still were yours,
    This trifle that delights you so.'

The owner, acting wrath, cries, 'Brother,
    What's this? Are my deserts so small
You'd give me trifles?' But the other
    Smiles, 'Brother, you may take my all.'

He then enraged with one so meek,
    So unresponsive to his mood,
Most soundly smites the martyr cheek
    And rends the island quietude.

The martyr, who till now has feigned
    In third degree of craftiness
That meekness is so deep ingrained
    No taunt or slight can make it less,

Spits out the tooth in honest wrath,
    'You hit too hard, old fool,' cried he.
They grapple on the rocky path
    That zigzags downward to the sea.

In rising fury strained and stiff
    They lunge across the narrow ground;
They topple headlong from the cliff
    And murderously embraced are drowned.

*   *   *   *   *   *

Here Peter sits: two spirits reach
    To sound the knocker at his Gate.
They shower forgiveness each on each,
    Beaming triumphant and elate.

But oh, their sweats, their secret fears
    Lest clod-souled witnesses may rise
To set a tingling at their ears
    And bar the approach to Paradise!

THE SIBYL

Her hand falls helpless: thought amazements fly
    Far overhead, they leave no record mark –
Wild swans urged whistling across dazzled sky,
    Or Gabriel hounds* in chorus through the dark.

Yet when she prophesies, each spirit swan,
    Each spectral hound from memory's windy zones,
Flies back to inspire one limb-strewn skeleton
    Of thousands in her valley of dry bones.

There as those life-restored battalions shout,
    Succession flags and Time goes maimed in flight:
From each live gullet twenty swans glide out
    With hell-packs loathlier yet to amaze the night.

* Gabriel hounds, a spectral pack hunting the souls of the damned through the air at night: the origin of this belief some find in the strange noise made by the passage of flocks of wild geese or swans.

A CRUSADER

Death, eager always to pretend
   Himself my servant in the land of spears,
Humble allegiance at the end
   Broke where the homeward track your castle nears:
Let his white steed before my red steed press
And rapt you from me into quietness.

A NEW PORTRAIT OF JUDITH OF BETHULIA

She trod the grasses grey with dew,
   She hugged the unlikely head;
Avenging where the warrior Jew
   Incontinent had fled.

The bearded lips writhed ever more
   At this increase of shame –
Killed by a girl, pretending whore,
   Gone scatheless as she came!

His doom yet loathlier that he knew
   Hers was no nation-pride,
No high religion snatched and slew
   Where he lay stupefied.

Nebuchadnezzar's duke enticed
   To pay a megrim's fee?
Assyrian valour sacrificed
   For a boudoir dignity?

'Only for this, that some tall knave
   Had scorned her welcoming bed,
For this, the assault, the stroke, the grave,'
   Groaned Holofernes' head.

A REVERSAL

The old man in his fast car
    Leaves Achilles lagging,
The old man with his long gun
    Outshoots Ulysses' bow,
Nestor in his botched old age
    Rivals Ajax bragging,
To Nestor's honeyed courtship
    Could Helen say 'No'?

Yet, ancient, since you borrow
    From youth the strength and speed,
Seducing as an equal
    His playmates in the night,
He, robbed, assumes your sceptre,
    He overgoes your rede,
And with his brown and lively hairs
    Out-prophesies your white.

THE MARTYRED DECADENTS:
A SYMPATHETIC SATIRE

We strain our strings thus tight,
    Our voices pitch thus high,
A song to indite
    That nevermore shall die.

The Poet being divine
    Admits no social sin,
Spurring with wine
    And lust the Muse within.

Finding no use at all
    In arms or civic deeds,
Perched on a wall
    Fulfilling fancy's needs.

Let parents, children, wife,
    Be ghosts beside his art,
Be this his life
    To hug the snake to his heart.

Sad souls, the more we stress
    The advantage of our crown,
So much the less
    Our welcome by the Town,

By the gross and rootling hog
    Who grunts nor lifts his head,
By jealous dog
    Or old ass thistle-fed.

By so much less their praise,
    By so much more our glory.
Grim pride outweighs
    The anguish of our story.

We strain our strings thus tight,
    Our voices pitch thus high,
To enforce our right
    Over futurity.

EPIGRAMS

ON CHRISTOPHER MARLOWE

Here ranted Isaac's elder son,
The proud shag-breasted godless one,
From whom observant Smooth-Cheek stole
Birthright, blessing, hunter's soul.

A VILLAGE FEUD

The cottage damson, laden as could be,
Scowls at the Manor House magnolia-tree
That year by year within its thoughtless powers
Yields flowers and leaves and flowers and leaves and flowers,
While the Magnolia shudders as in fear:
'*Figurez-vous!* two sackfuls every year!'

DEDICATORY

Dolon, analyst of souls,
   To the Graces hangs up here
His shrimp-net rotting into holes
   And oozy from the infernal mere;
He wreathes his gift around with cress,
Lush harvest of the public cess.

TO MY COLLATERAL ANCESTOR, REV. R. GRAVES, THE FRIEND OF THE POET SHENSTONE AND AUTHOR OF THE SPIRITUAL QUIXOTE: ON RECEIPT OF A PRESS-CUTTING INTENDED FOR HIM.

O friend of Shenstone, do you frown
   In realms remote from me
When Messrs Durrant send you down
   By inadvertency
Clippings identifying you
   With some dim man in the moon,
A Spiritual Quixote, true,
   But friend of S. Sassoon?

'A VEHICLE, TO WIT, A BICYCLE'

(Dedicated, without permission, to my friend P.C. Flowers)

'My front-lamp, constable? Why, man, the moon!
   My rear-lamp? Shining there ten yards behind me,
Warm parlour lamplight of *The Dish and Spoon!*'
   But for all my fancy talk, they would have fined me,
Had I not set a rather sly half-crown
   Winking under the rays of my front lamp:
Goodwill towards men disturbed the official frown,
   My rear-light beckoned through the evening's damp.

MOTTO TO A BOOK OF EMBLEMS

Though you read these, but understand not, curse not!
    Or though you read and understand, yet praise not!
What poet weaves a better knot or worse knot
    Untangling which, your own lives you unbrace not?

THE BOWL AND RIM

The bearded rabbi, the meek friar,
    Linked by their ankles in one cell,
Through joint distress of dungeon mire
    Learned each to love his neighbour well.

When four years passed and five and six,
    When seven years brought them no release,
The Jew embraced the crucifix,
    The friar assumed phylacteries.

Then every Sunday, keeping score,
    And every Sabbath in this hymn
They reconciled an age-long war
    Between the platter's bowl and rim.

'Man-like he lived, but God-like died,
    All hatred from His thought removed,
Imperfect until crucified,
    In crucifixion well-beloved.

'If they did wrong, He too did wrong,
    (For love admits no contraries)
In blind religion rooted strong
    Both Jesus and the Pharisees.

'"Love all men as thyself," said He.
    Said they, "Be just with man or dog",
"But only loathe a Pharisee",
    "But crucify this demagogue".

'He died forgiving on the Tree
    To make amends for earlier spite;
They raised Him up their God to be,
    And black with black accomplished white.

'When He again descends on man
    As chief of Scribes and Pharisees,
With loathing for the Publican,
    The maimed and halt His enemies,

'And when a not less formal fate
    Than Pilate's justice and the Rood
His righteous angers expiate,
    To make men think Him wholly good,

'Then He again will have done wrong,
    If God be Love for every man,
For lewd and lettered, weak and strong,
    For Pharisee or Publican,

'But like a God He will have died,
    All hatred from His thought removed,
Imperfect until crucified,
    In crucifixion well-beloved.'

A FORCED MUSIC

Of Love he sang, full-hearted one.
But when the song was done,
The King demanded more,
Ay, and commanded more.
The boy found nothing for encore,
Words, melodies, none:
Ashamed the song's glad rise and plaintive fall
Had so charmed King and Queen and all.

He sang the same verse once again,
But urging less Love's pain,
With altered time and key
He showed variety,
Seemed to refresh the harmony
Of his only strain,
So still the glad rise and the plaintive fall
Could charm the King, the Queen, and all.

He of his song then wearying ceased,
But was not yet released;
The Queen's request was 'More',
And her behest was 'More'.
He played of random notes some score,
He found his rhymes at least –
Then suddenly let his twangling harp down fall
And fled in tears from King and Queen and all.

THE TURN OF A PAGE

'He suddenly,' the page read as it turned,
'Died.'
          The indignant eye discerned
No sense. 'Good page, turn back,' it cried,
(Happily evermore was cheated).
'After these things he suddenly died,'
The truthful page repeated.

'Turn back you earlier pages, nine or ten,
To "Him she loved" and "He alone of men".
Now change the sentence, page!' But still it read
'He suddenly died: they scarce had time to kiss.'
'Read on, ungentle reader,' the book said,
'Resign your hopes to this.'

The eye could not resign, restless in grief,
But darting forward to a later leaf
Found 'Him she loved' and 'He alone of men'.
Oh, who this He was, being a second He,
Confused the plan; the book spoke sternly then,
'Read page by page and see!'

THE MANIFESTATION IN THE TEMPLE

On the High Feast Day in that reverent space
Between the Sacrifice and the word of Grace,
I, come to town with a merry-making throng
To pay my tithes and join in the season's song,
Closing my eyes, there prayed – and was hurried far

Beyond what ages I know not, or what star,
To a land of thought remote from the breastplate glint
And the white bull's blood that flows from the knife of flint,
Then, in this movement, being not I but part
In the fellowship of the universal heart,
I sucked a strength from the primal fount of strength,
I thought and worked omnipotence. At length
Hit in my high flight by some sorry thought
Back to the sweat of the soil-bound I was caught
And asked in pique what enemy had worked this,
What folly or anger thrust against my bliss?
Then I grew aware of the savour of sandal-wood
With noise of a distant fluting, and one who stood
Nudging my elbow breathed 'Oh, miracle! See!'
The folk gape wonder, urge tumultuously,
They fling them down on their faces every one,
Some joyfully weep, others for anguish moan.
Lo, the tall gilt image of God at the altar niche
Wavers and stirs, we see his raiment twitch.
Now he stands and signs benediction with his rod.
The courtyard quakes, the fountains gush with blood.
The whistling scurry and throb of spirit wings
Distresses man and child. Now a bird-voice sings,
And a loud throat bellows, that every creature hears,
A sign to himself he must lay aside his fears.
It babbles an antique tongue, and threatening, pleads
Prompt sacrifice and a care for priestly needs,
Wholeness of heart, the putting away of wrath,
A generous measure for wine, for oil, for cloth,
A holding fast to the law that the Stones ordain,
And the rites of the Temple watch that ye maintain
Lest fire and ashes down from the mountain rain!
With expectance of goodly harvest and rain in Spring
To such as perform the will of the Jealous King.
To his priestly servants hearken!

                                    The syllables die.
Now up from the congregation issues a sigh
As of stopped breath slow released. But here stands one
Who has kept his feet though the others fell like stone,
Who prays with outstretched palms, standing alone,
To a God who is speechless, not to be known by touch,
By sight, sound, scent. And I cry, 'Not overmuch
Do I love this juggling blasphemy, O High Priest.
Or do you deny your part here? Then, at least,

An honest citizen of this honest town
May preach these nightmare apparitions down,
These blundering, perfumed noises come to tell
No more than a priest-instructed folk knows well.
Out, meddlesome Imps, whatever Powers you be,
Break not true prayer between my God and me.'

TO ANY SAINT

You turn the unsmitten other cheek,
    In silence welcoming God's grace,
Disdaining, though they scourge, to speak,
    Smiling forgiveness face to face.

You plunge your arms in tyrant flame,
    From ravening beasts you do not fly,
Calling aloud on one sweet Name,
    Hosannah-singing till you die.

So angered by your undefeat,
    Revenge through Christ they meditate,
Disciples at the bishop's feet
    They learn this newer sort of hate,

This unresisting meek assault
    On furious foe or stubborn friend,
This virtue purged of every fault
    By furtherance of the martyr's end,

This baffling stroke of naked pride,
    When satires fail and curses fail
To pierce the justice's tough hide,
    To abash the cynics of the jail.

Oh, not less violent, not less keen
    And barbèd more than murder's blade!
'The brook,' you sigh, 'that washes clean,
    The flower of love that will not fade!'

A DEWDROP

The dewdrop carries in its eye
Snowdon and Hebog, sea and sky,
Twelve lakes at least, woods, rivers, moors,
And half a county's out-of-doors:
Trembling beneath a wind-flower's shield
In this remote and rocky field.

But why should man in God's Name stress
The dewdrop's inconspicuousness
When to lakes, woods, the estuary,
Hebog and Snowdon, sky and sea,
This dewdrop falling from its leaf
Can spread amazement near to grief,
As it were a world distinct in mould
Lost with its beauty ages old?

A VALENTINE

The hunter to the husbandman
Pays tribute since our love began,
And to love-loyalty dedicates
The phantom hunts he meditates.
Let me pursue, pursuing you,
Beauty of other shape and hue,
Retreating graces of which none
Shone more than candle to your sun,
Your well-loved shadow beckoning me
In unfamiliar imagery –
Smile your forgiveness; each bright ghost
Dives in love's glory and is lost,
Yielding your comprehensive pride
A homage, even to suicide.

THE FEATHER BED

(1923)

THE WITCHES' CAULDRON

In sudden cloud that, blotting distance out,
Confused the compass of the traveller's mind,
Biased his course: three times from the hill's crest
Trying to descend but with no track to follow,
Nor visible landmark – three times he had struck
The same sedged pool of steaming desolation,
The same black monolith rearing up before it.
This third time then he stood and recognized
The Witches' Cauldron, only known before
By hearsay, fly-like on whose rim he had crawled
Three times and three times dipped to climb again
Its uncouth sides, so to go crawling on.

By falls of scree, moss-mantled slippery rock,
Wet bracken, drunken gurgling watercourses
He escaped, limping, at last, and broke the circuit –
Travelling down and down; but smooth descent
Interrupted by new lakes and ridges,
Sprawling unmortared walls of boulder granite,
Marshes; one arm hung bruised where he had fallen;
Blood in a sticky trickle smeared his cheek;
Sweat, gathering at his eyebrows, ran full beads
Into his eyes, which made them smart and blur.

At last he blundered on some shepherd's hut –
He thought, the hut took pity and appeared –
With mounds of peat and welcome track of wheels
Which he now followed to a broad green road
That ran from right to left; but still at fault,
The mist being still on all, with little pause
He chose the easier way, the downward way.
Legs were dog-tired already, but this road,
Gentle descent with some relief of guidance,
Maintained his shambling five miles to the hour

Coloured with day-dreams. Then a finger-post
Moved through the mist, pointing into his face,
Yet when he stopped to read gave him no comfort.
Seventeen miles to – somewhere, God knows where –
The paint was weathered to a puzzle
Which cold-unfocused eyes could not attempt –

And jerking a derisive thumb behind it
Up a rough stream-wet path: 'The Witches' Cauldron,
One mile.' Only a mile
For two good hours of stumbling steeplechase!
There was a dead snake by some humorous hand
Twined on the pointing finger; far away
A bull roared hoarsely, but all else was mist.

Then anger overcame him…

THE FEATHER BED

'Goodbye, but now forget all that we were
Or said, or did to each other, here's goodbye.
Send no more letters now, only forget
We ever met…' and the letter maunders on
In the unformed uncompromising hand
That witnesses against her, yet provides
Extenuation and a grudging praise.
Rachel to be a nun! Postulate now
For her noviciate in a red brick convent:
Praying, studying, wearing uniform,
She serves the times of a tyrannic bell,
Rising to praise God in the early hours
With atmosphere of filters and stone stairs,
Distemper, crucifixes and red drugget,
Dusty hot-water pipes, a legacy-library…

Sleep never comes to me so tired as now
Leg-chafed and footsore with my mind in a blaze
Troubling this problem over, vexing whether
To beat Love down with ridicule or instead
To disregard new soundings and still keep
The old course by the uncorrected chart,
(The faithful lover, his unchanging heart)

Rachel, before goodbye
Obscures you in your sulky resignation
Come now and stand out clear in mind's eye
Giving account of what you were to me
And what I was to you and how and why,
Saying after me, if you can say it, 'I loved.'

Rachel so summoned answers thoughtfully
But painfully, turning away her head,
'I lived and thought I loved, for I had gifts
Of most misleading, more than usual beauty,
Dark hair, grey eyes, capable fingers, movement
Graceful and certain; my slow puzzled smile
Accusing of too much ingenuousness
Yet offered more than I could hope to achieve,
And if I thought I loved, no man would doubt it.'
So speaks the image as I read her mind,
Or is it my pride speaks on her behalf,
Ventriloquizing to deceive myself?
Anger, grief, jealousy, shame confuse the issue,
Her beauty is a truth I can not blink
However angry, jealous, sad, ashamed.

Dissolve, image, dissolve!
Make no appeal to the hunter in my nature,
Leave me to self-reproach in my own time;
If I too promised more than you could meet,
Your beauty overrode my sense of fate
And fitness, with extravagant pretence.
Is it true that we were lovers once, or nearly?
Lovers should sleep together on one pillow
Clasped in each other's arms with lip to lip,
Their bed should be a masterpiece of ease,
A mother-of-pearl embrace for its twin pearls.
But where do you sleep now, and where am I?
Disdaining all the comforts of old use
We fall apart, are made ridiculous.
You in your cell toss miserably enough
Under thin blankets on a springless couch,
And I two hundred miles away or further
Wallow in this feather bed,
With nothing else to rest my gaze upon
Than flowery wall-paper, bulging and stained,
And two stern cardboard signals: '*God is love*', and

'I was a stranger and ye took Me in',
Ye took me in, took me in, took me in,….

The train of my thought straggles, loses touch,
Piles in confusion, takes the longer road,
Runs anyhow, heads true only by chance.
Sacred Carnivals trundle through my mind,
With Rhyme-compulsion motting each waggon.
God's Love, the Holy Dove, and *Heaven above*
Sin, deadly Sin, Begin, the Fight to Win
Ye took me in; inn; inn; – and now a jolt
Returns me consciousness, and weary Logic
Gathers her snapped threads up. A mouldy inn
Offensive with cockchafers, sour and musty,
All night the signboard creaks and the blinds bang,
The cupboards groan, the draught under the door
Flurries the carpets of this inn, this inn.
How I came here? Where else could I be bettered?
Loneliness drew me here and cloudy weather
With cold Spring rains to chill me through and through
Pelting across the mountains, purging away
Affection for a fault, restoring faith ….
So God is Love? Admitted; still the thought
Is Dead Sea fruit to angry baffled lovers
Lying sleepless and alone in double beds,
Shaken in mind, harassed with hot blood fancies.
Break the ideal, and the animal's left
Which this ideal stood as mask to hide.
Then the hot blood with no law hindering it
Drums and buffets suddenly at the heart
And seeks a vent with what lies first to hand.

But yet no earthbound evil spirit comes
Taking advantage of my unwrought mind,
Tempting me to a gay concubinage,
In likeness of some ancient queen of heaven
Ardent and ever young. The legends say
They come to hermits so, and holy saints,
Disguised in a most blinding loveliness;
Disrobe about the good man's bed and twitch
His blankets off and make as if to kiss him
With sighs of passion irresistibly sweet.
Yet he has power to turn on them, to cry
'In the name of Christ begone!' and go they must.

If I were a hermit now – but being myself
I never give them challenge, never bend
Kneeling at my bedside for hours together
Praying aloud for chastity – that's the bait
Certain to draw them from their shadowy caves,
Their broken shrines and rockbound fastnesses –
Praying against the World, the Flesh, the Devil,
But pausing most on Flesh – that praying against,
Proposing yet denying the fixed wish!
Closest expressed it's the most dangerous ....

How would I *say my prayers* now, if I tried,
Using what formula? Would instinct turn
To
                    Gentle Jesus meek and mild
                    Look upon thy little child
To Gentle Jesus and the entrancing picture
Of *Pretty mice in Plicity* (where, alas,
Is County Plicity now? Beyond what skyline?
I climbed in vain to-day) .... When Rachel prays,
Does she still dreamily speak to Gentle Jesus,
The shepherd in that Nürnberg oleograph
Hanging above the nursery mantelpiece?
Her God? Anthropomorphic surely. One
Bearded like Moses, straddled on the clouds,
Armed with thunderbolts and shaggy eyebrows.
'Bless me, dear God, and make me a good child.'
Her childishness obscures her womanhood.
When was I ever conscious in her presence
That she was bodily formed like other women
With womb for bearing and with breasts for suckling,
With power, when she desired, to rouse in me
By but the slightest art in diminution
Of her accustomed childish truthfulness,
A word or gesture hinting doubtfulness,
The angry stream flooding beyond restraint?
And yet no frisky wraith has come to-night
Assuming Rachel's body, goading me
With false presentment of her honest person
To mutiny and to utter overthrow;
No wanton Venus, no bold Helen of Troy.

For look, a different play performs to-night!
See how come crowding in, with a bold air

Of pertinence I do not dare to question
This odd rag-tag-and-bobtail of lost souls,
Ecclesiastical, furtive, dim, far gone
In their *dementia praecox*! Doctor Hornblow
On the Pentateuch, Dean Dogma upon Ruth
(Ay, Ruth; the alien corn was not the worst)
Keble and Pusey, Moody and Sankey griddling,
And one most strange Victorian apparition,
The ghost of Gladstone, with his stickout collars,
Goes hand in hand with Señor Monkey-brand,
Comrades who, printed on a paper cover,
Gladstone in front and Monkey on the back,
Made the *Impregnable Rock of Holy Scripture*
Tacit defence of Darwin's blasphemies.
There go the ghosts of Mason, Martin Tupper,
Dean Farrar, South, Cautionary Mrs. Turner,
Butterfield with a spotted senior clerk,
And a long rabble of confusing figures,
Nuns, deacons, theologians, commentators,
Spikes in birettas, missionaries like apes
Hairy and chattering, bald; with, everyone,
A book in the left hand tight clasped, the right
Free to point scorn.

           My cauliflower-wicked candle
Gutters and splutters on the chair beside me,
Over two books and a letter; the crowd passing
Groans for reproach, confident in their numbers.
But I, long used to crowds and their cowardly ways,
Return these insults with the cold set eye
That breaks their corporate pride –

                  What? those are plays.
Yes, dramas by John Ford – *Love's Sacrifice*,
The Broken Heart, *'Tis Pity She's a Whore*.
The titles shock? These things are 'not convenient'?
Well, try this other by (ah) Canon Trout,
The Wisest Course of Love – why do you smile?
The book of plays I bought, this was a present,
Sent me with Rachel's letter – but you smile,
You're smiling still? Then I apologize,
Ladies and Lords. Indeed I never guessed
Humour was a luxury you admitted.
''Tis pity she's a…postulant'. Is it that?
Malicious hearts! but you still nod, laugh, point,
Pointing what joke? *The Wisest Course of Love*?

Yes?

     I don't see. I'll buy it for a forfeit.
Then a red-haired beaky-nosed burly nun
Called Sister Agatha, so I tell myself,
Comes nearer, throws her veil aside, takes up
The envelope of the letter. Now she lays
A manicured finger on the office post-mark,
Leering down in my face.
                 I see it now,
You ugly she-bear. Wisest Course of Love
Is *Maidenhead*? Then you have read the letter?
Dictated it quite likely? You, then, you!
I know you, nun-official set to guide
The postulants through their long penances
And stern soul-searchings – with the twisted grin
Of a bawd mistress, none too well concealed,
You greeted Rachel in the Convent Hall,
And peered and saw that she was beautiful,
Giving her welcome with a sisterly kiss.

Mother Superior was quite satisfied
After inquiry in Burke's *Landed Gentry*
That the newcomer was a suitable
Candidate for the Order of Seven Sorrows.
It's *so important* to have *ladies only*!
You twirl dear Mother round a little finger;
You know her weaknesses, emotionalism,
Snobbery, love of ritual; quite content
To let her have her way in formal matters
If you may mould the spirit of the place
By due control of youthful aspirants,
Postulants and novices – with the glow
Of great devotion, honesty itself,
You teach them hatred of their woman-flesh
Eyeing their bodies with flagellant gaze
Approving shame's rebellion. *Maidenhead*!
A well spiced joke! The carnal maidenhead
Untaken, but the maidenhead of spirit
Stolen away. Rachel in your good care!

She says three years' probation. For three years
Humiliation, then she takes the veil
And goes for ever ... 'But of course, dear Friend,
(Where did she learn 'Dear Friend'?)

Should I discover when I search my heart
That God has sealed me for some other life,
That my intended vow of resignation
Is only pride, why then I'm free again.
I pray for you,' etc., and etc.
Dear Friend? lover or nothing it must be.
I'm tired of friends, I'm past the need of friends.

We never talked religion till that day.
I took for granted Rachel used her sense,
Thought for herself without the aid of priests
On spiritual matters: I? I never trouble
About such talk one year's end to the next,
But one day argument began; she started
On Christian meekness, the low slavish virtue
'Tapeinophrosune', obsequiousness,
Which I called nonsense. 'Nonsense?' (with wide eyes)
'Or call it poetry. Christ was never meek.
Let meekness crawl below in catacombs,
Pride drives the money-changers with a scourge,
Keeps silence to accusers, chooses death
When an escape is more acceptable
To justice than embarrassment of killing.
I'm talking paradox? I never meant it.'
(Here I grew nettled at her wooden look)
'And as for "feeling Jesus in my heart"
What *does* that mean? explain!
I might acknowledge that historically
All generous action flows from the prime source
Of Jesus' teaching (though give Plato credit
And Aristotle). But Jesus as a power
Alive, praying, pleading like a ouija spirit,
Or *Laughing Eyes* the séance influence,
That's stupid and unnecessary, in my mind.
I am a man, I am proud, Jesus was man and proud;
He died fulfilling, and his soul found peace.
I greet him friendly down the gulf of years.'
'But no!' she said. 'There *is* a Spirit of Jesus
Say what you like, there *is* a Spirit of Jesus.'
So I allowed her that, changing my front
Saying, 'If Jesus died on Cross, He's dead,
In so far as Mary's son, the prophet, died.
But hardly was He dead,
Than up this elemental demon sprang

Assuming mastership of Jesus' school
Using his body, even, so it's told
Calling himself by name of *Jesus Risen*.
Who was he? Some poor godling, fallen through pride
And greed of human flesh, on evil days.
He changed his heart and once more stood for power,
A roaring lion in the white lamb's fleece,
So by a long campaign of self-abasement
And self-effacement grown mob-strong at length
He overturned high Heaven, now rules the world.
Yes, he's a powerful devil; we are his sons
Got on she-furies of our Northern gales.
We hate the inheritance entailed on us
And the outlandish family coat we blazon,
The tell-tale features also; would deny
His fatherhood, but for that eye, that nose,
Betraying Galilee our Father's land.
There's no escape from him. Midwife Tradition
Has knotted Jesus in our navel strings
Never to be undone this side the grave.'
But that was one stage worse than blasphemy.
And when we parted, she smiled grudgingly.
I had said too much and cut her to the quick.
She thought, poor child, she had her choice to make
Between God's way and my way. And so she chose…
This letter…But she writes of Christian love.
What *is* that? It's a most annoying habit,
A warm blood-teasing smile, an open look,
A recognition – thinks I to myself,
Boy, this is fine! Love at first sight! True love!
But then the disillusionment – by God
She turns the same look of those clear kind eyes
On a bootblack, on some fool behind a counter.
She calls that, Love? But what *is* Love to me?
Love; it's a two-part game, I'd say, not merely
The searching radiations from one eye,
That fly about with indiscriminate force –
Sometimes unthinking in a public place
I stare at girls sitting sideface to me
And wonder at their beauty, summing it up,
Then being innocent girls (I'd never look
At others so) they grow aware of the heat
That pours out from my eyes; but do not see me.
(I may be fifty feet away or more)

They fidget in their seats, uncross their knees,
Pull down their skirts to hide even their ankles,
Blush furiously and gaze about, in trouble;
Then I start guiltily, rise and walk away;
But that's not Love, the searching and the heat;
Love is an act of God, akin to Faith,
Call it the union of two prayers by Faith
(Here we come back to prayer by a long circuit
And back to 'God is Love')
But to explain again what's Faith, what's prayer,
That's the teaser! much too hard for me.

Still, these are not Christian monopolies.
What's Faith but power stripped of its ornaments,
Grants, title-deeds and suchlike accidentals;
Force won by disentangling from the mind
All hampering ties of luxury and tradition,
Possessions, loyalties and hobby-horses?
Cast all these overboard, and Faith is left,
Faith potent through its prayer to miracles,
Whether in name of Jesus or Jim Crow.
Prayer: Rachel seems to think the collects prayer,
And Mother Superior, I make no doubt,
Will teach her scores of neatly turned devotions
Couched in diminutives and pastoral terms,
(Lord, how I hate the *literary* prayer),
Little white lambs indeed – O baa baa black sheep
Have you any wool? – And Rachel in return
Flushing with shame impetuously confesses,
And holds half back, but crafty eyes are watching
To drag all out, so Rachel has to tell
How on the river bank one morning early
The water was so clear, the sun so warm,
She kissed me suddenly and was kissed by me –
Lip kisses, that was all, and fingers clasped.
Mother Superior then demanding further
Will cross-examine her on how and why.
'To tell it now will mortify the passion,
Then when you make your general confession
To Father James, your mind will have found peace.'
(A good excuse) 'What then were your sensations,
The physical joy, tell me, my erring lamb!
Tell me, I beg, but as the sin was pleasant
So must confession of the sin be pain...'

''Tis pity she's a whore'. Rachel told all.
Whore, traitress to the secret rites of love,
Publisher of the not-communicable.
If she refused the vows? If her heart changed?
Rachel and I? This meek ex-novice rifled
Of her love-secrets? medals and images
Sewn in her skirts, Birmingham images
From the totem-factory, niched in her heart?
No, Love is fusion of Prayer, and prayer must be
The flash of faith, unformulated words
Demanding an accomplishment of Love
With noise of thunder, against circumstance,
And Rachel forfeits there all power to love.

Who's this? For now the rabble have passed through,
Going unnoticed out; Mother Superior
Secretly with one finger at her lips,
Re-enters, carefully locks my bedroom door,
Now she disrobes with fingers trembling so
They tear the fastenings – naked she steps out
To practise with her long-past-bearing body
The wiles of the Earthbound (Ah, the fine young man,
The hot young man whose kisses tasted sweet
To our new postulant!) Madam, I beg you!
You have mistaken the room; no, next door sleeps
A lusty bagman, he's the man to embrace you
And welcome you with every brisk refinement
Of passion. But while *you* rumple his sheets,
The innocent and unhappy eyes of Rachel
Bewilder me – Oh then in spite of Faith
I am cast down – You nuns, but if I needed,
As I no longer need, I'd challenge you
To contest of hard praying, one against all.
I could wrest Rachel back even to this bed
To-night. But Faith, and Prayer that's born of Faith
Find her slow mind impediment to their power,
So I resign her – Agatha, do your worst.

The wisest course of Love? Yes, maidenhead.
For me? Love's Sacrifice? It was not love.
The Broken Heart? Not mine. I'll say no more
Than mere *goodbye.* Go, get you to your nunnery,
And out the candle! Darkness absolute
Surrounds me, sleepy mother of good children

Who drowse and drowse and cry not for the sun,
Content and wisest of their generation.

I AM THE STAR OF MORNING

I am the Star of Morning poised between
The dead night and the coming of the sun,
Yet neither relic of the dark nor pointing
The angry day to come. My virtue is
My own, a mild light, an enduring courage;
And the remembering ancient tribe of birds
Sing blithest at my showing; only Man
Sleeps on and stirs rebellious in his sleep.
Lucifer, Lucifer, am I, millstone-crushed
Between conflicting powers of doubleness,
By envious Night lost in her myriad more
Counterfeit glints, in day-time quite overwhelmed
By tyrant blazing of the warrior sun.
Yet some, my prophets who at midnight held me
Fixedly framed in their observant glass,
By daylight also, sinking well-shafts deep
For water and for coolness of pure thought,
Gaze up and far above them see me shining,
Me, single natured, without gender, one,
The only spark of Godhead unresolved.

MOCK BEGGAR HALL

(1924)

DIPLOMATIC RELATIONS

King George, still powder-grimed from Dettingen,
Called in thick tones: 'My Lord, fetch ink and pen.
I'll write a threatening note in my own hand.
This Chinese potentate must understand
That Britons have a boundless fame to brag.
No insult shall defile our glorious flag.
Two Bristol ships at Hankow fetching tea,
Boarded and robbed, at wharfside as they lay,
Of a costly cargo? Ha, Sir! Let me boast
My fleet stands ready to bombard your coast.
If meek apologies be not forthcoming
My fusiliers must through Pekin go drumming.
You shall eat dirt, d'ye hear, you knavish fellow,
Or we must tan your hide a deeper yellow.
Ten ships shall yearly visit your chief ports
With mirrors, beads, and clothing of all sorts,
Carrying decorum to your savage parts
With civilization, learning and the arts.
But if so much as a rattle's robbed or broke
Your Chinese territory flies up in smoke.
You then, beware! Signed, GEORGIUS REX. So, so.
Our Foreign Minister sends this. Take it, go!'

The Foreign Minister, reading the piece through,
Swore by his wig, why, this would never do.
'Our Sovereign trips on all the finer points
Of English speech, confuses, blurs, disjoints.
To send this note, 's blood, it were most unwise.
Suppose it intercepted by French spies?
"La langue du roi…" (I hear their mocking tone)
"Dunce-cap instead of crown, dunce-stool for throne!"
Why, even in China, men would laugh to read
This halting, odd, mis-spelt, improbable screed.
But stay! Our Sovereign we would surely please,

Translating him his Note into Chinese.
Li-Chung will do't, then there can be no call
To pawn our honour with the original.'

Li-Chung, the Bond Street tea-man with meek eyes
Performed the service, showing no surprise,
Though inwardly enraged and jealous for
The sacred majesty of his Emperor...
How faithful his translation, who can say?
George signed it readily, and it reached Cathay.

The Emperor from his Summer terraces
Claps hands for ink and sable paint-brushes
And writes with care a special declaration
To the Loyal Governor of the British Nation,
Commiserating with that luckless one
By seas exiled from his Imperial Sun
On such outcast and pariah-like condition:
'We note the abject tone of your petition
And sorry excuses for your impudence
In thus soliciting our Magnificence,
Then, though we cannot in the atlas hit on
A Chinese province (or sub-province) *Britain*,
We graciously will none the less allow
Ten yearly junks to harbour at Hankow
With skins, blubber, oil or suchlike pelting stuff –
Indeed five junk-loads would be quite enough.
Formal permission signed, YOUR GOD. So, so.
Our Foreign Minister sends this. Take it! Go!'

The Foreign Minister, reading the piece through,
Swore by his pigtail, this would never do.
'Our Emperor neglects the niceties,
Indeed the major rules, of Court Chinese.
Our iron-helmed Manchu God in battle's shock
Or warrior council sits as firm as rock,
But as for drafting edict, Note or letter...
My six-year-old could do as well, aye, better.
Can I permit my Sovereign's reputation
To sink even in a heathen's estimation?
I'll tactfully propose it more correct
To send this note in British dialect.
Ned Gunn the boxing-teacher at Nanking
Will soon translate the odd fantastic thing.'

Ned Gunn, a stolid sailor with bold eyes,
Performed the service, showing no surprise
Though, loyal to the death, he felt his gorge
Mount at this insult to victorious George.
His English version (which he owned was free)
The Emperor signed, frowned, sent oversea.

George read the note, puffed out his cheeks, began:
'He takes his medicine like a sensible man,
Apologizes humbly, swears to behave
With fawning loyalty of dog or slave,
Sadly admits his colour far from white
And trusts this missive is not impolite,
Longs for our British cargoes rich and strange,
Has only trash to offer in exchange.
"May your Red, White and Blue still rule the main
And countless Dettingens be fought again!
God Save the King! Kow Tow! Success to barter."'
George swore: 'We must reward him with the Garter.'

HEMLOCK

*(Fragment of a late-Greek satire, probably Gadarene,
here for the first time done into English)*

Socrates on the seventh day
Sneezed and stretched and went his way,
Then stood bare-headed in the sun
Till seven times seventy days had run.
An equal count of days from these
The exiled Alcibiades
Beheld him in the Chersonese
Yet spectre-faint: the Master said
Plainly, that, far from striking dead,
The hemlock acting inwardly
Gave him invisibility
And life prolonged ten thousand years
With such discerning eyes, with ears
So tuned by music of the Spheres,
He could see through brick and stone,
Could hear the unborn infant groan,
Could catch the plotting, piece by piece,

In Persian courts against fair Greece,
Yea, read the yet unspoken mind
Of Aethiopes or men of Ind.
The Athenian *Thirty* he forgave
Who thought to end him in his grave
And 'Athens' genius I shall be,'
He said, 'While Athens follows me.'
All this and more did Socrates
Unfold to Alcibiades,
Then slowly disappeared from sight,
Bald head and beard and mantle white.
But Alcibiades for hate
Of his own Athenian state
Until his deathbed gasp concealed
The wondrous message thus revealed.
So Socrates walks here to-day,
In Porch and School and Agorâ
He watches us, all jealousy,
While we exchange our sophistry
Discoursing his philosophy,
He frowns when we omit his mode
Dialecticè – truth's only road –
He prods us with a touch like ice
If ever falsely we premise,
He weeps glad tears of sacred scent
When we prevail in argument
Against some un-Greek jack-in-the-box
Defending a new paradox –
We kneel to clasp thy phantom knees,
Mouthpiece of wisdom, Socrates,
And while we work thy god-like will
Athens shall be Athens still!

Scepticos heard this popular
Figment in the spice-bazaar,
And good Pisteuon started, shocked
To see the way his neighbour mocked,
Grimacing that 'this Platonism
Is meshed in sentimentalism,
Encouraging such absolute
Value for a dissolute
Mulberry-nosed philosopher
(A very Plague of Athens, sir)
That if his system is to thrive

They *must* assume him still alive,
Spying demoniac, brushing them
With his unseen garment's hem.
Of all religious forms,' said he,
'I most detest Necrophily.
Now too the enthusiastic kind
Will so get Hemlock on their mind,
They'll drink small potions on the sly
And gradually stiffening, die,
To stalk among us afterwards
Flaunting invisible rewards.
A phantom hierarchy, friend,
That is the logical and only end.'

FULL MOON

As I walked out that sultry night,
    I heard the stroke of One.
The moon, attained to her full height,
    Stood beaming like the sun:
She exorcized the ghostly wheat
To mute assent in love's defeat,
    Whose tryst had now begun.

The fields lay sick beneath my tread,
    A tedious owlet cried,
A nightingale above my head
    With this or that replied –
Like man and wife who nightly keep
Inconsequent debate in sleep
    As they dream side by side.

Your phantom wore the moon's cold mask,
    My phantom wore the same;
Forgetful of the feverish task
    In hope of which they came,
Each image held the other's eyes
And watched a grey distraction rise
    To cloud the eager flame –

To cloud the eager flame of love,
    To fog the shining gate;
They held the tyrannous queen above
    Sole mover of their fate,
They glared as marble statues glare
Across the tessellated stair
    Or down the halls of state.

And now warm earth was Arctic sea,
    Each breath came dagger-keen;
Two bergs of glinting ice were we,
    The broad moon sailed between;
There swam the mermaids, tailed and finned,
And love went by upon the wind
    As though it had not been.

MYRRHINA

Ambergris from John Whale's moans,
Pearls from Jane Oyster's groans
    Who knew no beauty:
Groaning Oyster, moaning Whale,
Myrrhina thinks a merry tale,
    Confident in her beauty.

Yet must Myrrhina pay the fee
If she would wear old misery
    To enhance her beauty,
Twined at her throat, sweet on her dress
Exhaling innocent carelessness
    Of all but maiden beauty.

A pang for every several pang
That round her neck in clusters hang
    Of seeming beauty,
Despair for John's uncouth despair
Breathed from her dancing yellow hair –
The Nessus-robe that beauties wear
    Burning away their beauty.

Now must Myrrhina groaning say
She knew not there were bills to pay
    For simple beauty,
But pay she must, and on the nail,
Giddied with tears, distraught, death-pale,
Jane Oyster's debt and John the Whale.
    This done, there's room for beauty.

TWIN SOULS

    The hermit on his pillar top
      Shuddering lean and bare;
    The glutton in his rowdy-shop
      With velvet clothes to wear.

    The hermit with his finger-nails
      Growing through his palms;
    The glutton in his swallow-tails
      Humming hell-fire psalms.

Glutton: 'By day I am a glutton,
      But (this is my complaint)
    In dreams I groan upon your stone
      A parched and giddy saint.'

Hermit: 'By day I am a hermit,
      But (this is my complaint)
    In dreams a glutton of beef and mutton
      Kissing powder and paint.'

    Then each began to say and see,
      Which cut him like a knife,
    'Visions of dark are more to me
      Than this my waking life.'

Glutton: 'My body is feeble and fat,
      My head has never been strong,
    If I were to stand on your pillar
      I doubt I would stand for long.

    'Heigh me! I am growing old
      And gone too far on my way,
    In dreams of midnight, bold,
      But a coward at break of day.'

Hermit: 'My body is feeble and thin,
                  My head has never been strong,
              If I were to drink in your manner
                  I doubt I would drink for long.

              'My eyes are a frosted glass,
                  My fists are clenched like buckles:
              Could I please your saucy lass
                  With a hand that is only knuckles?'

              The glutton on his pillar top
                  Shuddering cold and bare,
              The hermit in his rowdy-shop
                  Groaning hot despair,

              They died and they are buried,
                  Both on the Easter Day,
              Now joined as one in spirit,
                  Who lived apart in clay.

THE NORTH WINDOW

When the chapel is lit and sonorous with ploughmen's praise,
When matron and child crouch low to the Lord of Days,
When the windows are shields of greyness all about,
For the glowing lamps within and the storm without;
On this Eve of All Souls (suicides too have souls)
The damned to the Northward rise from their tablets and scrolls,
With infants unbaptized that lie without ease,
With women betrayed, their mothers, who murdered these,
They make them a furious chapel of wind and gloom
With, Southward, one stained window *The Hour of Doom*
Lit up by the lamp of the righteous beaming through
With the scene reversed, and the legend backwards too,
Displaying in scarlet and gold the Creator who damns
Who has thrust on His Left the bleating sheep and the lambs,
Who has fixed on His Right the goats and kids accursed,
With *Omega : Alpha* restoring the last as first:
Then the psalms to God that issue hence or thence
Ring blasphemy each to the other's Omnipotence.

ATTERCOP: THE ALL-WISE SPIDER

James derided Walter,
Twisting him a halter
Of argument and synthesis,
'Hang yourself, Poet, in this.'
Walter, whistling on a reed
'Sweet Melancholy', took no heed;
He lolled against a finger-post,
Preening Fancy's pinion,
He summoned bogle, elf and ghost
With other trivial sprites that most
Resent the sour dominion
Of James, renowned philosopher;
He clothed each airy minion
With cobwebs, with gossamer,
He bade them cast in bonfire flames
All the writings of this James
To smoke with yon green rubbish, sir!

Myself, not bound by James' view
Nor Walter's, in a vision saw these two
Like trapped and weakening flies
In toils of the same hoary net;
I seemed to hear ancestral cries
Buzzing 'To our All-Wise, Omnivorous
Attercop glowering over us,
Whose table we have set
With blood and bones and sweat.'
These old cries echo plainly yet
Though James sits calmer now
Composed, with spectacles on brow,
Explaining why and how,
Telling on the fingers of his hands
And seldom losing count, the strands
Of intricate silk entangling both his feet.
He points 'Here this and that web meet,
Yet, I surmise,
A different combination might arise
If that or this worked otherwise.'
He ponders where the Primal Den can be,
He holds the web to have no finity
And boldly adds, 'Attercop has no base
In any sure discoverable place,

Lost in his own complexities of lace;
A most capricious Beast
Whose tricks need not concern us in the least.
He's mad or possibly long years deceased;
But this web serves as flooring for us flies.
Who disregards this web binding the skies,
That man himself denies.
The Web! Life! Liberty! All else is lies!'

Lyrical Walter cannot speak
Philosophy, nor use the same technique,
But listen to his natural-magic charm
Potent, as he thinks, for harm
Against the tyrant Attercop.
  'Brush down the cobwebs from the cupboard-top
  With a long feather-mop.
  Go, cheerily stride at dawn
  With careless feet about the lawn
  Breaking the threads of gossamer;
  This, then, shall prove a token
  Of Liberty, my sapient sir,
  Attercop, whose proud name with hate be spoken,
  His net too shall be broken.'

ANTINOMIES

Lying in long grass one hot afternoon,
Between two eighteenth-century garden statues,
'Furor Poeticus' and 'Phryne Judged',
I observed my muse in likeness of a grasshopper
Trilling 'Sing, Sing, child!' So I answered her,
'What can I sing, Muse?' And she told me plainly,
'Always the first thing floating in your mind.
A formless, lumpish, nothing-in-particular.
You take, toss, catch it, turn it inside out,
Do new things with it; wean it, breech it, school it,
Bring it to man's estate; in your old age
It should support you out of filial duty.'

My mind was empty as the summer sky,
And sleepy with the hum of bees and midges,
Until a sudden clashing clamour began,

The church bells ringing up for evensong.
They checked my natural-magic reveries,
Tuning the mind to more parochial thought,
To Mrs. Ames, the widow, and Miss Bold,
Setting their caps, if gossip may be trusted,
At Cutt, the rector, very bitter rivals.
Red-gowned and surpliced, sawing with his hands,
This Cutt pours rhetoric from my mental pulpit.
The text about the flesh warring with spirit,
Spirit with flesh. Cutt takes the spirit's part,
Poor, baffled soul; though why he speaks through me
I dare not tempt my curious muse to enquire.
'Sing, Sing!' the grasshopper warning comes again.
'I'll sing, but here's fair Phryne's nakedness
Demands inclusion; let the *Sculptor's Mistress*
Plead with a sympathetic voice for flesh.
Now, listen, Muse, what will you make of this?'

> His gorgon eyes make stone
> Of sweetest flesh and bone;
> Resigning true-love's part
> He lets a pedant art
> Academize his heart.
> For him my body is
> A thing of surfaces
> For chisels to uncover;
> Mathematician-lover
> He lets love-splendour pass
> In thoughts of line and mass,
> And craftsman-like observes
> The straightenings and the curves
> Of my young excellence
> Making its fond expense.
> Go, fool! be done with this!
> Let steel and marble kiss,
> Transcribing the disgrace
> Of our untrue embrace,
> Let the brisk flakes that fly
> Beneath your careful eye
> Disclose for all to see
> Love's virtuosity,
> Your mind in terms of me,
> On either part the same,
> Scorned beauty, deadness, shame.

'That's well enough,' my muse said, 'yet what of it?
A biased history, purporting no more;
Craftily written, rather too precise;
Strung on the thread of an experience
Too sympathetic to the heroine's case.'
'Muse,' I said, 'Muse! wait, let the theme develop!
We'll speak a sympathetic word for Spirit.
Here, then! the sculptor's talking.'

> She came as my true friend,
> This art our common end.
> Who could have guessed at first,
> Seeing her so demure,
> Wistful and seeming pure,
> I'd fixed my love secure
> In a strumpet of the worst,
> A fly-by-night accurst,
> A most malignant slut,
> Whose mouth I could not shut
> Nor long evade her call?
> Flesh was her all-in-all;
> I fell, and in this fall
> Here, woman, you shall view
> This marble ruined too,
> My mind in terms of you,
> On either part the same,
> Scorned beauty, passion, shame.

'That's very well,' my muse said, 'yet what of it?
Here's plaintiff and defendant, Roe with Doe,
Cunningly balanced; rather too precise.
A clear antinomy, purporting no more.
Where does it lead us? Mutual ruination,
Deadlock, but have you nothing to suggest,
No swift solution of these tangled knots
By Alexander's way, or Solomon's?'
'Muse,' I said, 'Muse, when were you ever content?
I gave you wronged Othello, Shakespeare-like,
And you said "Well enough," or "None too bad,"
But asked for wronged Iago; that I gave you,
Plainer than Shakespeare, proving very clearly
Misunderstanding never makes a villain.
There was a definite wrong Iago suffered
From this same Moor. I gave that wrong in full.

What did you tell me then? "A mere antinomy,
Cunningly balanced, rather too precise,
Strung on the thread of an experience
Not sympathetic to Iago's case."
I tell you, Muse, you'll have to stay content
This great while yet with such antinomies.
Until all history's written in that style
(Absolutism made ridiculous),
There's no room for constructing newer forms.
Be content, Muse, you're driving me too hard.'

Yet, still, among the clashing noise of bells
And buzzing brazen echoes when they ceased,
My grass-hid muse whirred her dissatisfaction,
'Critical Box and Cox, Roe against Doe,
Unsolved antinomies, have you nothing else?
Sing, child, a fuller song. Sing, Sing,' she trilled.
'A fuller song? Sweet Muse, how can that be,
While I must yet continue implicate
With life half-strangled by its own free-will?
Always, when I am called to approve the rights
Of one or other side in any brawl,
To hold both claims at fault can make no sense.
How can the plaintiff hear me, still recalling
The old wrong done, the insult unavenged,
Drowning my saws with shrill reiteration?
It's then I brief myself as advocate
For the defence, I advance counter-claims
Raising my voice as loud as his or louder.
"Deny it, plaintiff, nevertheless it's true."
He'll bite on that, distasteful though it be,
And the quarrel marches one step nearer peace.
No one loves conflict on its own account,
But for the hoped-for triumphs it entails.
Then since I hold that, though no conflict ends
Except in ruin of opposing views,
Yet till antinomies plainly stand opposed
Truth cannot rise to knock the swords aside,
What's to be done? The immediate action's plain,
To throw my weight the other side of the scales.
Trimming? Contrariness? Equivocation?
Nothing of that. Muse, here's a novel turn
To Aesop's fable of the Man and Satyr: —
      Blow hot to warm your hands, cold for your porridge.

Then though the simple Satyr stands aghast
Warning his brethren to beware your mouth,
Not even a Satyr could deny this much
That hands need warming, porridge demands cooling,
Rather than frost-bite or the scalded tongue.'

NORTHWARD FROM OXFORD

(An Architectural Progress)

First from Beaumont Street:
Do you know Beaumont Street in Oxford, city of ghosts and damps?
　　The eighteenth century curves up, broadly, from Worcester College,
And apart from the 'Cave of Forty Thieves'* lit by Ruskin's Lamps
　　The street has an air of knowledge, strength and confidence in
　　　　　knowledge,
Not the knowledge and strength, admitted, that delights me best,
　　But politeness, grand proportions, decorum and the rest:
　　Pass on, then, from Beaumont Street; gloomy but impressed.

Next to Banbury Road,
Leaving St. Giles's, passing the old bounds of the city.
　　It begins with the young Victoria, and ends with Edward's age,
And the middle compromises, solid state with pretty-pretty,
　　Oh, the Struggle-for-Existence-God's-in-His-Heaven-Art-for-Art's-
　　　　　sake stage,
Red brick and gables, Gothic spires, freestone and knick-knackery,
　　Steep, narrow stairs, dark kitchens, the greenhouse, the rockery,
　　Beards, bustles, black silk dresses, and the glazed art crockery!

So to Summertown,
By 'bus, to a row of post-war villas, neurotically built,
　　Standing each at different curious angles to the road,
Each with the most extravagantly individualistic shrug and tilt
　　Of roof, wall, porch and gutter, as though each abode,
Rosslyn, Sans Souci, Mons defied the serjeant-major, *would not*
　　　　　dress,
　　Dumbly blaspheming Banbury Road's ordered pretentiousness,
　　The semi-detached pairs writhing in a loveless caress.

So on from Oxford:

Come home with me these three miles beyond Summertown –
    If the Cherwell does not flood the fields between –
Our house is older than Beaumont Street, at first sight rather tumble-
        down
    But solid enough; and the windows open, and floors are easy to
        clean:
A house self-certain, not divided, with a good *feng shwee*.§
    Beaumont Street, Banbury Road and Summertown cannot come to
        see,
    Whom I can no more understand than they can me.

* The local name for an important establishment in this neighbourhood; architecturally the
first-fruits of Ruskin's Oxford lectures.

§ *Feng shwee.* I do not know if this is a correct transliteration of the convenient Chinese term
meaning the feeling about the house, its ghost, aroma, genius.

WITCHES

These churchyard witches in pursuit
    Of magics most abominate
Urge out their sieves from the cliff's foot
    The midnight seas to navigate,
Or high in air through roaring glooms
    With brooms their covens levitate.

I have watched their Sabbath pack –
    North Berwickward in flight they came –
Nutcracker face and knobbled back,
    Or young breasts bare and eyes like flame,
Twelve to the coven, with one more;
    Him they adore in Hell's own name.

Wedgewise by thirteens they flew,
    Each devil sounding his Jews' trump,
The witches chanting psalms thereto
    Mouthing and clapping hand on rump,
That we who watched from Tweed's far brink
    Felt the heart sink like a lead lump.

Such feats on oath we testify
    To whom like powers have long been known,
But we for love the cold heavens fly
    Which other whiles for lust are flown,
We walk the swellings of the sea
    Dryshod and free, for love alone.

Do you, my cribbed empiricist,
    Judge these things false, then false they'll be
For all who never swooped and kissed
    Above the moon, below the sea;
Yet set no tangles in their place
    Of Time and Space and Gravity.

For Space and Time have only sense
    Where these are flattered and adored;
And there sit many parliaments
    Where clock and compass have no word,
Where gravity makes levity,
    Where reason snaps her blunted sword.

Be wary, lest on unbelief
    The cloak of dark one day be spread,
Time shall be grief and Space be grief
    And Love in accidie lie dead,
And broomstick rites alone remain
    To lend your cramping pain relief.

[The King himself examined Agnes Sampsown: she confessed that upon the night of Allhallow E'en last she was accompanied as well as with the persons aforesaid, as also with a great many other witches to the number of two hundred, and that all went together to sea, each one in a riddle or sieve and went into the same with flagons of wine making merry and drinking by the way in the same riddles or sieves to the kirk of North Berwick in Lothian, and that after they had landed, took hands on the land, and danced this reel or short dance, singing with one voice. Giles Duncan went before them playing this reel or dance upon a small trump, called a Jew's trump, until they entered into the kirk of North Berwick. These confessions made the King in a wonderful admiration, and sent for the said Giles Duncan, who upon the like trump did play the said dance before the King's Majesty.]

[*A True Discourse of the Apprehension of Sundry Witches lately taken in Scotland; 1591.*]

ANTIGONUS: AN ECLOGUE

James, *a literary historian;*   John, *a poet.*

John.   Why, James!
James.   Well, John? What are you writing now?
            Letters?
John.   A poem.
James.   Are you? Then I'll go.
            If I had guessed...
John.   'Person from Porlock,'* stay!
            If you don't know my only rule for writing
            It's this, to welcome all disturbances
            As bearing somehow on the work in hand,
            Supplying an unguessed material need.
James.   Convenient rule! If you resent disturbance
            As you must sometimes do, in spite of rules,
            What happens?
John.   Then resentment shapes the poem.
            And if the scheme was cheerful at the start,
            And if my mind swings back to cheerfulness
            It takes some time to check the damage done:
            My rule is economical in the end.
            But, James, what have you walked out here to tell me?
            You always spring some literary surprise –
            Keats' early punctuation? or the name
            Of Marvell's wet-nurse, and her views on God?
James.   Nothing particular; oh, yes, there was.
            Do you recall Antigonus and the bear?
John.   'Antigonus, crux of the *Winter's Tale*,
            Running the drama past the accepted mark
            That separates the comic from the tragic.'
            Or, that's the verdict that your school upholds.
James.   You've got the point, then listen! Yesterday
            A knowledgeable student of research,
            But never mind the name –
John.   From Aberystwyth?
James.   That's right – convinced me, giving chapter and verse
            That Shakespeare's story of Antigonus
            Besides its knockabout popular appeal,
            Hides a discreet political allusion,
            Caviare for the courtiers in the stalls.
John.   Who was Antigonus, then?
James.   Philip of Spain.

John.	Philip was dead a dozen years or more.
James.	True, but now Spain was pressing Italy,
	And England sympathetically aghast
	Recalled the Armada threat. When Shakespeare's Clown
	Relates 'Antigonus roared and the bear roared
	The Tempest roaring even louder still.'
	And grins 'The bear wrenched out his shoulderblade,
	And the vessel, how the sea flap-dragoned it!'
	(Or words to that effect, a comic turn)
	Philip was this Antigonus (of the Jews),
	A nickname lent him by the pamphleteers.
	Dutch, Huguenots, Italians they all used it.
	The shoulderblade was actual shoulderblade
	Relic of Philip's favourite saint, St. Laurence,
	In faith of which the Armada had been launched:
	So, when the tempest and our English guns,
	Drake's *Bear* leading the van, broke Philip's hopes,
	A savage gust of merriment convulsed
	Protestant Europe, with this caricature
	'The Bear tears out Antigonus' shoulderblade'
	Which jest, revived to hearten sixteen-ten
	Preserves the comic unities, my friend holds.§
John.	I hardly know whether you're serious.
	To accept this correspondence of ideas
	Will damage your Shakespearean reputation.
	Once you begin it, this political tack
	Involves a most unorthodox position.
	Couldn't you try to explain it all away?
James.	No mockery!
John.	James, I'll take you one street further.
	I'll tell you more about Antigonus
	Than you or Aberystwyth ever guessed.
James (drily).	The scientific method aptly used
	Can yield results of most romantic flavour.
John.	James, if I swear that Julio Romano
	Whose fame lives golden in the *Winter's Tale*,
	Published a pamphlet – fifteen-ninety-three,
	It's most important to invent a date –
	Of covert anti-Catholic imagery;
	That one torn copy of this book survives
	Though not for public reading, at Madrid;
	That in this book, Antigonus and the bear
	The tempest and the shoulderbone occur
	With a deal more about this grim encounter

Than Shakespeare with his fine selective sense
Included – if I tell you this, believe it.
I'll make it circumstantially convincing,
Though, as you'd say, 'in point of fact, a lie.'
But does your scientific claim deter me
By its confirmed absolutism? No.
In any case there'll be no libel action.
No one can copyright Antigonus,
Not even Sydney Lee, or Clemence Dane.

James.   Is there much fun in forging history?
Nothing you write can ever alter facts.

John.   When you say 'history', what does that imply?
The logical or the psychological?
Logical? but there's history that refers
To another context with new premises
Not bound by challenge of empiric proof.
One day this history may become supreme
As your empiric kind succeeded myth,
And then who'll be the forger, you or I?

James.   John, I don't follow you: it sounds like nonsense.
I can't believe you mean half what you say.
Must we revert to myth?

John.   No, not to myth
In the dimmer sense, but a new form of myth
Alert, with both eyes open, self-aware –
This is my point, the past is always past
And what the present calls past history
Springs new, capricious, unforeseeable
Not pinned to this or that structure of thought;
Then what the structural classification
Of Bruce and Spider, Washington and Hatchet,
Alfred and Cakes, may prove in time to come,
Or how such tales may alter in essentials
By new research in one vein or the next,
Do you dare prophesy?

James.   No, but meanwhile
The empiric structure stands. John, tell your story.
So long as you admit there's no pretence
Of conformation to what I still call
Absolute truth, I'll hear you out. Remember
The scientist off-duty loves a lie
When monstrous or fantastical enough,
Or else a lie plausible in technique
So long as he's admitted to the secret,

> But not a lie that blunders near the truth
> And trips up over every nicety.
> Despite the lavish bounty of their isle
> For which they thanked God much, but not enough,
> *Swiss Family Robinson* drove me half-mad.

John. But how?

James.   The pious author plumed himself
> On his zoology and his botany.
> One page he's quite informative, the next…

John. He's tied his Wallace Line in loops and bows
> And croquet-hooped his lines of longitude.

James. It makes my head ache.

John.   I'll respect your head.
> Now then: –
>   Antigonus, Romano writes,
> Was not the sole Sicilian lord entrusted
> With the marooning of young Perdita.
> There was another gallant, of Sigunto,
> Fernando Campi, 'who in schools of fence
> Where foils are tipped with buttons, had such fame
> For quickness with his thrust, parry, quart and tierce
> That, had he burst upon the field of war
> Single against whole companies of swordsmen
> (So went the common rumour through the Land)
> He would have spitted them as cooks do larks,
> And borne away the spoils of victory.'
> But somehow there was peace in Sicily
> And since Fernando never picked a quarrel,
> And since he shone so bright in feats of fence
> He'd fought no duels with the naked sword.
> Fernando landed with Antigonus
> On the sea-coast of wild Bohemia's isle.
> Falling behind his friend, to lace a shoe,
> He saw the bear charge from a bramble thicket.
> Antigonus, bold hero, stood his ground,
> Unarmed alack, save for a toyish dagger
> And roared defiance. But Fernando turned,
> Aye, rapier in hand, he turned and ran.
> Bawling for help he pelted from the wood:
> And came by chance upon a simple clown
> Reclined in a green dell two miles away
> Playing at cards with one Autolycus.

James. Autolycus? I seem to know that name.

John. Don't cramp my neo-Elizabethan manner.

James.	I thought John never minded being disturbed.
John.	He bade them follow speedily to the rescue.
	They had no arms, they said. He found them arms,
	Cutting stout quarter-staves from an oak hedge.
	Forward! alas, they found the ravenous bear
	Scarce finished dining on the gentleman.
James.	What then?
John.	Antigonus had two bold brothers

Marco and Cassio, a wife Paulina,
And a dear friend, Clement, a learned friar.
The finish of the story lies with these.
From mouth to mouth rambling circuitously,
News reached them how Antigonus had perished,
And of the coward part Fernando played.
But no one could believe it of Fernando.
Some three years later, back the traitor comes:
He makes complete admission of the facts,
With lame excuses palliating these;
He suffered from a sickness of the bowels,
He had no skill with bears, his wrist was numbed,
He thought he heard men's voices coming near
So ran to call them, but they came too late.
Now offers to expend ten thousand crowns
In reverent masses for his dear friend's soul.
Paulina spat and smote the coward's cheek,
Her brothers challenged him to mortal duel
But he reneged, flying for sanctuary
To the same chapel where this Clement was.
Now Clement who had loved Antigonus
More than his own life, loved these brothers too,
And held Paulina in sincere affection
And for Fernando's parts had great esteem.
What should he do, but plead 'Forgive the traitor,
Forgive, forget, receive him back again,
Think how he suffers in black self-reproach.'
They would not hear him. Clement told them then
'Forgive Fernando, or cast Clement off.'
So choosing hotly, they cast Clement off.
Clement, to prove his spirit of forgiveness,
Though, true enough, Fernando used him coldly
Admitting neither cowardice nor shame,
Dedicated him a friendship's garland
(Fernando took it as a covert sneer)
His life's work, a text-book on Garden Pests....

	I'll give the fifth act of the tale in brief:
	At last Fernando in revenge of slights
	Betrayed his island to the Turkish Fleet,
	Ravished Paulina from her second husband,
	Had Cassio and Marco maimed and branded
	And Clement perished in Sigunto's sack.
James.	An edifying tale; but I can't follow
	The ramifications of your allegory.
	Who was Fernando, to the pamphleteer?
	Medina-Sidonia? or the Duke of Parma?
John.	Scholastic James, I haven't yet considered
	Romano's dark political references:
	If you'll decide Fernando's prototype
	In Philip's day, I'll re-arrange the details.
	Meanwhile, a simple tragedy of manners,
	An ethical tangle, for your comment, James.
James.	I find that simple: Clement was a Christian.
John.	But are you satisfied with Clement's fate?
James.	Satisfied with its probability, yes.
	He acted as his Saviour would have acted,
	He suffered as his Saviour would have suffered.
John.	Do you approve his action?
James.	Yes, I do.
John.	And you condemn Fernando?
James.	Very strongly.
John.	Marco and Cassio?
James.	Deserved their fate.
John.	Paulina?
James.	What else happened to Paulina?
	You left your fifth act in the air, I think.
John.	She died by her own hand, but killed Fernando.
James.	I like Paulina, in the tragic style.
John.	And I dislike them all impartially.
James.	What, Clement too?
John.	Certainly, Clement too.
James.	Well, what do you think Clement should have done?
John.	Disliking Clement is not blaming him.
	I told you, Clement was a Christian friar
	And his whole life centred in Christian doctrine.
	He had no option: as he did, he did.
James.	Well, what would you advise Clement to do
	If ever you met a man in Clement's case?
John.	Nothing I could advise a Christian saint
	Would ever touch him: I should hold my tongue.

James. Put it another way, then, logic-chopper,
        If you were Clement, in a general sense
        But bound by no particular monkish ties,
        How would you wish to act towards either party?
        Which side would you support? Paulina's side?

John.   Never; Fernando too had been my friend,
        And though he acted in an ugly way,
        (Break-downs are always ugly) could he help it?
        It was his first experience of danger,
        And there's no bear like a Bohemian bear,
        For size of paw, or length of claw, or strength of jaw.

James. Would you support Fernando, then, like Clement,
        But not with Clement's full extravagance?

John.   No, could I so offend my oldest friends?
        Think what Fernando's conduct meant for them.
        Courage, among Sicilian noble houses,
        Courage and loyalty were the two prime virtues.
        Forgiveness came a bad third on the list.
        Forgive your foe – but only a brave foe,
        Acquainted with the laws of chivalry.
        Forgive your friend – but not the traitor sort,
        Only the headstrong, 'Come, then, fight me!' friend.
        That was the strict Siguntine code of manners.

James. Well, then? If you would neither blame Fernando
        To please Paulina and her brothers-in-law,
        Nor yet reproach Paulina to Fernando,
        Fernando cursing her, what follows then?
        You have lost everything, antagonized all
        And thrown away even this satisfaction,
        'I acted as my Saviour approves action.'

John.   If I had strictly kept from taking sides
        I would conclude that both my former loves,
        Affection for Paulina and the brothers
        And admiration for Fernando's parts,
        Were tainted with a strong self-interest,
        Therefore the better for complete suspension.

James. So you would still abstain from taking sides?

John.   So far as it were possible to abstain.
        But with this trust, that before many months
        A change would come on either side; Fernando
        Would play the hero on the field, perhaps.
        Paulina and her brothers by the play
        Of quick political changes might be found
        Cowardly and disloyal in their turn

In spite of every virtuous resolution:
Then from the ruin of opposing views
Securer friendship might again be borne
And with the changing sides, I too would change.
James. Do you find Providence always runs so slick?
John. I do, but leave it as a mere assumption,
The philosophical 'why' can wait its turn.
Let this bear dine on its Antigonus
And inwardly digest him undisturbed.
James. Tell me, what was the poem you were writing?
John. Only an eclogue between you and me:
Or, that's its newest phase: its past is past.
As for its future; when I've done, you'll say,
'Well, John, it might have better stayed in prose.'
And with your grim scholastic mind, you'll add,
'Why eclogue? Eclogues treat of goats, not bears.'
James. Then you'll dance off into psychology,
And 'psychologic truth' and verbal quags.

* The reference is to the interruption of Coleridge's 'Kubla Khan'.

§ My friend Miss Winstanley, of Aberystwyth University, had given me this explanation of Antigonus, promising chapter and verse from the pamphleteers. I used it, without the question of its accuracy arising, as a type of a surprising development of literary history.

ESSAY ON CONTINUITY

With unvexed certainty
Historians trace their line
Of continuity
To plot the march of wine
From vineyard, press, tun, bin,
To throats of church or inn.

But after? But before?
Your logic baffles me
That this line runs no more,
True continuity,
Back to the soil, or on
To life in flesh and bone.

For, unless men are wine,
As you deny they be,
Unless you stretch the vine
In continuity
Back to the darksome, dead,
Prone earth on which it fed,

There shines no sense at all
From your cramped history
Of rise, endurance, fall:
Discontinuity
Havocks your central claim,
Disturbs your every aim.

Yet, if wine's progress stands
Forever sure, made free
Of hampering laws and bands
In perpetuity,
By logic it would seem
Bacchus is God supreme.

Not so? You have ears, eyes,
And other senses three,
Wherewith to recognize
True continuity
Of proven forms and shapes?
Wine's wine, and grapes are grapes?

'Old knowledge of these forms,
As all but fools agree,'
You say, 'survives the storms
Of contrariety?
The lexicon defines
Such knowledge with close lines?'

What witness have you found,
What faith or warranty,
That these forms must abound
In perpetuity?
If grapes defy the press?
If wine lose tastiness?

Must wine proceed from vine?
Cana of Galilee
Saw water turned to wine,
Then continuity
In blank amazement stops
Where grapes are water-drops.

Illusion? Miracle? Dream?
Whatever cause you see,
There's something checks the stream
Of continuity,
Reneges, annihilates,
Knowledge of modes and states.

Then stretch what lines you please
In the name of history,
(For men must live by these)
Yet continuity
Shall yet demand in vain
Absolute right to reign.

So, the moving pictures flick
In continuity.
Charles Chaplin twirls a stick
And leers at you and me.
Scene chases hard on scene
Denying gaps between.

So, the trimmed poem runs
As facile as can be
Though it acknowledged once
No continuity,
A scrawling impotence
That knew not its own sense,

Darting from this to that,
Champagne to Galilee,
Kant's tome to Chaplin's hat,
Yet continuity
Appears awhile and is,
And again perishes.

Perishes, springs again,
In perpetuity;
No smallest rags remain
Of its past history:
New knowledge comes, new shapes,
New wine, new lips, new grapes.

KNOWLEDGE OF GOD

So far from praising he blasphemes
    Who says that God has been or is,
Who swears he met with God in dreams
Or face to face in woods and streams,
    Meshed in their boundaries.

'Has been' and 'is' the seasons bind,
    (Here glut of bread, there lack of bread).
The mill-stones grumble as they grind
That if God is, he must be blind,
    Or if he was, is dead.

Can God with Danäe sport and kiss,
    Or God with rebel demons fight,
Making a proof as Jove or Dis,
Force, Essence, Knowledge, that or this,
    Of Godhead Infinite?

The caterpillar years-to-come
    March head to tail with years-that-were
Round and around the cosmic drum;
To time and space they add their sum,
    But how is Godhead there?

Weep, sleep, be merry, vault the gate
    Or down the evening furrow plod,
Hate and at length withhold your hate,
Rule, or be ruled by certain fate,
    But cast no net for God.

MOCK BEGGAR HALL: A PROGRESSION

I

Poet.   Last night I dreamed about a haunted house: it was hardly a frightening dream or a gloomy dream, though I have for a long while been vexed by that kind of nightmare, but a disturbing problem-ridden affair demanding the comments of a moralist. The setting was something like that of Mock Beggar Hall at Oxford, once a leper-house outside the city walls, then a parsonage, now a private house where undergraduates lodge.

Philosopher.   Have you ever heard whether the Hall is actually haunted?

Poet.   No, but it occurred to me when I last visited there that it had every excuse for being so. In the dream I saw lepers and a parson and other odd ghosts alternately invading the rooms: thereupon a voice informed me that the lepers once used to haunt the parson and were themselves once haunted by these other nameless bearded ghosts, and now both parson, lepers and the bearded ones quarrel for turns to haunt the present occupants. I was asked in all seriousness what was to be done about it, but I could make no suggestion.

Philosopher.   You discovered the sense of the allegory?

Poet.   The dream follows naturally on the discussion we began yesterday. The ghosts represent the antisocial impulses in the individual. The new element which the dream has added is an observation that as social systems evolve, new modes of behaviour are expected from the individual and the old modes are discountenanced. But certain individuals cling to tradition, then as each mode claims complete liberty of action at the expense of other interests there follows continual friction. Is there any solution for these troubles? The name Mock Beggar Hall promises little hope.

Philosopher.   Now that the problem is stated in this completer form, I shall be interested to hear your dreams tomorrow morning. I expect them to bring you to some sort of conclusion: it will not be the first time that our dreams and our philosophy have developed concurrently.

II
THE NEXT DAY

Philosopher. Well, what were your dreams?

Poet. Forgotten. But last night I began writing a poem and this morning I finished it; and as apparently my dreams provided something that enabled me to finish this morning, quite easily, what seemed an impossible problem last night; and as poetry and dreams are closely allied and sometimes identical, your expectations have been more or less satisfied.

Philosopher. Well then, read!

Poet.
  You, landlord, when your tenants make complaint
  Of uncouth doings in the black of night,
  And even in decent sunlit hours of day;
  Of choristers who practise doleful anthems
  And the grey vicar, candlestick in hand,
  Hunting his spectacles from room to room;
  Or when they speak of eviller visitations
  Of faces silver-white, noseless and earless,
  Outcry of clappers, inarticulate moans;
  Or tell how always on a Saturday
  Come gaunt old men, with beards and parchment rolls
  And long-drawn Babylonian misereres
  Trailing procession through the solid walls;
  Or when they chance on scenes of solemn passion
  Where, cloak and toga duly hung on nails,
  Breast kisses breast and thighs are joined with thighs
  While incense burns beside the rose-wreathed couch –
  Be then the historian concealing nothing,
  Inform them of the age of this foundation,
  Registry-office now, once parsonage,
  Before that lazar-house; farther back yet
  Synagogue (in the reign of good King John)
  And even before, a shrine to Roman Venus;
  Whose tenants in each stern successive age
  Had variance with their ghostly predecessors,
  Each making claim for undisturbed possession.
  Relate how once with candle, bell and book
  The surly vicar strove to exorcize
  Ghosts of the lepers, but they stayed to plague him,

Being blind, stone-deaf and obstinate in grief.
Tell them, these lepers when they lived in flesh
Saw phantoms too, they cowered in palsied fear
From the rabbi and his fur-capped congregation.
Nor had these Jews enjoyed possessive peace,
They had called the vengeance of their angels down
On ghost defilers of God's chosen place,
The Venus-worshippers; archangels even
Proved powerless to evict them. And these Romans,
Had they no strange incursions at their shrine
Of Druid knives and basket-sacrifices
Breaking the sacred raptures of the kiss?
Was not their temple founded here to mask
The lopped oakgrove of aboriginal gods?
Then let your tenants, duly warned, consider
Their duty as the present occupants
Or their advantage, if that touches nearer,
Of being the first to practise tolerance,
Allotting private times to every faction
Inviolable by others, quick or dead;
Reserving for themselves, free from all trespass
Such office-hours as business may demand,
Lest, failing to deal fairly, they themselves
May century-long be doomed to walk these rooms.
Then let them think it more than possible
That future tenants may resent intrusion
At casual moments of the night or day
Of Gretna marriages, proud fatherhood
And red-eyed notifications of decease.

There it finishes: but I did not recognize until after the poem
was written why I had made the haunted house a registry-
office, though I was aware that during the war Mock Beggar
Hall had been used as a Government office-building: it
evidently symbolizes European civilization, officialdom
attempting to control the individual from the cradle to the
coffin. The allegory has broadened from the conflicts within
the individual to the conflicts between groups of individ-
uals. I had only recognized, before I began writing, that the
Romans and the Jews were standing respectively for flesh
and spirit: it seems now that they also symbolize the two
main historic streams, often conflicting, to which Europe
owes her legal and religious development.

Philosopher.   If you are waiting for my comment, it is this. The poem has only just begun its broader allegory. While I approve the idea of tolerance, as you know, I question your solution: it appears too much like a compromise, and compromises can by their nature only lead to further conflict. The registrar draws up his very characteristic time-table and gives himself all the best hours of every day but Sunday; will the ghosts be satisfied?

Poet.   I appreciate your point. I am afraid that this *Haunted House* is going to haunt us for a great while yet.

III
A WEEK LATER

Philosopher.   Are there any new developments of the poem you read me?

Poet.   Mock Beggar Hall? Yes. A lawyer and the landlord have started an ethical dialogue. The lawyer after beginning with the poem more or less as I read it you has been answered as follows: –

> *I must confess myself vastly surprised*
> *To hear a lawyer recognizing ghosts*
> *Possessed of individual rights and feelings,*
> *Instead of taking the old legal stand*
> *'Once the estate is settled, the man's dead.'*
> *Your lyrical presentation, too, was fine.*
> *And I admire your sense in recognizing*
> *There's a commercial and a legal question*
> *Bound up with hauntings.*
>
> (Then the lawyer says complacently):
>   *That's sound common sense.*
>
> (The landlord picks him up quickly):
> *Yet common sense, the Anglo-Saxon flair*
> *Seems weakest on its vaunted practical side,*
> *Compromise, managing the unruly factions*
> *With 'You stay here' and 'You keep over there'.*
> *Only advice at first, no hint of arms.*
> *'We have no greed for power, desiring only*
> *Business connections, order, progress, Peace.*
> *Trust us; we can restore your fainting land.*
> *We'll be your servants, stewards and managers.'*
> *For awhile, admitted, things go well enough.*

At first mere arbitration, registration,
Statistics, scientific service, steam,
Development of minerals, harbours, roads.
'Responsibility weighs most heavy on us.
Not central power, mere central agency
For news, views, experts on one thing or other.'
Yet gradually by slow degrees appears
A small police well drilled with guns and rods,
A loyal stern Praetorian Guard, abets
The rising tyranny; soon Augustan splendour,
The pink Protectorate grown Empire-red,
Army and Navy, Laws, poll-taxes, fines,
History written as 'Divide and Rule'
By loyal Virgils, 'Tu regere imperio
Populos, Romane' and the rest of it,
Clipped powers of movement for the native tribes,
Still a pretence of representative rule
With general fatness, general acquiescence.
National debit swings across to credit,
And every weak dissenting voice goes dumb.
The Jews enjoy each Saturday for Sabbath,
Christians enjoy each Sunday for their Sabbath,
And all goes well until some Christian Feast
Falls on a holy Jewish Saturday.
Then the new power, foreseeing grave events
Calls out the lathi-wallahs to line the streets.
Order must be preserved whatever the cost.
Then 'Head Cut', 'Fork Cut', 'Belly Point', 'Charge Lathis'
Where two processions take converging routes.
They drive both backward to their starting points,
Killing a few, breaking some arms and legs,
With a complacent 'But for us, of course
Things would have been far worse', which pleases no one.
Then 'Those ungrateful swine'; 'These arrogant bullies'
Whispered at first, soon shouted in the squares
When distant Rome outlasts her conquering noon,
Next, boycotts, massacre, non-co-operation,
And the play drags to its anarchic end.
No, sir, though I admit the attempt will come
In much the manner you have just outlined
Towards settling the disputes between these factions,
I'll take no part in hurrying on events.
No arbitration I could give would lull
Suspicions of an interested motive.

I sailed along easily so far, but then grounded: now I have come to talk it over with you.

Philosopher.   How it broadens! but why this satire on British imperialism? How does it rise out of the former version of the poem and the original dream? I believe I see the connexion but please reassure me.

Poet.   Surely this, that efforts to exploit one mode of behaviour in the individual at the expense of all others is a form of imperialism comparable with a political imperialism, and though at first it is the ready solution of former difficulties, all imperialism as such is bound in its later stages to run a certain unhappy course. Besides, British Imperialism is not singled out for illustration; Roman imperialism is hinted too, and at one point I was considering the origins of the recent tyranny in Russia; although not invaders from outside and honestly communistic the Bolsheviks started and developed along the usual imperialistic lines. All imperialisms, Tartar, Mogul, Rajput, Aztec, Spanish; there is no difference in the outline of their rise and fall.

Philosopher.   That part will stand, then. But I am not happy about the relations between your lawyer and your landlord. If the landlord is really a landlord, he cannot afford to criticize the legal methods that maintain him. How did he become landlord except approving and approved by the lawyer? I make this criticism not in any formal scholastic sense. I do not mind whether poems continue the single-strand logic of the Classicist or the metamorphic logic of the Romantic method – I am just continuing your allegory.

Poet.   I know that, but I can hardly follow yet. Probably this is the sandbank where I ran aground.

Philosopher.   Did you see what General … what General *Dunkel* said about the Indian question at Cascara Colony in Africa?

Poet.   Tell me. I have always been taught to regard Dunkel as the one honest man in world-politics; since his insistence on the rights of European subject races when the map was being arranged four years ago, and his recent outburst at the Imperial Conference.

Philosopher. His comment was something to this effect. 'Why should the Cascara Indians, with their tradition of an exclusive caste system, object to us English becoming the military and administrative caste, which in a modern state takes precedence of all others?' He pointed out that the white races have obviously developed the sciences of government and war further than either the brown or black races.

Poet. I don't blame Dunkel, he could hardly have taken any other view. A verbal question by the way; I believe that it would add greatly to the amity of nations if the word *pink* were substituted for *white*, and *blue* for *black* as you talk of a *blue* Persian cat: there is a powerful symbolic suggestion in white and black, white for honour and purity, black for dishonour and devilry.

Philosopher. Neither do I blame Dunkel; and the apparent inconsistency of his attitude is easy to explain. It is possible for him to be generous to European subject races where he is not personally concerned and where it is only a case of pink against pink, but in his own continent the hegemony of the pink races over the blue and brown must be assured. It is an interesting comment on your lawyer character that Dunkel began his career as most politicians do by practising law.

Poet. Enlarge on the imperialistic question, please.

Philosopher. Although not pink myself, I can sympathize with the Pinks – as you know I spent some years in one of the few surviving Brown tyrannies outside the Pink Raj. These Pinks, then, once they are firmly enough established on Brown territory explain themselves thus. 'Here we are, and here by fate, we stay. We hate our exile and we hate your climate, but we are forced to maintain ourselves here because, for one thing, there is not enough scope at home for the military and administrative professions to which we have been educated. In the wider sense, we stay here because our country is organized for trade and industry and is dependent on yours for a steady supply of raw materials and a steady market for our admirable manufactured goods. You Easterners have a proverb "First, the Bible, then the enamel basin, then the bayonet." It is unhappily true about the bayonet, but a minority is always at the mercy of the majority unless it controls the administrative offices, and these finally depend on bayonet power. We act only in self-defence and I think you will agree that we manage very efficiently. As for certain disagreements that have arisen between us, you must recognize that being Pink we cannot afford to live in these unhealthy coast-cities and plain-cities all the year round. Our families have joined us here now and in the heats we must all take our turn for going up to the hills; to stay where we are would kill us quickly. Therefore whether by Bible, basin or bayonet we intend to possess ourselves of the hill-stations which you formerly occupied and to keep these safe for Pinks. You are Browns, some of you even Blues, therefore you can, though with difficulty, survive the summer on the plains and in the coast-cities: we are sorry for you, but life is as a struggle for existence, and by this arrangement we can both just survive. Remember that if ever there is a famine in the land, our administrative genius will alleviate it as usual; that is to say, after we have taken our share of the rice supply and after the usual quantity has been shipped home and paid for by the money that covers our salaries, we will then equitably distribute what is left among you. If there is only just enough rice for us to eat we will not send any home (we can get our salaries by simple land taxes) but we will equitably share among your provinces the rice-water in which our rice has been boiled: and you can drink it out of our admirable enamel basins.' That genuinely well-disposed attitude is what the subject races call 'mocking the beggar'.

Poet.   I see. Then Dunkel will only be able to support the League of Nations' ideals when his own basin of rice is not threatened. Similarly the Pink Americans are up against a Blue Problem in the South. The pink minority there found that it could not survive when the blue majority had been given the franchise by well-meaning but unintelligent Dunkels in the North: there followed the original Klu Klux Klan revolt, and pink hegemony was restored under a legal fiction of democracy, that is, Blue voted, Pink voted, but the Blue votes were left uncounted in the Ballot box: or it amounted to that.

Philosopher.   Again, the Struggle for Existence way of looking at human relationships insures that, where an imperialism is tottering, the ancient honest virtues approved by a Cato or a Cincinnatus tend to disappear in political circles. You will find the central government of a province spending an annual sum of millions, through its secret service, on keeping one subject-race at loggerheads with another. This enables them to point out the necessity of their continued government, if the country is not to be torn in pieces. Meanwhile the subject races, who have developed each in their own communities the moral code of schoolboys, prisoners or prostitutes, that lies and low cunning are commendable when directed against the system that holds them down, begin to abandon their former technique for a sort of mutinous self-righteousness corresponding with the changed technique of their oppressors.

Poet. I'll put the poem away for a bit.

IV
A MONTH LATER

Poet. Do you remember Mock Beggar Hall?

Philosopher. I have been expecting some more news: read it as it stands now.

Poet. I am not at all satisfied with it as a final version of the poem, but a new point has emerged: that you cannot talk about the *Voice of India* or the *Voice of England* or the *Voice of Civilization* or the *Voice of the Individual,* even, where these are not any longer entities but storm-centres, rough houses of acute conflict. So in the poem as I read it to you last time, though the lawyer still makes his lawyer speech, and gets the same answer, the man who answers him is not called the landlord but just 'The Other', because as landlord he cannot co-exist with the lawyer. He represents the hope of reintegration in these groups. He has no contact with the lawyer's practical suggestions because the law is fed by litigation and because he cannot realize himself as owner of the property until the rival claims to the estate disappear and the tenants quit.

Philosopher. Well, then.

Poet reads:
  LAWYER. My card, sir.

THE OTHER.   *(reads).* John B. League of *League and Action,*
                         Solicitors, late *Liberty and Action.*

LAWYER.   I have come to speak about some real estate
                         Between King Street and Martyr Avenue.
                         I understand that's yours, or we could prove
                         Your legal title if you cared to employ us.
                         May I continue, sir?

THE OTHER.   Then, Mr. League
                         Let this be talk and not a consultation;
                         Nothing you say must prejudice my purse.
                         I'm not the landlord yet.

LAWYER.   Quite so.

THE OTHER.   Remember
                         I never dealt with Liberty and Action
                         Nor feel disposed to deal with League and Action
                         Though Mr. Liberty, I hear, is dead.

LAWYER.   Poor man, he got the firm in disrepute.
                         A most efficient lawyer in his day
                         He suffered from delusions towards the finish,
                         Undertook business far beyond his means
                         And drove the office-staff nearly distracted.
                         He left us terrible liabilities
                         (I make no secret). Now he's dead, however,
                         We have regained the confidence of the Banks.
                         Business increases nicely, every day
                         We get new clients...still if you mistrust...

THE OTHER.   No, talk by all means.

LAWYER.   Well, sir, I hear rumours,
                         Deterioration of the property,
                         Domestic differences, complaints and so on.
                         Let us assume your title, for the moment,
                         And now suggest a method of improving
                         The rentable value of this fine estate.
                         If you approve this, we would ask the favour
                         Of taking legal steps on your behalf.

(Then he continues with the passage).
                         'Then landlord when your tenants make
                                    complaint
                         As I have ample evidence that they will.'

The Other answers him as before
                         'I must confess myself vastly surprised', et cetera,

But goes on:
                         Then too, though you assume my landlord's
                                    claim

I'm not a landlord in the legal sense,
Nor do I wish to press a legal claim.
My ancestors last held that property
By arch-druidic right in Celtic times.
So I possess no title deeds to show
Beyond a hopeful old prophetic verse
Engraved on a bronze bowl in Ogham writing,
That says, this property was one time ours
And will eventually be ours again –
Two thousand years is mentioned, from what
    date
Does not appear exactly – 'Then', it runs,
'The existent legal titles will fall through
Confirmed by whatsoever authority.'

LAWYER.   My dear sir, if this bowl is genuine,
And if your genealogy runs down true...

THE OTHER.   No! understand that I prefer to wait.
Then Mr. League, when these two thousand
    years
Expire, and the whole property reverts
Either to me or to my heirs-at-blood,
Then, on the day that we resume the house,
In a most real sense we become the house,
A house that's continuity of the tenants
Through whom by slow accretion it evolved,
Taking the individual stamp of each,
Often at odds, room against room divided,
Waiting the landlord-absentee's return,
Long while despaired of such reintegration.
We being the house then, a house whole and free,
Become the continuity of these ghosts,
And there can be no question of annoyance
Or hauntings in the former vicious mode.
No one will claim possession; if ghosts come
They'll come as guests laughing at ancient frays
And what new conflicts rise in future years
Between my heirs, or my heirs' assignees
Those we can leave trustfully to their fate:
That man's a monument of discontent
Who grieves beyond the next millennium's
    promise.

LAWYER.   There's nothing to be done, you say, but wait?
Deterministic sloth! what place is left
For self-control and social betterment

                          If you leave conflicts to be solved by fate?
                          Settle the house, *now*: show them who is landlord.
                          (We'll arm you with imposing parchment deeds
                          To prove their lease is held from you direct)
                          Where diplomatic tact has failed, use force,
                          Threaten eviction, hint a legal loophole
                          By which their lease can be foreclosed at will.
THE OTHER.   Such restlessness can spare no time for thought.
                          It's do, do, do! Hack through, or muddle through!
                          But my mind runs ahead to consequences.
                          How can I oust the present landlordry
                          (There are three rival claims to this estate)
                          Without ill-will all round? as for the tenants
                          How can I hope to impose my dominant will
                          Without the unavoidable repercussion
                          Of subjugation to another's will?
                          And what's the end of muddling through, but
                              muddle?
                          As for your self-control, when have you tried it?
                          When have you ever yet refused a brief
                          Even though you knew your client had no case?
                          When have you ever abstained from good advice
                          Even though you knew it could not be accepted?
                          Does litigation make for social peace?
                          Go your own way, sir, with your files and ledgers,
                          Support the likeliest of these rival claimants.
                          I'll stand aside.
LAWYER.   You'll not impede our action?
THE OTHER.   I'll give you that assurance.
LAWYER.   Come! In writing?
THE OTHER. *(writes it out).* Now leave me to my hopeful feats of
                              sloth,
                          The absentee's profession that you loathe.

Philosopher.   I am not sure whether you have seen one point that for me comes out clearly. That while there are several claimants to the position of landlord, the domestic troubles between the tenants and the ghosts can hope for no solution. In fact, while the friction continues between political groups the moral conflicts within the individual cannot disappear. We noticed in the European War how the breakdown of the Ten Commandments in their regulation of the political conduct of nations involved the weakening of these commandments in the individual or small group. I believe that all these problems of conflict can only find a settlement together, and that League of Nations ideals which are as old as human society, and not a new discovery of 1919, must in practice always be defeated so long as the idea embodied in the word *Nation* remains. I think we are seeing things more clearly now: but your poem is not ended yet.

Poet.   That may be, but let us record it so far and put a book-mark in until next week or next month, or next year, or ten years hence. Neither are you ended or I ended: but as in each phase of our life we are self-sufficient and complete, so these different stages of the poem.

Philosopher.   In your next version what perhaps ought to be made clear is that we are raising no objection to imperialists as being villainous, or more villainous than the people they oppress. As you have shown, in its beginnings imperialism has its positive value: though not a permanent solution of political difficulties between those groups whom the imperial power discovers at odds, intervention is a relief, and an inevitable step towards final harmony. Further, we are holding that wherever unpleasant traits appear in imperialism we cannot judge the subject races to be innocent; where a Gandhi and a Dyer come in conflict it would be ridiculous to claim that either is an angel while his opposite is a demon. Our point is that either they are both angels or both devils. Beggary is as offensive to mockers as mockery to beggars.

Poet.   To make an analogy from painting; if we decide 'in this painting yellow is going to stand for white,' then nobody need object to the relation between two objects appearing in the painting, one of which has hitherto appeared bright blue and is now shown as bright green, and another which has hitherto appeared dark blue and is now shown as dark green; the relation between the two objects remains virtually the same. But to paint the first object *bright* green and the second *dark* blue, that causes popular confusion unless many people are involved in the same sort of conflict that has altered the painter's conventional colour-values.

Philosopher.   Yes, what we are trying to point out is this, I believe, that hitherto attempted solutions of political and individual conflicts have always taken the form of judging one party or one mode of behaviour to be better or worse than the opposing party according as it conforms to a code of ethics,

pretending to be absolute, adopted by the dominant polit-
ical group or culture. The 'better' interest has been
rewarded, the 'worse' punished. That is a matter of history,
and it is also a matter of history that, so to speak, the swing
of the quintain has always knocked the tilter off his horse.
You and I are not condemning the lawyer for believing that
laws can be absolute; if we could understand the history of
human relationships before any moral codes were formu-
lated, we would sympathize with him wholeheartedly. All
that we are suggesting is that the time must come, now that
the absolutist claim has been recognized and questioned
and an alternative proposed, when there will be no further
use for the lawyer or imperialist of tradition, when human
relationships can be conducted according to a different
system: that is, mutual abstention from conflict when
conflict is recognized as obtaining, and a positive faith that
the very fact of abstention and endurance will introduce a
new element to solve existing differences.

Poet.   I agree; but I hope that I have already made it clear that
between the lawyer and the Other (that is, I suppose, the
traditional view and the view that we are holding) there is
no conflict. The lawyer has his important part to play in
history; but so have we.

THE RAINBOW AND THE SCEPTIC

'Decrees of God? Of One Prime Cause?
    Predestinate for men,
Whose only knowledge of such laws
    Is change and change again?

'Made free or fated, what care I
    In truth's grand overthrow?
Since knowledge is but folly's spy
    It is not sane to know.

'For Fate's a word of trivial sense
    And Freedom is knocked blind,
If there is nowhere permanence,
    If God can change His mind.'

Disconsolate and strange enough
    He walked the forest side,
The sun blazed out, the shower drew off,
    The rainbow straddled wide.

It stained with red the chalky road,
    It leapt from sea to hill;
A second arch more faintly showed,
    A third arch faintlier still.

The black blaspheming furious mood
    Passed from him gradually:
Wry-mouthed in cynic pause he stood
    And smiled: 'The Golden Key.

'The elf-key at the rainbow's rise:
    Watch it and walk with care!
It vanishes beneath your eyes,
    It passes on elsewhere.

'So laws like rainbows move and mock,
    So wisdom never brings
The airy treasure to unlock
    The essential heart of things.'...

A spirit of air in answer spoke
    With strange and solemn sense:
Music and light about him broke
    In seven-toned effluence.

'Man, Man, accept this new degree
    Of beauty as you go;
Observe the march of what must be,
    The bend of each new bow.

'Then since laws move in rainbow-light
    Let faith be therefore strong,
That change can never prove you right,
    Nor either prove you wrong.

'Shall Time-the-present judge Time-past
    Once blotted from its view?
Each key must vary from the last,
    Because each lock springs new.

'Knowledge of changing lock and key,
    So much the FINITE is;
Let the bow beckon "Follow me,
    Whose hopes are certainties";

'Yet beyond all this, rest content
    In dumbness to revere
INFINITE God without event,
    Causeless, not there, not here,

'Neither eternal nor time-bound,
    Not certain, nor in change,
Uncancelled by the cosmic round,
    Nor crushed within its range.'

WELCHMAN'S HOSE

(1925)

ALICE

When that prime heroine of our nation, Alice,
Climbing courageously in through the Palace
Of Looking Glass, found it inhabited
By chessboard personages, white and red,
Involved in never-ending tournament,
She being of a speculative bent
Had long foreshadowed something of the kind,
Asking herself: 'Suppose I stood behind
And viewed the fireplace of Their drawing-róom
From hearthrug level, why must I assume
That what I'd see would need to correspond
With what I now see? And the rooms beyond?'
Proved right, yet not content with what she had done,
Alice decided to prolong her fun:
She set herself, with truly British pride
In being a pawn and playing for her side,
And simple faith in simple stratagem,
To learn the rules and moves and perfect them.
So prosperously there she settled down
That six moves only and she'd won her crown –
A triumph surely! But her greater feat
Was rounding these adventures off complete:
Accepting them, when safe returned again,
As queer but true – not only in the main
True, but as true as anything you'd swear to,
The usual three dimensions you are heir to.
For Alice though a child could understand
That neither did this chance-discovered land
Make nohow or contrariwise the clean
Dull round of mid-Victorian routine,
Nor did Victoria's golden rule extend
Beyond the glass: it came to the dead end
Where empty hearses turn about; thereafter
Begins that lubberland of dream and laughter,

The red-and-white-flower-spangled hedge, the grass
Where Apuleius pastured his Gold Ass,
Where young Gargantua made whole holiday....
But farther from our heroine not to stray,
Let us observe with what uncommon sense –
Though a secure and easy reference
Between Red Queen and Kitten could be found –
She made no false assumption on that ground
(A trap in which the scientist would fall)
That queens and kittens are identical.

BURRS AND BRAMBLES

Discourse, bruised heart, on trivial things
    With laughter vague and hollow,
Conceal the sudden tear that stings,
    The lump that's hard to swallow;
These are mere manners, these no part
Of the self-deceiver's art,
    And rankly here grow nettles
    With burrs and brambles prickly,
Here slide snakes across the brakes
    Whose tongues do murder quickly.

Make light of that embrace you lost
    And the long anguish sequent,
Prove it was bought at slender cost,
    A light romance, be frequent
With every subterfuge and lie
That masks the soul of misery,
    For rankly here grow nettles
    With burrs and brambles prickly,
Here slide snakes across the brakes
    Whose tongues do murder quickly.

Choose any way of countless ways
    To ease the jealous gnawing,
Fire, if you must, that angry blaze
    From which there's no withdrawing:
Let all Hell's demons guide your hate:
Or, if you must, be mean and wait,
    For rankly here grow nettles

With burrs and brambles prickly,
Here slide snakes across the brakes
    Whose tongues do murder quickly.

Do what you must, yet nevermore
    Think, when this torment ceases
That warned before is armed before
    Against false-love's caprices,
Never by any force withstood,
So unforeseen and sly and rude,
    For rankly here grow nettles
    With burrs and brambles prickly,
Here slide snakes across the brakes
    Whose tongues do murder quickly.

FROM OUR GHOSTLY ENEMY

The fire was already white ash
    When the lamp went out,
And the clock at that signal stopped:
The man in the chair held his breath
    As if Death were about.

The moon shone bright as a lily
    On his books outspread.
He could read in that lily light:
'When you have endured your fill,
    Kill!' the book read.

The print being small for his eyes,
    To ease their strain
A hasty candle he lit,
Keeping the page with his thumb.
    'Come, those words again!'

But the book he held in his hand
    And the page he held
Spelt prayers for the sick and needy,
'By God, they are wanted here,'
    With fear his heart swelled.

'I know of an attic ghost,
    Of a cellar ghost,
And of one that stalks in the meadows,
But here's the spirit I dread,'
    He said, 'the most;

'Who, without voice or body,
    Distresses me much,
Twists the ill to holy, holy to ill,
Confuses me, out of reach
    Of speech or touch;

'Who works by moon or by noon,
    Threatening my life.
I am sick and needy indeed.'
He went then filled with despairs
    Upstairs to his wife.

He told her these things, adding
    'This morning alone,
Writing, I felt for a match-box;
It rose up into my hand,
    Understand, on its own.

'In the garden yesterday
    As I walked by the beds,
With the tail of my eye I caught
"Death within twelve hours"
    Written in flowers' heads.'

She answered him, simple advice
    But new, he thought, and true.
'Husband, of this be sure,
That whom you fear the most,
    This ghost, fears you.

'Speak to the ghost and tell him,
    "Whoever you be,
Ghost, my anguish equals yours,
Let our cruelties therefore end.
    Your friend let me be."'

He spoke, and the ghost, who knew not
   How he plagued that man,
Ceased, and the lamp was lit again,
And the dumb clock ticked again,
   And the reign of peace began.

DEATH OF THE FARMER

'What ails the Master, do I think?
Undoubtedly,' the Ox cried, 'drink,
That stupefies the spirit, dims
The reason, dulls the limbs.'

'He's done no good about the farm
These fifteen years, but only harm.
As well you know,' the old Ass said,
'We often wish him dead.

'How hopefully at his Son's birth
We preached the reign of Heaven on Earth
And sang him praises high and low.
Ay, that was long ago!

'Still, to ensure domestic peace,
We tell the turkeys, ducks and geese:
"He rules, omniscient and great,
Proof-armoured against fate."

'"Granted," we say, "he's no more seen
Tending fat sheep in pastures green,
Or scattering at the break of morn
Largesse, profuse, of corn.

'"Yet, from some glorious inner room,
He guides the cowman, steward or groom,
And posts his ledger, page by page,
In joy or solemn rage.

'"Our feeding and our water-time,
Our breeding and our slaughter-time,
The dyke, the hedge, the plough, the cart –
These thoughts lie next his heart."

'The simple birds believe it true,
What now, poor poultry, will they do,
Dazed to confusion, when the glum
Gloved undertakers come,

'Tilting the coffin past the pond,
The ricks, the clamps, the yard beyond,
Skirting the midden-heap with care,
Then out, we know not where?'

OVID IN DEFEAT

The grammar of Love's Art
   Ovid still teaches,
Grotesque in Pontic snows
   And bearskin breeches.*

'Let man be ploughshare,
   Woman his field;
Flatter, beguile, assault,
   And she must yield.

'Snatch the morning rose
   Fresh from the wayside,
Deflower it in haste
   Ere the dew be dried.'

Ovid instructs you how
   Neighbours' lands to plough;
'Love smacks the sweeter
   For a broken vow.'

Follows his conclusion
   Of which the gist is
The cold '*post coitum*
   Homo tristis'.

Thereat despairing,
   Other Ovids hallow
Ploughshare in rust
   And field left fallow,

Or, since in Logic books
    Proposed they find,
'Where two ride together,
    One rides behind',

This newer vision
    Of love's revealed,
Woman as the ploughshare,
    Man, her field.

Man as the plucked flower
    Trampled in mire,
When his unfair fair
    Has eased desire.

One sort of error
    Being no worse than other,
O, hug this news awhile,
    My amorous brother,

That the wheel of Fortune
    May be turned complete,
Conflict, domination,
    Due defeat.

Afterwards, when you weary
    Of false analogy,
Offending both philosophy
    And physiology,

You shall see in woman
    Neither more nor less
Than you yourself demand
    As your soul's dress.

Thought, though not man's thought,
    Deeds, but her own,
Art, by no comparisons
    Shaken or thrown.

Plough then salutes plough
    And rose greets rose:
While Ovid in toothache goes
    Stamping through old snows.

---

*   Pellibus et sutis arcent mala frigora braccis.

DIVERSIONS

TO AN EDITOR

(A Satiric Complaint in the Old Style)

John Cole, Esquire,
It is my desire,
If it be your pleasure,
To be paid full measure*
For the poetic fire
And the fantastic treasure
Which the Muses inspire:
So much of it as I
Committed last July
To your mercurial eye.

You accepted those verses
Neither with sneers nor curses,
But with hearty laudations,
Jolly recommendations
Of all my late creations.
And I thought this strange, for you
Never publish a review,
Even with faint damnations,
Of the work I now do.
Was this a changed view?

I would have you remember
That poem grave and sober
Which you printed in October
(No, indeed, in September),
About a Glass Palace,
And the curious rambles
Of a girl named Alice;
Also *Burrs and Brambles,*
How the venomous snakes
Slide in the prickly brakes
With cunning and malice.
It was then my desire,
Had it been your pleasure,
To be paid full measure.
I was worthy of my hire,
John Cole, Esquire!

But, indeed, you must remember
How, when November
To its close had run,
I sent you a dun.
(For the butcher and baker
And candlestick-maker
Had me on the run.)
You sent me back fair phrases,
Like roses and daisies,
But of guineas not one.

Out went November,
In came December,
And you printed my verse
Of the ghostly curse,
Blown lamp and cold ember,
In phrase simple and terse.
John Cole, Esquire,
It was then my desire,
Had it been your pleasure,
To be paid in just measure:
I swear I am no liar.

Now the old year is gone,
Spring is drawing on,
And what season is worse
For a poet's purse?
I tell you, none.
The milkmen, the coalman,
And the oilman, a droll man,
Are knocking at my door
Louder and worse and more;
And had I the courage
I would charge you demurrage
On the poems yet sleeping
In your close keeping:
That one of the farm ditches,
Of the straw and the fitches,
Where the elder beasts, unweeping,
Scorn on their god are heaping,
And that of *Ovid's Breeches*,
With the strife that vexes
The embattled sexes
When arrogance itches –
John Cole, Esquire,
I no longer desire

To await your pleasure,
With 'At your leisure!'
Pay me now my hire!

I hear on every part
That you have a kind heart
And a lofty soul,
And passions in control;
But though your heart be kind,
Though your soul be wed to Art,
Though your honour be whole,
Does that help *me* to find
My bread, meat, and coal,
My coffee and my roll,
My candlesticks and oil?
No one can call me lazy,
For I toil when I toil:
I keep from any broil,
I am merry and easy,
A Johnny-pluck-the-daisy;
But even good tempers spoil.

Sir, though it may appear
An easy thing to rear
Four children on a clear
Two hundred pounds a year,
I think this is no reason
Why at the present season
You should praise my verse,
But draw tight your purse.
For your private commendations
Or secret approbations
Are scant fare to live at ease on:
They make the case worse.

Then John Cole, Esquire,*
If it be your pleasure,
It is now my desire
To be paid in full measure,
According to my hire.

Addressed to John Lynn Cole, Esquire, From The World's End, Islip, Oxfordshire.

Mr. 'John Cole' took the above in good part, and after a time replied with a cheque and acceptable explanations of the delays of which the poem complains.

* 'Payment is customarily made at the close of the month in which the contributions appear....' – *The Trade of Authorship.*

THE KINGFISHER'S RETURN

A song for the children at Field Place, where Shelley was born; made to celebrate the Kingfisher's return from being stuffed. This is a variation on a simpler version by my friend, Molly Adams.

Long had our Kingfisher been
Barred from his meadows green,
From green waters running deep
Where the dumb fish glide and sleep;
Reeds in their ranks keep
The banks on either side,
Weeds divide and surge wide
As the miller's boat goes by;
Kingfishers, when they die,
To far Cloud-Cuckoo pastures fly,
But this Kingfisher makes a home
Where little children go and come,
With nosegays welcoming
The advent of their King,
This ancient regent
Of an excellent
Rainbow Land.
Join we hand in hand
By the river strand,
To dance for our playmate
Till the day grows late,
Greeting him with this song
A long while planned.

LOVE WITHOUT HOPE

Love without hope, as when the young bird-catcher
Swept off his tall hat to the Squire's own daughter,
So let the imprisoned larks escape and fly
Singing about her head, as she rode by.

TRAVELLER'S CURSE AFTER MISDIRECTION

(from the Welsh)

May they stumble, stage by stage
On an endless pilgrimage,
Dawn and dusk, mile after mile,
At each and every step, a stile;
At each and every stile, withal,
May they catch their feet and fall;
At each and every fall they take
May a bone within them break;
And may the bone that breaks within
Not be, for variation's sake,
Now rib, now thigh, now arm, now shin,
But always, without fail, THE NECK.

TILLY KETTLE

His name was Tilly Kettle,
A painter of Joshua Reynolds' school.
It was he consolidated Plassey,
It was he consolidated Plassey
And enlarged the English Rule.

He despised the Mughal painters.
Their work, he avowed, was incorrect;
Thus he consolidated Plassey,
Thus he consolidated Plassey
And won Lord Clive's respect.

He painted Rajahs and Begums,
He asked and obtained a huge commission.
It was he consolidated Plassey,
It was he consolidated Plassey
And killed a great tradition.

Full-length Rajahs in their robes,
He measured them both with rule and eye
As he consolidated Plassey,
As he consolidated Plassey
And worked his palette dry.

'Hand on hip,' said Tilly Kettle,
'And drapery in the Italian style,
For you learned a lesson at Plassey,
For you learned a lesson at Plassey,
Must last you a little while.'

He was not a Reynolds nor a Gainsborough,
His art, he confessed, was of baser metal,
But he consolidated Plassey,
But he consolidated Plassey,
And his name was Tilly Kettle.

The conclusion of this ballad,
Indian wit, not mine, should settle;
But the moral, if any, of Plassey,
But the moral, if any, of Plassey,
Is the moral of Tilly Kettle.

THE COLLEGE DEBATE

'That this House approves the Trend of Modern Poetry.'
(From a Letter addressed to Edith Sitwell)

So, as I say, the Dean of Saul Hall, shuffling
His centenarian slippered feet and snuffling
(He attends all these debates with grim devotion),
Spoke somewhat heatedly against the motion.
With the same working of his Adam's apple
That spells 'You sir, why were you not in Chapel?'
He gibed at modern poets, 'Show me one
Knee-high in stature to a Tennyson,
Shoe-high to a Wordsworth. No, for decadence
Restless and mean rots the whole present tense.
What has there been written worth a reader's while
These thirty years? Young coxcombs, dare you smile,
Neglectful of those grandlier looming shapes?
Yours is an age of pigmies, dwarfs and apes.'
With condemnatory gesture his speech ran,
A dangerous outburst for so frail a man.

With snowy beard half thawed in streaks of yellow,
The Head Librarian rose; I like the old fellow.

He sympathized with much the Dean had said,
Yet doubted Albion's glory was quite dead.
True, Hardy was no poet: to his mind,
'A clumsier craftsman you could scarcely find,'
And Housman's gift was slight and his thought weak,
And Doughty's metric sense was far to seek,
'Yet two grand singers,' he said, 'still survive:
Watson still writes, Bridges is yet alive –
Two perfect lyrists; but, sir, I'll agree,
These two removed, farewell to Poesie.'

A junior don takes up the argument;
He ventures, quite politely, to dissent.
Hardy and Housman he defends, aware
Further of Brooke, Squire, Flecker, De la Mare,
Masefield: thus far most cordially, but then
He has no patience with the younger men,
This post-war group. Sassoon is crude and queer,
And Eliot's mad or wholly insincere,
And Free Verse isn't Poetry, that's clear,
Blunden shows promise, but he's quite small beer,
There's D. H. Lawrence doesn't write a bit well,
While as for that fantastic…

When they reached you, Edith, I couldn't wait
To hear the accustomed end of such debate,
But I saw champions bouncing from their seats
Prepared to justify your wickedest feats:
First to dispose of Tennyson and his peers,
Then pressing their attack through recent years
To point where Watson failed, where Bridges failed,
Hardy and Housman, one by one detailed,
Sniping at Brooke and Masefield like as not,
Sadly backnumbered, hardly worth their shot,
With patronage for doting De la Mare,
Since newer Genius dawns. Lo here! Lo there!

On calm days, Edith, I don't give a curse
For this poetic better, equal, worse,
Not quick to side with don or head-librarian
Or undergraduate or centenarian
In their fixed laws of Taste (which disagree).
I only know what poetry sorts with me
From mood to mood, and sometimes know the reason:

But poems alter by the clock and season
As men do, with the same caprice as they
Towards hate or concord. Tennyson, did they say?
I admit he gratified his age, but blame
The pseudo-Tennyson who outlives the same
With greed of incense and prolonged restriction
Of metrics, matter, ethical outlook, diction,
And critics who compare rotten with ripe,
The modern Alfred with his prototype,
Holding I don't know which in pained abhorrence
Because he never wrote like D. H. Lawrence;
Cursing the 'sixties for not eulogizing
The mournful star of Hardy, then first rising.
(Engrossed with what emasculate revision
Of open bawdry, bold manslaughter, Vision?)
Now Hardy's honoured? Though I've not forgotten
The Elizabethan tag, 'Medlars when rotten
Most fit for eating', that's not true of peaches
Like Tennyson was, and though old Hardy reaches
A hand back to his boyhood, who can claim
That this young Hardy lives and moves, the same,
Unshaken both in purpose and technique,
When Swinburne droops and Browning's phantom-weak
And 'Gentlemen, the bower we shrined to Tennyson
Lies roof-wracked' and 'the spider is sole denizen';*
Who knows, this dour old Hardy whom we preach
May rot, with us, like the most juicy peach!

Well, that's my calmer mood, and where's the man
Will not abstain from curses while he can?
But once I start in anger to defend
The reputation of a poet-friend,
Yours for example, I forget all that.
Often, indeed quite recently, I have sat
Sceptered and orbed the absolutist throne,
Have upped this favourite, downed that other one,
This absolutely good, that utterly bad.
Playing the god, what merry times I have had!
But afterwards paid for each proud excess
With change of heart, fatigue, mere foolishness.

* From Mr. Hardy's Poem, 'An Ancient to Ancients'.

SERGEANT-MAJOR MONEY

(1917)

It wasn't our battalion, but we lay alongside it,
    So the story is as true as the telling is frank.
They hadn't one Line-officer left, after Arras,
    Except a batty major and the Colonel, who drank.

'B' Company Commander was fresh from the Depôt,
    An expert on gas drill, otherwise a dud;
So Sergeant-Major Money carried on, as instructed,
    And that's where the swaddies began to sweat blood.

His Old Army humour was so well-spiced and hearty
    That one poor sod shot himself, and one lost his wits;
But discipline's maintained, and back in rest-billets
    The Colonel congratulates 'B' Company on their kits.

The subalterns went easy, as was only natural
    With a terror like Money driving the machine,
Till finally two Welshmen, butties from the Rhondda,
    Bayoneted their bugbear in a field-canteen.

Well, we couldn't blame the officers, they relied on Money;
    We couldn't blame the pitboys, their courage was grand;
Or, least of all, blame Money, an old stiff surviving
    In a New (bloody) Army he couldn't understand.

A LETTER FROM WALES

(Richard Rolls to his friend, Captain Abel Wright)

This is a question of identity
Which I can't answer. Abel, I'll presume
On your good-nature, asking you to help me.
I hope you will, since you too are involved
As deeply in the problem as myself.
Who are we? Take down your old diary, please,
The one you kept in France, if you are you
Who served in the Black Fusiliers with me.
That is, again, of course, if I am I –
This isn't Descartes' philosophic doubt,
But, as I say, a question of identity,

And practical enough. – Turn up the date,
July the twenty-fourth, nineteen-sixteen,
And read the entry there:

> 'To-day I met
> *Meredith, transport-sergeant of the Second.*
> *He told me that Dick Rolls had died of wounds.*
> *I found out Doctor Dunn, and he confirms it;*
> *Dunn says he wasn't in much pain, he thinks.'*

Then the first draft of a verse-epitaph,
Expanded later into a moving poem.
'Death straddled on your bed: you groaned and tried
To stare him out, but in that death-stare died.'
Yes, died, poor fellow, the day he came of age.
But then appeared a second Richard Rolls
(Or that's the view that the facts force on me),
Showing Dick's features to support his claim
To rank and pay and friendship, Abel, with you.
And you acknowledged him as the old Dick,
Despite all evidence to the contrary,
Because, I think, you missed the dead too much.
You came up here to Wales to stay with him
And I don't know for sure, but I suspect
That you were dead too, killed at the Rectangle
One bloody morning of the same July,
The time that something snapped and sent you Berserk:
You ran across alone, with covering fire
Of a single rifle, routing the Saxons out
With bombs and yells and your wild eye; and stayed there
In careless occupation of the trench
For a full hour, reading, by all that's mad,
A book of pastoral poems! Then, they say,
Then you walked slowly back and went to sleep
Without reporting; that was the occasion,
No doubt, they killed you: it was your substitute
Strolled back and laid him down and woke as you,
Showing your features to support his claim
To rank and pay and friendship, Abel, with me.
So these two substitutes, yours and my own
(Though that's an Irish way of putting it,
For the I now talking is an honest I,
Independent of the I's now lost,
And a live dog's as good as a dead lion),

So, these two friends, the second of the series,
Came up to Wales pretending a wild joy
That they had cheated Death: they stayed together
At the same house and ate and drank and laughed
And wrote each other's poems, much too lazy
To write their own, and sat up every night
Talking and smoking almost until dawn.
Yes, they enjoyed life, but unless I now
Confound my present feeling, with the past,*
They felt a sense of unreality
In the proceedings – stop! that's good, *proceedings*,
It suggests ghosts. – Well, then I want to ask you
Whether it really happened. Eating, laughing,
Sitting up late, writing each other's verses,
I might invent all that, but one thing happened
That seems too circumstantial for romance.
Can you confirm it? Yet, even if you can,
What does that prove? for who are you? or I?
Listen, it was a sunset. We were out
Climbing the mountain, eating blackberries;
Late afternoon, the third week in September,
The date's important: it might prove my point,
For unless Richard Rolls had really died
Could he have so recovered from his wounds
As to go climbing less than two months later?
And if it comes to that, what about you?
How had you come on sick-leave from the Line?
I don't remember you, that time, as wounded.
Anyhow…We were eating blackberries
By a wide field of tumbled boulderstones
Hedged with oaks and nut-trees. Gradually
A glamour spread about us, the low sun
Making the field unreal as a stage,
Gilding our faces with heroic light;
Then oaks and nut-boughs caught this golden flood,
Sending it back in a warm flare of green…
There was a mountain-ash among the boulders,
But too full-clustered and symmetrical
And highly coloured to convince as real.
We stopped blackberrying and someone said
(Was it I or you?) 'It is good for us to be here.'
The other said, 'Let us build Tabernacles'
(In honour of a new Transfiguration;
It was that sort of moment); but instead

I climbed up on the massive pulpit stone,
An old friend, but unreal with the rest,
And prophesied – not indeed of the future,
But declaimed poetry, and you climbed up too
And prophesied. The next thing I remember
Was a dragon scaly with fine-weather clouds
Poised high above the sun, and the sun dwindling
And then the second glory.
                                    You'll remember
That we were not then easily impressed
With pyrotechnics, whether God's or Man's.
We had seen the sun rise daily, weeks on end,
And watched the nightly rocket-shooting, varied
With red and green, and livened with gun-fire
And the loud single-bursting overgrown squib
Thrown from the minen-werfer: and one night
From a billet-window some ten miles away
We had watched the French making a mass-attack
At Notre Dame de Lorette, in a thunderstorm.
That was a grand display of all the Arts,
God's, Man's, the Devil's: in the course of which,
So lavishly the piece had been stage-managed,
A Frenchman was struck dead by a meteorite,
That was the sort of gala-show it was!
But this Welsh sunset, what shall I say of it?
It ended not at all as it began,
An influence rather than a spectacle
Raised to a strange degree beyond all wonder.
And I remember that we looked and found
A region of the sky below the dragon
Where we could gaze behind all time and space
And see as it were the colour of pure thought,
The texture of emptiness, and at that sight
We came away, not daring to see more:
Death was the price, we knew, of such perfection
And walking home…
                                    fell in with Captain Todd,
The Golf-Club Treasurer; he greeted us
With '*Did* you see that splendid sunset, boys?
Magnificent, was it not? I wonder now,
What writer could have done real justice to it
Except, of course, my old friend Walter Pater?
Ruskin perhaps? Yes, Ruskin might have done it.'

Well, *did* that happen, or am I just romancing?
And then again, one has to ask the question
What happened after to that *you* and *me*?
I have thought lately that they too got lost.
My representative went out once more
To France, and so did yours, and yours got killed,
Shot through the throat while bombing up a trench
At Bullecourt; if not there, then at least
On the thirteenth of July, nineteen eighteen,
Somewhere in the neighbourhood of Albert,
When you took a rifle bullet through the skull
Just after breakfast on a mad patrol.
But still you kept up the same stale pretence
As children do in nursery battle-games,
'No, I'm not dead. Look, I'm not even wounded.'
And I admit I followed your example,
Though nothing much happened that time in France.
I died at Hove after the Armistice,
Pneumonia, with the doctor's full consent.

I think the I and you who then took over
Rather forgot the part we used to play;
We wrote and saw each other often enough
And sent each other copies of new poems,
But there was a constraint in all our dealings,
A doubt, unformulated, but quite heavy
And not too well disguised. Something we guessed
Arising from the War, and yet the War
Was a forbidden ground of conversation.
Now *why*, can you say *why*, short of accepting
My substitution view? Then yesterday,
After five years of this relationship,
I found a relic of the second Richard,
A pack-valise marked with his name and rank…
And a sunset started, most unlike the other,
A pink-and-black depressing sort of show
Influenced by the Glasgow School of Art.
It sent me off on a long train of thought
And I began to feel badly confused,
Being accustomed to this newer self;
I wondered whether you could reassure me.
Now I have asked you, do you see my point?
What I'm asking really isn't 'Who am I?'
Or 'Who are you?' (you see my difficulty?)

But a stage before that, *'How am I to put*
The question that I'm asking you to answer?'

* A reminiscence from Wordsworth's 'Nutting'.

THE PRESENCE

Why say 'death'? Death is neither harsh nor kind:
Other pleasures or pains could hold the mind
If she were dead. For dead is gone indeed,
Lost beyond recovery and need,
Discarded, ended, rotted underground –
Of whom no personal feature could be found
To stand out from the soft blur evenly spread
On memory, if she were truly dead.

But living still, barred from accustomed use
Of body and dress and motion, with profuse
Reproaches (since this anguish of her grew
Do I still love her as I swear I do?)
She fills the house and garden terribly
With her bewilderment, accusing me,
Till every stone and flower, table and book,
Cries out her name, pierces me with her look,
'You are deaf, listen!
You are blind, see!'
                    How deaf or blind,
When horror of the grave maddens the mind
With those same pangs that lately choked her breath,
Altered her substance, and made sport of death?

THE CLIPPED STATER

(To Aircraftman 338171, T. E. Shaw)

King Alexander had been deified
By loud applause of the Macedonian phalanx,
By sullen groans of the wide worlds lately conquered.
Who but a god could have so engulphed their pride?

He did not take a goddess to his throne
In the elder style, remembering what disasters
Juno's invidious eye brought on her Consort.
Thaïs was fair; but he must hold his own.

Nor would he rank himself a common god
In fellowship with those of Ind or Egypt
Whom he had shamed; even to Jove his father
Paid scant respect (as Jove stole Saturn's nod).

Now meditates: 'No land of all known lands
Has offered me resistance, none denied me
Infinite power, infinite thought and knowledge;
What yet awaits the assurance of my hands?'

Alexander, in a fever of mind,
Reasons: 'Omnipotence by its very nature
Is infinite possibility and purpose,
Which must embrace *that it can be confined*.

'Then finity is true godhead's final test,
Nor does it dim the glory of free being.
I must fulfil myself by self-destruction.'
The curious phrase renews his conquering zest.

He assumes man's flesh. Djinn catch him up and fly
To a land of yellow folk beyond his knowledge,
And that he does not know them, he takes gladly
For surest proof he has put his godhead by.

In Macedonia shortly it is said:
'Alexander, our god, has died of a fever;
Demi-gods parcel out his huge dominions.'
So Alexander, as god, is duly dead.

But Alexander the man, whom yellow folk
Find roving naked, armed with a naked cutlass,
Has death, which is the stranger's fate, excused him.
Joyfully he submits to the alien yoke.

He is enrolled now in the frontier-guard
With gaol-birds and the press-gang's easy captures;
Where captains who have felt the Crown's displeasure,
But have thought suicide too direct and hard,

Teach him a new tongue and the soldier's trade,
To which the trade *he* taught has little likeness.
He glories in his foolish limitations:
At every turn his hands and feet are stayed.

'Who was your father, friend?' He answers: 'Jove.'
'His father?' 'Saturn.' 'And *his* father?' 'Chaos.'
'And *his*?' Thus Alexander loses honour:
Ten fathers is the least that a man should prove.

Stripes and bastinadoes, famine and thirst –
All these he suffers, never in resolution
Shaken, nor in his heart enquiring whether
Gods by their fiats can be self-accursed.

Thus he grows grey and eats his frugal rice,
Endures his watch on the fort's icy ramparts,
Staring across the uncouth leagues of desert,
Furbishes leather and steel; or shakes the dice.

He will not dream Olympianly, nor stir
To enlarge himself with comforts or promotion,
Nor yet evade the rack when, sour of temper,
He has tweaked a corporal's nose and called him 'cur'.

His comrades mutinously demand their pay –
'We have had none since the Emperor's Coronation.
At one gold piece a year there are fifteen owing.
One-third that sum would buy us free,' say they.

The pay-sack came at length, when hope was cold,
Though much reduced in bulk since its first issue
By the Chief Treasurer; and he, be certain,
Kept back one third of the silver and all the gold.

Every official hand had dipped in the sack;
And the frontier captains, themselves disappointed
Of long arrears, took every doit remaining;
But from politeness put a trifle back.

They informed the men: 'Since no pay has come through,
We will advance from our too lavish purses
To every man of the guard, a piece of silver.
Let it be repaid when you get your overdue.'

The soldiers, grumbling but much gratified
By hopes of a drink and a drab, accept the favour;
And Alexander, advancing to the pay-desk,
Salutes and takes his pittance without pride.

The coin is bored, to string with the country's bronze
On a cord, and one side scraped to glassy smoothness;
But the head, clipped of its hair and neck, bears witness
That it had a broad, more generous mintage once.

Alexander, gazing at it then,
Greets it as an Alexandrian stater
Coined from the bullion taken at Arbela.
How came it here among these slant-eyed men?

He stands in a troubled reverie of doubt
Till a whip stings his shoulders and a voice bellows:
'Are you dissatisfied, you spawn of the ditches?'
So he salutes again and turns about,

More than uncertain what the event can mean.
Was his lost Empire, then, not all-embracing?
And how can the stater, though defaced, owe service
To a power that is as if it had never been?

'Must I renew my godhead?' But well he knows
Nothing can change the finite course resolved on;
He spends the coin on a feast of fish and almonds
And back to the ramparts briskly enough he goes.

THE POETIC STATE

'How is it,' I was asked, 'to be a poet?'
And since the question had been simply put
There were no suave evasions on my part.

The title does not rouse me to emotion.
I see no virtue in bland deprecation,
The 'I, sir? No, you flatter me' tradition.

Poetry is, I said, my father's trade,
Familiar since my childhood; I have tried
Always to annul the curse of that grim triad

Which holds it death to mock and leave a poet
In mockery, death likewise to love a poet,
But death above all deaths to live a poet.

I will not see myself the desolate bard,
His natural friendships cast and his loves buried,
Auguring doom like some black carrion bird.

I seek no strength in the well-formed cabbala,
In runic practice or loud alleluiah,
In conference with spirits high or low.

But mocked, I see my weakness in that mocking,
And loved, I charge myself with that love-making,
Nor am I marked with beast's or angel's marking.

VANITY

Be assured, the Dragon is not dead
But once more from the pools of peace
Shall rear his fabulous green head.

The flowers of innocence shall cease
And like a harp the wind shall roar
And the clouds shake an angry fleece.

'Here, here is certitude,' you swore,
'Below this lightning-blasted tree.
Where once it struck, it strikes no more.

'Two lovers in one house agree.
The roof is tight, the walls unshaken.
As now, so must it always be.'

Such prophecies of joy awaken
The toad who dreams away the past
Under your hearth-stone, light forsaken,

Who knows that certitude at last
Must melt away in vanity –
No gate is fast, no door is fast –

That thunder bursts from the blue sky,
That gardens of the mind fall waste,
That fountains of the heart run dry.

AT THE GAMES *

Two quiet sportsmen, this an Englishman,
That French, seated one crowded afternoon
In the Paris amphitheatre at the Games,
And curiously eyeing each the other,
Found voice together, 'We have met before,'
Then clasped hands on the memory.

Fr.   Still alive,
        Old friend? How did you manage to endure
        Those three worst years of War after we met?
        Where, tell me! show me that you too remember.

Eng.   In a field near Albert.

Fr.   The occasion?

Eng.   Sport.

Fr.   Bravo! the occasion then as now, *le sport!*
        A football match between allied battalions
        1915, mid-August. You remember?

Eng.   Yes, I recall it well, the famous match –
        One goal apiece at half-time, still a draw
        When the whistle blew to end it, two goals all.

Fr.   'Shall we play overtime to find the victors?
        No, no, leave it a draw for friendship's sake.
        We'll play it out,' we cried, '*après la guerre.*'

Eng.   That second goal you Frenchmen got was fine.
        Your left-outside, the big man, swerved across,
        Beat both the backs and scored with a stinging volley.
        He left our young goalkeeper standing dazed.

Fr.   Maurice, his name was.

Eng.   Norris was our boy.

Fr.   Maurice was killed before Verdun.

Eng.   Young Norris
            At Passchendaele; I wouldn't dare to reckon
            How many of that team still boot the ball.

Fr.   Brave fellows, no *embusqués* in that class.

Eng.   You played right-back that day.

Fr.   You, left-inside.
            Your company took over billets from us,
            I have kept the slip you gave me for receipt.

Eng.   But come, how are you now? *Blessé?*

Fr.   *Bien blessé.*
            Both lungs, also this leg at La Fille Morte.

Eng.   I at Cambrai, the lungs, this shoulder too.
            My friend, there was a time in hospital
            I used to calculate what chance remained
            Of playing any game when I came out.
            At first, my best hopes were for bowls and croquet.
            Curling, perhaps, and billiards. I despaired
            At first, even of playing village cricket
            With a boy to run for me when I went in,
            And as for Rugby football or rock climbing,
            Those were my sports by preference...what? yours too?...
            But health flowed back far stronger than I dreamed.
            How much can you do now?

Fr.   More than I hoped.
            Tennis, indeed, but three sets are too much.

Eng.   Ah, three sets are beyond my limit too.
            What brings you here to-day?

Fr.   A younger brother.

Eng.   *La boxe?* My younger brother's boxing too
            In the middle weights.

Fr.   Then they should meet!

Eng. }
Fr.   The rascals!

Eng.   He boxes well?

Fr.   I've staked big money on him.

Laughter from both, but then a doubtful silence.

Fr.   You are thinking, my old comrade?

Eng.   Many thoughts:
           The personal, the philosophical,
           But banded in a close fantastic medley.
           We English and you French have different modes
           Of thought; you think in logical progression,
           We in a coloured flurry of images,
           Neither more perfect than the other mode,
           For Action springs from both alike.

Fr.   Well said!
           Voltaire and Shakespeare! yes, it staggers me
           That nations bred on genius so diverse
           Can ever meet and parley at one board,
           Can ever league against a common foe,
           Play the same sports, use the same sporting code,
           Agree on the same virtue, sportsmanship!

Eng.   Agree, you say? do we, can we afford it?
           But *à nos moutons!* Logic has demanded
           Account of my fantastics.
                                      Yes! these brothers,
           What could they think of our new meeting here
           After three years of war and six of peace?
           How could they understand, though we explained?
           They were too young to serve in France like us,
           They still have their knight-bachelor blood to cool,
           The same young heat of blood we cooled in War.
           Victory would be sweet for them; yet note!
           Whichever wins, we stand to lose.

Fr.   *Vous dites?*

Eng.   I mean, here we two sit linked once again
        By common pleasures, common sufferings,
        The same despairs and reassurances,
        Blood-bonded also by the name of Sport.

Fr.   Then?

Eng.   All at once to end this harmony
        A cross wind rises from two younger brothers,
        Each braced by hopes of the same famous prize,
        Each backed to win by an elder brother's purse.
        One must be beaten, what of his elder brother?

Fr.   He twists a wry smile in the name of Sport,
        And shakes a fist with his old comrade here,
        Consoled by boastings of good sportsmanship.

Eng.   But friendship, is that quite the same again,
        Especially if one disputes the verdict?
        '*Après la guerre.*' Is this the sequel then,
        Our football match decided by *la boxe*?
        I never wanted that decision made.
        Leave it a draw, because our friends are dead!

Fr.   I hope these brothers never meet at all,
        I hope both beaten in the earlier bouts,
        So we can join in amicable wrath
        Against the unknown who bears off the prize.

          .   .   .   .   .

        Silence again? You are thinking, my old comrade?

Eng.   Yes, lost in thought as in a maze of trenches.
        Once more to Logic, then. You have in France
        As many, I dare say, as we in England,
        Enthusiasts who wish to end all War,
        To wipe it from the world with 'never again'?

Fr.   I have wished the same myself, in hospital
        While waiting for my thirteenth operation.

Eng.   So too have I, and in the trenches even,
        When the barrage rolled forward, wreathed in gas.
        But now, I am doubting whether War, as such,
        War, even modern War, is man's worst fault.

Is conflict so much uglier seen in War
When patent, more dramatically staged,
Than seen in Commerce, Social life, the Arts,
Disguised in their official mask of Peace?
Listen to a story, and then answer!
When my grandfather, fighting in New Zealand,
Was captured with his company of foot,
Surprised at dawn by a bold Maori tribe,
Disarmed and ignominiously trussed up,
Those Maoris handed them their bayonets back
On this condition, they should fight it out,
Cold steel against cold steel, with equal sides,
In a pitched battle on the open plain.

Fr.   Those were the sportsmen!

Eng.   And a rare fight followed.
Yet my grandfather, wounded and sent home,
Was shamefully ill-used by his own country,
Discharged without a pension: he died cursing,
Not the brave sportsmen who had wounded him,
But General Ostrich Feathers of Whitehall,
And Bloggs, a bullying landlord of the worst,
And Noggs, the lawyer who supported Bloggs.

Fr.   There are wars and wars: often a war's a sport,
And stays a sport until one side plays foul,
Uses a new advantage, breaks conventions.

Eng.   Exactly: and sometimes a sport's a war,
In its worst sense of cruelty, lies and shame.

Fr.   Even within the framed rules of the sport.

Eng.   In Rugby football I have killed more men,
Playing full-back and tackling with ill will,
Killed them, I mean, in murderous intention,
Than ever I killed at Loos or Passchendaele.
At Loos I saw them running, shot them down
With a sportsman's instinct as he marks down birds.
At Passchendaele I bayoneted a man
As one might pink a fencer with the foil.

Fr.   No hate? We too had little hatred there,

Unless quite seldom we were losing heart.
But see, the middle weights are drawn for now –
Soon we shall know how long our friendship lasts.
You have boxed yourself, my friend?

Eng.   Yes, I have boxed
And known the loving-kindness of the victor
For the man he's knocked to pieces, afterwards
Shaking his hand and complimenting him.

Then narrowly each watched the other's face.

Fr.   Those ringside manners, I too know them well.
Agreeing always on the term 'good sport',
Did you ever fight a man you could not trust,
A man who had set upon you unawares
Once before, and smashed you? Then again,
Hearing him come behind you with a rush,
Have you floored him and been forced to hammer him,
Though he still kept one knee upon the ground,
Yes, knocked him down and had to punch him silly
Against all rules of boxing? Then, to make sure
That he was done, have you been forced to kick him?
Have you felt his ribs to make sure they were smashed,
Because that man had always played you foul?

Eng.   Thank God, I have not: I can truly say
My sportsmanship was never tested so.

Fr.   So may it never be, my English friend!

Eng.   I understand, respecting you the more
That you can face facts and explain your mind.
But did you ever see two scowling neighbours
Threaten each other in a public place?
One, the bigger and stronger, waits his time
And when the smaller fellow turns his back,
Leaps on him, hooks him sideways on the jaw,
So that he staggers? Then in the name of sport,
But also anxious in mere self-defence,
To lay that bullying fellow on his back,
Have you too leaped in, striking at his face,
And kept on striking? When the smaller man
Rises again, returning blow for blow,

The man who struck him first cries out, alarmed,
'Two against one! Is this good sportsmanship,
Is this *la boxe*? No, since you break the rules,
I'll call for *la savate;* I'll use my feet.'
A rough-house follows, all three men get hurt,
But the end is, the big lout groans 'Enough.'
You, then, feeling your wrongs avenged, stand off
And taking stock of bruises, cuts and sprains,
Remind yourself 'When he called *la savate*
I also used my feet, yes, to good purpose.
Granted he was a bully at the start,
He's learned a lesson not forgotten soon
And he fought gamely. Come, I'll be a sportsman,
I'll go and shake hands, help him to his feet.'
By this time there's a big ring gathered round,
And look, your ally, seated on the foe,
Batters him senseless. 'My dear friend,' cry you,
'Are you a sportsman? then stop hurting him.'
He answers, 'This great coward only shams.
If once I loose him, up he'll jump again,
As twice he's done before, and knock me spinning.
You talk of sport, but I with Aesop's frogs
Reply, "What's sport to you is death to me."'
At this the crowd groans, hisses, cheers: disputes
Which is the better sportsman, you or he –
Then between loyalty to your brave ally
And pride in your much vaunted sportsmanship
Have you been torn in mind, left standing helpless,
Charged with hypocrisy, shame, perfidy?

Fr.   Thank Heaven, I have not, I can say truly
          My self-respect was never tested so.

Eng.   So may it never be, my brave French friend!

Fr.   And doctor's fees; let us not speak of those…
          Instead to joke about the long delay
          Of our Academy in the compilation
          Of their Grande Dictionnaire de la Langue Française,
          The full, the final, never-to-be-gainsaid:
          Always, perhaps, they shirk the letter 's',
          Since no one dares define *le sportsmanship*?
          Yet there's a word they cannot well omit
          Now that the State so warmly fosters sport.

There *is* no final definition?

Eng.   None.
To speak again of War, 'The Sport of Kings',
Telling a tale this time against ourselves:
The same grandfather, in the same campaign
Against the Maoris, lately Christianized,
Attacked one Sunday morning in full force;
He found the Maoris not expecting him,
Devoutly praying in their tribal church.
Captured and scandalized, the Maoris asked
For explanation of this gross abuse.
They quoted Rule 4 of the Christian code.
Grandfather stoutly pleaded precedent:
Cromwell, Napoleon, Gustaf-Adolf
All fought their bloodiest battles on a Sunday.
That noble savage would have pleased Rousseau:
Dismissing precedent as a lame excuse,
He asked for sportsmanship in its pure form.

Fr.   Ah! the pure form! could we recover that!
But where in history lies that golden age?

          .   .   .   .   .
Soon in the understanding pause that followed
They watched their younger brothers mount the ring,
Matched together by caprice of Fate,
Each proudly girded in his country's colours.
With first a most perfunctory glove-clasp,
They dodged, sparred, side-stepped, fell into a clinch,
Breaking away with heavy body punches,
Battering each other till the bruises showed.
One scowled, the other's lips moved in a threat;
Panting hard, they boxed more cunningly;
Each recognized that he had met his match.
'Goodbye, friend, we are foes now,' said their brothers.
But at that word a strange experience!
Whom should they see, walking between the tiers
Arm in arm and chattering volubly,
But Norris and Maurice! They grinned, passed, vanished,
A pair of daylight ghosts, plain as could be.
Then brotherhood and country were no more:
Up jumped those elder brothers from their seats,
'Let the best boxer win,' they cried as one,
'We take no sides, we forfeit both our bets.

Maurice and Norris! That was strange, by Heaven!'
'Here,' cried the Frenchman, 'here there's closer bond
Than between any brothers. Here we meet,
Two honest soldiers, old philosophers,
Thinking in different modes, but thinking straight;
We speak the truth when we can speak the truth,
Hate when we must hate, find sport where we can,
And keep from sentimental juggleries,
Ready to face new conflicts as they rise,
Yet honouring our good comrades who are dead.'
Then, on my oath, they left those boxers boxing:
Arm in arm they wandered towards the gates,
Snug in a café absent-mindedly
Played dominoes, and kept no score who won;
Maurice and Norris chaffing from the shadows,
Feinting at each other with clenched fists.

---

*   Written in January, 1924, but prophetic of the Mallin-Brousse boxing episode and the
ill-feeling that followed. This poem was awarded a medal at the Olympic Games themselves.

THE MARMOSITE'S MISCELLANY

(1925)

TO M. IN INDIA

In India you, cross-legged these long years waiting
Beneath your peepul tree, the spread of thought
That canopies your loneliness and mine,
You, watching the resistless moving water,
The wide warm holy flood of Mother Ganges
Nourish her young ones. And in England I,
Waiting, chin to knee, hands moodily clasped
At my accustomed seat, refuge for silence,
The old cleft pollard willow leaning
Where two streams flow together, tributary
To little boastful Thames; where buttercups
Streak the white daisy pasture and moorhens
Cluck in the rising sedge. In India you
Exiled at your own home as I at mine,
Aghast at the long cruelty of tradition
At so much pain yet to be harvested
With the old instruments. In England I
Bruised, battered, crushed often in mind and spirit
But soon revived again like the torn grass
When, after battle, broken guns and caissons
Are hauled off and the black swoln corpses burnt.
I, the historian from hour to hour
As you are, though few letters pass between us
(For these things are beyond the scope of words)
Of such calamities as whelm us both,
The dragon darkness that piece-meal devours us,
The sun that sucks our life; and of those rare
Moments of peace when nothing hurts or broods
When music sounds across the tranquil fields
And light falls golden.
                          You with no ambition
As I have none, nor the few friends we share,
Except this only, to have no ambition;
With no sure knowledge but that knowledge changes

Beyond all local proof or local disproof;
With no support but friendship that makes light
Of broad dividing seas, broad continents,
That thrives on absence, that denies the force
Of scandal, contrariety, jealousies,
Friendship that springs unsown by precedent
Or purpose from the salted fields of hate,
That swells and ripens, drawing greater strength
Not only from sweet air but from soured earth.
Wait now a little longer by your peepul:
It is my willow if you make it so,
For I rest here by Ganges. Then in waiting
Watch the clear morning waters for a sign,
And when you see it, laugh, and I'll see mine.

THE MARMOSITE'S MISCELLANY

1   As I happened one day in a World Exhibition,
      I watched a troop of monkeys in a wire cage.
They seemed little troubled by their cramped condition,
      Agreeing to regard it as a needful stage,
      And not too unhappy, of life's pilgrimage.
They had monkey nuts in plenty (a nut is a nut)
And privacy at nightfall when the gates shut.

2   Among those nimble monkeys, an old Marmosite.
      I knew him at once for a creature of thought.
He moved a piece of looking-glass in the sunlight,
      And smiled a little sadly as his fellows caught
      At the bright round reflection and scuffled and fought,
But when he extinguished it with a sly paw,
Pretended to be tussling for a tassel of straw.

3   'The critics,' I remarked; 'The critics,' he agreed.
      'I was a scholar's monkey. I read his books through.
My reading reminds me how sadly they need
      These constant adventures after something new.
      On us, then, as artists, on myself and you,
Devolves the dull task of springing the surprise,
Of aiding their digestions by sharp exercise.'

4   I was astounded to hear the creature's voice,
        But there at Larissa, that Thessalian town,
     Things happen most oddly by chance or by choice:
        The least confusion shown would prove me a clown.
        I talked to him calmly, I took his words down:
     If any doubt my story, here is proof indeed,
     The monkey's views in long-hand for the world to read.

5   'How can you bear it, Marmosite, in this cribbed cage,
        Exposed to the gaze of the garrulous crowd?
     Five minutes for me would provoke such a rage
        I would rattle the bars, I would scream aloud.'
        'I earn my living by it,' he answered and bowed.
     'I find it no hardship; after all, I see
     At least as much of mankind as they do of me.'

6   I questioned him further. 'Learned Marmosite,
        Confess, are you agnostic, are you atheist,
     Or have you honest faith in any creed or rite?
        Do arguments amuse you, does the Idealist
        Combating, thrust with twist, the bald Materialist?'
     He answered: 'In Joe Miller recorded we find,
     "What is Mind? No matter. What is Matter? Never mind."

7   'I am a mere monkey, having no soul,
        But a heart and a head, and they console me much:
     With no immoral appetites to keep in control.
        I read the learned journals in Spanish or Dutch,
        I adorn, may I say? whatever I touch.
     Theology beguiles me in my soulless state,
     And I mouth metaphysics early and late.

8   'What the locusts of Athens could not devour,
        What passed the Alexandrian caterpillar's teeth,
     The rank spiny grass and the remotest flower
        That the canker-worm of Germany doubted beneath,
        I am garlanding together in a glorious wreath
     To fletcherize at leisure: one day you'll see
     I shall be proved the palmer-worm of Philosophy.

9   'I would pour out my musings from A to final Z
        Into your cordial ear were time not so brief –
     The moody machinations of my heated head,
        But one letter even shall afford relief.

And Truth is not constant, it comes like a thief,
  It blooms for a moment like the wild rose,
  Then storms break above it, and away it goes.

10   '*M* shall be the letter to head my confession,
        M stands in the middle of the learned line,
      M is the magistrate of the mental session,
        He titles the triumvirs myself, me and mine,
        He mediates in all things common or divine,
      He stewards the multiplicity of a rich house,
      Mousetraps and muchness, like the Dormouse.'

11   'Sing then, merry monkey, of the Muses' choir,
        Of Mormons and Mandarins, of Moll-Cut-the-Purse,
      Of Moses and his Ministry to the Cloud of Fire,
        Of many other matters both better and worse –
        Let them all be threaded and strung in your verse.
      Let *M* be the Movement, the Magnet, the Magician,
      The Monk, the Merry Andrew, the Mathematician.'

12   He said: 'I cock my mirror above the cage wires,
        And through the side window what visions I see!
      The whole world of men and their dismal desires,
        Fortune tellers, feather ticklers, the crystal sea,
        Corky angels twanging the tunes of Tennessee,
      Pearly gates, golden streets, a cokernut shy,
      The moral peepshow pandering to the prurient eye.

13   'I can see men moving in the Great Maze,
        Who reaches the middle expects a rich prize:
      Dead-ends confound them and returning ways.
        Some trust in a system, some close their eyes,
        Some hack at the hedges, some report it wise
      To camp at a crosspath, staunchly to sit,
      "Let the prize come to them, not they to it."

14   'Melchizedek had neither father nor mother,
        He was the first cartographer of the Great Maze.
      Moses was the next, I read of no other
        Who pierced the holy puzzle in those dark days.
        Melchizedek was mute, but Moses could raise
      Apparitions of the Inmate, a mad Minotaur
      From Horeb's holy mountain his precepts to roar.

15   'Mnevis in the likeness of a Golden Calf
        Disputing for power with Jehovah the Just,
    Moses takes Mnevis and hews him in half,
        Burns him with charcoal and grinds him to dust,
        The Hebrews drink Mnevis, drink him they must.
    Inwardly rotting, they decline and die:
    Moses was the Minister of the Most High.

16   'Moloch, Mars, Modo and many more again
        Swore vengeance for Mnevis on Jehovah's power.
    Michael did battle on the Heavenly plain,
        He broke them to rout in a ruinous hour.
        In that Pyrrhic victory fell the fine flower
    Of the guardian angels, without number then,
    Who police the appetites and desires of men.

17   'Magic and Mockery sprang up like weeds,
        Obscuring the clean track that Moses had shown.
    Philosophers and poets scattered the seeds
        Of idling and argument, no sooner sown
        Than topping the hedges with buds overblown,
    And flowering into sciences from whose fruit rose
    A race of demi-demons, Jehovah's new foes.

18   'The Messiah came down as a sweet dispensation
        To redeem the ravages of that Great War.
    He went, as was fittest, to Jehovah's nation
        With a hairy herald trumping before.
        Many a baleful insult this Messiah bore.
    He was a mild martyr where His Father was wroth,
    But Man was a monster, blaspheming both.

19   'He was the son of Mary, in a manger born;
        Between two malefactors on a mount He died,
    For the pains of sinful man His heart sadly torn.
        The world must bow and wonder, or woe betide!
        To hear of His humility and the Priests' pride.
    Yet I can view Him calmly in a clearer light:
    The Messiah died for Man and not for Marmosite.

20   'I met a titled Manchu, a tall Mandarin.
        He intended his sons for a Missionary School.
    He was a pagan rooted in ancestral sin,
        But a man of discernment, no wise a fool.

He wanted them generals to conquer and rule.
On the Methodist Mission his heart was long set:
"The Christians are the boldest with the bayonet."

21   'Let us pass to Mahomet, the mouthpiece of God;
          The Moors and the Mongols know his name well.
      In Arabian Mecca Mahomet's feet trod,
          Superstition trembled when he tolled the bell.
          He unriddled the Maze, his books clearly tell.
      More learned than Moses, more holy than Christ,
      And every honest Mussulman loves sherbet iced.

22   'Of Muggleton, the tailor, and his inward Light!
          He stood for the one God, great and unfriended!
      None who came before him had led men aright.
          He charted the Maze before he had ended:
          What Muggleton ordained could not be amended.
      All were duly damned but for one saving grace,
      They must yield to Muggleton the Messiah's place.

23   'Were I a merry tailor I would bless his commission,
          A staunch Muggletonian, true to my trade.
      With state or with church I would make no condition,
          In the public pillory chanting unafraid:
          On my dumb tailor's goose his hand would be laid,
      To testify in Latin, to glory and groan,
      "Quam verus propheta Lodowick Muggleton."

24   'The Mormons bear witness to the golden plates,
          To the glasses of crystal set on Smith's nose.
      Mormon and Mosiah guiding their fates,
          They made the salt Wilderness bloom like the rose.
          They had little mercy on their Gentile foes,
      They massacred their warriors once and again,
      The Midianite militia on the parched plain.

25   'Morgan was a Buccaneer on the Spanish Main,
          Vice-Admiral to Mansvelt of the pirate fleet;
      Mansvelt was murdered, beginning Morgan's reign.
          He was a fierce fighter, he knew no defeat,
          He delighted in torture, he drank arrack neat,
      He captured Panama with its jewels and plate,
      But made small pretension to prophetic state.

26   'Mull'd Sack was a rogue deserving the Wreath.
            He began chimney sweeper at Mary-le-Bow,
        He picked Cromwell's pocket upon Hounslow Heath;
            But thence to Cologne, little favour to show,
            He robbed from King Charles all his bags at a blow.
        His mistress, a merchant's wife, lived in Mark's Lane.
        He pretended no piety, his plunders were plain.

27   'Moll-Cut-the-Purse was Mercury's bitch,
            Prostitute, procuress, pickpocket, thief;
        On the spoils of the public she grew very rich,
            Wasting no time in repentance and grief.
            A pipe of tobacco was her joy in chief.
        Morgan, Mull'd Sack and this Moll-Cut-the-Purse
        Dishonoured the prophets, but died none the worse.

28   'In the Middle Ages it was *memento mori*.
            Vivere memento, is the modern cry.
        "We are all one kindred" was the old story,
            The Struggle for Existence gives that the lie,
            Competition is loud at the Cokernut shy.
        What with Marx and Malthus and the Millionaires,
        The Angel of Death has been kicked down the stairs.

29   'Movements are judged by their monied results;
            The days of Revelation are not yet done.
        The Middle West and Manchester welcome new cults,
            Mary Baker Eddy enjoys a rich run,
            There are millions to be made in a new form of fun,
        Uncovering a cypher, say, in Matthew or Mark
        For the sacrifice of bull-calves in the pitch dark.'

30   'Mischievous monkey, do not tell me more.
            What further you imagine, I do not dare think.
        Have you, then, no principles to praise and adore?
            Is folly your food, and is laughter your drink?'
            He answered me gravely, without a smile or blink:
        'Go-cart in the Lexicon has an honoured place,
        Being next before *God*, with a lien on His Grace.

31   'Principles I have, but only one or two,
            Firm enough foundation for a busy mind.
        First to reverence God, but not from any pew;
        No Frankenstein monster of a furious mind.

If God be Omnipotent, can a creature find
Satisfaction in serving a Classification,
A singling out of qualities, God in separation?

32   'Next, to myself and my neighbours at once
          I owe this respect without favour or fear,
      That he may be a doctor, I a mere dunce,
          He may be a pauper, a Pope, or a peer,
          But unless as an equal I shall not go near.
      I will not kiss his great toe except he kiss mine,
      Nor swell in self-importance at his flattering whine.

33   'The maunderings of the maniac signifying nothing
          I hold in respect; I hear his tale out.
      Thought comes often clad in the strangest clothing.
          So Kekulé, the chemist, watched the weird rout
          Of eager atom-serpents winding in and out,
      And walzing tail to mouth; in that absurd guise
      Appeared benzene and anilin, their drugs and their dyes.

34   'The Moon is the Mistress of escape and pity,
          Her regions are portalled by an ivory gate.
      There are fruit-plats and fountains in her silver city,
          With honeysuckle hedges where true lovers mate,
          With undisputed thrones where beggars hold state,
      With smooth hills and fields where in freedom may run
      All men maimed and manacled by the cruel sun.

35   'Her madness is musical, kindly her mood,
          She is Dian no more when the sun quits the skies.
      She is the happy Venus of the hushed wood.
          So artless Actaeon may banquet his eyes
          At the crisp hair curling on her naked thighs,
      At her shapely shoulders, her breasts and her knees,
      She will kiss him pleasantly under tall trees.'

PART II

36   'You ask me of the Muses. What shall I say?
          To talk of my friends is no easy affair.
      They treat me, be sure, in a cousinly way;
          I coax them, I tease them, I tangle their hair.
          Melpomené, my favourite, finds me a chair.
      She tempts me with tit-bits in a tasty row.
      I am like a learned parrot she loved long ago.

37   'Often I mock them, "you mannerly minxes,
       The way you dress for drawing-rooms makes me laugh loud.
  To see your flowing skirts, your front like the Sphinx's.
       You stop your fine noses at the foetid crowd.
       I flush and I tremble to see you so proud."
  "Aristotle has invited us to afternoon tea.
  You are jealous, my marmosite," smiles Melpomené.

38   'Last night as the Muses and I sat together,
       Conversing in riddles from reason remote,
  I begged pretty Pegasus for a wing feather,
       I cut it to a quill and in a book wrote.
       Melpomené was drowsy, she took little note.
  Then a copy of *Erewhon* on the table near
  Provoked me to the poem in parts you shall hear.

39   'I title it *The Safe, Erewhon Redivivus*,
       The odd phantasmagoria of a restless night.
  We poets drift about where the mad winds drive us;
       We shoot our urgent arrows far out of sight,
       Only when we find them can we guess their flight.
  This, then, is Samuel Butler, moving alive,
  Vicariously nerved in nineteen twenty-five.

THE SAFE, OR EREWHON REDIVIVUS

40   *'I was dreaming a dream that was not of Merry May,*
  With Flora and Venus and white lambs at play.
     Nor yet of plague and famine, oil wells aflame.
       But across a world in little,
       An arras strained and brittle,
     The rending progression of an angry Name.

41   *'Blunden wore the sunset hues of a stranded bream,*
  A shoal of Oxford minnows followed upstream,
     Edward Marsh was poised on the edge of a sofa,
       Hardy dribbled his umbrella,
       Belloc danced a tarantella,
     Aldous Huxley juggled up a skull and a loofah.

42   'Then I wrote of Bridges and the English tongue,
       He reported it furry, prescribing a purge;
  How Lawrence, with dark robes of destiny hung,
       Defied the volcano from its deadly verge;

How Wells tramped Utopia with ambitious urge;
How, far in the background, a great scarp up-reared
For Doughty, the old bard, with owls in his beard.

43   'Then of Masefield, astride on his notable nag,
         Its name was Right Royalty, out of Grand Slam;
Of Bennett eating ortolans from a paper bag;
         Of Davies at play with a lodging-house lamb;
         Of Shaw's manifestos signed with "I am."
And *"Yonder blandly blinking in the warm sunshine,*
Little David Garnett, a cage-mate of mine."

44   *'But, O, the Fitzwilliam, and, O, Samuel Butler,*
      Subtlest of writers, by death made subtler,
            He's bequeathing a safe from the Musical Banks,
                 And Mr. Sydney Cockerell,
                 To whom I dedicate this doggerel,
            Is accepting it with thanks.

45   *'No knob here nor handle, keyhole nor key,*
      Butler has vanished with a gleam of glee;
            "Open Sesame, Open Lilies"; they did no such thing.
                 The bearded curators
                 And literary spectators
            Drone: "Ichabod, Ichabod," in the voice of Dean Inge.

46   *'Follows discussion and Gossip and trouble,*
      Babel and lobby-talk, confused hubble bubble.
            Force the lock, how, why? Why not, or whether?
                 But Messrs. Ellis and Yeats
                 Observed two curious copper plates,
            Which courtly Gosse slid back with an oiled goose-feather.

47   *'Two keyholes were revealed*
      By these covering plates concealed.
            With tantalizing promise for futurity,
                 Sir Sidneys Colvin and Lee
                 Raised up a mottled calf to see;
            Which, peering in, remarked on a profound obscurity.

48   *'Keyless, but not hopeless, even at this impasse,*
      The faithful murmured rapidly, Ça passe, Ça passe, Ça passe!
            (Here I apologize for a somewhat sleepy rhyme)
                 While Mr. Lytton Strachey,

> *With his skeleton latchkey,*
> *Picked first one lock, then t'other, in less than no time.*

49   *'We rushed, pushed, looked in – but as I saw myself,*
> *Not even a camphor marble on a bottom shelf,*
> > *Not even a torn sheet of an empty notebook found,*
> > > *Until T. S. Eliot, from an upper bracket,*
> > > *Pulled down a stud and a dusty ping-pong racquet,*
> > *And Joyce pinged one on the other with a dismal sound.*

50   *'I rose at the noise of this priapic pinging,*
> *Tom-toms beaten distantly for Handelian singing.*
> > *Then the voice of Middleton Murry*
> > > *Said "He ought to have looked higher",*
> > > *And the voice of J. C. Squire*
> > *Came blurred and thick and furry.*

51   *The disciples of Freud*
> > > *Were quite overjoyed*
> > > *At this typical bit*
> > > *Of tendency wit;*
> > > *The disciples of Jung*
> > > *All put out their tongue*
> > > *At this symbological misfit.*

> *Where are the straighteners that Erewhon prophesies?*
> > *Analyze, gentles, analyze!*
> *Fish for the Society's annual prize.'*

52   'Melpomené caught up the poem to read.
> Down she threw it, furious. And at once I said:
> "It is nonsense, dear mistress, nonsense indeed,
> > Obscure, local, spiteful, not to be read;
> > But if you destroy it, I swear by Pope's head
> I'll burn your long bookshelves of Augustan verse,
> No duller than mine are, written much worse."

53   'She pinched my ear for me, saying all was well,
> But forbade me to trespass on her goodwill.
> Apollo would curse me, candle, book and bell,
> > If I could not study to control my quill:
> > He would banish me for ever from their high hill.
> I heard her lecture out, I took it in good part,
> But Apollo, I knew well, is divided at heart.

54   'His people are stiff-necked, steely their hearts,
          Holding pure Helycon in the lowest scorn;
      Square-headed merchants of practical parts.
          And where is the poet? in what city born?
          Shall charm them with lutestring or rouse them with horn,
      To delight in abstractions or in high-flung thought?
      With what hook let down is Leviathan caught?

55   'We serve a lost cause: does any pride remain
          In prolonging tradition beyond its due time,
      Giving it lip-service, mumbling and vain,
          With a measured metre and expected rhyme?
          Morning and evening our ancient bells chime,
      Yet the whole congregation could sit in one pew,
      The sexton, the verger, and old folk one or two.

56   'Then while our dead church is not yet disendowed,
          While I still am preacher and the pulpit's wide,
      I shall roar what I will to the sprinkled crowd,
          Shall drive them hobbling forth aghast and horrified.
          The noise of my hurricane shall be heard outside.
      There are many young lost things passing our way
      Who will turn in to listen, and, puzzled, stay.

57   'The beginning of wisdom is laughter and song,
          The furtherance of wisdom, scholarship and groans.
      Between first and second, reactions are strong;
          The disputants wrangle in no playful tones,
          Dream against waking, blood against bones:
      Let poetry, then, enter on its third degree,
      In grammar of unreason marching close and free.'

58   At this point the monkey paused in his speech,
          Breaking off short half-way through a line.
      Squatting in a corner he began to reach
          For the small of his back, why, I could not divine.
          'A flea,' he informed me, 'an old friend of mine.
      He knows there's no comfort in this life to match
      Sunshine, sleep, solitude and a good scratch.'

59   This was a gentle hint, I must go on my way;
          He was quietly scratching and settling for sleep.
      I raised my hat to him, he grunted 'Good day',
          So curled at his corner, in a hairy heap;

> Soon his quick breathing came steady and deep.
> Then the sounder he slept, the more wakeful grew I:
> Till up rose the red sun in the Eastern sky.

TAIL PIECE

> A sniff at every flask
>   And a lick at every stopper:
> In these quick days, in this odd maze
>   It is neither just nor proper,

> Neither just nor proper
>   For more than this to ask:
> A lick at every stopper,
>   And a sniff at every flask.

NOTES

Stanza 2. – '... who can/Call Tullia's ape a marmosite or Leda's goose a swan.'

Stanza 4. – See Apuleius' *Golden Ass: The Story of Thelyphron.*

Stanza 6. – This generation is curiously unaware of Joe Miller's one-time pre-eminence as the father of Jests and god-father of Chestnuts. The recent early-Victorian revival would have done well to exhume him.

Stanza 8. – To fletcherize is to chew thirty times to each mouthful. Horace Fletcher, the inventor, was born in America in 1849. The Old Testament prophecy to which this stanza refers should not need a note. [Joel 1. 4, 2. 25 *Ed.*]

Stanza 16. – Modo. 'The Prince of Darkness is a gentleman. Modo he's called, and Mahu.' *King Lear.*

Stanza 22. – Lodowick Muggleton, born 1609, died 1697. He enjoyed a numerous following about the times of the Civil War. His works, among them *Milk for Babes*, were burnt by the common hangman.

Stanza 24. – See *The Book of Mormon* and text-books of American military history.

Stanza 25. – Morgan's feat at Panama was remarkable. With only twelve hundred men he defeated the Spanish Governor at the head of two squadrons of horse, four regiments of foot, and a great number of wild bulls driven by Indian slaves.

Stanza 26. – See Caulfield's *Remarkable Persons*. Mull'd Sack's baptismal name was John Cottington; hanged at Smithfield in 1659, after a prosperous career.

Stanza 27. – Mary Frith, an associate of Mull'd Sack. An old print has this motto:

> 'See here the Presidress of the pilfering trade,
>   Mercury's second, Venus's only maid.'

Stanza 36. – 'Melpomené, that fair maid, she burnished my beak.
> I pray you let Parrot have liberty to speak.'

Skelton's *Speke, Parrot.*

Stanza 40 *et seq.* – *The Safe* was first published in the *Winter Owl*. It is an attempt to use the mechanism of the fantastic dream with all its absurd interlacing themes for the purpose of a satiric history of contemporary events. These themes may be particularized as follows. The principal one is given in the introductory stanza, the development in 1925 of Butler's critical method. The Safe from the Musical Banks occurs in *Erewhon*, and around it there is continuation of the struggle that Butler's restless and ingenious mind carried on with the critics of his day, whom he accused of deliberately obscuring the truth. The Fitzwilliam Museum at Cambridge possesses many Butler relics, though not so many as the Library of St. John's College at the same University, which can show a wide range of very personal *Butleriana*, from his paint-box to his kettle-holder. The stud and the ping-pong racquet refer partly to this.

Another theme interwoven is the state of poetry in the years immediately following the war. Mr. Blunden's fish poems, of which he has written many, are linked up with the *London Mercury* school of poetry and criticism, the *Mercury* having been first published at Bream's Buildings. There are many similar plays on words in the piece. 'Open Sesame, Open Lilies' refers to Butler's quarrel with Ruskin; the 'arras strained and brittle' hides a reference to the Arras fighting, in which Mr. Blunden himself took part, and is equivalent to the strained post-war structure of Society and Literature. Mr. Blunden is taken as representative of the best of this *London Mercury* school; his ruralities are real, a form of war-convalescence distinguished from the mere fatuity of his imitators. He is the one big fish in that stream of Natural History verse; the undergraduate contributors to Mr. Squire's journal are mere minnows in comparison, but the sunset hues suggest that Mr. Blunden is the last dying glory of the party, and at the time of writing Mr. Blunden is on a foreign strand. Mr. Marsh poised on the edge of a sofa, as the author once saw him in a drawing-room, represents the Georgian movement poised between the soft cushions of tradition and the hard floor of modernism.

Messrs. Ellis and Yeats's enquiry, sincere, but largely negative in result, into the meaning of Blake's Prophetic Books is recollected; engraved plates are associated in Jewish, Mormon and other religions with sacred mystery, but Blake's copper-plate cover-designs to the Prophetic Books are particularly referred to. Sir Sidneys Colvin and Lee have both recently been assailed, whether justly or not I do not know, as obscurers of literary truth. Sir Sidney Lee for his treatment of Shakespeare's Sonnets (Butler quarrelled with him over this very thing), and Sir Sidney Colvin for his treatment of Keats's and Robert L. Stevenson's early amours. The mottled calf suggests literary scholarship; the raising up of a calf is a Biblical reminiscence and emblematic of setting up a false god. Mr. Lytton Strachey, whose *Queen Victoria* and *Eminent Victorians* are books that Butler would have much enjoyed, won his successes by a bold research in sacrosanct records, such as the Greville Memoirs, which had hitherto been kept locked away from the public. Messrs Strachey, Eliot and James Joyce are, in the author's opinion, Samuel Butler's literary and critical heirs; but a lot of things have changed since Butler's death; these are typified by the Negroid influence in art and music and the sex obsession which to-day characterize the *enfant terrible* school which Butler founded. Judged from a modern standpoint, Butler was fairly conventional in his aesthetic tastes. In music Handel was his hero: he gave him the same pre-eminence as he gave Shakespeare in dramatic poetry. The end of *The Safe* refers to Butler's prophecy of the psycho-analytic movement; his 'straighteners' of *Erewhon*, an absurdity in 1872, are now a common feature of professional life. Perhaps, were Butler alive now, his would be the sort of mind to set in order the extravagance of the Central European School of psychoanalysis, as in his scientific books, *Luck, or Cunning?* and *Life and Habit*, he soundly criticized the detail of Darwin's evolutionary theory. The last lines of the poem refer both to the new psychologists and to the Georgians, whom the author invites to fish for the Society's annual prize, presumably the Hawthornden Prize, which has been awarded to two or three Georgians;

Georgians shrink from psychological analysis in any form.

Note the 'gentles', which are piscatorially intended. The reference to the Poet Laureate is to his admirable work with the Society of Pure English. 'Prescribing' because Doctor Bridges was once in practice as a physician. Other references to Messrs. Shaw, Doughty, Bennett, D. H. Lawrence, Davies, Masefield need little explanation. David Garnett is a 'cage-mate' partly, but not entirely, on account of the *Man in the Zoo*.

FINAL STANZAS . – A zoologist informs me that monkeys do not have fleas: what they pick off their bodies is only scurf. But the popular proverb about a monkey and his fleas justifies the error.

THE MOMENT OF WEAKNESS

Let us at last be dull
And heavy, battered hull
Becalmed, like hogs in clover
Let us roll, our labours over.
These moments justify
Terrors of destiny,
Black waves and broken sky,
Lost cargo and men's lives;
The better part survives –
You, boy and I, content
In self-abandonment,
So broken is our mood,
To discount fortitude
And hate adventurous weather.
Here let us loll together,
Do nothing and be nothing
And hold all thought in loathing.
The too large-hearted gale
That stript our tops of sail,
That havocked yards and deck,
Driving us half in wreck
Seven hundred miles at least
On our set course, due East,
Has dwindled to a breeze
And failed in sunny seas,
Leaving us, none too soon,
To enjoy this temperate noon
And quiet sleep, past hope,
To forget rigging and rope
And set no damage straight,
To toss the dice and bait

Fish-hooks, to smoke and joke
With heads, not hearts, of oak.

Herrings from the Bay,
Fresh herrings from the Bay,
The handbells are ringing,
The fishwives are gay.
But last night as my laden boat
The landing-stage neared,
A drowned man went by afloat,
With bubbles in his beard.

Sow what you would sow
But another shall reap;
To-morrow night you go
Into bellies of the deep.
Before crabs tear your gaping lips,
Or fish suck your eyes,
Get the most play from the shining day,
Eat, drink, and be not wise.

From POEMS (1914–26)

(1927)

THE COUNTRY DANCE

More slowly the sun travels West,
    Earth warming beneath,
Man's heart swelling tight in his breast
    As a bud in the sheath.

For the tender and unquiet season,
    The Spring, drawing on
Kindles flame in the eye, chokes the reason
    And silvers the swan.

Leap high, jealous Ralph; jet it neat,
    Merry Jill, and remove
By employment of elbows and feet
    The green sickness of love.

THE ROSE AND THE LILY

The Rose and the Lily
Were loving and silly,
The Goat and the Ass
Would let little pass.
Then the Ass blamed the Goat
For devouring the Lily
And the Goat blamed the Ass
For devouring the Rose.
So hoof against horn
They raged through the corn,
They stamped it to ruin,
And round the world goes.

AN OCCASION

'The trenches are filled in, the houseless dead
Disperse and on the rising thunder-storm
Cast their weak limbs, are whirled up overhead
In clouds of fear....'

                    Then suddenly as you read,
As we sat listening there, and cushioned warm,
War-scarred yet safe, alive beyond all doubt,
The blundering gale outside faltered, stood still:
Two bolts clicked at the glass doors, and a shrill
Impetuous gust of wind blew in with a shout,
Fluttering your poems. And the lamp went out.

A DEDICATION OF THREE HATS

This round hat I devote to Mars,
   Tough steel with leather lined.
My skin's my own, redeemed by scars
From further still more futile wars
   The God may have in mind.

Minerva takes my square of black
   Well-tasselled with the same;
Her dullest nurselings never lack
With hoods of scarlet at their back
   And letters to their name.

But this third hat, this foolscap sheet,
   (For there's a strength in three)
Unblemished, conical and neat
I hang up here without deceit
   To kind Euphrosyne.

Goddess, accept with smiles or tears
   This gift of a gross fool
Who having sweated in death fears
With wounds and cramps for three long years
   Limped back, and sat for school.

ANCESTORS

My New Year's drink is mulled to-night
    And hot sweet vapours roofward twine.
The shades cry *Gloria!* with delight
    As down they troop to taste old wine.

They crowd about the crackling fire,
    Impatient as the rites begin;
Mulled porto is their souls' desire –
    Porto well aged with nutmeg in.

'Ha,' cries the first, 'my Alma wine
    Of one-and-seventy years ago!'
The second cheers 'God bless the vine!'
    The third and fourth like cockerels crow:

They crow and clap their arms for wings,
    They have small pride or breeding left –
Two grey-beards, a tall youth who sings,
    A soldier with his cheek-bone cleft.

O Gloria! for each ghostly shape,
    That whiffled like a candle smoke,
Now fixed and ruddy with the grape
    And mirrored in the polished oak.

I watch their brightening boastful eyes,
    I hear the toast their glasses clink:
'May this young man in drink grown wise
    Die, as we also died, in drink!'

Their reedy voices I abhor,
    I am alive at least, and young.
I dash their swill upon the floor:
    Let them lap grovelling, tongue to tongue.

THE CORNER KNOT

I was a child and overwhelmed: Mozart
Had snatched me up fainting and wild at heart
To a green land of wonder, where estranged
I dipped my feet in shallow brooks, I ranged
Rough mountains, and fields yellow with small vetch:
Of which, though long I tried, I could not fetch
One single flower away, nor from the ground
Pocket one pebble of the scores I found
Twinkling enchanted there. So for relief
'I'll corner-knot,' said I, 'this handkerchief,
Faithful familiar that, look, here I shake
In these cool airs for proof that I'm awake.'
I tied the knot, the aspens all around
Heaved, and the river-banks were filled with sound;
Which failing presently, the insistent loud
Clapping of hands returned me to the crowd.
I felt and, fumbling, took away with me
The knotted witness of my ecstasy,
Though flowers and streams were vanished past recall,
The aspens, the bright pebbled reach and all.

But now, grown older, I suspect Mozart
Himself had been snatched up by curious art
To my green land: estranged and wild at heart
He too had crossed the brooks, essayed to pick
That yellow vetch with which the plains are thick;
And being put to it (as I had been)
To smuggle back some witness of the scene,
Had knotted up his cambric handkerchief
With common music, rippling, flat and brief;
And home again, had sighed above the score
'Ay, a remembrancer, but nothing more.'

VIRGIL THE SORCERER

Virgil, as the old Germans have related,
    Meaning a master-poet of wide fame –
And yet their Virgil stands dissociated
    From the suave hexametrist of that name,

Maro, whose golden and lick-spittle tongue
   Served Caesar's most un-Roman tyrannies,
Whose easy-flowing Georgics are yet sung
   As declamations in the academies –

Not Mantuan Virgil but another greater
   Who at Toledo first enlarged his spells,
Virgil, sorcerer, prestidigitator,
   Armed with all power that flatters or compels.

He, says the allegory, once was thrown
   By envious dukes into a dungeon keep
Where, vermin-scarred and wasting to the bone,
   Men crouched in year-old filth and could not sleep.

He beckoned then his bond-mates to his side,
   Commanding charcoal; from a rusty grate
Charcoal they fetched him. Once again he cried
   'Where are the lordly souls, unbowed by fate,

'Eager to launch with me on midnight air
   A ship of hope, through the cold clouds to skim?'
They gazed at Virgil in a quick despair
   Thinking him mad; yet gently humoured him,

And watched his hand where on the prison wall
   He scratched a galley, buoyant and well-found.
'Bring sticks for oars!' They brought them at his call.
   'Up then and row!' They stepped from solid ground,

Climbed into fantasy and with a cheer
   Heaved anchor, bent their oars, pulled without stop.
Virgil was captain, Virgil took the steer
   And beached them, presently, on a mountain-top.

Here, without disillusion, all were free:
   Wrenching their fetters off, they went their ways.
A feat, they swore, that though it could not be,
   Was, in effect, accomplished beyond praise.

'Did Virgil do what legend has related?
   Is poetry in truth the queen of arts?
Can we hope better than a glib, bald-pated
   Self-laurelled Maro of agreeable parts?'

Ah, fellow-captives, must you still condone
    The stench of evil? On a mound of mud
You loll red-eyed and wan, whittling a bone,
    .Vermined, the low gaol-fever in your blood.

RECENT POEMS: 1925–26

PYGMALION TO GALATEA

As you are woman, so be lovely:
Fine hair afloat and eyes irradiate,
Long crafty fingers, fearless carriage,
And body lissom, neither short nor tall.
So be lovely!

As you are lovely, so be merciful:
Yet must your mercy abstain from pity:
Prize your self-honour, leaving me with mine.
Love if you will; or stay stone-frozen.
So be merciful!

As you are merciful, so be constánt:
I ask not you should mask your comeliness,
Yet keep our love aloof and strange,
Keep it from gluttonous eyes, from stairway gossip.
So be constant!

As you are constant, so be various:
Love comes to sloth without variety.
Within the limits of our fair-paved garden
Let fancy like a Proteus range and change.
So be various!

As you are various, so be woman:
Graceful in going as well armed in doing.
Be witty, kind, enduring, unsubjected:
Without you I keep heavy house.
So be woman!

As you are woman, so be lovely:
As you are lovely, so be various,
Merciful as constant, constant as various.
So be mine, as I yours for ever.

IN COMMITTEE

As the committee musters,
'Silence for Noisy, let Noisy orate.'
Noisy himself blusters,
Shouldering up, mounting the dais,
And baritonely opens the debate
With cream-bun fallacies
With semi-nudes of platitudes
And testamentary feuds
Rushed at a slap-stick rate
To a jangling end.
Immediately he
Begins again, pleads confidentially:
'Be grateful to your Noisy,
The old firm, your old friend –'
Whose bagpipe lungs express
Emphatic tunelessness.
How could we draft a fair report
Till all old Noisy's variants have been aired,
His complimentary discords paired,
Bellowing and squealing sort by sort
In Noah's Ark fashion;
Noisy's actual invalidation?

Applause. Up jumps Hasty. 'Excellent Hasty,
Three cheers for Hasty,' sings out Hearty,
And is at once ejected
As he expected.
Hasty speaks. Hasty is diabetic,
Like a creature in spasms, pathetic, out of joint,
Stammers, cannot clear the point,
Only as he sinks back, from his seat
Spits out, 'Noisy you dog, you slug, you cheat.'
Enter the Chairman, late,
Gathers the threads of the debate,
Raps for order,

'Ragman, will you speak next, sir?'
Ragman pulls out his latest clippings,
Potsherds, tags of talk, flint chippings,
Quotations happy and miserable,
Various careless ologies, half a skull,
Commonplace books, blue books, cook books
And artificial flies with tangled hooks.
'All genuine,' lamely says Ragman,
'Draw your own deductions, gentlemen,
I offer nothing.'

Critic crosses the floor, snuffling,
Draws casually from Ragman's bag
Two judgements, a fossil, a rag, a thread,
Compares them outspread.
'Here Noisy cheated, as Hasty said,
Though not as Hasty meant.
Use your discernment.
These objects prove both speakers lied:
One side first, then the other side.
We can only say this much: –
So and So clearly is not such and such.
And the point is…' Critic wrinkles his nose.
'Use your discernment.'

Re-enter Hearty, enthusiastically repentant,
Cries of 'Order, Order!' Uproar.
Chairman raps, is impotent.
Synthesis smoking in a corner
Groans, pulls himself together,
Holds his hand up, takes the floor,
'Gentlemen, only a half-hour more
And nothing done. What's to be blamed?
No, no. Let us agree
First, that the motion's wrongly framed,
Two senses are confused, indeed three,
Next, the procedure's upside-down.
Pray, Mr. Chairman, Mr. Secretary…
Let us hear Pro and Con
On the reconstituted motion.'

Pro and Con speak. Noisy makes no objection,
Busy recalling his oration
For instant publication.

Hasty makes no objection,
Busy clicking the blind-cords up and down,
Nor Ragman (Ragman consults a Hebrew Lexicon),
Nor Critic (Critic drums with a pencil on the table),
Nor Hearty (Hearty is affable
In bubbling praise of Ragman's knowledge).

Synthesis sums up, nerves on edge.
Critic amends a small detail.
Synthesis accepts it, not too proud.
Chairman reads the draft-report aloud,
'Resolved that this day fortnight without fail…'

All vote, all approve
With show of brotherly love,
And the clock strikes, just in time.
Hearty proposes in pun-strewn rhyme
A vote of thanks to all the officers.
Cheers drown Hasty's angry bark.
Noisy begins: 'Gentlemen and Philosophers…'
Critic hums: 'Not too ill a morning's work.'
Ragman's on all fours after scraps and crumbs.
Chairman turns out the gas: 'Come, Ragman!'
     Ragman comes;
Synthesis left sitting in the dark:
'I shall resign to-morrow, why stay
Flattered as indispensable
By this odd rabble,
Not indispensable: and going grey?'

A LETTER TO A FRIEND

Gammon to Spinach,
Kentucky to Greenwich,
'Neither have I met you,
Nor can I forget you
While the world's round.'
Spinach in reply,
'Fool! but more fool I.
Neither do I know you
Nor shall I forgo you.
Here's occasion found

For a graver meeting
For a blunter greeting
Spinach with Gammon,
Jacksnipe with Salmon
In the deserts of Ammon
Thus to live nearly,
Thus to love dearly
On unexplored ground.'

IN SINGLE SYLLABLES

Since I was with you last, at one with you,
Twelve hours have passed. Can I now swear it true
That love rose up in wrath to make us blind,
And stripped from us all powers of heart and mind,
So we were mad and had no pulse or thought
But love, love, love, in the one bale-fire caught?

You pass, you smile: yet is that smile I see
Of love, and of your all-night gift to me?
Now I too smile, for doubt, and own the doubt,
And wait in fear for night to root it out,
And doubt the more; but take heart to be true,
Each time of change, to a fresh hope of you,
That love may prove his worth once more and be
Fierce as the tides of Spring in you and me,
And bear with us till dawn shall break, though soon
With dreams of doubt to vex me at high noon.

THE TIME OF DAY

Here some sit restless asking the time of day,
Waiting the miracle. 'What miracle's that?' I ask.
'The triumph of one confident hour,' they say,
'Over its team-mates in the century's task.'

'An event, be sure,' I say, 'that shall never be,
Nor was nor could be, unless as mere denial
Of some huge timely eventuality
That promised more than it later brought to trial.

'For the hour must always cry for a certain date
As a glass to gaze in, a charter of true succession,
Consent each time to bow to the legal fate
Of quaintness, which is the end of self-possession.'

Even while I spoke, they shivered white as sheets
Muttering 'The Comforter is about to speak.
He will exalt the mighty to their usual seats
And kick the cringing buttocks of the humble and meek.

'For while the miracle waits of which we have spoken
The Comforter's here to confirm the ancestral story,
How the teeth of all the ungodly shall be broken
And the flag of Virtue flaunt its tattered glory.'

Then the Comforter eyed the niche where I was sitting.
'Well pleaded, fanciful spirit,' he laughed, and named
My early sweetnesses. Coward! I found it fitting
To blush my deprecations, but I was truly shamed.

BLONDE OR DARK?

Who calls for women, drink and snuff
In the one breath, has said enough
To give the scientist his answer
To 'How came pox and gout and cancer?'
Undifferentiated 'women
And drink and snuff' in time of famine
Become materialized, remain
Real when plenty comes again,
And pox, gout, cancer are the price
Of this continued artifice,
A self-abusive make-believe
That wears its heart not on its sleeve
Merely, but flips it in the palm
Of any business-like *madame*
Whose 'Blonde or dark, sir?' says enough
Whether of women, drink, or snuff.

BOOTS AND BED

Here in this wavering body, now brisk, now dead,
Rules the long struggle between boots and bed,
Empiric boots distrusting all that seems,
And quietistic bed, my ship of dreams.
Each laid a wager in my infancy
Himself would have me when I came to die,
And still the stakes are raised as I appear
More stalwart or more sickly, year by year;
Until I lie afield, and keep my toes
Naked and nimble as a monkey goes.
Yet something always baulking this evasion,
Glass under foot or frost or irritation
Of gnats and midges in the summer hay,
Once more begins my accustomed day-to-day
With pride of boots, and closes in delight
Of ghoulish bed gloating 'Perhaps to-night':
So nothing's left but to dull-weary them
And out-Methusalem Methusalem.

THE TAINT

Being born of a dishonest mother
Who knew one thing and thought the other,
A father too whose golden touch
Was 'Think small, please all, compass much',
He was hard put to it to unwind
The early swaddlings of his mind.

'Agree, it is better to confess
The occasion of my rottenness
Than in a desperation try
To cloak, dismiss or justify
The inward taint: of which I knew
Not much until I came to you
And saw it then, furred on the bone,
With as much horror as your own.

'You were born clean; and for the sake
Of your strict eyes I undertake
(If such disunion be allowed
To speak a sentence, to go proud
Among the miseries of to-day)
No more to let mere doing weigh
As counterbalance in my mind
To being rotten-boned and blind,
Nor leave the honesty and love
Of both only for you to prove.'

DUMPLINGS' ADDRESS TO GOURMETS

King George who asked how was the dumpling packed
With apple, seeing the crust was yet intact,
Was no more royal fool than you who show
Our lives in terms of raw fruit and raw dough
Or make our dumplingdom mere aggregate
Of heat, fruit, sugar, dough and china plate,
Who criticize our beneath-crust condition
Before the crust is cracked, from a position
Blankly outside, or more unfairly still,
Cracking the crust and doing what you will
With spoon and fingers, claim at last to find
The proof of dumplingdom – study defined
Without regard for the unstudied whole –
In your digestion and your finger-bowl.

Either be dumplings and be wise of us
Or be content, as men, not to discuss
What is not us so soon as you begin
To let our steam out and your noses in.

SORROW

There is a you, a you yourself, denies
All predicates that admit contraries.
Therefore I spare you *love* because of *hate*,
Or *life* because of *death*. *Joy* cannot state
Such joy I have in you, because of *grief*.
No, let me name you *sorrow*: sorrow, in brief,
Is a full thought with no contrasting sense
But sorrow. Grief will cloud an innocence
Or wholeness, which in turn love's rebel hates
Blacken, which death-of-life annihilates,
But sorrow quickens to transparency.
Be not even beauty to me through your beauty,
But singly through your sorrow: that will ease me.

THE NAPE OF THE NECK

To speak of the hollow nape where the close chaplet
Of thought is bound, the loose-ends lying neat
In two strands downward, where the shoulders open
Casual and strong below, waiting their burden,
And the long spine begins its downward journey:
The hair curtains this postern silkily,
This secret stairway by which thought will come
More personally, with a closer welcome,
Than through the latticed eyes or portalled ears;
Where kisses and all unconsidered whispers
Go smoother in than by the very lip,
And more endeared because the head's asleep
Or grieving, the face covered with the hands.

'But equally,' you say, 'to these neck-ribbands —'

To be near napeless, headsunk, simian
Forgoes the privilege of man and woman.
The tighter bound the chaplet, the more easy
The door moves on its hinges; the more free
The stair, then the more sure the tenancy —'

'But equally,' you say, 'to these neck-ribbands
May come one night the hypocrite assassin
With show of love or wisdom thrusting in
And, prompted in the watchword of the day,
Run up and stab and walk unseen away.'
But there's no need to use such melodrama,
For each betrayer only can betray
Once and the last effect of violation
Need be no ruin, no grief or contrition
(Despite tradition)
But a clear view: 'I was betrayed indeed,
Yet to a strictness and a present need.'
And it should come to this, to wear with pride
The knife scars that it would be shame to hide,
And once more without shuddering or hardness
Loll down the head to any chosen kiss.

A VISIT TO STRATFORD

And was he innocent as you protest
Of these hot wheels, this tide, this trade, this sawdust?
No, there was weakness in him that foreknew,
Even claimed it with a brazen *non sans droict*,
And here's his pedigree which pardon me
I do not mean to read, *found in his closet*.
His rival playwrights nudged and laughed at this,
For patronage busy among the heralds
In gratitude for secret service rendered
Had cut all tangled genealogic knots
And sealed the lie – linking the generations
We also laugh at him, in spite of love.

To go no further than the tanner's son.
The tannery failed, beginning the long turmoil:
Turmoil brought settled grief, grief, fear of death:
This fear postponed itself in architecture:
Architecture spelt itself sweet death;
After death the abstraction of the body
(Protected by the merest formal curse)
Freeing the massy tomb for commendation,
For commentaries, for mere scholiasm:
And scholiasm bred strange heresies

Which thinned and spread in chatter through the schools:
Chatter brought pilgrims flocking, therefore trade:
Trade, this false history, this word-worn patter:
So, timber from the mulberry that he planted
Miraculously multiplied, enough
To plank and roof a great memorial hall
For summer festivals: his eight least plays,
The *Shrew* and *Merry Wives* starring the bill:
Matinees, Saturdays and Wednesdays: stalls
And sideshows valeted by the Concordance.
Oh, he foreknew the frequence of the sequence –
Sixpence a ticket, sixpence, sixpence,
School-children with their teachers, twopence.
The hackney rides, quotation to quotation,
To be or not to be. The bubble reputation.
A grievous fault (for one so rich of wit)
And grievously has Caesar answered it.

PURE DEATH

We looked, we loved, and therewith instantly
Death became terrible to you and me.
By love we disenthralled our natural terror
From every comfortable philosopher
Or tall, grey doctor of divinity:
Death stood at last in his true rank and order.

It happened soon, so wild of heart were we,
Exchange of gifts grew to a malady:
Their worth rose always higher on each side
Till there seemed nothing but ungivable pride
That yet remained ungiven, and this degree
Called a conclusion not to be denied.

Then we at last bethought ourselves, made shift
And simultaneously this final gift
Gave: each with shaking hands unlocks
The sinister, long, brass-bound coffin-box,
Unwraps pure death, with such bewilderment
As greeted our love's first acknowledgement.

THE COOL WEB

Children are dumb to say how hot the day is,
How hot the scent is of the summer rose,
How dreadful the black wastes of evening sky,
How dreadful the tall soldiers drumming by.

But we have speech, to chill the angry day,
And speech, to dull the rose's cruel scent.
We spell away the overhanging night,
We spell away the soldiers and the fright.

There's a cool web of language winds us in,
Retreat from too much joy or too much fear:
We grow sea-green at last and coldly die
In brininess and volubility.

But if we let our tongues lose self-possession,
Throwing off language and its watery clasp
Before our death, instead of when death comes,
Facing the wide glare of the children's day,
Facing the rose, the dark sky and the drums,
We shall go mad no doubt and die that way.

THE COOL WEB

Children are dumb to say how hot the day is,
How hot the scent is of the summer rose,
How dreadful the black wastes of evening sky,
How dreadful the tall soldiers drumming by.

But we have speech, to chill the angry day,
And speech, to dull the rose's cruel scent.
We spell away the overhanging night,
We spell away the soldiers and the fright.

There's a cool web of language winds us in,
Retreat from too much joy or too much fear:
We grow sea-green at last and coldly die
In brininess and volubility.

But if we let our tongues lose self-possession,
Throwing off language and its watery clasp
Before our death, instead of when death comes,
Facing the wide glare of the children's day,
Facing the rose, the dark sky and the drums,
We shall go mad no doubt and die that way.

II

From *POEMS (1914–27)*

(1927)

THE PROGRESS

There is a travelling fury in his feet
   (Scorn for the waters of his native spring)
   Which proves at last the downfall of this king:
Shame will not let him sound the long retreat.

Tormented by his progress he displays
   An open flank to the swarmed enemy
   Who, charging through and through, set his pride free
For death's impossible and footless ways.

HELL

Husks, rags and bones, waste-paper, excrement,
   Denied a soul whether for good or evil
And casually consigned to unfulfilment,
   Are pronged into his bag by the great-devil.

Or words repeated, over and over and over,
   Until their sense sickens and all but dies,
These the same fellow like a ghoulish lover
   Will lay his hands upon and hypnotize.

From husks and rags and waste and excrement
   He forms the pavement-feet and the lift-faces;
He steers the sick words into parliament
   To rule a dust-bin world with deep-sleep phrases.

When healthy words or people chance to dine
    Together in this rarely actual scene,
There is a love-taste in the bread and wine,
    Nor is it asked: 'Do you mean what you mean?'

But to their table-converse boldly comes
    The same great-devil with his brush and tray,
To conjure plump loaves from the scattered crumbs,
    And feed his false five thousands day by day.

THE FURIOUS VOYAGE

So, overmasterful, to sea!
But hope no distant view of sail,
No growling ice, nor weed, nor whale,
Nor breakers perilous on the lee.

Though you enlarge your angry mind
Three leagues and more about the ship
And stamp till every puncheon skip,
The wake runs evenly behind.

And it has width enough for you,
This vessel, dead from truck to keel,
With its unmanageable wheel,
A blank chart and a surly crew,

In ballast only due to fetch
The turning point of wretchedness
On an uncoasted, featureless
And barren ocean of blue stretch.

O JORROCKS, I HAVE PROMISED

Sprung of no worthier parentage than sun
In February, and fireside and the snow
Streaked on the north side of each wall and hedge,
And breakfast late, in bed, and a tall puppy
Restless for sticks to fetch and tussle over,
And Jorrocks bawling from the library shelf,

And the accumulation of newspapers
And the day-after-judgement-day to face –
This poem (only well bred on one side,
Father a grum, mother a lady's maid)
Asked for a style, a place in literature.
So, since the morning had been wholly spoilt
By sun, by snow, breakfast in bed, the puppy,
By literature, a headache and their headaches;
Throwing away the rest of my bad day
I gave it style, let it be literature
Only too well, and let it talk itself
And me to boredom, let it draw lunch out
From one o'clock to three with nuts and smoking
While it went talking on, with imagery,
Why it was what it was, and had no breeding
But waste things and the ambition to be real;
And flattered me with puppy gratitude.
I let it miss the one train back to town
And stay to tea and supper and a bed
And even bed-in-breakfast the next morning.
More thanks.
       The penalty of authorship;
Forced hospitality, an impotence
Expecting an impossible return
Not only from the plainly stupid chance
But from impossible caddishness, no less.
I answered leading questions about Poe
And let it photograph me in the snow
And gave it a signed copy of itself
And 'the nursery money-box is on the shelf,
How kind of you to give them each a penny.'

    O Jorrocks I have promised
      To serve thee to the end,
    To entertain young Indians,
      The pupils of my friend,
    To entertain Etonians
      And for their sake combine
    The wit of T.S. Eliot,
      The grace of Gertrude Stein.
    Be thou forever near me
      To hasten or control,
    Thou Literary Supplement,
      Thou Guardian of my soul.

I shall not fear the battle
    While thou art by my side,
Nor wander from the pathway
    If thou shalt be my guide.
                                        Amen.

LOST ACRES

These acres, always again lost
    By every new ordnance-survey
And searched for at exhausting cost
    Of time and thought, are still away.

They have their paper-substitute –
    Intercalation of an inch
At the so-many-thousandth foot –
    And no one parish feels the pinch.

But lost they are, despite all care,
    And perhaps likely to be bound
Together in a piece somewhere,
    A plot of undiscovered ground.

Invisible, they have the spite
    To swerve the tautest measuring-chain
And the exact theodolite
    Perched every side of them in vain.

Yet, be assured, we have no need
    To plot these acres of the mind
With prehistoric fern and reed
    And monsters such as heroes find.

Maybe they have their flowers, their birds,
    Their trees behind the phantom fence,
But of a substance without words:
    To walk there would be loss of sense.

GARDENER

Loveliest flowers, though crooked in their border,
And glorious fruit, dangling from ill-pruned boughs –
Be sure the gardener had not eye enough
To wheel a barrow between the broadest gates
Without a clumsy scraping.

Yet none could think it simple awkwardness;
And when he stammered of a garden-guardian,
Said the smooth lawns came by angelic favour,
The pinks and pears in spite of his own blunders,
They nudged at this conceit.

Well, he had something, though he called it nothing –
An ass's wit, a hairy-belly shrewdness
That would appraise the intentions of an angel
By the very yard-stick of his own confusion,
And bring the most to pass.

TO A CHARGE OF DIDACTICISM

Didactic, I shall be didactic
   When I have hit on something new
Else dons unborn will be didactic
   On undidacticism too.

Didactic, they will be didactic
   With 'excellently's' and 'absurd's':
Let me make sure that they're didactic
   On my own words on my own words.

THE PHILATELIST-ROYAL

The Philatelist-Royal
Was always too loyal
To say what he honestly
Thought of Philately.

Must it rank as a Science?
Then he had more reliance,
(As he told the Press wittily),
In Royal Philately
Than in all your geologies,
All your psychologies,
Bacteriologies,
Physics and such.
It was honester, much,
Free of mere speculations
And doubtful equations,
So therefore more true
From a pure science view
Than other school courses:
For Nature's blind forces
Here alone, they must own,
Played no meddlesome part.
It was better than Art:
It enforced education,
It strengthened the nation
In the arts of mensuration
And colour-discrimination,
In cleanliness, in hope,
In use of the microscope,
In mercantile transactions,
In a love of abstractions,
In geography and history:
It was a noble mystery.
So he told them again
That Philately's reign,
So mild and humane,
Would surely last longer,
Would surely prove stronger
Than the glory of Greece,
Than the grandeur of Rome.
It brought goodwill and peace
Wherever it found a home.

It was more democratic,
More full, more ecstatic,
Than the Bible, the bottle,
The Complete Works of Aristotle,
And worthierer and betterer
And etceterier and etcetera.

The Philatelist-Royal
Was always too loyal
To say what he honestly
Thought of Philately.

SONG: TO BE LESS PHILOSOPHICAL

Listen, you theologians,
Give ear, you rhetoricians,
Hearken, you Aristotelians:
Of the Nature of God, my song shall be.

Our God is infinite,
Your God is infinite,
Their God is infinite,
Of infinite variety.

God, he is also finite,
God, she is also definite,
He, she; we, they; you, each and it –
Of finite omnipresence.

He is a bloody smart sergeant
And served in the Royal Artillery:
For gallantly exposing his person
He won the Victoria Cross.

She is also divorced,
From a Russian count in exile,
And paints a little and sings a little –
And won a little prize in Paris.

It has also the character of a soap
And may be employed quite freely
For disinfecting cattle trucks
And the very kine in the byre.

You are also mad, quite mad,
To imagine you are not God.
Goddam it, aren't you a Spirit,
And your ministers a flaming fire?

We are also gradually tending
To be less philosophical,
We talk through hats more personally,
With madness more divine.

They are a very smart Goddam Cross
With the character of a soap, a little:
They disinfect more personally,
To be less philosophical.

Each is a very smart Paris hat
And may be divorced quite freely,
Freely, freely in the Royal Artillery,
To be each less philosophical.

POEMS 1929

(1929)

SICK LOVE

O Love, be fed with apples while you may,
And feel the sun and go in royal array,
A smiling innocent on the heavenly causeway,

Though in what listening horror for the cry
That soars in outer blackness dismally,
The dumb blind beast, the paranoiac fury:

Be warm, enjoy the season, lift your head,
Exquisite in the pulse of tainted blood,
That shivering glory not to be despised.

Take your delight in momentariness,
Walk between dark and dark – a shining space
With the grave's narrowness, though not its peace.

IN NO DIRECTION

To go in no direction
    Surely as carelessly,
Walking on the hills alone,
    I never found easy.

Either I sent leaf or stick
    Twirling in the air,
Whose fall might be prophetic,
    Pointing 'there',

Or in superstition
    Edged somewhat away
From a sure direction,
    Yet could not stray,

Or undertook the climb
   That I had avoided
Directionless some other time,
   Or had not avoided,

Or called as companion
   An eyeless ghost
And held his no direction
   Till my feet were lost.

IN BROKEN IMAGES

He is quick, thinking in clear images;
I am slow, thinking in broken images.

He becomes dull, trusting to his clear images;
I become sharp, mistrusting my broken images.

Trusting his images, he assumes their relevance;
Mistrusting my images, I question their relevance.

Assuming their relevance, he assumes the fact;
Questioning their relevance, I question the fact.

When the fact fails him, he questions his senses;
When the fact fails me, I approve my senses.

He continues quick and dull in his clear images;
I continue slow and sharp in my broken images.

He in a new confusion of his understanding;
I in a new understanding of my confusion.

THIEF

To the galleys, thief, and sweat your soul out
With strong tugging under the curled whips,
That there your thievishness may find full play.
Whereas, before, you stole rings, flowers and watches,
Oaths, jests and proverbs,
Yet paid for bed and board like an honest man,
This shall be entire thiefdom: you shall steal
Sleep from chain-galling, diet from sour crusts,
Comradeship from the damned, the ten-year-chained –
And, more than this, the excuse for life itself
From a craft steered toward battles not your own.

WARNING TO CHILDREN

Children, if you dare to think
Of the greatness, rareness, muchness,
Fewness of this precious only
Endless world in which you say
You live, you think of things like this:
Blocks of slate enclosing dappled
Red and green, enclosing tawny
Yellow nets, enclosing white
And black acres of dominoes,
Where a neat brown paper parcel
Tempts you to untie the string.
In the parcel a small island,
On the island a large tree,
On the tree a husky fruit.
Strip the husk and pare the rind off:
In the kernel you will see
Blocks of slate enclosed by dappled
Red and green, enclosed by tawny
Yellow nets, enclosed by white
And black acres of dominoes,
Where the same brown paper parcel –
Children, leave the string alone!
For who dares undo the parcel
Finds himself at once inside it,
On the island, in the fruit,
Blocks of slate about his head,

Finds himself enclosed by dappled
Green and red, enclosed by yellow
Tawny nets, enclosed by black
And white acres of dominoes,
With the same brown paper parcel
Still unopened on his knee.
And, if he then should dare to think
Of the fewness, muchness, rareness,
Greatness of this endless only
Precious world in which he says
He lives – he then unties the string.

DISMISSAL

If you want life, there's no life here.
    Whatever trust you held for me
Or I for you in some such year,
    Is ended as you see.
I forced this quarrel; it was not
    So much disgust with all you did
As sudden doubt of whom and what
    My easy friendship hid;
    I carefully offended.
It would be best if you too broke
Acquaintance, with a monstrous look,
    Rather than stay to temporize
    Or steal away with brimming eyes
Like old friends in a book.
So if a man of you can be
    Regretful of the time that's gone
He must now imperturbably
    Accept this antic kick from one
    Who used to be his father's son
    Discreet in blind devotion.

GUESSING BLACK OR WHITE

Guessing black or white,
　Guessing white, guessing black.
Guessing black or white.
　Guessing white, guessing black.

His mother was a terrier bitch,
His father a Dalmatian,
　Guessing black or white:
Not black because white
Because black because white;
Not white because black
Because white because black,
　Guessing black or white.

His mother was from Renfrew,
His father was a Zulu,
　Guessing black or white:
Not black because black
Because white because white;
Not white because white
Because black because black,
　Guessing black or white.

His mother was a domino,
His father was a dice-box,
　Guessing black or white:
Not white because white
Because white because white;
Not black because black
Because black because black,
　Guessing black or white.

HECTOR

The persons in the thought, like shapes, waver.
Not to forget them, forge a history
Of squarenesses and narrownesses, saying
'Thus ticket Hector with his fishing-rod
To the dungeon of the ticket Princess came,
Gave her a ticket.' Or what you will.
The shapes are neither this nor that,
Not Hectors and princesses, rods and dungeons,
Nor indeed shapes but, as I say, persons
Who look 'remember me and know me',
And so are lost under the many tickets.
But what the devil to do with ticket Hector
Who is no more person than he was a squareness
Or squareness was a shape? He stands, mock-Hector,
Fishing with his forged rod through the false grille
From the false moat outside the forged dungeon,
(The ticket princess standing by) –
The dull what's left of ticketing a ticket.
Let them close-ticket at their princely leisure
To please what girls and boys may read the myth.
The persons in the thought are long dead.

AGAINST KIND

Become invisible by elimination
    Of kind in her, she none the less persisted
    Among kind with no need to find excuses
For choosing this and not some alien region.

Invisibility was her last kindness:
    She might have kept appearance, had she wished;
    Yet to be seen living against all kind,
That would be monstrous; she permitted blindness.

She asked and she permitted nothing further,
    She went her private and eventless way
    As uncompanioning as uncompanioned;
And for a while they did not think to mourn her.

But soon it vexed them that her name still stood
    Plain on their registers, and over-simple,
    Not witnessed to by laundry, light or fuel,
Or even, they wondered most, by drink and food.

They tried rebuttal; it was not for long:
    Pride and curiosity raised a whisper
    That swelled into a legend and the legend
Confirmed itself in terror and grew strong.

It was not that they would prefer her presence
    To her room (now hating her), but that her room
    Could not be filled by any creature of kind,
It gaped; they shook with sudden impotence.

Sleeplessness and shouting and new rumours
    Tempted them nightly; dulness wore their days;
    They waited for a sign, but none was given;
She owed them nothing, they held nothing of hers.

They raged at her that being invisible
    She would not use that gift, humouring them
    As Lilith, or as an idiot poltergeist,
Or as a Gyges turning the ring's bezel.

She gave no sign; at last they tumbled prostrate
    Fawning on her, confessing her their sins;
    They burned her the occasion's frankincense,
Crying 'Save, save!', but she was yet discrete.

And she must stay discrete, and they stay blind
    Forever, or for one time less than ever –
    If they, despaired and turning against kind,
Become invisible too, and read her mind.

MIDWAY

Between insufferable monstrosities
And exiguities insufferable,
Midway is man's own station. We no longer
Need either hang our heads or lift them high
But for the fortunes of finance or love.
We have no truck either with the forebeings
Of Betelgeux or with the atom's git.
Our world steadies: untrembling we renew
Old fears of earthquakes, adders, floods, mad dogs
And all such wholesomes. Nothing that we do
Concerns the infinities of either scale.
Clocks tick with our consent to our time-tables,
Trains run between our buffers. Time and Space
Amuse us merely with their rough-house turn,
Their hard head-on collision in the tunnel.
A dying superstition smiles and hums
'Abide with me' – God's evening prayer, not ours.
So history still is written and is read:
The eternities of divine commonplace.

CABBAGE PATCH

Green cabbage-wit, only by trying,
    Flew as bird-wit;
But flocking for the season's flying,
Restless perching and prying,
    Could not content it.

As lightning-wit therefore it struck
    And split the rocks indeed,
Fusing their veins, but in the instant's luck
    Was spilt by its own speed.

Back therefore to green cabbage-wit
In the old plot with glass and grit.
Tenth-in-the-line for kings and cabbages
Has honourable privileges
For which no rocks are split.

THE CASTLE

Walls, mounds, enclosing corrugations
Of darkness, moonlight on dry grass.
Walking this courtyard, sleepless, in fever;
Planning to use – but by definition
There's no way out, no way out –
Rope-ladders, baulks of timber, pulleys,
A rocket whizzing over the walls and moat –
Machines easy to improvise.
                      No escape,
No such thing; to dream of new dimensions,
Cheating checkmate by painting the king's robe
So that he slides like a queen;
Or to cry, 'Nightmare, nightmare!'
Like a corpse in the cholera-pit
Under a load of corpses;
Or to run the head against these blind walls,
Enter the dungeon, torment the eyes
With apparitions chained two and two,
And go frantic with fear –
To die and wake up sweating by moonlight
In the same courtyard, sleepless as before.

WELSH INCIDENT

'But that was nothing to what things came out
From the sea-caves of Criccieth yonder.'
'What were they? Mermaids? dragons? ghosts?'
'Nothing at all of any things like that.'
'What were they, then?'
                      'All sorts of queer things,
Things never seen or heard or written about,
Very strange, un-Welsh, utterly peculiar
Things. Oh, solid enough they seemed to touch,
Had anyone dared it. Marvellous creation,
All various shapes and sizes, and no sizes,
All new, each perfectly unlike his neighbour,
Though all came moving slowly out together.'
'Describe just one of them.'
                      'I am unable.'
'What were their colours?'

                                  'Mostly nameless colours,
Colours you'd like to see; but one was puce
Or perhaps more like crimson, but not purplish.
Some had no colour.'
                                  'Tell me, had they legs?'
'Not a leg nor foot among them that I saw.'
'But did these things come out in any order?
What o'clock was it? What was the day of the week?
Who else was present? How was the weather?'
'I was coming to that. It was half-past three
On Easter Tuesday last. The sun was shining.
The Harlech Silver Band played *Marchog Jesu*
On thirty-seven shimmering instruments,
Collecting for Caernarvon's (Fever) Hospital Fund.
The populations of Pwllheli, Criccieth,
Portmadoc, Borth, Tremadoc, Penrhyndeudraeth,
Were all assembled. Criccieth's mayor addressed them
First in good Welsh and then in fluent English,
Twisting his fingers in his chain of office,
Welcoming the things. They came out on the sand,
Not keeping time to the band, moving seaward
Silently at a snail's pace. But at last
The most odd, indescribable thing of all,
Which hardly one man there could see for wonder,
Did something recognizably a something.'
'Well, what?'
                                  'It made a noise.'
                                                    'A frightening noise?'
'No, no.'
                                  'A musical noise? A noise of scuffling?'
'No, but a very loud, respectable noise –
Like groaning to oneself on Sunday morning
In Chapel, close before the second psalm.'
'What did the mayor do?'
                                                    'I was coming to that.'

BACK DOOR

For bringing it so far, thank you,
Though they seem very light ones, thank you;
Who gave you my address and rank?
It may prove so-so in the end;
That would depend on what else stays so.
Easy to blend all together
But the devil to know whether or not
And how to keep it fresh in taste:
They hang on the air like rot
And are blown to waste in the end.
Still this, I own, seems steady, thanks,
Four or five of them already,
Just what the store-rooms need.
For bringing it so far, thanks.
I recognized your pranks at once, indeed
Almost before I heard the gate slam.
Of course, it's all a gamble really:
First it's the finding, then the picking,
Then the minding, then the dressing,
Guessing them over the awkward stage,
(I was in the trade myself, you see,
When I was on the stage;
I had several made for me
When I was in the trade,
When I was on the stage),
Then it's those naked-light instructions
That the muctions plaster up,
Destruction take them,
In the room where the stuff's folded
On which the whole lay's laid.
Always the same, these crews, these crows –
Lousy! Not interested? No? The shame!
Then how much must I owe you?
Many thanks, again, many francs,
Many pranks, many thanks, again.
Good day!

FRONT DOOR SOLILOQUY

'Yet from the antique heights or deeps of what
Or which was grandeur fallen, sprung or what
Or which, beyond doubt I am grandeur's grandson
True to the eagle nose, the pillared neck,
(Missed by the intervening generation)
Whom large hands, long face, and long feet sort out
From which and what, to wear my heels down even,
To be connected with all reigning houses,
Show sixteen quarterings or sixty-four
Or even more, with clear skin and eyes clear
To drive the nails in and not wound the wood,
With lungs and heart sound and with bowels easy:
An angry man, heaving the sacks of grain
From cart to loft and what and what and which
And even thus, and being no Rousseauist,
Nor artists-of-the-world-unite, or which,
Or what, never admitting, in effect,
Touch anything my touch does not adorn –
Now then I dung on my grandfather's doorstep,
Which is a reasonable and loving due
To hold no taint of spite or vassalage
And understood only by him and me –
But you, you bog-rat-whiskered, you psalm-griddling,
Lame, rotten-livered, which and what canaille,
You, when twin lackeys, with armorial shovels,
Unbolt the bossy gates and bend to the task,
Be off, work out your heads from between the railings,
Lest we unkennel the mastiff and the Dane –
This house is jealous of its nastiness.'

ANAGRAMMAGIC

Anagrammatising
TRANSUBSTANTIATION,
Slyly deputising
For old Copopulation
SIN SAT ON A TIN TAR TUB
And did with joy his elbows rub.

Art introseduced him
To females dull and bad,
Flapper flappings, limb-slim,
From his blonde writing-pad,
The river-girlgling drained of blood –
Post-card flower of kodak mud.

By such anagrammagic
And mansturbantiation
They fathered then this tragic
Lustalgia on the nation,
And after that, and after that,
ON A TIN SIN TUB ART SAT.

VISION IN THE REPAIR-SHOP

Be sure the crash was worse than ever.
In, flying out, collapsed with music;
Out, flying in, roared up in flames.
The blast was non-continuous.
But what matter? The force generated
At every point of impact
Was, you remarked, dispersed for other uses.
In this you saw the well-geared mind
Of the garage-man-in-chief,
Prime corpse of each new speed-track,
Who by unequalled salesmanship
Engines a car for every son and daughter
In a city of twelve millions –
What prettier traffic-block imaginable
Lasting, day in, day out, for centuries,
While life flows easily down the gutters
Or swings in the air on ropes,
And you and I, stuffing this cotton-wool
Closer into our ears, from habit,
Lie in plaster of Paris on our backs
And drink the drip of many radiators?

NATURE'S LINEAMENTS

When mountain rocks and leafy trees
And clouds and things like these,
With edges,

Caricature the human face,
Such scribblings have no grace
Nor peace –

The bulbous nose, the sunken chin,
The ragged mouth in grin
Of cretin.

Nature is always so: you find
That all she has of mind
Is wind,

Retching among the empty spaces,
Ruffling the idiot grasses,
The sheep's fleeces.

Whose pleasures are excreting, poking,
Havocking and sucking,
Sleepy licking.

Whose griefs are melancholy,
Whose flowers are oafish,
Whose waters, silly,
Whose birds, raffish,
Whose fish, fish.

SEA SIDE

Into a gentle wildness and confusion,
Of here and there, of one and everyone,
Of windy sandhills by an unkempt sea,
Came two and two in search of symmetry,
Found symmetry of two in sea and sand,
In left foot, right foot, left hand and right hand.

The beast with two backs is a single beast,
Yet by his love of singleness increased
To two and two and two and two again,
Until, instead of sandhills, see, a plain
Patterned in two and two, by two and two –
And the sea parts in horror at a view
Of rows of houses coupling, back to back,
While love smokes from their common chimney-stack
With two-four-eight-sixteenish single same
Re-registration of the duple name.

WM. BRAZIER

At the end of Tarriers' Lane, which was the street
We children thought the pleasantest in Town
Because of the old elms growing from the pavement
And the crookedness, when the other streets were straight,
[They were always at the lamp-post round the corner,
Those pugs and papillons and in-betweens,
Nosing and snuffling for the latest news]
Lived Wm. Brazier, with a gilded sign,
'Practical Chimney Sweep'. He had black hands,
Black face, black clothes, black brushes and white teeth;
He jingled round the town in a pony-trap,
And the pony's name was Soot, and Soot was black.
But the brass fittings on the trap, the shafts,
On Soot's black harness, on the black whip-butt,
Twinkled and shone like any guardsman's buttons.
Wasn't that pretty? And when we children jeered:
'Hello, Wm. Brazier! Dirty-face Wm. Brazier!'
He would crack his whip at us and smile and bellow,
'Hello, my dears!' [If he were drunk, but otherwise:
'Scum off, you damned young milliners' bastards, you!']

Let them copy it out on a pink page of their albums,
Carefully leaving out the bracketed lines.
It's an old story – f's for s's –
But good enough for them, the suckers.

A FORMER ATTACHMENT

And glad to find, on again looking at it,
It meant even less to me than I had thought –
You know the ship is moving when you see
The boxes on the quayside slide away
And become smaller – and feel a calm delight
When the port's cleared and the coast out of sight,
And ships are few, each on its proper course,
With no occasion for approach or discourse.

RETURN FARE

And so to Ireland on an Easter Tuesday
To a particular place I could not find.
A sleeping man beside me in the boat-train
Sat whistling Liliburlero in his sleep;
Not, I had thought, a possible thing, yet so.
And through a port-hole of the Fishguard boat,
That was the hospital-boat of twelve years back,
Passengered as before with doubt and dying,
I saw the moon through glass, but a waning moon –
Bad luck, self-doubtful, so once more I slept.
And then the engines woke me up by stopping.
The piers of the quay loomed up. So I went up.
The sun shone rainily and jokingly,
And everyone joked at his own expense,
And the priest declared 'nothing but fishing tackle,'
Laughing provokingly. I could not laugh.
And the hard cackling laughter of the men
And the false whinnying laughter of the girls
Grieved me. The telegraph-clerk said, grieving too,
'St Peter, he's two words in the Free State now,
So that's a salmon due.' I paid the fish.
And everyone I asked about the place
Knew the place well, but not its whereabouts,
And the black-shawled peasant woman asked me then,
Wasn't I jaded? And she grieved to me
Of the apple and the expulsion from the garden.
Ireland went by, and went by as I saw her
When last I saw her for the first time
Exactly how I had seen her all the time.
And I found the place near Sligo, not the place,
So back to England on the Easter Thursday.

SINGLE FARE

By way of Fishguard, all the lying devils
Are back to Holy Ireland whence they came.
Each took a single fare: which cost them less
And brought us comfort. The dumb devils too
Take single fares, return by rail to Scotland
Whence they came. So the air is cool and easy.
And if, in some quarter of some big city,
A little Eire or a little Scotland
Serves as a rallying-point for a few laggards,
No matter, we are free from taint of them.
And at the fire-side now (drinking our coffee),
If I ask, 'But to what township did they book,
Those dumb devils of Scotland?' you will answer:
'There's the Bass Rock, once more a separate kingdom,
Leagued with Ireland, the same cold grey crag
Screamed against by the gulls that are all devils.'
And of the Irish devils you will answer:
'In Holy Ireland many a country seat
Still stands unburned – as Cooper's Hill, Lisheen,
Cloghan Castle, or Killua in County Galway –
For the devils to enter, unlock the library doors
And write love-letters and long threatening letters
Even to us, if it so pleases them.'

IT WAS ALL VERY TIDY

When I reached his place,
The grass was smooth,
The wind was delicate,
The wit well timed,
The limbs well formed,
The pictures straight on the wall:
It was all very tidy.

He was cancelling out
The last row of figures,
He had his beard tied up in ribbons,
There was no dust on his shoe,
Everyone nodded:
It was all very tidy.

Music was not playing,
There were no sudden noises,
The sun shone blandly,
The clock ticked:
It was all very tidy.

'Apart from and above all this,'
I reassured myself,
'There is now myself.'
It was all very tidy.

Death did not address me,
He had nearly done:
It was all very tidy.

They asked, did I not think
It was all very tidy?

I could not bring myself
To laugh, or untie
His beard's neat ribbons,
Or jog his elbow,
Or whistle, or sing,
Or make disturbance.
I consented, frozenly,
He was unexceptionable:
It was all very tidy.

A SHEET OF PAPER

Then was blank expectation,
Was happening without incident,
Was thinking without images,
Was speaking without words,
Was being without proof,
Happiness not signalized,
Sorrow without cause,
And place for nothing further.

Now is a sheet of paper,
A not blank expectation,
A happening, but with incident,
A thinking, but with images,
A speaking, but with words,
A being, over-proved,
A report of happiness,
A cause for sorrow,
Place for the signature
And for the long post-script.

TEN POEMS MORE

(1930)

THE READER OVER MY SHOULDER

You, reading over my shoulder, peering beneath
My writing arm – I suddenly feel your breath
   Hot on my hand or on my nape,
So interrupt my theme, scratching these few
Words on the margin for you, namely you,
   Too-human shape fixed in that shape: –

All the saying of things against myself
And for myself I have well done myself.
   What now, old enemy, shall you do
But quote and underline, thrusting yourself
Against me, as ambassador of myself,
   In damned confusion of myself and you?

For you in strutting, you in sycophancy,
Have played too long this other self of me,
   Doubling the part of judge and patron
With that of creaking grind-stone to my wit.
Know me, have done: I am a proud spirit
   And you for ever clay. Have done!

HISTORY OF THE WORD

The Word that in the beginning was the Word
For two or three, but elsewhere spoke unheard,
Found Words to interpret it, which for a season
Prevailed until ruled out by Law and Reason
Which, by a lax interpretation cursed,
In Laws and Reasons logically dispersed;
These, in their turn, found they could do no better
Than fall to Letters and each claim a letter.
In the beginning then, the Word alone,
But now the various tongue-tied Lexicon

In perfect impotence the day nearing
When every ear shall lose its sense of hearing
And every mind by knowledge be close-shuttered –
But two or three, that hear the Word uttered.

INTERRUPTION

If ever against this easy blue and silver
Hazed-over countryside of thoughtfulness,
Far behind in the mind and above,
Boots from before and below approach trampling,
Watch how their premonition will display
A forward countryside, low in the distance –
A picture-postcard square of June grass;
Will warm a summer season, trim the hedges,
Cast the river about on either flank,
Start the late cuckoo emptily calling,
Invent a rambling tale of moles and voles,
Furnish a path with stiles.
Watch how the field will broaden, the feet nearing,
Sprout with great dandelions and buttercups,
Widen and heighten. The blue and silver
Fogs at the border of this all-grass.
Interruption looms gigantified,
Lurches against, treads thundering through,
Blots the landscape, scatters all,
Roars and rumbles like a dark tunnel,
Is gone.
      The picture-postcard grass and trees
Swim back to central: it is a large patch,
It is a modest, failing patch of green,
The postage-stamp of its departure,
Clouded with blue and silver, closing in now
To a plain countryside of less and less,
Unpeopled and unfeatured blue and silver,
Before, behind, above.

SURVIVAL OF LOVE

We love, and utterly,
Unnaturally:
From nature lately
By death you freed me,
Yourself free already.

Proof that we are unnatural:
This purposeful
And straining funeral,
Nature's unnatural,
Now become unfunereal.

And indeed merriest when
The gasp and strain
Will twitch like pain,
Clouding the former brain
Of us, the man and woman.

NEW LEGENDS

Content in you,
Andromeda serene,
Mistress of air and ocean
And every fiery dragon,
Chained to no cliff,
Asking no rescue of me.

Content in you,
Mad Atalanta,
Stooping unpausing,
Ever ahead,
Acquitting me of rivalry.

Content in you
Who made King Proteus marvel,
Showing him singleness
Past all variety.

Content in you,
Niobe of no children,
Of no calamity.

Content in you,
Helen, foiler of beauty.

SAINT

This Blatant Beast was finally overcome
And in no secret tourney: wit and fashion
Flocked out and for compassion
Wept as the Red Cross Knight pushed the blade home.

The people danced and sang the paeans due,
Roasting whole oxen on the public spit;
Twelve mountain peaks were lit
With bonfires; yet their hearts were doubt and rue.

Therefore no grave was deep enough to hold
The Beast, who after days came thrusting out,
Wormy from rump to snout,
His yellow cere-cloth patched with the grave's mould.

Nor could sea hold him: anchored with huge rocks,
He swelled and buoyed them up, paddling ashore
As evident as before
With deep-sea ooze and salty creaking bones.

Lime could not burn him, nor the sulphur fire:
So often as the good Knight bound him there,
With stink of singeing hair
And scorching flesh the corpse rolled from the pyre.

In the city-gutter would the Beast lie
Praising the Knight for all his valorous deeds:
'Ay, on those water-meads
He slew even me. These death-wounds testify.'

The Knight governed that city, a man shamed
And shrunken: for the Beast was over-dead,
With wounds no longer red
But gangrenous and loathsome and inflamed.

Not all the righteous judgements he could utter,
Nor mild laws frame, nor public works repair,
Nor wars wage, in despair,
Could bury that same Beast, crouched in the gutter.

A fresh remembrance-banquet to forestall,
The Knight turned hermit, went without farewell
To a far mountain-cell;
But the Beast followed as his seneschal,

And there drew water for him and hewed wood
With vacant howling laughter; else all day
Noisome with long decay
Sunning himself at the cave's entry stood.

Would bawl to pilgrims for a dole of bread
To feed the sick saint who once vanquished him
With spear so stark and grim;
Would set a pillow of grass beneath his head,
Would fetch him fever-wort from the pool's brim –
And crept into his grave when he was dead.

TAP ROOM

Believe me not a dolt: I would invent
No proverbs; but considering them
I need to state them:

Beauty impracticable,
Strength undemonstrable;
Lives without end await them.

Yet know me able and quick
To force an ending. How?
Finding a dolt to have begun them.

Finding him where?
On Halfpenny Island where they milk the cats.
Where may that lie?
Near Farthing Island where they milk mice.

How shall he have begun them?
O how indeed, but
Cracking the nut against the hammer.
What nut? Why, sir, the nut …

Believe me not a dolt: I have invented
No proverbs …

THE TERRACED VALLEY

In a deep thought of you and concentration
I came by hazard to a new region:
The unnecessary sun was not there,
The necessary earth lay without care –
For more than sunshine warmed the skin
Of the round world that was turned outside-in.

Calm sea beyond the terraced valley
Without horizon easily was spread,
As it were overhead,
Washing the mountain-spurs behind me:
The unnecessary sky was not there,
Therefore no heights, no deeps, no birds of the air.

Neat outside-inside, neat below-above,
Hermaphrodizing love.
Neat this-way-that-way and without mistake:
On the right hand could slide the left glove.
Neat over-under: the young snake
Through an unyielding shell his path could break.
Singing of kettles, like a singing brook,
Made out-of-doors a fireside nook.

But you, my love, where had you then your station?
Seeing that on this counter-earth together
We go not distant from each other;
I knew you near me in that strange region,
So searched for you, in hope to see you stand
On some near olive-terrace, in the heat,
The left-hand glove drawn on your right hand,
The empty snake's egg perfect at your feet –

But found you nowhere in the wide land,
And cried disconsolately, until you spoke
Immediate at my elbow, and your voice broke
This trick of time, changing the world about
To once more inside-in and outside-out.

OAK, POPLAR, PINE

The temple priests though using but one sign
For TREE, distinguish poplar, oak and pine:
Oak, short and spreading – poplar, tall and thin –
Pine, tall, bunched at the top and well inked in.
Therefore in priestly thought all various trees
Must be enrolled, in kind, as one of these.
The fir, the cedar and the deodar
Are pines, so too the desert palm-trees are;
Aspens and birches are of poplar folk
But chestnut, damson, elm and fig are oak.
All might be simple, did the priests allow
That apple-blossom dresses the oak bough,
That dates are pines-cones; but they will not so,
Well taught how pine and oak and poplar grow:
In every temple-court, for all to see
Flourishes one example of each tree
In tricunx. Your high-priest would laugh to think
Of oak boughs blossoming in pagan pink,
Or numerous cones, hung from a single spine,
Sticky yet sweeter than the fruit of vine,
(For vine's no tree; vine is a creeping thing,
Cousin to snake, that with its juice can sting).
Confront your priest with evident apple-blossom;
Will faith and doubt, conflicting, heave his bosom?
Force dates between his lips, will he forget
That there's no date-palm in the alphabet?
Turn apostate? Even in secret? No,
He'll see the blossom as mere mistletoe.
The dates will be as grapes, good for his needs:
He'll swallow down their stones like little seeds.
And here's no lie, no hypocritic sham:
Believe him earnest-minded as I am.
His script has less, and mine more, characters
Than stand in use with lexicographers.

They end with palm, I see and use the sign
For tree that is to palm as palm to pine,
As apple-bough to oak-bough in the spring:
It is no secrecy but a long looking.

ACT V, SCENE 5

You call the old nurse and the little page
To act survivors on your tragic stage –
You love the intrusive extra character.
'But where's the tragedy,' you say, 'if none
Remains to moralize on what's been done?
There's no catharsis in complete disaster.
Tears purge the soul – the nurse's broken line:
"O mistress, pretty one, dead!" the page's whine:
"Thou too? Alas, fond master!"'

No purge for my disgusted soul, no tears
Will wash away my bile of tragic years,
No sighs vicariously abate my rancour –
If nurse and page survive, I'd have them own
Small sorrow to be left up-stage alone,
And on the bloodiest field of massacre
Either rant out the anti-climax thus:
' 'A's dead, the bitch!' 'So's Oscar! Joy for us!'
Then fall to rifling pocket, belt and purse
With corky jokes and pantomime of sin;
Or let the feud rage on, page against nurse –
His jewelled dirk, her thund'rous rolling-pin.

SONG: LIFT-BOY

Let me tell you the story of how I began:
I began as the boot-boy and ended as the boot-man,
With nothing in my pockets but a jack-knife and a button,
With nothing in my pockets but a jack-knife and a button,
With nothing in my pockets.

Let me tell you the story of how I went on:
I began as the lift-boy and ended as the lift-man,
With nothing in my pockets but a jack-knife and a button,
With nothing in my pockets but a jack-knife and a button,
With nothing in my pockets.

I found it very easy to whistle and play
With nothing in my head or my pockets all day,
With nothing in my pockets.

But along came Old Eagle, like Moses or David;
He stopped at the fourth floor and preached me Damnation:
'Not a soul shall be savèd, not one shall be savèd.
The whole First Creation shall forfeit salvation:
From knife-boy to lift-boy, from ragged to regal,
Not one shall be savèd, not you, not Old Eagle,
No soul on earth escapeth, even if all repent –'
So I cut the cords of the lift and down we went,
With nothing in our pockets.

From POEMS 1926–1930

(1931)

BROTHER

It's odd enough to be alive with others,
But odder still to have sisters and brothers:
To make one of a characteristic litter –
The sisters puzzled and vexed, the brothers vexed and bitter
That this one wears, though flattened by abuse,
The family nose for individual use.

BAY OF NAPLES

The blind man reading Dante upside-down
And not in Braille frowned an admiring frown;
He sniffed, he underscored the passage read,
'One nose is better than both eyes,' he said.
'Here's a strong trace of orange-peel and sweat
And palate-scrapings on the rock, still wet,
And travellers' names carved on the sappy tree –
Old Ugolino's grief! Sublime!' said he.

FLYING CROOKED

The butterfly, a cabbage-white,
(His honest idiocy of flight)
Will never now, it is too late,
Master the art of flying straight,
Yet has – who knows so well as I? –
A just sense of how not to fly:
He lurches here and here by guess
And God and hope and hopelessness.
Even the aerobatic swift
Has not his flying-crooked gift.

REASSURANCE TO THE SATYR

The hairs of my beard are red and black mingled,
With white now frequent in the red and black.
My finger-nails, see here, are ill-assorted;
My hands are not a pair, nor are my brows;
My nose is crooked as my smile.

'How?' says the Satyr. 'Dare I trust a monster
Who cannot match his left hand with his right,
Who wears three several colours in his beard?'
Satyr, the question is well asked.

Nevertheless I am as trustworthy
As any shepherd in this wide valley.
I touch the doubtful with the left hand first,
Then with the right, under right brow and left
Peer at it doubtfully.
I am red-bearded wild, white-bearded mild,
Black-bearded merry.

And what the other shepherds know but singly
And easily at the first sight or touch
(Who follow a straight nose and who smile even)
I know with labour and most amply:
I know each possible lie and bias
That crookedness can cozen out of straightness.
Satyr, you need not shrink.

SYNTHETIC SUCH

'The sum of all the parts of Such –
   Of each laboratory scene –
Is Such.' While Science means this much
   And means no more, why, let it mean!

But were the science-men to find
   Some animating principle
Which gave synthetic Such a mind
   Vital, though metaphysical –

To Such, such an event, I think
    Would cause unscientific pain:
Science, appalled by thought, would shrink
    To its component parts again.

DRAGONS

These ancient dragons not committed yet
To any certain manner,
To any final matter,
Ranging creation recklessly,
Empowered to overset
Natural form and fate,
Freaking the sober species,
Smoothing rough accident to be
Level in a long series
And, each new century,
Forging for God a newer signet –
To these wild monsters boasting
Over and over
Their unchecked tyranny,
The only not a monster
In a small voice calling
Answered despitefully:
'Dragons, you count for nothing:
You are no more than weather,
The year's unsteadfastness
To which, now summer-basking,
To which, now in distress
Midwinter-shivering,
The mind pays no honour.'

THE NEXT TIME

And that inevitable accident
    On the familiar journey – roughly reckoned
By miles and shillings – in a cramped compartment
    Between a first hereafter and a second?

And when we passengers are given two hours,
   The wheels failing once more at Somewhere-Nowhere,
To climb out, stretch our legs and pick wild flowers –
   Suppose that this time I elect to stay there?

TO WHOM ELSE?

(1931)

LARGESSE TO THE POOR

I had been God's own time on travel
From stage to stage, guest-house to guest-house,
And at each stage furnished one room
To my own comfort, hoping God knows what,
Most happy when most sure that no condition
Might ever last in God's own time –
Unless to be death-numb, as I would not.

Yet I was always watchful at my choices
To change the bad at least for a no worse,
And I was strict nowhere to stay long.
In turn from each new home passing
I locked the door and pocketed the key,
Leaving behind goods plainly mine
(Should I return to claim them legally)
Of which I kept particular register –
In nightly rooms and chattels of the occasion
I was, to my own grief, a millionaire.

But now at last, out of God's firmament,
To break this endless journey –
Homeless to come where that awaits me
Which in my mind's unwearying discontent
I begged as pilgrim's due –
To fling my keys as largesse to the poor,
The always travel-hungry God-knows-who,
With, 'Let them fatten on my industry
Who find perfection and eternity
In might-be-worse, a roof over the head,
And any half-loaf better than no bread,
For which to thank God on their knees nightly.'

THE FELLOE'D YEAR

The pleasure of summer was its calm success
Over winter past and winter sequent:
The pleasure of winter was a warm counting,
'Summer comes again, when, surely.'
This pleasure and that pleasure touched
In a perpetual spring-with-autumn ache,
A creak and groan of season,
In which all moved,
In which all move yet – I the same, yet praying
That the twelve spokes of this round-felloe'd year
Be a fixed compass, not a turning wheel.

TIME

The vague sea thuds against the marble cliffs
And from their fragments age-long grinds
Pebbles like flowers.

Or the vague weather wanders in the fields,
And up spring flowers with coloured buds
Like marble pebbles.

The beauty of the flowers is Time, death-grieved;
The pebbles' beauty too is Time,
Life-wearied.

It is easy to admire a blowing flower
Or a smooth pebble flower-like freaked
By Time and vagueness.

Time is Time's lapse, the emulsive element coaxing
All obstinate locks and rusty hinges
To loving-kindness.

And am I proof against that lovesome pair,
Old age and childhood, twins in Time,
In sorrowful vagueness?

And will I not pretend the accustomed thanks:
Humouring age with filial flowers,
Childhood with pebbles?

ON RISING EARLY

Rising early and walking in the garden
Before the sun has properly climbed the hill –
His rays warming the roof, not yet the grass
That is white with dew still.

And not enough breeze to eddy a puff of smoke,
And out in the meadows a thick mist lying yet,
And nothing anywhere ill or noticeable –
Thanks indeed for that.

But was there ever a day with wit enough
To be always early, to draw the smoke up straight
Even at three o'clock of an afternoon,
To spare dullness or sweat?

Indeed, many such days I remember
That were dew-white and gracious to the last,
That ruled out meal-times, yet had no more hunger
Than was felt by rising a half-hour before breakfast,
Nor more fatigue – where was it that I went
So unencumbered, with my feet trampling
Like strangers on the past?

ON DWELLING

Courtesies of good-morning and good-evening
From rustic lips fail as the town encroaches:
Soon nothing passes but the cold quick stare
Of eyes that see ghosts, yet too many for fear.

Here I too walk, silent myself, in wonder
At a town not mine though plainly coextensive
With mine, even in days coincident:
In mine I dwell, in theirs like them I haunt.

And the green country, should I turn again there?
My bumpkin neighbours loom even ghostlier:
Like trees they murmur or like blackbirds sing
Courtesies of good-morning and good-evening.

ON NECESSITY

Dung-worms are necessary. And their certain need
Is dung, more dung, much dung and on such dung to feed.
And though I chose to sit and ponder for whole days
On dung-worms, what could I find more to tell or praise
Than their necessity, their numbers and their greed
To which necessity in me its daily tribute pays?

THE FOOLISH SENSES

Feverishly the eyes roll for what thorough
Sight may hold them still,
And most hysterically strains the throat
At the love song once easy to sing out
In minstrel serfdom to the armoured ill –
Let them cease now.

The view is inward, foolish eye: your rolling
Flatters the outward scene
To spread with sunset misery. Foolish throat,
That ill was colic, love its antidote,
And beauty, forced regret of who would sing
Of loves unclean.

No more, senses, shall you so confound me,
Playing your pageants through
That have outlived their uses in my mind –
Your outward staring that is inward blind
And the mad strummings of your melancholy,
Let them cease now.

DEVILISHLY PROVOKED

Devilishly provoked
  By my officious pen –
Where I demand one word
  It scrawls me nine or ten;
But each surviving word
  Resentfully I make
Sweat for those nine or ten
  I blotted for its sake.

And even more provoked
  By my officious heart
Whose emblems of desire
  From every corner start:
So little joy I find
  In their superfluous play
I curse the spell that drives
  My only love away.

THE LEGS

There was this road,
And it led up-hill,
And it led down-hill,
And round and in and out.

And the traffic was legs,
Legs from the knees down,
Coming and going,
Never pausing.

And the gutters gurgled
With the rain's overflow,
And the sticks on the pavement
Blindly tapped and tapped.

What drew the legs along
Was the never-stopping,
And the senseless, frightening
Fate of being legs.

Legs for the road,
The road for legs,
Resolutely nowhere
In both directions.

My legs at least
Were not in that rout:
On grass by the roadside
Entire I stood,

Watching the unstoppable
Legs go by
With never a stumble
Between step and step.

Though my smile was broad
The legs could not see,
Though my laugh was loud
The legs could not hear.

My head dizzied, then:
I wondered suddenly,
Might I too be a walker
From the knees down?

Gently I touched my shins.
The doubt unchained them:
They had run in twenty puddles
Before I regained them.

OGRES AND PYGMIES

Those famous men of old, the Ogres –
They had long beards and stinking arm-pits,
They were wide-mouthed, long-yarded and great-bellied
Yet not of taller stature, Sirs, than you.
They lived on Ogre-Strand, which was no place
But the churl's terror of their vast extent,
Where every foot was three-and-thirty inches
And every penny bought a whole hog.
Now of their company none survive, not one,
The times being, thank God, unfavourable

To all but nightmare shadows of their fame;
Their images stand howling on the hill
(The winds enforced against those wide mouths),
Whose granite haunches country-folk salute
With May Day kisses, and whose knobbed knees.

So many feats they did to admiration:
With their enormous throats they sang louder
Than ten cathedral choirs, with their grand yards
Stormed the most rare and obstinate maidenheads,
With their strong-gutted and capacious bellies
Digested stones and glass like ostriches.
They dug great pits and heaped huge mounds,
Deflected rivers, wrestled with the bear
And hammered judgements for posterity –
For the sweet-cupid-lipped and tassel-yarded
Delicate-stomached dwellers
In Pygmy Alley, where with brooding on them
A foot is shrunk to seven inches
And twelve-pence will not buy a spare rib.
And who would judge between Ogres and Pygmies –
The thundering text, the snivelling commentary –
Reading between such covers he will marvel
How his own members bloat and shrink again.

TO WHOM ELSE?

To whom else other than,
To whom else not of man
Yet in human state,
Standing neither in stead
Of self nor idle godhead,
Should I, man in man bounded,
Myself dedicate?

To whom else momently,
To whom else endlessly,
But to you, I?
To you who only,
To you who mercilessly,
To you who lovingly,
Plucked out the lie?

To whom else less acquaint,
To whom else without taint
Of death, death-true?
With great astonishment
Thankfully I consent
To my estrangement
From me in you.

AS IT WERE POEMS

I

In the legend of Reynard the Fox, Isegrim the Wolf, Grymbart the
Brock, Tybert the Cat, Cuwart the Hare, Bellyn the Ram, Baldwin the
Ass, Rukenawe the She-Ape and the rest of that company, where was I?

I was in the person of Bruin the Bear. And through the spite of Reynard
and my own greed and credulity I left behind my ears and the claws of
my fore-feet wedged in the trunk of a honey-tree.

In the legend of Troy where was I?

I was in the person of Ajax the son of Telamon. And Odysseus cheated
me of the prize of dead Achilles' arms. For he suborned Trojan captives
to testify that it was he who of us all had done their city the most harm.
Angered by this, I drove Troy's whole forces single-handed from the field.
But he covertly disposed slaughtered sheep in the place of the dead men
that I had strewn behind me and so fastened on me the name of madman.

In the legend of Robin Hood and his Merry Men, where was I?

I would prefer to be written down for the Sheriff of Nottingham, Robin's
enemy. But the natural truth is that I played the part of jolly Friar Tuck.
I took and gave great buffets. I was the gross fool of the greenwood.

In the legend of Jesus and his companions, where was I?

I was not Jesus himself, I was not John the Baptist, nor Pontius Pilate,
nor Judas Iscariot, nor even Peter. I was Lazarus sickening again in old
age long after the Crucifixion, and knowing that this time I could not cheat
death.

In the legend of Tobit, where was I?

I was not old Tobit himself, nor his kinsman Raguel, nor Sarah, Raguel's
daughter, nor the angel Raphael, nor the devil Asmodaeus. I was Tobias,
in sight of the towers of Ecbatana, with the gall, heart and liver of the fish
in a pouch by my side.

In the legend of that Lucius whom a witch of Thessaly turned into a dumb ass and who after many cruel adventures was restored to human shape by the intervention of the goddess Isis, where was I?

I was that impassioned ass in the gold trappings.

In the legend of Isis, of Python the destroyer, and of Osiris yearly drowned, where was I?

I was the drowned Osiris.

II

A sick girl went from house to house fitting people into legends of her own making. For you and for me she made a legend of the Christ and of King West the Shepherd and of the Golden Seal of Solomon long hidden in a cave of a hill at Jerusalem. You were the Christ-Woman and I was King West and she was Queen East with whom King West takes ship to Palestine: to find the Golden Seal. You as of old nursed the souls of the dead; she and I led the living.

But you reasoned with the sick girl: in the legend of the Christ there is no room for a sequel, it is a page covered with writing on both sides. Whoever would take the story further must find a clean page.

And I scolded angrily: Jesus, the Christ-Man, was a timid plagiarist. He made no new legends but said over the old ones, fitting himself into them. He was the Child foretold by Isaiah and the other prophets. Born at Bethlehem, equivocally of the seed of David, riding through Zion in prophesied glory on an ass's colt, stiffnecked to eschew love that he might be duly rejected and despised, busying himself vexatiously with the transgressions of others – he was true to the smallest articles of the legend and was drawn at last miserably to a well-documented death.

III

And how shall I call you, between the name concealed in the legends and that open name by which reason calls you and in which you reasonably answer – your name to whosoever would not have his fellow levelheads say, 'Look, he is mad, he is talking with a familiar spirit'?

'Call me,' you say, 'by my open name, so that you do not call upon any of those false spirits of the legends, those names of travesty. For in my open name I am jealous for my hinder name, that it should not be belied in drunken mystifications: am I not the most levelheaded of all your fellows? So let my open name be my closed name, and my closed name, my open name.'

To which I answer, 'And so the names of the travesty vanish into a single name against the meddling of men with the unchangeable import of the name: Isis, the secrecy of the import. In Egypt she was the holy name of the year of holy months: she was known to her priests as the invisible removed one, and to her people as the manifoldly incomprehensible. Every new moon crowned her with its peculiar head-dress – a rose, a star, an ear of barley, the horns of a goat: and she became the Moon itself, the single head of variety, Hecate by name. And Lilith, the owl of wisdom, because her lodges were held in stealthy darkness. At length the priests themselves forgot whom they meant in Isis. They even confounded her with the cowish Demeter, the blind force of Nature, and made her wife to Osiris.

'Now let all the false goddesses sprung from Isis – Pallas, Diana, Juno, Ceres and the rest – return to Isis, the greatly unnamed and greatly unseen and greatly unspoken with. Had but a single man seen her in Egypt, face to face, and known her for herself, then she would have been human woman, for other men to pass by and not know.

'So likewise Osiris was myself greatly meddling, Osiris the triple-named. He was Apollo in bright strength who dries up the floods. He was Dionysus, the growth of the vine. And he was Pluto, the dead man of the pit, the flooded Egypt to which life ever returns. Every year he rose again from the dead, but every year returned to the dead again. For she was only Isis, a closed name.'

ON PORTENTS

If strange things happen where she is,
So that men say that graves open
And the dead walk, or that futurity
Becomes a womb and the unborn are shed,
Such portents are not to be wondered at,
Being tourbillions in Time made
By the strong pulling of her bladed mind
Through that ever-reluctant element.

From *POEMS 1930–1933*

(1933)

THE BARDS

The bards falter in shame, their running verse
Stumbles, with marrow-bones the drunken diners
Pelt them for their delay.
It is a something fearful in the song
Plagues them – an unknown grief that like a churl
Goes commonplace in cowskin
And bursts unheralded, crowing and coughing,
An unpilled holly-club twirled in his hand,
Into their many-shielded, samite-curtained,
Jewel-bright hall where twelve kings sit at chess
Over the white-bronze pieces and the gold;
And by a gross enchantment
Flails down the rafters and leads off the queens –
The wild-swan-breasted, the rose-ruddy-cheeked
Raven-haired daughters of their admiration –
To stir his black pots and to bed on straw.

ULYSSES

To the much-tossed Ulysses, never done
    With woman whether gowned as wife or whore,
Penelope and Circe seemed as one:
She like a whore made his lewd fancies run,
    And wifely she a hero to him bore.

Their counter-changings terrified his way:
    They were the clashing rocks, Symplegades,
Scylla and Charybdis too were they;
Now angry storms frosting the sea with spray
    And now the lotus island's drunken ease.

They multiplied into the Sirens' throng,
   Forewarned by fear of whom he stood bound fast
Hand and foot helpless to the vessel's mast,
Yet would not stop his ears: daring their song
   He groaned and sweated till that shore was past.

One, two and many: flesh had made him blind,
   Flesh had one pleasure only in the act,
Flesh set one purpose only in the mind –
Triumph of flesh and afterwards to find
   Still those same terrors wherewith flesh was racked.

His wiles were witty and his fame far known,
Every king's daughter sought him for her own,
   Yet he was nothing to be won or lost.
   All lands to him were Ithaca: love-tossed
He loathed the fraud, yet would not bed alone.

DOWN, WANTON, DOWN!

Down, wanton, down! Have you no shame
That at the whisper of Love's name,
Or Beauty's, presto! up you raise
Your angry head and stand at gaze?

Poor bombard-captain, sworn to reach
The ravelin and effect a breach –
Indifferent what you storm or why,
So be that in the breach you die!

Love may be blind, but Love at least
Knows what is man and what mere beast;
Or Beauty wayward, but requires
More delicacy from her squires.

Tell me, my witless, whose one boast
Could be your staunchness at the post,
When were you made a man of parts
To think fine and profess the arts?

Will many-gifted Beauty come
Bowing to your bald rule of thumb,
Or Love swear loyalty to your crown?
Be gone, have done! Down, wanton, down!

THE PHILOSOPHER

Three blank walls, a barred window with no view,
A ceiling within reach of the raised hands,
A floor blank as the walls.

And, ruling out distractions of the body –
Growth of the hair and nails, a prison diet,
Thoughts of escape –

Ruling out memory and fantasy,
The distant tramping of a gaoler's boots,
Visiting mice and such,

What solace here for a laborious mind!
What a redoubtable and single task
One might attempt here:

Threading a logic between wall and wall,
Ceiling and floor, more accurate by far
Than the cob-spider's.

Truth captured without increment of flies:
Spinning and knotting till the cell became
A spacious other head

In which the emancipated reason might
Learn in due time to walk at greater length
And more unanswerably.

THE SUCCUBUS

Thus will despair
In ecstasy of nightmare
Fetch you a devil-woman through the air,
    To slide below the sweated sheet
And kiss your lips in answer to your prayer
    And lock her hands with yours and your feet with her feet.

Yet why does she
Come never as longed-for beauty
Slender and cool, with limbs lovely to see,
    (The bedside candle guttering high)
And toss her head so the thick curls fall free
    Of halo'd breast, firm belly and long, slender thigh?

Why with hot face,
With paunched and uddered carcase,
Sudden and greedily does she embrace,
    Gulping away your soul, she lies so close,
Fathering brats on you of her own race?
    Yet is the fancy grosser than your lusts were gross?

NOBODY

Nobody, ancient mischief, nobody,
Harasses always with an absent body.

Nobody coming up the road, nobody,
Like a tall man in a dark cloak, nobody.

Nobody about the house, nobody,
Like children creeping up the stairs, nobody.

Nobody anywhere in the garden, nobody,
Like a young girl quiet with needlework, nobody.

Nobody coming, nobody, not yet here,
Incessantly welcomed by the wakeful ear.

Until this nobody shall consent to die
Under his curse must everyone lie –

The curse of his envy, of his grief and fright,
Of sudden rape and murder screamed in the night.

DANEGELD

When I ceased to be a child
   I had great discontent
With a not-me unreconciled
   To what I thought and meant.

Some told me this, or that, or this –
   No counsel was the same:
Some preached God's holy purposes,
   Some used the Devil's name.

I made my truce with foreignness,
   As seemed the easiest plan:
The curious hauntings should express
   A me complete as man.

But this enlargement only spelt
   To see and yet be blind –
A pirate flesh allowed Danegeld
   By an unready mind.

Had I but held my truth apart
   And granted greed no say
In what I saw, deep in my heart,
   Must be my body way!

TRUDGE, BODY!

Trudge, body, and climb, trudge and climb,
But not to stand again on any peak of time:
Trudge, body!

I'll cool you, body, with a hot sun, that draws the sweat,
I'll warm you, body, with ice-water, that stings the blood,
I'll enrage you, body, with idleness, to do
And having done to sleep the long night through:
Trudge, body!

But in such cooling, warming, doing or sleeping,
No pause for satisfaction: henceforth you make address
Beyond heat to the heat, beyond cold to the cold,
Beyond enraged idleness to enraged idleness.
With no more hours of hope, and none of regret,
Before each sun may rise, you salute it for set:
Trudge, body!

MUSIC AT NIGHT

Voices in gentle harmony
Rise from the slopes above the midnight sea,
And every sound comes true and clear,
And the song's old:
It charms the wisest ear –

Night and the sea and music bind
Such forced perfection on the darkened mind
That, ah now, with that dying fall
All truth seems told
And one light shines for all –

The Moon, who from the hill-top streams
On each white face and throat her absent beams.
The song-enchanted fellows send
Their chords of gold
Rippling beyond time's end.

They link arms and all evils fly:
The flesh is tamed, the spirit circles high.
Each angel softly sings his part
Not proud, not bold,
Dream-ecstasied in heart.

But lamp-light glitters through the trees:
Lamp-light will check these minor harmonies,
And soon the busy Sun will rise
And blaze and scold
From the same hill-top skies.

WITHOUT PAUSE

Without cause and without
Pause blankness follows, turning
Man once more into
An autumn elm or
Ash in autumn mist,
His arms upraised, no
Heart or head, moreover
Nothing heard but now
This constant dropping always
Of such heavy drops
Distilled on finger-tips
From autumn mist and
Nowhere immanence or end
Or pause or cause,
But all is blankness
Seeming headache, yet not
Headache, yet not heartache:
Wanting heart and head,
The tree man – false,
Because the angry sap
Has faded down again
To tree roots dreading
Cold, and these abandoned
Leaves lie fallen flat
To make mould for
The pretty primroses that
Spring again in Spring
With little faces blank,

And sap again then
Rising proves the pain
Of Spring a fancy
Not attempted, no: so,
Until the frantic trial,
Blankness only made for
Pondering and tears against
That sudden lurch-away.

THE CLOCK MAN

The clocks are ticking with good will:
    They make a cheerful sound.
I am that temporizer still
    Who sends their hands around,
By fresh experiments with birth and age
Teasing the times each time to further courage.

You who are grateful for your birth
    To hours that ticked you free
(And gratefully relapse to earth)
    Your thanks are due to me –
Which I accept, inured to shame, and mock
My vows to timelessness, sworn with the clock.

THE COMMONS OF SLEEP

That ancient common-land of sleep
Where the close-herded nations creep
    On all fours, tongue to ground –
Be sure that every night or near
I, sheep-like too, go wandering there
    And wake to have slept sound.

How comfortable can be misrule
Of dream that whirls the antic spool
    Of sense-entangling twist,
Where proud in idiot state I sit
At skirmish of ingenious wit,
    My nape by fairies kissed.

'From the world's loving-cup to drink,
In sleep, can be no shame,' I think.
  'Sleep has no part in shame.'
But to lie down in hope to find
Licence for devilishness of mind –
  Will sleeping bear the blame?

For at such welcome dream extends
Its hour beyond where sleeping ends
  And eyes are washed for day,
Till mind and mind's own honour seem
That nightmare dream-within-the-dream
  Which brings the most dismay.

Then lamps burn red and glow-worm green
And naked dancers grin between
  The rusting bars of love.
Loud and severe the drunken jokes
Go clanging out in midnight strokes.
  I weep: I wake: I move.

WHAT TIMES ARE THESE?

Against the far slow fields of white,
A cloud came suddenly in sight
  And down the valley passed,
Compact and grey as bonfire smoke –
This one cloud only, like a joke,
  It flew so fast.

And more: the shape, no inexact
Idle half-likeness but a fact
  Which all my senses knew,
Was a great dragon's and instead
Of fangs it had the scoffing head
  Of an old Jew.

What times are these that visions bear
So plainly down the morning air
  With wings and scales and beard?
I stared, and quick, a swirl of wind
Caught at his head: he writhed and thinned,
  He disappeared.

The last that stayed were the wide wings
And long tail barbed with double stings:
   These drifted on alone
Over the watch-tower and the bay
So out to open sea, where they
   Did not fade soon.

I knew him well, the Jew, for he
Was honest Uncle Usury
   Who lends you blood for blood:
His dragon's claws were keen and just
To bleed the body into dust,
   As the bond stood.

What times are these – to be allowed
This ancient vision of grey cloud
   Gone in a casual breath?
The times of the torn dragon-wing
Still threatening seaward and the sting
   Still poised for death.

From *COLLECTED POEMS*

(1938)

THE CHRISTMAS ROBIN

The snows of February had buried Christmas
Deep in the woods, where grew self-seeded
The fir-trees of a Christmas yet unknown,
Without a candle or a strand of tinsel.

Nevertheless when, hand in hand, plodding
Between the frozen ruts, we lovers paused
And 'Christmas trees!' cried suddenly together,
Christmas was there again, as in December.

We velveted our love with fantasy
Down a long vista-row of Christmas trees,
Whose coloured candles slowly guttered down
As grandchildren came trooping round our knees.

But he knew better, did the Christmas robin –
The murderous robin with his breast aglow
And legs apart, in a spade-handle perched:
He prophesied more snow, and worse than snow.

CERTAIN MERCIES

Now must all satisfaction
Appear mere mitigation
Of an accepted curse?

Must we henceforth be grateful
That the guards, though spiteful,
Are slow of foot and wit?

That by night we may spread
Over the plank bed
A thin coverlet?

That the rusty water
In the unclean pitcher
Our thirst quenches?

That the rotten, detestable
Food is yet eatable
By us ravenous?

That the prison censor
Permits a weekly letter?
(We may write: 'We are well.')

That, with patience and deference,
We do not experience
The punishment cell?

That each new indignity
Defeats only the body,
Pampering the spirit
With obscure, proud merit?

THE CUIRASSIERS OF THE FRONTIER

Goths, Vandals, Huns, Isaurian mountaineers,
Made Roman by our Roman sacrament,
We can know little (as we care little)
Of the Metropolis: her candled churches,
Her white-gowned pederastic senators,
The cut-throat factions of her Hippodrome,
The eunuchs of her draped saloons.

Here is the frontier, here our camp and place –
Beans for the pot, fodder for horses,
And Roman arms. Enough. He who among us
At full gallop, the bowstring to his ear,
Lets drive his heavy arrows, to sink
Stinging through Persian corslets damascened,
Then follows with the lance – he has our love.

The Christ bade Holy Peter sheathe his sword,
Being outnumbered by the Temple guard.
And this was prudence, the cause not yet lost
While Peter might persuade the crowd to rescue.
Peter renegued, breaking his sacrament.
With us the penalty is death by stoning,
Not to be made a bishop.

In Peter's Church there is no faith nor truth,
Nor justice anywhere in palace or court.
That we continue watchful on the rampart
Concerns no priest. A gaping silken dragon,
Puffed by the wind, suffices us for God.
We, not the City, are the Empire's soul:
A rotten tree lives only in its rind.

CALLOW CAPTAIN

The sun beams jovial from an ancient sky,
    Flooding the round hills with heroic spate.
A callow captain, glaring, sword at thigh,
    Trots out his charger through the camp gate.
Soon comes the hour, his marriage hour, and soon
    He fathers children, reigns with ancestors
Who, likewise serving in the wars, won
    For a much-tattered flag renewed honours.

A wind ruffles the book, and he whose name
    Was mine vanishes; all is at an end.
Fortunate soldier: to be spared shame
    Of chapter-years unprofitable to spend,
To ride off into reticence, nor throw
    Before the story-sun a long shadow.

THE STRANGER

He noted from the hill top,
Fixing a cynic eye upon
The stranger in the distance
Up the green track approaching,
She had a sure and eager tread;
He guessed mere grace of body
Which would not for unloveliness
Of cheek or mouth or other feature
Retribution pay.

He watched as she came closer,
And half-incredulously saw
How lovely her face also,
Her hair, her naked hands.
Come closer yet, deception!
But closer as she came, the more
Unarguable her loveliness;
He frowned and blushed, confessing slowly,
No, it was no cheat.

To find her foolish-hearted
Would rid his baffled thought of her;
But there was wisdom in that brow
Of who might be a Muse.
Then all abashed he dropped his head:
For in his summer haughtiness
He had cried lust at her for whom
Through many deaths he had kept vigil,
Wakeful for her voice.

THE SMOKY HOUSE

He woke to a smell of smoke.
    The house was burning.
His room-mates reassured him:
    'Smouldering, not burning.'

'Break no window,' they warned,
    'Make no draught:
Nobody wants a blaze.'
    Choking, they laughed

At such a stubborn fellow
   Unresigned to smoke,
To sore lungs and eyes –
   For them a joke –

Yet who would not consent,
   At a cry or curse,
That water on the smoulder
   Made the smoke worse.

VARIABLES OF GREEN

Grass-green and aspen-green,
Laurel-green and sea-green,
Fine-emerald-green,
And many another hue:
As green commands the variables of green
So love my loves of you.

THE GOBLET

From this heroic skull buried
Secretly in a tall ant-castle,
Drawn out, stripped of its jawbone, blanched
In sun all the hot summer,
Mounted with bands of hammered gold,
The eye-holes paned with crystal –
From this bright skull, a hero's goblet now,
What wine is to drink?

A dry draught, medicinal,
Not the sweet must that flowed
Too new between these lips
When here were living lips,
That pampered tongue
When here was tasting tongue.

But who shall be the drinker?
That passionate man, his rival
In endless love and battle,
Who overcame him at the end?
Or I, the avenging heir? I taste
Wine from a dead man's head
Whose griefs were not my own?

If I this skull a goblet made
It was a pious duty, nothing more.
Here is clean bone, and gold and crystal,
So may the ghost sigh gratitude
To drink his death, as I would mine.

FIEND, DRAGON, MERMAID

The only Fiend, religious adversary,
Ceased in the end to plague me, dying
By his own hand on a scarred mountain-top
Full in my sight. His valedictory
Was pity for me as for one whose house,
Swept and garnished, now lay open
As hospice for a score of lesser devils:
I had no better friend than him, he swore.
His extreme spasms were of earthquake force –
They hurled me without sense on the sharp rocks;
The corpse, ridiculous – that long, thin neck,
Those long, thin, hairy legs, the sawdust belly –
This same was Hell's prince in his prime,
And lamed me in his fall.

Next of the ancient dragon I was freed
Which was an emanation of my fears
And in the Fiend's wake followed always.
An acid breeze puffed at his wings: he flew
Deathward in cloudy blue and gold, frightful,
Yet showing patches of webbed nothingness
Like soap-bubbles before they burst –
Which was a cause for smiling.
Furious, he glared: 'Confess, my dragon glory
Was a resplendency that seared the gaze –
All else mere candle-light and glowing ember!'

The mermaid last, with long hair combed and coiled
And childish-lovely face, swam slowly by.
She called my name, pleading an answer,
Yet knew that though my blood is salty still
It swings to other tides than the old sea.
'Greedy mermaid, are there no mariners
To plunge into green water when you sing,
That you should stretch your arms for me?
Fain to forget all winds and weathers
And perish in your beauty?' So she turned
With tears, affecting innocence:
'Proud heart, where shall you find again
So kind a breast as pillow for your woes,
Or such soft lips? Your peace was my love's care.'
'Peace is no dream of mariners,' I said.
She dived; and quit of dragon, Fiend and her
I turned my gaze to the encounter of
The later genius, who of my pride and fear
And love
No monster made but me.

FRAGMENT OF A LOST POEM

O the clear moment, when from the mouth
A word flies, current immediately
Among friends; or when a loving gift astounds
As the identical wish nearest the heart;
Or when a stone, volleyed in sudden danger,
Strikes the rabid beast full on the snout!

Moments in never....

GALATEA AND PYGMALION

Galatea, whom his furious chisel
From Parian stone had by greed enchanted,
Fulfilled, so they say, Pygmalion's longings:
   Stepped from the pedestal on which she stood,
Bare in his bed laid her down, lubricious,
With low responses to his drunken raptures,
   Enroyalled his body with her demon blood.

Alas, Pygmalion had so well plotted
The articulation of his woman monster
That schools of eager connoisseurs beset
   Her single person with perennial suit;
Whom she (a judgement on the jealous artist)
Admitted rankly to a comprehension
   Of themes that crowned her own, not his repute.

THE DEVIL'S ADVICE TO STORY-TELLERS

Lest men suspect your tale to be untrue,
Keep probability – some say – in view.
But my advice to story-tellers is:
Weigh out no gross of probabilities,
Nor yet make diligent transcriptions of
Known instances of virtue, crime or love.
To forge a picture that will pass for true,
Do conscientiously what liars do –
Born liars, not the lesser sort that raid
The mouths of others for their stock-in-trade:
Assemble, first, all casual bits and scraps
That may shake down into a world perhaps;
People this world, by chance created so,
With random persons whom you do not know –
The teashop sort, or travellers in a train
Seen once, guessed idly at, not seen again;
Let the erratic course they steer surprise
Their own and your own and your readers' eyes;
Sigh then, or frown, but leave (as in despair)
Motive and end and moral in the air;
Nice contradiction between fact and fact
Will make the whole read human and exact.

LUNCH-HOUR BLUES

His ears discount the ragged noise,
   His nose, the tangled smell;
His eyes when prodigies go past
   Look up, but never dwell.

His tongue not even registers
   The juices of his plate,
His hands (some other eater's hands?)
   Will not communicate.

He's thrown the senses from their seat,
   As Indian heroes do –
An act more notable were not
   The mind unseated too.

O yogey-bogey lunching man,
   Lunch on, against the bill –
Your service to the ascetic rule
   And to the chiming till.

HOTEL BED AT LUGANO

Even in hotel beds the hair tousles.
But this is observation, not complaint –
'Complaints should please be dropped in the complaint-box' –
'Which courteously we beg you to vacate
In that clean state as you should wish to find it.'

And the day after Carnival, today,
I found, in the square, a crimson cardboard heart:
'Anna Maria', it read. Otherwise, friends,
No foreign news – unless that here they drink
Red wine from china bowls; here anis-roots
Are stewed like turnips; here funiculars
Light up at dusk, two crooked constellations;
And if bells peal a victory or great birth,
That will be cows careering towards the pail.

'It is not yet the season,' pleads the Porter,
'That comes in April, when the rain most rains.'
Trilingual Switzer fish in Switzer lakes
Pining for rain and bread-crumbs of the season,
In thin reed-beds you pine!

                                  A-bed drowsing,
(While the hair slowly tousles) uncomplaining …
Anna Maria's heart under my pillow
Provokes no furious dream. Who is this Anna?
A Switzer maiden among Switzer maidens,
Child of the children of that fox who never
Ate the sour grapes: her teeth not set on edge.

PROGRESSIVE HOUSING

At history's compulsion
A welcome greeted once
All gross or trivial objects
That reached, by grand endurance,
Their bicentenary year.

But not two thousand years
Could sanctify this building
With bat-and-ivy ruin,
Or justify these furnishings
As woe-begone antiques.

No doubt it is good news
That the spell of age is lifted,
The museums' greed rebuked:
Yet might this not have come about
Less nastily perhaps?

LEDA

Heart, with what lonely fears you ached,
    How lecherously mused upon
That horror with which Leda quaked
    Under the spread wings of the swan.

Then soon your mad religious smile
    Made taut the belly, arched the breast,
And there beneath your god awhile
    You strained and gulped your beastliest.

Pregnant you are, as Leda was,
    Of bawdry, murder and deceit;
Perpetuating night because
    The after-languors hang so sweet.

THE FLORIST ROSE

This wax-mannequin nude, the florist rose,
She of the long stem and too glossy leaf,
Is dead to honest greenfly and leaf-cutter:
Behind plate-glass watches the yellow fogs.

Claims kin with the robust male aeroplane
Whom eagles hate and phantoms of the air,
Who has no legend, as she breaks from legend –
From fellowship with sword and sail and crown.

Experiment's flower, scentless (he its bird);
Is dewed by the spray-gun; is tender-thorned;
Pouts, false-virginal, between bud and bloom;
Bought as a love-gift, droops within the day.

BEING TALL

Long poems written by tall men
Wear a monstrous look; but then
Would these do better to write short
Like poets of the midget sort?

Here is no plea for medium height
In poets or what poets write:
Only a trifle to recall
The days when I had grown too tall,

When jealous dwarfs leered up at me
From somewhere between shoe and knee.
I grinned them my contempt and fear,
Stooping till our heads came near.

Then all I wrote, until in rage
I whipped them off the path and page,
Bent like a hook this way and that —
And who could guess what I was at?

But rage was not enough to teach
My natural height and breadth and reach:
It wanted love with kindly phlegm
To shrink my bones and straighten them.

AT FIRST SIGHT

'Love at first sight,' some say, misnaming
Discovery of twinned helplessness
Against the huge tug of procreation.

But friendship at first sight? This also
Catches fiercely at the surprised heart
So that the cheek blanches and then blushes.

RECALLING WAR

Entrance and exit wounds are silvered clean,
The track aches only when the rain reminds.
The one-legged man forgets his leg of wood,
The one-armed man his jointed wooden arm.
The blinded man sees with his ears and hands
As much or more than once with both his eyes.
Their war was fought these twenty years ago
And now assumes the nature-look of time,
As when the morning traveller turns and views
His wild night-stumbling carved into a hill.

What, then, was war? No mere discord of flags
But an infection of the common sky
That sagged ominously upon the earth
Even when the season was the airiest May.
Down pressed the sky, and we, oppressed, thrust out
Boastful tongue, clenched fist and valiant yard.
Natural infirmities were out of mode,
For Death was young again: patron alone
Of healthy dying, premature fate-spasm.

Fear made fine bed-fellows. Sick with delight
At life's discovered transitoriness,
Our youth became all-flesh and waived the mind.
Never was such antiqueness of romance,
Such tasty honey oozing from the heart.
And old importances came swimming back –
Wine, meat, log-fires, a roof over the head,
A weapon at the thigh, surgeons at call.
Even there was a use again for God –
A word of rage in lack of meat, wine, fire,
In ache of wounds beyond all surgeoning.

War was return of earth to ugly earth,
War was foundering of sublimities,
Extinction of each happy art and faith
By which the world had still kept head in air,
Protesting logic or protesting love,
Until the unendurable moment struck –
The inward scream, the duty to run mad.

And we recall the merry ways of guns –
Nibbling the walls of factory and church
Like a child, piecrust; felling groves of trees
Like a child, dandelions with a switch.
Machine-guns rattle toy-like from a hill,
Down in a row the brave tin-soldiers fall:
A sight to be recalled in elder days
When learnedly the future we devote
To yet more boastful visions of despair.

X

Detective, criminal or corpse –
Who is the I of the story?
Agreed, the first stage of a narrative
Permits mystification – the I
Rainbowing clues and fancies.
That is the time of drawing-room charades:
Each mask resembles every other mask,
And every beard is false.
But now the story hardens and grows adult:
By the beginning of the final chapter

Holmes and Moriarty are distinct,
The corpse at least not either's –
I joins merrily in the man-hunt
With a key to the code.

The great K.C. is briefed at last,
The Judge is trying on his sternest wig,
The public queueing up with camp-stools.
Do you dare to tell us, I, at this late hour,
That who you are still waits decision?
Malice Aforethought or Unfit to Plead?

PARENT TO CHILDREN

When you grow up, are no more children,
Nor am I then your parent:
The day of settlement falls.

'Parent', mortality's reminder,
In each son's mouth or daughter's
A word of shame and rage!

I, who begot you, ask no pardon of you;
Nor may the soldier ask
Pardon of the strewn dead.

The procreative act was blind:
It was not you I sired then –
For who sires friends, as you are mine now?

In fear begotten, I begot in fear.
Would you have had me cast fear out
So that you should not be?

TO CHALLENGE DELIGHT

Living is delight –
Lovers, even, confess it;
And what could compare
With the pain these suffer?
Delight is all repeating –
Doves coo, cats purr, men sing.

'Challenge delight, of purpose,
And you pull Nature's nose
In self-spite, you slap her face
In the portico of her palace,
Exchange her sportive sun
For a black perfection.'

Thus hardly anybody
Will make delight his study.
Its meaning to know
Would be emptier than sorrow,
That Sunday morning respite
From a hard week of delight.

TO WALK ON HILLS

To walk on hills is to employ legs
As porters of the head and heart
Jointly adventuring towards
Perhaps true equanimity.

To walk on hills is to see sights
And hear sounds unfamiliar.
When in wind the pine-tree roars,
When crags with bleatings echo,
When water foams below the fall,
Heart records that journey
As memorable indeed;
Head reserves opinion,
Confused by the wind.

A view of three shires and the sea!
Seldom so much at once appears
Of the coloured world, says heart.
Head is glum, says nothing.

Legs become weary, halting
To sprawl in a rock's shelter,
While the sun drowsily blinks
On head at last brought low –
This giddied passenger of legs
That has no word to utter.

Heart does double duty,
As heart, and as head,
With portentous trifling.
A castle, on its crag perched,
Across the miles between is viewed
With awe as across years.

Now a daisy pleases,
Pleases and astounds, even,
That on a garden lawn could blow
All summer long with no esteem.

And the buzzard's cruel poise,
And the plover's misery,
And the important beetle's
Blue-green-shiny back....

To walk on hills is to employ legs
To march away and lose the day.
Tell us, have you known shepherds?
And are they not a witless race,
Prone to quaint visions?
Not thus from solitude
(Solitude sobers only)
But from long hilltop striding.

TO BRING THE DEAD TO LIFE

To bring the dead to life
Is no great magic.
Few are wholly dead:
Blow on a dead man's embers
And a live flame will start.

Let his forgotten griefs be now,
And now his withered hopes;
Subdue your pen to his handwriting
Until it prove as natural
To sign his name as yours.

Limp as he limped,
Swear by the oaths he swore;
If he wore black, affect the same;
If he had gouty fingers,
Be yours gouty too.

Assemble tokens intimate of him –
A seal, a cloak, a pen:
Around these elements then build
A home familiar to
The greedy revenant.

So grant him life, but reckon
That the grave which housed him
May not be empty now:
You in his spotted garments
Shall yourself lie wrapped.

TO EVOKE POSTERITY

To evoke posterity
Is to weep on your own grave,
Ventriloquizing for the unborn:
'Would you were present in flesh, hero!
What wreaths and junketings!'

And the punishment is fixed:
To be found fully ancestral,
To be cast in bronze for a city square,
To dribble green in times of rain
And stain the pedestal.

Spiders in the spread beard;
A life proverbial
On clergy lips a-cackle;
Eponymous institutes,
Their luckless architecture.

Two more dates of life and birth
For the hour of special study
From which all boys and girls of mettle
Twice a week play truant
And worn excuses try.

Alive, you have abhorred
The crowds on holiday
Jostling and whistling – yet would you air
Your death-mask, smoothly lidded,
Along the promenade?

ANY HONEST HOUSEWIFE

Any honest housewife could sort them out,
Having a nose for fish, an eye for apples.
Is it any mystery who are the sound,
And who the rotten? Never, by her lights.

Any honest housewife who, by ill-fortune,
Ever engaged a slut to scrub for her
Could instantly distinguish from the workers
The lazy, the liars, and the petty thieves.

Does this denote a sixth peculiar sense
Gifted to housewives for their vestal needs?
Or is it failure of the usual five
In all unthrifty writers on this head?

DEFEAT OF THE REBELS

The enemy forces are in wild flight.
Poor souls (you say), they were intoxicated
With rhetoric and banners, thought it enough
To believe and to blow trumpets, to wear
That menacing lie in their shakos.

Enough: it falls on us to shoot them down,
The incorrigibles and cowards,
Where they shiver behind rocks, or in ditches
Seek graves that have no headstones to them –
Such prisoners were unprofitable.

Now as our vanguard, pressing on,
Dislodges them from village and town,
Who yelling abandon packs and cloaks,
Their arms and even the day's rations,
We are not abashed by victory,

We raise no pitying monument
To check the counter-stroke of fortune.
These are not spoils: we recognize
Our own strewn gear, that never had been robbed
But for our sloth and hesitancy.

THE GRUDGE

Judging the gift, his eye of greed
Weighed resentment against need.
Resentment won, for to receive
Is not so blessèd as to give:
To give is to undo a lack.
Nor could the gift be deeded back
But with vile ingratitude –
And gifts, like embassies, he viewed
As if enclaves of foreign ground.
Nor could a compromise be found
Between the giver's thoughtfulness
And his own more-than-thanklessness.
The gift held neither bribe nor blame
But with cruel aptness came,

Disproving self-sufficiency –
That cloaked-in-silence misery
Which had, itself, no gifts to make,
Grudged to bend, and would not break.

NEVER SUCH LOVE

Twined together and, as is customary,
For words of rapture groping, they
'Never such love,' swore, 'ever before was!'
Contrast with all loves that had failed or staled
Registered their own as love indeed.

And was this not to blab idly
The heart's fated inconstancy?
Better in love to seal the love-sure lips,
For truly love was before words were,
And no word given, no word broken.

When the name 'love' is uttered
(Love, the near-honourable malady
With which in greed and haste they
Each other do infect and curse)
Or, worse, is written down....

Wise after the event, by love withered,
A 'never more!' most frantically
Sorrow and shame would proclaim
Such as, they'd swear, never before were:
True lovers even in this.

THE HALFPENNY

His lucky halfpenny after years of solace
Mixed with the copper crowd, was gone.
He grieved all day, a comic grief
But by next morning sadly verified:
His face was not his own!

A man as like his neighbours, you would say,
As halfpenny like halfpence, yet
Marked from among them by the luck
This halfpenny of halfpence brought him,
Disfigured by its loss.

Made by luck, by lack of luck unmade –
A bankrupt sameness was his doom:
To have had luck and now to have none,
To have no face but what he borrowed
From neighbours' charity.

Begging at the kerb-side, he won it back,
The very coin – fit for a fob
If such he had, but all was rags now.
'To be my ill-luck token,' he rejoiced,
'My ill luck now my own!'

Pride of differentiated face:
'And what are rags and broken shoes
When I can boast myself to strangers,
Leaping face-forward from their high roofs,
My ill luck in my hand?'

THE FALLEN SIGNPOST

The signpost of four arms is down,
But one names your departure-town:
With this for guide you may replant
Your post and choose which road you want –

Logic that only seems obscure
To those deliberately not sure
Whether a journey should begin
With cross-roads or with origin.

The square post, and the socket square –
Now which way round to set it there?
Thus from the problem coaxing out
Four further elements of doubt,

They make the simple cross-roads be
A crux of pure dubiety
Demanding how much more concern
Than to have taken the wrong turn!

THE CHINA PLATE

From a crowded barrow in a street-market
The plate was ransomed for a few coppers,
Was brought gleefully home, given a place
On a commanding shelf.

'Quite a museum-piece,' an expert cries
(Eyeing it through the ready pocket-lens) –
As though a glass case would be less sepulchral
Than the barrow-hearse!

For weeks this plate retells the history
Whenever an eye runs in that direction:
'Near perdition I was, in a street-market
With rags and old shoes.'

'A few coppers' – here once again
The purchaser's proud hand lifts down
The bargain, displays the pot-bank sign
Scrawled raggedly underneath.

Enough, permit the treasure to forget
The emotion of that providential purchase,
Becoming a good citizen of the house
Like its fellow-crockery.

Let it dispense sandwiches at a party
And not be noticed in the drunken buzz,
Or little cakes at afternoon tea
When cakes are in demand.

Let it regain a lost habit of life,
Foreseeing death in honourable breakage
Somewhere between the kitchen and the shelf –
To be sincerely mourned.

IDLE HANDS

To-day, all day, for once he did nothing –
A proud report from one whose hands,
Of Satan warned when young, engross him
Always with over-busyness. Nothing –
Pleasure unposted in the journal.

This is for eyes that ask no illustration,
Not for those poor adepts at less than nothing
Who would enquire: Was it town-idleness,
Or did he drink the sun by the calm sea
Until the sunset washed upon his daze,
Then home to supper, and the bedside lamp?

He did nothing; tells you plainly so.

Where he did nothing is no part of this:
Whether by the wild sea or the calm sea
Or where the pavement-coloured dog befouls
The pavement-kerb. It is enough that
He did nothing, neither less nor more,
Leaving the day, for a remembrance,
A clear bubble in Time's chalky glass.

THE LAUREATE

Like a lizard in the sun, though not scuttling
When men approach, this wretch, this thing of rage,
Scowls and sits rhyming in his horny age.

His time and truth he has not bridged to ours,
But shrivelled by long heliotropic idling
He croaks at us his out-of-date humours.

Once long ago here was a poet; who died.
See how remorse twitching his mouth proclaims
It was no natural death, but suicide.

Arrogant, lean, unvenerable, he
Still turns for comfort to the western flames
That glitter a cold span above the sea.

A JEALOUS MAN

To be homeless is a pride
To the jealous man prowling
Hungry down the night lanes,

Who has no steel at his side,
No drink hot in his mouth,
But a mind dream-enlarged,

Who witnesses warfare,
Man with woman, hugely
Raging from hedge to hedge:

The raw knotted oak-club
Clenched in the raw fist,
The ivy-noose well flung,

The thronged din of battle,
Gaspings of the throat-snared,
Snores of the battered dying,

Tall corpses, braced together,
Fallen in clammy furrows,
Male and female,

Or, among haulms of nettle
Humped, in noisome heaps,
Male and female.

He glowers in the choked roadway
Between twin churchyards,
Like a turnip ghost.

(Here, the rain-worn headstone,
There, the Celtic cross
In rank white marble.)

This jealous man is smitten,
His fear-jerked forehead
Sweats a fine musk;

A score of bats bewitched
By the ruttish odour
Swoop singing at his head;

Nuns bricked up alive
Within the neighbouring wall
Wail in cat-like longing.

Crow, cocks, crow loud,
Reprieve the doomed devil –
Has he not died enough?

Now, out of careless sleep,
She wakes and greets him coldly,
The woman at home,

She, with a private wonder
At shoes bemired and bloody –
His war was not hers.

THE CLOAK

Into exile with only a few shirts,
Some gold coin and the necessary papers.
But winds are contrary: the Channel packet
Time after time returns the sea-sick peer
To Sandwich, Deal or Rye. He does not land,
But keeps his cabin; so at last we find him
In humble lodgings maybe at Dieppe,
His shirts unpacked, his night-cap on a peg,
Passing the day at cards and swordsmanship
Or merry passages with chambermaids,
By night at his old work. And all is well –
The country wine wholesome although so sharp,
And French his second tongue; a faithful valet
Brushes his hat and brings him newspapers.
This nobleman is at home anywhere,
His castle being, the valet says, his title.
The cares of an estate would incommode
Such tasks as now his Lordship has in hand.
His Lordship, says the valet, contemplates
A profitable absence of some years.
Has he no friend at Court to intercede?
He wants none: exile's but another name
For an old habit of non-residence
In all but the recesses of his cloak.
It was this angered a great personage.

THE HALLS OF BEDLAM

Forewarned of madness:
In three days' time at dusk
The fit masters him.

How to endure those days?
(Forewarned is foremad)
' – Normally, normally.'

He will gossip with children,
Argue with elders,
Check the cash account.

'I shall go mad that day –'
The gossip, the argument,
The neat marginal entry.

His case is not uncommon,
The doctors pronounce;
But prescribe no cure.

To be mad is not easy,
Will earn him no more
Than a niche in the news.

Then to-morrow, children,
To-morrow or the next day
He resigns from the firm.

His boyhood's ambition
Was to become an artist –
Like any City man's.

To the walls and halls of Bedlam
The artist is welcome –
Bold brush and full palette.

Through the cell's grating
He will watch his children
To and from school.

'Suffer the little children
To come unto me
With their Florentine hair!'

A very special story
For their very special friends –
They burst in the telling:

Of an evil thing, armed,
Tap-tapping on the door,
Tap-tapping on the floor,
'On the third day at dusk.'

Father in his shirt-sleeves
Flourishing a hatchet –
Run, children, run!

No one could stop him,
No one understood;
And in the evening papers....

(Imminent genius,
Troubles at the office,
Normally, normally,
As if already mad.)

OR TO PERISH BEFORE DAY

The pupils of the eye expand
And from near-nothings build up sight;
The pupil of the heart, the ghost,
Swelling parades the dewy land:

With cowardice and with self-esteem
Makes terror in the track that through
The fragrant spotted pasture runs;
And a bird wails across the dream.

Now, if no heavenly window shines
Nor angel-voices cheer the way,
The ghost will overbear the man
And mark his head with fever-signs.

The flowers of dusk that he has pulled
To wonder at when morning's here
Are snail-shells upon straws of grass –
So easily the eye is gulled.

The sounding words that his mouth fill
Upon to-morrow's lip shall droop;
The legs that slide with skating ease
Be stiff to the awakened will.

Or, should he perish before day,
He leaves his lofty ghost behind
Perpetuating uncontrolled
This hour of glory and dismay.

A COUNTRY MANSION

This ancient house so notable
For its gables and great staircase,
Its mulberry-trees and alleys of clipped yew,
Humbles the show of every near demesne.

At the beginning it acknowledged owners –
Father, son, grandson –
But then, surviving the last heirs of the line,
Became a place for life-tenancy only.

At the beginning, no hint of fate,
No rats and no hauntings;
In the garden, then, the fruit-trees grew
Slender and similar in long rows.

A bedroom with a low ceiling
Caused little fret at first;
But gradual generations of discomfort
Have bred an anger there to stifle sleep.

And the venerable dining-room,
Where port in Limerick glasses
Glows twice as red reflected
In the memory-mirror of the waxed table –

For a time with paint and flowered paper
A mistress tamed its walls,
But pious antiquarian hands, groping,
Rediscovered the grey panels beneath.

Children love the old house tearfully,
And the parterres, how fertile!
Married couples under the testers hugging
Enjoy carnality's bliss as nowhere else.

A smell of mould from loft to cellar,
Yet sap still brisk in the oak
Of the great beams: if ever they use a saw
It will stain, as cutting a branch from a green tree.

... Old Parr had lived one hundred years and five
(So to King Charles he bragged)
When he did open penance, in a sheet,
For fornication with posterity.

Old Parr died; not so the mansion
Whose inhabitants, bewitched,
Pour their fresh blood through its historic veins
And, if a tile blow from the roof, tremble.

The last-born of this race of sacristans
Broke the long spell, departed;
They lay his knife and fork at every meal
And every evening warm his bed;

Yet cannot draw him back from the far roads
For trifling by the lily-pool
Or wine at the hushed table where they meet,
The guests of genealogy.

It was his childhood's pleasure-ground
And still may claim his corpse,
Yet foster-cradle or foster-grave
He will not count as home.

This rebel does not hate the house,
Nor its dusty joys impugn:
No place less reverend could provoke
So proud an absence from it.

He has that new malaise of time:
Gratitude choking with vexation
That he should opulently inherit
The goods and titles of the extinct.

THE EREMITES

We may well wonder at those bearded hermits
Who like the scorpion and the basilisk
Couched in the desert sands, to undo
Their scurfy flesh with tortures.

They drank from pools fouled by the ass and camel,
Chewed uncooked millet pounded between stones,
Wore but a shame-rag, dusk or dawn,
And rolled in thorny places.

In the wilderness there are no women;
Yet hermits harbour in their shrunken loins
A penitential paradise,
A leaping-house of glory.

Solomons of a thousand lusty love-chants,
These goatish men, burned Aethiopian black,
Kept vigil till the angelic whores
Should lift the latch of pleasure.

And what Atellan orgies of the soul
Were celebrated then among the rocks
They testify themselves in books
That rouse Atellan laughter.

Haled back at last to wear the ring and mitre,
They clipped their beards and, for their stomachs' sake,
Drank now and then a little wine,
And tasted cakes and honey.

Observe then how they disciplined the daughters
Of noble widows, who must fast and thirst,
Abjure down-pillows, rouge and curls,
Deform their delicate bodies:

Whose dreams were curiously beset by visions
Of stinking hermits in a wilderness
Pressing unnatural lusts on them
Until they wakened screaming.

Such was the virtue of our pious fathers:
To refine pleasure in the hungry dream.
Pity for them, but pity too for us –
Our beds by their leave lain in.

ADVOCATES

Fugitive firs and larches for a moment
Caught, past midnight, by our headlight beam
On that mad journey through unlasting lands
I cannot put a name to, years ago,
(And my companions drowsy-drunk) – those trees
Resume again their sharp appearance, perfect
Of spur and tassel, claiming memory,
Claiming affection: 'Will we be included
In the catalogue? Yes, yes?' they plead.

Green things, you are already there enrolled.
And should a new resentment gnaw in me
Against my dear companions of that journey
(Strangers already then, in thought and deed)
You shall be advocates, charged to deny
That all the good I lived with them is lost.

SELF-PRAISE

No, self-praise does not recommend.
    What shall I do with mine
When so few Englishmen pretend
    Not to be dogs or swine,

That to assume the peacock's part,
    To scream and spread the tail,
Is held a doom-defying art
    And witnesses turn pale?

But praise from fellow-creatures is
    (All Englishmen agree)
The sweetest of experiences
    And confers modesty,

And justifies the silent boast
    Of a bemedalled line:
The most dog-true of dogs, the most
    Egregious swine of swine.

O, let me suffer in self-praise,
    Unfit to occupy
The kennel, for my headstrong ways,
    Too squeamish for the sty.

THE CHALLENGE

In ancient days a glory swelled my thighs,
And sat like fear between my shoulder-blades,
And made the young hair bristle on my poll.

Sun was my crown, green grassflesh my estate,
The wind a courtier, fanning at my cheek,
And plunged I in the stream, its waters hissed.

Queens I had to try my glory on,
And glory-princes my queens bore to me.
Royally I swept off all caitiff crowns.

Were the queens whores? the princes parricides?
Or were the tumbled crowns again worn high?
No, I was king then, if kings ever were.

O cousin princes, glory is hard put by,
And green grassflesh is lovely to a king.
My hawks were lightning darted from my fist.

Time was my chronicler, my deeds age-new,
And death no peril, nor decay of powers.
Glory sat firmly in my body's thrones.

Only, at midnight, rose another crown
That drained the wholesome colour from my realm,
That stilled the wind and froze the headlong stream.

I said: A challenge not to be endured,
A shadow clouding the sweet drunken hour
When with my queens in love I company.

I left the palace sleeping, I rode out,
I flew my hawk at that thin, mocking crown,
I emptied my full quiver at the sky.

Where went my hawk? He came not home again.
What ailed my horse? He cast me like a sack.
The crown moved ghostly off against the dawn.

And from that hour, though the sun burned as fierce,
Though the wind brought me frequency of spice,
Glory was gone, and numb was all my flesh.

Whose weakling is the vanquished of the Moon?
His own heart's weakling: thievishly he longs
To diadem his head with stolen light.

The Moon's the crown of no high-walled domain
Conquerable by angry reach of pride:
Her icy lands welcome no soldiery.

Thus I was shamed, I wandered in the fields,
I let my nails grow long and my hair long,
Neglecting all the business of my day.

No lovely queen nor wisest minister
Could medicine me out of my wretchedness:
The palace fell in ruins, the land smoked.

In my lost realm, if grass or flower yet grew,
It sprouted from the shade of broken walls.
I threw the walls flat, crushing flower and grass.

At length in my distemper's latest hour
I rose up shuddering, reckless to live
An idiot pawn of that inhuman power.

Over the mountain peak I watched her glide
And stood dumbfoundered by her reasoned look.
With answering reason my sick heart renewed.

So peace fell sudden, and in proof of peace
There sat my flown hawk, hooded on my fist,
And with my knees I gripped my truant horse.

Toward that most clear, unscorching light I spurred.
Whiter and closer shone the increasing disc,
Until it filled the sky, scattering my gaze.

When I might see once more, the day had come
And I was riding through gold harvest-fields,
Toward a rebuilded city, and my home.

Here then in majesty I rule again,
And grassflesh pays me tribute as of old;
In wind and sun and stream my joys I take,
Bounded by white horizons beyond touch.

TO THE SOVEREIGN MUSE

Debating here one night we reckoned that
Between us we knew all the poets
Who bore that sacred name: none bore it clear,
Not one. Some we commended
For being all they might be in a day
To which poetry was a shrouded emblem,
And some we frowned upon for lawyers' clerks
Drafting conveyances on moral sheepskin,
Or for pantomimists making parody
Of a magnificence they feared to acclaim.

This was to praise you, Sovereign muse,
And to your love our pride devote,
Who pluck the speech-thread from a jargon-tangled
Fleece of a thousand tongues, wills, voices,
To be a single speech, twisted fine;
Snapping it short like Fate then –
'Thus much, no more –'

Thereafter, in acknowledgement of you
We might no longer feign and stutter
As poets of the passionate chance,
Nor claim the indulgence of the hour.
Our tongues must prompter be than those
That wagged with modish lamentation –
Or lost men, otherwise, and renegades
To our confession, maudlin-sane must die
Suicides on the stair of yesterday.

THE AGES OF OATH

To find a garden-tulip growing
Among wild primroses of a wild field,
Or a cuckoo's egg in a blackbird's nest,
Or a giant mushroom, a whole basketful –
The memorable feats of childhood!
Once, by the earthworks, scratching in the soil,
My stick turned up a Roman amber bead....

The lost, the freakish, the unspelt
Drew me: for simple sights I had no eye.
And did I swear allegiance then
To wildness, not (as I thought) to truth –
Become a virtuoso, and this also,
Later, of simple sights, when tiring
Of unicorn and upas?

Did I forget how to greet plainly
The especial sight, how to know deeply
The pleasure shared by upright hearts?
And is this to begin afresh, with oaths
On the true book, in the true name,
Now stammering out my praise of you,
Like a boy owning his first love?

LIKE SNOW

She, then, like snow in a dark night,
Fell secretly. And the world waked
With dazzling of the drowsy eye,
So that some muttered 'Too much light',
And drew the curtains close.
Like snow, warmer than fingers feared,
And to soil friendly;
Holding the histories of the night
In yet unmelted tracks.

THE CLIMATE OF THOUGHT

The climate of thought has seldom been described.
It is no terror of Caucasian frost,
Nor yet that brooding Hindu heat
For which a loin-rag and a dish of rice
Suffice until the pestilent monsoon.
But, without winter, blood would run too thin;
Or, without summer, fires would burn too long.
In thought the seasons run concurrently.

Thought has a sea to gaze, not voyage, on;
And hills, to rough the edge of the bland sky,
Not to be climbed in search of blander prospect;
Few birds, sufficient for such caterpillars
As are not fated to turn butterflies;
Few butterflies, sufficient for such flowers
As are the luxury of a full orchard;
Wind, sometimes, in the evening chimneys; rain
On the early morning roof, on sleepy sight;
Snow streaked upon the hilltop, feeding
The fond brook at the valley-head
That greens the valley and that parts the lips;
The sun, simple, like a country neighbour;
The moon, grand, not fanciful with clouds.

END OF PLAY

We have reached the end of pastime, for always,
Ourselves and everyone, though few confess it
Or see the sky other than, as of old,
A foolish smiling Mary-mantle blue;

Though life may still seem to dawdle golden
In some June landscape among giant flowers,
The grass to shine as cruelly green as ever,
Faith to descend in a chariot from the sky –

May seem only: a mirror and an echo
Mediate henceforth with vision and sound.
The cry of faith, no longer mettlesome,
Sounds as a blind man's pitiful plea of 'blind'.

We have at last ceased idling, which to regret
Were as shallow as to ask our milk-teeth back;
As many forthwith do, and on their knees
Call lugubriously upon chaste Christ.

We tell no lies now, at last cannot be
The rogues we were – so evilly linked in sense
With what we scrutinized that lion or tiger
Could leap from every copse, strike and devour us.

No more shall love in hypocritic pomp
Conduct its innocents through a dance of shame,
From timid touching of gloved fingers
To frantic laceration of naked breasts.

Yet love survives, the word carved on a sill
Under antique dread of the headsman's axe;
It is the echoing mind, as in the mirror
We stare on our dazed trunks at the block kneeling.

THE FALLEN TOWER OF SILOAM

Should the building totter, run for an archway!
We were there already – already the collapse
Powdered the air with chalk, and shrieking
Of old men crushed under the fallen beams
Dwindled to comic yelps. How unterrible
When the event outran the alarm
And suddenly we were free –

Free to forget how grim it stood,
That tower, and what wide fissures ran
Up the west wall, how rotten the under-pinning
At the south-eastern angle. Satire
Had curled a gentle wind around it,
As if to buttress the worn masonry;
Yet we, waiting, had abstained from satire.

It behoved us, indeed, as poets
To be silent in Siloam, to foretell
No visible calamity. Though kings
Were crowned and gold coin minted still and horses
Still munched at nose-bags in the public streets,
All such sad emblems were to be condoned:
An old wives' tale, not ours.

THE GREAT-GRANDMOTHER

That aged woman with the bass voice
And yellowing white hair: believe her.
Though to your grandfather, her son, she lied
And to your father disingenuously
Told half the tale as the whole,
Yet she was honest with herself,
Knew disclosure was not yet due,
Knows it is due now.

She will conceal nothing of consequence
From you, her great-grandchildren
(So distant the relationship,
So near her term),
Will tell you frankly, she has waited
Only for your sincere indifference
To exorcize that filial regard
Which has estranged her, seventy years,
From the folk of her house.

Confessions of old distaste
For music, sighs and roses –
Their false-innocence assaulting her,
Breaching her hard heart;
Of the pleasures of a full purse,
Of clean brass and clean linen,
Of being alone at last;
Disgust with the ailing poor
To whom she was bountiful;
How the prattle of young children
Vexed more than if they whined;
How she preferred cats.

She will say, yes, she acted well,
Took such pride in the art
That none of them suspected, even,
Her wrathful irony
In doing what they asked
Better than they could ask it....
But, ah, how grudgingly her will returned
After the severance of each navel-cord,
And fled how far again,
When again she was kind!

She has outlasted all man-uses,
As was her first resolve:
Happy and idle like a port
After the sea's recession,
She does not misconceive the nature
Of shipmen or of ships.
Hear her, therefore, as the latest voice;
The intervening generations (drifting
On tides of fancy still), ignore.

NO MORE GHOSTS

The patriarchal bed with four posts
Which was a harbourage of ghosts
Is hauled out from the attic glooms
And cut to wholesome furniture for wholesome rooms;

Where they (the ghosts) confused, abused, thinned,
Forgetful how they sighed and sinned,
Cannot disturb our ordered ease
Except as summer dust tickles the nose to sneeze.

We are restored to simple days, are free
From cramps of dark necessity,
And one another recognize
By an immediate love that signals at our eyes.

No new ghosts can appear. Their poor cause
Was that time freezes, and time thaws;
But here only such loves can last
As do not ride upon the weathers of the past.

LEAVING THE REST UNSAID

Finis, apparent on an earlier page,
With fallen obelisk for colophon,
Must this be here repeated?

Death has been ruefully announced
And to die once is death enough,
Be sure, for any life-time.

Must the book end, as you would end it,
With testamentary appendices
And graveyard indices?

But no, I will not lay me down
To let your tearful music mar
The decent mystery of my progress.

So now, my solemn ones, leaving the rest unsaid,
Rising in air as on a gander's wing
At a careless comma,

From *NO MORE GHOSTS*

(1940)

THE GLUTTON

Beyond the Atlas roams a glutton
Lusty and sleek, a shameless robber,
Sacred to Aethiopian Aphrodite;
The aborigines harry it with darts,
And its flesh is esteemed, though of a fishy tang
Tainting the eater's mouth and lips.

Ourselves once, wandering in mid-wilderness
And by despair drawn to this diet,
Before the meal was over sat apart
Loathing each other's carrion company.

A LOVE STORY

The full moon easterly rising, furious,
Against a winter sky ragged with red;
The hedges high in snow, and owls raving –
Solemnities not easy to withstand:
A shiver wakes the spine.

In boyhood, having encountered the scene,
I suffered horror: I fetched the moon home,
With owls and snow, to nurse in my head
Throughout the trials of a new Spring,
Famine unassuaged.

But fell in love, and made a lodgement
Of love on those chill ramparts.
Her image was my ensign: snows melted,
Hedges sprouted, the moon tenderly shone,
The owls trilled with tongues of nightingale.

These were all lies, though they matched the time,

And brought me less than luck: her image
Warped in the weather, turned beldamish.
Then back came winter on me at a bound,
The pallid sky heaved with a moon-quake.

Dangerous it had been with love-notes
To serenade Queen Famine.
In tears I recomposed the former scene,
Let the snow lie, watched the moon rise, suffered the owls,
Paid homage to them of unevent.

THE THIEVES

Lovers in the act dispense
With such meum-tuum sense
As might warningly reveal
What they must not pick or steal,
And their nostrum is to say:
'I and you are both away.'

After, when they disentwine
You from me and yours from mine,
Neither can be certain who
Was that I whose mine was you.
To the act again they go
More completely not to know.

Theft is theft and raid is raid
Though reciprocally made.
Lovers, the conclusion is
Doubled sighs and jealousies
In a single heart that grieves
For lost honour among thieves.

TO SLEEP

The mind's eye sees as the heart mirrors:
Loving in part, I did not see you whole,
Grew flesh-enraged that I could not conjure
A whole you to attend my fever-fit
In the doubtful hour between a night and day
And be Sleep that had kept so long away.

Of you sometimes a hand, a brooch, a shoe
Wavered beside me, unarticulated –
As the vexed insomniac dream-forges;
And the words I chose for your voice to speak
Echoed my own voice with its dry creak.

Now that I love you, now that I recall
All scattered elements of will that swooped
By night as jealous dreams through windows
To circle above the beds like bats,
Or as dawn-birds flew blindly at the panes
In curiosity rattling out their brains –

Now that I love you, as not before,
Now you can be and say, as not before:
The mind clears and the heart true-mirrors you
Where at my side an early watch you keep
And all self-bruising heads loll into sleep.

From WORK IN HAND

(1942)

DAWN BOMBARDMENT

Guns from the sea open against us:
The smoke rocks bodily in the casemate
And a yell of doom goes up.
We count and bless each new, heavy concussion –
Captives awaiting rescue.

Visiting angel of the wild-fire hair
Who in dream reassured us nightly
Where we lay fettered,
Laugh at us, as we wake – our faces
So tense with hope the tears run down.

THE WORMS OF HISTORY

On the eighth day God died; his bearded mouth
That had been shut so long flew open.
So Adam's too in a dismay like death –
But the world still rolled on around him,
Instinct with all those lesser powers of life
That God had groaned against but not annulled.

'All-Excellent', Adam had titled God,
And in his mourning now demeaned himself
As if all excellence, not God, had died;
Chose to be governed by those lesser powers,
More than inferior to excellence –
The worms astir in God's corrupt flesh.

God died, not excellence his name:
Excellence lived, but only was not God.
As for those lesser powers who played at God,
Bloated with Adam's deferential sighs
In mourning for expired divinity,
They reigned as royal monsters upon earth.

Adam grew lean, and wore perpetual black;
He made no reaching after excellence.
Eve gave him sorry comfort for his grief
With birth of sons, and mourning still he died.
Adam was buried in one grave with God
And the worms ranged and ravaged in between.

Into their white maws fell abundance
Of all things rotten. They were greedy-nosed
To smell the taint out and go scavenging,
Yet over excellence held no domain.
Excellence lives; they are already dead –
The ages of a putrefying corpse.

A WITHERING HERB

Ambition in the herb denied his root.
In dreams of the dark he whispered:
'O to be all flower, and to star the sky –
True brother to the moon, that stemless flower
Who long has cherished me!'

Disdained the happy sun of morning,
Held it gross rival to the sovereign moon –
Thus for ambition cast his cloak of leaves
Yet could not snap the stem, to float upward
And from his roots be free:
So withered staunchly.

THE SHOT

The curious heart plays with its fears:
To hurl a shot through the ship's planks,
Being assured that the green angry flood
Is charmed and dares not dance into the hold –
Nor first to sweep a lingering glance around
For land or shoal or cask adrift.
'So miracles are done; but madmen drown.'

O weary luxury of hypothesis –
For human nature, honest human nature
(Which the fear-pampered heart denies)
Knows its own miracle: not to go mad.
Will pitch the shot in fancy, hint the fact,
Will bore perhaps a meagre auger hole
But stanch the spurting with a tarred rag,
And will not drown, nor even ride the cask.

DREAM OF A CLIMBER

Watch how this climber raises his own ladder
From earth to heaven, and not in a night
Nor from the secret, stony pillow.
(World patents pending; tested in the shops.)

Here's quality timber, nosings of pure brass,
The perfect phallo-spiritual tilt,
A fuzzy puff of cloud on top –
Excellent lure for angels and archangels!

Come, climber, with your scientific hat
And beady gambler's eye, ascend!
He pauses, poses for his camera-man:
'Well-known Climber About to Ascend.'

But in the published print, we may be sure,
He will appear, not on the lowest rung
But nearly out of view, almost in the cloud,
Leaning aside for an angel to pass,
His muscular broad hands a-glint in the sun,
And crampons on his feet.

LOLLOCKS

By sloth on sorrow fathered,
These dusty-featured Lollocks
Have their nativity in all disordered
Backs of cupboard drawers.

They play hide and seek
Among collars and novels
And empty medicine bottles,
And letters from abroad
That never will be answered.

Every sultry night
They plague little children,
Gurgling from the cistern,
Humming from the air,
Skewing up the bed-clothes,
Twitching the blind.

When the imbecile agèd
Are over-long in dying
And the nurse drowses,
Lollocks come skipping
Up the tattered stairs
And are nasty together
In the bed's shadow.

The signs of their presence
Are boils on the neck,
Dreams of vexation suddenly recalled
In the middle of the morning,
Languor after food.

Men cannot see them,
Men cannot hear them,
Do not believe in them –
But suffer the more
Both in neck and belly.

Women can see them –
O those naughty wives
Who sit by the fireside
Munching bread and honey,
Watching them in mischief
From corners of their eyes,
Slily allowing them to lick
Honey-sticky fingers.

Sovereign against Lollocks
Are hard broom and soft broom,
To well comb the hair,
To well brush the shoe,
And to pay every debt
As it falls due.

DESPITE AND STILL

Have you not read
The words in my head,
And I made part
Of your own heart?
We have been such as draw
The losing straw –
You of your gentleness,
I of my rashness,
Both of despair –
Yet still might share
This happy will:
To love despite and still.
Never let us deny
The thing's necessity,
But, O, refuse
To choose
Where chance may seem to give
Loves in alternative.

THE SUICIDE IN THE COPSE

The suicide, far from content,
Stared down at his own shattered skull:
Was this what he meant?

Had not his purpose been
To liberate himself from duns and dolts
By a change of scene?

From somewhere came a roll of laughter:
He had looked so on his wedding-day,
And the day after.

There was nowhere at all to go,
And no diversion now but to peruse
What literature the winds might blow

Into the copse where his body lay:
A year-old sheet of sporting news,
A crumpled schoolboy essay.

FRIGHTENED MEN

We were not ever of their feline race,
Never had hidden claws so sharp as theirs
In any half-remembered incarnation;
Have only the least knowledge of their minds
Through a grace on their part in thinking aloud;
And we remain mouse-quiet when they begin
Suddenly in their unpredictable way
To weave an allegory of their lives,
Making each point by walking round it –
Then off again, as interest is warmed.
What have they said? Or unsaid? What?
We understood the general drift only.

They are punctilious as implacable,
Most neighbourly to those who love them least.
A shout will scare them. When they spring, they seize.
The worst is when they hide from us and change
To something altogether other:
We meet them at the door, as who returns
After a one-hour-seeming century
To a house not his own.

A STRANGER AT THE PARTY

For annoyance, not shame,
    Under their covert stares
She would not give her name
    Nor demand theirs.

Soon everyone at the party,
    Who knew everyone,
Eyed her with plain envy
    For knowing none –

Such neighbourly mistrust
    Breathed across the floor,
Such familiar disgust
    With what they were and wore –

Until, as she was leaving,
    Her time out-stayed,
They tried to say they loved her;
    But pride forbade.

THE OATH

The doubt and the passion
Falling away from them,
    In that instant both
Take timely courage
From the sky's clearness
    To confirm an oath.

Her loves are his loves,
His trust is her trust;
    Else all were grief
And they, lost ciphers
On a yellowing page,
    Death overleaf.

Rumour of old battle
Growls across the air;
    Then let it growl
With no more terror
Than the creaking stair
    Or the calling owl.

She knows, as he knows,
Of a faithful-always
    And an always-dear
By early emblems
Prognosticated,
    Fulfilled here.

LANGUAGE OF THE SEASONS

Living among orchards, we are ruled
By the four seasons necessarily:
This from unseasonable frosts we learn
Or from usurping suns and haggard flowers –
Legitimist our disapproval.

Weather we knew, not seasons, in the city
Where, seasonless, orange and orchid shone,
Knew it by heavy overcoat or light,
Framed love in later terminologies
Than here, where we report how weight of snow,
Or weight of fruit, tears branches from the tree.

MID-WINTER WAKING

Stirring suddenly from long hibernation,
I knew myself once more a poet
Guarded by timeless principalities
Against the worm of death, this hillside haunting;
And presently dared open both my eyes.

O gracious, lofty, shone against from under,
Back-of-the-mind-far clouds like towers;
And you, sudden warm airs that blow
Before the expected season of new blossom,
While sheep still gnaw at roots and lambless go –

Be witness that on waking, this mid-winter,
I found her hand in mine laid closely
Who shall watch out the Spring with me.
We stared in silence all around us
But found no winter anywhere to see.

THE ROCK AT THE CORNER

The quarrymen left ragged
A rock at the corner;
But over it move now
The comforting fingers
Of ivy and briar.

Nor will it need assurance
Of nature's compassion
When presently it weathers
To a noble landmark
Of such countenance

That travellers in winter
Will see it as a creature
On guard at the corner
Where deep snows ingratiate
The comforts of death.

From POEMS 1938–1945

(1945)

THE BEACH

Louder than gulls the little children scream
Whom fathers haul into the jovial foam;
But others fearlessly rush in, breast high,
Laughing the salty water from their mouths –
Heroes of the nursery.

The horny boatman, who has seen whales
And flying fishes, who has sailed as far
As Demerara and the Ivory Coast,
Will warn them, when they crowd to hear his tales,
That every ocean smells alike of tar.

THE VILLAGERS AND DEATH

The Rector's pallid neighbour at The Firs,
Death, did not flurry the parishioners.
Yet from a weight of superstitious fears
Each tried to lengthen his own term of years.
He was congratulated who combined
Toughness of flesh and weakness of the mind
In consequential rosiness of face.
This dull and not ill-mannered populace
Pulled off their caps to Death, as they slouched by,
But rumoured him both atheist and spy.
All vowed to outlast him (though none ever did)
And hear the earth drum on his coffin-lid.
Their groans and whispers down the village street
Soon soured his nature, which was never sweet.

THE DOOR

When she came suddenly in
It seemed the door could never close again,
Nor even did she close it – she, she –
The room lay open to a visiting sea
Which no door could restrain.

Yet when at last she smiled, tilting her head
To take her leave of me,
Where she had smiled, instead
There was a dark door closing endlessly,
The waves receded.

UNDER THE POT

Sulkily the sticks burn, and though they crackle
    With scorn under the bubbling pot, or spout
Magnanimous jets of flame against the smoke,
    At each heel end a dirty sap breaks out.

Confess, creatures, how sulkily ourselves
    We hiss with doom, fuel of a sodden age –
Not rapt up roaring to the chimney stack
    On incandescent clouds of spirit or rage.

THROUGH NIGHTMARE

Never be disenchanted of
That place you sometimes dream yourself into,
Lying at large remove beyond all dream,
Or those you find there, though but seldom
In their company seated –

The untameable, the live, the gentle.
Have you not known them? Whom? They carry
Time looped so river-wise about their house
There's no way in by history's road
To name or number them.

In your sleepy eyes I read the journey
Of which disjointedly you tell; which stirs
My loving admiration, that you should travel
Through nightmare to a lost and moated land,
Who are timorous by nature.

TO LUCIA AT BIRTH

Though the moon beaming matronly and bland
    Greets you, among the crowd of the new-born,
With 'welcome to the world' yet understand
    That still her pale, lascivious unicorn
And bloody lion are loose on either hand:
    With din of bones and tantarará of horn
Their fanciful cortège parades the land –
    Pest on the high road, wild-fire in the corn.

Outrageous company to be born into,
    Lunatics of a royal age long dead.
Then reckon time by what you are or do,
    Not by the epochs of the war they spread.
    Hark how they roar; but never turn your head.
Nothing will change them, let them not change you.

DEATH BY DRUMS

If I cried out in anger against music,
    It was not that I cried
Against the wholesome bitter arsenic
    Necessary for suicide:
For suicide in the drums' racking riot
    Where horned moriscoes wailing to their bride
Scare every Lydian songster from the spot.

SHE TELLS HER LOVE WHILE HALF ASLEEP

She tells her love while half asleep,
    In the dark hours,
        With half-words whispered low:
As Earth stirs in her winter sleep
    And puts out grass and flowers
        Despite the snow,
        Despite the falling snow.

INSTRUCTIONS TO THE ORPHIC ADEPT

[In part translated from the *Timpone Grande* and *Campagno*
Orphic tablets.]

So soon as ever your mazed spirit descends
From daylight into darkness, Man, remember
What you have suffered here in Samothrace,
What you have suffered.

After your passage through Hell's seven floods,
Whose fumes of sulphur will have parched your throat,
The Halls of Judgement shall loom up before you,
A miracle of jasper and of onyx.
To the left hand there bubbles a black spring
Overshadowed with a great white cypress.
Avoid this spring, which is Forgetfulness;
Though all the common rout rush down to drink,
Avoid this spring!

To the right hand there lies a secret pool
Alive with speckled trout and fish of gold;
A hazel overshadows it. Ophion,
Primaeval serpent straggling in the branches,
Darts out his tongue. This holy pool is fed
By dripping water; guardians stand before it.
Run to this pool, the pool of Memory,
Run to this pool!

Then will the guardians scrutinize you, saying:
'Who are you, who? What have you to remember?
Do you not fear Ophion's flickering tongue?
Go rather to the spring beneath the cypress,
Flee from this pool!'

Then you shall answer: 'I am parched with thirst.
Give me to drink. I am a child of Earth,
But of Sky also, come from Samothrace.
Witness the glint of amber on my brow.
Out of the Pure I come, as you may see.
I also am of your thrice-blessèd kin,
Child of the three-fold Queen of Samothrace;
Have made full quittance for my deeds of blood,
Have been by her invested in sea-purple,
And like a kid have fallen into milk.
Give me to drink, now I am parched with thirst,
Give me to drink!'

But they will ask you yet: 'What of your feet?'
You shall reply: 'My feet have borne me here
Out of the weary wheel, the circling years,
To that still, spokeless wheel: – Persephone.
Give me to drink!'

Then they will welcome you with fruit and flowers,
And lead you toward the ancient dripping hazel,
Crying: 'Brother of our immortal blood,
Drink and remember glorious Samothrace!'
Then you shall drink.

You shall drink deep of that refreshing draught,
To become lords of the uninitiated
Twittering ghosts, Hell's countless populace –
To become heroes, knights upon swift horses,
Pronouncing oracles from tall white tombs
By the nymphs tended. They with honey water
Shall pour libations to your serpent shapes,
That you may drink.

THESEUS AND ARIADNE

High on his figured couch beyond the waves
He dreams, in dream recalling her set walk
Down paths of oyster-shell bordered with flowers,
Across the shadowy turf below the vines.
He sighs: 'Deep sunk in my erroneous past
She haunts the ruins and the ravaged lawns.'

Yet still unharmed it stands, the regal house
Crooked with age and overtopped by pines
Where first he wearied of her constancy.
And with a surer foot she goes than when
Dread of his hate was thunder in the air,
When the pines agonized with flaws of wind
And flowers glared up at her with frantic eyes.
Of him, now all is done, she never dreams
But calls a living blessing down upon
What he supposes rubble and rank grass;
Playing the queen to nobler company.

LAMENT FOR PASIPHAË

Dying sun, shine warm a little longer!
My eye, dazzled with tears, shall dazzle yours,
Conjuring you to shine and not to move.
You, sun, and I all afternoon have laboured
Beneath a dewless and oppressive cloud –
A fleece now gilded with our common grief
That this must be a night without a moon.
Dying sun, shine warm a little longer!

Faithless she was not: she was very woman,
Smiling with dire impartiality,
Sovereign, with heart unmatched, adored of men,
Until Spring's cuckoo with bedraggled plumes
Tempted her pity and her truth betrayed.
Then she who shone for all resigned her being,
And this must be a night without a moon.
Dying sun, shine warm a little longer!

THE TWELVE DAYS OF CHRISTMAS

The impassioned child who stole the axe of power,
Debauched his virgin mother
And vowed in rage he would be God the Father,

Who, grown to strength, strangled her lion twins
And from a cloud, in chains,
Hung her with anvils at her ankle bones,

Who whipped her daughters with a bull's pizzle,
Forced them to take the veil
And heard their loveless prayers with a lewd smile –

Senile at last the way of all flesh goes:
Into the kitchen where roast goose,
Plum-pudding and mince-pies his red robes grease.

She from the tree-top, true to her deserts,
With wand and silver skirts
Presides unravished over all pure hearts.

COLD WEATHER PROVERB

Fearless approach and puffed feather
In birds, famine bespeak;
In man, belly filled full.

TO JUAN AT THE WINTER SOLSTICE

There is one story and one story only
That will prove worth your telling,
Whether as learned bard or gifted child;
To it all lines or lesser gauds belong
That startle with their shining
Such common stories as they stray into.

Is it of trees you tell, their months and virtues,
Or strange beasts that beset you,
Of birds that croak at you the Triple will?
Or of the Zodiac and how slow it turns
Below the Boreal Crown,
Prison of all true kings that ever reigned?

Water to water, ark again to ark,
From woman back to woman:
So each new victim treads unfalteringly
The never altered circuit of his fate,
Bringing twelve peers as witness
Both to his starry rise and starry fall.

Or is it of the Virgin's silver beauty,
All fish below the thighs?
She in her left hand bears a leafy quince;
When with her right she crooks a finger, smiling,
How may the King hold back?
Royally then he barters life for love.

Or of the undying snake from chaos hatched,
Whose coils contain the ocean,
Into whose chops with naked sword he springs,
Then in black water, tangled by the reeds,
Battles three days and nights,
To be spewed up beside her scalloped shore?

Much snow is falling, winds roar hollowly,
The owl hoots from the elder,
Fear in your heart cries to the loving-cup:
Sorrow to sorrow as the sparks fly upward.
The log groans and confesses:
There is one story and one story only.

Dwell on her graciousness, dwell on her smiling,
Do not forget what flowers
The great boar trampled down in ivy time.
Her brow was creamy as the crested wave,
Her sea-grey eyes were wild
But nothing promised that is not performed.

SATIRES AND GROTESQUES

THE PERSIAN VERSION

Truth-loving Persians do not dwell upon
The trivial skirmish fought near Marathon.
As for the Greek theatrical tradition
Which represents that summer's expedition
Not as a mere reconnaissance in force
By three brigades of foot and one of horse
(Their left flank covered by some obsolete
Light craft detached from the main Persian fleet)
But as a grandiose, ill-starred attempt
To conquer Greece – they treat it with contempt;
And only incidentally refute
Major Greek claims, by stressing what repute
The Persian monarch and the Persian nation
Won by this salutary demonstration:
Despite a strong defence and adverse weather
All arms combined magnificently together.

THE WEATHER OF OLYMPUS

Zeus was once overheard to shout at Hera:
    'You hate it, do you? Well, I hate it worse –
East wind in May, sirocco all the Summer.
    Hell take this whole impossible Universe!'

A scholiast explains his warm rejoinder,
    Which sounds too man-like for Olympic use,
By noting that the snake-tailed Chthonian winds
    Were answerable to Fate alone, not Zeus.

APOLLO OF THE PHYSIOLOGISTS

Despite this learned cult's official
And seemingly sincere denial
That they either reject or postulate
God, or God's scientific surrogate,
Prints of a deity occur *passim*
Throughout their extant literature. They make him
A dumb, dead-pan Apollo with a profile
Drawn in Victorian-Hellenistic style –
The pallid, bald, partitioned head suggesting
Wholly abstract cerebral functioning;
Or nude and at full length, this deity
Displays digestive, venous, respiratory
And nervous systems painted in bold colour
On his immaculate exterior.
Sometimes, *in verso*, a bald, naked Muse,
His consort, flaunts her arteries and sinews,
While, upside-down, crouched in her chaste abdomen,
Adored by men and wondered at by women,
Hangs a Victorian-Hellenistic foetus –
Fruit of her academic god's afflatus.

THE OLDEST SOLDIER

The sun shines warm on seven old soldiers
    Paraded in a row,
Perched like starlings on the railings –
    Give them plug-tobacco!

They'll croon you the Oldest-Soldier Song:
    Of Harry who took a holiday
From the sweat of ever thinking for himself
    Or going his own bloody way.

It was arms-drill, guard and kit-inspection,
    Like dreams of a long train-journey,
And the barrack-bed that Harry dossed on
    Went rockabye, rockabye, rockabye.

Harry kept his rifle and brasses clean,
    But Jesus Christ, what a liar!
He won the Military Medal
    For his coolness under fire.

He was never the last on parade
    Nor the first to volunteer,
And when Harry rose to be storeman
    He seldom had to pay for his beer.

Twenty-one years, and out Harry came
    To be odd-job man, or janitor,
Or commissionaire at a picture-house,
    Or, some say, bully to a whore.

But his King and Country calling Harry,
    He reported again at the Depôt,
To perch on this railing like a starling,
    The oldest soldier of the row.

GROTESQUES

I

My Chinese uncle, gouty, deaf, half-blinded,
And more than a trifle absent-minded,
Astonished all St James's Square one day
By giving long and unexceptionably exact directions
To a little coolie girl, who'd lost her way.

II

The Lion-faced Boy at the Fair
And the Heir Apparent
Were equally slow at remembering people's faces.
But whenever they met, incognito, in the Brazilian
Pavilion, the Row and such-like places,
They exchanged, it is said, their sternest nods –
Like gods of dissimilar races.

III

Dr Newman with the crooked pince-nez
Had studied in Vienna and Chicago.
Chess was his only relaxation.
And Dr Newman remained unperturbed
By every nastier manifestation
Of pluto-democratic civilization:
All that was cranky, corny, ill-behaved,
Unnecessary, askew or orgiastic
Would creep unbidden to his side-door (hidden
Behind a poster in the Tube Station,
Nearly half-way up the moving stairs),
Push its way in, to squat there undisturbed
Among box-files and tubular steel-chairs.

He was once seen at the Philharmonic Hall
Noting the reactions of two patients,
With pronounced paranoiac tendencies,
To old Dutch music. He appeared to recall
A tin of lozenges in his breast-pocket,
Put his hand confidently in –
And drew out a black imp, or sooterkin,
Six inches long, with one ear upside-down,
Licking at a vanilla ice-cream cornet –
Then put it back again with a slight frown.

IV

A Royal Duke, with no campaigning medals
To dignify his Orders, he would speak
Nostalgically at times of Mozambique
Where once the ship he cruised in ran aground:
How he drank cocoa, from a sailor's mug,
Poured from the common jug,
While loyal toasts went round.

V

Sir John addressed the Snake-god in his temple,
Which was full of bats, not as a votary
But with the somewhat cynical courtesy,
Just short of condescension,
He might have paid the Governor-General

Of a small, hot, backward colony.
He was well versed in primitive religion,
But found this an embarrassing occasion:
The God was immense, noisy and affable,
Began to tickle him with a nervous chuckle,
Unfobbed a great gold clock for him to listen,
Hissed like a snake, and swallowed him at one mouthful.

VI

All horses on the racecourse of Tralee
   Have four more legs in gallop than in trot –
   Two pairs fully extended, two pairs not;
And yet no thoroughbred with either three
   Or five legs but is mercilessly shot.
I watched a filly gnaw her fifth leg free,
Warned by a speaking mare since turned silentiary.

THE EUGENIST

Come, human dogs, interfertilitate –
   Blackfellow and white lord, brown, yellow and red!
Accept the challenge of the lately bred
   Newfoundland terrier with the dachshund gait.[1]

Breed me gigantic pygmies, meek-eyed Scots,
   Phlegmatic Irish, perfume-hating Poles,
Poker-faced, toothy, pigtailed Hottentots,
   And Germans with no envy in their souls.

---

[1] *See:* Charles R. Stockard and collaborators: *The genetic and endocrinic basis for differences in form and behaviour, as elucidated by studies of contrasted pure-line dogbreeds and their hybrids.* (Philadelphia, 1941.)

1805

At Viscount Nelson's lavish funeral,
    While the mob milled and yelled about St Paul's,
A General chatted with an Admiral:

'One of your Colleagues, Sir, remarked today
    That Nelson's *exit*, though to be lamented,
Falls not inopportunely, in its way.'

'He was a thorn in our flesh,' came the reply –
    'The most bird-witted, unaccountable,
Odd little runt that ever I did spy.

'One arm, one peeper, vain as Pretty Poll,
    A meddler, too, in foreign politics
And gave his heart in pawn to a plain moll.

'He would dare lecture us Sea Lords, and then
    Would treat his ratings as though men of honour
And play at leap-frog with his midshipmen!

'We tried to box him down, but up he popped,
    And when he'd banged Napoleon at the Nile
Became too much the hero to be dropped.

'You've heard that Copenhagen "blind eye" story?
    We'd tied him to Nurse Parker's apron-strings –
By G–d, he snipped them through and snatched the glory!'

'Yet,' cried the General, 'six-and-twenty sail
    Captured or sunk by him off Tráfalgár –
That writes a handsome *finis* to the tale.'

'Handsome enough. The seas are England's now.
    That fellow's foibles need no longer plague us.
He died most creditably, I'll allow.'

'And, Sir, the secret of his victories?'
    'By his unServicelike, familiar ways, Sir,
He made the whole Fleet love him, damn his eyes!'

AT THE SAVOY CHAPEL

[From *World's Press News*, 22 February, 1945. 'Alexander Clifford, the war correspondent, is today marrying Flight Officer Jenny Nicholson, daughter of Robert Graves. They met in the front line.']

Up to the wedding, formal with heirloom lace,
Press-cameras, carnations out of season,
Well-mellowed priest and well-trained choristers,

The relatives come marching, such as meet
Only at weddings and at funerals,
The elder generation with the eldest.

Family features for years undecided
What look to wear against a loveless world
Fix, as the wind veers, in the same grimace.

Each eyes the others with a furtive pity:
'Heavens, how she has aged – and he,
Grey hair and sunken cheeks, what a changed man!'

They stare wistfully at the bride (released
From brass buttons and the absurd salute)
In long white gown, bouquet and woman's pride.

'How suitable!' they whisper, and the whisper
'How suitable!' rustles from pew to pew;
To which I nod suitably grave assent.

Now for you, loving ones, who kneel at the altar
And preside afterwards at table –
The trophy sword that shears the cake recalling

What god you entertained last year together,
His bull neck looped with guts,
Trampling corpse-carpet through the villages –

Here is my private blessing: so to remain
As today you are, with features
Resolute and unchangeably your own.

From COLLECTED POEMS
(1914–1947)
(1948)

TO POETS UNDER PISCES

Until the passing years establish
Aquarius who with fruitful spate
All dried pools will at last replenish,
Resign yourselves to celebrate,
Poets, with grief or hate,
These gasping rainbowed flurries of the Fish.

JUNE

June, the jolly season of most bloodshed:
Soldiers with roses in their rifle barrels
And children, cherries bobbing at their ears,
Who roar them on like furious adjutants
Where the broad oak its feathered bonnet rears.

THE LAST DAY OF LEAVE

(1916)

We five looked out over the moor
At rough hills blurred with haze, and a still sea:
Our tragic day, bountiful from the first.

We would spend it by the lily lake
(High in a fold beyond the farthest ridge),
Following the cart-track till it faded out.

The time of berries and bell-heather;
Yet all that morning nobody went by
But shepherds and one old man carting turfs.

We were in love: he with her, she with him,
And I, the youngest one, the odd man out,
As deep in love with a yet nameless muse.

No cloud; larks and heath-butterflies,
And herons undisturbed fishing the streams;
A slow cool breeze that hardly stirred the grass.

When we hurried down the rocky slope,
A flock of ewes galloping off in terror,
There shone the waterlilies, yellow and white.

Deep water and a shelving bank.
Off went our clothes and in we went, all five,
Diving like trout between the lily groves.

The basket had been nobly filled:
Wine and fresh rolls, chicken and pineapple –
Our braggadocio under threat of war.

The fire on which we boiled our kettle
We fed with ling and rotten blackthorn root;
And the coffee tasted memorably of peat.

Two of us might stray off together
But never less than three kept by the fire,
Focus of our uncertain destinies.

We spoke little, our minds in tune –
A sigh or laugh would settle any theme;
The sun so hot it made the rocks quiver.

But when it rolled down level with us,
Four pairs of eyes sought mine as if appealing
For a blind-fate-aversive afterword: –

'Do you remember the lily lake?
We were all there, all five of us in love,
Not one yet killed, widowed or broken-hearted.'

TO BE CALLED A BEAR

Bears gash the forest trees
   To mark the bounds
   Of their own hunting grounds;
They follow the wild bees
   Point by point home
   For love of honeycomb;
They browse on blueberries.

Then should I stare
If I am called a bear,
And it is not the truth?
Unkempt and surly with a sweet tooth
I tilt my muzzle toward the starry hub
Where Queen Callisto guards her cub;

But envy those that here
   All winter breathing slow
   Sleep warm under the snow,
That yawn awake when the skies clear,
   And lank with longing grow
No more than one brief month a year.

A CIVIL SERVANT

While in this cavernous place employed
   Not once was I aware
Of my officious other-self
   Poised high above me there,

My self reversed, my rage-less part,
   A slimy yellowish cone –
Drip, drip; drip, drip – so down the years
   I stalagmized in stone.

Now pilgrims to the cave, who come
   To chip off what they can,
Prod me with child-like merriment:
   'Look, look! It's like a man!'

GULLS AND MEN

The naturalists of the Bass Rock
  On this vexatious point agree:
That sea-birds of all sorts that flock
  About the Bass, repeatedly
    Collide in mid-flight,

And neither by design, in play,
  Nor by design, in shrewd assault,
But (as these patient watchers say,
  Eyes that are seldom proved at fault)
    By lack of foresight.

Stupidity, which poor and rich
  Hold the recognizance of man,
Precious stupidity, of which
  Let him denude himself who can
    And stand at God's height –

Stupidity that brings to birth
  More, always more, than to the grave,
The burden of all songs on earth,
  And by which men are brave
    And women contrite –

This jewel bandied from a cliff
  By gulls and razor-bills and such!
Where is man's vindication if
  Perfectibility's as much
    Bird-right as man-right?

MAGICAL POEMS

THE ALLANSFORD PURSUIT

[As danced by North-country witches at their Sabbaths. A
restoration of the fragmentary seventeenth-century text.]

Cunning and art he did not lack
But aye her whistle would fetch him back.

O, I shall go into a hare
With sorrow and sighing and mickle care,
And I shall go in the Devil's name
Aye, till I be fetchèd hame.
  – Hare, take heed of a bitch greyhound
  Will harry thee all these fells around,
  For here come I in Our Lady's name
  All but for to fetch thee hame.

Cunning and art, etc.

Yet I shall go into a trout
With sorrow and sighing and mickle doubt,
And show thee many a crooked game
Ere that I be fetchèd hame.
  – Trout, take heed of an otter lank
  Will harry thee close from bank to bank,
  For here come I in Our Lady's name
  All but for to fetch thee hame.

Cunning and art, etc.

Yet I shall go into a bee
With mickle horror and dread of thee,
And flit to hive in the Devil's name
Ere that I be fetchèd hame.
  – Bee, take heed of a swallow hen
  Will harry thee close, both butt and ben,
  For here come I in Our Lady's name
  All but for to fetch thee hame.

Cunning and art, etc.

Yet I shall go into a mouse
And haste me unto the miller's house,
There in his corn to have good game
Ere that I be fetchèd hame.
> – Mouse, take heed of a white tib-cat
> That never was baulked of mouse or rat,
> For I'll crack thy bones in Our Lady's name:
> Thus shalt thou be fetchèd hame.

Cunning and art, etc.

AMERGIN'S CHARM

[The text restored from mediaeval Irish and Welsh variants.]

I am a stag: *of seven tines,*
I am a flood: *across a plain,*
I am a wind: *on a deep lake,*
I am a tear: *the Sun lets fall,*
I am a hawk: *above the cliff,*
I am a thorn: *beneath the nail,*
I am a wonder: *among flowers,*
I am a wizard: *who but I*
Sets the cool head aflame with smoke?

I am a spear: *that roars for blood,*
I am a salmon: *in a pool,*
I am a lure: *from paradise,*
I am a hill: *where poets walk,*
I am a boar: *renowned and red,*
I am a breaker: *threatening doom,*
I am a tide: *that drags to death,*
I am an infant: *who but I*
Peeps from the unhewn dolmen arch?

I am the womb: *of every holt,*
I am the blaze: *on every hill,*
I am the queen: *of every hive,*
I am the shield: *for every head,*
I am the grave: *of every hope.*

THE SIRENS' WELCOME TO CRONOS

Cronos the Ruddy, steer your boat
Toward Silver Island whence we sing;
Here you shall pass your days.

Through a thick-growing alder-wood
We clearly see, but are not seen,
Hid in a golden haze.

Our hair the hue of barley sheaf,
Our eyes the hue of blackbird's egg,
Our cheeks like asphodel.

Here the wild apple blossoms yet;
Wrens in the silver branches play
And prophesy you well.

Here nothing ill or harsh is found.
Cronos the Ruddy, steer your boat
Across these placid straits,

With each of us in turn to lie
Taking your pleasure on young grass
That for your coming waits.

No grief nor gloom, sickness nor death,
Disturbs our long tranquillity;
No treachery, no greed.

Compared with this, what are the plains
Of Elis, where you ruled as king?
A wilderness indeed.

A starry crown awaits your head,
A hero feast is spread for you:
Swineflesh, milk and mead.

DICHETAL DO CHENNAIB

'Today it is by the finger ends that the poet effects the *Dichetal do chennaib*, and this is the way he does it. When he sees the required person or object before him he at once makes a poem with his finger tips, or in his mind without reflexion, composing and repeating simultaneously.'

(Mediaeval Irish scholiast on the *Senchus Mor*.)

Tree powers, finger tips,
First pentad of the four,
Discover all your poet asks
Drumming on his brow.

Birch-peg, throbbing thumb,
By power of divination,
Birch, bring him news of love;
Loud knocks the heart.

Rowan-rod, forefinger,
By power of divination,
Unriddle him a riddle;
The key's cast away.

Ash, middle finger,
By power of divination
Weather-wise, fool otherwise,
Mete him out the winds.

Alder, physic finger,
By power of divination
Diagnose all maladies
Of a doubtful mind.

Willow-wand, earfinger,
By power of divination
Force confessions from the mouth
Of a mouldering corpse.

Finger-ends, five twigs,
Trees, true-divining trees,
Discover all your poet asks
Drumming on his brow.

THE BATTLE OF THE TREES

[Text reassembled and restored from the deliberately
confused mediaeval Welsh poem-medley, *Câd Goddeu*, in
the *Red Book of Hergest*, hitherto regarded as nonsensical.]

The tops of the beech tree
    Have sprouted of late,
Are changed and renewed
    From their withered state.

When the beech prospers,
    Though spells and litanies
The oak tops entangle,
    There is hope for trees.

I have plundered the fern,
    Through all secrets I spy,
Old Math ap Mathonwy
    Knew no more than I.

With nine sorts of faculty
    God has gifted me:
I am fruit of fruits gathered
    From nine sorts of tree –

Plum, quince, whortle, mulberry,
    Raspberry, pear,
Black cherry and white
    With the sorb in me share.

From my seat at Fefynedd,
    A city that is strong,
I watched the trees and green things
    Hastening along.

Retreating from happiness
    They would fain be set
In forms of the chief letters
    Of the alphabet.

Wayfarers wondered,
    Warriors were dismayed
At renewal of conflicts
    Such as Gwydion made,

Under the tongue root
  A fight most dread,
And another raging
  Behind, in the head.

The alders in the front line
  Began the affray.
Willow and rowan-tree
  Were tardy in array.

The holly, dark green,
  Made a resolute stand;
He is armed with many spear points
  Wounding the hand.

With foot-beat of the swift oak
  Heaven and earth rung;
'Stout Guardian of the Door',
  His name in every tongue.

Great was the gorse in battle,
  And the ivy at his prime;
The hazel was arbiter
  At this charmed time.

Uncouth and savage was the fir,
  Cruel the ash-tree –
Turns not aside a foot-breadth,
  Straight at the heart runs he.

The birch, though very noble,
  Armed himself but late:
A sign not of cowardice
  But of high estate.

The heath gave consolation
  To the toil-spent folk,
The long-enduring poplars
  In battle much broke.

Some of them were cast away
  On the field of fight
Because of holes torn in them
  By the enemy's might.

Very wrathful was the vine
    Whose henchmen are the elms;
I exalt him mightily
    To rulers of realms.

Strong chieftains were the blackthorn
    With his ill fruit,
The unbeloved whitethorn
    Who wears the same suit,

The swift-pursuing reed,
    The broom with his brood,
And the furze but ill-behaved
    Until he is subdued.

The dower-scattering yew
    Stood glum at the fight's fringe,
With the elder slow to burn
    Amid fires that singe,

And the blessed wild apple
    Laughing in pride
From the *Gorchan* of Maelderw
    By the rock side.

In shelter linger
    Privet and woodbine,
Inexperienced in warfare,
    And the courtly pine.

But I, although slighted
    Because I was not big,
Fought, trees, in your array
    On the field of Goddeu Brig.

THE SONG OF BLODEUWEDD

[Text reassembled and restored from the same poem-
medley as the foregoing.]

Not of father nor of mother
Was my blood, was my body.
I was spellbound by Gwydion,
Prime enchanter of the Britons,
When he formed me from nine blossoms,
   Nine buds of various kind:
From primrose of the mountain,
Broom, meadow-sweet and cockle,
   Together intertwined,
From the bean in its shade bearing
A white spectral army
   Of earth, of earthy kind,
From blossoms of the nettle,
Oak, thorn and bashful chestnut –
Nine powers of nine flowers,
   Nine powers in me combined,
      Nine buds of plant and tree.
Long and white are my fingers
     As the ninth wave of the sea.

INTERCESSION IN LATE OCTOBER

How hard the year dies: no frost yet.
On drifts of yellow sand Midas reclines,
Fearless of moaning reed or sullen wave.
Firm and fragrant still the brambleberries.
On ivy-bloom butterflies wag.

Spare him a little longer, Crone,
For his clean hands and love-submissive heart.

THE TETRAGRAMMATON

[A magical gloss on Numbers vi, 23-27.]

Light was his first day of Creation,
Peace after labour was his seventh day,
Life and the Glory are his day of days.

He carved his law on tables of sapphirus,
Jerusalem shines with his pyrope gates,
Four cherubs fetch him amber from the north.

Acacia yields her timber for his ark,
Pomegranate sanctifies his priestly hem,
His hyssop sprinkles blood at every door.

Holy, Holy, Holy, is his name.

NUNS AND FISH

Circling the circlings of their fish
   Nuns walk in white and pray;
    For he is chaste as they,
   Who was dark-faced and hot in Silvia's day,
And in his pool drowns each unspoken wish.

THE DESTROYER

Swordsman of the narrow lips,
Narrow hips and murderous mind
Fenced with chariots and ships,
By your joculators hailed
The mailed wonder of mankind,
Far to westward you have sailed.

You it was dared seize the throne
Of a blown and amorous prince
Destined to the Moon alone,
A lame, golden-heeled decoy,
Joy of hens that gape and wince
Inarticulately coy.

You who, capped with lunar gold
Like an old and savage dunce,
Let the central hearth go cold,
Grinned, and left us here your sword
Warden of sick fields that once
Sprouted of their own accord.

Gusts of laughter the Moon stir
That her Bassarids now bed
With the ignoble usurer
While an ignorant pale priest
Rides the beast with a man's head
To her long-omitted feast.

RETURN OF THE GODDESS

Under your Milky Way
    And slow-revolving Bear
Frogs from the alder thicket pray
In terror of your judgement day,
    Loud with repentance there.

The log they crowned as king
    Grew sodden, lurched and sank;
An owl floats by on silent wing,
Dark water bubbles from the spring;
    They invoke you from each bank.

At dawn you shall appear,
    A gaunt red-leggèd crane,
You whom they know too well for fear,
Lunging your beak down like a spear
    To fetch them home again.

> *Sufficiunt*
> *Tecum,*
> *Caryatis,*
> *Domnia*
> *Quina.*

From POEMS AND SATIRES 1951

(1951)

THE WHITE GODDESS

All saints revile her, and all sober men
Ruled by the God Apollo's golden mean –
In scorn of which we sailed to find her
In distant regions likeliest to hold her
Whom we desired above all things to know,
Sister of the mirage and echo.

It was a virtue not to stay,
To go our headstrong and heroic way
Seeking her out at the volcano's head,
Among pack ice, or where the track had faded
Beyond the cavern of the seven sleepers:
Whose broad high brow was white as any leper's,
Whose eyes were blue, with rowan-berry lips,
With hair curled honey-coloured to white hips.

Green sap of Spring in the young wood a-stir
Will celebrate the Mountain Mother,
And every song-bird shout awhile for her;
But we are gifted, even in November
Rawest of seasons, with so huge a sense
Of her nakedly worn magnificence
We forget cruelty and past betrayal,
Heedless of where the next bright bolt may fall.

THE CHINK

A sunbeam on the well-waxed oak,
   In shape resembling not at all
The ragged chink by which it broke
   Into this darkened hall,
Swims round and golden over me,
The sun's plenipotentiary.

So may my round love a chink find:
  With such address to break
Into your grief-occluded mind
  As you shall not mistake
  But, rising, open to me for truth's sake.

COUNTING THE BEATS

You, love, and I,
(He whispers) you and I,
And if no more than only you and I
What care you or I?

Counting the beats,
Counting the slow heart beats,
The bleeding to death of time in slow heart beats,
Wakeful they lie.

Cloudless day,
Night, and a cloudless day,
Yet the huge storm will burst upon their heads one day
From a bitter sky.

Where shall we be,
(She whispers) where shall we be,
When death strikes home, O where then shall we be
Who were you and I?

Not there but here,
(He whispers) only here,
As we are, here, together, now and here,
Always you and I.

Counting the beats,
Counting the slow heart beats,
The bleeding to death of time in slow heart beats,
Wakeful they lie.

THE JACKALS' ADDRESS TO ISIS

Grant Anup's children this:
To howl with you, Queen Isis,
Over the scattered limbs of wronged Osiris.
What harder fate than to be woman?
She makes and she unmakes her man.
In Jackal-land it is no secret
Who tempted red-haired, ass-eared Set
To such bloody extreme; who most
Must therefore mourn and fret
To pacify the unquiet ghost.
And when Horus your son
Avenges this divulsion,
Sceptre in fist, sandals on feet,
We shall return across the sand
From loyal Jackal-land
To gorge five nights and days on ass's meat.

THE DEATH ROOM

Look forward, truant, to your second childhood.
The crystal sphere discloses
Wall-paper roses mazily repeated
In pink and bronze, their bunches harbouring
Elusive faces, under an inconclusive
Circling, spidery, ceiling craquelure,
And, by the window-frame, the well-loathed, lame,
Damp-patch, cross-patch, sleepless L-for-Lemur
Who, puffed to giant size,
Waits jealously till children close their eyes.

THE YOUNG CORDWAINER

She: Love, why have you led me here
   To this lampless hall,
  A place of despair and fear
   Where blind things crawl?

He: Not I, but your complaint
   Heard by the riverside
  That primrose scent grew faint
   And desire died.

She: Kisses had lost virtue
   As yourself must know;
  I declared what, alas, was true
   And still shall do so.

He: Mount, sweetheart, this main stair
   Where bandogs at the foot
  Their crooked gilt teeth bare
   Between jaws of soot.

She: I loathe them, how they stand
   Like prick-eared spies.
  Hold me fast by the left hand;
   I walk with closed eyes.

He: Primrose has periwinkle
   As her mortal fellow:
  Five leaves, blue and baleful,
   Five of true yellow.

She: Overhead, what's overhead?
   Where would you take me?
  My feet stumble for dread,
   My wits forsake me.

He: Flight on flight, floor above floor,
   In suspense of doom
  To a locked secret door
   And a white-walled room.

She: Love, have you the pass-word,
       Or have you the key,
    With a sharp naked sword
     And wine to revive me?

He: Enter: here is starlight,
       Here the state bed
    Where your man lies all night
     With blue flowers garlanded.

She: Ah, the cool open window
       Of this confessional!
    With wine at my elbow,
    And sword beneath the pillow,
     I shall perfect all.

YOUR PRIVATE WAY

Whether it was your way of walking
Or of laughing moved me,
At sight of you a song wavered
Ghostly on my lips; I could not voice it,
Uncertain what the notes or key.

Be thankful I am no musician,
Sweet Anonymity, to madden you
With your own private walking-laughing way
Imitated on a beggar's fiddle
Or blared across the square on All Fools' Day.

MY NAME AND I

The impartial Law enrolled a name
  For my especial use:
My rights in it would rest the same
Whether I puffed it into fame
  Or sank it in abuse.

Robert was what my parents guessed
    When first they peered at me,
And *Graves* an honourable bequest
With Georgian silver and the rest
    From my male ancestry.

They taught me: 'You are *Robert Graves*
    (Which you must learn to spell),
But see that *Robert Graves* behaves,
Whether with honest men or knaves,
    Exemplarily well.'

Then though my I was always I,
    Illegal and unknown,
With nothing to arrest it by –
As will be obvious when I die
    And *Robert Graves* lives on –

I cannot well repudiate
    This noun, this natal star,
This gentlemanly self, this mate
So kindly forced on me by fate,
    Time and the registrar;

And therefore hurry him ahead
    As an ambassador
To fetch me home my beer and bread
Or commandeer the best green bed,
    As he has done before.

Yet, understand, I am not he
    Either in mind or limb;
My name will take less thought for me,
In worlds of men I cannot see,
    Than ever I for him.

CONVERSATION PIECE

By moonlight
At midnight,
Under the vines,
A hotel chair
Settles down moodily before the headlines
Of a still-folded evening newspaper.

The other chair
Of the pair
Lies on its back,
Stiff as in pain,
Having been overturned with an angry crack;
And there till morning, alas, it must remain.

On the terrace
No blood-trace,
No sorry glitter
Of a knife, nothing:
Not even the fine-torn fragments of a letter
Or the dull gleam of a flung-off wedding-ring.

Still stable
On the table
Two long-stemmed glasses,
One full of drink,
Watch how the rat among the vines passes
And how the moon trembles on the crag's brink.

THE GHOST AND THE CLOCK

About midnight my heart began
    To trip again and knock.
The tattered ghost of a tall man
Looked fierce at me as in he ran,
    But fiercer at the clock.

It was, he swore, a long, long while
    Until he'd had the luck
To die and make his domicile
On some ungeographic isle
    Where no hour ever struck.

'But now, you worst of clocks,' said he,
    'Delayer of all love,
In vengeance I've recrossed the sea
To jerk at your machinery
    And give your hands a shove.'

So impotently he groped and peered
    That his whole body shook!
I could not laugh at him; I feared
This was no ghost but my own weird,
    And closer dared not look.

ADVICE ON MAY DAY

Never sing the same song twice
    Lest she disbelieve it.
Though reproved as over-nice,
Never sing the same song twice –
Unobjectionable advice,
    Would you but receive it:
Never sing the same song twice
    Lest she disbelieve it.

Never sing a song clean through,
    You might disenchant her;
Venture on a verse or two
(Indisposed to sing it through),
Let that seem as much as you
    Care, or dare, to grant her;
Never sing your song clean through,
    You might disenchant her.

Make no sermon on your song
    Lest she turn and rend you.
Fools alone deliver long
Sermons on a May-day song;
Even a smile may put you wrong,
    Half a word may end you:
Make no sermon on your song
    Lest she turn and rend you.

FOR THE RAIN IT RAINETH EVERY DAY

Arabs complain – or so I have been told –
   Interminably of heat, as Lapps complain
Even of seasonable Christmas cold;
   Nor are the English yet inured to rain
Which still, my angry William, as of old
   Streaks without pause your birthday window pane.
      But you are English too;
      How can I comfort you?

Suppose I said: 'Those gales that eastward ride
   (Their wrath portended by a sinking glass)
With good St George of England are allied'?
   Suppose I said: 'They freshen the Spring grass,
Arab or Lapp would envy a fireside
   Where such green-fingered elementals pass'?
      No, you are English too;
      How could that comfort you?

QUESTIONS IN A WOOD

The parson to his pallid spouse,
   The hangman to his whore,
Do both not mumble the same vows,
   Both knock at the same door?

And when the fury of their knocks
   Has waned, and that was that,
What answer comes, unless the pox
   Or one more parson's brat?

Tell me, my love, my flower of flowers,
   True woman to this man,
What have their deeds to do with ours
   Or any we might plan?

Your startled gaze, your restless hand,
   Your hair like Thames in flood,
And choked voice, battling to command
   The insurgence of your blood:

How can they spell the dark word said
   Ten thousand times a night
By women as corrupt and dead
   As you are proud and bright?

And how can I, in the same breath,
   Though warned against the cheat,
Vilely deliver love to death
   Wrapped in a rumpled sheet?

Yet, if from delicacy of pride
   We choose to hold apart,
Will no blue hag appear, to ride
   Hell's wager in each heart?

THE PORTRAIT

She speaks always in her own voice
Even to strangers; but those other women
Exercise their borrowed, or false, voices
Even on sons and daughters.

She can walk invisibly at noon
Along the high road; but those other women
Gleam phosphorescent – broad hips and gross fingers –
Down every lampless alley.

She is wild and innocent, pledged to love
Through all disaster; but those other women
Decry her for a witch or a common drab
And glare back when she greets them.

Here is her portrait, gazing sidelong at me,
The hair in disarray, the young eyes pleading:
'And you, love? As unlike those other men
As I those other women?'

DARIEN

It is a poet's privilege and fate
To fall enamoured of the one Muse
Who variously haunts this island earth.

She was your mother, Darien,
And presaged by the darting halcyon bird
Would run green-sleeved along her ridges,
Treading the asphodels and heather-trees
With white feet bare.

Often at moonrise I had watched her go,
And a cold shudder shook me
To see the curved blaze of her Cretan axe.
Averted her set face, her business
Not yet with me, long-striding,
She would ascend the peak and pass from sight.
But once at full moon, by the sea's verge,
I came upon her without warning.

Unrayed she stood, with long hair streaming,
A cockle-shell cupped in her warm hands,
Her axe propped idly on a stone.

No awe possessed me, only a great grief;
Wanly she smiled, but would not lift her eyes
(As a young girl will greet the stranger).
I stood upright, a head taller than she.
'See who has come,' said I.

She answered: 'If I lift my eyes to yours
And our eyes marry, man, what then?
Will they engender my son Darien?
Swifter than wind, with straight and nut-brown hair,
Tall, slender-shanked, grey-eyed, untameable;
Never was born, nor ever will be born
A child to equal my son Darien,
Guardian of the hid treasures of your world.'

I knew then by the trembling of her hands
For whom that flawless blade would sweep:
My own oracular head, swung by its hair.

'Mistress,' I cried, 'the times are evil
And you have charged me with their remedy.
O, where my head is now, let nothing be
But a clay counterfeit with nacre blink:
Only look up, so Darien may be born!

'He is the northern star, the spell of knowledge,
Pride of all hunters and all fishermen,
Your deathless fawn, an eaglet of your eyrie,
The topmost branch of your unfellable tree,
A tear streaking the summer night,
The new green of my hope.'

                                   Lifting her eyes,
She held mine for a lost eternity.
'Sweetheart,' said I, 'strike now, for Darien's sake!'

THE SURVIVOR

To die with a forlorn hope, but soon to be raised
By hags, the spoilers of the field, to elude their claws
And stand once more on a well-swept parade-ground,
Scarred and bemedalled, sword upright in fist
At head of a new undaunted company:

Is this joy? – to be doubtless alive again,
And the others dead? Will your nostrils gladly savour
The fragrance, always new, of a first hedge-rose?
Will your ears be charmed by the thrush's melody
Sung as though he had himself devised it?

And is this joy: after the double suicide
(Heart against heart) to be restored entire,
To smooth your hair and wash away the life-blood,
And presently seek a young and innocent bride,
Whispering in the dark: 'for ever and ever'?

PROMETHEUS

Close bound in a familiar bed
All night I tossed, rolling my head;
Now dawn returns in vain, for still
The vulture squats on her warm hill.

I am in love as giants are
That dote upon the evening star,
And this lank bird is come to prove
The intractability of love.

Yet still, with greedy eye half shut,
Rend the raw liver from its gut:
Feed, jealousy, do not fly away –
If she who fetched you also stay.

SATIRES

QUEEN-MOTHER TO NEW QUEEN

Although only a fool would mock
The secondary joys of wedlock
(Which need no recapitulation),
The primary's the purer gold,
Even in our exalted station,
For all but saint or hoary cuckold.

Therefore, if ever the King's eyes
Turn at odd hours to your sleek thighs,
Make no delay or circumvention
But do as you should do, though strict
To guide back his bemused attention
Towards privy purse or royal edict,

And stricter yet to leave no stain
On the proud memory of his reign –
You'll act the wronged wife, if you love us.
Let them not whisper, even in sport:
'His Majesty's turned parsimonious
And keeps no whore now but his Consort.'

SECESSION OF THE DRONES

These drones, seceding from the hive,
    In self-felicitation
That henceforth they will throng and thrive
    Far from the honeyed nation,

Domesticate an old cess-pit,
    Their hairy bellies warming
With buzz of psychologic wit
    And homosexual swarming.

Engrossed in pure coprophily,
    Which makes them mighty clever,
They fabricate a huge King Bee
    To rule all hives for ever.

DAMOCLES

Death never troubled Damocles,
    Nor did the incertitude
When the sword, swung by a light breeze,
    Cast shadows on his food –
        'A thread is spun
        For every son,'
    Said he, 'of Pyrrha's brood.'

But great Zeus cursed him, none the less,
    With foresight to deplore
The end of that day's childishness,
    And he could eat no more:
        His fame would float
        Through anecdote
    Into dead metaphor.

Then orators from every land,
    Caught by the same disease,
With thump of fist or saw of hand
    Or sinking to their knees,
        Would madly boom
        Of the world's doom
    And swords of Damocles.

HOMAGE TO TEXAS

It's hardly wise to generalize
    About a state or city;
But Texan girls are decent girls
    And bold as they are pretty.

Who dared the outrageous unicorn
    Through lonely woods a-leaping?
Who made him halt and lower his horn
    And couch beside her, weeping?

Not Helen (wonder of her sex)
    Nor Artemis, nor Pallas;
No, sir: a girl from Houston, Tex.,
    Though some claim it was Dallas.

He told her: 'Ma'am, your Lone Star State,
    Though maybe short on schooling,
Outshines the whole bright forty-eight' –
    And so it did, no fooling.

THE DILEMMA

When Time, though granting scope enough
    For any conversationalist,
Gives the sworn poet a rebuff,
    Should he indeed desist?

Should he to timeless bogs retreat,
    His pace slowed to an old man's pace,
Where antique histories interlace
    Around a hearth of peat?

Or, rather, take revenge on Time,
    Stalking into those flood-lit stews:
Drown conversation with a crime,
    · Pause, yell and blow the fuse?

Sadist and masochist in me,
    Each boasting himself more than half,
Press the dilemma feverishly
    And raise hell if I laugh.

GENERAL BLOODSTOCK'S LAMENT FOR ENGLAND

'This image (seemingly animated) walks with them in the fields in broad Day-light; and if they are employed in delving, harrowing, Seed-sowing or any other Occupation, they are at the same time mimicked by the ghostly Visitant. Men of the Second Sight … call this reflex-man a Co-walker, every way like the Man, as his Twin-brother and Companion, haunting as his Shadow.'

Kirk's *Secret Commonwealth*, 1691.

Alas, England, my own generous mother,
One gift I have from you I hate,
The second sight: I see your weird co-walker,
Silver-zoned Albion, stepping in your track,
Mimicking your sad and doubtful gait,
Your clasped hands, your head-shakings, your bent back.

The white hem of a winding sheet
Draws slowly upward from her feet;
Soon it will mount knee-high, then to the thigh.
It crackles like the parchment of the treaties,
Bonds, contracts and conveyances,
With which, beggared and faint and like to die,
You signed away your island sovereignty
To rogues who learned their primer at your knees.

'¡WELLCOME, TO THE CAVES OF ARTÁ!'

'They are hollowed out in the see coast at the muncipal terminal of Capdepera, at nine kilometer from the town of Artá in the Island of Mallorca, with a suporizing infinity of graceful colums of 21 meter and by downward, wich prives the spectator of all animacion and plunges in dumbness. The way going is very picturesque, serpentine between style mountains, til the arrival at the esplanade of the vallee called "The Spider". There are good enlacements of the railroad with autobuses of excursion, many days of the week, today actually Wednesday and Satturday. Since many centuries renown foreing visitors have explored them and wrote thier eulogy about, included Nort-American geoglogues.'

From a Tourist leaflet.

Such subtile filigranity and nobless of construccion
    Here fraternise in harmony, that respiracion stops.
While all admit thier impotence (though autors most formidable)
    To sing in words the excellence of Nature's underprops,
Yet stalactite and stalagmite together with dumb language
    Make hymnes to God wich celebrate the stregnth of water drops.

¿You, also, are you capable to make precise in idiom
 Consideracions magic of ilusions very wide?
Alraedy in the Vestibule of these Grand Caves of Artá
 The spirit of the human verb is darked and stupefyed;
So humildy you trespass trough the forest of the colums
 And listen to the grandess explicated by the guide.

From darkness into darkness, but at measure, now descending
 You remark with what esxactitude he designates each bent;
'The Saloon of Thousand Banners', or 'The Tumba of Napoleon',
 'The Grotto of the Rosary', 'The Club', 'The Camping Tent'.
And at 'Cavern of the Organ' there are knocking streange
   formacions
 Wich give a nois particular pervoking wonderment.

¡Too far do not adventure, sir! For, further as you wander,
 The every of the stalactites will make you stop and stay.
Grand peril amenaces now, your nostrills aprehending
 An odour least delicious of lamentable decay.
It is some poor touristers, in the depth of obscure cristal,
 Wich deceased of thier emocion on a past excursion day.

TO A POET IN TROUBLE

Cold wife and angry mistress
And debts: all three?
Though they combine to kill you
Be grateful to the Goddess,
(Our cruel patroness),
For this felicity:
Your poems now ring true.

From *POEMS 1953*

(1953)

TO CALLIOPE

Permit me here a simple brief aside,
    Calliope,
You who have shown such patience with my pride
    And obstinacy:

Am I not loyal to you? I say no less
    Than is to say;
If more, only from angry-heartedness,
    Not for display.

But you know, I know, and you know I know
    My principal curse:
Shame at the mounting dues I have come to owe
    A devil of verse,

Who caught me young, ingenuous and uncouth,
    Prompting me how
To evade the patent clumsiness of truth –
    Which I do now.

No: nothing reads so fresh as I first thought,
    Or as you could wish –
Yet must I, when far worse is eagerly bought,
    Cry stinking fish?

THE STRAW

Peace, the wild valley streaked with torrents,
A hoopoe perched on his warm rock. Then why
This tremor of the straw between my fingers?

What should I fear? Have I not testimony
In her own hand, signed with her own name
That my love fell as lightning on her heart?

These questions, bird, are not rhetorical.
Watch how the straw twitches and leaps
As though the earth quaked at a distance.

Requited love; but better unrequited
If this chance instrument gives warning
Of cataclysmic anguish far away.

Were she at ease, warmed by the thought of me,
Would not my hand stay steady as this rock?
Have I undone her by my vehemence?

THE FOREBODING

Looking by chance in at the open window
    I saw my own self seated in his chair
With gaze abstracted, furrowed forehead,
    Unkempt hair.

I thought that I had suddenly come to die,
    That to a cold corpse this was my farewell,
Until the pen moved slowly upon paper
    And tears fell.

He had written a name, yours, in printed letters:
    One word on which bemusedly to pore –
No protest, no desire, your naked name,
    Nothing more.

Would it be tomorrow, would it be next year?
    But the vision was not false, this much I knew;
And I turned angrily from the open window
    Aghast at you.

Why never a warning, either by speech or look,
    That the love you cruelly gave me could not last?
Already it was too late: the bait swallowed,
    The hook fast.

CRY FAUGH!

Caria and Philistia considered
Only pre-marital adventures wise;
The bourgeois French argue contrariwise.

Socrates and Plato burked the issue
(Namely, how man-and-woman love should be)
With homosexual ideology.

Apocalyptic Israelites, foretelling
The Imminent End, called only for a chaste
Sodality: all dead below the waist.

Curious, various, amoral, moral –
Tell me, what elegant square or lumpish hamlet
Lives free from nymphological disquiet?

'Yet males and females of the lower species
Contrive to eliminate the sexual problem,'
Scientists ponder: 'Why not learn from them?'

Cry faugh! on science, ethics, metaphysics,
On antonyms of sacred and profane –
Come walk with me, love, in a golden rain

Past toppling colonnades of glory,
The moon alive on each uptilted face:
Proud remnants of a visionary race.

HERCULES AT NEMEA

Muse, you have bitten through my fool's-finger.
Fierce as a lioness you seized it
In your white teeth most amorously;
And I stared back, dauntless and fiery-eyed,
Challenging you to maim me for my pride.

See me a fulvous hero of nine fingers –
Sufficient grasp for bow and arrow.
My beard bristles in exultation:
Let all Nemea look and understand
Why you have set your mark on this right hand.

DIALOGUE ON THE HEADLAND

She: You'll not forget these rocks and what I told you?
He: How could I? Never: whatever happens.
She: What do you think might happen?
        Might you fall out of love? – did you mean that?
He: Never, never! 'Whatever' was a sop
        For jealous listeners in the shadows.
She: You haven't answered me. I asked:
        'What do you think might happen?'
He: Whatever happens: though the skies should fall
        Raining their larks and vultures in our laps –
She: 'Though the seas turn to slime' – say that –
        'Though water-snakes be hatched with six heads.'
He: Though the seas turn to slime, or tower
        In an arching wave above us, three miles high –
She: 'Though she should break with you' – dare you say that?
        'Though she deny her words on oath.'
He: I had that in my mind to say, or nearly;
        It hurt so much I choked it back.
She: How many other days can't you forget?
        How many other loves and landscapes?
He: You are jealous?
She: Damnably.
He: The past is past.
She: And this?
He: Whatever happens, this goes on.
She: Without a future? Sweetheart, tell me now:
        What do you want of me? I must know that.
He: Nothing that isn't freely mine already.
She: Say what is freely yours and you shall have it.
He: Nothing that, loving you, I could dare take.
She: O, for an answer with no 'nothing' in it!
He: Then give me everything that's left.
She: Left after what?
He: After whatever happens:
        Skies have already fallen, seas are slime,
        Watersnakes poke and peer six-headedly –
She: And I lie snugly in the Devil's arms.
He: I said: 'Whatever happens.' Are you crying?
She: You'll not forget me – ever, ever, ever?

LOVERS IN WINTER

The posture of the tree
  Shows the prevailing wind;
And ours, long misery
  When you are long unkind.

But forward, look, we lean –
  Not backward as in doubt –
And still with branches green
  Ride our ill weather out.

ESAU AND JUDITH

Robbed of his birthright and his blessing
Esau sought refuge in the wilderness,
An outlaw girding at the world's deceit.
He took to wife Judith, daughter of Heth,
Tall and grey-eyed, a priestess of her grove.
The curse lay heavy on their marriage-couch.

She was that sea which God had held corrupt;
Her tides he praised and her curvetting fish,
Though with no comprehension of their ways;
As a man blind from birth fondly adores
Fantasies of imagined gold and blue –
The curse lay heavy on their marriage-couch.

For how might Esau strive against his blood?
Had Isaac and Rebekah not commanded:
'Take thee a daughter from thy father's house!' –
Isaac who played the pander with Rebekah,
Even as Abraham had done with Sarah?
The curse lay heavy on their marriage-couch.

THE MARK

If, doubtful of your fate,
You seek to obliterate
And to forget
The counter-mark I set
In the warm blue-veined nook
Of your elbow crook,
How can you not repent
The experiment?

No knife nor fang went in
To lacerate the skin;
Nor may the eye
Tetter or wen descry:
The place which my lips pressed
Is coloured like the rest
And fed by the same blood
Of womanhood.

Acid, pumice-stone,
Lancings to the bone,
Would be in vain.
Here must the mark remain
As witness to such love
As nothing can remove
Or blur, or hide,
Save suicide.

WITH THE GIFT OF A RING

If one of thy two loves be wroth
And cry: 'Thou shalt not love us both,
Take one or 'tother!', O then choose
Him that can nothing thee refuse!
Only a rogue would tear a part,
How small soever, from thy heart;
As Adam sought to plunder Eve's
(What time they clad themselves in leaves),
Conjuring her to make an end
Of dalliance with her cursèd friend –
Too late, now she had learned to tell
False love from true, and ill from well.

LIADAN AND CURITHIR

Even in childhood
Liadan never would
    Accept love simply,
But stifled longing
And went away to sing
    In strange company.

Alas, for Liadan!
To fear perfection
    Was her ill custom:
Choosing a scruple
That might seem honourable,
    For retreat therefrom.

Herself she enticed
To be nunned for Christ,
    Though in marriage sought
By a master-poet
On whom her heart was set –
    Curithir of Connaught;

And raised a wall
As it were of crystal
    Her grief around.
He might not guess
The cause of her fickleness
    Nor catch one sound.

She was walled soon after
Behind stones and mortar,
    From whence too late
He heard her keening,
Sighing and complaining
    Of her dire self-hate.

THE SEA HORSE

Since now in every public place
Lurk phantoms who assume your walk and face,
You cannot yet have utterly abjured me
Nor stifled the insistent roar of sea.

Do as I do: confide your unquiet love
(For one who never owed you less than love)
To this indomitable hippocamp,
Child of your element, coiled a-ramp,
Having ridden out worse tempests than you know of;
Under his horny ribs a blood-red stain
Portends renewal of our pain.
Sweetheart, make much of him and shed
Tears on his taciturn dry head.

THE DEVIL AT BERRY POMEROY

Snow and fog unseasonable,
The cold remarkable,
Children sickly;
Green fruit lay thickly
Under the crab-tree
And the wild cherry.
I heard witches call
Their imps to the Hall:
'Hey, Ilemauzar,
Sack-and-Sugar,
Peck-in-the-Crown,
Come down, come down!'
I heard bells toll
For a monster's soul
That was born, half dead,
With a double head;
I saw ghosts leap
From the ruined keep;
I saw blows thwack
On the raw back
Of a dying ass.
Blight was on the grass,
Poison in the cup

(Lover, drink up!),
With envy, slander,
Weasels a-wander,
Incest done
Between mother and son,
Murder of hags
For their money-bags,
Wrath, rape,
And the shadowy ape
Which a lady, weeping,
Leads by a string
From first twilight
Until past midnight
Through the Castle yard –
'Blow winds, blow hard!'
So the Devil snaps his chain
And renews his reign
To the little joy
Of Berry Pomeroy.

REPROACH TO JULIA

Julia: how Irishly you sacrifice
Love to pity, pity to ill-humour,
Yourself to love, still haggling at the price.

DETHRONEMENT

With pain pressing so close about your heart,
Stand (it behoves you), head uncovered,
To watch how she enacts her transformations –
Bitch, vixen, sow – the laughing, naked queen
Who has now dethroned you.

Hymns to her beauty or to her mercy
Would be ill-conceived. Your true anguish
Is all that she requires. You, turned to stone,
May not speak nor groan, shall stare dumbly,
Grinning dismay.

But as the play ends, or in its after-hush,
O then, deluded, flee! Her red-eared hounds
Scramble upon your track; past either cheek
Swan-feathered arrows whistle, or cruelly comb
Long furrows in your scalp.

Run, though you hope for nothing: to stay your foot
Would be ingratitude, a sour denial
That the life she bestowed was sweet.
Therefore be fleet, run gasping, draw the chase
Up the grand defile.

They will rend you to rags assuredly
With half a hundred love-bites –
Your hot blood an acceptable libation
Poured to Persephone, in whose domain
You shall again find peace.

CAT-GODDESSES

A perverse habit of cat-goddesses –
Even the blackest of them, black as coals
Save for a new moon blazing on each breast,
With coral tongues and beryl eyes like lamps,
Long-leggèd, pacing three by three in nines –
This obstinate habit is to yield themselves,
In verisimilar love-ecstasies,
To tatter-eared and slinking alley-toms
No less below the common run of cats
Than they above it; which they do for spite,
To provoke jealousy – not the least abashed
By such gross-headed, rabbit-coloured litters
As soon they shall be happy to desert.

THE BLUE-FLY

Five summer days, five summer nights,
The ignorant, loutish, giddy blue-fly
Hung without motion on the cling peach,
Humming occasionally: 'O my love, my fair one!'
    As in the *Canticles*.

Magnified one thousand times, the insect
Looks farcically human; laugh if you will!
Bald head, stage-fairy wings, blear eyes,
A caved-in chest, hairy black mandibles,
　　Long spindly thighs.

The crime was detected on the sixth day.
What then could be said or done? By anyone?
It would have been vindictive, mean and what-not
To swat that fly for being a blue-fly,
　　For debauch of a peach.

Is it fair, either, to bring a microscope
To bear on the case, even in search of truth?
Nature, doubtless, has some compelling cause
To glut the carriers of her epidemics –
　　Nor did the peach complain.

RHEA

On her shut lids the lightning flickers,
Thunder explodes above her bed,
An inch from her lax arm the rain hisses;
Discrete she lies,

Not dead but entranced, dreamlessly
With slow breathing, her lips curved
In a half-smile archaic, her breast bare,
Hair astream.

The house rocks, a flood suddenly rising
Bears away bridges: oak and ash
Are shivered to the roots – royal green timber.
She nothing cares.

(Divine Augustus, trembling at the storm,
Wrapped sealskin on his thumb; divine Gaius
Made haste to hide himself in a deep cellar,
Distraught by fear.)

Rain, thunder, lightning: pretty children.
'Let them play,' her mother-mind repeats;
'They do no harm, unless from high spirits
Or by mishap.'

THE HERO

This prince's immortality was confirmed
With envious rites paid him by such poor souls
As, dying, were condemned to flit like bats
In endless caverns of oblivion:
For he alone, amid excessive keening,
Might voyage to that island paradise,
In the red West,
Where bees come thronging to the apple flow
And thrice three damsels in a tall house
Tend the mead-vat of inspiration.

They feel no envy now, those poor souls.
Did not some bald Cilician sell them
Mansions in Heaven, and at a paltry price:
Offering crowns of gold for scabbed heads,
Robes of state for vitiliginous backs?
No blood is poured now at the hero's tomb,
No prayers intoned,
The island paradise is unfrequented,
And neither Finn, nor Ogier, nor Arthur,
Returns to prophesy our common doom.

MARGINAL WARNING

Prejudice, as the Latin shows,
Means that you follow your own nose
Like an untutored spaniel; hence,
A nose being no good evidence
That Farmer Luke hangs from a limb
With cart-rope tightly trussing him,
Till twelve unblinking pairs of eyes
Can view the corpse and authorize
A coroner to shake his head
For: 'Gentlemen, this man is dead',
Your blind prognostication is
Roundly condemned as prejudice;
And should you further speculate,
Snuffing once more, upon what date
His cowman strung him to the tree:
The case being now *sub judice*,

Contempt of court will be the cry
To challenge and arrest you by –
What will your children think of you,
Docked of your nose and your ears too?

THE ENCOUNTER

Soon after dawn in hottest June (it may
For all I know, have been Midsummer's Day)
An hour at which boulevardiers are few,
From either end of the grand avenue
Flanked with basilicas and palaces
And shaded by long rows of ancient trees,
A man drew near, his lips in rage compressed,
Marching alone, magnificently dressed –
This, rose on green; that, mulberry on gold –
Two tall unyielding men of the same mould
Who wore identical helmets, cloaks and shoes
And long straight swords they had well learned to use,
Both being luckless fellows, paired by fate
In bonds of irremediable hate.

Closer they steered: although the walk was wide,
A scant inch served as margin to their pride.
The encounter surely could but end in blows;
Yet neither thought to tweak his enemy's nose,
Or jostle him, or groan, or incur guilt
By a provocative grasp at the sword hilt,
Each setting such reliance on mischance
He sauntered by without a sidelong glance.

I'M THROUGH WITH YOU FOR EVER

The oddest, surely, of odd tales
    Recorded by the French
Concerns a sneak thief of Marseilles
    Tried by a callous Bench.

His youth, his innocency, his tears –
    No, nothing could abate
Their sentence of 'One hundred years
    In galleys of the State.'

Nevertheless, old wives affirm
    And annalists agree,
He sweated out the whole damned term,
    Bowed stiffly, and went free.

Then come, my angry love, review
    Your sentence of today.
'For ever' was unjust of you,
    The end too far away.

Give me four hundred years, or five –
    Can rage be so intense? –
And I will sweat them out alive
    To prove my impenitence.

WITH HER LIPS ONLY

This honest wife, challenged at dusk
At the garden gate, under a moon perhaps,
In scent of honeysuckle, dared to deny
Love to an urgent lover: with her lips only,
Not with her heart. It was no assignation;
Taken aback, what could she say else?
For the children's sake, the lie was venial;
'For the children's sake', she argued with her conscience.

Yet a mortal lie must follow before dawn:
Challenged as usual in her own bed,
She protests love to an urgent husband,
Not with her heart but with her lips only;
'For the children's sake', she argues with her conscience,
'For the children' – turning suddenly cold towards them.

THE BLOTTED COPY-BOOK

He broke school bounds, he dared defy
The Master's atrabilious eye,
Diced, swigged raw brandy, used foul oaths,
Wore shamelessly Corinthian clothes,
And taught St Dominic's to mock
At gown and hood and whipping-block.

The boy's a nabob now, retired
With wealth enough to be admired
Even by the School Governors
(Benignly sycophantic bores)
Who call on him to give away
Prize-medals on Foundation Day.

Will he at last, or will he not,
His yellowing copy-book unblot:
Accede, and seriously confess
A former want of seriousness,
Or into a wild fury burst
With: 'Let me see you in Hell first!'?

THE SACRED MISSION

The ungainsayable, huge, cooing message
Hurtles suddenly down the dawn streets:
Twenty loudspeakers, twenty lovesick voices
Each zealous to enlarge his own range
And dominate the echoing border-zones.

Now the distressed whimper of little children,
The groans of sick men cheated in their hope
Of snatching a light sleep from the jaws of pain,
The curses, even, of the unregenerate –
All are submerged in the rising sea of noise
Which floods each room and laps round every pillow,
Roaring the mercy of Christ's limitless love.

FROM THE EMBASSY

I, an ambassador of Otherwhere
To the unfederated states of Here and There
Enjoy (as the phrase is)
Extra-territorial privileges.
With heres and theres I seldom come to blows
Or need, as once, to sandbag all my windows.
And though the Otherwhereish currency
Cannot be quoted yet officially,
I meet less hindrance now with the exchange
Nor is my garb, even, considered strange;
And shy enquiries for literature
Come in by every post, and the side door.

SIROCCO AT DEYÁ

How most unnatural-seeming, yet how proper;
The sea like a cat with fur rubbed the wrong way,
As the sirocco with its furnace flavour
Dashes at full tilt around the village
['From every-which-a-way, hot as a two-buck pistol']
Stripping green olives from the blown-back boughs,
Scorching the roses, blinding the eyes with sand;
While slanderous tongues in the small cafés
And in the tightly-shuttered limestone houses
Clack defamation, incite and invite
Knives to consummate their near-murders....
Look up, a great grey cloud broods nonchalant
On the mountain-top nine hundred feet above us,
Motionless and turgid, blotting out the sun,
And from it sneers a supercilious Devil:
'Mere local wind: no messenger of mine!'

PENTHESILEIA

Penthesileia, dead of profuse wounds,
Was despoiled of her arms by Prince Achilles
Who, for love of that fierce white naked corpse,
Necrophily on her committed
In the public view.

Some gasped, some groaned, some bawled their indignation,
Achilles nothing cared, distraught by grief,
But suddenly caught Thersites' obscene snigger
And with one vengeful buffet to the jaw
Dashed out his life.

This was a fury few might understand,
Yet Penthesileia, hailed by Prince Achilles
On the Elysian plain, pauses to thank him
For avenging her insulted womanhood
With sacrifice.

POETS' CORNER

De ambobus mundis ille
Convoravit diligens ...

The Best of Both Worlds being Got
Between th'Evangel and the Pot,
He, though Exorbitantly Vice'd,
Had Re-discover'd Thirst for Christ
And Fell a Victim (Young as This)
To Ale, God's Love and Syphilis.

Here then in Triumph See Him Stand,
Laurels for Halo, Scroll in Hand,
Whyle Ganymeds and Cherubim
And Squabby Nymphs Rejoyce with Him:
Aye, Scroll Shall Fall and Laurels Fade
Long, Long before his Debts are Pay'd.

CORONATION ADDRESS

I remember, Ma'am, a frosty morning
When I was five years old and brought ill news,
Marching solemnly upstairs with the paper
Like an angel of doom; knocked gently.
'Father, the *Times* has a black border. Look!
The Queen is dead.'
                                        Then I grew scared
When big tears started, ran down both his cheeks
To hang glistening in the red-grey beard –
A sight I had never seen before.

My mother thought to comfort him, leaned closer,
Whispering softly: 'It was a ripe old age....
She saw her century out.' The tears still flowed,
He could not find his voice. My mother ventured:
'We have a King once more, a real King.
"God Save the King" is in the Holy Bible.
Our Queen was, after all, only a woman.'

At that my father's grief burst hoarsely out.
'Only a woman! You say it to my face?
Queen Victoria only a woman! What?
Was the orb nothing? Was the sceptre nothing?
To cry "God Save the King" is honourable,
But to serve a Queen is lovely. Listen now:
Could I have one wish for this son of mine ... '

A wish fulfilled at last after long years.

Think well, Ma'am, of your great-great-grandmother
Who earned love, who bequeathed love to her sons,
Yet left one crown in trust for you alone.

BEAUTY IN TROUBLE

Beauty in trouble flees to the good angel
    On whom she can rely
To pay her cab-fare, run a steaming bath,
    Poultice her bruised eye;

Will not at first, whether for shame or caution,
    Her difficulty disclose;
Until he draws a cheque book from his plumage,
    Asking how much she owes.

(Breakfast in bed: coffee and marmalade,
    Toast, eggs, orange-juice,
After a long, sound sleep – the first since when? –
    And no word of abuse.)

Loves him less only than her saint-like mother,
    Promises to repay
His loans and most seraphic thoughtfulness
    A million-fold one day.

Beauty grows plump, renews her broken courage
    And, borrowing ink and pen,
Writes a news-letter to the evil angel
    (Her first gay act since when?):

The fiend who beats, betrays and sponges on her,
    Persuades her white is black,
Flaunts vespertilian wing and cloven hoof;
    And soon will fetch her back.

Virtue, good angel, is its own reward:
    Your guineas were well spent.
But would you to the marriage of true minds
    Admit impediment?

A LOST JEWEL

Who on your breast pillows his head now,
Jubilant to have won
The heart beneath on fire for him alone,

At dawn will hear you, plagued by nightmare,
Mumble and weep
About some blue jewel you were sworn to keep.

Wake, blink, laugh out in reassurance,
Yet your tears will say:
'It was not mine to lose or give away.

'For love it shone – never for the madness
Of a strange bed –
Light on my finger, fortune in my head.'

Roused by your naked grief and beauty,
For lust he will burn:
'Turn to me, sweetheart! Why do you not turn?'

THE WINDOW SILL

Presage and caveat not only seem
To come in dream,
But do so come in dream.

When the cock crew and phantoms floated by,
This dreamer I
Out of the house went I,

Down long unsteady streets to a queer square;
And who was there,
Or whom did I know there?

Julia, leaning on her window sill.
'I love you still,'
She said, 'O love me still!'

I answered: 'Julia, do you love me best?'
'What of this breast,'
She mourned, 'this flowery breast?'

Then a wild sobbing spread from door to door,
And every floor
Cried shame on every floor,

As she unlaced her bosom to disclose
Each breast a rose,
A white and cankered rose.

SPOILS

When all is over and you march for home,
The spoils of war are easily disposed of:
Standards, weapons of combat, helmets, drums
May decorate a staircase or a study,
While lesser gleanings of the battlefield –
Coins, watches, wedding-rings, gold teeth and such –
Are sold anonymously for solid cash.

The spoils of love present a different case,
When all is over and you march for home:
That lock of hair, these letters and the portrait
May not be publicly displayed; nor sold;
Nor burned; nor returned (the heart being obstinate) –
Yet never dare entrust them to a safe
For fear they burn a hole through two-foot steel.

From *THE CROWNING PRIVILEGE*

(1955)

THE CLEARING

Above this bramble-overarched long lane
Where an autochthonous owl flits to and fro
    In silence,
Above these tangled trees – their roots encumbered
By strawberries, mushrooms, pignuts, flowers' and weeds'
    Exuberance –
The planetary powers gravely observe
    With what dumb patience
You stand at twilight in despair of love,
Though the twigs crackling under a light foot
    Declare her immanence.

THE THREE PEBBLES

(*In thirty of these burials, the black deposit of fragmentized pots contained a small white quartz pebble associated with two pieces of alien ware, one red porphyry, the other a greenish stone, probably porphyry also. Their presence was clearly intentional.* – Proceedings of the Cumberland and Westmorland Archaeological Society, New Series, vol. xiv.)

Is red the ghost of green? and green, of red?
And white, the impartial light upon them shed?
And I, my own twin warring against me?

Then, woman, take two jewels of porphyry,
Well matched in weight, one green, one angry red:
To light them with yourself, a pure moon-crystal,
And lay them on my bier when I am dead.

POSSIBLY

Possibly is not a monosyllable;
    Then answer me
At once if possible
    Monosyllabically,
No will be good, *Yes* even better
Though longer by one letter.

Possibly is not a monosyllable,
    And my heart flies shut
At the warning rumble
    Of a suspended *But* ...
O love, be brief and exact
In confession of simple fact.

END OF THE WORLD

When, at a sign, the Heavenly vault entire
Founders and your accustomed world of men
Drops through the fundament – too vast a crash
To register as sound – and you plunge with it,
Trundling, head over heels, in dark confusion
Of trees, churches, elephants, railway trains,
And the cascading seven seas:

It cannot signify how deep you fall
From everything to nothing. Nothingness
Cushions disaster, and this much is sure:
A buoyant couch will bear you up at last,
Aloof, alone – but for the succuba.

TO A PEBBLE IN MY SHOE

I cannot pity you,
Poor pebble in my shoe,
    Now that the heel is sore;
You planned to be a rock
And a stumbling block,
    Or was it perhaps more?

But now be grateful if
You vault over the cliff,
    Shaken from my shoe;
Where lapidary tides
May scour your little sides
    And even polish you.

THE TENANTS

Pictures and books went off ahead this morning:
    The furniture is sold (and tells you so);
Both trunks are packed, and seven suit-cases;
    A cat glides petulantly to and fro,
        Afraid to leave us.

Now massive walls and stairs, for so long certain,
    Retreat and fade like a mirage at sea;
Your room and mine lose their established meanings –
    By dawn tomorrow let them cease to be
        Or to concern us!

We faced a scowl from window, door and fireplace,
    Even in the kitchen, when we first were here;
It cost us years of kindness to placate them.
    But now each scowl resolves into a leer
        With which to speed us.

How dared we struggle with a house of phantoms,
    Soaked in ill luck? And when we go away,
Confess, can you and I be certain whether
    The ghost of our unhappiness will stay
        Or follow with us?

MY MORAL FORCES

My moral forces, always dissipated
    If I condone the least
Fault that I should have hated
    In (say)
Politician, prostitute, or priest,

Appear fanatical to a degree
    If ever I dispute
Claims of integrity
    Advanced (say)
By politician, priest, or prostitute.

But though your prostitute, priest, or politician
    Be good or bad
As such, I waive the ambition
    To curl (say)
Chameleon-like on a Scots tartan plaid.

INTERVIEW

Sixty bound books, an entire bookcase full,
All honest prose, without one duplicate.

Why written? *Answer:* for my self-support –
I was too weak to dig, too proud to beg.

Worth reading? *Answer:* this array of titles
Argues a faithful public following.

Will I not add to the above statement,
Touching (however lightly) on my verse?

Answer: this question makes me look a fool,
As who breeds dogs because he loves a cat.

From 5 PENS IN HAND

(1958)

THE FACE IN THE MIRROR

Grey haunted eyes, absent-mindedly glaring
From wide, uneven orbits; one brow drooping
Somewhat over the eye
Because of a missile fragment still inhering,
Skin deep, as a foolish record of old-world fighting.

Crookedly broken nose – low tackling caused it;
Cheeks, furrowed; coarse grey hair, flying frenetic;
Forehead, wrinkled and high;
Jowls, prominent; ears, large; jaw, pugilistic;
Teeth, few; lips, full and ruddy; mouth, ascetic.

I pause with razor poised, scowling derision
At the mirrored man whose beard needs my attention,
And once more ask him why
He still stands ready, with a boy's presumption,
To court the queen in her high silk pavilion.

FORBIDDEN WORDS

There are some words carry a curse with them:
Smooth-trodden, abstract, slippery vocables.
They beckon like a path of stepping stones;
But lift them up and watch what writhes or scurries!

Concepts barred from the close language of love –
Darling, you use no single word of the list,
Unless ironically in truth's defence
To volley it back against the abstractionist.

Which is among your several holds on my heart;
For you are no uninstructed child of Nature,
But passed in schools and attained the laurel wreath:
Only to trample it on Apollo's floor.

SONG FOR NEW YEAR'S EVE

Chill moonlight flooding from chill sky
  Has drowned the embers' glow.
Your pale hands glitter; you and I
  Out in the fields must go,

Where cat-ice glazes every rut
  And firs with snow are laced,
Where wealth of bramble, crab and nut
  Lies tumbled into waste.

The owlets raise a lovely din,
  The fox has his desire,
And we shall welcome New Year in
  With frost instead of fire.

ALEXANDER AND QUEEN JANET

On Janet come so late
To their banquet of state
  The angels nobly smile;
But Alexander thrusts away his plate.

'Janet, where have you been?
Janet, what have you seen?
  Your lover is abashed:
For want of you we have sat down thirteen.'

'I have nowhere been,
And nothing have I seen.
  Were it not for Alexander
You had no reason to sit down thirteen.'

Sweet wine for Janet now,
Fresh costards from the bough
    Of Paradise, white bread
Which they must force between her lips somehow.

'I could not wish,' says she,
'For prettier company,
    Angels of light, than yours,
Yet crystal cups and dishes are not for me.

'Though Alexander dine
On Heaven's own bread and wine,
    And Paradisal fruit,
Such delicacies are not for me or mine.

'Do you approve the grace
Of my form or my face?
    It springs from earth,' says Janet,
'And must be welcomed in a greener place.'

At this the angels hide
Their proud heads, mortified;
    Being deep in love with Janet
And jealous, too, for Alexander's pride.

Queen Janet softly goes
Treading on her tip toes
    To the bright table head;
She lays before her man a damask rose.

'Is it still your desire
To shiver at my fire?
    Then come now, Alexander,
Or stay and be a monk, or else a friar.'

'My lambkin, my sweet,
I have dined on angels' meat,
    And in you I had trusted
To attend their call and make my joy complete.'

'Do you come? Do you stay?
Alexander, say!
    For if you will not come
This gift rose I must surely snatch away.'

'Janet, how can I come?
Eat only a crumb
    Of bread, essay this wine!
In God's name sit beside me; or be dumb.'

Her back Janet turns,
Dumbly she spurns
    The red rose with her shoe;
But in each cheek another red rose burns.

The twelve angels, alas,
Are brought to a sad pass:
    Their lucent plumage pales,
Their glittering sapphire eyes go dull as glass.

Now Alexander's soul
Flies up from the brain hole,
    To circle like a bat
Above his body threshing past control.

It was Queen Janet's power
Turned the sweet wine sour,
    Shrivelled the apples' bloom,
And the bread crumbled into dusty flour.

THE CORAL POOL

It was a hippocamp addressed her darling,
    Perched on the coral branches of a pool
Where light reflected back from violet moss
    And fishes veered above in a tight school:

'Daughter, no sea is deep enough for drowning;
    Therefore let none seem broad enough for you,
My foal, my fledgeling bird, my dragon-imp,
    Or understand a tithe of what you do.

'To wanton fish never divulge your secret,
    But only to our mistress of the tides
Whose handy-men are octopus and crab,
    At whose white heel the amorous turtle glides.'

GRATITUDE FOR A NIGHTMARE

His appearances are incalculable,
His strength terrible,
I do not know his name.

Huddling pensive for weeks on end, he
Gives only random hints of life, such as
Strokes of uncomfortable coincidence.

To eat heartily, dress warmly, lie snugly
And earn respect as a leading citizen
Granted long credit at all shops and inns –

How dangerous! I had feared this shag demon
Would not conform with my conformity
And in some leaner belly make his lair.

But now in dream he suddenly bestrides me....
'All's well,' I groan, and fumble for a light,
Brow bathed in sweat, heart pounding.

FRIDAY NIGHT

Love, the sole Goddess fit for swearing by,
Concedes us graciously the little lie:
The white lie, the half-lie, the lie corrective
Without which love's exchange might prove defective,
Confirming hazardous relationships
By kindly *maquillage* of Truth's pale lips.

This little lie was first told, so they say,
On the sixth day (Love's planetary day)
When, meeting her full-bosomed and half dressed,
Jove roared out suddenly: 'Hell take the rest!
Six hard days of Creation are enough' –
And clasped her to him, meeting no rebuff.

Next day he rested, and she rested too.
The busy little lie between them flew:
'If this be not perfection,' Love would sigh,
'Perfection is a great, black, thumping lie.... '
Endearments, kisses, grunts, and whispered oaths;
But were her thoughts on breakfast, or on clothes?

THE NAKED AND THE NUDE

For me, the naked and the nude
(By lexicographers construed
As synonyms that should express
The same deficiency of dress
Or shelter) stand as wide apart
As love from lies, or truth from art.

Lovers without reproach will gaze
On bodies naked and ablaze;
The Hippocratic eye will see
In nakedness, anatomy;
And naked shines the Goddess when
She mounts her lion among men.

The nude are bold, the nude are sly
To hold each treasonable eye.
While draping by a showman's trick
Their dishabille in rhetoric,
They grin a mock-religious grin
Of scorn at those of naked skin.

The naked, therefore, who compete
Against the nude may know defeat;
Yet when they both together tread
The briary pastures of the dead,
By Gorgons with long whips pursued,
How naked go the sometime nude!

WOMAN AND TREE

To love one woman, or to sit
    Always beneath the same tall tree,
Argues a certain lack of wit
    Two steps from imbecility.

A poet, therefore, sworn to feed
    On every food the senses know,
Will claim the inexorable need
    To be Don Juan Tenorio.

Yet if, miraculously enough,
    (And why set miracles apart?)
Woman and tree prove of a stuff
    Wholly to glamour his wild heart?

And if such visions from the void
    As shone in fever there, or there,
Assemble, hold and are enjoyed
    On climbing one familiar stair … ?

To change and chance he took a vow,
    As he thought fitting. None the less,
What of a phoenix on the bough,
    Or a sole woman's fatefulness?

DESTRUCTION OF EVIDENCE

You neigh and flaunt your coat of sorrel-red,
O long-winged Pegasus sprung from my head,
Walking the lawn so lively and complete
That, like a wolf, my after-birth I eat –
Must he be told, the astonished passer-by,
I did not draw you down from a clear sky?

THE SECOND-FATED

My stutter, my cough, my unfinished sentences,
Denote an inveterate physical reluctance
To use the metaphysical idiom.
Forgive me: what I am saying is, perhaps this: –

Your accepted universe, by Jove's naked hand
Or Esmun's, or Odomankoma's, or Marduk's –
Choose which name jibes – formed scientifically
From whatever there was before Time was,
And begging the question of perfect consequence,
May satisfy the general run of men
(If 'run' be an apt term for patent paralytics)
That blueprints destine all they suffer here,
But does not satisfy certain few else.

Fortune enrolled me among the second-fated
Who have read their own obituaries in *The Times*,
Have heard 'Where, death, thy sting? Where, grave, thy victory?'
Intoned with unction over their still clay,
Have seen two parallel red-ink lines drawn
Under their manic-depressive bank accounts,
And are therefore strictly forbidden to walk in grave-yards
Lest they scandalize the sexton and his bride.

We, to be plain with you, taking advantage
Of a brief demise, visited first the Pit,
A library of shades, completed characters;
And next the silver-bright Hyperborean Queendom,
Basking under the sceptre of Guess Whom?
Where pure souls matrilineally foregather.
We were then shot through by merciful lunar shafts
Until hearts tingled, heads sang, and praises flowed;
And learned to scorn your factitious universe
Ruled by the death which we had flouted;
Acknowledging only that from the Dove's egg hatched
Before aught was, but wind – unpredictable
As our second birth would be, or our second love:
A moon-warmed world of discontinuance.

A SLICE OF WEDDING CAKE

Why have such scores of lovely, gifted girls
    Married impossible men?
Simple self-sacrifice may be ruled out,
    And missionary endeavour, nine times out of ten.

Repeat 'impossible men': not merely rustic,
    Foul-tempered or depraved
(Dramatic foils chosen to show the world
    How well women behave, and always have behaved).

Impossible men: idle, illiterate,
    Self-pitying, dirty, sly,
For whose appearance even in City parks
    Excuses must be made to casual passers-by.

Has God's supply of tolerable husbands
    Fallen, in fact, so low?
Or do I always over-value woman
    At the expense of man?
                        Do I?
                                It might be so.

A PLEA TO BOYS AND GIRLS

You learned Lear's *Nonsense Rhymes* by heart, not rote;
    You learned Pope's *Iliad* by rote, not heart;
These terms should be distinguished if you quote
    My verses, children – keep them poles apart –
And call the man a liar who says I wrote
    All that I wrote in love, for love of art.

A BOUQUET FROM A FELLOW ROSEMAN

Oh, what does the roseman answer
    On receiving a gift bouquet
Of raddled and blowsy roses
    From the garden across the way,
        From a fellow roseman?

If the roseman is a roseman is a roseman,
    And nothing other at all,
He flings that bouquet of roses
    Clear over his garden wall
        Like a proper roseman.

But, if only a week-end roseman,
  He does what he has to do:
'What beautiful blooms,' he answers,
  'How exceedingly kind of you!'
    To the flattered roseman;

And never escapes the insistent
  Arrival of new bouquets,
All equally damned and dismal,
  All hankering for his praise
    As a fellow roseman.

YES

The Romans had no word for YES,
  So mean they were, and stiff;
With SI the Spaniards make you guess
  (Their YES conceals an IF);
OUI means no more than 'so I hear';
  JA sounds a little coarse;
Then, child, say YES, polite and clear –
  Not UH-HUH, like a horse.

THE OUTSIDER

Glandular change provokes a vague content,
  St Martin's summer blossoms warm and sweet.
Frail, balding, toothless, yet benevolent
  The outsider has attained the inside seat
Which once he scorned; all angry passion spent,
  And twelve disciples prostrate at his feet.

Now that his once outrageous heresies
  Stand firmly in the schools' curriculum,
Should he be vexed if young fools think him wise
  Whom their grandfathers prayed to be struck dumb?
And should he disavow old truth as lies,
  Which on obsequious lips it has become?

From *STEPS*

(1958)

THE ENLISTED MAN

Yelled Corporal Punishment at Private Reasons:
   'Rebels like you have no right to enlist –
   Or to exist!'
Major Considerations leered approval,
   Clenching his fist,
   And gave his fierce moustache a fiercer twist.
So no appeal, even to General Conscience,
   Kept Private Reasons' name off the defaulter-list.

MIKE AND MANDY

Mandy: O, I'd like to be a Rug
           Basking by the fireside
           In a farm-house parlour.

Mike: If you were the Rug,
           I'd like to be a Hard Broom
           And scratch you all over.

Mandy: If you were the Hard Broom,
           I'd like to be a Kitchen Maid
           And toss you in a corner.

Mike: If you were a Kitchen Maid,
           I'd like to be the Farmer
           And show you who was master.

Mandy: If you were the Farmer,
           I'd like to be his Wife
           And strike you with a poker.

Mike: If you were his Wife,
I'd like to be the Constable
And grab you by the shoulder.

Mandy: If you were the Constable,
I'd like to be a Rug,
Lying by the fireside
In that farm-house parlour –
To slide and trip you up
And make you bang your head
On the corner of the firegrate
And kill you stone dead.

NOTHING

NOTHING is circular,
Like the empty centre
Of a smoke-ring's shadow:
That colourless zero
Marked on a bare wall –
Nothing at all
And reflected in a mirror.

Then need you wonder
If the trained philosopher
Who seeks to define NOTHING
As absence of anything,
A world more logistically
Than, above, I
(Though my terms are cosier),

And claims he has found
That NOTHING is not round
Or hardly ever,
Will run a brain-fever
To the precise degree
Of one hundred and three
On Fahrenheit's thermometer?

CALL IT A GOOD MARRIAGE

Call it a good marriage –
For no one ever questioned
Her warmth, his masculinity,
Their interlocking views;
Except one stray graphologist
Who frowned in speculation
At her h's and her s's,
His p's and w's.

Though few would still subscribe
To the monogamic axiom
That strife below the hip-bones
Need not estrange the heart,
Call it a good marriage:
More drew those two together,
Despite a lack of children,
Than pulled them apart.

Call it a good marriage:
They never fought in public,
They acted circumspectly
And faced the world with pride;
Thus the hazards of their love-bed
Were none of our damned business –
Till as jurymen we sat upon
Two deaths by suicide.

READ ME, PLEASE!

If, as well may happen,
    On an autumn day
When white clouds go scudding
    And winds are gay,

Some earth-bound spirit,
    A man lately dead,
(Your fellow-clerk) should take it
    Into his crazed head

To adopt a more venturesome
　Shape than a dead leaf
And wish you a 'good morning'
　Abrupt and brief,

He will come disguised
　As a sheet of newspaper
Charging across the square
　With a clumsy caper,

To flatten himself out
　Across your shins and knees
In a suppliant posture:
　'Read me, please!'

Then scanning every column
　On both sides, with care,
You will find that clerk's name
　Printed somewhere –

Unless, perhaps, in warning
　The sheet comes blown
And the name which you stumble on
　Is, alas, your own.

THE TWIN OF SLEEP

Death is the twin of Sleep, they say:
　For I shall rise renewed,
Free from the cramps of yesterday,
　Clear-eyed and supple-thewed.

But though this bland analogy
　Helps other folk to face
Decrepitude, senility,
　Madness, disease, disgrace,

I do not like Death's greedy looks:
　Give me his twin instead –
Sleep never auctions off my books,
　My boots, my shirts, my bed.

AROUND THE MOUNTAIN

Some of you may know, others perhaps can guess
    How it is to walk all night through summer rain
(Thin rain that shrouds a beneficent full moon),
    To circle a mountain, and then limp home again.

The experience varies with a traveller's age
    And bodily strength, and strength of the love affair
That harries him out of doors in steady drizzle,
    With neither jacket nor hat, and holds him there.

Still, let us concede some common elements:
    Wild-fire that, until midnight, burns his feet;
And surging rankly up, strong on the palate,
    Scents of July, imprisoned by long heat.

Add: the sub-human, black tree-silhouettes
    Against a featureless pale pall of sky;
Unseen, gurgling water; the bulk and menace
    Of entranced houses; a wraith wandering by.

Milestones, each one witness of a new mood –
    Anger, desperation, grief, regret;
Her too-familiar face that whirls and totters
    In memory, never willing to stay set.

Whoever makes the desired turning-point,
    Which means another fifteen miles to go,
Learns more from dawn than love, so far, has taught him:
    Especially the false dawn, when cocks first crow.

Those last few miles are easy: being assured
    Of the truth, why should he fabricate fresh lies?
His house looms up; the eaves drip drowsily;
    The windows blaze to a resolute sunrise.

III

From FOOD FOR CENTAURS

(1960)

TWICE OF THE SAME FEVER

No one can die twice of the same fever?
    Tell them it is untrue:
Have we not died three deaths, and three again,
    You of me, I of you?

The chill, the frantic pulse, brows burning,
    Lips broken by thirst –
Until, in darkness, a ghost grieves:
    'It was I died the first.'

Worse than such death, even, is resurrection.
    Do we dare laugh away
Disaster, and with a callous madrigal
    Salute the new day?

ESTABLISHED LOVERS

The established lovers of an elder generation
Dead from the waist down, every man of them,
Have now expired for sure
And, after nine days' public threnody,
Lapse to oblivion, or literature …
Clerks of Establishment must therefore search
For faces fit to people the blank spaces.

Faces enough are found, to pretend modesty
And mask their yearning for the public call:
Pluperfect candidates
Having long ceased to live as lovers do …
Clerks of Establishment, checking the dates,
Can feel no qualm in recommending Orders,
Titles and honorary love-doctorates.

Observe him well, the scarlet-robed academician
Stalled with his peers, an Order on his breast,
And (who could doubt it?) free
Of such despairs and voices as attended
His visits to the grotto below sea
Where once he served a glare-eyed Demoness
And swore her his unswerving verity.

THE QUIET GLADES OF EDEN

All such proclivities are tabulated –
By trained pathologists, in detail too –
The obscener parts of speech compulsively
Shrouded in Classic Latin.

But though my pleasure in your feet and hair
Is ungainsayable, let me protest
(Dear love) I am no trichomaniac
And no foot-fetichist.

If it should please you, for your own best reasons,
To take and flog me with a rawhide whip,
I might (who knows?) surprisedly accept
This earnest of affection.

Nothing, agreed, is alien to love
When pure desire has overflowed its baulks;
But why must private sportiveness be viewed
Through public spectacles?

Enough, I will not claim a heart unfluttered
By these case-histories of aberrancy;
Nevertheless a long cool draught of water,
Or a long swim in the bay,

Serves to restore my wholesome appetite
For you and what we do at night together:
Which is no more than Adam did with Eve
In the quiet glades of Eden.

HEROES IN THEIR PRIME

Theseus: was he an old, bald King of Athens
    By folly forced into self-banishment,
Who cursed his own twelve tribes from Mount Gargettus
    And sailed for Scyros, glowering discontent?

No, but that tall youth who laid low Procrustes,
    Sinis and Scyron, bandits of repute,
And in a labyrinthine lair at Cnossus
    The Minotaur by night did execute.

Bellerophon: was he a tattered outcast
    Seldom descried on the rough Xanthian plain,
Whom Pegasus had pitched into a thorn-bush,
    Thus rudely closing his presumptuous reign?

No, but that hero, smiled on by Athene,
    Scourge both of Amazons and Solymi,
Who quenched Chimaera's fiery exhalations
    With arrows shot at her from a clear sky.

Jason: was Jason a chap-fallen beggar
    Whom the prophetic prow of Argo slew
When back he crawled to die in shame at Corinth
    Loathed by the gods, and by his shipmates too?

No, but that single-sandalled young Magnesian,
    Fearless and fond, the cynosure of Greece,
Who by your kindly aid, Queen Aphrodite,
    Seduced Medea and fetched home the Fleece.

And Nestor: was he Agamemnon's Nestor,
    Whose grey beard wagged beside the walls of Troy
And wagged still more, long after Troy had fallen,
    Anent his exploits as a beardless boy?

Yes, that was he: revered by Prince Achilles,
    Odysseus, Diomede and many more –
Not the young braggart quaking at the tree-top
    In terror of a Calydonian boar.

CATKIND

Through the window,
Listening carefully,
I overheard a low
Moonlight murmur from an olive-tree –
Three cats rehearsed the virtues of catkind:
Catkind's silky tread and devious mind,
Catkind's quiet economy
(Cleansing itself with wash of its own body),
Catkind's nonchalance,
Catkind's persistence,
Catkind's circumambulance,
Its fealty to the Queen of Cats above –
'But when we love,' they wailed, 'alas, we LOVE!'

TWO CHILDREN

You were as venturesome as I was shy:
Eager and inquisitive your eye.
        You set a nap on the plum, a haze on the rose,
And shooting stars across the wintry sky
        Flashed by in volleys for me when you chose.

None spoke with you, I alone worshipped you,
Child of the wave, child of the morning dew,
And in my dreams went chasing here and there
A fugitive beacon – your moon-yellow hair.

HERE LIVE YOUR LIFE OUT!

Window-gazing, at one time or another
In the course of travel, you must have startled at
Some coign of true felicity. 'Stay!' it beckoned,
'Here live your life out!' If you were simple-hearted
The village rose, perhaps, from a broad stream
Lined with alders and gold-flowering flags –
Hills, hay-fields, orchards, mills – and, plain to see,
The very house behind its mulberry-tree
Stood, by a miracle, untenanted!

Alas, you could not alight, found yourself jolted
Viciously on; public conveyances
Are not amenable to casual halts,
Except in sternly drawn emergencies –
Bandits, floods, landslides, earthquakes or the like –
Nor could you muster resolution enough
To shout: 'This is emergency, let me out!'
Rushing to grasp their brakes; so the whole scene
Withdrew forever. Once at the terminus
(As your internal mentor will have told you),
It would have been pure folly to engage
A private car, drive back, sue for possession.
Too far, too late:
Already bolder tenants were at the gate.

JOAN AND DARBY

My friends are those who find agreement with me
In large measure, but not absolutely.
Little children, parasites and God
May flatter me with absolute agreement –
For no one lives more cynical than God.

As for my love, I gifted my heart to her
Twenty years ago, without proviso,
And in return she gifted hers to me;
Yet still they beat as two, unyielding in
Their honest, first reluctance to agree.

Other seasons, other thoughts and reasons,
Other fears or phases of the moon:
In loving-kindness we grow grey together –
Like Joan and Darby in their weather-lodge
Who never venture out in the same weather.

SUPERMAN ON THE RIVIERA

Looked tough, was tall and permanently bronzed
(I should guess Berkeley, do not quote me, though)
Not an ounce above the statutory weight,
Two hundred pounds, most of it bone and muscle;
Blue-eyed, with jutting chin and jutting brows.
The nose, however, did not command the chin.
Myself, I would rather have no chin at all
Than one that dared be wiser than its boss.
As for his mouth, a man-sized Cupid bow,
Curved for kissing a diminutive mother
And flashing teen-age smiles of high intent:
Was that the cause, or was it one more symptom,
Of his twin habits – equally repulsive
To us inveterate Western Europeans –
Downing a midday pint of raw cow's milk
And treating France's noblest vintages
Like bath-tub gin whenever he got high?

THE PICTURE NAIL

I brought a Death of Nelson home, where I
Hung it, by inadvertence, on a fly.
    Down crashed the heavy frame, off the fly flew,
And how my curses rang! Frankly, I own
To a sad lack of humour when alone –
    Like you, by God, and you, and even you!

OLD WORLD DIALOGUE

'Is this,' she asked, 'what the lower orders call … ?'
'Yes, yes,' replied her lover, Lord Whitehall,
'But, hush!, the expression is a trifle crude – '
'*Much* too good for them,' cried Lady Ermintrude.

'Nevertheless,' resumed the tactless peer,
'Those who excel at it – pray, do not sneer –
Are, by and large, of obscure parentage.
One girl I knew – '
                            'Take that!' she shouted, red with rage.

THE WERE-MAN

Alone, alone and well alone at last,
Sentries by stealth outwitted, frontiers passed!
Yet walking alien thoroughfares you brood
Fearfully on the man by this feat rescued.

Never before, though trusted friends were few,
Though your own love of loves her oath outgrew,
Though off to the loud wars your children ran,
Never before closeted with a were-man.

Loathing his sylvan company, unable
To bed with him or set his place at table,
A savage life you lead, condemned to share
Your hearth with one whose habitat is nowhere.

THE PERSON FROM PORLOCK

... At that moment the Author was unfortunately called out by a person
on business from Porlock and on his return found to his mortification that
though he retained some vague recollection of his vision, yet with the excep-
tion of eight or ten scattered lines and images, all the rest had passed away.
Coleridge's preface to *Kubla Khan: A Fragment*

Unkind fate sent the Porlock person
To collect fivepence from a poet's house;
Pocketing which old debt he drove away,
Heedless and gay, homeward bound for Porlock.

O Porlock person, habitual scapegoat,
Should any masterpiece be marred or scotched,
I wish your burly fist on the front door
Had banged yet oftener in literature!

From *THE PENNY FIDDLE*

(1960)

THE PENNY FIDDLE

Yesterday I bought a penny fiddle
 And put it to my chin to play,
But I found that the strings were painted,
 So I threw my fiddle away.

A gipsy girl found my penny fiddle
 As it lay abandoned there;
When she asked me if she might keep it,
 I told her I did not care.

Then she drew such music from the fiddle
 With help of a farthing bow,
That I offered five shillings for the secret.
 But, alas, she would not let it go.

ROBINSON CRUSOE

Robinson Crusoe cut his coats
 Not too narrow, not too big,
From the hides of nanny-goats;
 Yet he longed to keep a pig.

Robinson Crusoe sat in grief,
 All day long he sometimes sat,
Gazing at the coral reef,
 Grumbling to his favourite cat.

'Queen of Pussies,' he would say,
 'Two things I am sure about:
Bacon should begin the day,
 "Pork!" should put the candle out.'

THE SIX BADGERS

As I was a-hoeing, a-hoeing my lands,
Six badgers walked up, with white wands in their hands.
They formed a ring round me and, bowing, they said:
'Hurry home, Farmer George, for the table is spread!
There's pie in the oven, there's beef on the plate:
Hurry home, Farmer George, if you would not be late!'

So homeward went I, but could not understand
Why six fine dog-badgers with white wands in hand
Should seek me out hoeing, and bow in a ring,
And all to inform me so common a thing!

JOCK O' BINNORIE

King Duncan had a fool called Leery
    And gave him very high pay
To tell him stories after dinner,
    A new one every day;
But if the stories failed him
    (As Leery did agree)
The King would call his merry men all
    And hang him from a tree.

Leery began with Jim o' Binnorie
    Who danced on Stirling Rock
And emptied a peck of pickled eels
    All over his brother Jock;
Yet Jock refrained from unkind words
    That many a lad might use,
And while Jim slept on a load of hay
    Put five live eels in his shoes.

Leery had told nine hundred tales
    And found no others to tell,
He started from the first once more –
    King Duncan knew it well.
'Old friends are best, dear Fool,' he cried,
    'And old yarns heard again.
You may tell me the story of Jock o' Binnorie
    Every night of my reign!'

From *MORE POEMS 1961*

(1961)

LYCEIA

All the wolves of the forest
Howl for Lyceia,
Crowding together
In a close circle,
Tongues a-loll.

A silver serpent
Coiled at her waist
And a quiver at knee,
She combs fine tresses
With a fine comb:

Wolf-like, woman-like,
Gazing about her,
Greeting the wolves;
Partial to many,
Yet masked in pride.

The young wolves snarl,
They snap at one another
Under the moon.
'Beasts, be reasonable,
My beauty is my own!'

Lyceia has a light foot
For a weaving walk.
Her archer muscles
Warn them how tightly
She can stretch the string.

I question Lyceia,
Whom I find posted
Under the pine trees
One early morning:
'What do the wolves learn?'

'They learn only envy,'
Lyceia answers,
'Envy and hope,
Hope and chagrin.
Would you howl too
In that wolfish circle?'
She laughs as she speaks.

SYMPTOMS OF LOVE

Love is a universal migraine,
A bright stain on the vision
Blotting out reason.

Symptoms of true love
Are leanness, jealousy,
Laggard dawns;

Are omens and nightmares –
Listening for a knock,
Waiting for a sign:

For a touch of her fingers
In a darkened room,
For a searching look.

Take courage, lover!
Could you endure such grief
At any hand but hers?

THE SHARP RIDGE

Since now I dare not ask
Any gift from you, or gentle task,
Or lover's promise – nor yet refuse
Whatever I can give and you dare choose –
Have pity on us both: choose well
On this sharp ridge dividing death from hell.

UNDER THE OLIVES

We never would have loved had love not struck
Swifter than reason, and despite reason:
Under the olives, our hands interlocked,
We both fell silent:
Each listened for the other's answering
Sigh of unreasonableness –
Innocent, gentle, bold, enduring, proud.

THE VISITATION

Drowsing in my chair of disbelief
I watch the door as it slowly opens –
A trick of the night wind?

Your slender body seems a shaft of moonlight
Against the door as it gently closes.
Do you cast no shadow?

Your whisper is too soft for credence,
Your tread like blossom drifting from a bough,
Your touch even softer.

You wear that sorrowful and tender mask
Which on high mountain tops in heather-flow
Entrances lonely shepherds;

And though a single word scatters all doubts
I quake for wonder at your choice of me:
Why, why and why?

FRAGMENT

Are you shaken, are you stirred
By a whisper of love?
Spell-bound to a word
Does Time cease to move,
Till her calm grey eye
Expands to a sky
And the clouds of her hair
Like storms go by?

APPLE ISLAND

Though cruel seas like mountains fill the bay,
Wrecking the quayside huts,
Salting our vineyards with tall showers of spray;

And though the moon shines dangerously clear,
Fixed in another cycle
Than the sun's progress round the felloe'd year;

And though I may not hope to dwell apart
With you on Apple Island
Unless my breast be docile to the dart –

Why should I fear your element, the sea,
Or the full moon, your mirror,
Or the halved apple from your holy tree?

THE FALCON WOMAN

It is hard to be a man
Whose word is his bond
In love with such a woman,

When he builds on a promise
She lightly let fall
In carelessness of spirit.

The more sternly he asks her
To stand by that promise
The faster she flies.

But is it less hard
To be born such a woman
With wings like a falcon
And in carelessness of spirit
To love such a man?

TROUGHS OF SEA

'Do you delude yourself?' a neighbour asks,
Dismayed by my abstraction.
But though love cannot question love
Nor need deny its need,

Pity the man who finds a rebel heart
Under his breastbone drumming
Which reason warns him he should drown
In midnight wastes of sea.

Now as he stalks between tormented pines
(The moon in her last quarter)
A lissom spectre glides ahead
And utters not a word.

Waves tasselled with dark weed come rearing up
Like castle walls, disclosing
Deep in their troughs a ribbed sea-floor
To break his bones upon.

 – Clasp both your hands under my naked foot
And press hard, as I taught you:
A trick to mitigate the pangs
Either of birth or love.

THE LAUGH

Your sudden laugh restored felicity –
Everything grew clear that before would not:
The impossible genies, the extravagants,
Swung in to establish themselves fairly
As at last manageable elements
In a most daylight-simple plot.
It was the identity of opposites
Had so confused my all too sober wits.

THE DEATH GRAPPLE

Lying between your sheets, I challenge
A watersnake in a swoln cataract
Or a starved lioness among drifts of snow.

Yet dare it out, for after each death grapple,
Each gorgon stare borrowed from very hate,
A childish innocent smile touches your lips,
Your eyelids droop, fearless and careless,
And sleep remoulds the lineaments of love.

THE STARRED COVERLET

A difficult achievement for true lovers
Is to lie mute, without embrace or kiss,
Without a rustle or a smothered sigh,
Basking each in the other's glory.

Let us not undervalue lips or arms
As reassurances of constancy,
Or speech as necessary communication
When troubled hearts go groping through the dusk;

Yet lovers who have learned this last refinement –
To lie apart, yet sleep and dream together
Motionless under their starred coverlet –
Crown love with wreaths of myrtle.

THE INTRUSION

Going confidently into the garden
Where she made much of you four hours ago
You find another person in her seat.

If your scalp crawls and your eyes prick at sight
Of her white motionless face and folded hands
Framed in such thunderclouds of sorrow,

Give her no word of consolation, man,
Dissemble your own anguish,
Withdraw in silence, gaze averted –
This is the dark edge of her double-axe:
Divine mourning for what cannot be.

PATIENCE

Almost I could prefer
A flare of anger
To your dumb signal of displeasure.

Must it be my task
To assume the mask
Of not desiring what I may not ask?

On a wide bed,
Both arms outspread,
I watch the spites do battle in my head,

Yet know this sickness
For stubborn weakness
Unconsonant with your tenderness.

O, to be patient
As you would have me patient:
Patient for a thousand nights, patient!

THE CURE

No lover ever found a cure for love
Except so cruel a thrust under the heart
(By her own hand delivered)
His wound was nine long years in healing,
Purulent with dead hope,
And ached yet longer at the moon's changes ...
More tolerable the infection than its cure.

HAG-RIDDEN

I awoke in profuse sweat, arms aching,
Knees bruised and soles cut to the raw –
Preserved no memory of that night
But whipcracks and my own voice screaming.
Through what wild, flinty wastes of fury,
Hag of the Mill,
Did you ride your madman?

TURN OF THE MOON

Never forget who brings the rain
In swarthy goatskin bags from a far sea:
It is the Moon as she turns, repairing
Damages of long drought and sunstroke.

Never count upon rain, never foretell it,
For no power can bring rain
Except the Moon as she turns; and who can rule her?

She is prone to delay the necessary floods,
Lest such a gift might become obligation,
A month, or two, or three; then suddenly
Not relenting but by way of whim
Will perhaps conjure from the cloudless west
A single rain-drop to surprise with hope
Each haggard, upturned face.

Were the Moon a Sun, we would count upon her
To bring rain seasonably as she turned;
Yet no one thinks to thank the regular Sun
For shining fierce in summer, mild in winter –
Why should the Moon so drudge?

But if one night she brings us, as she turns,
Soft, steady, even, copious rain
That harms no leaf nor flower, but gently falls
Hour after hour, sinking to the tap roots,
And the sodden earth exhales at dawn
A long sigh scented with pure gratitude,
Such rain – the first rain of our lives, it seems,
Neither foretold, cajoled, nor counted on –
Is woman giving as she loves.

THE SECRET LAND

Every woman of true royalty owns
A secret land more real to her
Than this pale outer world:

At midnight when the house falls quiet
She lays aside needle or book
And visits it unseen.

Shutting her eyes, she improvises
A five-barred gate among tall birches,
Vaults over, takes possession.

Then runs, or flies, or mounts a horse
(A horse will canter up to greet her)
And travels where she will;

Can make grass grow, coax lilies up
From bud to blossom as she watches,
Lets fish eat from her palm;

Has founded villages, planted groves
And hollowed valleys for brooks running
Cool to a land-locked bay.

I never dared question my love
About the government of her queendom
Or its geography,

Nor followed her between those birches,
Setting one leg astride the gate,
Spying into the mist.

Yet she has pledged me, when I die,
A lodge beneath her private palace
In a level clearing of the wood
Where gentians grow and gillyflowers
And sometimes we may meet.

SELDOM YET NOW

Seldom yet now: the quality
Of this fierce love between us –
Seldom the encounter,
The presence always,
Free of oath or promise.

And if we were not so
But birds of similar plumage caged
In the peace of every day,
Would we still conjure wildfire up
From common earth, as now?

TO MYRTO OF MYRTLES

Goddess of Midsummer, how late
    You let me understand
My lines of head, life, fate
        And heart: a broad M brand
        Inerasable from either hand.

ANCHISES TO APHRODITE

Your sceptre awes me, Aphrodite,
    The knot-of-wisdom in your grasp.
Though you have deigned my couch to warm
    And my firm neck in love to clasp,

How am I more than a man-lion
    To you a goddess, the world's queen?
Ten thousand champions of your choice
    Are gone as if they had not been.

Yet while you grant me power to stem
    The tide's unalterable flow,
Enroyalled I await your pleasure
    And starve if you would have it so.

A LOST WORLD

'Dear love, why should you weep
        For time's remorseless way?
Though today die in sleep
        And be called yesterday,
        We love, we stay.'

'I weep for days that died
        With former love that shone
On a world true and wide
        Before this newer one
        Which yours shines on.'

'Is this world not as true
        As that one ever was
Which now has fled from you
        Like shadows from the grass
        When the clouds pass?'

'Yet for that would I weep
        Kindly, before we kiss:
Love has a faith to keep
        With past felicities
        That weep for this.'

THE DANGEROUS GIFT

Were I to cut my hand
    On that sharp knife you gave me
    (That dangerous knife, your beauty),
I should know what to do:
    Bandage the wound myself
And hide the blood from you.

A murderous knife it is,
    As often you have warned me:
    For if I looked for pity
Or tried a wheedling note
    Either I must restore it
Or turn it on my throat.

SURGICAL WARD: MEN

Something occurred after the operation
To scare the surgeons (though no fault of theirs),
Whose reassurance did not fool me long.
Beyond the shy, concerned faces of nurses
A single white-hot eye, focusing on me,
Forced sweat in rivers down from scalp to belly.
I whistled, gasped or sang, with blanching knuckles
Clutched at my bed-grip almost till it cracked:
Too proud, still, to let loose Bedlamite screeches
And bring the charge-nurse scuttling down the aisle
With morphia-needle levelled....
                        Lady Morphia –
Her scorpion kiss and dark gyrating dreams –
She in mistrust of whom I dared out-dare,
Two minutes longer than seemed possible,
Pain, that unpurposed, matchless elemental
Stronger than fear or grief, stranger than love.

NIGHTFALL AT TWENTY THOUSAND FEET

A black wall from the east, toppling, arches the tall sky over
To drown what innocent pale western lights yet cover
Cloud banks of expired sunset; so goodbye, sweet day!
From earliest green you sprang, in green tenderly glide away ...
Had I never noticed, on watch before at a humbler height,
That crowding through dawn's gate come night and dead of night?

THE SIMPLETON

To be defrauded often of large sums,
A whole year's income, even,
By friends trusted so long and perfectly
He never thought to ask receipts from them:
Such had been his misfortune.

He did not undervalue money, sighed for
Those banknotes, warm in the breast pocket,
For want of which his plans were baulked;
But could not claim that any man had left him
In complete poverty.

Easier to choke back resentment,
Never to sue them, never pit in court
His unsupported oath against theirs;
Easier not to change a forsworn friend
For a sworn enemy.

Easier, too, to scoff at legal safeguards,
Promissories on pale-blue foolscap
Sealed, signed, delivered before witnesses.
What legal safeguard had a full wallet
Carried among a crowd?

But though he preened himself on calmly
Cancelling irrecoverable debts,
It vexed him not to know
Why all his oldest, dearest friends conspired
To pluck him like a fowl.

TWO RHYMES ABOUT FATE AND MONEY

'Neighbour, neighbour, don't forget:
 Thirty shillings due tomorrow!'
Fate and mammon rule us yet,
In the midst of life we are in debt,
 Here to pay and gone to borrow.

*

How and why
Poets die,
 That's a dismal tale:
Some take a spill
On Guinea Hill,
 Some drown in ale,

Some get lost
At sea, or crossed
 In love with cruel witches,
But some attain
Long life and reign
 Like Popes among their riches.

THE TWO WITCHES

O sixteen hundred and ninety-one,
Never was year so well begun,
Backsy-forsy and inside out,
The best of years to ballad about.

On the first fine day of January
I ran to my sweetheart Margery
And tossed her over the roof so far
That down she fell like a shooting star.

But when we two had frolicked and kissed
She clapped her fingers about my wrist
And tossed me over the chimney stack,
And danced on me till my bones did crack.

Then, when she had laboured to ease my pain,
We sat by the stile of Robin's Lane,
She in a hare and I in a toad
And puffed at the clouds till merry they glowed.

We spelled our loves until close of day.
I wished her good-night and walked away,
But she put out a tongue that was long and red
And swallowed me down like a crumb of bread.

BURN IT!

Fetch your book here.
That you have fought with it for half a year
(Christmas till May)
Not intermittently but night and day
Need but enhance your satisfaction
In swift and wholesome action.

Write off the expense
Of stationery against experience,
And salvage no small beauties or half-lines.
You took the wrong turn, disregarded signs
Winking along your track,
Until too close-committed to turn back.

Fetch the book here
And burn it without fear,
Grateful at least that, having gone so far,
You still know what truth is and where you are,
With better things to say
In your own bold, unmarketable way.

SONG: COME, ENJOY YOUR SUNDAY!

Into your outstretched hands come pouring
Gifts by the cornucopiaful –
    What else is lacking?
Come, enjoy your Sunday
While yet you may!

Cease from unnecessary labours,
Saunter into the green world stretching far,
    Light a long cigar,
Come, enjoy your Sunday
While yet you may!

What more, what more? You fended off disaster
In a long war, never acknowledging
    Any man as master;
Come, enjoy your Sunday
While yet you may!

Are you afraid of death? But death is nothing:
The leaden seal set on a filled flask.
    If it be life you ask,
Come, enjoy your Sunday
While yet you may!

On a warm sand dune now, sprawling at ease
With little in mind, learn to despise the sea's
    Unhuman restlessness:
Come, enjoy your Sunday
While yet you may!

RUBY AND AMETHYST

Two women: one as good as bread,
     Bound to a sturdy husband.
Two women: one as rare as myrrh,
     Bound only to herself.

Two women: one as good as bread,
     Faithful to every promise.
Two women: one as rare as myrrh,
     Who never pledges faith.

The one a flawless ruby wears
     But with such innocent pleasure
A stranger's eye might think it glass
     And take no closer look.

Two women: one as good as bread,
     The noblest of the city.
Two women: one as rare as myrrh,
     Who needs no public praise.

The pale rose-amethyst on her breast
     Has such a garden in it
Your eye could trespass there for hours,
     And wonder, and be lost.

About her head a swallow wheels
     Nor ever breaks the circuit:
Glory and awe of womanhood
     Still undeclared to man.

Two women: one as good as bread,
     Resistant to all weathers.
Two women: one as rare as myrrh,
     Her weather still her own.

THE MILLER'S MAN

The imperturbable miller's man
Whose help the boy implored, drowning,
Drifting slowly past the mill,
Was a stout swimmer, yet would not come between
The river-god and his assured victim.

Soon he, too, swimming in the sun,
Is caught with cramp; and the boy's ghost
Jeers from the reeds and rushes.
But he drowns valiantly in silence,
This being no one's business but his own.

Let us not reckon the miller's man
With Judas or with Jesus,
But with the cattle, who endure all weathers,
Or with the mill-wheel foolishly creaking,
Incurious of the grain in the bins.

JULY 24TH

July the twenty-fourth, a day
Heavy with clouds that would not spill
On the disconsolate earth.

Across the road in docile chorus
School-children raised their morning hymn to God
Who still forgot their names and their petitions.

'What an age to be born in!' cried old Jamboree.
'Two world wars in one generation!'
'However,' said I, 'the plum crop should be heavy!'

What was the glass doing? The glass was low.
The Germans claimed to have stormed the town of Rostov.
Sweden dismissed the claim as premature.

Not a single painter left in the neighbourhood –
All were repainting ruined Exeter.
We had no earthly right to grumble … No?

I was reading a book about bone artifacts
In the age of the elk or woolly rhinoceros.
Already, it seems, man had a high culture.

A clerk wrote from the Ministry of Labour
To ask what reasons (if any) would prevent me
From serving in the Devonshire Home Guard.

Soon the Americans would be here: the patter
Of their rubber heels sounding like summer rain.
So pleasantly passed my forty-seventh birthday.

SAFE RECEIPT OF A CENSORED LETTER

As the war lengthened, the mail shrank:
And now the Military Censor's clerk
Caught up with correspondence twelve months old –
But letters in a foreign language waited
Five months more.

'Time,' he said, 'is the best Censor:
Secret movements of troops and guns, even,
Become historical, cease to concern.
These uninterpretable items may be
Passed at last.'

Your letter was among the favoured –
Dateless familiar gossip of the village.
Thus you (who died a year ago) succeed,
Old rogue, in circumventing a more rigid
Censorship.

From NEW POEMS 1962

(1962)

RECOGNITION

When on the cliffs we met, by chance,
    I startled at your quiet voice
And watched the swallows round you dance
    Like children that had made a choice.

Simple it was, as I stood there,
    To penetrate the mask you wore,
Your secret lineage to declare
    And your lost dignities restore.

Yet thus I earned a poet's fee
    So far out-distancing desire
That swallows yell in rage at me
    As who would set their world on fire.

THE WATCH

Since the night in which you stole
    Like a phantom to my bed,
Seized my throat and from it wrung
    Vows that could not be unsaid,

Here beneath my arching ribs
    Red-hot embers, primed to be
Blown upon by winds of love,
    Scorch away mortality.

Like sledgehammers my two fists,
    My broad forehead grim with pride,
Muscles corded on my calves
    And my frame gigantified.

Yet your watching for an hour
    That our mutual stars will bless
Proves you more entranced than I
    Who go parched in hope of less.

NAME DAY

Tears of delight that on my name-day
She gave me nothing, and in return
Accepted every gift I heaped upon her –
Call me the richest poet alive!

UNCALENDARED LOVE

The first name cut on a rock, a King's,
Marked the beginning of time's annals;
And each new year would recapitulate
The unkind sloughings and renewals
Of the death-serpent's chequered coat.

But you with me together, together, together,
Survive ordeals never before endured:
We snatch the quill out of Enoch's hand
To obliterate our names from his black scroll –
Twin absentees of time.

Ours is uncalendared love, whole life,
As long or brief as befalls. Alone, together,
Recalling little, prophesying less,
We watch the serpent, crushed by your bare heel,
Rainbow his scales in a deathward agony.

THE MEETING

We, two elementals, woman and man,
Approached each other from far away:
I on the lower wind, she on the upper.

And the faith with which we came invested
By the blind thousands of our twin worlds
Formed thunder clouds about us.

Never such uproar as when we met,
Nor such forked lightning; rain in a cataract
Tumbled on deserts dry these thousand years.

What of the meteorologists?
They said nothing, turned their faces away,
Let the event pass unrecorded.

And what of us? We also said nothing.
Is it not the height of silent humour
To cause an unknown change in the earth's climate?

LACK

Born from ignoble stock on a day of dearth
He tramps the roads, trailing his withered branch,
And grudges every beauty of the wide earth.

Lack is his name, and although in gentleness
You set him honourably at the high table
And load his plate with luxury of excess,

Crying: 'Eat well, brother, and drink your fill',
Yet with hunger whetted only, he boasts aloud:
'I have never begged a favour, nor ever will!'

His clothes are sad, but a burly wretch is he,
Of lustreless look, slack mouth, a borrowed wit,
And a sigh that would charm the song-bird from her tree.

Now he casts his eye in greed upon your demesne
With open mockery of a heart so open
It dares this gallows-climber to entertain.

NOT AT HOME

Her house loomed at the end of a Berkshire lane,
Tall but retired. She was expecting me;
And I approached with light heart and quick tread,
Having already seen from the garden gate
How bright her knocker shone – in readiness
For my confident rap? – and the steps holystoned.
I ran the last few paces, rapped and listened
Intently for the rustle of her approach....

No reply, no movement. I waited three long minutes,
Then, in surprise, went down the path again
To observe the chimney stacks. No smoke from either.
And the curtains: were they drawn against the sun?
Or against what, then? I glanced over a wall
At her well-tended orchard, heavy with bloom
(Easter fell late that year, Spring had come early),
And found the gardener, bent over cold frames.

'Her ladyship is not at home?'
                                                        'No, sir.'
'She was expecting me. My name is Lion.
Did she leave a note?'
                                        'No, sir, she left no note.'
'I trust nothing has happened...?'
                                                        'No, sir, nothing....
And yet she seemed preoccupied: we guess
Some family reason.'
                                '*Has* she a family?'
'That, sir, I could not say.... She seemed distressed –
Not quite herself, if I may venture so.'
'But she left no note?'
                                        'Only a verbal message:
Her ladyship will be away some weeks
Or months, hopes to return before midsummer,
And, please, you are not to communicate.
There was something else: about the need for patience.'

The sun went in, a bleak wind shook the blossom,
Dust flew, the windows glared in a blank row....
And yet I felt, when I turned slowly away,
Her eyes boring my back, as it might be posted
Behind a curtain slit, and still in love.

HORIZON

On a clear day how thin the horizon
Drawn between sea and sky,
Between sea-love and sky-love;
And after sunset how debatable
Even for an honest eye.

'Do as you will tonight,'
Said she, and so he did
By moonlight, candlelight,
Candlelight and moonlight,
While pillowed clouds the horizon hid.

Knowing-not-knowing that such deeds must end
In a curse which lovers long past weeping for
Had heaped upon him: she would be gone one night
With his familiar friend,
Granting him leave her beauty to explore
By moonlight, candlelight,
Candlelight and moonlight.

GOLDEN ANCHOR

Gone: and to an undisclosed region,
Free as the wind, if less predictable.
Why should I grieve, who have no claim on her?
My ring circles her finger, from her neck
Dangles my powerful jade. All is not lost
While still she wears those evident tokens
And no debts lie between us except love.

Or does the golden anchor plague her
As a drag on woman's liberty? Longing
To cut the cable, run grandly adrift,
Is she warned by a voice what wide misfortune
Ripples from ill faith? – therefore temporizes
And fears to use the axe, although consorting
With lovelessness and evil?

What should I say or do? It was she chose me,
Not contrariwise. Moreover, if I lavished
Extravagant praise on her, she deserved all.
I have been honest in love, as is my nature;
She secret, as is hers. I cannot grieve
Unless for having vexed her by unmasking
A jewelled virtue she was loth to use.

LION LOVER

You chose a lion to be your lover –
Me, who in joy such doom greeting
Dared jealously undertake
Cruel ordeals long foreseen and known,
Springing a trap baited with flesh: my own.

Nor would I now exchange this lion heart
For a less furious other,
Though by the Moon possessed
I gnaw at dry bones in a lost lair
And, when clouds cover her, roar my despair.

Gratitude and affection I disdain
As cheap in any market:
Your naked feet upon my scarred shoulders,
Your eyes naked with love,
Are all the gifts my beasthood can approve.

IBYCUS IN SAMOS

The women of Samos are lost in love for me:
Nag at their men, neglect their looms,
And send me secret missives, to my sorrow.

I am the poet Ibycus, known by the cranes,
Each slender Samian offers herself moon-blanched
As my only bride, my heart's belovèd;

And when I return a calm salute, no more,
Or a brotherly kiss, will heap curses upon me:
Do I despise her warm myrrh-scented bosom?

She whom I honour has turned her face away
A whole year now, and in pride more than royal
Lacerates my heart and hers as one.

Wherever I wander in this day-long fever,
Sprigs of the olive-trees are touched with fire
And stones twinkle along my devious path.

Who here can blame me if I alone am poet,
If none other has dared to accept the fate
Of death and again death in the Muse's house?

Or who can blame me if my hair crackles
Like thorns under a pot, if my eyes flash
As it were sheets of summer lightning?

POSSESSED

To be possessed by her is to possess –
Though rooted in this thought
Build nothing on it.

Unreasonable faith becomes you
And mute endurance
Even of betrayal.

Never expect to be brought wholly
Into her confidence.
Being natural woman

She knows what she must do, not why;
Balks your anticipation
Of pleasure vowed;

Yet, no less vulnerable than you,
Suffers the dire pangs
Of your self-defeat.

THE WINGED HEART

Trying to read the news, after your visit,
When the words made little sense, I let them go;
And found my heart suddenly sprouting feathers.

Alone in the house, and the full honest rain
After a devil's own four-day sirocco
Still driving down in sheets across the valley –

How it hissed, how the leaves of the olives shook!
We had suffered drought since earliest April;
Here we were already in October.

I have nothing more to tell you. What has been said
Can never possibly be retracted now
Without denial of the large universe.

Some curse has fallen between us, a dead hand,
An inhalation of evil sucking up virtue:
Which left us no recourse, unless we turned

Improvident as at our first encounter,
Deriding practical care of how or where:
Your certitude must be my certitude.

And the tranquil blaze of sky etherializing
The circle of rocks and our own rain-wet faces,
Was that not worth a lifetime of pure grief?

IN TRANCE AT A DISTANCE

It is easy, often, and natural even,
To commune with her in trance at a distance;
To attest those deep confessionary sighs
Otherwise so seldom heard from her;
To be assured by a single shudder
Wracking both hearts, and underneath the press
Of clothes by a common nakedness.

Hold fast to the memory, lest a cold fear
Of never again here, of nothing good coming,
Should lure you into self-delusive trade
With demonesses who dare masquerade
As herself in your dreams, and who after a while
Skilfully imitate her dancing gait,
Borrow her voice and vocables and smile.

It is no longer – was it ever? – in your power
To catch her close to you at any hour:
She has raised a wall of nothingness in between
(Were it something known and seen, to be torn apart,
You could grind its heartless fragments into the ground);
Yet, taken in trance, would she still deny
That you are hers, she yours, till both shall die?

THE WREATH

A bitter year it was. What woman ever
Cared for me so, yet so ill-used me,
Came in so close and drew so far away,
So much promised and performed so little,
So murderously her own love dared betray?
Since I can never be clear out of your debt,
Queen of ingratitude, to my dying day,
You shall be punished with a deathless crown
For your dark head, resist it how you may.

IN HER PRAISE

This they know well: the Goddess yet abides.
Though each new lovely woman whom she rides,
Straddling her neck a year or two or three,
Should sink beneath such weight of majesty
And, groping back to humankind, gainsay
The headlong power that whitened all her way
With a broad track of trefoil – leaving you,
Her chosen lover, ever again thrust through
With daggers, your purse rifled, your rings gone –
Nevertheless they call you to live on
To parley with the pure, oracular dead,
To hear the wild pack whimpering overhead,
To watch the moon tugging at her cold tides.
Woman is mortal woman. She abides.

THE ALABASTER THRONE

This tall lithe Amazon armed herself
With all the cunning of a peasant father
Who, fled to Corinth from starved Taenarum,
Had cherished her, the child of his new wealth,
Almost as though a son.

From Corinth she embarked for Paphos
Where white doves, circling, settled on her palms
And a sudden inspiration drew us
To heap that lap with pearls, almost as though
Ignorant of her antecedents.

Which was the Goddess, which the woman?
Let the philosophers break their teeth on it!
She had seized an empty alabaster throne
And for two summers, almost, could deny
Both Taenarum and Corinth.

A RESTLESS GHOST

Alas for obstinate doubt: the dread
Of error in supposing my heart freed,
All care for her stone dead!
Ineffably will shine the hills and radiant coast
Of early morning when she is gone indeed,
Her divine elements disbanded, disembodied
And through the misty orchards in love spread –
When she is gone indeed –
But still among them moves her restless ghost.

BETWEEN MOON AND MOON

In the last sad watches of night
Hardly a sliver of light will remain
To edge the guilty shadow of a waned moon
That dawn must soon devour.

                        Thereafter, another
Crescent queen shall arise with power –
So wise a beauty never yet seen, say I:
A true creature of moon, though not the same
In nature, name or feature –
Her innocent eye rebuking inconstancy
As if Time itself should die and disappear.

So was it ever. She is here again, I sigh.

BEWARE, MADAM!

Beware, madam, of the witty devil,
The arch intriguer who walks disguised
In a poet's cloak, his gay tongue oozing evil.

Would you be a Muse? He will so declare you,
Pledging his blind allegiance,
Yet remain secret and uncommitted.

Poets are men: are single-hearted lovers
Who adore and trust beyond all reason,
Who die honourably at the gates of hell.

The Muse alone is licensed to do murder
And to betray: weeping with honest tears
She thrones each victim in her paradise.

But from this Muse the devil borrows an art
That ill becomes a man. Beware, madam:
He plots to strip you bare of woman-pride.

He is capable of seducing your twin-sister
On the same pillow, and neither she nor you
Will suspect the act, so close a glamour he sheds.

Alas, being honourably single-hearted,
You adore and trust beyond all reason,
Being no more a Muse than he a poet.

THE CLIFF EDGE

Violence threatens you no longer:
It was your innocent temerity
Caused us to tremble: veterans discharged
From the dirty wars of life.

Forgive us this presumption: we are abashed –
As when a child, straying on the cliff's edge,
Turns about to ask her white-faced brothers:
'Do you take me for a child?'

ACROBATS

Poised impossibly on the high tight-rope
        Of love, in spite of all,
They still preserve their dizzying balance
And smile this way or that,
        As though uncertain on which side to fall.

OUZO UNCLOUDED

Here is ouzo (she said) to try you:
Better not drowned in water,
Better not chilled with ice,
Not sipped at thoughtfully,
Nor toped in secret.
Drink it down (she said) unclouded
At a blow, this tall glass full,
But keep your eyes on mine
Like a true Arcadian acorn-eater.

THE BROKEN GIRTH

Bravely from Fairyland he rode, on furlough,
Astride a tall bay given him by the Queen
From whose couch he had leaped not a half-hour since,
Whose lilies-of-the-valley shone from his helm.

But alas, as he paused to assist five Ulstermen
Sweating to raise a recumbent Ogham pillar,
Breach of a saddle-girth tumbled Oisín
To common Irish earth. And at once, it is said,
Old age came on him with grief and frailty.

St Patrick asked: would he not confess the Christ? –
Which for that Lady's sake he loathed to do,
But northward loyally turned his eyes in death.
It was Fenians bore the unshriven corpse away
For burial, keening.
                    Curse me all squint-eyed monks
Who misconstrue the passing of Finn's son:
Old age, not Fairyland, was his delusion.

INKIDOO AND THE QUEEN OF BABEL

When I was a callant, born far hence,
You first laid hand on my innocence,
But sent your champion into a boar
That my fair young body a-pieces tore.

When I was a lapwing, crowned with gold,
Your lust and liking for me you told,
But plucked my feathers and broke my wing –
Wherefore all summer for grief I sing.

When I was a lion of tawny fell,
You stroked my mane and you combed it well,
But pitfalls seven you dug for me
That from one or other I might not flee.

When I was a courser, proud and strong,
That like the wind would wallop along,
You bated my pride with spur and bit
And many a rod on my shoulder split.

When I was a shepherd that for your sake
The bread of love at my hearth would bake,
A ravening wolf did you make of me
To be thrust from home by my brothers three.

When I tended your father's orchard close
I brought you plum, pear, apple, and rose,
But my lusty manhood away you stole
And changed me into a grovelling mole.

When I was simple, when I was fond,
Thrice and thrice did you wave your wand,
But now you vow to be leal and true
And softly ask, will I wed with you?

THREE SONGS FOR THE LUTE

I

TRUTH IS POOR PHYSIC

A wild beast falling sick
Will find his own best physic –
    Herb, berry, root of tree
Or wholesome salt to lick –
    And so run free.

But this I know at least
Better than a wild beast:
    That should I fall love-sick
And the wind veer to East,
    Truth is poor physic.

II

IN HER ONLY WAY

When her need for you dies
    And she wanders apart,
Never rhetoricize
    On the faithless heart,

But with manlier virtue
    Be content to say
She both loved you and hurt you
    In her only way.

III

HEDGES FREAKED WITH SNOW

No argument, no anger, no remorse,
    No dividing of blame.
There was poison in the cup – why should we ask
    From whose hand it came?

No grief for our dead love, no howling gales
    That through darkness blow,
But the smile of sorrow, a wan winter landscape,
    Hedges freaked with snow.

THE AMBROSIA OF DIONYSUS AND SEMELE

Little slender lad, toad-headed,
For whom ages and leagues are dice to throw with,
Smile back to where entranced I wander
Gorged with your bitter flesh,
Drunk with your Virgin Mother's lullaby.

Little slender lad, lightning engendered,
Grand master of magicians:
When pirates stole you at Icaria
Wild ivy gripped their rigging, every oar
Changed to a serpent, panthers held the poop,
A giant vine sprouted from the mast crotch
And overboard they plunged, the whey-faced crew!

Lead us with your song, tall Queen of earth!
Twinned to the god, I follow comradely
Through a first rainbow-limbo, webbed in white,
Through chill Tyrrhenian grottoes, under water,
Where dolphins wallow between marble rocks,
Through sword-bright jungles, tangles of unease,
Through halls of fear ceilinged with incubi,
Through blazing treasure-chambers walled with garnet,
Through domes pillared with naked Caryatids –
Then mount at last on wings into pure air,
Peering down with regal eye upon
Five-fruited orchards of Elysium,
In perfect knowledge of all knowledges.

And still she drowsily chants
From her invisible bower of stars.
Gentle her voice, her notes come linked together
In intricate golden chains paid out
Slowly across brocaded cramoisy,
Or unfold like leaves from the jade-green shoot
Of a rising bush whose blossoms are her tears....
O, whenever she pauses, my heart quails
Until the sound renews.

Little slender lad, little secret god,
Pledge her your faith in me,
Who have ambrosia eaten and yet live.

THE UNNAMED SPELL

Let us never name that royal certitude,
That simultaneous recognition
When first we stood together,

When I saw you as a child astonished,
Years before, under tall trees
By a marching sound of wind:

Your heart sown with a headlong wisdom
Which every grief or joy thereafter
Rooted still more strongly.

Naming is treacherous, names divide
Truth into lesser truths, enclosing them
In a coffin of counters –

Give the spell no name, liken it only
To the more than tree luxuriating
Seven ells above earth:

All heal, golden surprise of a kiss,
Wakeful glory while the grove winters,
A branch Hell-harrowing,

Of no discoverable parentage,
Strangeling scion of varied stocks
Yet true to its own leaf,

Secret of secrets disclosed only
To who already share it,
Who themselves sometimes raised an arch –
Pillared with honour; its lintel, love –
And passed silently through.

From *MAN DOES, WOMAN IS*

(1964)

A TIME OF WAITING

The moment comes when my sound senses
Warn me to keep the pot at a quiet simmer,
Conclude no rash decisions, enter into
No random friendships, check the runaway tongue
And fix my mind in a close caul of doubt –
Which is more difficult, maybe, than to face
Night-long assaults of lurking furies.

The pool lies almost empty; I watch it nursed
By a thin stream. Such idle intervals
Are from waning moon to the new – a moon always
Holds the cords of my heart. Then patience, hands;
Dabble your nerveless fingers in the shallows;
A time shall come when she has need of them.

EXPECT NOTHING

Give, ask for nothing, hope for nothing,
Subsist on crumbs, though scattered casually
Not for you (she smiles) but for the birds.
Though only a thief's diet, it staves off
Dire starvation, nor does she grow fat
On the bread she crumbles, while the lonely truth
Of love is honoured, and her word pledged.

NO LETTER

Be angry yourself, as well you may,
But why with her? She is no party to
Those avaricious dreams that pester you.
Why knot your fists as though plotting to slay
Even our postman George (whose only due
Is a small Christmas box on Christmas Day)
If his delivery does not raise the curse
Of doubt from your impoverished universe?

THE WHY OF THE WEATHER

Since no one knows the why of the weather
Or can authoritatively forecast
More than twelve hours of day or night, at most,
Every poor fool is licensed to explain it
As Heaven's considered judgement on mankind,
And I to account for its vagaries, Myrto,
By inklings of your unaccountable mind.

IN TIME

In time all undertakings are made good,
All cruelties remedied,
Each bond resealed more firmly than before –
Befriend us, Time, Love's gaunt executor!

FIRE WALKER

To be near her is to be near the furnace.
Fortunate boy who could slip idly through,
Basket in hand, culling the red-gold blossom,
Then wander on, untaught that flowers were flame,
With no least smell of scorching on his clothes!
I, at a greater distance, charred to coal,
Earn her reproach for my temerity.

DEED OF GIFT

After close, unembittered meditation
    She gave herself to herself, this time for good;
    Body and heart re-echoed gratitude
For such a merciful repudiation
    Of debts claimed from them by the neighbourhood –

Not only friends, and friends of friends, but lovers
    Whom in the circumstances few could blame
    (Her beauty having singed them like a flame)
If they had hoarded under legal covers
    Old promissory notes signed with her name.

And though to stand once more on the firm road
    From which by misadventure she had strayed,
    So that her journey was that much delayed,
Justified the default of duties owed,
    What debt of true love did she leave unpaid?

AT BEST, POETS

Woman with her forests, moons, flowers, waters,
And watchful fingers:
We claim no magic comparable to hers –
At best, poets; at worst, sorcerers.

SHE IS NO LIAR

She is no liar, yet she will wash away
Honey from her lips, blood from her shadowy hand,
And, dressed at dawn in clean white robes will say,
Trusting the ignorant world to understand:
'Such things no longer are; this is today.'

A LAST POEM

A last poem, and a very last, and yet another –
O, when can I give over?
Must I drive the pen until blood bursts from my nails
And my breath fails and I shake with fever,
Or sit well wrapped in a many-coloured cloak
Where the moon shines new through Castle Crystal?
Shall I never hear her whisper softly:
'But this is truth written by you only,
And for me only; therefore, love, have done'?

THE PEARL

When, wounded by her anger at some trifle,
I imitate the oyster, rounding out
A ball of nacre about the intrusive grit,
Why should she charge me with perversity
As one rejoicing in his own torn guts
Or in the lucent pearl resultant
Which she disdainfully strings for her neck?
Such anger I admire; but could she swear
That I am otherwise incorrigible?

THE LEAP

Forget the rest: my heart is true
And in its waking thought of you
Gives the same wild and sudden leap
That jerks it from the brink of sleep.

BANK ACCOUNT

Never again remind me of it:
There are no debts between us.
Though silences, half-promises, evasions
Curb my impatient spirit
And freeze the regular currency of love,
They do not weaken credit. Must I demand
Sworn attestations of collateral,
Forgetting how you looked when first you opened
Our joint account at the Bank of Fate?

JUDGEMENT OF PARIS

What if Prince Paris, after taking thought,
Had not adjudged the apple to Aphrodite
But, instead, had favoured buxom Hera,
Divine defendress of the marriage couch?
What if Queen Helen had been left to squander
Her beauty upon the thralls of Menelaus,
Hector to die unhonoured in his bed,
Penthesileia to hunt a poorer quarry,
The bards to celebrate a meaner siege?
Could we still have found the courage, you and I,
To embark together for Cranaë
And consummate our no less fateful love?

MAN DOES, WOMAN IS

Studiously by lamp-light I appraised
The palm of your hand, its heart-line
Identical with its head-line;
And you appraised the approving frown.

I spread my cards face-upwards on the table,
Not challenging you for yours.
Man does; but woman is –
Can a gamester argue with his luck?

THE AMPLE GARDEN

However artfully you transformed yourself
Into bitch, vixen, tigress,
I knew the woman behind.

Light as a bird now, you descend at dawn
From the poplar bough or ivy bunch
To peck my strawberries,

And have need indeed of an ample garden:
All my fruits, fountains, arbours, lawns
In fief to your glory.

You, most unmetaphorically you:
Call me a Catholic, so devout in faith
I joke of love, as Catholics do of God,
And scorn all exegesis.

TO MYRTO ABOUT HERSELF

Fierce though your love of her may be,
    What man alive can doubt
I love her more? Come now, agree
Not to turn rivalrous of me,
    Lest you and I fall out!

And should her law make little sense
    Even at times to you,
Love has its own sure recompense:
To love beyond all reason – hence
    Her fondness for us two.

What she pursues we neither know
    Nor can we well inquire;
But if you carelessly bestow
A look on me she did not owe
    It comes at her desire.

THE THREE-FACED

Who calls her two-faced? Faces, she has three:
The first inscrutable, for the outer world;
The second shrouded in self-contemplation;
The third, her face of love,
Once for an endless moment turned on me.

DAZZLE OF DARKNESS

The flame guttered, flared impossibly high,
Went out for good; yet in the dazzle of darkness
I saw her face ashine like an angel's:
Beauty too memorable for lamentation,
Though doomed to rat and maggot.

MYRRHINA

O, why judge Myrrhina
As though she were a man?
She obeys a dark wisdom
(As Eve did before her)
Which never can fail,
Being bound by no pride
Of armorial bearings
Bequeathed in tail male.

And though your blood brother
Who dared to do you wrong
In his greed of Myrrhina
Might plead a like wisdom
The fault to excuse,
Myrrhina is just:
She has hanged the poor rogue
By the neck from her noose.

FOOD OF THE DEAD

Blush as you stroke the curves – chin, lips and brow –
Of your scarred face, Prince Orpheus: for she has called it
Beautiful, nor would she stoop to flattery.
Yet are you patient still, when again she has eaten
Food of the dead, seven red pomegranate seeds,
And once more warmed the serpent at her thighs
For a new progress through new wards of hell?

EURYDICE

'*I am oppressed, I am oppressed, I am oppressed*' –
Once I utter the curse, how can she rest:
No longer able, weeping, to placate me
With renewed auguries of celestial beauty?

Speak, fly in her amber ring; speak, horse of gold!
What gift did I ever grudge her, or help withhold?
In a mirror I watch blood trickling down the wall –
Is it mine? Yet still I stand here, proud and tall.

Look where she shines, with a borrowed blaze of light
Among the cowardly, faceless, lost, unright,
Clasping a naked imp to either breast –
Am I not oppressed, oppressed, three times oppressed?

She has gnawn at corpse-flesh till her breath stank,
Paired with a jackal, grown distraught and lank,
Crept home, accepted solace, but then again
Flown off to chain truth back with an iron chain.

My own dear heart, dare you so war on me
As to strangle love in a mad perversity?
Is ours a fate can ever be forsworn
Though my lopped head sing to the yet unborn?

TO BEGUILE AND BETRAY

To beguile and betray, though pardonable in women,
Slowly quenches the divine need-fire
By true love kindled in them. Have you not watched
The immanent Goddess fade from their brows
When they make private to her mysteries
Some whip-scarred rogue from the hulks, some painted clown
From the pantomime – and afterwards accuse you
Of jealous hankering for the mandalot
Rather than horror and sick foreboding
That she will never return to the same house?

I WILL WRITE

He had done for her all that a man could,
And, some might say, more than a man should.
Then was ever a flame so recklessly blown out
Or a last goodbye so negligent as this?
'I will write to you,' she muttered briefly,
Tilting her cheek for a polite kiss;
Then walked away, nor ever turned about....

Long letters written and mailed in her own head –
There are no mails in a city of the dead.

BIRD OF PARADISE

At sunset, only to his true love,
The bird of paradise opened wide his wings
Displaying emerald plumage shot with gold
Unguessed even by him.
                                        True, that wide crest
Had blazoned royal estate, and the tropic flowers
Through which he flew had shown example
Of what brave colours gallantry might flaunt,
But these were other. She asked herself, trembling:
'What did I do to awake such glory?'

THE METAPHOR

The act of love seemed a dead metaphor
For love itself, until the timeless moment
When fingers trembled, heads clouded,
And love rode everywhere, too numinous
To be expressed or greeted calmly:
O, then it was, deep in our own forest,
We dared revivify the metaphor,
Shedding the garments of this epoch
In scorn of time's wilful irrelevancy;
So at last understood true nakedness
And the long debt to silence owed.

SECRECY

Lovers are happy
When favoured by chance,
But here is blessedness
Beyond all happiness,

Not to be gainsaid
By any gust of chance,
Harvest of one vine,
Gold from the same mine:

To keep which sacred
Demands a secrecy
That the world might blame
As deceit and shame;

Yet to publish which
Would make a him and her
Out of me and you
That were both untrue.

Let pigeons couple
Brazenly on the bough,
But royal stag and hind
Are of our own mind.

JOSEPH AND MARY

They turned together with a shocked surprise –
He, old and fabulous; she, young and wise –
Both having heard a newborn hero weep
In convalescence from the stroke of sleep.

AN EAST WIND

Beware the giddy spell, ground fallen away
Under your feet, wings not yet beating steady:
An ignorant East Wind tempts you to deny
Faith in the twofold glory of your being –
You with a thousand leagues or more to fly.

'Poised in air between earth and paradise,
Paradise and earth, confess which pull
Do you find the stronger? Is it of homesickness
Or of passion? Would you be rather loyal or wise?
How are these choices reconcilable?'

Turn from him without anger. East Wind knows
Only one wall of every foursquare house,
Has never viewed your northern paradise
Nor watched its queen tending her jewelled boughs,
But always from the same sick quarter blows.

DANCE OF WORDS

To make them move, you should start from lightning
And not forecast the rhythm: rely on chance,
Or so-called chance for its bright emergence
Once lightning interpenetrates the dance.

Grant them their own traditional steps and postures
But see they dance it out again and again
Until only lightning is left to puzzle over –
The choreography plain, and the theme plain.

A BLIND ARROW

Though your blind arrow, shot in time of need
Among the shadowy birches, did indeed
Strike, as you knew it must, the assassin's heart,
Never disparage a trained bowman's art.

THE OLEASTER

Each night for seven nights beyond the gulf
A storm raged, out of hearing, and crooked flashes
Of lightning animated us. Before day-break
Rain fell munificently for the earth's need....

No, here they never plant the sweet olive
As some do (bedding slips in a prepared trench),
But graft it on the club of Hercules
The savage, inexpugnable oleaster
Whose roots and bole bunching from limestone crannies
Sprout impudent shoots born only to be lopped
Spring after Spring. Theirs is a loveless berry....

By mid-day we walk out, with naked feet,
Through pools on the road, gazing at waterfalls
Or a line of surf, but mostly at the trees
Whose elegant branches rain has duly blackened
And pressed their crowns to a sparkling silver.

Innumerable, plump with promise of oil,
The olives hang grass-green, in thankfulness
For a bitter sap and bitter New Year snows
That cleansed their bark....

                        Forgive me, dearest love,
If nothing I can say be strange or new.
I am no child of the hot South like you,
Though in rock rooted like an oleaster.

THE SEPTUAGENARIAN

Youth is the ruggedest burden that can score
Your septuagenarian shoulder:
If you should threaten, as before, to powder
Rocks with bare heels, or rend the oak asunder
With naked fingers, you can now no more
Plead youthful benefit of metaphor.
Such unsubstantiated boasts will be
Substantial evidence of senility.

NON COGUNT ASTRA

Come, live in Now and occupy it well.
Prediction's no alternative to forethought
Despite at least four hundred arts of scrying
The dubious future, such as to study birds,
Or bull's guts, or sheep droppings, or wine lees
In an alabaster cup. True, the most ancient,
Most exact discipline, astrology,
Comes hallowed by a college of gowned mantics
Who still cast horoscopes only by stars
Apparent to the still unaided eye –
And of whom a few, the best, focus their powers
On exact horary configurations, then
At an agreed moment brusquely sweep away
Zodiacal signs, conjunctions, trines,
And reinduce a pure, archaic vision;
Yet disregard all false astrologers
Who dare lay greedy or compulsive hands
On the stars you sped at your nativity
Along their courses and forbad to canker
The rose of love or blunt the blade of honour:
No public hangmen these, but servants chosen
To wear bright livery at your house gate;
And favour you the more, the less you fear them.

SONG: SWORD AND ROSE

The King of Hearts a broadsword bears,
    The Queen of Hearts, a rose –
Though why, not every gambler cares
    Or cartomancer knows.

Be beauty yours, be honour mine,
    Yet sword and rose are one:
Great emblems that in love combine
    Until the dealing's done;

For no card, whether small or face,
    Shall overtrump our two
Except that Heart of Hearts, the Ace,
    To which their title's due.

ENDLESS PAVEMENT

In passage along an endless, eventless pavement,
None but the man in love, as he turns to stare
At the glazed eyes flickering past, will remain aware
Of his own, assured, meticulous, rustic tread –
As if pavement were pebbles, or rocks overgrown by grasses;
And houses, trees with birds flying overhead.

IN DISGUISE

Almost I welcome the dirty subterfuges
Of this unreal world closing us in,
That present you as a lady of high fashion
And me as a veteran on the pensioned list.

Our conversation is infinitely proper,
With a peck on either cheek as we meet or part –
Yet the seven archons of the heavenly stair
Tremble at the disclosure of our seals.

A MEASURE OF CASUALNESS

Too fierce the candlelight; your gentle voice
Roars as in dream: my shoulder-nooks flower;
A scent of honeysuckle invades the house,
And my fingertips are so love-enhanced
That sailcloth feels like satin to them.
Teach me a measure of casualness
Though you stalk into my room like Venus naked.

IN TIME OF ABSENCE

Lovers in time of absence need not signal
With call and answering call:
By sleight of providence each sends the other
A clear, more than coincidental answer
To every still unformulated puzzle,
Or a smile at a joke harboured, not yet made,
Or power to be already wise and unafraid.

THE GREEN CASTLE

The first heaven is a flowery plain;
The second, a glass mountain;
The third, likewise terrestrial,
Is an orchard-close unclouded
By prescience of death or change
Or the blood-sports of desire:
Our childhood paradise.

The next three heavens, known as celestial,
Are awkward of approach.
Mind is the prudent rider; body, the ass
Disciplined always by a harsh bit,
Accepts his daily diet of thorns
And frugal, brackish water;
Holds converse with archangels.

The seventh heaven, most unlike those others,
We once contrived to enter
By a trance of love; it is a green castle
Girdled with ramparts of blue sea
And silent but for the waves' leisured wash.
There Adam rediscovered Eve:
She wrapped him in her arms.

An afterglow of truth, still evident
When we had fallen earthward,
Astonished all except the born blind.
Strangers would halt us in the roadway:
'Confess where you have been.'
And, at a loss, we replied stumblingly:
'It was here, it was nowhere –
Last night we lodged at a green castle,
Its courtyard paved with gold.'

NOT TO SLEEP

Not to sleep all the night long, for pure joy,
Counting no sheep and careless of chimes,
Welcoming the dawn confabulation
Of birds, her children, who discuss idly
Fanciful details of the promised coming –
Will she be wearing red, or russet, or blue,
Or pure white? – whatever she wears, glorious:
Not to sleep all the night long, for pure joy,
This is given to few but at last to me,
So that when I laugh and stretch and leap from bed
I shall glide downstairs, my feet brushing the carpet
In courtesy to civilized progression,
Though, did I wish, I could soar through the open window
And perch on a branch above, acceptable ally
Of the birds still alert, grumbling gently together.

THE HEARTH

Here it begins: the worm of love breeding
Among red embers of a hearth-fire
Turns to a chick, is slowly fledged,
And will hop from lap to lap in a ring
Of eager children basking at the blaze.

But the luckless man who never sat there,
Nor borrowed live coals from the sacred source
To warm a hearth of his own making,
Nor bedded lay under pearl-grey wings
In dutiful content,

How shall he watch at the stroke of midnight
Dove become phoenix, plumed with green and gold?
Or be caught up by jewelled talons
And haled away to a fastness of the hills
Where an unveiled woman, black as Mother Night,
Teaches him a new degree of love
And the tongues and songs of birds?

THAT OTHER WORLD

Fatedly alone with you once more
As before Time first creaked:
Sole woman and sole man.

Others admire us as we walk this world:
We show them kindliness and mercy,
So be it none grow jealous
Of the truth that echoes between us two,
Or of that other world, in the world's cradle,
Child of your love for me.

THE BEDS OF GRAINNE AND DIARMUID

How many secret nooks in copse or glen
We sained for ever with our pure embraces,
No man shall know; though indeed master poets
Reckon one such for every eve of the year,
To sain their calendar.
                         But this much is true:
That children stumbling on our lairs by chance
In quest of hazel-nuts or whortleberries
Will recognize the impress of twin bodies
On the blue-green turf, starred with diversity
Of alien flowers, and shout astonishment.
Yet should some amorous country pair, presuming
To bask in joy on any bed of ours,
Offend against the love by us exampled,
Long ivy roots will writhe up from beneath
And bitterly fetter ankle, wrist and throat.

RAIN OF BRIMSTONE

Yet if they trust by lures or spells
    To exorcize the tall angel,
Love, from this ancient keep by us
    Now long frequented,

And if frustration turns their wits,
    So that they bawl in hell's fury
Battering at our gate all night
    With oaken cudgels,

Are we to blame for sparing them
    The voice of truth which they deny us?
Should we not darkly leave the town
    To its rain of brimstone?

CONSORTIUM OF STONES

The stones you have gathered, of diverse shapes,
Chosen from sea strand, lake strand, mountain gully:
Lay them all out on a basalt slab together
But allow intervals for light and air,
These being human souls; and reject any
With crumpled calceous edges and no feature
That awakes loving correspondence.

Start at this pair: blue flint, grey ironstone,
Which you ring around with close affinities
In every changeless colour, hatched, patched, plain –
Curve always answering curve; and angle, angle.

Gaps there may be, which next year or the next
Will fill to a marvel: never jog Time's arm,
Only narrow your eyes when you walk about
Lest they miss what is missing. The agreed intent
Of each consortium, whether of seven stones,
Or of nineteen, or thirty-three, or more,
Must be a circle, with firm edges outward,
Each various element aware of the sum.

THE BLACK GODDESS

Silence, words into foolishness fading,
Silence prolonged, of thought so secret
We hush the sheep-bells and the loud cicada.

And your black agate eyes, wide open, mirror
The released firebird beating his way
Down a whirled avenue of blues and yellows.

Should I not weep? Profuse the berries of love,
The speckled fish, the filberts and white ivy
Which you, with a half-smile, bestow
On your delectable broad land of promise
For me, who never before went gay in plumes.

BROKEN NECK

'Some forty years ago or maybe more,'
Pronounced the radiologist, 'you broke
Your neck: that is to say, contrived to fracture
Your sixth cervical vertebra – see here,
The picture's clear – and between sixth and seventh
Flattened this cartilage to uselessness:
Hence rheumatism. Surely you recall
Some incident? We all do foolish things
While young, and obstinately laugh them off –
Till they catch up with us in God's good time.
Let me prescribe you a Swiss analgesic
Which should at least....'

                          Love, I still laugh it off
And all Swiss mercenary alleviations,
For though I broke my neck in God's good time
It is in yours alone I choose to live.

O

'*O per se O, O per se O!*',
The moribund grammarian cried
To certain scholars grouped at his bedside,
Spying the round, dark pit a-gape below:
'*O per se O!*'

WOMAN OF GREECE

By your knees they rightly clasp you,
    Strong sons of your bed,
Whom you get, kneeling; and bear, kneeling;
    Kneeling, mourn for dead.

THE COLOURS OF NIGHT

The Moon never makes use of the Sun's palette.
Admire her silvery landscapes, but abstain
From record of them: lest you be later tempted
To counterfeit the dangerous colours of Night
Which are man's blood spurted on moving cloud.

BETWEEN TRAINS

Arguing over coffee at the station,
Neither of us noticed her dark beauty,
Though she sat close by, until suddenly
Three casual words – does it matter what they were? –
Spoken without remarkable intonation
Or accent, so bewildered him and me,
As it were catching the breath of our conversation,
That each set down his coffee-cup, to stare.
'You have come for us?' my lips cautiously framed –
Her eyes were almost brighter than I could bear –
But she rose and left, unready to be named.

TO THE TEUMESSIAN VIXEN

Do not mistake me: I was never a rival
    Of that poor fox who pledged himself to win ·
Your heart by gnawing away his brush. Who ever
    Proved love was love except by a whole skin?

THE HUNG WU VASE

With women like Marie no holds are barred.
Where do they get the gall? How can they do it?

She stormed out, slamming the hall door so hard
That a vase on the gilt shelf above – you knew it,
Loot from the Summer Palace at Pekin
And worth the entire contents of my flat –
Toppled and fell....

               I poured myself straight gin,
Downing it at a gulp. 'So that was that!'

The bell once more.... Marie walked calmly in,
Observed broken red porcelain on the mat,
Looked up, looked down again with condescension,
Then, gliding past me to retrieve a glove
(Her poor excuse for this improper call),
Muttered: 'And one thing I forgot to mention:
Your Hung Wu vase was phoney, like your love!'

How can they do it? Where do they get the gall?

LA MEJICANA

Perfect beneath an eight-rayed sun you lie,
   Rejoiced at his caresses. Yours is a land
For pumas, chillis, and men dark of eye;
   Yet summon me with no derisive hand
From these remote moon-pastures drenched in dew –
And watch who burns the blacker: I or you.

LAMIA IN LOVE

Need of this man was her ignoble secret:
Desperate for love, yet loathing to deserve it,
She wept pure tears of sorrow when his eyes
Betrayed mistrust in her impeccable lies.

AFTER THE FLOOD

Noah retrieves the dove again,
   Which bears him in its bill
A twig of olive to explain
That, if God sends them no more rain,
   The world may prosper still.

Shem, Ham and Japheth raise a shout,
   But weeks on end must wait
Till Father Noah, venturing out,
Can view the landscape all about
   And prophesy their fate.

'Where have the waters of God's Flood
   Dispersed?' God only knew.
What Noah saw was miles of mud,
Drowned rogues, and almond trees in bud
   With blossom peeping through.

'Bold lads, in patience here abide!
   This mire around the ark
By wind or sun must well be dried
Before we set against her side
   The planks to disembark.'

Obedient sons, a virtuous wife,
   Flocks, cattle, jars of seeds,
Crook, coulter, halter, pruning-knife –
Noah forecasts a brave new life
   Agreeable to his needs.

Exult with him at the clear sky,
   Proud Noahs of today,
For though we here and there descry
Morasses that no sun can dry
   (Regret them how we may),

God's rainbow is a glorious toy,
   His wine a cheerful drink,
And since He chooses to destroy
Folk better dead, we wish Him joy,
   While choking at the stink.

A LATE ARRIVAL

A Libyan pilgrim-ship tied up at Joppa
Twenty-four hours late, on a Wednesday morning.
The poor Jew from Cyrene hired no ass
But trudged, by way of Gimzo and Beth Horon,
Three hundred stadia to Jerusalem.

That Friday morning, close to the Western Gate
Where his son Alexander welcomed him,
He was tapped on the wrist by a Roman sergeant
And, though with little on his conscience, jumped
In excusable fright. The grinning sergeant said:
'A work of charity awaits you, sir!'

Foot-sore Simon, thus impressed to shoulder
The eight-foot oaken cross-piece of a cross
Towards Jeremiah's grotto – now already
Late for a family gathering and, far worse,
Contaminated by this unclean baulk –
Vented his rage on the condemned bandit:

'Poor fool! Betrayed to those Boethan traitors
By one of your own men, my son reports!
How long had you known Judah of Cherioth?
Seven years, or more? Alas, what innocence!
So long, and never peered into his heart?
I heard him once, far too loud in your praise
(Three Passovers ago, it must have been),
And all but naming you the Appointed King ...
I am told that Judah, jealous for your honour
Yet jealous of you, boasting he knew best,
Pleaded for your protective custody;
Loved you, he said, but loved our nation more.'

Since the poor stumbling felon made no answer,
Though his lips moved, as it might be in prayer,
Simon thought pityingly of Alexander:
What a disgrace for his own son to see him
Hauled off to attend a Roman crucifixion!
Why had God's hand delayed that Lybian ship?

Later the man spoke in a small, dry voice:
'May God forgive me and my servant too –
We both thought we knew better than our lord.'

SONG: WITH NO RETURN

If you keep your heart so true
    That her oaks take fire and burn,
And her foxes dance for you
All together in full view,
    Paradise is here to earn,
    Peace to learn:
She will pledge you, as she must,
To a trust beyond all trust
    With no manner of return.

ALL I TELL YOU FROM MY HEART

I begged my love to wait a bit
    Although the sky was clear:
'I smell a shower of rain,' said I,
    'And you'll be caught, I fear.'
'You want to keep me trapped,' she said,
    'And hold my hand again....'
But not ten minutes had she gone
    When how the rain did rain!

'Alas, dear love, so wet you are –
    You should have trusted me!
For all I tell you from my heart
    Is sure as prophecy.'

I begged my love to wait a bit
    And watch the faggots blaze.
'There's music on the march,' said I,
    'To cheer whoever stays.'
'You want to keep me trapped,' she said,
    'O, every night's the same....'
But not ten minutes had she gone
    When in the fiddlers came!

'Alas, dear love, what tunes they played –
    You should have trusted me!
For all I tell you from my heart
    Is sure as prophecy.'

I begged my love to take good heed
   When walking through the wood,
And warned her of a random rogue
   Who brought the world no good.
'You want to keep me trapped,' she said,
   'And roll me in your bed....'
But scarce a hundred yards from home
   She lost her maidenhead.

'Alas, dear love, it is too late –
   You should have trusted me!
For all I told you from my heart
   Was sure as prophecy.'

THE UNDEAD

To be the only woman alive in a vast hive of death
Is a strange predicament, granted! Innumerable zombies
With glazed eyes shuffle around at their diurnal tasks,
Keep the machines whirring, drudge idly in stores and bars,
Bear still-born zombie children, pack them off to school
For education in science and the dead languages,
Divert themselves with moribund travesties of living,
Lay mountainous bets on horses never seen to run,
Speed along highways in conveyor-belt automobiles
But, significantly enough, often dare overshoot
The traffic signals and *boing!* destroy themselves again,
Earning expensive funerals. (These, if at last they emerge
From the select green cemetery plots awarded them
On their twenty-first death-days by sombre uncles and aunts,
Will become zombies of the second degree, reverenced
Nationwide in church or synagogue.)
                               Nevertheless,
Let none of this daunt you, child! Accept it as your fate
To live, to love, knowingly to cause true miracles,
Nor ever to find your body possessed by a cold corpse.
For one day, as you choose an unfamiliar side-street
Keeping both eyes open, alert, not apprehensive,
You shall suddenly (this is a promise) come to a brief halt:
For striding towards you on the same sidewalk will appear
A young man with the halo of life around his head,
Will catch you reassuringly by both hands, asseverating

In phrases utterly unintelligible to a zombie
That all is well: you are neither diseased, deranged, nor mistaken,
But merely undead. He will name others like you, no less alive:
Two girls and a man, all moneyless immigrants arrived
Lately at a new necropolitan conurbation.
'Come with me, girl, and join them! The dead, you will observe,
Can exercise no direct sanctions against the living
And therefore doggedly try to omit them from all the records.
Still, they cannot avoid a certain morbid fascination
With what they call our genius. They will venture questions
But never wait for an answer – being doubtless afraid
That it will make their ears burn, or their eyes prick with tears –
Nor can they countermand what orders we may issue.'

Nod your assent, go with him, do not even return to pack!
When five live people room together, each rates as a million –
But encourage the zombies to serve you, the honest creatures,
For though one cannot ameliorate their way of death
By telling them true stories or singing them real songs,
They will feel obscurely honoured by your warm presence.

From *ANN AT HIGHWOOD HALL*

(1964)

ANN AT HIGHWOOD HALL

Ann ran away from home, where she had been
The third-but-youngest child of seventeen;
Since her poor mother's death that drunken man,
Ann's father, had thrown cups and plates at Ann
And once – he saw her polishing the stairs –
Asked, who was *she* to give herself such airs?

Ann, dressed in rags and an old tattered shawl,
Marched resolutely off to Highwood Hall,
Making herself invisible (for she
Had learned this trick from harsh necessity),
Then stole past valets, footmen, pages, grooms,
White marble statues, chambermaids with brooms,
And up the curving staircase carpeted
In green, down corridors all hung in red,
To the Duke's private room where twin fire-dogs
Crouched under a huge pile of crackling logs.

Ann entered calmly, chose a book, sat down
And began reading with a thoughtful frown.
In flounced the Duchess. Ann gave her a smile
But still continued reading a long while
Until the Duchess, watched by the Duke's cat,
Rang for the butler: 'Browne, remove this brat,
His Grace the Duke's latest discovery,
And bring her back attired more decently.'

The butler, Browne, led Ann to a large tub
Full of hot water. She enjoyed her scrub
And having her fair tresses tied in braids
Most elegantly by two lady's maids,
And being dressed in muslin. Thereupon
She sauntered back, but found the Duchess gone.

Now, Ann had learned at home: SILENCE IS BEST,
And since the Duke was seldom told what guest
His Duchess had invited – this gay pair
Let half the English peerage picnic there –
Ann took for granted she was welcome too,
And later felt it neither strange nor new
That now she dined in state at the Duke's board
As though the heiress of some powerful lord.

She sang to her own lute, lay long a-bed,
Swooned fashionably, embroidered with gold thread,
Danced, rode to hounds, was held in high regard,
Refused two Earls …
                                But here her story (starred
With royal visits, royal compliments,
Odes to her beauty, duels, tournaments,
Portraits by rival painters) dims at last
With the Duke's execution and a vast
Ruin engulfing all his relatives …

Thieves plundered Highwood Hall. Yet Ann still lives:
A lovely lady in her attic room
Working, folk say, by starlight at a loom,
Invisible to most eyes, but not all,
And well content with rags and tattered shawl.

ST VALENTINE'S DAY

Tell me truly, Valentine,
        What you most require.
Off I'll hurry, back I'll fetch
        All your heart's desire:

Stockings for your jaunty legs,
        Staddles for your ricks,
String to tie the pickle-jar,
        Straw to make bricks,

Silver salvers for your board,
        Satin for your bed,
And scented suds to blow you bubbles,
        Green, blue, yellow and red.

I HAVE A LITTLE COUGH, SIR

'I have a little cough, sir,
     In my little chest, sir,
All night long I cough, sir,
     I can never rest, sir,
And every time I cough, sir,
     It leaves a little pain, sir –
Cough, cough, cough, sir:
     There it is again, sir!'

'O Doctor Millikan,
     I shall surely die!'
'Yes, pretty Susan –
     So one day shall I.'

JOSEPH AND JESUS

(from the Spanish)

Said Joseph unto Mary,
     'Be counselled by me:
Fetch your love child from the manger,
     For to Egypt we must flee.'

As Mary went a-riding
     Up the hill out of view,
The ass was much astonishèd
     How like a dove he flew.

Said Jesus unto Joseph,
     Who his soft cheek did kiss:
'There are thorns in your beard, good sir.
     I askèd not for this.'

Then Joseph brought to Jesus
     Hot paps of white bread
Which, when it burned that pretty mouth,
     Joseph swallowed in his stead.

LOVE RESPELT

(1965)

THE RED SHOWER

Live sparks rain from the central anvil
   In a red shower. Let all beware
Who read the event as history, frowning at
   What they may find of madness there:
   Felicity endangering despair.

ABOVE THE EDGE OF DOOM

Bats at play taunt us with 'guess how many',
And music sounds far off, tempered by sea.
Above the edge of doom sits woman
Communing with herself. 'Dear love,' says she,
As it were apostrophizing cat or dog,
'Sometimes by a delicate glance and gesture
You almost seem to understand me,
Poor honest creature of the blue eyes,
Having crept closer to my sealed bosom
With your more desperate faith in womankind
Than any other since I first flowered.

It may be best you cannot read my mind.'

WILD CYCLAMEN

'What can I do for you?' she asked gently.
I reached for pen and paper: 'Draw me flowers!'

She pursed her lips – O the smooth brown forehead,
The smooth lids drooped, intent on their task –
And drew me wild Majorcan cyclamen
(Not yet in season) extravagantly petalled,
Then laughed and tossed me back the picture.

'It is nothing,' she said; yet that cyclamen odour
Hung heavy in the room for a long while;
And when she was gone, I caught myself smiling
In her own crooked way, trying to make my eyes
Sparkle like hers, though ineffectually,
Till I fell asleep; for this was my sick-bed
And her visits brief, by order.

GIFT OF SIGHT

I had long known the diverse tastes of the wood,
Each leaf, each bark, rank earth from every hollow;
Knew the smells of bird's breath and of bat's wing;
Yet sight I lacked: until you stole upon me,
Touching my eyelids with light finger-tips.
The trees blazed out, their colours whirled together,
Nor ever before had I been aware of sky.

BATXÓCA

Firm-lipped, high-bosomed, slender Queen of Beanstalk Land,
Who are more to me than any woman upon this earth
Though you live from hand to mouth, keeping no certain hours,
Disguising your wisdom with unpracticality
And your elusiveness with hugs for all and sundry,
Flaunting green, yellow and scarlet, suddenly disappearing
In a whirlwind rage and flurry of skirts, always alone
Until found, days later, asleep on a couch of broom
And incommunicable until you have breakfasted –
By what outrageous freak of dissimilarity
Were you forced, noble Batxóca, to fall so deep in love
With me as to demand marriage, despite your warning
That you and I must on no account be seen together –
A Beanstalk Queen, no less, paired with a regular man!

Did you wistfully, perhaps, expect me to say 'no'?

THE SNAP-COMB WILDERNESS

Magic is tangled in a woman's hair
For the enlightenment of male pride.
To slide a comb uxoriously
Through an even swell of tresses undisturbed
By their cascade from an exact parting
Could never hearten or enlighten me –
Not though her eyes were bluer than blue sea.
Magic rules an irreducible jungle
Dark as eclipse and scented with despair,
A stubborn snap-comb wilderness of hair,
Each strand a singular, wild, curling tree.

CHANGE

'This year she has changed greatly' – meaning you –
My sanguine friends agree,
And hope thereby to reassure me.

No, child, you never change; neither do I.
Indeed all our lives long
We are still fated to do wrong,

Too fast caught by care of humankind,
Easily vexed and grieved,
Foolishly flattered and deceived;

And yet each knows that the changeless other
Must love and pardon still,
Be the new error what it will:

Assured by that same glint of deathlessness
Which neither can surprise
In any other pair of eyes.

A COURT OF LOVE

Were you to break the vow we swore together,
The vow, I said, would break you utterly:
Despite your pleas of duty elsewhere owed,
You could no longer laugh, work, heal, do magic,
Nor in the mirror face your own eyes.

They have summoned me before their Court of Love
And warned me I must sign for your release
Pledging my word never again to draft
A similar pact, as one who has presumed
Lasting felicity still unknown in time.
What should I do? Forswear myself for you?
No man in love, plagued by his own scruples
Will ever, voluntarily, concede
That women have a spirit above vows.

BLACK

Black drinks the sun and draws all colours to it.
I am bleached white, my truant love. Come back,
And stain me with intensity of black.

BETWEEN HYSSOP AND AXE

To know our destiny is to know the horror
Of separation, dawn oppressed by night:
Is, between hyssop and axe, boldly to prove
That gifted, each, with singular need for freedom
And haunted, both, by spectres of reproach,
We may yet house together without succumbing
To the low fever of domesticity
Or to the lunatic spin of aimless flight.

GOLD AND MALACHITE

After the hour of illumination, when the tottering mind
Has been by force delivered from its incubus of despair,
When all the painted, papier mâché, Mexican faces
Of demons grinning at you from hell's vaulted roof
Fade and become angelic monitors of wisdom –
Slowly the brisk intelligence wakes, to mutter questions
Of when, where, how; and which should be the first step forward....

Now is the crucial moment you were forewarned against.
Stop your ears with your fingers, guard unequivocal silence
Lest you discuss wisdom in the language of unwisdom;
Roam instead through the heaped treasury of your heart:
You will find her, from whom you have been so long estranged,
Chin to knees, brooding apart on gold and malachite.
But beware again: even a shy embrace would be too explicit –
Let her learn by your gait alone that you are free at last.

AMBIENCE

The nymph of the forest, only in whose honour
These birds perform, provides an ambience
But never leads the chorus: even at dawn
When we awake to whistle, flute and pipe,
Astonished they can so extemporize
Their own parts, as it were haphazard
Each in his own time, yet avoid discordance
Or domineering, however virtuose
Or long sustained each voluntary of love.
The rare silences, too, appear like sound
Rather than pause for breath or meditation....
Nor is the same piece ever given twice.

THE VOW

No vow once sworn may ever be annulled
Except by a higher law of love or mercy –
Search your heart well: is there a lie hidden
Deep in its convolutions of resolve?

For whom do you live? Can it be yourself?
For whom then? Not for this unlovely world,
Not for the rotting waters of mischance,
Nor for the tall, eventual catafalque.

You live for her who alone loves you,
Whose royal prerogative can be denied
By none observant of the awakening gasps
That greet her progress down whatever hall.

Your vow is to truth, not practicality;
To honour, not to the dead world's esteem;
To a bed of rock, not to a swan's-down pillow;
To the tears you kiss away from her black eyes.

They lament an uninstructible world of men
Who dare not listen or watch, but challenge proof
That a leap of a thousand miles is nothing
And to walk invisibly needs no artifice.

THE FROG AND THE GOLDEN BALL

She let her golden ball fall down the well
    And begged a cold frog to retrieve it;
For which she kissed his ugly, gaping mouth –
    Indeed, he could scarce believe it.

And seeing him transformed to his princely shape,
    Who had been by hags enchanted,
She knew she could never love another man
    Nor by any fate be daunted.

But what would her royal father and mother say?
    They had promised her in marriage
To a cousin whose wide kingdom marched with theirs,
    Who rode in a jewelled carriage.

'Our plight, dear heart, would appear past human hope
    To all except you and me: to all
Who have never swum as a frog in a dark well
    Or have lost a golden ball.'

'What then shall we do now?' she asked her lover.
  He kissed her again, and said:
'Is magic of love less powerful at your Court
  Than at this green well-head?'

THOSE WHO CAME SHORT

Those who came short of love for me or you,
Where are they now? Ill-starred and bitter-mouthed,
Cursing us for their own contrariness,
Each having fallen in turn, head over heels,
From that illusive heaven at which they flew.

Are we then poison of love-perfection
To all but our own kind? Should we beware
Of handling such intemperate shaggy creatures
As leap on us like dogs to be cosseted
And, after, claim full rights of jealousy?

At once too simple and too various
Except for ourselves, should we awhile conceal
Our studies from the world, in cool forbearance
Watching each night for another dawn to break
And the last guest to straggle home?

WHOLE LOVE

Every choice is always the wrong choice,
Every vote cast is always cast away –
How can truth hover between alternatives?

Then love me more than dearly, love me wholly,
Love me with no weighing of circumstance,
As I am pledged in honour to love you:

With no weakness, with no speculation
On what might happen should you and I prove less
Than bringers-to-be of our own certainty.
Neither was born by hazard: each foreknew
The extreme possession we are grown into.

THIS HOLY MONTH

The demon who throughout our late estrangement
Followed with malice in my footsteps, often
Making as if to stumble, so that I stumbled
And gashed my head against a live rock;
Who tore my palms on butcher's broom and thorn,
Flung me at midnight into filthy ditches
And multiplied the horrors of this house
When back I limped again to a hard bed;
Who simultaneously plagued you too
With sleeplessness, dismay and darkness,
Paralysed your hands, denied you air –
We both know well he was the same demon,
Arch-enemy of rule and calculation,
Who lives for our love, being created from it,
Astonishes us with blossom, silvers the hills
With more than moonlight, summons bees in swarms
From the Lion's mouth to fill our hives with honey,
Turns flesh into fire, and eyes into deep lakes;
And so may do once more, this holy month.

THE BLOW

You struck me on the face and I, who strike
Only to kill, stood in confusion like
Death's fool: your ugly blow
Had fallen soft as snow.

Love me for what I am, with liberty
To curb my rage; I love you for what will be –
Your urgent sun – therefore
Acquitting you of error.

Laughter becomes us: gift of the third eye
That passes nothing by.

THE IMPOSSIBLE

Dear love, since the impossible proves
    Our sole recourse from this distress,
Claim it: the ebony ritual-mask of no
    Cannot outstare a living yes.

Claim it without despond or hate
    Or greed; but in your gentler tone
Say: 'This is ours, the impossible,' and silence
    Will give consent it is ours alone.

The impossible has wild-cat claws
    Which you would rather meet and die
Than commit love to time's curative venom
    And break our oath; for so would I.

THE FETTER

Concerned, against our wish, with a sick world,
Self-neglectful, tuned to knock or summons,
We make amends for follies not our own.

We have taken love through a thousand deaths;
Should either try to slip our iron fetter,
It bites yet deeper into neck and arm.

As for that act of supererogation,
The kiss in which we secretly concur,
Let laughter mitigate its quiet excess.

Could we only be a simple, bickering pair
In the tied cottage of a small estate,
With no tasks laid on us except to dig,
Hoe, fatten geese and scrape the quarter's rent,
How admirable our close interdependence;
Our insecurity how fortunate!

IRON PALACE

We stood together, side by side, rooted
At the iron heart of circumambient hills,
Parents to a new age, weeping in awe
That the lot had fallen, of all mankind, on us
Now sealed as love's exemplars.

We could not prevaricate or argue,
Citing involvement in some alien scene,
Nor plead unworthiness: none else would venture
To live detached from force of circumstance
As history neared its ending.

We told no one. These were not strange dreams
Recalled at breakfast with a yawning smile,
Nor tales for children, on the verge of sleep,
Who ask no questions. Our predicament
Remained a silent burden.

We had no token or proof, and needed none
Of what we learned that day; but laughed softly
Watching our hands engage, in co-awareness
That these red hills warned us, on pain of death,
Never to disengage them.

Woman, wild and hard as the truth may be,
Nothing can circumvent it. We stand coupled
With chains, who otherwise might live apart
Conveniently paired, each with another,
And slide securely graveward.

TRUE JOY

Whoever has drowned and awhile entered
The adamantine gates of afterwards,
Stands privileged to reject heavenly joy
(Though without disrespect for God's archangels)
With 'never again' – no moon, no herbs, no sea,
No singular love of women.

True joy, believe us, is to groan and wake
From the hallelujah choir on Fiddler's Green,
With lungs now emptied of salt water,
With gradual heat returning to clammed veins
In the first flicker of reanimation,
Repossession of now, awareness
Of her live hands and lips, her playful voice,
Her smooth and wingless shoulders.

TOMORROW'S ENVY OF TODAY

Historians may scorn the close engagement
Of Moon with Lion that we have witnessed
Here in this lair, here in this numinous grove,
May write me down as imbecile, or presume
A clot of madness festering in your heart –
Such is tomorrow's envy of today.

Today we are how we are, and how we see:
Alive, elate, untrimmed, without hazard
Of supersession: flowers that never fade,
Leaves that never shrivel, truth persistent
Not as a prophecy of bliss to fall
A thousand generations hence on lovers
More fortunately circumstanced than we,
But as a golden interlock of power
Looped about every bush and branching tree.

THE HIDDEN GARDEN

Nor can ambition make this garden theirs,
Any more than birds can fly through a window pane.
When they hint at passwords, keys and private stairs,
We are tempted often to open the front gate,
Which has no lock, and haul them bodily in,
Abashed that there they wait, disconsolate.

And yet such pity would be worse than pride:
Should we admit as love their vain self-pity,
The gate must vanish and we be left outside.

THE WEDDING

When down I went to the rust-red quarry
I was informed, by birds, of your resolve
To live with me for ever and a day –
The day being always new and antecedent.
What could we ask of Nature? Nothing more
Than to outdo herself in our behalf.

Blossoms of caper, though they smell sweet,
Have never sailed the air like butterflies
Circling in innocent dance around each other
Over the cliff and out across the bay;
Nor has broom-blossom scorched a man's finger
With golden fire, kindled by sun.

Come, maids of honour and pages chosen
To attend this wedding, charged to perform
Incomparable feats – dance, caper-blossom!
Scorch, blossom of broom, our married fingers –
Though crowds of almost-men and almost-women
Howl for their lost immediacy.

WHAT WILL BE, IS

Manifest reason glared at you and me
Thus ringed with love. Entire togetherness
Became for us the sole redress.

Together in heart, but our over-eager bodies
Distrained upon for debt, we shifted ground;
Which brought mistiming. Each cried out in turn,
And with a complementary delusion:
'I am free; but you? Are you still bound?'

In blood the debts were paid. Hereafter
We make no truce for manifest reason
From this side of the broad and fateful stream
Where wisdom rules from her dark cave of dream
And time is corrigible by laughter.

Moon and Sun are one. Granted, they ride
Paths unconformable to the calendar,
And seldom does a New Moon coincide
With a New Year; yet we agree:
'What will be, is' – rejoicing at a day
Of dolphins jostling in the blue bay,
Eagles in air, and flame on every tree.

SON ALTESSE

Alone, you are no more than many another
Gay-hearted, greedy, passionate noblewoman;
And I, alone, no more than a slow-witted
Passionate, credulous knight, though skilled in fight.

Then if I hail you as my Blessed Virgin
This is no flattery, nor does it endow you
With private magics which, when I am gone,
May flatter rogues or drunken renegades.

Name me your single, proud, whole-hearted champion
Whose feats no man alive will overpass;
But they must reverence you as I do; only
Conjoined in fame can we grow legendary.

Should I ride home, vainglorious after battle,
With droves of prisoners and huge heaps of spoil,
Make me dismount a half-mile from your door;
To walk barefoot in dust, as a knight must.

Yet never greet me carelessly or idly,
Nor use the teasing manners learned at Court,
Lest I be ambushed in a treacherous pass –
And you pent up in shame's black nunnery.

EVERYWHERE IS HERE

By this exchange of eyes, this encirclement
You of me, I of you, together we baffle
Logic no doubt, but never understanding;
And laugh instead of choking back the tears
When we say goodbye.

                  Fog gathers thick about us
Yet a single careless pair of leaves, one green, one gold,
Whirl round and round each other skippingly
As though blown by a wind; pause and subside
In a double star, the gold above the green.

Everywhere is here, once we have shattered
The iron-bound laws of contiguity,
Blazoning love as an eagle with four wings
(Their complementary tinctures counterchanged)
That scorns to roost in any terrene crag.

SONG: THE FAR SIDE OF YOUR MOON

The far side of your moon is black,
   And glorious grows the vine;
Ask anything of me you lack,
   But only what is mine.

Yours is the great wheel of the sun,
   And yours the unclouded sky;
Then take my stars, take every one,
   But wear them openly,

Walking in splendour through the plain
   For all the world to see,
Since none alive shall view again
   The match of you and me.

DELIVERANCE

Lying disembodied under the trees
(Their slender trunks converged above us
Like rays of a five-fold star) we heard
A sudden whinnying from the dark hill.

Our implacable demon, foaled by love,
Never knew rein or saddle; though he drank
From a stream winding by, his blue pastures
Ranged far out beyond the stellar mill.

He had seared us two so close together
That death itself might not disjoin us;
It was impossible you could love me less,
It was impossible I could love you more.

We were no calculating lovers
But gasped in awe at our deliverance
From a too familiar prison,
And vainly puzzled how it was that now
We should never need to build another,
As each, time after time, had done before.

CONJUNCTION

What happens afterwards, none need enquire:
They are poised there in conjunction, beyond time,
At an oak-tree top level with Paradise:
Its leafy tester unshaken where they stand
Palm to palm, mouth to mouth, beyond desire,
Perpetuating lark song, perfume, colour,
And the tremulous gasp of watchful winds,

Past all unbelief, we know them held
By peace and light and irrefragable love –
Twin paragons, our final selves, resistant
To the dull pull of earth dappled with shade:
Myself the forester, never known to abandon
His vigilant coursing of the greenwood's floor,
And you, dryad of dryads, never before
Yielding her whole heart to the enemy, man.

NOTHING NOW ASTONISHES

A month of vigilance draws to its close
With silence of snow and the Northern Lights
In longed-for wordlessness.

This rainbow spanning our two worlds
Becomes more than a bridge between them:
They fade into geography.

Variegated with the seven colours
We twist them into skeins for hide and seek
In a lovers' labyrinth.

Can I be astonished at male trembling
Of sea-horizons as you lean towards them?
Nothing now astonishes.

You change, from a running drop of pure gold
On a silver salver, to the white doe
In nut-groves harbouring.

Let me be changed now to an eight-petalled
Scarlet anemone that will never strain
For the circling butterfly.

Rest, my loud heart. Your too exultant flight
Had raised the wing-beat to a roar
Drowning seraphic whispers.

I'D DIE FOR YOU

I'd die for you, or you for me,
So furious is our jealousy –
And if you doubt this to be true
Kill me outright, lest I kill you.

From COLLECTED POEMS 1965

(1965)

GRACE NOTES

It was not the words, nor the melody,
    Not the beat, nor the pace;
It was that slow suspension of our breathing
    As we watched your face,
And the grace-notes, unrecordable on the clef,
    Sung only by a spirit in grace.

GOOD NIGHT TO THE OLD GODS

Good night, old gods, all this long year so faint
You propped your heavy eyelids up with shells!
Though once we honoured you who ruled this land
One hundred generations and ten more,
Our mood has changed: you dribble at the mouth,
Your dark-blue fern-tattoos are faded green,
Your thunderous anger wanes to petulance,
And love to groanings of indifference.
What most you crave is rest in a rock-cave,
Seasonally aroused by raucous gulls
Or swallows, nodding off once more to sleep.

We lay you in a row with cool palm wine
Close at your elbows, should you suffer thirst,
And breadfruit piled on rushes by your feet;
But will not furnish you a standing guard –
We have fish to net and spear, taro to hoe,
Pigs to fatten, coco-trees to climb;
Nor are our poets so bedulled in spirit
They would mount a platform, praising in worn verse
Those fusillades of lightning hurled by you
At giants in a first day-break of time:
Whom you disarmed and stretched in a rock-cave
Not unlike this – you have forgotten where.

THE SWEET-SHOP ROUND THE CORNER

The child dreaming along a crowded street
Lost hold of his mother, who had turned to greet
Some neighbour, and mistakenly matched his tread
With a strange woman's. 'Buy me sweets,' he said,
Waving his hand, which he found warmly pressed;
So dragged her on, boisterous and self-possessed:
'The sweet-shop's round the corner!' Both went in,
And not for a long while did the child begin
To feel a dread that something had gone wrong:
Were Mother's legs so lean, or her shoes so long,
Or her skirt so patched, or her hair tousled and grey?
Why did she twitter in such a ghostly way?
'O Mother, are you dead?'

                    What else could a child say?

DOUBLE BASS

He coils so close about his double-bass,
Serpentine and entranced,
That they form a single creature:
Which man-instrument writhes and complains,
Mouth of disaster, skeleton limbs a-twitch,
Cavernous belly booming,
Insistent fingers torturing us to love,
Its deep-gulped fumes of marihuana
Blinding our eyes with scarlet streamers....

Again I turn, for your laugh-nod to lend me
Measured reassurance of sanity.

DESCENT INTO HELL

Christ harrowed Hell in pity for all damned souls
Who had perverted innocence and honour –
It was a Sabbath, the day given to rest –
But none rose with him, and his journey grieved
The hearts even of such as loved him best.

THE PARDON

Should not the white lie and the unkept promise,
    Though distant from black lie and broken vow,
Demand a kiss of pardon afterwards
    From the sworn lover? So I kiss you now,
Counting on my own pardon: who but I
    Provoked both unkept promise and white lie?

POINT OF NO RETURN

When the alcoholic passed the crucial point
Of no return, he sold his soul to priests
Who, mercifully, would not deny him drink
But remitted a thousand years of purgatory
On this condition: that he must now engage
A woman's pity, beseeching her to cure him,
Wearing her down with betterment and relapse,
Till he had won a second soul for glory,
At the point of no return.

A SHIFT OF SCENE

To lie far off, in bed with a foul cough,
And a view of elms and roofs and six panes' worth
Of clear sky; here to watch, all the day long,
For a dove, or a black cat, or a puff of smoke
To cause a shift of scene – how could it do so? –
Or to take a pen and write – what else is there
To write but: 'I am not dead, not quite, as yet
Though I lie far off, in bed with a foul cough
And a view of elms and roofs and six panes' worth
Of clear sky'? Tell me, love, are you sick too
And plagued like me with a great hole in the mind
Where all those towers we built, and not on sand,
Have been sucked in and lost; so that it seems
No dove, and no black cat, nor puff of smoke
Can cause a shift of scene and fetch us back
To where we lie as one, in the same bed?

From *SEVENTEEN POEMS MISSING FROM 'LOVE RESPELT'*

(1966)

COCK IN PULLET'S FEATHERS

Though ready enough with beak and spurs,
You go disguised, a cock in pullet's feathers,
Among those crowing, preening chanticleers.
But, dear self, learn to love your own body
In its full naked glory,
Despite all blemishes of moles and scars –
As she, for whom it shines, wholly loves hers.

DEAD HAND

Grieve for the loveless, spiritless, faceless men
Without alternative but to protract
Reason's mortmain on what their hearts deny –
Themselves – and owed small courtesy beyond
The uncovered head, as when a hearse goes by.

ARREARS OF MOONLIGHT

My heart lies wrapped in red under your pillow,
My body wanders banished among the stars;
On one terrestrial pretext or another
You still withhold the extravagant arrears
Of moonlight that you owe us,
Though the owl whoops from a far olive branch
His brief, monotonous, night-long reminder.

WHAT DID YOU SAY?

She listened to his voice urgently pleading,
So captivated by his eloquence
She saw each word in its own grace and beauty
Drift like a flower down that clear-flowing brook,
And draw a wake of multicoloured bubbles.
But when he paused, intent on her reply,
She could stammer only: 'Love, what did you say?' –
As loath as ever to hold him in her arms
Naked, under the trees, until high day.

LURE OF MURDER

A round moon suffocates the neighbouring stars
With greener light than sun through vine-leaves.
Awed by her ecstasy of solitude
I crouch among rocks, scanning the gulf, agape,
Whetting a knife on my horny sole.

Alas for the lure of murder, dear my love!
Could its employment purge two moon-vexed hearts
Of jealousy more formidable than death,
Then each would stab, stab, stab at secret parts
Of the other's beloved body where unknown
Zones of desire imperil full possession.

But never can mortal dagger serve to geld
This glory of ours, this loving beyond reason –
Death holds no remedy or alternative:
We are singled out to endure his lasting grudge
On the tall battlements of nightfall.

THE GORGE

Yonder beyond all hopes of access
Begins your queendom; here is my frontier.
Between us howl phantoms of the long dead,
But the bridge that I cross, concealed from view
Even in sunlight, and the gorge bottomless,
Swings and echoes under my strong tread
Because I have need of you.

ECSTASY OF CHAOS

When the immense drugged universe explodes
In a cascade of unendurable colour
And leaves us gasping naked,
This is no more than ecstasy of chaos:
Hold fast, with both hands, to that royal love
Which alone, as we know certainly, restores
Fragmentation into true being.

STOLEN JEWEL

You weep whole-heartedly – your shining tears
Roll down for sorrow, not like mine for joy.
Dear love, should we not scorn to treat each other
With palliatives and with placebos?

Under a blinding moon you took from me
This jewel of wonder, but unaware
That it was yielded only on condition
Of whole possession; that it still denies you
Strength or desire for its restitution.

What do you fear? My hand around your throat?
What do I fear? Your dagger through my heart?
Must we not rage alone together
In lofts of singular high starriness?

THE EAGRE

Suddenly the Eagre mounts upstream
And a tall youth on dolphin back
Outdares my blue eyes and your black.

THE SNAPPED THREAD

Desire, first, by a natural miracle
United bodies, united hearts, blazed beauty;
Transcended bodies, transcended hearts.

Two souls, now unalterably one
In whole love always and for ever,
Soar out of twilight, through upper air,
Let fall their sensuous burden.

Is it kind, though, is it honest even,
To consort with none but spirits –
Leaving true-wedded hearts like ours
In enforced night-long separation,
Each to its random bodily inclination,
The thread of miracle snapped?

FORTUNATE CHILD

For fear strangers might intrude upon us
You and I played at being strangers,
But lent our act such verisimilitude
That when at last, by hazard, we met alone
In a secret glen where the badger earths
We had drawn away from love: did not prepare
For melting of eyes into hearts of flowers,
For a sun-aureoled enhancement of hair,
For over-riding of death on an eagle's back –
Yet so it was: sky shuddered apart before us
Until, from a cleft of more than light, we both
Overheard the laugh of a fortunate child
Swung from those eagle talons in a gold cloth.

LOVING TRUE, FLYING BLIND

How often have I said before
That no soft 'if', no 'either-or',
Can keep my obdurate male mind
From loving true and flying blind? –

Which, though deranged beyond all cure
Of temporal reason, knows for sure
That timeless magic first began
When woman bared her soul to man.

Be bird, be blossom, comet, star,
Be paradisal gates ajar,
But still, as woman, bear you must
With who alone endures your trust.

THE NEAR ECLIPSE

Out shines again the glorious round sun –
After his near-eclipse when pools of light
Thrown on the turf between leaf shadows
Grew crescent-shaped like moons – dizzying us
With paraboles of colour: regal amends
To our own sun mauled barbarously
By the same wide-mouthed dragon.

DANCING FLAME

Pass now in metaphor beyond birds,
Their seasonal nesting and migration,
Their airy gambols, their repetitive song;
Beyond the puma and the ocelot
That spring in air and follow us with their eyes;
Beyond all creatures but our own selves,
Eternal genii of dancing flame
Armed with the irreproachable secret
Of love, which is: never to turn back.

BIRTH OF ANGELS

Never was so profound a shadow thrown
On earth as by your sun: a black roundel
Harbouring an unheard-of generation
Fledged by the sun ablaze above your own –
Wild beyond words, yet each of them an angel.

ON GIVING

Those who dare give nothing
Are left with less than nothing;
Dear heart, you give me everything,
Which leaves you more than everything –
Though those who dare give nothing
Might judge it left you nothing.

Giving you everything,
I too, who once had nothing,
Am left with more than everything
As gifts for those with nothing
Who need, if not our everything,
At least a loving something.

THE P'ENG THAT WAS A K'UN

(Adapted from the Chinese of Lao Tse)

In Northern seas there roams a fish called K'un,
Of how many thousand leagues in length I know not,
Which changes to a bird called P'eng – its wing-span
Of how many thousand leagues in width I know not.
Every half-year this P'eng, that was a K'un,
Fans out its glorious feathers to the whirlwind
And soars to the most Southerly pool of Heaven.

The Finch and Sparrow, thus informed, debated:
'We by our utmost efforts may fly only
To yonder elm. How can the P'eng outdo us?'
Though, indeed, neither started as a fish.

LIKE OWLS

The blind are their own brothers; we
Form an obscure fraternity
Who, though not destitute of sight
Know ourselves doomed from birth to see,
Like owls, most clearly in half light.

IN PERSPECTIVE

What, keep love in *perspective*? – that old lie
Forced on the Imagination by the Eye
Which, mechanistically controlled, will tell
How rarely table-sides run parallel;
How distance shortens us; how wheels are found
Oval in shape far oftener than round;
How every ceiling-corner's out of joint;
How the broad highway tapers to a point –
Can all this fool us lovers? Not for long:
Even the blind will sense that something's wrong.

THE UTTER RIM

But if that Cerberus, my mind, should be
Flung to earth by the very opiate
That frees my senses for undared adventure,
Waving them wide-eyed past me to explore
Limitless hells of disintegrity,
Endless, undifferentiatable fate
Scrolled out beyond the utter rim of nowhere,
Scrolled out ......
                    who on return fail to surrender
Their memory trophies, random wisps of horror
Trailed from my shins or tangled in my hair?

BOWER-BIRD

The Bower-bird improvised a cool retreat
For the hen he honoured, doing his poor best
With parrot-plumage, orchids, bones and corals,
To engage her fancy.
                    But this was no nest ...
So, though the Penguin dropped at his hen's feet
An oval stone to signal: 'be my bride',
And though the Jackdaw's nest was glorified
With diamond rings and brooches massed inside,
It was the Bower-bird who contented me
By not equating love with matrimony.

MIST

Fire and Deluge, rival pretenders
To ruling the world's end; these cannot daunt us
Whom flames will never singe, nor floods drown,
While we stand guard against their murderous child
Mist, that slily catches at love's throat,
Shrouding the clear sun and clean waters
Of all green gardens everywhere –
The twitching mouths likewise and furtive eyes
Of those who speak us fair.

THE WORD

The Word is unspoken
Between honest lovers:
They substitute a silence
Or wave at a wild flower,
Sighing inaudibly.

That it exists indeed
Will scarcely be disputed:
The wildest of conceptions
Can be reduced to speech –
Or so the Schoolmen teach.

You and I, thronged by angels,
Learned it in the same dream
Which startled us by moon-light,
And that we still revere it
Keeps our souls aflame.

'God' is a standing question
That still negates an answer.
The Word is not a question
But simple affirmation,
The antonym of 'God'.

Who would believe this Word
Could have so long been hidden
Behind a candid smile,
A sweet but hasty kiss
And always dancing feet?

PERFECTIONISTS

Interalienation of their hearts
It was not, though both played resentful parts
In proud unwillingness to share
One house, one pillow, the same fare.
It was perfectionism, they confess,
To know the truth and ask for nothing less.

Their fire-eyed guardians watched from overhead:
'These two alone have learned to love,' they said,
'But neither can forget
They are not worthy of each other yet.'

PRISON WALLS

Love, this is not the way
To treat a glorious day:
To cloud it over with conjectured fears,
Wiping my eyes before they brim with tears
And, long before we part,
Mourning the torments of my jealous heart.

That you have tried me more
Than who else did before,
Is no good reason to prognosticate
My last ordeal: when I must greet with hate
Your phantom fairy prince
Conjured in childhood, lost so often since.

Nor can a true heart rest
Resigned to second best –
Why did you need to temper me so true
That I became your sword of swords, if you
Must nail me on your wall
And choose a painted lath when the blows fall?

Because I stay heart-whole,
Because you bound your soul
To mine, with curses should it wander free,
I charge you now to keep full faith with me
Nor can I ask for less
Than your unswerving honest-heartedness.

Then grieve no more, but while
Your flowers are scented, smile
And never sacrifice, as others may,
So clear a dawn to dread of Judgement Day –
Lest prison walls should see
Fresh tears of longing you let fall for me.

A DREAM OF HELL

You reject the rainbow
Of our Sun castle
As hyperbolic;

You enjoin the Moon
Of our pure trysts
To condone deceit;

Lured to violence
By a lying spirit,
You break our troth.

Seven wide, enchanted
Wards of horror
Lie stretched before you,

To brand your naked breast
With impious colours,
To band your thighs.

How can I discharge
Your confused spirit
From its chosen hell?

You who once dragged me
From the bubbling slime
Of a tidal reach,

Who washed me, fed me,
Laid me in white sheets,
Warmed me in brown arms,

Would you have me cede
Our single sovereignty
To your tall demon?

OUR SELF

When first we came together
It was no chance foreshadowing
Of a chance happy ending.
The case grows always clearer
By its own worse disorder:
However reasonably we oppose
That unquiet integer, our self, we lose.

BITES AND KISSES

Heather and holly,
Bites and kisses,
A courtship-royal
On the hill's red cusp.
Look up, look down,
Gaze all about you –
A livelier world
By ourselves contrived:

Swan in full course
Up the Milky Way,
Moon in her wildness,
Sun ascendant
In Crab or Lion,
Beyond the bay
A pride of dolphins
Curving and tumbling
With bites and kisses …

Or dog-rose petals
Well-starred by dew,
Or jewelled pebbles,
Or waterlilies open
For the dragon-flies
In their silver and blue.

SUN-FACE AND MOON-FACE

We twin cherubs above the Mercy Seat,
Sun-face and Moon-face,
Locked in the irrevocable embrace
That guards our children from defeat,
Are fire not flesh; as none will dare deny
Lest his own soul should die.

FREEHOLD

Though love expels the ugly past
Restoring you this house at last –
This generous-hearted mind and soul
Reserved from alien control –
How can you count on living free
From sudden jolts of history,
From interceptive sigh or stare
That heaves you back to how-things-were
And makes you answerable for
The casualties of bygone war?
Yet smile your vaguest: make it clear
That then was then, but now is here.

THE NECKLACE

Variegated flowers, nuts, cockle-shells
And pebbles, chosen lovingly and strung
On golden spider-webs with a gold clasp
For your neck, naturally: and each bead touched
By a child's lips as he stoops over them:
Wear these for the new miracle they announce –
All four cross-quarter-days beseech you –
Your safe return from shipwreck, drought and war,
Beautiful as before, to what you are.

A BRACELET

A bracelet invisible
For your busy wrist,
Twisted from silver
Spilt afar,
From silver of the clear Moon,
From her sheer halo,
From the male beauty
Of a shooting star.

BLACKENING SKY

Lightning enclosed by a vast ring of mirrors,
Instant thunder extravagantly bandied
Between red cliffs no hawk may nest upon,
Triumphant jetting, passion of deluge: ours –
With spray that stuns, dams that lurch and are gone....

But against this insensate hubbub of subsidence
Our voices, always true to a fireside tone,
Meditate on the secret marriage of flowers
Or the bees' paradise, with much else more;
And while the sky blackens anew for rain,
On why we love as none ever loved before.

BLESSED SUN

Honest morning blesses the Sun's beauty;
Noon, his endurance; dusk, his majesty;
Sweetheart, our own twin worlds bask in the glory
And searching wisdom of that single eye –
Why must the Queen of Night on her moon throne
Tear up their contract and still reign alone?

LION-GENTLE

Love, never disavow our vow
Nor wound your lion-gentle:
Take what you will, dote on it, keep it,
But pay your debts with a grave, wilful smile
Like a woman of the sword.

SONG: THE PALM TREE

Palm-tree, single and apart
    In your serpent-haunted land,
Like the fountain of a heart
    Soaring into air from sand –
None can count it as a fault
That your roots are fed with salt.

Panniers-full of dates you yield,
    Thorny branches laced with light,
Wistful for no pasture-field
    Fed by torrents from a height,
Short of politics to share
With the damson or the pear.

Never-failing phoenix tree
    In your serpent-haunted land,
Fount of magic soaring free
    From a desert of salt sand;
Tears of joy are salty too –
Mine shall flow in praise of you.

SPITE OF MIRRORS

O what astonishment if you
Could see yourself as others do,
Foiling the mirror's wilful spite
That shows your left cheek as the right
And shifts your lovely crooked smile
To the wrong corner! But meanwhile
Lakes, pools and puddles all agree
(Bound in a vast conspiracy)
To reflect only your stern look
Designed for peering in a book –
No easy laugh, no glint of rage,
No thoughts in cheerful pilgrimage,
No start of guilt, no rising fear,
No premonition of a tear.

How, with a mirror, can you keep
Watch on your eyelids closed in sleep?
How judge which profile to bestow
On a new coin or cameo?
How, from two steps behind you, stare
At your firm nape discovered bare
Of ringlets as you bend and reach
Transparent pebbles from the beach?
Love, if you long for a surprise
Of self-discernment, hold my eyes
And plunge deep down in them to see
Sights never long withheld from me.

PRIDE OF LOVE

I face impossible feats at your command,
Resentful at the tears of love you shed
For the faint-hearted sick who flock to you;
But since all love lies wholly in the giving,
Weep on: your tears are true,
Nor can despair provoke me to self-pity
Where pride alone is due.

HOODED FLAME

Love, though I sorrow, I shall never grieve:
Grief is to mourn a flame extinguished;
Sorrow, to find it hooded for the hour
When planetary influences deceive
And hope, like wine, turns sour.

INJURIES

Injure yourself, you injure me:
Is that not true as true can be?
Nor can you give me cause to doubt
It works the other way about;
So what precautions must I take
Not to be injured for love's sake?

HER BRIEF WITHDRAWAL

'Forgive me, love, if I withdraw awhile:
It is only that you ask such bitter questions,
Always another beyond the extreme last.
And the answers astound: you have entangled me
In my own mystery. Grant me a respite:
I was happier far, not asking, nor much caring,
Choosing by appetite only: self-deposed,
Self-reinstated, no one observing.
When I belittled this vibrancy of touch
And the active vengeance of these folded arms
No one could certify my powers for me
Or my saining virtue, or know that I compressed
Knots of destiny in a careless fist,
I who had passed for a foundling from the hills
Of innocent and flower-like phantasies,
Though minting silver by my mere tread ....
Did I not dote on you, I well might strike you
For implicating me in your true dream.'

THE CRANE

The Crane lounes loudly in his need,
    And so for love I loune:
Son to the sovereign Sun indeed,
    Courier of the Moon.

STRANGENESS

You love me strangely, and in strangeness
I love you wholly, with no parallel
To this long miracle; for each example
Of love coincidence levels a finger
At strangeness undesigned as unforeseen.

And this long miracle is to discover
The inmost you and never leave her;
To show no curiosity for another;
To forge the soul and its desire together
Gently, openly and for ever.

Seated in silence, clothed in silence
And face to face – the room is small
But thronged with visitants –
We ask for nothing: we have all.

From THE POOR BOY WHO FOLLOWED HIS STAR

(1968)

HIDE AND SEEK

The trees are tall, but the moon small,
My legs feel rather weak,
For Avis, Mavis and Tom Clarke
Are hiding somewhere in the dark
And it's my turn to seek.

Suppose they lay a trap and play
A trick to frighten me?
Suppose they plan to disappear
And leave me here, half-dead with fear,
Groping from tree to tree?

Alone, alone, all on my own
And then perhaps to find
Not Avis, Mavis and young Tom
But monsters to run shrieking from,
Mad monsters of no kind?

THE HERO

Slowly with bleeding nose and aching wrists
After tremendous use of feet and fists
He rises from the dusty schoolroom floor
And limps for solace to the girl next door,
Boasting of kicks and punches, cheers and noise,
And far worse damage done to bigger boys.

AT SEVENTY-TWO

At seventy-two,
Being older than you,
I can rise when I please
Without slippers or shoes
And go down to the kitchen
To eat what I choose –
Jam, tomatoes and cheese –
Then I visit the garden
And wander at ease
Past the bed where what grows is
A huge clump of roses
And I swing in the swing
Set up under the trees
My mouth full of biscuits,
My hat on my knees.

From *POEMS 1965–1968*

(1968)

SONG: HOW CAN I CARE?

How can I care whether you sigh for me
    While still I sleep alone swallowing back
The spittle of desire, unmanned, a tree
    Pollarded of its crown, a dusty sack
    Tossed on the stable rack?

How can I care what coloured frocks you wear,
    What humming-birds you watch on jungle hills,
What phosphorescence wavers in your hair,
    Or with what water-music the night fills –
    Dear love, how can I care?

SONG: THOUGH ONCE TRUE LOVERS

Though once true lovers,
    We are less than friends.
What woman ever
    So ill-used her man?
That I played false
    Not even she pretends:
May God forgive her,
    For, alas, I can.

SONG: CHERRIES OR LILIES

Death can have no alternative but Love,
Or Love but Death.
Acquaintance dallying on the path of Love,
Sickness on that of Death,
Pause at a bed-side, doing what they can
With fruit and flowers bought from the barrow man.

Death can have no alternative but Love,
Or Love but Death.
Then shower me cherries from your orchard, Love,
Or strew me lilies, Death:
For she and I were never of that breed
Who vacillate or trifle with true need.

SONG: CROWN OF STARS

Lion-heart, you prowl alone
True to Virgin, Bride and Crone;
None so black of brow as they
Now, tomorrow, yesterday.
Yet the night you shall not see
Must illuminate all three
As the tears of love you shed
Blaze about their single head
And a sword shall pierce the side
Of true Virgin, Crone and Bride
Among mansions of the dead.

SONG: FIG TREE IN LEAF

One day in early Spring
Upon bare branches perching
  Great companies of birds are seen
  Clad all at once in pilgrim green
Their news of love to bring:

Their fig tree parable,
For which the world is watchful,
  Retold with shining wings displayed:
  Her secret flower, her milk, her shade,
Her scarlet, blue and purple.

SONG: DEW-DROP AND DIAMOND

The difference between you and her
(Whom I to you did once prefer)
Is clear enough to settle:
She like a diamond shone, but you
Shine like an early drop of dew
Poised on a red rose-petal.

The dew-drop carries in its eye
Mountain and forest, sea and sky,
With every change of weather;
Contrariwise, a diamond splits
The prospect into idle bits
That none can piece together.

SONG: JUST FRIENDS

Just friend, you are my only friend –
You think the same of me
And swear our love must never end
Though lapped in secrecy,
As all true love should be.
They ask us: 'What about you two?'
I answer 'Only friends' and you:
'Just friends' gently agree.

SONG: OF COURSE

No, of course we were never
        Off course in our love,
Being nourished by manna
        That dripped from above,

And our secret of loving
        Was taught us, it seems,
By ravens and owlets
        And fast-flowing streams.

We had sealed it with kisses,
        It blazed from our eyes,
Yet all was unspoken
        And proof against lies.

For to publish a secret
        Once learned in the rain
Would have meant to lose course
        And not find it again.

So this parting, of course,
        Is illusion, not fate,
And the love in your letters
        Comes charged overweight.

SONG: THREE RINGS FOR HER

Flowers remind of jewels;
Jewels, of flowers;
Flowers, of innocent morning;
Jewels, of honest evening –
Emerald, moonstone, opal –
For so I mean, and meant.
Jewels are longer lasting –
Emerald, moonstone, opal;
Opal, emerald, moonstone:
Moonstone, opal, emerald –
And wear a livelier scent.

SINCÈREMENT

J'étais confus à cet instant.
Quelle honte d'avoir écrit
L'adverbe aveugle 'sincèrement' –
'Je t'aime' m'aurait suffi
Sans point et sans souci.

DANS UN SEUL LIT

Entre deux belles femmes dans un seul lit
Cet homme, se sentant interdit,
Des convenances n'ose pas faire foin
Mais opte pour elle qu'il aime le moins.

Entre deux beaux hommes en pareil cas,
Une dame sans mœurs si délicats
Mais sans s'exprimer en termes crus,
Se penche vers lui qu'elle aime le plus.

IS NOW THE TIME?

If he asks, 'Is now the time?', it is not the time.
She turns her head from his concern with time
As a signal not to haste it;
And every time he asks: 'Is now the time?'
A hundred nights are wasted.

TWINS

Siamese twins: one, maddened by
The other's moral bigotry,
Resolved at length to misbehave
And drink them both into the grave.

SAIL AND OAR

Woman sails, man must row:
Each, disdainful of a tow,
Cuts across the other's bows
Shame or fury to arouse –
And evermore it shall be so,
Lest man sail, or woman row.

GOOSEFLESH ABBEY

Nuns are allowed full liberty of conscience.
Yet might this young witch, when she took the veil,
Count on an aged Abbess's connivance
At keeping toad-familiars in her cell?
Some called it liberty; but others, licence –
And how was she to tell?

THE HOME-COMING

At the tangled heart of a wood I fell asleep,
Bewildered by her silence and her absence –
As though such potent lulls in love were not
Ordained by the demands of pure music.

A bird sang: 'Close your eyes, it is not for long –
Dream of what gold and crimson she will wear
In honour of your oak-brown.'

It was her hoopoe. Yet, when the spread heavens
Of my feast night glistened with shooting stars
And she walked unheralded up through the dim light
Of the home lane, I did not recognize her –
So lost a man can be
Who feeds on hopes and fears and memory.

WITH THE GIFT OF A LION'S CLAW

Queen of the Crabs, accept this claw
Plucked from a Lion's patient paw;
It shall propel her forward who
Ran sideways always hitherto.

WIGS AND BEARDS

In the bad old days a bewigged country Squire
Would never pay his debts, unless at cards,
Shot, angled, urged his pack through standing grain,
Horsewhipped his tenantry, snorted at the arts,
Toped himself under the table every night,
Blasphemed God with a cropful of God-damns,
Aired whorehouse French or lame Italian,
Set fashions of pluperfect slovenliness
And claimed seigneurial rights over all women
Who slept, imprudently, under the same roof.

Taxes and wars long ago ploughed them under –
'And serve the bastards right' the Beards agree,
Hurling their empties through the café window
And belching loud as they proceed downstairs.
Latter-day bastards of that famous stock,
They never rode a nag, nor gaffed a trout,
Nor winged a pheasant, nor went soldiering,
But remain true to the same hell-fire code
In all available particulars
And scorn to pay their debts even at cards.
Moreunder (which is to subtract, not add),
Their ancestors called themselves gentlemen
As they, in the same sense, call themselves artists.

PERSONAL PACKAGING, INC.

Folks, we have zero'd in to a big break-thru:
Our boys are learning how to package *people*
By a new impermeable-grading process
In cartons of mixed twenties – all three sexes!

Process involves molecular adjustment
To micro-regulated temperatures,
Making them unexpendable time-wise
Thru a whole century … Some clients opt for
Five thousand years, or six, in real deep freeze –
A chance what sensible guy would kick against
To pile up dollars at compound interest?
Nor do we even propose that they quit smoking
Or, necessarily, be parted from their wives.

WORK ROOM

Camp-stool for chair once more and packing case for table;
All histories of doubt extruded from this room
With its menacing, promising, delusive, toppling bookshelves;
Nothing now astir but you in my fresh imagination,
And no letters but yours ever demanding answers.
To start all over again; indeed, why should I not? –
With a new pen, clean paper, full inkpot.

THE ARK

Beasts of the field, fowls likewise of the air,
Came trooping, seven by seven or pair by pair;
And though from Hell the arch-fiend Samael
Bawled out 'Escapist!' Noah did not care.

ALL EXCEPT HANNIBAL

Trapped in a dismal marsh, he told his troops:
'No lying down, lads! Form your own mess-groups
And sit in circles, each man on the knees
Of the man behind; then nobody will freeze.'

They obeyed his orders, as the cold sun set,
Drowsing all night in one another's debt,
All except Hannibal himself, who chose
His private tree-stump – he was one of those!

THE BEGGAR MAID AND KING COPHETUA

To be adored by a proud Paladin
Whom the wide world adored,
To queen it over countless noblewomen:
What fame was hers at last,
What lure and envy!

Yet, being still a daughter of the mandrake
She sighed for more than fame;
Not all the gold with which Cophetua crowned her
Could check this beggar-maid's
Concupiscence.

Sworn to become proverbially known
As martyred by true love,
She took revenge on his victorious name
That blotted her own fame
For woman's magic.

True to her kind, she slipped away one dawn
With a poor stable lad,
Gaunt, spotted, drunken, scrawny, desperate,
Mean of intelligence
As bare of honour.

So pitiable indeed that when the guards
Who caught them saw the green
Stain on her finger from his plain brass ring
They gaped at it, too moved
Not to applaud her.

FOR EVER

Sweetheart, I beg you to renew and seal
With a not supererogatory kiss
Our contract of 'For Ever'.
                         Learned judges
Deplore the household sense 'interminable':
True love, they rule, never acknowledges
Future or past, only a perfect now....
But let it read 'For Ever', anyhow!

JUGUM IMPROBUM

Pyrrha, jugo tandem vitulum junges-ne leoni?
Sit tibi dilectus, num stricto verbere debet
Compelli pavitans medium moriturus in ignem?

DE ARTE POETICA

De minimis curat non Lex, utcumque poeta.

SIT MIHI TERRA LEVIS

Ante mortem qui defletus
        Solis lucem repperit
Ante Mortem perquietus,
        Erato, domum redit.

ASTYMELUSA*

'Astymelusa!'
                Knees at your approach
Suddenly give, more than in sleep or death –
As well they may; such love compels them.
'Astymelusa!'
                But no answer comes.
Crowned with a leafy crown, the girl passes
Like a star afloat through glittering sky,
Or a golden flower, or drifted thistledown.

* A fragment by the Dorian Greek poet Alcman, seventh
century B.C., found among the Oxyrhynchus papyri.

TOUSLED PILLOW

She appeared in Triad – Youth, Truth, Beauty –
Full face and profiles whispering together
All night at my bed-foot.
                And when dawn came
At last, from a tousled pillow resolutely
I made my full surrender:
'So be it, Goddess, claim me without shame
And tent me in your hair.'
                Since when she holds me
As close as candlewick to candleflame
And from all hazards free,
My soul drawn back to its virginity.

TO BE IN LOVE

To spring impetuously in air and remain
Treading on air for three heart-beats or four,
Then to descend at leisure; or else to scale
The forward-tilted crag with no hand-holds;
Or, disembodied, to carry roses home
From a Queen's garden – this is being in love,
Graced with *agilitas* and *subtilitas*
At which few famous lovers ever guessed
Though children may foreknow it, deep in dream,
And ghosts may mourn it, haunting their own tombs,
And peacocks cry it, in default of speech.

FACT OF THE ACT

On the other side of the world's narrow lane
You lie in bed, your young breasts tingling
With imagined kisses, your lips puckered,
Your fists tight.

Dreaming yourself naked in my arms,
Free from discovery, under some holm oak;
The high sun peering through thick branches,
All winds mute.

Endlessly you prolong the moment
Of your delirium: a first engagement,
Silent, inevitable, fearful,
Honey-sweet.

Will it be so in fact? Will fact mirror
Your virginal ecstasies:
True love, uncircumstantial,
No blame, no shame?

It is for you, now, to say 'come';
It is for you, now, to prepare the bed;
It is for you as the sole hostess
Of your white dreams –

It is for you to open the locked gate,
It is for you to shake red apples down,
It is for you to halve them with your hands
That both may eat.

Yet expectation lies as far from fact
As fact's own after-glow in memory;
Fact is a dark return to man's beginnings,
Test of our hardihood, test of a wilful
And blind acceptance of each other
As also flesh.

TO OGMIAN HERCULES

Your Labours are performed, your Bye-works too,
Your ashes gently drift from Oeta's peak.
Here is escape then, Hercules, from empire.

Lithe Hebë, youngest of all Goddesses,
Who circles on the Moon's broad threshing-floor
Harboured no jealousy for Megara,
Augë, Hippolytë, Deianeira,
But grieved for each in turn. You broke all hearts,
Burning too Sun-like for a Grecian bride.

Rest your immortal head on Hebë's lap;
What wars you started let your sons conclude.
Meditate a new Alphabet, heal wounds,
Draw poets to you with long golden chains
But still go armed with club and lion's pelt.

ARROW SHOTS

Only a madman could mistake,
        When shot at from behind a tree,
The whizz and thud that arrows make –
        Yours, for example, fired at me.

Some bows are drawn to blind or maim,
    I have known others drawn to kill,
But truth in love is your sole aim
    And proves your vulnerary skill.

Though often, drowsing at mid-day,
    I wince to find myself your mark,
Let me concede the hit, but say:
    'Your hand is steadiest after dark.'

SHE TO HIM

To have it, sweetheart, is to know you have it
Rather than think you have it;
To think you have it is a wish to take it,
Though afterwards you would not have it –
And thus a fear to take it.
Yet if you know you have it, you may take it
And know that still you have it.

WITHIN REASON

You have wandered widely through your own mind
And your own perfect body;
Thus learning, within reason, gentle one,
Everything that can prove worth the knowing.

A concise wisdom never attained by those
Bodiless nobodies
Who travel pen in hand through others' minds,
But without reason,
Feeding on manifold contradiction.

To stand perplexed by love's inconsequences
Like fire-flies in your hair
Or distant flashes of a summer storm:
Such are the stabs of joy you deal me
Who also wander widely through my mind
And still imperfect body.

THE YET UNSAYABLE

It was always fiercer, brighter, gentler than could be told
Even in words quickened by Truth's dark eye:
Its absence, whirlpool; its presence, deluge;
Its time, astonishment; its magnitude,
A murderous dagger-point.
                              So we surrender
Our voices to the dried and scurrying leaves
And choose our own long-predetermined path
From the unsaid to the yet unsayable
In silence of love and love's temerity.

NONE THE WISER

They would be none the wiser, even could they overhear
My slurred ecstatic mumbling or grow somehow aware
Of eyes ablaze behind shut lids in the attic gloom.

Even if they adjured me on pain of death to disclose
All that I see and am when I so absent myself,
What would they make of steady, somnolent light-rings
Converging, violet-blue or green hypnotic gold,
Upon a warded peep-hole, as it were a rift in Space,
Through which I peer, as it might be into your eyes,
And pass disembodied, a spiral wisp or whorl
Tall, slanted, russet-red, crowned with a lunar nimbus? –
To you the central flow, the glow, the ease, the hush
Of music drawn through irrecoverable modes.
And then such after-glory, meteors across the heart
When I awake, astonished, in the bed where once you dreamed.

'Metaphysical', they would comment lamely, 'metaphysical';
But you would smile at me for leaving so much out.

THE NARROW SEA

With you for mast and sail and flag,
And anchor never known to drag,
Death's narrow but oppressive sea
Looks not unnavigable to me.

THE OLIVE-YARD

Now by a sudden shift of eye
The hitherto exemplary world
Takes on immediate wildness
And birds, trees, winds, the very letters
Of our childhood's alphabet, alter
Into rainbowed mysteries.

Flesh is no longer flesh, but power;
Numbers, no longer arithmetical,
Dance like lambs, fly like doves;
And silence falls at last, though silken branches
Gently heave in the near olive-yard
And vague cloud labours on.

Whose was the stroke of summer genius
Flung from a mountain fastness
Where the griffon-vulture soars
That let us read our shrouded future
As easily as a book of prayer
Spread open on the knee?

BEYOND GIVING

(1969)

PART I

SONG: TO A ROSE

Queen of Sharon in the valley,
Clasp my head your breasts between:
Darkly blind me to your beauty –
Rose renowned for blood-red berries
Ages earlier than for fragrant
Blossom and sweet hidden honey,
Save by studious bees.

SONG: DREAM WARNING

A lion in the path, a lion;
A jewelled serpent by the sun
Hatched in a desert silence
And stumbled on by chance;
A peacock crested with green fire,
His legs befouled in mire;
Not less, an enlacement of seven dreams
On a rainbow scale returning
To the drum that throbs against their melodies
Its dark insistent warning.

SONG: BEYOND GIVING

There is a giving beyond giving:
        Yours to me
Who awoke last night, hours before the dawn,
        Set free
By one intolerable lightning stroke
        That ripped the sky
To understand what love withholds in love,
        And why.

TRIAL OF INNOCENCE

Urged by your needs and my desire,
I first made you a woman; nor was either
Troubled by fear of hidden evil
Or of temporal circumstance;
For circumstances never alter cases
When lovers, hand in hand, face trial
Pleading uncircumstantial innocence.

POISONED DAY

The clouds dripped poisonous dew to spite
A day for weeks looked forward to. True love
Sickened that evening without remedy:
We neither quarrelled, kissed, nor said good-night
But fell asleep, our arms around each other,
And awoke to the gentle hiss of rain on grass
And thrushes calling that the worst was over.

SUPERSTITION

Forget the foolishness with which I vexed you:
Mine was a gun-shy superstition
Surviving from defeat in former loves
And banished when you stood staring aghast
At the replacement of your sturdy lover
By a disconsolate waif.

Blame the foul weather for my aching wounds,
Blame ugly history for my wild fears,
Nor ever turn from your own path; for still
Despite your fancies, your white silences,
Your disappearances, you remain bound
By this unshakeable trust I rest in you.

Go, because inner strength ordains your journey,
Making a necessary occasion seem
No more than incidental. Love go with you
In distillation of all past and future –
You, a clear torrent flooding the mill-race,
Forcing its mill to grind
A coarse grain into flour for angels' bread.

IN THE NAME OF VIRTUE

In the name of Virtue, girl,
Why must you try so hard
In the hard name of Virtue?
Is not such trying, questioning?
Such questioning, doubting?
Such doubting, guessing?
Such guessing, not-knowing?
Such not-knowing, not-being?
Such not-being, death?
Can death be Virtue?

Virtue is from listening
To a private angel,
An angel overheard
When the little-finger twitches –
The bold little-finger
That refused education:
When the rest went to college
And philosophized on Virtue,
It neither went, nor tried.

Knowing becomes doing
When all we need to know
Is how to check our pendulum
And move the hands around
For a needed golden instant
Of the future or past –
Then start time up again
With a bold little-finger
In Virtue's easy name.

WHAT WE DID NEXT

What we did next, neither of us remembers....
Still, the key turned, the wide bronze gate creaked open
And there before us in profuse detail
Spread Paradise: its lawns dappled with petals,
Pomegranate trees in quincunx, corn in stooks;
Plantations loud with birds, pools live with fish,
And unborn children blue as bonfire-smoke
Crouching entranced to see the grand serpent
Writhe in and out of long rock-corridors,
Rattling his coils of gold –
Or the jewelled toad from whose immense mouth
Burst out the four great rivers.... To be there
Was always to be there, without grief, always,
Superior to all chance, or change, or death....

What we did next, neither of us remembers.

COMPACT

My love for you, though true, wears the extravagance of centuries;
Your love for me is fragrant, simple and millennial.
Smiling without a word, you watch my extravagances pass;
To check them would be presumptuous and unmaidenly –
As it were using me like an ill-bred schoolboy.

Dear Live-apart, when I sit confused by the active spites
Tormenting me with too close sympathy for fools,
Too dark a rage against hidden plotters of evil,
Too sour a mind, or soused with sodden wool-bales –
I turn my eyes to the light smoke drifting from your fire.

Our settled plan has been: never to make plans –
The future, present and past being already settled
Beyond review or interpretative conjecture
By the first decision of truth that we clasped hands upon:
To conserve a purity of soul each for the other.

SONG: NEW YEAR KISSES

Every morning, every evening,
Kisses for my starving darling:
On her brow for close reflection,
On her eyes for patient watching,
On her ears for watchful listening,
On her palms for careful action,
On her toes for fiery dancing –
Kisses that outgo perfection –
On her nape for secrecy,
On her lips for poetry,
On her bosom bared for me
Kisses more than three times three.

SONG: THE CLOCKS OF TIME

The clocks of time divide us:
You sleep while I wake –
No need to think it monstrous
Though I remain uneasy,
Watchful, albeit drowsy,
Communing over wastes of sea
With you, my other me.

Too strict a concentration,
Each on an absent self,
Distracts our prosecution
Of what this love implies:
Genius, with its complexities
Of working backwards from the answer
To bring a problem near.

But when your image shortens
(My eyes thrown out of focus)
And fades in the far distance –
Your features indistinguishable,
Your gait and form unstable –
Time's heart revives our closeness
Hand in hand, lip to lip.

GOLD CLOUD

Your gold cloud, towering far above me,
Through which I climb from darkness into sleep
Has the warmth of sun, rain's morning freshness
And a scent either of wood-smoke or of jasmine;
Nor is the ascent steep.

Our creature, Time, bends readily as willow:
We plan our own births, that at least we know,
Whether in the lovely moment of death
Or when we first meet, here in Paradise,
As now, so years ago.

SONG: BASKET OF BLOSSOM

Jewels here lie heaped for you
Under jasmine, under lilac –
Leave them undisclosed awhile;
If the blossoms be short-lasting
Smile, but with your secret smile.

I have always from the first
Made my vow in honour's name
Only thus to fetch you jewels,
Never vaunting of the same.

SONG: WHEREVER WE MAY BE

Wherever we may be
There is mindlessness and mind,
There is lovelessness and love,
There is self, there is unself,
Within and without;
There is plus, there is minus;
There is empty, there is full;
There is God, the busy question
In denial of doubt.

There is mindlessness and mind,
There is deathlessness and death,
There is waking, there is sleeping,
There is false, there is true,
There is going, there is coming,
But upon the stroke of midnight
Wherever we may be,
There am I, there are you.

WHAT IS LOVE?

But what is love? Tell me, dear heart, I beg you.
Is it a reattainment of our centre,
A core of trustful innocence come home to?

Is it, perhaps, a first wild bout of being,
The taking of our own extreme measure
And for a few hours knowing everything?

Or what is love? Is it primeval vision
That stars our course with oracles of danger
And looks to death for timely intervention?

SONG: THE PROMISE

While you were promised to me
But still were not yet given,
There was this to be said:
Though wishes might be wishes,
A promise was a promise –
Like the shadow of a cedar,
Or the moon overhead,
Or the firmness of your fingers,
Or the print of your kisses,
Or your lightness of tread,
With not a doubt between us
Once bats began their circling
Among the palms and cedars
And it was time for bed.

SONG: YESTERDAY ONLY

Not today, not tomorrow,
Yesterday only:
A long-lasting yesterday
Devised by us to swallow
Today with tomorrow.

When was your poem hidden
Underneath my pillow,
When was your rose-bush planted
Underneath my window –
Yesterday only?

Green leaves, red roses,
Blazoned upon snow,
A long-lasting yesterday,
Today with tomorrow,
Always and only.

PART II

SEMI-DETACHED

Her inevitable complaint or accusation
Whatever the Major does or leaves undone,
Though, being a good wife, never before strangers,
Nor, being a good mother, ever before their child ...
With no endearments except for cats and kittens
Or an occasional bird rescued from cats ...
Well, as semi-detached neighbours, with party-walls
Not altogether sound-proof, we overhear
The rare explosion when he retaliates
In a sudden burst of anger, although perhaps
(We are pretty sure) apologizing later
And getting no forgiveness or reply.

He has his own resources – bees and gardening –
And, we conclude, is on the whole happy.
They never sleep together, as they once did
Five or six years ago, when they first arrived,
Or so we judge from washing on their line –
Those double sheets are now for guests only –
But welcome streams of visitors. How many
Suspect that the show put on by both of them,
Of perfect marital love, is apology
In sincere make-believe, for what still lacks?

If ever she falls ill, which seldom happens,
We know he nurses her indefatigably,
But this she greets, we know, with sour resentment,
Hating to catch herself at a disadvantage,
And crawls groaning downstairs to sink and oven.
If he falls ill she treats it as affront –
Except at the time of that car-accident
When he nearly died, and unmistakable grief
Shone from her eyes for almost a whole fortnight,
But then faded ...

              He receives regular airmail
In the same handwriting, with Austrian stamps.
Whoever sends it, obviously a woman,
Never appears. Those are his brightest moments.
Somehow they take no holidays whatsoever
But are good neighbours, always ready to lend

And seldom borrowing. Our child plays with theirs;
Yet we exchange no visits or confidences.
Only once I penetrated past their hall –
Which was when I fetched him in from the wrecked car
And alone knew who had caused the accident.

IAGO

Iago learned from that old witch, his mother,
How to do double murder
On man and woman fallen deep in love;
Lie first to her, then lie again to him,
Make each mistrustful of the honest other.
Guilt and suspicion wear the same sick face –
Two deaths will follow in a short space.

AGAINST WITCHCRAFT

No smile so innocent or angelic
As when she nestled to his wounded heart,
Where the slow poison worked within
And eggs of insane fever incubated …

Out, witch, out! Here are nine cloves of garlic
That grew repellent to the Moon's pull;
Here too is every gift you ever gave him,
Wrapped in a silken cloth.
Your four-snake chariot awaits your parting
And here I plant my besom upside down.

TROUBLESOME FAME

To be born famous, as your father's son,
    Is a fate troublesome enough, unless
Like Philip's Alexander of Macedon
    You can out-do him by superb excess
Of greed and profligacy and wantonness.

To become famous as a wonder-child
    Brings no less trouble, with whatever art
You toyed precociously, for Fame had smiled
    Malevolence at your birth … Only Mozart
Played on, still smiling from his placid heart.

To become famous while a raw young man
    And lead Fame by the nose, to a bitter end,
As Caesar's nephew did, Octavian
    Styling himself Augustus, is to pretend
Peace in the torments that such laurels lend.

To become famous in your middle years
    For merit not unblessed by accident –
Encountering cat-calls, missiles, jeers and sneers
    From half your uncontrollable parliament –
Is no bad fate, to a good sportsman sent.…

But Fame attendant on extreme old age
    Falls best. What envious youth cares to compete
With a lean sage hauled painfully upstage,
    Bowing, gasping, shuffling his frozen feet –
A ribboned hearse parked plainly down the street?

TOLLING BELL

'But why so solemn when the bell tolled?'
'Did you expect me to stand up and caper?'
'Confess, what are you trying to hide from me?
Horror of death?'
             'That seventeenth-century
Skeletal effigy in the Church crypt?'
'Or is it fear, perhaps, of a second childhood?
Of incurable sickness? Or of a strange someone
Seated in your own chair at your own table?
Or worse, of that chair gone?'
             'Why saddle me
With your own nightmares?'
             'Fear of the other world?'
'Be your own age! What world exists but ours?'
'Distaste for funerals?'
             'Isn't it easier

To play the unweeping corpse than the pall-bearer?'
'Why so mysterious?'
                              'Why so persistent?'
'I only asked why you had looked solemn
When the bell tolled.'
                              'Angered, not solemn, angered
By all parochially enforced grief.
Death is a private, ungainsayable act.'
'Privately, then, what does Death mean to you?'
'Only love's gentle sigh of consummation,
Which I have little fear of drawing too soon.'

BLANKET CHARGE

This fever doubtless comes in punishment
For crimes discovered by your own conscience:
You lie detained here on a blanket charge
        And between blankets lodged.

So many tedious hours of light and dark
To weigh the incriminatory evidence –
With your head somewhat clearer by midday
        Than at its midnight worst.

Ignorance of the Law is no defence
In any Court; but can you plead 'not guilty
Of criminal intent' without a lawyer
        To rise on your behalf?

However long the sentence passed on you,
The term served here will, you assume, be taken
Into consideration; you have proved,
        Surely, a model prisoner?

The worst is finding where your fault lay
In all its pettiness; do you regret
It was not some cardinal, outrageous sin
        That drew crowds to the gibbet?

THE STRAYED MESSAGE

Characteristic, nevertheless strange:
Something went badly wrong at the Exchange,
And my private message to you, in full detail,
Got broadcast over eleven frequencies
With the usual, though disquieting, consequences
Of a torrential amatory fan-mail.

SONG: THE SUNDIAL'S LAMENT

(*Air: The Groves of Blarney*)

Since much at home on
My face and gnomon,
The sun refuses
Daylight to increase;
Yet certain powers dare
Miscount my hours there
Though sun and shadow
Still collogue in peace.

These rogues aspire
To act Hezekiah
For whom Isaiah
In a day of trial,
All for delaying
His end by praying
Turned back the shadow
On my honest dial.

Nay, Sirs, though willing
To abase the shilling
From noble twelvepence
To the half of ten,
Pray go no further
On this path of murther:
If hours be Dismalized,
Sure, I'm finished then.

POEM: A REMINDER

Capital letters prompting every line,
Lines printed down the centre of each page,
Clear spaces between groups of these, combine
In a convention of respectable age
To mean: 'Read carefully. Each word we chose
Has rhythm and sound and sense. This is not prose.'

                              poem: a reminder

capitallett
                    -ers prompting ev
                                        -eryline lines printed down the
                                        cen
                                        -tre of each page clear

                              spaces between

                              groups of these combine in a con

v
       e
                n
                     t
                          i
                               o
                                    n
                                        of respectable age to mean read
care
                                        -fully each word we chose has

                                                  rhythm and
                                                  sound and
                                                  sense this is
notprose

ANTORCHA Y CORONA, 1968

Píndaro no soy, sino caballero
De San Patricio; y nuestro santo
Siglos atrás se hizo mejicano.

Todos aquí alaban las mujeres
Y con razón, como divinos seres –
Por eso entrará en mis deberes

A vuestra Olimpiada mejicana
El origen explicar de la corona:
En su principio fué femenina....

Antes que Hercules con paso largo
Metros midiera para el estadio
Miles de esfuerzos así alentado –

Ya antes, digo, allí existia
Otra carrera mas apasionada
La cual presidia la Diosa Hera.

La virgen que, a su fraternidad
Supero con maxima velocidad
Ganaba el premio de la santidad:

La corona de olivo.... Me perdonará
El respetable, si de Atalanta
Sueño, la corredora engañada

Con tres manzanas, pero de oro fino....
Y si los mitos griegos hoy resumo
Es que parecen de acuerdo pleno,

A la inventora primeval del juego,
A la Santa Madre, más honores dando
Que no a su portero deportivo.

En tres cientas trece Olimpiadas
Este nego la entrada a las damas
Amenazandolas, ai, con espadas!

Aquí, por fin, brindemos por la linda
Enriqueta de Basilio: la primera
Que nos honra con antorcha y corona.*

* This poem, with its English translation, was read at the Mexican Cultural Olympiads and awarded the Gold Medal for Poetry.

TORCH AND CROWN, 1968

(English translation of the foregoing)

No Pindar, I, but a poor gentleman
Of Irish race. Patrick, our learned saint,
Centuries past made himself Mexican.

All true-bred Mexicans idolize women
And with sound reason, as divine beings,
I therefore owe it you as my clear duty

At your Olympics, here in Mexico,
To explain the origin of the olive crown:
In the Golden Age women alone could wear it.

Long before Hercules with his huge stride
Paced out the circuit of a stadium,
Provoking men to incalculable efforts,

Long, long before, in Argos, had been run
Even more passionately, a girls' foot race
Under the watchful eye of Mother Hera.

The inspired runner who outstripped all rivals
Of her sorority and finished first
Bore off that coveted and holy prize –

The olive crown. Ladies and gentlemen,
Forgive me if I brood on Atalanta,
A champion quarter-miler tricked one day

By three gold apples tumbled on her track;
And if I plague you with these ancient myths
That is because none of them disagrees

In paying higher honours to the foundress
Of all competitive sport – the Holy Mother –
Than to her sportive janitor, Hercules.

Three hundred and thirteen Olympic Games
Hercules held, though warning off all ladies,
Even as audience, with the naked sword!

So homage to Enriqueta de Basilio
Of Mexico, the first girl who has ever
Honoured these Games with torch and olive crown!

ARMISTICE DAY, 1918

What's all this hubbub and yelling,
    Commotion and scamper of feet,
With ear-splitting clatter of kettles and cans,
    Wild laughter down Mafeking Street?

O, those are the kids whom we fought for
    (You might think they'd been scoffing our rum)
With flags that they waved when we marched off to war
    In the rapture of bugle and drum.

Now they'll hang Kaiser Bill from a lamp-post,
    Von Tirpitz they'll hang from a tree....
We've been promised a 'Land Fit for Heroes' –
    What heroes we heroes must be!

And the guns that we took from the Fritzes,
    That we paid for with rivers of blood,
Look, they're hauling them down to Old Battersea Bridge
    Where they'll topple them, souse, in the mud!

But there's old men and women in corners
    With tears falling fast on their cheeks,
There's the armless and legless and sightless –
    It's seldom that one of them speaks.

And there's flappers gone drunk and indecent
    Their skirts kilted up to the thigh,
The constables lifting no hand in reproof
    And the chaplain averting his eye....

When the days of rejoicing are over,
    When the flags are stowed safely away,
They will dream of another wild 'War to End Wars'
    And another wild Armistice day.

But the boys who were killed in the trenches,
    Who fought with no rage and no rant,
We left them stretched out on their pallets of mud
    Low down with the worm and the ant.

THE MOTES

You like to joke about young love
    Because (let me be just)
In your dead courts and corridors
Motes dance upon no sunbeams
    But settle down as dust.

From *POEMS ABOUT LOVE*

(1969)

IF AND WHEN

She hates an *if*, know that for sure:
Whether in cunning or self-torture,
Your *ifs* anticipate the *when*
That womankind conceals from men.

From POEMS 1968–1970

(1970)

SONG: THE SIGIL

Stumbling up an unfamiliar stairway
   Between my past and future
And overtaken by the shadowy mind
    Of a girl dancing for love,
    I glanced over my shoulder.

She had read my secret name, that was no doubt,
   For which how could I blame her?
Her future paired so gently with my own,
    Her past so innocently,
    It flung me in a fever.

Thereupon, as on every strange occasion,
   The past relived its future
With what outdid all hopes and fantasies –
    How could I not concede
    My sigil in its favour?

SONG: TWINNED HEART

Challenged once more to reunite,
    Perfect in every limb
But screened against the intrusive light
    By ghosts and cherubim,

I call your beauty to my bed,
    My pride you call to yours
Though clouds run maniac overhead
    And cruel rain down pours,

With both of us prepared to wake
        Each in a bed apart,
True to a spell no power can break:
        The beat of a twinned heart.

SONG: OLIVE TREE

Call down a blessing
On that green sapling,
A sudden blessing
For true love's sake
On that green sapling
Framed by our window
With her leaves twinkling
As we lie awake.
Two birds flew from her
In the eye of morning
Their folded feathers
In the sun to shake.

Augury recorded,
Vision rewarded
With an arrow flying
With a sudden sting,
With a sure blessing,
With a double dart,
With a starry ring,
With music from the mountains
In the air, in the heart
This bright May morning
Re-echoing.

SONG: ONCE MORE

These quiet months of watching for
An endless moment of once more
May not be shortened,

But while we share them at a distance,
In irreproachable persistence,
Are strangely brightened.

And these long hours of perfect sleep
When company in love we keep,
By time unstraitened,

Yield us a third of the whole year
In which to embrace each other here,
Sleeping together, watching for
An endless moment of once more
By dreams enlightened.

SONG: VICTIMS OF CALUMNY

Equally innocent,
Confused by evil,
Pondering the event,
Aloof and penitent,
With hearts left sore
By a cruel calumny,
With eyes half-open now
To its warped history,
But undeceivably
Both in love once more.

LOVE GIFTS

Though love be gained only by truth in love
Never by gifts, yet there are gifts of love
That match or enhance beauty, that indeed
Fetch beauty with them. Always the man gives,
Never the woman – unless flowers or berries
Or pebbles from the shore.
                        She welcomes jewels
To ponder and pore over tremblingly
By candlelight. 'Why does he love me so,
Divining my concealed necessities?'
And afterwards (there is no afterwards
In perfect love, nor further call for gifts)
Writes: 'How you spoil me!', meaning: 'You are mine',
But sends him cornflowers, pinks and columbine.

MANKIND AND OCEAN

You celebrate with kisses the good fortune
Of a new and cloudless moon
(Also the tide's good fortune),
Content with July fancies
To brown your naked bodies
On the slopes of a sea-dune.

Mankind and Ocean, Ocean and mankind:
Those fatal tricks of temper,
Those crooked acts of murder
Provoked by the wind –
I am no Ocean lover,
Nor can I love mankind.

To love the Ocean is to taste salt,
To drink the blood of sailors,
To watch the waves assault
Mast-high a cliff that shudders
Under their heartless hammers....
Is wind alone at fault?

VIRGIN MIRROR

Souls in virginity joined together
    Rest unassailable:
Ours is no undulant fierce rutting fever
    But clear unbroken lunar magic able
    To mirror loves illimitable.

When first we chose this power of being
    I never paused to warn you
What ruinous charms the world was weaving;
    I knew you for a child fostered in virtue
    And swore no hand could hurt you.

Then should I suffer nightmares now
    Lest you, grown somewhat older,
Be lured to accept a worldly where and how,
    Carelessly breathing on the virgin mirror,
    Clouding love's face for ever?

SECRET THEATRE

When from your sleepy mind the day's burden
Falls like a bushel sack on a barn floor,
Be prepared for music, for natural mirages
And for night's incomparable parade of colour.

Neither of us daring to assume direction
Of an unforeseen and fiery entertainment,
We clutch hands in the seventh row of the stalls
And watch together, quivering, astonished, silent.

It is hours past midnight now; a flute signals
Far off; we mount the stage as though at random,
Boldly ring down the curtain, then dance out our love:
Lost to the outraged, humming auditorium.

HOW IT STARTED

It started, unexpectedly of course,
At a wild midnight dance, in my own garden,
To which indeed I was not invited:
I read: 'Teen-agers only.'

In the circumstances I stayed away
Until you fetched me out on the tiled floor
Where, acting as an honorary teen-ager,
I kicked off both my shoes.

Since girls like you must set the stage always,
With lonely men for choreographers,
I chose the step, I even called the tune;
And we both danced entranced.

Here the narrator pauses circumspectly,
Knowing me not unpassionate by nature
And the situation far from normal:
Two apple-seeds had sprouted....

Recordable history began again
With you no longer in your late teens
And me socially (once more) my age –
Yet that was where it started.

BRIEF REUNION

Our one foreboding was: we might forget
How strangely close absence had drawn us,
How close once more we must be drawn by parting –
Absence, dark twin of presence!

Nor could such closeness be attained by practice
Of even the most heroic self-deceit:
Only by inbred faculties far wiser
Than any carnal sense –

Progress in which had disciplined us both
To the same doting pride: a stoicism
Which might confuse, at every brief reunion,
Presence with pangs of absence.

And if this pride should overshoot its mark,
Forcing on us a raw indifference
To what might happen when our hearts were fired
By renewed hours of presence?

Could we forget what carnal pangs had seized us
Three summers past in a burst of moonlight,
Making us more possessive of each other
Than either dared concede? – a prescience
Of the vast grief that each sublunary pair
Transmits at last to its chance children
With tears of violence.

THE JUDGES

Crouched on wet shingle at the cove
In day-long search for treasure-trove –
Meaning the loveliest-patterned pebble,
Of any colour imaginable,
Ground and smoothed by a gentle sea –
How seldom, Julia, we agree
On our day's find: the perfect one
To fetch back home when day is done,
Splendid enough to stupefy
The fiercest, most fastidious eye –
Tossing which back we tell the sea:
'Work on it one more century!'

LOVE AND NIGHT

Though your professions, ages and conditions
Might seem to any sober person
Irreconcilable,

Yet still you claim the inalienable right
To kiss in corners and exchange long letters
Patterned with well-pierced hearts.

When judges, dazzled by your blazing eyes,
Mistake you both for Seventh Day Adventists
(Heaven rest their innocent souls!)

You smile impassively and say no word –
The why and how of magic being tabu
Even in courts of Law.

Who could have guessed that your unearthly glow
Conceals a power no judgement can subdue,
Nor act of God, nor death?

Your love is not desire but certainty,
Perfect simultaneity,
Inheritance not conquest;

Long silences divide its delicate phases
With simple absence, almost with unbeing,
Before each new resurgence.

Such love has clues to a riddling of the maze:
Should you let fall the thread, grope for it,
Unawed by the thick gloom.

Such love illuminates the far house
Where difficult questions meet their answers
And lies get scoured away.

Your powers to love were forged by Mother Night –
Her perfect discipline of thought and breath –
Sleep is their sustenance.

You prophesy without accessories:
Her words run splashed in light across your walls
For reading as you wake.

But Night, no doubt, has deathless other secrets
Guarded by her unblinking owls against
All clumsy stumbling on them.

CHILD WITH VETERAN

You were a child and I your veteran;
An age of violence lay between us,
Yet both claimed citizenship of the same land
Conversing in our own soft, hidden language,
Often by signs alone.

Our eyelids closed, little by little,
And we fell chained in an enchantment
Heavier than any known or dreamed before,
Groping in darkness for each other's fingers
Lifting them to our lips.

Here brooded power beyond comparison,
Tremendous as a thousand bee-stings
Or a great volley of steel-tipped arrows
With which to take possession of a province
That no one could deny us,
For the swift regeneration of dead souls
And the pride of those undead.

PURIFICATION

'He numbed my heart, he stole away my truth,
He laid hands on my body.
Never had I known ecstasy like that:
I could have flown with him to the world's end
And thought of you no more.'

'Wake, dearest love, here in my own warm arms,
That was a nightmare only.
You kept the wall-side, leaving me the outer,
No demon slid between us to molest you.
This is a narrow bed.'

I would have brought her breakfast on a tray
But she seemed haunted still
By terror that in nine short months, maybe,
A demon's litter, twitching scaly tails
Would hang from either breast.

And still she shuddered inconsolably
All day; our true love-magic
Dwindled and failed. 'He swore to take me
The round of Paris, on his midnight tours,
Fiddling for me to dance.'

Thus to have murdered love even in dream
Called for purification;
And (as the Great Queen yearly did at Paphos)
Down to the sea she trod and in salt water
Renewed virginity.

POWERS UNCONFESSED

Diffidently, when asked who might I be,
I agreed that, yes, I ruled a small kingdom
Though, like yourself, free to wander abroad
Hatless, barefooted and incognito.

Abruptly we embraced – a strange event,
The casual passers-by taking less notice
Than had this been a chance meeting of cousins –
Nor did we argue over protocol.

You, from your queendom, answerable only
To royal virtue, not to a male code,
Knew me for supernatural, like yourself,
And fell at once head over heels in love;
As I also with you – but lamentably
Never confessed what wrathful powers attest
The Roman jealousy of my male genius.

PANDORA

But our escape: to what god did we owe it,
Pandora, my one love?
White-faced we lay, apart and all but dead.

In place of magic had you offered fancy
(Being still a girl and over-credulous)
To honour my poor genius? –
And with your careless innocence of death
Concealed the mischief and those unseen Spites
For long months haunting you and me, your Titan,
Chasing away the honey-bees of love?

Though my acute dream-senses, apprehending,
Warned me with fevers, chills and violences
That the postern gate was forced
And the keep in instant peril,
Why did my eyes stay blind and my ears deaf?

And this escape: to what god did we owe it,
Or to what unborn child?

SOLOMON'S SEAL

Peace is at last confirmed for us:
A double blessing, heavily priced,
Won back as we renew our maiden hearts
In a magic known to ourselves only,
Proof against furious tides of error
And bitter ironies of the self-damned:

Perfect in love now, though not sharing
The customary pillow – and our reasons
Appear shrouded in dark Egyptian dreams
That recreate us as a single being
Wholly in love with love.

Under each pyramid lies inverted
Its twin, the sister-bride to Pharaoh,
And so Solomon's seal bears witness.

Therefore we neither plead nor threaten
As lovers do who have lost faith –
Lovers not riven together by an oath
Sworn on the very brink of birth,
Nor by the penetrative ray of need
Piercing our doubled pyramid to its bed.

All time lies knotted here in Time's caress,
And so Solomon's seal bears witness.

TO PUT IT SIMPLY

Perfect reliance on the impossible
    By strict avoidance of all such conjecture
As underlies the so-called possible:
    That is true love's adventure.

Put it more simply: all the truth we need
    Is ours by curious preknowledge of it –
On love's impossibility agreed,
    Constrained neither by horoscope nor prophet.

Or put it still more simply: all we know
Is that love is and always must be so.

TO TELL AND BE TOLD

What is it I most want in all the world?
To be with you at last, alone in the world,
And as I kiss with you to tell and be told.

A child you no more are, yet as a child
You foresaw miracles when no more a child –
So spread a bed for us, to tell and be told.

You wear my promises on rings of gold,
I wear your promise on a chain of gold:
For ever and once more to tell and be told.

THE THEME OF DEATH

Since love is an astonished always
Challenging the long lies of history,
Yesterday when I chose the theme of death
You shook a passionate finger at me:
'Wake from your nightmare! Would you murder love?
Wake from your nightmare!'

No, sweetheart! Death is nightmare when conceived
As God's Last Judgement, or the curse of Time –
Its intransgressible bounds of destiny;
But love is an astonished always
With death as affidavit for its birth
And timeless progress.

What if these tombs and catafalques conspire,
Menacing us with gross ancestral fears,
To dissipate my living truth, and yours,
To induct us into ritual weeping?
Our love remains a still astonished always,
Pure death its witness.

AT THE WELL

To work it out even a thought better
Than ever before – yet a thought rare enough
To raise a sigh of wonder –
That is your art (he said) but mine also
Since first I fell upon the secret
And sighed for wonder that our dry mouths
After a world of travel
Were drawn together by the same spell
To drink at the same well.

Coincidence (she said) continues with us,
Secret by secret,
Love's magic being no more than obstinacy
In love's perfection –
Like the red apple, highest on the tree
Reserved for you by me.

LOGIC

Clear knowledge having come
Of an algebraic queendom,
Compulsive touch and tread
By a public voice dictated
Proclaims renewed loyalty
To a defunct geometry:
Blue-prints of logic –

Logic, tricking the tongue
With its fool's learning,
Prescribed excess,
Devoted emptiness,
With dull heart-burning
For a forgotten peace,
For work beyond employment,
For trust beyond allegiance,
For love beyond enjoyment,
For life beyond existence,
For death beyond decease.

ROBBERS' DEN

They have taken Sun from Woman
And consoled her with Moon;
They have taken Moon from Woman
And consoled her with Seas;
They have taken Seas from Woman
And consoled her with Stars;
They have taken Stars from Woman
And consoled her with Trees;
They have taken Trees from Woman
And consoled her with Tilth;
They have taken Tilth from Woman
And consoled her with Hearth;
They have taken Hearth from Woman
And consoled her with Praise –
Goddess, the robbers' den that men inherit
They soon must quit, going their ways,
Restoring you your Sun, your Moon, your Seas,
Your Stars, your Trees, your Tilth, your Hearth –
But sparing you the indignity of Praise.

THE ACCOMPLICE

Mercury, god of larceny
And banking and diplomacy,
Marks you as his accomplice.

No coins hang from his watch-chain
Where once he used to wear them:
He has done with toys like these.

Would you prove your independence
By entering some Order
Or taking your own life?

He will, be sure, divinely
Revenge the moral fervour
Of your disloyalties.

For his fistful of signed contracts
And million-dollar bank-notes
Bear witness to his credit
With your colleagues, friends, assistants
And your own faithful wife.

FIRST LOVE

Darling, if ever on some night of fever
But with your own full knowledge ...
Darling, confess how it will be if ever
You violate your true-love pledge
Once offered me unprompted,
Which I reciprocated
Freely, fully and without restraint
Nor ever have abjured since first we kissed?
Will that prove you a liar and me a saint,
Or me a fool and you a realist?

THROUGH A DARK WOOD

Together, trustfully, through a dark wood –
But headed where, unless to the ancient, cruel,
Inescapable, marital pitfall
With its thorny couch for the procreation
Of love's usurpers or interlopers?
Or worse by far, should each be trapped singly
But for true-love's sake gulp down a jealousy
And grief at not having suffered jointly....

Together, through a dark wood, trustfully.

IN THE VESTRY

It is over now, with no more need
For whispers, for brief messages posted
In the chestnut-tree, for blank avoidance
Of each other's eyes at festivals,
For hoarded letters, for blossom-tokens,
For go-betweens or confidants.

Well, are you glad that all is over now?
Be as truthful as you dare.
Posted at last as would-be man and wife
Behaving as the Lord Himself enjoined,
Repudiating your lascivious past,
Each alike swearing never to retrieve it,
Particularly (God knows) with someone else –
Marriage being for procreation only –
Are you both glad and sure that all is over?

WHEN LOVE IS NOT

'Where is love when love is not?'
   Asked the logician.
'We term it Omega Minus,'
   Said the mathematician.

'Does that mean marriage or plain Hell?'
   Asked the logician.
'I was never at the altar,'
   Said the mathematician.

'Is it love makes the world go round?'
   Asked the logician.
'Or you might reverse the question,'
   Said the mathematician.

THE REITERATION

The death of love comes from reiteration:
A single line sung over and over again –
No prelude and no end.

The word is not, perhaps, 'reiteration' –
Nature herself repunctuates her seasons
With the same stars, flowers, fruits –
Though love's foolish reluctance to survive
Springs always from the same mechanical fault:
The needle jumps its groove.

MAN OF EVIL

But should I not pity that poor devil,
Such a load of guilt he carries?
He debauched the daughter of his benefactor –
A girl of seventeen – her brother too,
At the same drunken picnic.

Pushes hard drugs, abstains from them himself;
His first wife ended in a mad-house,
The second was found drowned in a forest pool –
The Coroner, observing his distress,
Called for an open verdict.

And so on, oh and so on – why continue?
He complains always of his luckless childhood
And fills commiserating eyes with tears.
The truth is: he was evil from the womb
And both his parents knew it.

He cowers and sponges when his guilt is plain
And his bank-account runs dry.
O, that unalterable black self-pity,
Void of repentance or amendment,
Clouding his Universe!

But who can cast out evil? We can only
Learn to diagnose that natal sickness,
The one known cure for which, so far, is death.
Evil is here to stay unendingly;
But so also is Love.

THE RAFT

Asleep on the raft and forced far out to sea
By an irresistible current:
No good, no good!

O for a sister island! Ships were scarce
In that unhomely latitude,
And he lacked food.

No canoes would row out to his rescue;
No native ever called him brother –
What was brotherhood?

He asked another question: which to choose?
A drowning vision of damnation
Or slow starvation?

Even savages, hungry for his flesh,
Would offer him a happier exit;
And he need not fight.

Yet, having always drifted on the raft
Each night, always without provision,
Loathing each night,

So now again he quaked with sudden terror
Lest the same current, irresistibly
Reversed, should toss him back
Once more on the same shore –
As it did every night.

THE UNCUT DIAMOND

This is ours by natural, not by civil, right:
An uncut diamond, found while picnicking
Beside blue clay here on the open veldt!
It should carve up to a walnut-sized brilliant
And a score of lesser gems.

What shall we do? To be caught smuggling stones
Assures us each a dozen years in gaol;
And who can trust a cutting-agency?
So, do you love me?

                Or must I toss it back?

MY GHOST

I held a poor opinion of myself
When young, but never bettered my opinion
(Even by comparison)
Of all my fellow-fools at school or college.

Passage of years induced a tolerance,
Even a near-affection, for myself –
Which, when you fell in love with me, amounted
(Though with my tongue kept resolutely tied)
To little short of pride.

Pride brought its punishment: thus to be haunted
By my own ghost whom, much to my disquiet,
All would-be friends and open enemies
Boldly identified and certified
As me, including him in anecdotal
Autobiographies.

Love, should you meet him in the newspapers,
In planes, on trains, or at large get-togethers,
I charge you, disregard his foolish capers;
Silence him with a cold unwinking stare
Where he sits opposite you at table
And let all present watch amazed, remarking
On how little you care.

THE RISK

Though there are always doctors who advise
Fools on the care of their own foolish bodies,
And surgeons ready to rush up and set
Well-fractured arms or thighs, never forget
That you are your own body and alone
Can give it a true medical opinion
Drawn not from catalogued analogies
But from a sense of where your danger lies,
And how it obstinately defies the danger.

Your body, though yourself, can play the stranger
As when it falls in love, presuming on
Another's truth and perfect comprehension,
And fails to ask you: dare it run the risk
Of a mild cardiac lesion or slipped disk?

SOMETHING TO SAY

(*Dialogue between Thomas Carlyle and Lewis Carroll*)

T.C.   'Would you care to explain
           Why they fight for your books
           With already too many
           Tight-packed on their shelves
           (Many hundreds of thousands
           Or hundreds of millions)
           As though you had written
           Those few for themselves?'

    L.C.   'In reply to your query:
           I wrote for one reason
           And only one reason
           (That being my way):
           Not for fame, not for glory,
           Nor yet for distraction,
           But oddly enough
           I had something to say.'

    T.C.   'So you wrote for one reason?
           Be damned to that reason!
           It may sound pretty fine
           But relinquish it, pray!
           There are preachers in pulpits
           And urchins in playgrounds
           And fools in asylums
           And beggars in corners
           And drunkards in gutters
           And bandits in prisons
           With all the right reasons
           For something to say.'

OCCASIONALIA

RESEARCH AND DEVELOPMENT: CLASSIFIED

We reckon Cooke our best chemist alive
And therefore the least certain to survive
Even by crediting his way-out findings
To our Department boss, Sir Bonehead Clive.

Those Goblins, guessing which of us is what
(And, but for Cooke, we're far from a bright lot),
Must either pinch his know-how or else wipe him.
He boasts himself quite safe. By God, he's not!

In fact, we all conclude that Cooke's one hope
Is neither loud heroics nor soft soap:
Cooke must defect, we warn him, to the Goblins,
Though even they may grudge him enough rope.

THE IMMINENT SEVENTIES

Man's life is threescore years and ten,*
        Which God will surely bless;
Still, we are warned what follows then –
        Labour and heaviness –

And understand old David's grouch
        Though he (or so we're told)
Bespoke a virgin for his couch
        To shield him from the cold....§

Are not all centuries, like men,
        Born hopeful too and gay,
And good for seventy years, but then
        Hope slowly seeps away?

True, a new geriatric art
        Prolongs our last adventures
When eyes grow dim, when teeth depart:
        For glasses come, and dentures –

Helps which these last three decades need
        If true to Freedom's cause:
Glasses (detecting crimes of greed)
        Teeth (implementing laws).

* Psalms 40. 10.
§ I Kings 1. 1-15.

CAROL OF PATIENCE

Shepherds armed with staff and sling,
        Ranged along a steep hillside,
Watch for their anointed King
        By all prophets prophesied –
Sing patience, patience,
Only still have patience!

Hour by hour they scrutinize
 Comet, planet, planet, star,
Till the oldest shepherd sighs:
 'I am frail and he is far.'
Sing patience etc.

'Born, they say, a happy child;
 Grown, a man of grief to be,
From all careless joys exiled,
 Rooted in eternity.'
Sing patience etc.

Then another shepherd said:
 'Yonder lights are Bethlehem;
There young David raised his head
 Destined for the diadem.'
Sing patience etc.

Cried the youngest shepherd: 'There
 Our Redeemer comes tonight,
Comes with starlight on his hair,
 With his brow exceeding bright.'
Sing patience etc.

'Sacrifice no lamb nor kid,
 Let such foolish fashions pass;
In a manger find him hid,
 Breathed upon by ox and ass.'
Sing patience etc.

Dance for him and laugh and sing,
 Watch him mercifully smile,
Dance although tomorrow bring
 Every plague that plagued the Nile!
Sing patience, patience,
Only still have patience!

H

H may be N for those who speak
Russian, although long E in Greek;
And cockneys, like the French, agree
That H is neither N nor E
Nor Hate's harsh aspirate, but meek
And mute as in *Humanity*.

INVITATION TO BRISTOL

'Come as my doctor,
Come as my lawyer,
Or come as my agent
(First practise your lies)
For Bristol is a small town
Full of silly gossip
And a girl gets abashed by
Ten thousand staring eyes.'

'Yes, I'll come as your lawyer
Or as your god-father,
Or even as Father Christmas? –
Not half a bad disguise –
With a jingle of sleigh bells,
A sack full of crackers
And a big bunch of mistletoe
For you to recognize.'

THE PRIMROSE BED

The eunuch and the unicorn
    Walked by the primrose bed;
The month was May, the time was morn,
    Their hearts were dull as lead.

'Ah, unicorn,' the eunuch cried,
    'How tragic is our Spring,
With stir of love on every side,
    And loud the sweet birds sing.'

Then, arm and foreleg intertwined,
    Both mourned their cruel fate –
The one was single of his kind,
    The other could not mate.

THE STRANGLING IN MERRION SQUARE

None ever loved as Molly loved me then,
    With her whole soul, and yet
How might the patientest of Irishmen
    Forgive, far less forget
Her long unpaid and now unpayable debt?
There's scarce a liveried footman in the Square
But can detail you how and when and where.

THE AWAKENING

Just why should it invariably happen
That when the Christian wakes at last in Heaven
He finds two harassed surgeons watching by
In white angelic smocks and gloves, and why
Looking so cross and (as three junior nurses
Trundle the trolley off with stifled curses)
Why joking that the X-ray photograph
Must have been someone else's – what a laugh! – ?

Now they may smoke.... A message from downstairs
Says: 'Matron says, God's due soon after Prayers.'

From *THE GREEN-SAILED VESSEL*

(1971)

THE HOOPOE TELLS US HOW

Recklessly you offered me your all,
Recklessly I accepted,
Laying my large world at your childish feet
Beyond all bounds of honourable recall:
Wild, wilful, incomplete.

Absence reintegrates our pact of pacts –
The hoopoe tells us how:
With bold love-magic, Moon in *Leo*,
Sun in *Pisces*, blossom upon bough.

PART I

THE WAND

These tears flooding my eyes, are they of pain
Or of relief: to have done with other loves,
To abstain from childish folly?

It has fallen on us to become exemplars
Of a love so far removed from gallantry
That we now meet seldom in a room apart
Or kiss goodnight, or even dine together
Unless in casual company.

For while we walk the same green paradise
And confidently ply the same green wand
That still restores the wilting hopes of others
Far more distressed than we,
How can we dread the broad and bottomless mere
Of utter infamy sunk below us
Where the eggs of hatred hatch?

FIVE

Five beringed fingers of Creation,
Five candles blazing at a shrine,
Five points of her continuous pentagram,
Five letters in her name – as five in mine.
I love, therefore I am.

QUINQUE

Quinque tibi luces vibrant in nomine: quinque
    Isidis in stella cornua sacra deae.
Nonne etiam digitos anuli quinque Isidis ornant?
    Ornant te totidem, Julia.… Sum, quod amo.

ARROW ON THE VANE

Suddenly, at last, the bitter wind veers round
From North-East to South-West. It is at your orders;
And the arrow on our vane swings and stays true
To your direction. Nothing parts us now.
What can I say? Nothing I have not said,
However the wind blew. I more than love,
As when you drew me bodily from the dead.

GORGON MASK

When the great ship ran madly towards the rocks
An unseen current slewed her into safety,
A dying man ashore took heart and lived,
And the moon soared overhead, ringed with three rainbows,
To announce the birth of a miraculous child.
Yet you preserved your silence, secretly
Nodding at me across the crowded hall.

The ship carried no cargo destined for us,
Nor were her crew or master known to us,
Nor was that sick man under our surveillance,
Nor would the child ever be born to you,
Or by me fathered on another woman –
Nevertheless our magic power ordained
These three concurrent prodigies.

Stranger things bear upon us. We are poets
Age-old in love: a full reach of desire
Would burn us both to an invisible ash....
Then hide from me, if hide from me you must,
In bleak refuge among nonentities,
But wear your Gorgon mask of divine warning
That, as we first began, so must we stay.

TO BE POETS

We are two lovers of no careless breed,
Nor is our love a curiosity
(Like honey-suckle shoots from an oak tree
Or a child with two left hands) but a proud need
For royal thought and irreproachable deed;
What others write about us makes poor sense,
Theirs being a no-man's land of negligence.

To be poets confers Death on us:
Death, paradisal fiery conspectus
For those who bear themselves always as poets,
Who cannot fall beneath the ignoble curse
(Whether by love of self, whether by scorn
Of truth) never to die, never to have been born.

WITH A GIFT OF RINGS

It was no costume jewellery I sent:
True stones cool to the tongue, their settings ancient,
Their magic evident.
Conceal your pride, accept them negligently
But, naked on your couch, wear them for me.

CASSE-NOISETTE

As a scurrying snow-flake
Or a wild-rose petal
Carried by the breeze,
Dance your nightly ballet
On the set stage.

And although each scurrying
Snow-flake or rose-petal
Resembles any other –
Her established smile,
Her well-schooled carriage –

Dance to Rule, ballet-child;
Yet never laugh to Rule,
Never love to Rule!
Keep your genius hidden
By a slow rage.

So let it be your triumph
In this nightly ballet
Of snow-flakes and petals,
To present love-magic
In your single image –
With a low, final curtsey
From the set stage.

THE GARDEN

Enhanced in a tower, asleep, dreaming about him,
The twin buds of her breasts opening like flowers,
Her fingers leafed and wandering …

                                  Past the well
Blossoms an apple-tree, and a horde of birds
Nested in the close thickets of her hair
Grumble in dreamy dissonance,
Calling him to the garden, if he dare.

THE GREEN-SAILED VESSEL

We are like doves, well-paired,
Veering across a meadow –
Children's voices below,
Their song and echo;

Like raven, wren or crow
That cry and prophesy,
What do we not foreknow,
Whether deep or shallow?

Like the tiller and prow
Of a green-sailed vessel
Voyaging, none knows how,
Between moon and shadow;

Like the restless, endless
Blossoming of a bough,
Like tansy, violet, mallow,
Like the sun's afterglow.

Of sharp resemblances
What further must I show
Until your black eyes narrow,
Furrowing your clear brow?

DREAMING CHILDREN

They have space enough, however cramped their quarters,
    And time enough, however short their day,
In sleep to chase each other through dream orchards
    Or bounce from rafters into buoyant hay.

But midnight thunder rolls, with frequent flashes,
    Wild hail peppers the farm-house roof and walls,
Wild wind sweeps from the North, flattening the bushes
    As with a crash of doom chain-lightning falls.

Split to its tap-roots, their own favourite oak-tree
    Glows like a torch across the narrow heath.
She shudders: 'Take me home again! It scares me!
    Put your arms round me, we have seen death!'

THE PROHIBITION

You were by my side, though I could not see you,
Your beauty being sucked up by the moon
In whose broad light, streaming across the valley,
We could match colours or read the finest print,
While swart tree shadows rose from living roots
Like a stockade planted against intrusion.

But since dawn spread, birds everywhere wakeful
And the sun risen masterly from the East,
Where are you now? Not standing at my side
But gone with the moon, sucked away into daylight,
All magic vanished, save for the rare instant
When a sudden arrow-shot transfixes me.

Marry into your tribe, bear noble sons
Never to call me father – which is forbidden
To poets by the laws of moon magic,
The Goddess being forever a fierce virgin
And chastening all love with prohibition
Of what her untranslatable truth transcends.

SERPENT'S TAIL

When you are old as I now am
I shall be young as you, my lamb;
For lest love's timely force should fail
The Serpent swallows his own tail.

UNTIL WE BOTH ...

Until we both ...
                    Strolling across Great Park
With a child and a dog, greeting the guardian lions
At the royal entrance, slowly rounding the mere
Where boats are sailed all day, this perfect Sunday,
Counting our blessings peacefully enough ...

Until we both, at the same horrid signal,
The twelfth stroke of a clock booming behind us,
Sink through these nonchalant, broad, close-cut lawns
To a swirling no-man's land shrouded in smoke
That feeds our kisses with bright furnace embers,
And we beg anguished mercy of each other,
Exchanging vow for vow, our lips blistered ...

Until we both ...
                    Until we both at once ...
Have you more courage, love, even than I
Under this final torment?
Shall we ever again greet our guardian lions
And the boats on the Great Mere?

THE MIRACLE

No one can understand our habit of love
Unless, trudging perhaps across the moor
Or resting on a tree-stump, deep in thought,
He has been scorched, like me, by summer lightning
And every blade of grass etherialized.

Which must have happened at some sudden turn
Of love, neither invited nor foreseen,
Nor are such miracles ever repetitious
Unless in their long deep-drawn gasp of wonder
And fierce awareness of its origin.

Do they astonish always as renewal
Of truth after impossible variance,
With tongues of flame spurting from bush and tree?

THE ROSE

When was it that we swore to love for ever?
When did this Universe come at last to be?
The two questions are one.

Fetch me a rose from your rose-arbour
To bless this night and grant me honest sleep:
Sleep, not oblivion.

TESTAMENT

Pure melody, love without alteration,
Flame without smoke, cresses from a clean brook,
The sun and moon as it were casting dice
With ample falls of rain,
Then comes the peaceful moment of appraisal,
The first and last lines of our testament,
With you ensconced high in the castle turret,
Combing your dark hair at a silver mirror,
And me below, sharpening my quill again.

This body is now yours; therefore I own it.
Your body is now mine; therefore you own it.
As for our single heart, let it stay ours
Since neither may disown it
While still it flowers in the same dream of flowers.

THE CRAB-TREE

Because of love's infallibility,
Because of love's insistence –
And none can call us liars –
Spring heaps your lap with summer buds and flowers
And lights my mountain peaks with Beltane fires.

The sea spreads far below; its blue whale's-back
Forcing no limit on us;
We watch the boats go by
Beyond rain-laden ranks of olive trees
And, rising, sail in convoy through clear sky.

Never, yet always. Having at last perfected
Utter togetherness
We meet nightly in dream
Where no voice interrupts our confidences
Under the crab-tree by the pebbled stream.

THREE LOCKED HOOPS

Yourself, myself and our togetherness
Lock like three hoops, exempt from time and space.
Let preachers preach of sovereign trinities,
Yet can such ancient parallels concern us
Unless they too spelt He and She and Oneness?

CLIFF AND WAVE

Since first you drew my irresistible wave
To break in foam on your immovable cliff,
We occupy the same station of being –
Not as in wedlock harboured close together,
But beyond reason, co-identical.
Now when our bodies hazard an encounter,
They dread to engage the fury of their senses,
And only in the brief dismay of parting
Will your cliff shiver or my wave falter.

PART II

THOSE BLIND FROM BIRTH

Those blind from birth ignore the false perspective
Of those who see. Their inward-gazing eyes
Broaden or narrow no right-angle;
Nor does a far-off mansion fade for them
To match-box size.

Those blind from birth live by their four sound senses.
Only a fool disguises voice and face
When visiting the blind. Smell, tread and hand-clasp
Announce just why, and in what mood, he visits
That all-observant place.

FOOLS

There is no fool like an old fool,
    Yet fools of middling age
Can seldom teach themselves to reach
    True folly's final stage.

Their course of love mounts not above
    Some five-and-forty years,
Though God gave men threescore and ten
    To scald with foolish tears.

THE GATEWAY

After three years of constant courtship
Each owes the other more than can be paid
Short of a single bankruptcy.
                    Both falter
At the gateway of the garden; each advances
One foot across it, hating to forgo
The pangs of womanhood and manhood;
Both turn about, breathing love's honest name,
Too strictly tied by bonds of miracle
And lasting magic to be easily lured
Into acceptance of concubinage:
Its deep defraudment of their regal selves.

ADVICE FROM A MOTHER

Be advised by me, darling:
If you hope to keep my love,
Do not marry that man!

I cannot be mistaken:
There is murder on his conscience
And fear in his heart.

I knew his grandparents:
The stock is good enough,
Clear of criminal taint.

And I find no vice in him,
Only a broken spirit
Which the years cannot heal;

And gather that, when younger,
He volunteered for service
With a secret police;

That one day he had orders
From a number and a letter
Which had to be obeyed,

And still cannot confess,
In fear for his own life,
Nor make reparation.

The dead in their bunkers
Call to him every night:
'Come breakfast with us!'

No gentleness, no love,
Can cure a broken spirit;
I forbid you to try.

A REDUCED SENTENCE

They were confused at first, being well warned
That the Governor forbade, by a strict rule,
All conversation between long-term prisoners –
Except cell-mates (who were his own choice);
Also, in that mixed prison, the two sexes
Might catch no glimpse whatever of each other
Even at fire-drill, even at Church Service.

Yet soon – a most unusual case – this pair
Defied the spirit, although not the letter,
Of his harsh rules, using the fourth dimension
For passage through stone walls and cast-iron doors
As coolly as one strolls across Hyde Park:
Bringing each other presents, kisses, news.

By good behaviour they reduced their sentence
From life to a few years, then out they went
Through three-dimensional gates, gently embraced ...
And walked away together, arm in arm....
But, home at last, halted abashed and shaking
Where the stairs mounted to a double bed.

THE GENTLEMAN

That he knows more of love than you, by far,
And suffers more, has long been his illusion.
His faults, he hopes, are few – maybe they are
With a life barred against common confusion;
But that he knows far less and suffers less,
Protected by his age, his reputation,
His gentlemanly sanctimoniousness,
Has blinded him to the dumb grief that lies
Warring with love of love in your young eyes.

COMPLAINT AND REPLY

I

After our death, when scholars try
To arrange our letters in due sequence,
No one will envy them their task,
You sign your name so lovingly
So sweetly and so neatly
That all must be confounded by
Your curious reluctance,
Throughout this correspondence,
To answer anything I ask
Though phrased with perfect prudence ...
Why do you wear so blank a mask,
Why always baulk at a reply
Both in and out of sequence,
Yet sign your name so lovingly,
So sweetly and so neatly?

II

Oh, the dark future! I confess
Compassion for your scholars – yes.
Not being myself incorrigible,
Trying most gallantly, indeed,
To answer what I cannot read,
With half your words illegible
Or, at least, any scholar's guess.

SONG: RECONCILIATION

The storm is done, the sun shines out,
   The blackbird calls again
With bushes, trees and long hedgerows
   Still twinkling bright with rain.

Sweet, since you now can trust your heart
   As surely as I can,
Be still the sole woman I love
   With me for your sole man.

For though we hurt each other once
   In youthful blindness, yet
A man must learn how to forgive
   What women soon forget.

KNOBS AND LEVERS

Before God died, shot while running away,
He left mankind His massive hoards of gold:
Which the Devil presently appropriated
With the approval of all major trusts
As credit for inhumanizable
Master-machines and adequate spare-parts.

Men, born no longer in God's holy image,
Were graded as ancillary knobs or levers
With no Law to revere nor faith to cherish.
'You are free, Citizens,' old Satan crowed;
And all felicitated one another
As quit of patriarchal interference.

This page turns slowly: its last paragraph
Hints at a full-scale break-down implemented
By famine and disease. Nevertheless
The book itself runs on for five more chapters.
God died; clearly the Devil must have followed.
But was there not a Goddess too, God's mother?

THE VIRUS

We can do little for these living dead
Unless to help them bury one another
By an escalation of intense noise
And the logic of computers.
They are, we recognize, past praying for –
Only among the moribund or dying
Is treatment practical.

Faithfully we experiment, assuming
That death is a still undetected virus
And most contagious where
Men eat, smoke, drink and sleep money:
Its monstrous and unconscionable source.

DRUID LOVE

No Druid can control a woman's longing
Even while dismally foreboding
Death for her lover, anguish for herself
Because of bribes accepted, pledges broken,
Breaches hidden.
                    More than this, the Druid
May use no comminatory incantations
Against either the woman or her lover,
Nor ask what punishment she herself elects.

But if the woman be herself a Druid?
The case worsens: he must flee the land.
Hers is a violence unassessable
Save by herself – ultimate proof and fury
Of magic power, dispelling all restraint
That princely laws impose on those who love.

PROBLEMS OF GENDER

Circling the Sun, at a respectful distance,
Earth remains warmed, not roasted; but the Moon
Circling the Earth, at a disdainful distance,
Will drive men lunatic (should they defy her)
With seeds of wintry love, not sown for spite.

Mankind, so far, continues undecided
On the Sun's gender – grammars disagree –
As on the Moon's. Should Moon be god, or goddess:
Drawing the tide, shepherding flocks of stars
That never show themselves by broad daylight?

Thus curious problems of propriety
Challenge all ardent lovers of each sex:
Which circles which at a respectful distance,
Or which, instead, at a disdainful distance?
And who controls the regal powers of night?

CONFESS, MARPESSA

Confess, Marpessa, who is your new lover?
Could he be, perhaps, that skilful rough-sea diver
Plunging deep in the waves, curving far under
Yet surfacing at last with controlled breath?

Confess, Marpessa, who is your new lover?
Is he some ghoul, with naked greed of plunder
Urging his steed across the gulf of death,
A brood of dragons tangled close beneath?

Or could he be the fabulous Salamander,
Courting you with soft flame and gentle ember?
Confess, Marpessa, who is your new lover?

JUS PRIMAE NOCTIS

Love is a game for only two to play at,
Nor could she banish him from her soft bed
Even on her bridal night, *jus primae noctis*
Being irreversibly his. He took the wall-side
Long ago granted him. Her first-born son
Would claim his name, likeness and character.
Nor did we ask her why. The case was clear:
Even though that lover had been nine years dead
She could not banish him from her soft bed.

WORK DRAFTS

I am working at a poem, pray excuse me,
Which may take twenty drafts or more to write
Before tomorrow night,
But since no poem should be classed with prose,
I must not call it 'work', God knows –
Again, excuse me!

My poem (or non-poem) will come out
In the *New Statesman* first, no doubt,
And in hard covers gradually become
A handsome source of supplementary income,
Selected for *Great Poems* – watch the lists –
And by all subsequent anthologists.

Poems are not, we know, composed for money
And yet my work (or play)-drafts carefully
Hatched and cross-hatched by puzzling layers of ink
Are not the detritus that you might think:
They fetch from ten to fifty bucks apiece
In sale to Old Gold College Library
Where swans, however black, are never geese –
Excuse me and excuse me, pray excuse me!

HER BEAUTY

Let me put on record for posterity
The uniqueness of her beauty:
Her black eyes fixed unblinking on my own,
Cascading hair, high breasts, firm nose,
Soft mouth and dancer's toes.

Which is, I grant, cautious concealment
Of a new Muse by the Immortals sent
For me to honour worthily –
Her eyes brimming with tears of more than love,
Her lips gentle, moving secretly –

And she is also the dark hidden bride
Whose beauty I invoke for lost sleep:
To last the whole night through without dreaming –
Even when waking is to wake in pain
And summon her to grant me sleep again.

ALWAYS

Slowly stroking your fingers where they lie,
Slowly parting your hair to kiss your brow –
For this will last for always (as you sigh),
Whatever follows now.

Always and always – who dares disagree
That certainty hangs upon certainty?
Yet who ever encountered anywhere
So unendurably circumstanced a pair
Clasped heart to heart under a blossoming tree
With such untamable magic of despair,
Such childlike certainty?

DESERT FRINGE

When a live flower, a single name of names,
Thrusts with firm roots into your secret heart
Let it continue ineradicably
To scent the breeze not only on her name-day
But on your own: a hedge of roses fringing
Absolute desert strewn with ancient flints
And broken shards and shells of ostrich eggs –
Where no water is found, but only sand,
And yet one day, we swear, recoverable.

THE TITLE OF POET

Poets are guardians
Of a shadowy island
With granges and forests
Warmed by the Moon.

Come back, child, come back!
You have been far away,
Housed among phantoms,
Reserving silence.

Whoever loves a poet
Continues whole-hearted,
Her other loves or loyalties
Distinct and clear.

She is young, he is old
And endures for her sake
Such fears of unease
As distance provokes.

Yet how can he warn her
What natural disasters
Will plague one who dares
To neglect her poet? ...
For the title of poet
Comes only with death.

DEPTH OF LOVE

Since depth of love is never gauged
By proof of appetites assuaged,
Nor dare you set your body free
To take its passionate toll of me –
And with good reason –
What now remains for me to do
In proof of perfect love for you
But as I am continue,
The ecstatic bonds of monk or nun
Made odious by comparison?

BREAKFAST TABLE

Breakfast peremptorily closes
The reign of Night, her dream extravagances
Recalled for laughter only.

Yet here we sit at our own table,
Brooding apart on spells of midnight love
Long irreversible:

Spells that have locked our hearts together,
Never to falter, never again to stray
Into the fierce dichotomy of Day;
Night has a gentler laughter.

THE HALF-FINISHED LETTER

One day when I am written off as dead –
My works widely collected, rarely read
Unless as Literature (examiners
Asking each student which one he prefers
And how to classify it), my grey head
Slumped on the work-desk – they will find your name
On a half-finished letter, still the same
And in my characteristic characters:
That's one thing will have obdurately lasted.

THE HAZEL GROVE

To be well loved,
Is it not to dare all,
Is it not to do all,
Is it not to know all?
To be deep in love?

A tall red sally
Had stood for seventy
Years by the pool
(And that was plenty)
Before I could shape
My harp from her poll.

Now seven hundred
Years will be numbered
In our hazel grove
Before this vibrant
Harp falls silent –
For lack of strings,
Not for lack of love.

PITY

Sickness may seem a falling out of love,
With pleas for pity – love's lean deputy.
If so, refuse me pity, wait, love on:
Never outlaw me while I yet live.
The day may come when you too, falling sick,
Implore my pity. Let me, too, refuse it
Offering you, instead, my pitiless love.

SILENT VISIT

I was walking my garden
Judiciously, calmly,
Curved mattock in hand
Heavy basket on shoulder,
When all of a sudden

You kissed me most kindly
From forehead to chin,
Though arriving unseen
As a pledge of love-magic
And wordlessly even.

Had you come, long-announced,
Wearing velvets and silk
After travels of grandeur
From Greece to the Yemen,
Socotra and Aden

With no rapture of silence
Nor rapture of absence –
No poem to greet you,
No burst of green glory
From trees in my garden....

But you came, a grown woman,
No longer the child
Whom I loved well enough
When your age was just seven –
Who would enter alone
The close thickets of Eden
And there would run wild.

CORONET OF MOONLIGHT

Such was the circumstance of our first love:
Sea, silence, a full moon.
Nevertheless, even the same silence
Amended by a distant nightingale
From the same past, and gently heaving surf,
Brings me no sure revival of our dream –
For to be surely with you is to sleep,
Having well earned my coronet of moonlight
By no mere counting of processional sheep.

SONG: TO BECOME EACH OTHER

To love you truly
   I must become you,
And so to love you
   I must leave behind
All that was not you:
   All jewelled phantoms,
All fabrications
   Of a jealous mind.

For man and woman
   To become each other
Is far less hard
   Than would seem to be:
An eternal serpent
   With eyes of emerald
Stands curled around
   This blossoming tree.

Though I seem old
   As a castle turret
And you as young
   As the grass beneath
It is no great task
   To become each other
Where nothing honest
   Goes in fear of death.

HEAVEN

Laugh still, write always lovingly, for still
You neither will nor can deny your heart,
Which always was a poet's,
Even while our ways are cruelly swept apart.
But though the rose I gave you in your childhood
Has never crumbled yellowing into dust
Neither as yet have needles pricked your conscience,
Which also is a poet's,
To attempt the miracles which one day you must.

Meanwhile reject their Heaven, but guard our own
Here on this needle-point, immediately
Accessible, not sprawled like theirs across
Limitless outer space. If to those angels
We seem a million light-years yet unborn,
And cannot more concern them than they us,
Let our own Heaven, with neither choir nor throne
Nor janitor, rest inexpugnable
And private for our gentler love alone.

GROWING PAINS

My earliest love, that stabbed and lacerated,
Must I accept it as it seemed then –
Although still closely documented, dated
And even irreversibly annotated
By your own honest pen?

Love never lies, even when it most enlarges
Dimensions, griefs, or charges,
But, come what must, remains
Irrevocably true to its worst growing pains.

FRIDAY NIGHT

On the brink of sleep, stretched in a wide bed,
    Rain pattering at the windows
And proud waves booming against granite rocks:
    Such was our night of glory.

Thursday had brought us dreams only of evil,
    As the muezzin warned us:
'Forget all nightmare once the dawn breaks,
    Prepare for holy Friday!'

Friday brings dreams only of inward love
    So overpassing passion
That no lips reach to kiss, nor hands to clasp,
    Nor does foot press on foot.

We wait until the lamp has flickered out
    Leaving us in full darkness,
Each still observant of the other's lively
    Sighs of pure content.

Truth is prolonged until the grey dawn:
    Her face floating above me,
Her black hair falling cloudlike to her breasts,
    Her lovely eyes half-open.

THE PACT

The identity of opposites had linked us
In our impossible pact of only love
Which, being a man, I honoured to excess
But you, being woman, quietly disregarded –
Though loving me no less –
And, when I would have left you, envied me
My unassuageable positivity.

POOR OTHERS

Hope, not Love, twangles her single string
Monotonously and in broken rhythms.
Can Hope deserve praise?

I fell in love with you, as you with me.
Hope envies us for being otherwise
Than honest Hope should be.

No charm avails against the evil eye
Of envy but to spit into our bosoms
And so dissemble

That we are we and not such luckless others
As hope and tremble,
Shifting the blame to fathers or to mothers
For being themselves, not others:
Alas, poor others!

A TOAST TO DEATH

This is, indeed, neither the time nor the place
For victory celebrations. Victory over what?
Over Death, his grinning image and manifesto
Of which, as children, we have been forewarned
And offered a corpse's frigid hand to kiss.

Contrariwise, let me raise this unsteady glass
In a toast to Death, the sole deviser of life,
Our antenatal witness when each determined
Sex, colour, humour, religion, limit of years,
Parents, place, date of birth –
A full conspectus, with ourselves recognized
As viable capsules lodged in the fifth dimension,
Never to perish, time being irrelevant,
And the reason for which, and sole excuse, is love –
Tripled togetherness of you with me.

THE YOUNG SIBYL

The swing has its bold rhythm,
Yet a breeze in the trees
Varies the music for her
As down the apples drop
In a row on her lap.

Though still only a child
She must become our Sibyl,
A holder of the apple
Prophesying wild
Histories for her people.

Five apples in a row,
Each with ruddy cheeks,
So too her own cheeks glow
As the long swing creaks,
Pulsing to and fro.

RECORDS

Accept these records of pure love
With no end or beginning, written for
Yourself alone, not the abashed world,
Timeless therefore –

Whose exaltations clearly tell
Of a past pilgrimage through hell,
Which in the name of love I spare you.
Hell is my loneliness, not ours,
Else we should harrow it together.

Love, have you walked worse hells even than I,
Through echoing silence where no midge or fly
Buzzes – hells boundless, without change of weather?

THE FLOWERING ALOE

The century-plant has flowered, its golden blossom
Showering honey from seven times our height:
Now the stock withers fast and wonder ends.
Yet from its roots eventually will soar
Another stock to enchant your great-grandchildren
But vex my jealous, uninvited ghost,
These being no blood of mine.

CIRCUS RING

How may a lover draw two bows at once
Or ride two steeds at once,
Firm in the saddle?
Yet these are master-feats you ask of me
Who loves you crazily
When in the circus ring you rock astraddle
Your well-matched bay and grey –
Firing sharp kisses at me.

AGELESS REASON

We laugh, we frown, our fingers twitch
Nor can we yet prognosticate
How we shall learn our fate –
The occasion when, the country which –
Determined only that this season
Of royal tremulous possession
Shall find its deathless reason.

AS WHEN THE MYSTIC

To be lost for good to the gay self-esteem
That carried him through difficult years of childhood,
To be well stripped of all tattered ambitions
By his own judgement, now scorning himself
As past redemption –
                              this is anticipation
Of true felicity, as when the mystic
Starved, frightened, purged, assaulted and ignobled
Drinks Eleusinian ambrosia
From a gold cup and walks in Paradise.

UNPOSTED LETTER

(1963)

Do you still love, once having shared love's secret
With a man born to it?
Then sleep no more in graceless beds, untrue
To love, where jealousy of the secret
May scorch away your childlike sheen of virtue –
Did he not confer crown, orb and sceptre
On a single-hearted, single-fated you?

BIRTH OF A GODDESS

It was John the Baptist, son to Zechariah,
Who assumed the cloak of God's honest Archangel
And mouthpiece born on Monday, Gabriel,
And coming where his cousin Mary span
Her purple thread or stitched a golden tassel
For the curtain of the Temple Sanctuary,
Hailed her as imminent mother, not as bride –
Leaving the honest virgin mystified.

Nor would it be a man-child she must bear:
Foreseen by John as a Messiah sentenced
To ransom all mankind from endless shame –
But a Virgin Goddess cast in her own image
And bearing the same name.

BEATRICE AND DANTE

He, a grave poet, fell in love with her.
She, a mere child, fell deep in love with love
And, being a child, illumined his whole heart.

From her clear conspect rose a whispering
With no hard words in innocency held back –
Until the day that she became woman,

Frowning to find her love imposed upon:
A new world beaten out in her own image –
For his own deathless glory.

THE DILEMMA

Tom Noddy's body speaks, not so his mind;
    Or his mind speaks, not so Tom Noddy's body.
Undualistic truth is hard to find
    For the distressed Tom Noddy.

Mind wanders blindly, body misbehaves;
    Body sickens, mind at last repents,
Each calling on the heart, the heart that saves,
    Disposes, glows, relents.

Which of these two must poor Tom's heart obey:
    The mind seduced by logical excess
To misbehaviour, or its lonely prey –
    The unthinking body sunk in lovelessness?

THE WALL

A towering wall divides your house from mine.
You alone hold the key to the hidden door
That gives you secret passage, north to south,
Changing unrecognizably as you go.
The south side borders on my cherry orchard
Which, when you see, you smile upon and bless.
The north side I am never allowed to visit;
Your northern self I must not even greet,
Nor would you welcome me if I stole through.

I have a single self, which never alters
And which you love more than the whole world
Though you fetch nothing for me from the north
And can bring nothing back. To be a poet
Is to have no wall parting his domain,
Never to change. Whenever you stand by me
You are the Queen of poets, and my judge.
Yet you return to play the Mameluke
Speaking a language alien to our own.

WOMEN AND MASKS

Translated from Gábor Devecseri's Hungarian

Women and masks: an old familiar story.
Life slowly drains away and we are left
As masks of what we were. The living past
Rightly respects all countenances offered

As visible sacrifices to the gods
And clamps them fast even upon live faces.
Let face be mask then, or let mask be face –
Mankind can take its ease, may assume godhead.
Thus God from time to time descends in power
Graciously, not to a theologian's hell
But to our human hell enlaced with heaven.
Let us wear masks once worn in the swift circlings
And constant clamour of a holy dance
Performed always in prayer, in the ecstasy
Of love-hate murder – today's children always
Feeling, recording, never understanding.

Yet this old woman understands, it seems,
At least the unimportance of half-knowledge,
Her face already become mask, her teeth
Wide-gapped as though to scare us, her calm face
Patterned with wrinkles in unchanging grooves
That outlive years, decades and centuries.
Hers is a mask remains exemplary
For countless generations. Who may wear it?
She only, having fashioned it herself.
So long as memory lasts us, it was hers.
Behind it she assembles her rapt goodness,
Her gentle worth already overflooding
The mask, her prison, shaming its fierce, holy
Terror: for through its gaping sockets always
Peer out a pair of young and lovely eyes.

TILTH

('Robert Graves, the British veteran, is no longer in
the poetic swim. He still resorts to traditional metres
and rhyme, and to such out-dated words as *tilth*; with-
holding his 100% approbation also from contemporary
poems that favour sexual freedom.'

From a New York critical weekly)

Gone are the drab monosyllabic days
When 'agricultural labour' still was *tilth*;
And '100% approbation', *praise*;
And 'pornographic modernism', *filth* –
Yet still I stand by *tilth* and *filth* and *praise*.

THE LAST FISTFUL

He won her Classic races, at the start,
With a sound wind, strong legs and gallant heart;
Yet she reduced his fodder day by day
Till she had sneaked the last fistful away –
When, not unnaturally, the old nag died
Leaving her four worn horseshoes and his hide.

THE TRADITIONALIST

Respect his obstinacy of undefeat,
His hoarding of tradition,
Those hands hung loosely at his side
Always prepared for hardening into fists
Should any fool waylay him,
His feet prepared for the conquest of crags
Or a week's march to the sea.

If miracles are recorded in his presence
As in your own, remember
These are no more than time's obliquities
Gifted to men who still fall deep in love
With real women like you.

THE PREPARED STATEMENT

The Prepared Statement is a sure stand-by
For business men and Ministers. A lie
Blurted by thieves caught in the very act
Shows less regard, no doubt, for the act's fact
But more for truth; and all good thieves know why.

ST ANTONY OF PADUA

Love, when you lost your keepsake,
The green-eyed silver serpent,
And called upon St Antony
      To fetch it back again,
The fact was that such keepsakes
Must never become idols
And meddle with the magic
      That chains us with its chain:
Indeed the tears it cost you
By sliding from your finger
Was Antony's admonishment
      That magic must remain
Dependent on no silver ring
Nor serpent's emerald eyes
But equally unalterable,
      Acceptable and plain ...
Yet none the less St Antony
(A blessing on his honesty!)
Proved merciful to you and me
      And found that ring again.

BROKEN COMPACT

It was not he who broke their compact;
But neither had he dared to warn her
How dangerous was the act.
It might have seemed cruel blackmail,
Not mere foreknowledge, to confess
What powers protected and supported him
In his mute call for singleheartedness.

It was she indeed who planted the first kiss,
Pleading with him for true togetherness –
Therefore her faults might well be charged against him.
She dared to act as he had never dared.
Nor could he change: his heart remaining full,
Commanded by her, yet unconquerable,
Blinding her with its truth.
                              So, worse than blind,
He suffered more than she in body and mind.

A DREAM OF FRANCES SPEEDWELL

I fell in love at my first evening party.
You were tall and fair, just seventeen perhaps,
Talking to my two sisters. I kept silent
And never since have loved a tall fair girl,
Until last night in the small windy hours
When, floating up an unfamiliar staircase
And into someone's bedroom, there I found her
Posted beside the window in half-light
Wearing that same white dress with lacy sleeves.
She beckoned. I came closer. We embraced
Inseparably until the dream faded.
Her eyes shone clear and blue....

Who was it, though, impersonated you?

THE ENCOUNTER

Von Masoch met the Count de Sade
    In Hell as he strode by.
'Pray thrash me soundly, Count!' he begged.
    His lordship made reply:

'What? Strike a lacquey who *enjoys*
    Great blows that bruise and scar?'
'I love you, Count,' von Masoch sighed,
    'So cruel to me you are.'

AGE GAP

My grandfather, who blessed me as a child
Shortly before the Diamond Jubilee,
Was born close to the date of Badajoz
And I have grandchildren well past your age –
One married, with a child, expecting more.

How prudently you chose to be a girl
And I to be a boy! Contrary options
Would have denied us this idyllic friendship –
Boys never fall in love with great-grandmothers.

NIGHTMARE OF SENILITY

Then must I punish you with trustfulness
Since you can trust yourself no more and dread
Fresh promptings to deceive me? Or instead
Must I reward you by deceiving you,
By heaping coals of fire on my own head?
Are truth and friendship dead?

And why must I, turning in nightmare on you,
Bawl out my lies as though to make them true?
O if this Now were once, when pitifully
You dressed my wounds, kissed and made much of me,
Though warned how things must be!
　　　*　　*　　*　　*　　*　　*
Very well, then: my head across the block,
A smile on your pursed lips, and the axe poised
For a merciful descent. Ministering to you
Even in my torment, praising your firm wrists,
Your resolute stance.... How else can I protect you
From the curse my death must carry, except only
By begging you not to prolong my pain
Beyond these trivial years?
　　　　　　　　　　I am young again.
I watch you shrinking to a wrinkled hag.
Your kisses grow repulsive, your feet shuffle
And drag. Now I forget your name and forget mine ...
No matter, they were always equally 'darling'.
Nor were my poems lies; you made them so
To mystify our friends and our friends' friends.
We were the loveliest pair: all-powerful too,
Until you came to loathe me for the hush
That our archaic legend forced on you.

ABSENT CRUSADER

An ancient rule prescribed for true knights
Was: 'Never share your couch with a true lady
Whom you would not care in honour to acknowledge
As closest to your heart, on whose pure body
You most would glory to beget children
And acknowledge them your own.'

The converse to which rule, for fine ladies,
No knight could preach with firm authority;
Nor could he venture to condemn any
Who broke the rule even while still sharing
Oaths of love-magic with her absent knight,
Telling herself: 'This is not love, but medicine
For my starved animal body; and my right.
Such peccadilloes all crusades afford –
As when I yield to my own wedded Lord.'

DREAM RECALLED ON WAKING

The monstrous and three-headed cur
Rose hugely when she stroked his fur,
Using his metapontine tail
To lift her high across the pale.

Ranging those ridges far and near
Brought blushes to her cheek, I fear,
Yet who but she, the last and first
Could dare what lions never durst?

Proud Queen, continue as you are,
More steadfast than the Polar Star,
Yet still pretend a child to be
Gathering sea-wrack by the sea.

COLOPHON

Dutifully I close this book....
Its final pages, with the proud look
Of timelessness that your love lends it,
Call only for a simple Colophon
(Rose, key or shepherd's crook)
To announce it as your own
Whose coming made it and whose kiss ends it.

THE PROMISED BALLAD

This augurs well; both in their soft beds
Asleep, unwakably far removed,
Nevertheless as near as makes no odds –
Proud fingers twitching, all but touching.

What most engages him are his own eyes
Beautified by dreaming how one day
He will cast this long love-story as a ballad
For her to sing likewise –
How endless lovers will accept its marvels
As true, which they must be indeed:
Freed of dark witches and tall singing devils.

THE IMPOSSIBLE DAY

A day which never could be yesterday
Nor ever can become tomorrow,
Which framed eternity in a great lawn
Beside the appletrees, there in your garden –
We never shall dismiss it.

Threats of poverty, or of long absence,
Foreknowledge of ten thousand strokes
Threatened against our love by a blank world –
How suddenly they vanished and were gone;
We had fallen in love for ever.

Our proof of which, impossibility,
Was a test of such true magic
As no one but ourselves could answer for.
Both of us might be dead, but we were not,
Our light being still most needed.

And if some unannounced oppression breaks
To chase the governing stars from a clear sky,
Thunder rolling at once from west and east
What should we lovers fear from such a scene
Being incontestably a single heart?

Then say no more about eternity
That might compel us into fantasy:
One day remains our sure centre of being,
Substance of curious impossibility
At which we stand amazed.

THE POET'S CURSE

Restore my truth, love, or have done for good –
Ours being a simple compact of the heart
Guiding each obstinate body
And slow mind regularly –
Each always with a proud faith in the other's
Proud faith in love, though often wrenched apart
By the irresistible Nightmare that half-smothers –
But bound for ever by the poet's curse
Intolerably guarding ill from worse.

SEVEN YEARS

Where is the truth to indulge my heart,
These long years promised –
Truth set apart,
Not wholly vanished.
I still have eyes for watching,
Hands for holding fast,
Legs for far-striding,
Mouth for truth-telling –
Can the time yet have passed,
For loving and for listening?

LOVE AS LOVELESSNESS

What she refused him – in the name of love
And the hidden tears he shed –
She granted only to such soulless blades
As might accept her casual invitation
To a loveless bed.

Each year of the long seven gnawed at her heart,
Yet never would she lay
Tokens of his pure love under her pillow
Nor let him meet, by chance, her new bedfellow;
Thus suffering more than he.

Seven years had ended, the fierce truth was known.
Which of these two had suffered most?
Neither enquired and neither cared to boast:
'Not you, but I. It was myself alone.'
In loneliness true love burns to excess.

THE SCARED CHILD

It is seven years now that we first loved –
Since you were still a scared and difficult child
Confessing less than love prompted,
Yet one night coaxed me into bed
With a gentle kiss
And there blew out the candle.
Had you then given what your tongue promised,
Making no fresh excuses
And never again punished your true self
With the acceptance of my heart only,
Not of my body, nor offered your caresses
To brisk and casual strangers –
How would you stand now? Not in love's full glory
That jewels your fingers immemorially
And brines your eyes with bright prophetic tears.

AS ALL MUST END

All ends as all must end,
And yet cannot end
The way that all pretend,
Nor will it have been I
Who forged the obtrusive lie
But found sufficient wit
To contradict it.

Never was there a man
Not since this world began
Who could outlie a woman:
Nor can it have been you
Who tore our pact in two
And shaking your wild head
Laid a curse on my bed.

I hid in the deep wood,
Weeping where I stood,
Berries my sole food,
But could have no least doubt
That you would search me out,
Forcing from me a kiss
In its dark recesses.

TOUCH MY SHUT LIPS

Touch my shut lips with your soft forefinger,
Not for silence, but speech –
Though we guard secret words of close exchange,
Whispering each with each,
Yet when these cloudy autumn nights grow longer
There falls a silence stronger yet, we know,
Than speech: a silence from which tears flow.

THE MOON'S LAST QUARTER

So daylight dies.
The moon's in full decline,
Nor can those misted early stars outshine her.
But what of love, counted on to discount
Recurrent terror of the moon's last quarter?

Child, take my hand, kiss it finger by finger!
Can true love fade? I do not fear death
But only pity, with forgetfulness
Of love's timeless vocabulary

And an end to poetry
With death's mad aircraft rocketing from the sky.
Child, take my hand!

TRUE EVIL

All bodies have their yearnings for true evil,
A pall of darkness blotting out the heart,
Nor can remorse cancel luckless events
That rotted our engagements with Heaven's truth;
These are now history. Therefore once more
We swear perpetual love at love's own altar
And reassign our bodies, in good faith,
To faith in their reanimated souls.

But on our death beds shall our flaming passions
Revert in memory to their infantile
Delight of mocking the stark laws of love?
Rather let death concede a warning record
Of hells anticipated but foregone.

WHEN AND WHY

When and why we two need never ask –
It is not, we know, our task
Though both stand bound still to accept
The close faith we have always kept
With contradictions and the impossible:
To work indeed as one for ever
In rapt acknowledgment of love's low fever.

THE WINDOW PANE

To bed, to bed: a storm is brewing.
Three natural wonders – thunder, lightning, rain –
Test our togetherness. The window pane,
Regaling us with vistas of forked lightning,
Grants our mortality fair warning;
And every stroke reminds us once again
How soon true love curves round to its beginning.

PRIDE OF PROGENY

While deep in love with one another,
Those seven long earlier years, we two
Would often kiss, lying entranced together
Yet never do what simpler lovers do
In generous pride of generous progeny;
Counting ourselves as poets only,
We judged it false to number more than two.

THAT WAS THE NIGHT

That was the night you came to say goodnight,
Where from the roof hung gargoyles of protection
And our eyes ached, but not intolerably,
The scene for once being well:
We had no now that did not spell forever
Though traffic growled and wild cascades of rain
Rattled against each streaming window pane.

They had gone at last, we reassured each other,
Even those morbid untranslatable visions
Whose ancient terrors we were pledged to accept,
Whose broken past lay resolutely elsewhere.
Hell, the true worldly Hell, proved otherwise:
Dry demons having drunk our marshes dry.

SONG: THE QUEEN OF TIME

Two generations bridge or part us.
The case, we grant, is rare –
Yet while you dare, I dare:
Our curious love being age-long pledged to last,
Posterity, even while it ridicules,
Cannot disprove the past.

Neither of us would think to hedge or lie –
Too well we know the cost:
Should the least canon of love's law be crossed,
Both would be wholly lost –
You, queen of time, and I.

SHOULD I CARE?

'Should I care,' she asked, 'his heart being mine,
If his body be another's? –
Should I long for children and a full clothes-line?
Children, indeed, need mothers,
But do they still need fathers?
And now that money governs everything
Should a country need a king?'

TIMELESS MEETING

To have attained an endless, timeless meeting
By faith in the stroke which first engaged us,
Driving two hearts improbably together
Against all faults of history
And bodily disposition –

What does this mean? Prescience of new birth?
But one suffices, having paired us off
For the powers of creation –
Lest more remain unsaid.

Nor need we make demands or deal awards
Even for a thousand years:
Who we still are we know.

Exchange of love-looks came to us unsought
And inexpressible:

To which we stand resigned.

ENVOI

There is no now for us but always,
Nor any I but we –
Who have loved only and love only
From the hilltops to the sea
In our long turbulence of nights and days:
A calendar from which no lover strays
In proud perversity.

AT THE GATE

(1974)

OURS IS NO WEDLOCK

Ours is no wedlock, nor could ever be:
We are more, dear heart, than free.
Evil surrounds us – love be our eye-witness –
Yet while a first childish togetherness
Still links this magic, all terror of lies
Fades from our still indomitable eyes:
We love, and none dares gibe at our excess.

THE DISCARDED LOVE POEM

Should I treat it as my own
Though loth to recall
The occasion, the reason,
The scorn of a woman
Who let no tears fall?

It seems no mere exercise
But grief from a wound
For lovers to recognize:
A scar below the shoulder,
White, of royal size.

How did she treat the occasion?
In disdainful mood?
Or as death to her womanhood?
As the Devil's long tooth?
As the end of all truth?

EARLIER LOVERS

First came fine words softening our souls for magic,
Next came fine magic, sweetening hope with sex;
Lastly came love, training both hearts for grief –
Magical grief that no honour could vex.

Was it ever granted earlier true lovers –
Whether equally bruised need not concern us –
To anticipate such hand-in-hand conformity?
If so, how were they named? And was their glory
Fixed by an oath you never dared deny me?

FAST BOUND TOGETHER

Fast bound together by the impossible,
The everlasting, the contempt for change,
We meet seldom, we kiss seldom, seldom converse,
Sharing no pillow in no dark bed,
Knowing ourselves twin poets, man with woman,
A millennial coincidence past all argument,
All laughter and all wonder.

£. s. d.

When *Libra, Solidus, Denarius*
Ruled our metallic currency,
They satisfied and steadied us: –
Pounds, shillings, pence, all honest British money.

True, the gold *libra* weighed twelve ounces once.
The *solidus*, gold equally,
Worth twenty-five *denarii* –
Money that did not burn,
Money which in its turn ...

'What happened to the *solidus*?' you ask me.
Reduced at last to an unsilvered shilling
Of twelve *denarii* – 'pence', or bronze money –
It faded pitifully into the blue …
As for the *libra*, having done with gold,
It languished among paper promises
Based on hopes, lies and shrewd financial guesses.
But mourn for the French *sou*, as is most proper:
Three hundred ounces, once, all of pure copper.

THREE WORDS ONLY

Tears from our eyes
Start out suddenly
Until wiped away
By the gentle whisper
Of three words only.

And how should we stifle
Grief and jealousy
That would jerk us apart
Were it not for an oracle
Of three words only?

Three words only,
Full seven years waiting
With prolonged cruelty
Night by night endured
For three words only.

Sweetheart, I love you
Here in the world's eye
And always shall do
With a perfect faith
In three words only.

Let us boast ourselves
Still to be poets
Whose power and whose faith
Hang at this tall altar
Of three words only.

TRUE MAGIC

Love, there have necessarily been others
When we are forced apart
Into far-off continents and islands
Either to sleep alone with an aching heart
Or admit casual lovers ...

Is the choice murderous? Seven years have passed
Yet each remains the other's perfect love
And must continue suffering to the last ...
Can continence claim virtue in preserving
An oath hurtful and gruelling?

Patience! No firm alternative can be found
To absolute love; we therefore plead for none
And are poets, thriving all hours upon true magic
Distilled from poetry – such love being sacred
And its breach wholly beyond absolution.

THE TOWER OF LOVE

What demon lurked among those olive-trees,
Blackening your name, questioning my faith,
Raising sudden great flaws of desperate wind,
Making a liar of me?
Confess: was it the demon Jealousy?

Has there been any gift in these eight years
That ever you refused when gently asked?
Or that I ever chose to refuse you –
For fear of loving you too dearly –
However much I had failed to demand?

Forgive, and teach me to forgive myself.
This much we know: lifting our faith above
All argument and idle contradiction,
We have won eternity of togetherness
Here in this tall tower blessed for us alone.

THE LOVE LETTER

It came at last, a letter of true love,
Not asking for an answer,
Being itself the answer
To such perversities of absence
As day by day distress us –
Spring, summer, autumn, winter –
With due unhappiness and unease.

What may I say? What must I not say?
Ours is an evil age, afflicting us
With acts of unexampled cruelty
Even in this fast circle of friends,
Offering no choice between disease and death –
With love balanced above profound deeps …
Yet here is your love letter.

Why must we never sleep in the same bed
Nor view each other naked
Though our hearts and minds require it
In proof of honest love?
Can it be because poetic magic
Must mount beyond all sensual choosing
To a hidden future and forgotten past?

SONG: SEVEN FRESH YEARS

Two full generations
Had parted our births
Yet still I could love you
Beyond all concealment,
All fear, all reproach,
Until seven fresh years
Ruling distance and time
Had established our truth.

Love brooded undimmed
For a threatening new age,
So we travelled together
Through torment and error
Beyond jealousy's eras
Of midnight and dawn,
Until seven fresh years
Ruling distance and time
Had established our truth.

AS A LESS THAN ROBBER

You can scarcely grant me now
What was already granted
In bland self-deprivation
Only to other debtors
To whom you owed nothing.

And had I cause for complaint
After my honest absence
That for seven long years
I never dared insist
That you should keep faith?

Now in reward for waiting,
Being still a mere nobody,
Let me plead without reproach
As a less than robber
That I am owed nothing.

SINGLENESS IN LOVE

And the magic law long governing our lives
As poets, how should it be rightly phrased?
Not as injunction, not as interdiction,
But as true power of singleness in love
(The self-same power guarding the fifth dimension
In which we live and move
Perfect in time gone by and time foreknown)
Our endless glory to be bound in love,
Nor ever lost by cheating circumstance.

LOVE CHARMS

How closely these long years have bound us
Stands proved by constant imminence of death –
On land, on water, and in the sky –
As by our love-charms worn on the same finger
Against a broken neck or sudden drowning –
Should we debate them?

To have done with quarrels and misunderstandings
Seems of small import even though emphasizing
The impossibility of a fatal breach.
And yet how strange such charms may seem, how wanton,
And forced on us by what? Not by the present
Nor the past either, nor the random future:
Here we lie caught in love's close net of truth.

AT THE GATE

Where are poems? Why do I now write none?
This can mean no lack of pens, nor lack of love,
But need perhaps of an increased magic –
Where have my ancient powers suddenly gone?

Tonight I caught a glimpse of her at the gate
Grappling a monster never found before,
And jerking back its head. Had I come too late?
Her eyes blazed fire and I could look no more.

What could she hold against me? Never yet
Had I lied to her or thwarted her desire,
Rejecting prayers that I could never forget,
Stealing green leaves to light an alien fire.

THE MOON'S TEAR

Each time it happened recklessly:
No poet's magic could release her
From those feckless unfathomable demands
Of anger and imprudence,
Those pleas of cruelly injured innocence.

Why should he keep so strange a woman
Close at his elbow fitfully observing
The end of a world that was?
Must he fetch a moon's black tear to tame her
For ever and a day?

SONG: FROM OTHERWHERE OR NOWHERE

Should unknown messengers appear
From otherwhere or nowhere,
Treat them with courtesy,
Listen most carefully,
Never presume to argue.
Though the sense be unintelligible,
Accept it as true.

Otherwhere is a lonely past,
Nowhere a far future
To which love must have access
In time of loneliness.
Listen most carefully:
Though the sense be unintelligible,
Accept it as true.

A distant flower-garden,
A forgotten forest,
Islands on a lake
Teeming with salmon,
Its waters dark blue –
Though the sense be unintelligible,
Accept it as true.

NAME

Caught by the lure of marriage,
Casting yourself in prospect
As perfect wife and mother
Through endless years of joy,
Be warned by one who loves you
Never to name your first-born
Until you know the father
And: is it girl or boy?

Nine months in mortal darkness
Let it debate the future,
Reviewing its inheritance
Through three-score generations,
From both sides of the family,
A most exacting game;
Then, just before delivery,
Prepare for a soft whisper
As it reveals its name.

TWO DISCIPLINES

Fierce bodily control, constant routine,
Precision and a closely smothered rage
Alike at ballet-school and the manège:
These harden muscles, these bolster the heart
For glorious records of achievement
To glow in public memory apart.
Which disciplines (ballet and horsemanship)
Have proved no less reciprocally exclusive –
Note their strange differences in gait and carriage –
Than permissivity and Christian marriage.

THE UGLY SECRET

Grow angry, sweetheart, if you must, with me
Rather than with yourself. This honest shoulder
Will surely shrug your heaviest blow away,
So you can sleep the sounder.

As for the ugly secret gnawing at you
Which you still hide for fear of hurting me,
Here is my blank pledge of forgiveness –
Nor need you ever name the enemy,
Nor need I ever guess.

THREE YEARS WAITING

Have we now not spent three years waiting
For these preposterous longings to make sense –
Mine and what I divine to be your secret
Since gently you tighten your lips on its conclusion
Though never registering a copyright?

Since these are poems in their first making,
Let us refrain from secret consideration
Of their bewildered presence.
                                        What is a poem
Unless a shot in the night with a blind arrow
From a well-magicked bowstring?

From COLLECTED POEMS 1975

(1975)

THE CRYSTAL

Incalculably old,
True gift from true king –
Crystal with streaks of gold
For mounting in a ring –
Be sure this gem bespeaks
A sunrise love-making:
To kiss, to have, to hold.

A CHARM FOR SOUND SLEEPING

A charm for sound sleeping,
A charm against nightmares,
A charm against death –
Without rhyme, without music,
Yet short of deceit?

How to master such magic,
How acquire such deep knowledge,
How secure such full power?
Would you shrink from her answer?
Would you dare face defeat?

For to work out of time,
To endure out of space,
To live within her truth –
That alone is full triumph
And honour complete.

THE NEW ETERNITY

We still remain we;
The how and where now being stationary
Need not henceforth concern us;
Nor this new eternity
Of love prove dangerous
Even though it still may seem
Posted and hidden past all dream.

HISTORY OF THE FALL

But did not Adam, Eve's appointed playmate,
Honour her as his goddess and his guide,
Finding her ten times hardier than himself:
Resistant to more sickness and worse weather?
Did he not try his muscles in Eve's service –
Fell trees, shoulder vast boulders, run long errands?

Hers was a pure age, until humankind
Ate flesh like the wild beasts. Fruits, roots, and herbs
Had been their diet before world-wide drought
Forced famine on them: before witless Adam
Disobeyed orders, tossing sacred apples
From Eve's green tree, driving and butchering deer,
Teaching his sons to eat as now he ate.

Eve forced the family from their chosen Eden ...
And Cain killed Abel, battening on the corpse.

ELSEWHERE

Either we lodge diurnally here together
Both in heart and in mind,
Or awhile you lodge elsewhere –
And where, dear heart, is *Elsewhere*?

Elsewhere may be your casual breach of promise –
Unpunishable since unbound by oath –
Yet still awhile *Elsewhere*.

As a veteran I must never break my step,
As a poet I must never break my word,
Lest one day I should suddenly cease to love you
And remain unloved elsewhere.
Come, call on me tonight –
Not marching, love, but walking.

WHAT CAN WE NOT ASK?

What can we not ask you?
                              Being a woman
You still alert the world and, still being men,
We never dare gainsay you, nor yet venture
To descend the mountain when your bells chime
The midday feast and nature gives assent.

Whatever hours they strike, you are found true
To your lovely self and to yourself only:
Silent yet still uncontradictable.
Did we ever see you stumble, taking thought?

What rights have men in such divinity,
Widely though they may move within its shade,
Abstaining still from prayers?

TWO CRUCIAL GENERATIONS

Two crucial generations parted them,
Though neither chargeable as an offence –
Nor could she dare dismiss an honest lover
For no worse crime than mere senility,
Nor could he dare to blame her, being himself
Capable of a passionate end to love
Should she show signs of mocking at old age?
Then why debate the near impossible
Even in fitful bouts of honest rage?

TO COME OF AGE

At last we could keep quiet, each on his own,
Signalling silently though memorably
His news or latest unnews.

When younger we had spent those wintry evenings
In shoutings and wild laughter –
We dared not come of age.

Unless obsessed by love none of us changed.
How could we change? Has true love ever changed?
Not in our day, but only in another's.

Tell me, my heart of hearts, I still beseech you:
When dare we reasonably come of age?

SEPTEMBER LANDSCAPE

Olive-green, sky-blue, gravel-brown,
With a floor of tumbled locusts,
And along the country lane
Isabel dances dressed in red
Erect, thinking aloud,
Framed against sudden cloud
And its bold promise of much-needed rain.

CRUCIBLES OF LOVE

From where do poems come?
From workshops of the mind,
As do destructive armaments,
Philosophic calculations,
Schemes for man's betterment?

Or are poems born simply
From crucibles of love?
May not you and I together
Engrossed with each other
Assess their longevity?

For who else can judge merits
Or define demerits –
This remains a task for lovers
Held fast in love together
And for no others.

WOMAN POET AND MAN POET

Woman poet and man poet
Fell in love each with the other.
It was unsafe for either
To count on sunny weather,
The body being no poet.

Yet it had been the woman
Who drew herself apart,
Cushioned on her divan,
And lent some bolder man
Her body, not her heart.

When seven long years were over
How would their story end?
No change of heart for either,
Mere changes in the weather,
A lover being no friend.

THE FIELD-POSTCARD

475 *Graves (Robert)* AUTOGRAPH POST-
CARD signed (written in pencil), 1.R.W. Fus.
B.E.F. Nov 27, '15 to Edward Marsh, auto-
graph address panel on verso signed, Post
Office and Censor's postmarks   £30
'In the last few days I've been made a captain
and shifted here. I won't get any leave till
January at the earliest…'

Back in '15, when life was harsh
And blood was hourly shed,
I reassured Sir Edward Marsh
So far I was not dead.

My field-postcard duly arrived,
It seems, at Gray's Inn Square
Where Eddie, glad I still survived,
Ruffled his thinning hair ...

A full half century out of sight
It lay securely hid
Till Francis Edwards with delight
Sold it for thirty quid.
But who retained the copyright,
The invaluable copyright?
In common law *I* did.

IF NO CUCKOO SINGS

And if no cuckoo sings,
What can I care, or you?
Each heart will yet beat true
While outward happenings
Kaleidoscopically continue.

Year in, year out, we lie
Each in a lonely bed
With vows of true love read
Like prayers, though silently,
To a well-starred and open sky.

Fierce poems of our past –
How can they ever die,
Condemned by love to last
Word for word and exactly
Under a wide and changeful sky?

MOUNTAIN LOVERS

We wandered diligently and widely
On mountains by the sea,
Greeting no *now* that was not *always*,
Nor any *I* but *we*,
And braved a turbulence of nights and days
From which no honest lover strays,
However stark the adversity.

THREE TIMES IN LOVE

You have now fallen three times in love
With the same woman, first indeed blindly
And at her blind insistence;

Next with your heart alive to the danger
Of what hers might conceal, although such passion
Strikes nobly and for ever;

Now at last, deep in dream, transported
To her rose garden on the high ridge,
Assured that there she can deny you
No deserved privilege,
However controvertible or new.

THE SENTENCE

Is this a sentence passed upon us both
For too ambitious love in separation:
Not as an alien intervention or intrusion
But as heaviness and silence,
As a death in absence?

We have lived these seven years beyond recourse,
Each other's single love in separation:
A whispered name before sleep overtakes us
And before morning wakes us
At some far-distant station.

Let us not hold that either drew apart
In weariness or anger or adventure,
Or the resolve to nurse a single heart....
Call it an irresistible thunderbolt.
It was not my fault, love, nor was it your fault.

SPRING 1974

None yet have been good jocund days,
Clear dawning days,
Days of leisure and truth
Reflecting love's sharp gaze,
Being born, alas, in an evil month
By fetid marsh or by fouled river
Maligned in Hell, accursed in Heaven,
Always by love unshriven,
Void still of honest praise.

ADVENT OF SUMMER

You have lived long but over-lonely,
My grey-haired fellow-poet
Sighing for new melodies
In face of sullen grief,
With wanings of old friendship,
With sullen repetition –
For who can thrive in loneliness,
Accepting its cold needs?

Let love dawn with the advent
Of a cool, showery summer
With no firm, fallen apricots
Nor pods on any beanstalk,
Nor strawberries in blossom,
Nor cherries on the boughs.

Let us deny the absurdities
Of every true summer:
Let us never live ill-used
Or derided by new strangers;
Let us praise the vagrant thrushes
And listen to their songs.

THE UNPENNED POEM

Should I wander with no frown, these idle days,
My dark hair trespassing on its pale brow –
If so, without companionship or praise,
Must I revisit marshes where frogs croak
Like me, mimicking penitential ways?

Are you still anchored to my slow, warm heart
After long years of drawing nightly nearer
And visiting our haunted room, timely
Ruffling its corners with love's hidden mop?
And still must we not part?

What is a poem if as yet unpenned
Though truthful and emancipated still
From what may never yet appear,
From the flowery riches of still silent song,
From golden hours of a wakeful Spring?

Approach me, Rhyme; advise me, Reason!
The wind blows gently from the mountain top.
Let me display three penetrative wounds
White and smooth in this wrinkled skin of mine,
Still unacknowledged by the flesh beneath.

A poem may be trapped here suddenly,
Thrusting its adder's head among the leaves,
Without reason or rhyme, dumb –
Or if not dumb, then with a single voice
Robbed of its chorus.

Here looms November. When last did I approach
Paper with ink, pen, and the half truth?
Advise me, Reason!

THE GREEN WOODS OF UNREST

Let the weeks end as well they must
Not with clouds of scattered dust
But in pure certainty of sun –
And with gentle winds outrun
By the love that we contest
In these green woods of unrest.
You, love, are beauty's self indeed,
Never the harsh pride of need.

UNCOLLECTED POEMS

(1910–1974)

JUVENILIA: 1910–1914

A POT OF WHITE HEATHER

Thou, a poor woman's fairing, white heather,
Witherest from the ending
Of summer's bliss to the sting
Of winter's grey beginning.

Which is better, Dame Nature? A human
Woman's oft-uttered rapture
O'er thy dear gift, and the pure
Love that enshrines a treasure?

Or all the sweet plant loses, where grandly
A friendly mountain rises,
And a land of heather-trees
About its knees reposes?

THE MOUNTAIN SIDE AT EVENING

Now even falls
And fresh, cold breezes blow
Adown the grey-green mountain side
Strewn with rough boulders. Soft and low
Night speaks, her tongue untied
Darkness to Darkness calls.

'Tis now men say
From rugged piles of stones
Steal Shapes and Things that should be still;
Green terror ripples through our bones,
Our inmost heart-strings thrill
And yearn for careless day.

THE WILL O' THE WISP

See a gleam in the gloaming – out yonder
   It wand'reth bright flaming;
Its force – that is a fierce thing!
   It draweth men to drowning.

THE KING'S SON

Daintily stepped the son of the king
   Through the palace-gates flung wide,
He breathed of the fine fresh scents of Spring,
   As he walked by the river side;
But deep in his heart was blossoming
   The Tiger-lily of pride.

His eyes were a royal purple-grey,
   And his sweet lips harboured a smile,
As he dreamed of his kingdom far away,
   Of his wonderful Southern isle;
But evil lay in the purple-grey,
   And the smile was a tyrant's smile.

'The king, my sire, has given me
The fairest isle in all his lands;
Three-score stout vessels fringe her sands,
And seven-score guard the sea.

Thither I'll bid my captains bold
Bring droves of slaves, and thrice a day
A hundred heads I'll blow away
With my great gun of gold.

My squires will take the shattered skulls
And bind them with a golden chain,
To whiten in the sun and rain,
From my palace pinnacles.

O'er that fair isle my fancy roves,
She shall be clothed in majesty,
I'll pave her paths with ivory,
And gem-bedeck her groves.'

He mused by the river, foes forgot,
    While the wind in his love-locks blew;
But an hairy arm from the reeds upshot,
    And dragged him down by the shoe ....
The king's own brother plotted the plot,
    And the isle no boy-king knew.

THE MISER OF SHENHAM HEATH

A miser lived on Shenham Heath,
As lean and grey he was as death.
All children feared his long grey beard,
His toes peeped from the boots beneath.

Within the thatch he kept his store,
A thousand pounds of gold and more;
And every night by candle light
Would take and count them, o'er and o'er.

It chanced one chill November night,
He told the tale by candle light,
When sudden fled from heart and head
The lust for guineas round and bright.

He shivered, rose. Though he was old,
And though the waters glimmered cold,
A plunge he took in Shenham Brook
And washed away the taint of gold.

He cast his clouts and donned instead
A suit he'd worn when he was wed.
The cloth was new, of red and blue;
A feathered hat adorned his head.

He rose at dawning of the day,
That none might meet him on his way.
To Chert he went and money spent
But was not minded there to stay.

He bade a barber shave his chin,
And rode a-horse to Shenham Inn
In proper pride. The neighbours cried:
'A lord! A lord! but gruesome thin!'

Nor from that day forth did he cease
Feeding the countryside like geese:
He lavished gold on young and old –
Aye, even to his last gold piece!

A pauper lives on Shenham Heath,
As lean and grey he is as death;
All people fear to view him near,
His toes peep from his boots beneath.

RONDEAU

Word comes of a pursuing robber-band
From great Bokhara or from Samarkand.
          With tightened belly-girth and loosened rein
              The gallant, speedy dromedary-train
Pounds with broad feet the soft-embosomed sand;
And hearts are by such panic fear unmanned,
It hounds them onward while they yet can stand,
          With mingled snarl and cry and blow and strain,
                    Southward away.

So, as I watch from my far Northern strand,
High o'er the waves sweep by on either hand
          Great gibbous cloud-beasts, merchandized with rain
              From chilly Northern seas to thirsty Spain,
Wind-chased in frightened rout o'er sea, o'er land,
                    Southward away.

'AM AND ADVANCE: A COCKNEY STUDY

When we was wed my 'Erbert sed
   'Wot? Give 'em 'am? Good Lord!
Them wedding guests can beat their breasts,
   But 'am we can't afford.'

When 'Erbert died, Lord, 'ow I cried!
   But 'arf them tears was sham.
'At 'is bedside,' I thinks with pride,
   'The mourners they 'as 'Am.'

PEEPING TOM

I sat in my chamber yesternight;
I lit the lamp, I drew the blind,
And scratched with a quill at paper white;
With Mistress Bess was all my mind!
But stormy gusts had rent the blind
And you were peering from behind,
Peeping Tom in the skies afar –
Bold, inquisitive, impudent star!

Fair Bess was leaning o'er the well,
When down there dropped her store-room key.
A bucket lowered me where it fell;
Invisible, I yet could see
To blow her kisses secretly.
But down the shaft you laughed in glee,
Peeping Tom in the skies afar –
Bold, inquisitive, impudent star!

To-night I walk with Sweetheart Bess,
And love-glance follows love-glance swift;
I gather her in a soft caress,
With joy my eyes to heaven uplift.
But through the scudding vapour-drift
My mocker finds a fleeting rift,
Peeping Tom in the skies afar –
Bold, inquisitive, impudent star!

THE BALLAD OF THE WHITE MONSTER

We drave before a boisterous wind
   For twenty days and three.
Stout was the barque wherein we sailed,
   Shipmen from Normandie.

O carpenters, go take your tools
   To patch the good ship's side.
Ceased is the wind whereon we drave;
   The swelling waves subside.

The carpenters 'gan take their tools
   To patch the good ship's side:
They caulked the gaping seams also,
   To keep therefrom the tide.

But as they caulked the gaping seams
   With mighty craft and care,
Writhed from the oily sea beneath,
   White serpents everywhere.

Oh, be these worms or serpents strange
   Thus rising from the sea?
Nay, 'tis a terrible monstér
   Whose snaky arms they be.

The fish from out the oily waves
   Heaved forth his vast bodie,
And seized the hapless carpenters
   To pull them to the sea.

Come save us, save us, shipmates all,
   Save us from this monstér
That hath seizèd us with his white, white arms,
   An inch we may not stir.

'Tis they have ta'en their trusty swords
   And fought right valiantlie,
The creature twined about the mast,
   Most terrible to see.

> The mariners 'gan smite and hack
> 　　To save the carpenters,
> And swore their blows they'd not abate
> 　　For seven such monstérs.

> They hacked away the slimy flesh
> 　　And gared the monster flee,
> Who took with him the carpenters
> 　　To perish in the sea.

> He sank beneath the yeasty waves,
> 　　But erst a mariner
> Had gougèd out with a bony thumb
> 　　An eye of the monstér.

> A wind arose, and back we sailed
> 　　To France right merrilie,
> And thanked the Saints we fed no fish
> 　　At bottom of the sea.

THE FUTURE

Shepherd.　'Little Lamb of the Spring, in your pale-hued mountainy
　　　　　　　　　　　　　　　　　　　　　　　　meadow,
　　　　　By the rough wall bramble-bound mortarless couched in
　　　　　　　　　　　　　　　　　　　　　　　　the shadow,
　　　　　Lamb of the white hyacinthine fleece, give your heart to
　　　　　　　　　　　　　　　　　　　　　　　　this saying:
　　　　　Life for a lamb is a Year with his seasons. The Spring is for playing,
　　　　　Summer for love, and the Colds for decaying.

　　　　　'You will grow ere long, my delicate dainty creature –'
Lamb.　'As your Southdown Beast, not a sheep, but an insult to
　　　　　　　　　　　　　　　　　　　　　　　　nature,
　　　　　Loving the plains, large-trunked, foul, smutty-faced? I
　　　　　　　　　　　　　　　　　　　　　　　　such another?'
Shepherd.　'No, little friend, but a ewe, slim, gentle and fair as your
　　　　　　　　　　　　　　　　　　　　　　　　mother.'
Lamb.　'That would be good, to become like my mother.'

Shepherd.   'And the little white ram that is butting his fellow out yonder
             Will be lover and lord in the Summer: beside him you'll
                                                              wander
             Out o'er the open summer-clad hills through harebell and
                                                              heather ....
             I will recall this day: I will laugh to behold you together.'
Lamb.   'Love? What is Love, thus to keep us together?'

ALCAICS ADDRESSED TO MY STUDY FAUNA

Mine eye commends thee, Japanese elephant,
Bright body, proud trunk, wrought by a silver-smith:
Thee too, O swart-cheeked elfin rider,
Bought for a couple of Greek Iambics.

Fair wooden doe-deer, chiselled in Switzerland,
Why starest sad-eyed down from my cup-board top?
'Once, lord, a stag ten-tyned, tremendous
Shielded my side – now the dust-cart holds him!'

Green china kit-cat, hailing from Chester-town,
Sweet mouthed thou smilest after the Cheshire way,
Plumb o'er my gas-globe poised. I shudder
Reckoning out what thy fall would cost me.

I boast a three-legged dusty old desert-ship,
Red terra-cotta, native Egyptian;
Unlike the real true living camel,
Never he bites at the hand that bred him.

Next Summer Quarter sorrowing Charterhouse
Knows me no longer. Then sell I all my goods,
And Noah's ark long years in Studies
Slowly will circulate till decay comes.

THE CYCLONE

On Friday night the wind came, fumbling at my window,
Like a baby tapping, shaking, rapping, drumming
With tiny white fingers, delicate and strengthless;
Striving to gain entrance at key-hole and chimney,
All intent to learn what was harboured within.
Little I expected, awaking on Saturday,
To find the babe already weaned, already
Grown to a boy-hood curious, sturdy-limbed.
Grown pagan-hearted, wild, unconscionable,
Tumbling down the poplar, huge limbs tearing
From age-honoured elm-tree, slates from every house-top
Boy-like, in wantonness and fury overthrowing
Now the rich-man's villa, now the huts of the poor.
And ere he abated his frenzy equinoctial,
Thronged were the city-streets, thronged the country-lanes,
With maimed men, with women shrieking above the blast.

THE APE GOD

Her young one dead, some mother of the grey
    Wise apes that haunt the jungle-swallowed fane,
Had stolen from his ayah's arms away
    A rescued man-child of the English slain.
Myself once spied the tiny midget-shape
    'Mid glossy leaves of a scarlet-berried tree
Far out of man's reach, clinging like an ape,
    Grave-eyed, stark naked, dangling dizzily.
He has grown to youth and taught the ape-men fear;
    Provoked, he stares their eyes to bestial fright:
Climbs to sick heights where never man clomb near
    And leaps amazing leaps from height to height.
A vision strange! Amid his temple towers,
The wild free ape-god, crowned with crimson flowers!

LAMENT IN DECEMBER

December's come and all is dead:
Weep, woods, for Summer far has sped,
And leaves rot in the valley-bed.

Grey-blue and gaunt the oak-boughs spread
Mourn through a mist their leafage shed.
December, season of the dead!

Brown-golden, scarlet, orange-red,
Autumn's bright hues, are faded, fled.
December, season of the dead!

The goblins Fog and Dulness, wed
Breed ugly children in my head
And thought lags by with feet of lead.
December, season of the dead!

MERLIN AND THE CHILD

(Adapted from an early Cornish poem)

Merlin went up the mountain side.
A young boy stood above him and cried:
'Merlin, Merlin, where are you bound
Early, so early, with your black hound?
Your rod of hazel, well shaped and thin,
Do magic powers lie closed within?'

Merlin put two hands to his head,
Hiding his eyes in a terror, said:
'Lamb of thunder, avenging dove,
Dealer of wrath, High-king of love,
To search the way and the ways I am come
For a round red egg to carry home,
Blood-red egg of an ocean snake
From the hollowed stone where bright waves break,
To search if ever the valleys hold
Green watercress, or grass of gold,
By a woodland fountain-side to lop
The highest cluster from oak-tree top.
My hazel twig is a magic wand –
Magic of earth, and a power beyond.'

Close to Merlin the young boy stood,
Stretched his hand to the slender wood:
'Merlin, Merlin, turn now again!
Unharmed let the cluster of oak remain,
The cress in the valley where fresh brooks run,
The gold grass dancing below the sun,
And the smooth egg of your ocean snake
In the hollow where dappled waters shake.
Turn again in the steps you have trod:
There is no diviner, but only God!'

A DAY IN FEBRUARY

This foul February day
Dims all colour with dead grey.
Save where stumps of the sawn willow
Mark with shields of orange-yellow
The brown windings of the Wey,
This foul February day
Like a painter lean and sallow,
Dims all colour with dead grey.

THE WASP

I arose at dawn with this end in mind
To display in the wide world everywhere
The sable and gold that alternate
My corselet of proof to beautify.
In a cluster of scented meadow-sweet,
Off right good nectar breakfasting
And too well drunk to be quarrelsome,
I heard the booming buzz of bees,
Big black boisterous bumble-bees,
'Ziz iz zo zweet' from the fuchsias.
Each filled to bursting his honey-bag,
An appendage I've never been troubled with,
Bore it away, up-ended it
And sailed again through the morning air
On a bee-line back to the fuchsias.
As I marvelled to view their industry,

One travelled past me, homeward bound,
Humming 'Ziz iz ze zirty zird
Ztuffed zack of zweet ambrozia!'
Which seemed to me far from credible
And would have provoked my waspishness,
But I dared not give him the lie direct
And name him a nectar-bibbing drone,
For a bee has the pride of a gentleman,
The honour and pride of a gentleman,
And I never did hold with duelling,
And a bumble-bee stings outrageous.

FIVE RHYMES

MY HAZEL-TWIG

My hazel-twig is frail and thin
Yet mighty magic dwells therein,
Black magic, potent in the night,
The master-sorcerer's delight;
Whenas my rival witch appears
This wand will grow him asses' ears;
My hazel-twig is frail and thin
Yet mighty magic dwells therein.

AFTER THE RAIN

Now Earth has drunk her fill of rain
The thirsty common lives again,
And raindrops quivering argentine
'Mid new-born needles of the pine,
As through and through a fresh wind soughs,
Drop shining down to nether boughs.
Now Earth has drunk her fill of rain
The thirsty common lives again.

ENVY

'Envy' I'm loth to call the blight
That cankers all my day and night,
Yet when I see a villain shine
In glory that is rightly mine,
And when he says his taunting say
To me, his better, Envy – nay!
'Envy' I'm loth to call the blight
That cankers all my day and night.

THE KING'S HIGHWAY

The King's Highway is all too wide:
For me, the narrow street and dark,
Where houses lean from either side,
Where robbers lurk at eventide;
There let me wander unespied,
To plot and counter-plotting hark –
The King's Highway is all too wide:
For me, the narrow street and dark.

THE GLORIOUS HARSHNESS OF THE PARROT'S VOICE

Hateful are studied harmonies
Where shrills the parrot as he flies
And cranes his painted neck. 'Oho!
Through towering Jungletown I go!
With green and gold my plumage gleams,
The World is nought to me,' he screams –
Hateful are studied harmonies
Where shrills the parrot as he flies.

TWO MOODS

Of old this universe was born
From sorrow travailing forlorn.
Its highest joys serve but as foil
To toil and pain, to pain and toil;
The serpent chokes us, coil o'er coil;
Blind Cupid heaps our head with scorn.
Of old this universe was born
From sorrow travailing forlorn.

The peach-tree blossoms out
Confirming Winter's rout
And everywhere
One song is heard from amorous bird
'My love is fair!'

To me a wondrous thing,
The thrushes brown yet sing
The notes they sung
From laced treetops of a birchen copse
When I was young.

We had forgotten this
That Life may all be bliss
Devoid of pain.
Which lesson then, my fellow-men,
Come, learn again!

THE BRIAR BURNERS

The round breasted hill above
    Glows like a lamp-lit dome,
As hither with the seeds of fire
    The briar burners come.

Youths with torches flaring yellow
    Kindle the thickets dry,
The flames waxing clearer, clearer,
    Nearer, yet more nigh.

A pillar of illumined smoke
    Wavering skyward, marks
The silvered purple of the night
    With starbright fire-red sparks.

The oak leaves that but yesterday
    Thrust from their pregnant spike
Quiver in the fire-flare cruel,
    Transparent jewel-like.

Exultant silhouetted dark
    Against the golden glow
From brake to brake with brands a-fire
    The briar burners go.

THE TYRANNY OF BOOKS

Spring passes, summer's young,
Yet mute has been my tongue.
This is the seventh week
I have not sung.
And now I hear the verdant hillside speak
Chiding me for this wrong
That I have celebrated not in song
The new-come colour on her faded cheek,
The sap that inly swells,
The rooks, the lush bluebells,
The meadow-grasses shooting strong.
Spring airs are pleasant and the day is long;
The year is young,
And yet have I not sung.
For by my elbow lies a pile
Of books, of stern insistent books,
Big, broad, stout books
Crammed full of knowledge. Though it looks
As if I'd finish in a little while,
Still grows the pile.
The more I read the more they breed:
Books wed to books
Bear bookish progeny that bids me heed,
Denies my pen over the page to speed.
Outside, the rooks

Circle in air and mate and feed,
But I must read and read.
Can I afford to find my books
Only in running brooks?

THE EXHAUST-PIPE

The selfish poet, falling sick
Heals his disorder double quick
By taking pen in hand and cursing
His birth, conception, breeding, nursing,
His education, the fell strife
Between his nature and his life,
His love affairs, religion, health,
His art, his friendship-commonwealth,
Till those who read the verses groan
To think his case most like their own,
To find their own life pain and sorrow,
To see no hopes for their to-morrow,
And weep – but he who caused their grief,
Has found expression and relief.
If I indulged my naughtiest mood
And fostered melancholy's brood
Of wingèd spites, and sat me down
With clattered pen and furious frown
And forelock round my fingers curled,
Resolved to satirize the world,
Then after meditation long
My fevered brain would cram my wrong
Into a tiny verse so hot,
So full, so poison-tipped, 'twould rot
Man's faith in living and provide
Excuse for general suicide.
But do I frame this pregnant plaint?
No, I do *not*, sir!
                    ['What restraint!']

THE ORGAN GRINDER

Come along, gents: I'll play you a tune
That you won't 'ear twice in a blamed blue moon.
An' I bet that I'll simply give you fits
With me um-tum-tiddely twiddly bits.
I played this 'ere tune to a welchin' tout
An' a Baptist minister solemn an' swell:
One stood an' 'e laughed till 'is teeth shook out
An' 'tother one sang till 'e rang like a bell.
I played this 'ere tune to a jolly ole toff,
'Oo laughed an' quivered, and tears 'e shed
An' a smile went runnin' all round 'is 'ead
An' the upper 'alf of 'is face fell off ....
'Ey diddle diddle, the cat an' the fiddle!
I'll make you all giggle an' wriggle an' squiggle
An' stamp with your feet an' collapse in the middle!
Jingle jangle, 'ey diddle diddle!
You're 'oppin' about like peas on the griddle!
Tow row, rackety jangle – whirr!
That's the end of it.

> Thank you, sir!

1918–1927

THE TWO BROTHERS

(An Allegory)

Once two brothers, Joe and Will,
    Parted each to choose his home,
Joe on top of Windy Hill
    Where the storm clouds go and come
All day long, but Will the other
    In the plain would snugly rest
Low and safe yet near his brother:
    Low and safe he made his nest
At the foot of Windy Hill,
Built a clattering Watermill.

In the winter Joe would freeze,
    Will lay warm in his snug mill;
Through the summer Joe's cool breeze
    Filled with envy burning Will.
Yet to take all times together
    Both were portioned their fair due,
Joe enjoyed the fine warm weather,
    Will could smile in winter too;
Neither troubled nor complained,
Each in his own home remained.

These two brothers at first sight
    Made a pair of Heavenly Twins,
Two green peas, two birds in flight,
    Two fresh daisies, two new pins:
Yet the second time you'd seen 'em,
    Seen 'em close and watched 'em well,
You would find there lay between 'em
    All the span of Heaven and Hell,
Spring and Autumn, East and West,
And I know whom I liked best.

Listen: once when lofty Joe
    Climbing down to view the mill,
Wept to find Will lived so low
    Would not stop to dine with Will,
Will climbed back through the cloudy smother
    Laughed to feel he stood so high,
Tossed his hat up, kissed his brother,
    Drank old ale, ate crusty pie …
Will had no high soul, but oh
Give us Will, we all hate Joe!

PEACE

When that glad day shall break to match
'Before-the-War' with 'Since-the-Peace',
And up I climb to twist new thatch
Across my cottage roof, while geese
Stand stiffly there below and vex
The yard with hissing from long necks,
In that immense release,
That shining day, shall we hear said:
'New wars to-morrow, more men dead'?

When peace time comes and horror's over,
Despair and darkness like a dream,
When fields are ripe with corn and clover,
The cool white dairy full of cream,
Shall we work happily in the sun,
And think 'It's over now and done',
Or suddenly shall we seem
To watch a second bristling shadow
Of armed men move across the meadow?

Will it be over once for all,
With no more killed and no more maimed;
Shall we be safe from terror's thrall,
The eagle caged, the lion tamed;
Or will the young of that vile brood,
The young ones also, suck up blood
Unconquered, unashamed,
Rising again with lust and thirst?
Better we all had died at first,
Better that killed before our prime
      We rotted deep in earthy slime.

BAZENTIN, 1916

(A Reminiscence – Robert and David)

R. That was a curious night, two years ago,
     Relieving those tired Dockers at Bazentin.
     Remember climbing up between the ruins?
     The guide that lost his head when the gas-shells came,
     Lurching about this way and that, half-witted,
     Till we were forced to find the way ourselves?

D. Yes, twilight torn with flashes, faces muffled,
     In stinking masks, and eyes all sore and crying
     With lachrymatory stuff, and four men gassed.

R. Yet we got up there safely, found the trenches
     Untraversed shallow ditches, along a road
     With dead men sprawled about, some ours, some theirs –

D. Ours mostly, and those Dockers doing nothing,
     Tired out, poor devils; much too tired to dig,

Or to do anything but just hold the ground:
No touch on either flank, no touch in front,
Everything in the air. I cursed, I tell you.
Out went the Dockers, quick as we filed in,
And soon we'd settled down and put things straight,
Posted the guns, dug in, got out patrols,
And sent to right and left to restore touch.

R. There was a sunken road out on the right,
With rifle-pits half dug; at every pit
A dead man had his head thrust in for shelter.

D. Dawn found us happy enough; a funny day –
The strangest I remember in all those weeks.
German five-nines were bracketting down our trenches
Morning and afternoon.

R.   Why, yes; at dinner,
Three times my cup was shaken out of my hand
And filled with dirt: I had to pour out fresh.

D. That was the mug you took from the Boche gun.
Remember that field gun, with the team killed
By a lucky shot just as the German gunners
Were limbering up? We found the gunner's treasures
In a box behind, his lump of fine white chalk
Carefully carved, and painted with a message
Of love to his dear wife, and Allied flags,
A list of German victories, and an eagle.
Then his clean washing, and his souvenirs –
British shell-heads, French bullets, lumps of shrapnel,
Nothing much more. I never thought it lucky
To take that sort of stuff.

R.   Then a tame magpie –
German, we guessed – came hopping into the trench,
Picking up scraps of food. That's 'One for sorrow'
I said to little Owen.

D.   Not much mistaken
In the event, when only three days later
They threw us at High Wood and (mind, we got there!)
Smashed up the best battalion in the whole corps.
But, Robert, quite the queerest thing that day

Happened in the late afternoon. Worn out,
I snatched two hours of sleep; the Boche bombardment
Roared on, but I commended my soul to God,
And slept half through it; but as I lay there snoring
A mouse, in terror of all these wild alarms,
Crept down my neck for shelter, and woke me up
In a great sweat. Blindly I gave one punch
And slew the rascal at the small of my back.
That was a strange day!

R.   Yes, and a merry one.

THE DANCING GREEN

Girl.   What's that you're humming, gammer?
Grandmother.   A silly old song,
                They used to dance jigs to it in old Happy England
                    When *my* grandmother was young.

Girl.   Where did they dance it, gammer?
Grandmother.   Here where we stand,
                Kicking up their heels on the green daisy carpet,
                    Girls and boys, hand in hand.

                A blind man would make gay music
                    Perched on a cask,
                And bent old folk brought currant-cake and cider
                    Dancers never had to ask.

Girl.   Why did the jig end, gammer?
                None dance it now.
Grandmother.   Ninety years ago it was sent out of fashion:
                    Dance? we have forgotten how.

Girl.   Who was the spoilsport, gammer?
                Who stopped our play?
Grandmother.   The lawyers and the Mills and the base new gentry,
                    They stole our laughter away.

THE PERSONAL TOUCH

Cunning indeed Tom Fool must be to-day
    For us, who meet his verses in a book,
To cry 'Tom Fool wrote that … I know his way.…
    … Unsigned, yet eyed all over with Tom's look.…
    Why see! It's pure Tom Fool, I'm not mistook.…
Fine simple verses too; now who's to say
How Tom has charmed these worn old words to obey
    His shepherd's voice and march beneath his crook?'
Instead we ponder 'I can't name the man,
    But he's been reading Wilde', or 'That's the school
Of Coterie … Voices … Pound … the Sitwell clan … '
    '*He* "knows his Kipling"' … '*he* accepts the rule
Of Monro … of Lord Tennyson … of Queen Anne … ';
    How seldom, 'There, for a ducat, writes

TOM FOOL.'

SONG: THE RING AND CHAIN

Janet.   '*Where are those treasures that you promised me*
                If I should fetch and carry and bake your bread?
            Two years beyond my time I have laboured free
                And two on seven have worn me to a thread!'

Witch.   '*Ay, these nine winters you have lived by me,*
                No idler servant in the world than you:
            Two more again from now you must labour free
                And time shall bring reward if you serve me true.'

Janet.   '*Where are those trinkets that you tokened me,*
                The chain and ring if I should be your slave?
            Four years beyond my time I have laboured free
                And four on seven have brought me nigh the grave.'

Witch.   '*Ay, four on seven you have lived here by me,*
                But idler serving girl has never been mine;
            Your ring and chain lie deep below the sea,
                Where you may fish them up with hook and line.'

She was young and had a heart like steel,
    And scarcely had she set her feet on sand,
When up a herring swam and a crownèd eel
    And gave the jewels safe into her hand.

Janet has won the charm that makes unseen,
    Janet has won a great gold wishing ring.
This child of beauty shall be England's queen,
    And John the smith, her true-heart, shall be king.

THE OXFORD ENGLISH SCHOOL

1920

She's in the second row, see? No, not that one!
The girl in the green jersey, the pale fat one,
Taking few notes, sitting beatified,
Plump fingers locked, a large mouth open wide,
Eyes staring down.... Of course Professor Steel
Isn't a dried old haddock like Macneil,
The Chair of Anglo-Saxon, who'll admit
His period has no interest, not a bit,
Except to students ardent in research
For early records of our Laws or Church.
'Literature? No, nothing of the kind!
Still, Glosses need re-glossing you may find.' ...
But Steel (Parks Road Museum at midday,
Tuesdays and Fridays) points a happier way.
(Ascetic chin, smooth hair, persuasive gesture,
Smile, gentle Oxford voice setting at rest your
Rebel's mistrust of mortar-board and gown.)
He quotes, smiles, pauses. Itching pens rush down
Chapter and verse; for we sit tier on tier,
A girl from Roedean there, a Serbian here,
Two Reds from Ruskin next the Meat-King's daughter,
A one-armed Brigadier returned from slaughter,
A young Babu, the Nun from Foxcombe way,
All in a row we crouch, scribbling away.
But She sits still, her notebook shut, her pen
Idling. Steel treats of Beowulf's death, and then
Wrings a deep sigh from her, almost a tear,
With 'That old tale, the Snows of Yester-year.'

… What was the joke? I missed it, but they laughed;
A map of Syria shuddered with the draught.
She dimpled up, she laughed, she's grave again.
The stops are changed, now a cathedral strain
Peals out: –
                    'This Norman influence brought in
Fresh themes of Poetry and we first begin
To meet a new word, sweetened by new rhyme,
The great word, Love.'
                              I looked away this time,
Green Jersey; after all what right had I
To twitch aside the curtains, to play spy?
Still I could feel the sudden burst of red
Drench your pale face when glancing up, he said
Quoting most reverently: 'A crowned "A"
And after, AMOR VINCIT OMNIA.'

THE STEPMOTHER AND THE PRINCESS

Through fogs and magic spells
    All day I've guided you,
Through loud alarms and yells,
    Through scent of wizard stew,
    Through midday pools of dew,

Through crowds that moan and mock,
    Ogres at human feast,
Blood-streams and battleshock,
    Past phantom bird and beast,
    Monsters of West and East.

But this calm wood is hedged
    With the *set shape* of things;
Here is no phoenix fledged,
    No gryphon flaps his wings,
    No dragons wave their stings.

Nothing is here that harms,
    No toothed or spiny grass,
No tree whose clutching arms
    Drink blood when travellers pass,
    No poison-breathed Upas.

Instead the lawns are soft,
 The tree-stems grave and old:
Slow branches sway aloft,
 The evening air comes cold,
 The sunset scatters gold.

Nay, there's no hidden lair
 For tigers or for apes,
No dread of wolf or bear,
 No ghouls, no goblin shapes,
 No witches clad in capes.

My cloak, my ermine cloak,
 Shall keep you warm and dry;
Branches of elm I've broke
 To roof you as you lie
 Below the winking sky.

Sleep now and think no ill,
 No evil soul comes near.
The dreamy woods are still,
 Sigh, sleep, forget your fear,
 Sleep soundly, sleep, my dear.

CYNICS AND ROMANTICS

In club and messroom let them sit
At skirmish of ingenious wit;
Deriding Love, yet not with hearts
Accorded to those healthier parts
Of grim self-mockery, but with mean
And burrowing search for things unclean,
Pretended deafness, twisted sense,
Sharp innuendoes rising thence,
And affectation of prude-shame
That shrinks from using the short name.
We are not envious of their sour
Disintegrations of Love's power,
Their swift analysis of the stabs
Devised by virgins and by drabs
(Powder or lace or scent) to excite
A none-too-jaded appetite.

They never guess of Love as we
Have found the amazing Art to be,
Pursuit of dazzling flame, or flight
From web-hung blacknesses of night,
With laughter only to express
Care overborne by carelessness;
They never bridge from small to great,
From nod or glance to ideal Fate,
From clouded forehead or slow sigh
To doubt and agony looming by,
From shining gaze and hair flung free
To infinity and to eternity –
They sneer and poke a treacherous joke
With scorn for our rusticity.

RECORDS FOR WONDER

Once there came a mighty, furious wind
    (So old worthies tell).
It blew the oaks like nine-pins down,
And all the chimney-stacks in town
    Down together fell.
That was a wind – to write a record on,
        to hang a story on,
        to sing a ballad on,
    To ring the loud church bell!
But for one huge storm that cracks the sky
Come a thousand lesser winds rustling by,
And the only wind that will make me sing
Is breeze of summer or gust of spring,
But no more hurtful thing.

Once there came a mighty, thirsty drought
  (So old worthies tell).
The quags were drained, the brooks were dried,
Cattle and sheep and pigs all died,
  The Parson preached on Hell.
That was a drought – to write a record on,
     to hang a story on,
     to sing a ballad on,
  To ring the loud church bell!
But for one long drought of world-wide note
Come a thousand lesser ones on man's throat,
And the only drought for my singing mood
Is a thirst for the very best ale that's brewed,
Soon quenched, but soon renewed.

Once there came a mighty, biting frost
  (So old worthies tell).
It bound the never yet conquered lake
With ice that crow-bar scarce could break,
  It froze the deep draw-well.
That was a frost – to write a record on,
     to hang a story on,
     to sing a ballad on,
  To ring the loud church bell!
But for one black frost of strange alarm
Why, a thousand lesser ones bring no harm,
And the only frost that suits my strain
Is hoar-frost pattern on a latticed pane,
When Christmas comes again.

Once my sweetheart spoke an unkind word,
  As I myself must tell,
For none but I have seen or heard
My sweetheart to such cruelty stirred
  For one who loves her well.
That was a word – to write no record on,
     to hang no story on,
     to sing no ballad on,
  To ring no loud church bell!
Yet for one fierce word that has made me smart
Ten thousand gentle ones ease my heart,
So all the song that springs in me
Is 'Never a sweetheart born could be
So kind as only she!'

OLD LOB-LIE-BY-THE-FIRE

Henceforth old Lob shall sweat for no man's hire
On winter nights knee-deep in snow or mire,
Split no hard logs, nor shoulder no huge burden,
Since he has seen his nightly favours harden
To obligation, his cream-brimming vat
Thin to mere whey, scarce quarter filled at that.
From god to blackleg labourer being sunk,
Instead of reverent dues, old Lob has drunk
Sour grudging minimum-wage, working so hard,
And farmer's wife keeps her warm kitchen barred;
Then weary Lob, his job complete, may stand
In the muckyard.
                Oh, goodbye to this changed land!
To Canada or New Zealand or the Cape
He works his passage easily in the shape
Of a Dago stoker, or perhaps he hides
His matted shapelessness in a bale of hides.
Once over, he hopes cream and by some fire
To doze, yet shall he sweat for no man's hire,
Nor for ingratitude chore now never more.

MISGIVINGS, ON READING A POPULAR 'OUTLINE OF SCIENCE'

When man forswears *God* and dispels *taboo*
    Serving a butterfly expediency
    In ultimate anarchy,
Mating and murdering too
Regardless of who's who,
Only intent on doing what's to do –
    Will no one urge the sentimental plea
    For wise old savages like you and me,
His unsophisticated
Forbears of time undated?

THE TOADS

Do you wear away time
Over ballad and rhyme
Ecstatic in attic or basement,
Your difficult labours
The scorn of *Toad* neighbours
Who wink at your inky effacement?

O do you set Art
As a kingdom apart
Do you choose the sad Muses to bed with?
Then you shall have praise
At the close of your days
With bays to bedizen your head with.

But a *Toad* is a *Toad*
With so poisoned a mode
Of address that few dare to declare it.
He is crass, he is cruel,
He wears no hid jewel,
Despite worthy writers who swear it.

Your dearly bought fame
Will be dulled by the shame
Toads award any bard they call Master.
None such can go crowned
Or in purple robes gowned
But they spurt at him dirt and disaster.

For whatever your care
Or your secret despair
With scandal their hand'll unearth it.
Unlocking the locks
Of your intimate box
(Cry, pox on 'em! Is the praise worth it?)

They will prove that your brain
Never pleaded in vain
For cocaine-coloured dreams that enriched you,
That your wife was untrue
And your daughter a shrew
That a Jew and a Jesuit witched you.

They will show you complete
Lecher, liar and cheat,
A Job for ignoble diseases,
Ungentle, unwitty,
A sot without pity
Who preys and betrays as he pleases.

They will keep a sharp eye
On *Remains* when you die,
They will buy them for bagsfull of dollars.
Stray scraps that they find
Of old filth unrefined
They will bind up in books for the scholars.

They will oddly misquote
Whatsoever you wrote,
With a note on your 'exquisite manner':
And schoolmaster *Toads*
Will parade the long roads
With Centenary Odes and a banner.

And your unquiet ghost
Shall repent himself most
Of your boast for the bays and the laurels,
When Rose, Lily, Pink,
That in garlands you link
Shall stink of the *Toads* and their quarrels.

A HISTORY

The Palmist said: 'In your left hand, which shews your
inheritance, the Line of Head dips steeply towards Luna. In
your right hand, which shews your development, there is a
determined effort to escape into less melancholy thinking.'
I said nothing, but shewed him this sonnet: –

When in my first and loneliest love I saw
    The sun swim down in tears to meet the sea,
When woods and clouds and mountains massed their awe
    To whelm the house of torment that was me,
When spirits below the cromlech heard me pass,
    Belling their hate with such malignant cries
That horror and anguish rustled through the grass
    And the very flowers glared up with oafish eyes,

Then round I turned where rose the death-white Fay
    And knew her well that exercised her wand,
That spurred my heart with rowellings day by day
    To the very reach of madness, and beyond,
Thee, Moon, whom now I flout, by thought made bold,
    Naked, my Joseph's garment in thy hold.

FOUR CHILDREN

As I lay quietly in the grass,
    Half dreaming, half awake,
I saw four children barefoot pass
    Across the tufted brake:
The sky was glass, the pools were glass,
    And not a leaf did shake.

The autumn berries clustered thick,
    Seldom I met with more;
I thought these children come to pick,
    As many picked before;
Each had a long and crooked stick,
    And crowns of ash they wore.

But not one berry did they take;
    Gliding, I watched them go
Hand in hand across the brake
    With sallies to and fro.
So half asleep and half awake
    I guessed what now I know.

They were not children, live and rough,
    Nor phantoms of the dead,
But spirits woven of airy stuff
    By wandering fancy led,
Creatures of silence, fair enough
    No sooner seen than sped.

THE BARGAIN

The stable door was open wide:
I heard voices, looked inside.
Six candle-yellow birds were set
In a cage of silver net,
Shaking wing, preening feather,
Whistling loudly all together.
Two most ancient withered fairies
Bartered rings against canaries,
Haggled with a courteous cunning –
Hinting, boasting, teasing, punning
In a half-remembered tongue.
'Too low an offer!' 'Times are bad.'
'Too low!' 'By far the best you have had.'
'Raise it!' Then what a song was sung:
'Dicky is a pretty lad!
Dicky is a pretty lad!'
But diamonds twinkled with light flung
By twelve impatient golden wings,
The younger merchant took the rings,
Closed his bargain with a sigh,
And sadly wished his flock 'Goodbye.'
Goodbye, goodbye, in fairy speech
With a sugar-peck for each
Unsuspecting bright canary.
'Fare you well.'
                        A sudden airy
Gust of midnight slammed the door.
Out went the lights: I heard no more.

IN THE BEGINNING WAS A WORD

The difficulty was, it was
Simple, as simple as it seemed;
Needing no scrutinizing glass,
No intense light to be streamed

Upon it. It said what it said
Singly, without backthought or whim,
With all the strictness of the dead,
Past reason and past synonym.

But they, too dull to understand,
Laboriously improvised
A mystic allegory, and
A meaning at last recognized:

A revelation and a cause,
Crowding the cluttered stage again
With saints' and sinners' lies and laws
For a new everlasting reign.

THE BAIT

My wish, even my ambition
(For such ambition spells no diminution
Of virtue, strict in self-possession),
Is not, to deaden the mind
To be resigned
To take the insistent bait
To be hauled out, hooked and hulking;
Is not, to refuse the bait,
To be angry, to go hungry,
To lodge in the mud, to be sulking:
It is, I would surge toward these troubles
Trailing a row of easy bubbles;
Would gulp the bait, the hook, rod, reel,
Fisherman and creel,
Converting even the landing-net's tough mesh,
The spaced and regular knots, to wholesome flesh;
And would subside again, resume my occupation,
With 'yes and no' for what showed blank negation:
So, would remain just fish.
That, or something of that, is my wish.

AN INDEPENDENT

The warring styles both claim him as their man
    But undisturbed, resisting either pull
He paints each picture on its own right plan
    As unexpected as inevitable.

They while admitting that this treatment is
    Its own justification, take offence
At his unmodish daily practices:
    Granting him genius, they deny him sense.

He grinds his paints in his own studio,
    Has four legitimate children (odd!) and thinks
Of little else; he dresses like a crow,
    Keeps with his wife and neither smokes nor drinks.

When painting is discussed, he takes no part,
    Pretends he's dull; and who can call his bluff?
The styles protest, while honouring his art,
    He will not take Art seriously enough.

[THE UNTIDY MAN]

There was a man, a very untidy man,
    Whose fingers could nowhere be found to put in his tomb.
He had rolled his head far underneath the bed:
    He had left his legs and arms lying all over the room.

1934–1939

MIDSUMMER DUET*

First Voice
    O think what joy that now
    Have burst the pent grenades of summer
    And out sprung all the angry hordes
    To be but stuttering storm of bees
    On lisping swoon of flowers –
    That such winged agitation
    From midge to nightingale astir
    These lesser plagues of sting and song
    But looses on the world, our world.

---

* The First Voice is Laura Riding.

O think what peace that now
Our roads from house to sea go strewn
With fast fatigue – time's burning footsounds,
Devilish in our winter ears,
Cooled to a timeless standstill
As ourselves from house to sea we move
Unmoving, on dumb shores to pledge
New disbelief in ills to come
More monstrous than the old extremes.

Second Voice

And what regret that now
The dog-star has accomplished wholly
That promise April hinted with
Faint blossom on her hungry branches,
And pallid hedgerow shoots?
Exuberance so luscious
Of fruit and sappy briar
Disgusts: midsummer's passion chokes
'No more!' – a trencher heaped too high.

And O what dearth that now
We have sufficient dwelling here
Immune to hopes gigantical
That once found lodgement in our heart.
What if less shrewd we were
And the Dog's mad tooth evaded not –
But quick, the sweet froth on our lips,
Reached at fulfilments whose remove
Gave muscle to our faith at least?

First Voice

Let prophecy now cease
In that from mothering omens came
Neither the early dragon nor the late
To startle sleeping errantries
Or blaze unthinkable futures.
The births have not been strange enough;
Half-pestilential miseries
At ripeness failed of horrid splendour.
Our doomsday is a rabbit-age
Lost in the sleeve of expectation.

Let winter be less sharp
In that the heats of purpose
Have winter foreflight in their wings,
Shaking a frostiness of thought
Over those aestive fancies
Which now so inwardly belie
(Their fury tepid to our minds)
The outward boast of season –
We need not press the cold this year
Since warmth has grown so honest.

Second Voice

Let talk of wonders cease
Now that outlandish realms can hold
No prodigies so marvellous as once
The ten-years-lost adventurer
Would stretch our usual gaze with.
The golden apple's rind offends
Our parks, and dew-lapped mountaineers
Unbull themselves by common physic.
There comes no news can take us from
Loyalty to this latter sameness.

Let the bold calendar
Too garrulous in counting
Fortunes of solar accident
Weary, and festive pipes be soft.
Madness rings not so far now
Around the trysting-oak of time;
Midsummer's gentler by the touch
Of other tragic pleasures.
We need not write so large this year
The dances or the dirges.

First Voice

But what, my friend, of love –
If limbs revive to overtake
The backward miles that memory
Tracks in corporeal chaos?
Shall you against the lull of censoring mind
Not let the bones of nature run
On fleshlorn errands, journey-proud –
If ghosts go rattling after kisses,
Shall your firmed mouth not quiver with
Desires it once spoke beauty by?

And what of beauty, friend –
If eyes constrict to clear our world
Of doubt-flung sights and ether's phantom spaces
Cobwebbed where miserly conceit
Hoarded confusion like infinity?
If vision has horizon now,
Shall you not vex the tyrant eyes
To pity, pleading blindness?

Second Voice

But what, my friend, of death,
That has the dark sense and the bright,
Illumes the sombre hour of thought,
Fetches the flurry of bat-souls?
Shall you not at this shriven perfect watch
Survey my death-selves with a frown
And scold that I am not more calm?
Shall you not on our linking wisdoms
Loathe the swart shapes I living wear
In being dead, yet not a corpse?

And what of jest and play –
If caution against waggishness
(Lest I look backward) makes my mood too canting?
Shall you not mock my pious ways,
Finding in gloom no certain grace or troth,
And raise from moony regions of your smile
Light spirits, nimbler on the toe,
Which nothing are – I no one?

First Voice

Suppose the cock were not to crow
At whitening of night
To warn that once again
The spectrum of incongruence
Will reasonably unfold
From day's indulgent prism?

Second Voice

Suppose the owl were not to hoot
At deepening of sleep
To warn that once again
The gospel of oblivion
Will pompously be droned
From pulpit-tops of dream?

First Voice

And shall the world our world have end
In miracles of general palsy,
Abject apocalyptic trances
Wherein creature and element
Surrender being in a God-gasp?

Both Voices

Or shall the world our world renew
At worn midsummer's temporal ailing,
Marshal the season which senescence
Proclaimed winter but we now know
For the first nip of mind's hereafter?

MAJORCAN LETTER, 1935*

This year we are all back again in time –
For a year: excellent: in our zeal
We had abandoned, like new converts,
Certain practices which serve good sense
Under all cosmic flags. The later mind,
For instance, has a need of News as constant
As the earlier; strangers inhabit
Every liveable condition, and we cannot
Regulate our own affairs without at least
Such distancing (if not entire annulment)
Of theirs as with the reading of our papers
We had learnt to exert on foreign conduct.
A talent not to let lapse: the years
Increased the alien volume, few matters
Remained domestic. The need of privacy
Is as strong as ever, nor to be satisfied
Without a public universe to wall
The central reservations. Excellent then,
Those habits of concern with wars, politics,
Impromptu heroes, successes, tragedies,
All weather-mystic to the personal heart,
Substance of outer flush and evanescence;
Scientific rediscoveries of truths
Long known by natural names and numbers;

* With Laura Riding.

Theories of God, Finance, Verse and Diet
Called 'modern' because indeed many but now
First reflect on these primitive subjects,
As if wisdom had ceased to descend
And life were the amazed infant again.
It is well to look out from our discreet windows
With a still curious eye. It is well
To look upon the stale wonders and tumults
And, knowing the recent for ancient,
Remember how we are surrounded ever
As yesterday and once by the remote
Great populations of infinity;
And to keep advised how small-immediate
The space of final conference remains.

Communism is a mighty plan
For turning bread into a doctrine.
And each shall have as much doctrine
As bread: what could be simpler?
Religion was never so accurate.
But haven't they forgotten the wine?
Perhaps, after all, as they say,
Drinking is a lost art.
One still sees interesting recipes
For soups, but on the whole
The world is a drier place.
Ships do not merely no longer splash:
The very ocean has become
An abstraction whereon hotels
Convey the traveller to hotels
In the true spirit of competition,
Whose devices are more humane
Than Nature's, which after all
Is too literal-minded
For the comfortable accommodation
Of man's ubiquitous imagination.
In fact, water is an extinct element
Save for the quaint trickle in the taps
Wherewith they lay the ghosts
Of former hygienes, puny
To the present genii
Of vapours, creams and lotions.
Drinking is a lost art,
Baptism a lost rite,

Water a lost element.
Seaside balsam soothes away
The wetness sustained
In the exorcizing of wetness,
With the assistance of the sun.
And, the waves having by argument
Of logical progress from wet to dry
Undergone vigorous evaporation,
The world-at-large takes to the air-at-large,
In more generous fulfilment
Of the historic farewell
Governing the scattering of peoples
And senses: with a goodbye
More absolute than the mariner's
Salt tear and world-ho.
We are perfectly informed, you see,
In the character and manner
Of life as it is now lived
Around us and around us
And now and now and now
Along the ever-widening
Periphery of this modest
Memorial to coherence
Wherein ourselves have domicile.
(The three elements involved
In questions of this kind,
Our lawyer tells us,
Are Nationality, Residence
And Domicile. By Nationality
Is meant the political relationship
Existing between ourselves
And the sovereign states to which we owe –
But we, and our respective states,
Consider these formalities
Sacred to unpleasant incidents
Abroad, where our Consuls maintain us
In the liberty of feeling at home
Wherever the birth-days guaranteed
Mortal by our respective states
Find us in our post-national age.
Residence merely implies
The place we happen to dwell in
At a particular moment:
A word for the body absent

On the body's errands –
'A purely physical fact'
Our lawyer explicitly avows.
Each sleeps in many beds
During a lifetime of acquiring
Command over the limbs,
Till we are able, without regret,
To exact that permanence
Which our lawyer calls 'Domicil' –
He spells it without 'e', please note,
Terribly, insisting the spirit
Of the law before the letter.
'Domicil is a combination
Of facts and intention.'
We intend to remain thus
Resident in definite us
'For an indefinite time' –
Time, after the legal years
Have been passed, the numbers crossed out,
And no new counting can be done,
Becomes 'an indefinite time',
Which is to say we may safely
At any time go back, to consult
Our newspapers, lawyers or doctors,
Without being reported missing
From ourselves. Such is the credit
Of the extreme word 'Domicil'.)

And Anthony Eden is, we know,
A clever young man who, without
Other resources than tact and
A virile English education
And a flattering way of
Being at ease among the great
(So that the great exert themselves
To be greater, so that Anthony
May be still more at ease among them),
Has established the superior
Virtue of that which is charming.
In other times this would have caused
A complete paralysis of
Activity, not to mention wars,
All joining in the exaltation
Of the personal attractiveness

Of Anthony Eden.... Perhaps,
If he had been a woman ....
But the world has grown suspicious of
Solutions, everyone is anxious
For simple ways out of
Complicated situations
And simple ways back again:
Lest the trick of history-making
Be lost and life become the burden
Of those alive rather than, always,
The intact inheritance of
The unborn generation.
We know, you see, what is going on.
It is not as if we were living
On a desert island. When it is
A question of distance in time
Rather than in geography
It is easy to keep well-informed.
And there are no distances now
But in time, and time is a matter
Of print, we read neither by maps
Nor by dates; the works of T.S. Eliot
Are in no greater hurry to be read
Than the works of Homer –
It is this waiting-power, this
Going to sleep of the author
In the work, to be wakened after
An indefinite time, which makes
Literature the darling of
Leisure. 'Domicil' combines
The facts, intention, and leisure,
Homer is the God of leisure,
And T.S. Eliot its Christ.
One does not hesitate to mention
Homer heartily, he delights
In dozing off and hearing his name
Thunder, like a small boy letting
Sleep roll up the voice of breakfast.
But one is inclined to call softly on
T.S. Eliot, one is inclined, that is,
Not to wake him, to give him sleep
Of much soft calling; one feels
He would make breakfast a further
Occasion for martyrdom.

He is, you see, the Christ not risen
Of literature, leisure or domicil,
Whose glory is not to get up
Ever – thus the small boy becomes
The poet. We realize, you see,
The necessity of being
Back in time, at least for a year,
During which, of course, much may grow
Permanently unfit for interest;
Nevertheless, we mean not to lose
Interest. It is important
To cease looking, when one does,
Not merely because one is tired,
But because memory has succeeded
Observation by the ultimate
Yielding of contemporary
Life to the economic
Crisis: the expense of maintaining
A news-producing universe
For our benefit is gigantic,
Beyond the imagination
Of financiers, whose good-will depends
On the reasonable fantasticness
Of the investment. We do not,
Truly, require this lavish
Apparatus for impressing
On our minds what in any case
Our minds flash topically upon
The ever-paling screen of time:
It is a nice question whether
The whole dispatch of journalism
Is not, as far as we are concerned,
A work of supererogation.

Our regards to various people
   Who may happen to read this verse,
(We dare not make it much better
   For fear it may read much worse),

To the rich man in his castle
   And the poor man at the Spike,
And the patriot Lady Houston
   Whom personally we like,

And the new blue gentleman-bobby
  With his microscopes and such,
A radio-set in his helmet,
  And fluent in Czech and Dutch,

And fearless Admiral Philips –
  When the traffic light went red
He clapped his glass to his sightless eye
  And 'I can't see it,' he said,

And Number One Trunk-murderer
  And likewise Number Two,
And the fellow who left his legs behind
  In the train at Waterloo,

And the sixteen-year-old girl student
  Who wrote, with never a blot:
'The land of my birth is the best on Earth' –
  Which wasn't saying a lot,

And the hostesses of Mayfair
  Who do nothing out of season,
And the miners of the Rhondda
  Who are rebels within reason,

And men who fly to business,
  And women who fly to the Cape,
(But not that Viscount Castlerosse:
  We disapprove of his shape),

And the ex-ex-Rector of Stiffkey
  Who crouched in a barrel cozily,
And the ex-wild-life of Whipsnade
  And ex-Sir Oswald Mosley,

And almost-our-favourite author
  Who moderates loves and crimes
For *Shorter Notices: Fiction*
  In the supplement of the *Times*,

And W.H. Day-Spender,
  Who tries, and tries, and tries,
And the poet without initials –
  The Man with the Staring Eyes,

And the riveters of the Clyde
   And the coracle-men of Dee,
And the nightingale in the shady vale
   Who sings for the B.B.C. –

Now kindest regards to these
   And our love to all the rest,
And our homage to Mr. Baldwin
   (A Tory retort's the best),
And a warning frown to each little bird
   In somebody else's nest.

ASSUMPTION DAY

What was wrong with the day, doubtless,
Was less the unseasonable gusty weather
Than the bells ringing on a Monday morning
For a church-feast that nobody could welcome –
Not even the bell-ringers.

The pond had shrunk: its yellow lilies
Poked rubbery necks out of the water.
I paused and sat down crossly on a tussock,
My back turned on the idle water-beetles
That would not skim, but floated.

A wasp, a humble-bee, a blue-fly
Uncoöperatively at work together
Were sucking honey from the crowded blossom
Of a pale flower whose name someone once told me –
Someone to be mistrusted.

But, not far off, our little cow-herd
Made mud-cakes, with one eye on the cattle,
And marked each separate cake with his initials.
I was half-tempted by the child's example
To rescue my spoilt morning.

THE MOON ENDS IN NIGHTMARE

I had once boasted my acquaintance
With the Moon's phases: I had seen her, even,
Endure and emerge from full eclipse.
Yet as she stood in the West, that summer night,
The fireflies dipping insanely about me,
So that that the foggy air quivered and winked
And the sure eye was cheated,
In horror I cried aloud: for the same Moon
Whom I had held a living power, though changeless,
Split open in my sight, a bright egg shell,
And a double-headed Nothing grinned
All-wisely from the gap.

At this I found my earth no more substantial
Than the lower air, or the upper,
And ran to plunge in the cool flowing creek,
My eyes and ears pressed under water.
And did I drown, leaving my corpse in mud?
Yet still the thing was so.

I crept to where my window beckoned warm
Between the white oak and the tulip tree
And rapped – but was denied, as who returns
After a one-hour-seeming century
To a house not his own.

1952–1959

THE HOUSING PROJECT

Across the strand of no seaside
Will two waves similarly glide;
And always, from whatever strand,
The long horizon's drawn freehand.

Yet nature here must yield to art:
Look, these ten houses, kept apart
By the same exact interval,
Magnificently identical,
Whose ten same housewives, having now
Kissed ten same husbands on the brow
And sent them arm in arm away
To clock in, work, and draw their pay
At the same factory, which makes
Countless identical plum cakes,
Heave a light sigh in unison
And back to their same parlours run
With synchronized abandon, there
To put soap operas on the air.

ADVICE TO COLONEL VALENTINE

Romantic love, though honourably human,
Is comic in a girl or an old man,
Pathetic in a boy or an old woman.

'But counts as decent for how long?' Our nation
Allows a woman thirty years, tacks on
Ten more for men resolved on procreation.

Your decent years, alas, have lapsed? The comic
Come crowding, yet love gnaws you to the quick
As once when you were fifteen and pathetic?

What? Dye your hair, you ask? Dress natty,
Swing an aggressive cane, whistle and sigh?
No: that would be true comicality.

Honour your grey hairs, keep them out of fashion –
Even if a foolish girl, not yet full grown,
Confronts you with a scarcely decent passion.

HIPPOPOTAMUS'S ADDRESS TO THE FREUDIANS

*(He quotes Plutarch's OF ISIS AND OSIRIS 32,
pleading for the revision of the misnomer
'Oedipus Complex', which should be
'Hippopotamus Complex'. His own acts,
unlike those of the Theban King Oedipus,
were not committed in error, he asserts,
but prompted by a genuine infantile libido.)*

Deep in Nile mire,
　Jam etiam:
'I slew my sire,
　I forced my dam.
Plutarch's *Of Isis*
Dwells on my vices,
　Shameless I am:
Free from repression
Or urge to confession,
　Freud's little lamb.
I slew my sire,
In frantic desire
　I forced my dam –
I and not Oedipus,'
Roars Hippopotamus,
'You have confounded us
　Jam etiam!'

TWIN TO TWIN

Come, ancient rival, royal weird,
Who each new May must grip my beard
Till circling time shall cease to be:
Ground your red lance and mourn with me,
Though it were briefly –

Mourn that our wild-flower-breasted Fate,
Who locked us in this pact of hate,
Cuckolds us both as here we stand
And with unmagic mars the strand
Of her own island.

Yet, once again, your heart being true,
Our interrupted strife renew:
Reach for my beard with heaving breast
To roar: 'You lie! She loved me best',
And fight your fiercest.

CONSIDINE

'Why', they demand, 'with so much yet unknown
Anticipate the final colophon
Where the book fails among appendices
And indices?

'To count the tale almost as good as done
Would be intimidation by the Sun,
That tap-house bully with his mounting score
Chalked on the door.

'Look at Sam Shepherd, ruinously white,
With marrow in his bones to leap all night!'
Yet Considine sits dead from the neck down,
With not a tooth lost and a beard still brown,
Curse of the town.

THE JUGGLER

(for Henry Ringling North)

Posturing one-legged on a slack wire,
He is no illusionist (nor I a liar)
When his free foot tosses in sequence up,
To be caught confidently by the joggled head,
Saucer, cup,
        saucer, cup,
                saucer, cup,
                        saucer, cup,
Each to fall fair and square on its mounting bed.
Wonder enough? Or not?
                Not:
                    for a teapot
Floats up to crown them; item, following soon,
Supererogatory lump-sugar, and spoon.

Thus the possible is transcended
By a prankster's pride in true juggling,
Twice daily for weeks at Ringling's ring,
Until the seasonal circuit's ended –
An act one degree only less absurd
Than mine: of slipperily balancing
Word
      upon word
              upon word
                     upon word,
Each wanton as an eel, daft as a bird.

THE YOUNG WITCH

The moon is full,
   Forget all faith and me,
Go your own road,
   If your own road it be;
Below the girdle women are not wise.

Hecatë hounds you on,
   You dare not stay,
Nor will she lead you home
   Before high day –
Here is the truth, why taunt me with more lies?

BIRTH OF A GREAT MAN

Eighth child of an eighth child, your wilful advent
   Means, as they say, more water in the stew.
Tell us: why did you choose this year and month
   And house to be born into?

Were you not scared by Malthusian arguments
   Proving it folly at least, almost a sin,
Even to poke your nose around the door –
   Much more, come strutting in?

Yet take this battered coral in proof of welcome.
    We offer (and this is surely what you expect)
Few toys, few treats, your own stool by the fire,
    Salutary neglect.

Watch the pot boil, invent a new steam-engine;
    Daub every wall with inspirational paint;
Cut a reed pipe, blow difficult music through it;
    Or become an infant saint.

We shall be too short-handed for interference
    While you keep calm and tidy and never brag –
But evade the sesquipedalian school-inspector
    With his muzzle and his bag.

TO MAGDALENA MULET, MARGITA MORA & LUCIA GRAVES

Fairies of the leaves and rain,
One from England, two from Spain,
You who flutter, as a rule,
At Aina Jansons' Ballet School,
O what joy to see you go
Dancing at the **Lírico**:
Pirouetting, swaying, leaping,
Twirling, whirling, softly creeping,
To a most exciting din
Of French horn and violin!

These three bouquets which I send you
Show how highly I commend you,
And not only praise the bright
Brisk performance of tonight
(Like the audience), but far more
The practising that went before.
You have triumphed at the cost
Of week-ends in the country lost,
Aching toes from brand-new points,
Aching muscles, aching joints,
Pictures missed and parties too,
And suppers getting cold for you
With homework propped beside the plate,

Which meant you had to sit up late.
From dawn to midnight fairies run
To please both Aina and the Nun.

THE PUMPKIN

You may not believe it, for hardly could I –
I was cutting a pumpkin to put in a pie,
And on it was written most careful and plain:
'You may hack me in slices, but I'll grow again.'

I hacked it and sliced it and made no mistake
As, with dough rounded over, I set it to bake:
But down in the garden when I chanced to walk,
Why, there was my pumpkin entire on the stalk!

MAX BEERBOHM AT RAPALLO

The happiest of exiles he, who shakes
No dust from either shoe, who gently takes
His leave, discards his opera hat, but stows
Oxford and London in twin portmanteaux,
To be unpacked with care and loving eyes
Under the clear blue of Ligurian skies,
And becomes guardian of such excellence
As cannot fade nor lose its virtue!
                                              Hence,
After their long experience of decay
And damage, which had sent all wits astray,
The rueful English to Rapallo went;
Where Max, unaltered by self-banishment
Welcomed them to his vine, then (over tea)
Taught them what once they were, and still might be.

THE GRANDFATHER'S COMPLAINT

A Broadsheet Ballad

When I was ten years old
   And Grandfather would complain
To me and my two brothers –
   Would angrily maintain:
That beer was not so hearty,
   Nor such good songs sung,
Nor bread baked so wholesome
   As when himself was young,
Nor youth so respectful,
   We made no contradiction,
Though Grandfather was mistaken –
   Or we held that conviction.

Now fifty years have passed,
   But when likewise I complain
To my three rude young grandsons,
   And angrily maintain
That beer is not so hearty,
   Nor such good songs sung,
Nor bread baked so wholesome
   As when myself was young,
Nor youth so respectful,
   I meet with contradiction –
Though with fact, and solid fact,
   To support my conviction.

You may call me a liar,
   Grandchildren, without fear ...
Yet ask your nearest brewer
   If he still brews honest beer,
Or ask your nearest baker
   If he still bakes honest bread,
Then come back here to-morrow
   To tell me what they said;
Or sing me whatever
   You may think is still a song,
And I'll make no contradiction
   But leave you in the wrong.

SONG: A BEACH IN SPAIN

Young wives enjoy the statutory right
To slam the door, whether by day or night;
Young husbands, too, are privileged to spend
Long hours in bars, each with a chosen friend.
But tell me can such independence prove
More than a simple lack of love,
More than a simple lack of love?
O how can you regain
Love lost on honeymoon in sunny Spain?

Or though the nuptial contract, that deters
Adulteresses and adulterers,
May sweetly mortalize the venial sin
Of beach flirtation after too much gin,
Can such experiments in marriage prove
More than a simple lack of love,
More than a simple lack of love?
O how can you regain
Love lost on honeymoon in sunny Spain?

And if your OPERATION JEALOUSY
Should end with corpses tossing in the sea,
Both of you having sworn in hell's despite
Never to panic or break off the fight,
Can such heroic beach-head battles prove
More than a simple lack of love,
More than a simple lack of love?
O how can you regain
Love lost on honeymoon in sunny Spain?

BATHUNTS AT BATHURST

*(Australian fantasy provoked by a Spanish
compositor's end-of-line hyphens)*

Bat-
hurst's famed bath-
unts are led uph-
ill by
   Swart bat-
   hat-
   tendants, bold Jehos-
   hop-
   hats,
Toph-
eavily toffed up in tall toph-
ats,
   Who, in the sooth-
   ung top-
   het (where bats fly),
Clutc-
hing bath-
andles with poth-
unting glee,
   Hoth-
   eadedly do lat-
   her bats with bats.

TO A CARICATURIST, WHO GOT ME WRONG

Every gentleman knows
Just when to wear the wrong clo'es,
And naturally that
Will include the wrong hat.
Merchants (the bright ones)
Always wear the right ones;
As do also those asses,
The professional classes.
Beggars have no choice,
Convicts no voice,
Cads and kings go dressed
Always in their best;

And as for me
In my dubious category
Which, yes,
You need hardly press,
I wear (or do not wear)
Whatever I dare,
Or whatever comes to hand,
Sometimes pretty grand,
Sometimes just so,
Sometimes scare-crow,
But was never seen to choose
Either sandals or suede shoes,
No, sir, not I –
Nor an Old Carthusian tie.

IN JORROCKS'S WAREHOUSE

One hundred years ago, hard-riding Mr Jorrocks
Came an almighty purler at a five-barred gate,
Lapsed into science-fiction, and forgot his date.

Afterwards, in the warehouse, superficially healed
With a pair of bloody steaks, vinegar and brown paper,
Jorrocks addressed Bob Dubbs, sportsman and linen-draper:

'At Jorrocks's Super-Logistical Universo Mart
Sales traffic has been canalized, as from today;
Watch out for the amber-light, buyers, and on your way!

'Follow the desired illuminated moving band –
I 10 for Marine Insurance, I 12 for Isotopes –
All goods displayed from Samoyedes to Edible Soaps.

'No supererogatory thank you, welcome, or goodbye.
Our assistants are deaf mutes, robots, zombies and such;
Your duty is to choose, point, pay and never touch.

'Goods found defective cannot, of course, be replaced –
See *Conditions of Jorrocks's Universo Mart.*
Customers are warned to realistically play their part.

'Band C 305 will convey them to *Complaints*,
If they find the stock we carry is not, in fact, their meat,
And a greasy slide will deposit them, bonk! in the street.'

Bob Dubbs the linen-draper listened in wide-eyed horror.
It made worse sense than the Reverend Silas Phipp's
Dominical Exegesis of the Apocalypse.

Though I could, no doubt, invent a whip-crack ending,
This simple moral, reader, should be enough for you:
'Never charge at a five-barred gate on a broken-winded screw.'

A FEVER

Where the room may be, I do not know.
It is beamed and parquetted,
With yew-logs charring on a broad hearth,
Curtains of taffeta, chairs of cherry,
And a rough wolfskin to lie at ease upon
Naked before the fire in half-darkness;
The shadowy bed behind.

Who she may be I do not know,
Nor do I know her nation.
She is truthful, she is tender,
In everything a woman, but for the claws:
Her skin moon-blanched, her arms lissom,
Her tawny tresses hanging free,
Her frown eloquent.

What we do together, that I know;
But when, eludes me;
Whether long ago, one night, or never ...
Meaning? Meaning in some recess of Time,
Untemporal yet sure ...
Why should it irk me? Now I must sleep –
She says so with her frown.

AUGEIAS AND I

Now like the cattle byre of Augeias
   My work-room, Hercules, calls for the flood
Of Alpheus and Peneius, green as glass,
   To hurtle down in catastrophic mood
And free me from accumulated piles
Of books, trays, journals, bulging letter-files.

In memory often, I remount the stairs
   To that top room where once a sugar-case
Served me for chair – the house was poor in chairs –
   A broken wash-stand lent me writing space,
And one wax-candle cast a meagre light;
Where all I wrote was what I itched to write.

Augeias, though, if he had dunged the trees,
   Cornland, and pot-herb garden studiously,
Would not have needed help from Hercules;
   We stand accused of careless husbandry
When nothing less than floods or cleansing fire
Can purge my work-room and his cattle byre.

IS IT PEACE?

'What peace,' came Jehu's answering yell,
'While Jezebel is Jezebel?' –
But when the hungry pariahs cease
To gnaw her bones, will that bring peace?

Why (harlot though she were, or worse)
Could he not leave her to God's curse?
Rather than pamper their unclean
Bellies with blood of a live queen?

Two wars, world wars. I lost in one
My cousins; in the next, a son –
That scarcely finished with, I heard
Dismal prognoses of a third.

Yet – since no signed memorial,
Nor bannered march, nor crowded hall
Our Jehus can, it seems, restrain
From bawling 'Jezebel!' again –

Unrealistically (or not?)
I cultivate my garden plot
Where peppers, corn and sea kale sprout
Careless of strontium fallout.

FINGERS IN THE NESTING BOX

My heart would be faithless
If ever I forgot
My farm-house adventure
One day by the fowl run
When Phoebe (of the fringe
And the fairy-story face)
Incited me to forage
Under speckled feathers
For the first time.

Fabulous I thought it,
Fabulous and fateful
(Before familiarity
With the fond pastime
My feelings blunted),
To clasp in frightened fingers
A firm, warm, round ...
'Phoebe, dear Phoebe,
What have I found?'

BARABBAS'S SUMMER LIST

Barabbas, once a publisher
But currently Prime Minister,
Writes – not of course in his own fist –
'May we include you in our List'
(Across the *Times* in glory spread
With Baths and Garters at its head)?
'Your graceful lyric work,' says he,
'Fully deserves a C.B.E.'

I ask my agents, Messrs. Watt,
Whether I should accept or not.
Few agents are so tough as these
At battling with Barabbases:
The mongoose in his cobra-war
Provides a perfect metaphor.
'Barabbas ought to raise his price
By five per cent,' is Watt's advice.

STABLE DOOR

Watch how my lank team-fellow strains
    Home up the last incline!
His joints creak, but his heart remains
    As obdurate as mine.

Our crib may well contain no feed,
    The skies may be our roof,
Yet should two foundered horses need
    To clack an angry hoof

In their death-dream of oats and hay,
    A dry, well-littered floor,
And Sam the ostler, whistling gay,
    Drunk by the stable door?

FLIGHT REPORT

To be in so few hours translated from
Picking blood-oranges, mandarins, mimosa,
Roses and violets in my Spanish garden,
Where almonds also bloom like old men's polls
And olive twigs bow under wrinkled berries –
To be in so few hours translated here
Three miles above the frantic, chill Atlantic,
Is something monstrous.

                      Tell me, how should I act?
Bored (as do my seasoned fellow-birds),
Recalling equally sensational flights
I have taken in my mind's own empyrean?
Or should I register rustic amaze?

The captain in his cockpit tilts the craft
To enchant us with what Coleridge never saw:
An iceberg, towering up from grey pack ice,
Through which the sun, whose dawn we long delayed,
Shines green as emerald – or greener, even.

Fasten your belts! And down we drop at Gander,
In a snowstorm, among firs of Newfoundland,
Then battle against head-winds five hours more
To New York, is it?

                And this all began
Monstrously at a Barcelona counter
Where a suave clerk, his mind on smaller things,
Sold me my round-trip-ticket, with disdain
Checking the banknotes as I paid them out,
And grudged me even a formal *bon voyage!*

SCHOOL HYMN FOR ST TRINIAN'S

Allegro   Come, playmates, lift your girlish hands
                    In prayer to sweet St Trinian.
              With eyes like fiery brands, he stands –
                    Cleft hoof and bat-like pinion!
              He fosters all your little deeds
                    Of maidenly unkindness;
              His foul intentions flower like weeds;
                    He smites the Staff with blindness.
              With ink and stink-bomb be content,
                    Likewise the classroom rocket,
              His more conventional armament.
                    (An H-bomb bags the pocket.)

                    CHORUS
Maestoso   *Learning to be a be-utiful lay-aydee*
                    You can if you try;
              Learning to be a be-utiful lay-aydee
                    In the sweet by - and - by.

1960–1974

A PIEBALD'S TAIL

Fame is the tail of Pegasus
    (A piebald horse with wings),
One thought of which away will twitch
    The luck his colour brings.

It follows logically, of course,
    That poets always fail
Who try to catch their piebald horse
    By snatching at his tail.

THE INTRUDERS

I ask the young daughter
Of Jetto, a painter,
(Disclosing three faces,
Two bold and one fainter,
On Jetto's *Moon Chart*):
How dare these scapegraces,
These odd bodikins,
Who would once hide their grins
Among wall-paper roses
Or carved lambrequins,
Flaunt pantomime noses
And Carnival chins
In abstractionist art?

But Jetto's young daughter
Has drawn me apart
And pleads for the faces:
'Don't show them to Father!
He'll turn black as thunder
To see their grimaces –
He'll bury them under
Whole tubefuls of madder,
He'll widow my heart.'

TEIRESIAS

Courtship of beasts
And courtship of birds:
How delightful to witness
In fullness of Spring
When swallows fly madly
In chase of each other,
Prairie-dogs tumble,
Wild ponies cavort,
And the bower-bird proffers
Spectacular gifts
To the hen of his choice!

But as for the stark act
That consummates courtship:
Are not dusky rock-caverns
And desolate fastnesses,
Tangle of jungle
And blackness of night,
The refuges chosen
By all honest creatures
That pricked by love's arrow
Perform the said act?

Then despite curs or roosters,
Bulls, ganders or houseflies,
Or troops in sacked cities
Forgetful of shame,
It is surely a duty
Entailed in our beasthood
To turn and go dumbly
Averting the eye,
Should we blunder on lovers
Well couched in a forest
Who thought themselves free?

Courtship of beasts
And courtship of birds:
How delightful to witness
In fullness of Spring!
But be warned by Teiresias,
Thebes' elder prophet,
Who saw two snakes coupling
And crept up behind.
He for six years or seven
Was robbed of his manhood
But feigned to care nothing
And ended stark blind.

SONG: THE SMILE OF EVE

Her beauty shall blind you,
    Long as you live;
She will reap and grind you,
    Bolt you in a sieve,

Will blink her merry eyes,
    Set your brain a-fire,
Be womanly and wise,
    Thwart your desire.

Will trample you, skin you,
    Tear your flesh apart,
Slice nerve and sinew,
    Nestle at your heart.

Though her aspect alters
    Your pangs are the same;
Ready reason falters
    At sound of her name.

No serpent in his guile
    Nor no goatish man
Can rob her of the smile
    That with Eve began.

[VERSE COMPOSED OVER THE TELEPHONE]

Bullfight critics ranked in rows
    Crowd the enormous Plaza full;
But only one is there who *knows*
    And he's the man who fights the bull.

[FIR AND YEW]

Fir, womb of silver pain,
Yew, tomb of leaden grief –
Viragoes of one vein,
Alike in leaf –
With arms up-flung
Taunt us in the same tongue:
'Here Jove's own coffin-cradle swung'.

SONG: GARDENS CLOSE AT DUSK

City parks and gardens close
    Before day has ended,
To discourage crime for which
    They were not intended.

Yet when moonlight lawns resume
    The private peace they merit,
Why are boys and girls in love
    Told they may not share it?

[PRIVACY]

Privacy finds herself a nook
In bold print of an open book
Which few have eyes to read; the rest
(If studiously inclined) will look
For cypher or for palimpsest.

MATADOR GORED

A breeze fluttered the cape and you were caught:
One thrust under your jaw, one in the belly,
A third clean through the groin. Nevertheless,
As you lie stretched on the familiar slab
Comfort yourself by swearing to live on
In bloody vengeance on all bulls. It is
The heifer's horns that defy surgery.

CONFITEOR UT FAS

Alienae civitates
Quas inspexit voster vates,
Etsi tanto procul jacent,
Non tantum regresso placent
Quam (confiteor, ut fas)
Mitis Universitas
De qua nusquam linguae tacent,
Qua dicendi libertas.

NEW MOON THROUGH GLASS

I shall wrap myself in a many-coloured cloak
Where the moon shines new on Castle Crystal,
But make no boast of a passage forced
Through red flames, choking blizzard and black fog.
The extremest courtesy of love is silence.

DYNAMITE BARBEE

Dynamite Barbee, no clo'es on,
Rode on a lion whose name was John –
Dynamite Barbee, no! man, no!
She'll make trouble wherever she go.
'Short life only and a long time dead,
Got to be practical,' Barbee said.

Judged old lion was nigh to death,
Changed to a jackal, corpse on his breath –
Stink of corpse on her hands and hair,
Dynamite Barbee, she don't care:
'Short life only and a long time dead,
Got to be practical,' Barbee said.

Dynamite Barbee never got rich –
Things she done for that son of a bitch!
Pawned her ear-rings, pawned her fur,
And big gold watch that Lion gave her:
'Short life only and a long time dead,
Got to be practical,' Barbee said.

Sunk to the bottom, we guessed she would:
Three times down and she's gone for good.
Dynamite Barbee, no! man, no!
That mean jackal never let her go –
'Short life only and a long time dead,
Got to be practical,' Barbee said.

WHEN A NECKLACE BREAKS

Two lovers sat together under a tree
When suddenly he spoke in a loveless voice –
She answered him as a true woman should,
And the dog howled at their feet.

When a necklace breaks and the beads spill,
Bouncing and rolling across the parquet floor
That is no fatal sign, only a warning
To gather, count, rethread.

Common danger can knit together in love
Almost any desperate human pair;
But the danger gone, they will part silently,
To forget each other's names.

You are good, you are indeed a good sword,
True steel welded and tempered without flaw,
Fit only for a King at his coronation –
Must my scabbard wear a worse?

Up rose the sun, blazing in at the window:
If you honour me as you say, why do you spend
All night in talk and, at my first appearance
Sleep almost till I set?

A QUEEN

Let other women wrangle with their dooms,
A queen is doomed to self-sufficiency;
Shown herself at whatever age she will,
Tempestuous child, grand lady, gruesome hag,
Shifting her mask and dress continually;
Scatters benignant smiles on common folk
Who neither envy or impugn her powers;
Scoffs at all vauntings of nobility;
Summons to table jugglers, cardinals,
Assassins, dancing women, generals,
From whom she learns resource of policy;
And scars her chosen lover's innocent breast
With wounds that testify her royalty.

IF LOVE BECOMES A GAME

If love becomes a game the sweet young fool,
    Now both player and prize,
Learns to resist a gentlemanly rule,
    Against unsporting lies,

That draws her far-from-ladylike attack
    When, as a last resort,
She's kicked the table down, scattered the pack
    And turned to other sport –

To sport, alas, with some gay gambling boy
    Who, judging it no sin
Her sweet, young, foolish licence to enjoy,
    Can never help but win.

QUEEN SILVER AND KING GOLD

Queen Silver and King Gold for untold years
Held planetary sway
Over such common clay
As led its life in eulogy of theirs –

And are still fawned upon even today,
By Voucher, most astute of Ministers
With Town, Court, Bourse and Army in his pay,
Who, if he had his way …

LEARN THAT BY HEART

If there's a poem in this book
    To which I've put my name
And Teacher growls: 'Learn that by heart!',
    Don't let *me* bear the blame.

Tell Teacher there are certain things
    No one should ever do –
Say that I write to please myself,
    Not just to torture you.

Press Teacher's nose against the wall,
    Try not to seem unkind,
But say: 'Stop there till he forgives
    The deed you had in mind.'

SONG: ONE IN MANY

To be loved by many and to love many
Is never to die, is to live purely,
Never to lack for noble company;

But to be loved by many, and to love many
Is to be singled out by one only,
Of all those many, who can love truly.

'My doors are barred, my blinds are drawn; for surely
This is the end of love. I loved her wholly –
Now she is lost to me among the many.'

What! In despair for one whom you loved wholly,
You who love many and are loved by many,
Have you no eyes for her who lives purely,

With eyes unhooded, with no hate nor envy,
Singling you out to love wholly and surely
Nor ever lacks for noble company?

A LATE DAFFODIL FOR THE PRINCE OF GWYNEDD

Thrice fortunate is he who winneth
As heir to Maelgwyn Pendragon
Grand welcome at the heart of Gwynedd:
Setting his princely feet upon
Those golden streets of Sinadon
And guarded against evil will
By Dewi Sant's own daffodil.

1999

These are the good old days: appreciate them!
Hope has been lost, of course, but don't forget
We're still three to a bunk, beer is still drunk,
And ten bob buys a genuine cigarette.

ANGRY GARDENER

Gentle wild flowers, each with its own strange, twisting,
Graceful habit of growth and innocent aspect,
Find careless welcome to waste garden-corners.
Yet should some honey-gathering go-between
Dare to inaugurate miscegenation
On your parterres or even in waste-corners,
With what blind rage you tear the bastards out!

SONG: WEATHER

What rules the weather for your lover
Is neither wind nor rain nor mist;
Nor does his private climate alter,
Since the proud night when first you kissed;
For still the pulsing of his blood –
Young manhood awed by womanhood –
Makes love his weather-vane and weather
With neither wind, nor rain, nor mist.

FIERY ORCHARD

Will she ever need to fetch him home again
To man's beginnings, to that fiery orchard
Where frantic Adam lost himself in Eve?
Once in distress they drew together there,
Gasping, confused and blind,
Clasping and clasped in desperate make-believe;
Yet rose entire, each with a whole mind.

DEFEAT OF TIME

The omens being less than sympathetic,
    Love had recourse to its own magic
For the defeat of time.

This consummation (Love ruled briefly)
    Lies beyond all denial where both hearts burn
As in a single body.

Whether in distant past or future
    Who cares? Together sealed
Beyond all temporal favour.

SIX BLANKETS

How long is love, or how short is love,
    And what's the length of a string?
Nothing to something and back to nothing
    And around a small gold ring.

But to you I shall never, alas, be wed
    Though long I may mourn for you:
Across your bed six blankets are spread
    And I choke under more than two.

THE NOTE

And though your hasty note be bare
But for the secret sign you use,
I need no more – the essential news
Being instantly deciphered there:
That still you laugh, dance, dream and live,
That all you gave me you still give.

THE HEDGEPIG

The letter that you wrote me in your head,
    Last week, arrived at last by pigeon post,
Crumpled and smudged, but legible. It read:
    'Of all my countless worries I hate most
Pretending that your tickly-prickly foe
Sends you his love … He died three weeks ago.'

The nightmare flew me to you. First I hovered
    Over your bed, then I dropped into the shed
Where, with a smile of triumph, I discovered
    That you were wrong. Your hedgepig was not dead,
But hibernating in that cosy ball
Which all fat hedgepigs use when the leaves fall.

WHEN HE SAT WRITING

(Song for Shakespeare's Birthday, 1972)

When Will sat forging plays with busy friends
    He wrote no worse than they;
When he sat writing for his loves, and us,
    Such play outshone all play –
    And still it does today.

Comparisons are foolish: love alone
    Established Shakespeare's fame.
There's many a poet, laurelled on a throne,
    For whom the critics claim
    A like poetic flame.

Reject all rivals, even those richly blessed
    With histrionic art …
For groundlings he might jest, like all the rest,
    But suffered grief apart
    Mourning with his whole heart.

FOUR POEMS FROM *DEYA: A PORTFOLIO* (1972)

[OURS HAS NO BEARING ON QUOTIDIAN LOVE]

Ours has no bearing on quotidian love
And indeed how could it, while we live above
Quotidian circumstance, fitfully meeting,
Communing fitfully? Nor is ours bound
Like other loves to any common ground.

This is no marriage, nor must ever be –
We were both born more than free,
But our discovery of togetherness
Earned us a weight of silence, our charmed eyes
Lost in astonishment at such excess.

Silence, love's discipline by night or day –
Each time we meet, the occasion calls for silence
As at some unbelievable coincidence,
And, unbelievably, tomorrow will be Sunday:
Silence all but mistakable for absence.

[LOVE MAKES POOR SENSE IN EITHER SPEECH OR LETTERS]

Love makes poor sense in either speech or letters:
Its final truth cannot be told with words,
Only with grave and lengthening silences –
Such as might greet discoveries of truth.

Why then should I fall sick if weeks elapse
Without even a hasty scrawl from you?
Does this denote some fault in me, or merely
A woman's freedom from the snares of time?

And if I ceased to write, would you still love me?

[IS THERE ANOTHER MAN?]

Is there another man
Can claim what you deny me?
Is there another man?
The letters that you write me
Come seldom and invite me
To love you while I can –
Is there another man?

If there's another man
For whom you guard your beauty,
If there's another man,
Send no more letters to me
With kisses to renew me –
What kisses ever can,
If there's another man?

Yet where's the other man
Who loves you for your virtue,
Or where's the other man
Whose kiss of life can cure you?
Then let your pulse assure you
That there's no other woman
With me for other man.

[CONFESS, SWEETHEART, CONFESS]

Confess, sweetheart, confess
You cannot marry me:
Ours is no wedlock nor could ever be,
Though both live more than free –
Our childish greeting of togetherness
Grown to this weight of magic: our charmed eyes
Lost in bewilderment at love's excess.

Nor can we ever become otherwise
Than what love on the hillside made of us:
We scanned each other with close eyes,
We read fateful togetherness:
The door, the key, the power,
The unfolding flower.

And still we brood, our fingers twitch,
Nor can we yet prognosticate
The climax of our fate –
The occasion when, the country which –
Determined only that this brooding season
Of timeless love, this tremulous obsession,
Has its own fateful reason.

THE NOOSE

This is my own clear voice:
Sweetheart, keep faith with me.
A noose hangs from the rope;
I do not bring blind hope
But love in certainty.
Choose, for you have no choice:
Sweetheart, stand fast by me.

THE MORAL LAW

The moral law, being male, need not apply
To a true-hearted woman, though its breach
By such a woman wounds the male pride
Even of a lover loyal and wise enough
To condone her innocence –
Then proudly let him differentiate
Between tormented flesh and troubled spirit,
Resigned to nothingness in her defence.

BODIES ENTRANCED

Where poems, love also;
Where love, likewise magic
With powers indomitable,
Powers inexpendable,
Seasoned in love.

Whence come all true poems,
Their power and their magic
Of two souls as one?
From slow recognition
Of bodies entranced.

Which entrancement of bodies
Will rise from no impulse
To blind propagation,
But claim recognition
Of truth beyond love.

WHO MUST IT BE?

And if I suddenly die, will she have killed me,
    And must the wide world know it,
Gasping at mention of her name,
    My fellow poet,
Therefore the first to blame?

The child who years ago had mercy on me,
    Dragging me from the briars,
Thrusting this pen back in my hand,
    Hugging me close
For Love to understand?

And if I live will it be she who saved me
    From the tiger and the bear,
A reckless child among tall trees
    Balm on her fingers,
Her warm heart at ease?

THIS IS THE SEASON

This is the season
Of useless hunger,
Of strengthened reason,
Of more than danger,
Of endless drought,
Which Death, the stranger,
Has brought about.

This is the ending
Of promised plenty,
Of docile standing
Before God's throne,
The Goddess hidden
Beyond man's midden,
Proud and alone.

UNCO

The unco-guid and unco-ordinated
Walk hand in hand, closely related,
Being from birth so fated.

UNPUBLISHED AND POSTHUMOUSLY PUBLISHED POEMS

A Selection

THE FIRST POEM

No, not for me the lute or lyre!
A knight, I'll ride my thoughts of fire
And fly on wings for ever and aye
Through an unresisting starry sky,
Where the gleaming aether turns and sings
Its strange slow song of the Birth of Things.
And I cry: 'Oh, if I had never known
The cares of this petty world! Alone,
Alone I'd fly, unfettered, free,
Through the Garden of God, Infinity.'
>   And there lie paths that none have trod
>   And none again shall tread,
>   But I alone, with Rapture shod
>   With Triumph garlanded –

NIGHTMARE

Oh, some warlock's spell has bound me,
Myriad torches flare around me.
The warlock's shroud,
A misty cloud,
Swims before me. Sudden, loud,
In my ear some creature cries,
Something flutters in my eyes.
Up stands my hair,
I clutch at air,

I must wake. It's the nightmare!
No, some warlock's spell has bound me,
Creatures hop around, around me,
Hop and scream – it is a dream.
Dream and Life like brothers seem.
I must make the holy sign:
Warlocks waste away and pine
At the sign – they waste and pine.
Are these fingers thine or mine?
Move, you fingers, do my will;
Mark the sign for good or ill,
On my breast the crosses make.
At the sign, they waste, they pine.
God be praised! I am awake.

THE DRAGON-FLY

Who'd drag the yet unopened lily-bud
   Slim stalk far-trailing, from the lake-floor up,
   To desecrate the gold and silver cup
With oozy slime and black befouling mud?

Not I, by Hera! Like the dragon-fly
   In blue and sable would I skim instead
   Where lap the waves around the lily-bed,
Desiring nought but only to be nigh.

BOY-MORALITY

I have apples in a very pleasant orchard
   But I may not eat thereof.
I have shining fish in a blue-watered lake:
They are easily taken in the meshes of a net,
   But their flesh is poison.
I have deer in a scented pine-forest
It is good sport hunting them with bows:
Their venison is tender as the flesh of young lambs,
   But whoso eateth, dyeth.

The load that I dragged uphill has slipped backward:
The rope has run scorching through my hands.
I must now return to the hill's very bottom,
And the toil upward will be harder than ever before.
When to this spot I have again dragged my burden,
I shall remember my former folly, and all that ensued.
I shall strengthen my heart with a high endeavour,
And with my hands shall I take a surer hold.

I have apples in a very pleasant orchard,
I have shining fish in a blue-watered lake,
I have deer in a pine-scented forest,
    But I may not eat lest I die.

THE CORACLE

The youngest poet launched his boat
    A wattle-laboured coracle,
He sang for joy to feel it float:
    'A miracle! A coracle!
I have launched a boat, I feel it float,
And all the waves cry miracle.

'I wrenched the wattles from their tree
    For the weaving of my coracle,
I thumped the slimy clay, and see!
    A miracle! A coracle!
I have built a boat, I feel it float,
And all the land cries miracle.

'With patient care her ribs I wove,
    My beautiful new coracle,
With clumsy fingers taught by love –
    A miracle, my coracle!
I have built a boat, I feel it float,
And all the air cries miracle.'

1915–1919

THE LAST DROP

The fires are heated, watch Old Age
 Crowd up to hear the torture-cry:
In sacrifice for private rage
 He has sentenced Youth to die.
But Youth in love with fire and smoke
 Hugs the hot coals to his heart,
And dies still laughing at the joke
 That his delight shall make Age smart.
A moral, gentle sirs, who stop
At home and fight to the last drop!
For look, Old Age weeps for the dead,
Shivers and coughs and howls 'Bread, Bread!'

TRENCH LIFE†

Fear never dies, much as we laugh at fear
 For pride's sake and for other cowards' sakes,
And when we see some new Death, bursting near,
 Rip those that laugh in pieces, God ! it shakes
Sham fortitude that went so proud at first,
 And stops the clack of mocking tongues awhile
Until (o pride, pride!) at the next shell-burst
 Cowards dare mock again and twist a smile.

Yet we who once, before we came to fight,
 Drowned our prosperity in a waste of grief,
Contrary now find such perverse delight
 In utter fear and misery, that Belief
Blossoms from mud, and under the rain's whips,
Flagellant-like we writhe with laughing lips.

THROUGH THE PERISCOPE†

Trench stinks of shallow-buried dead
    Where Tom stands at the periscope,
Tired out. After nine months he's shed
    All fear, all faith, all hate, all hope.

Sees with uninterested eye
    Beyond the barbed wire, a gay bed
Of scarlet poppies and the lie
    Of German trench behind that red: –

Six poplar trees … a rick … a pond
    A ruined hamlet and a mine …
More trees, more houses and beyond
    La Bassée spire in gold sunshine.

The same thoughts always haunt his brain,
    Two sad, one scarcely comforting,
First second third and then again
    The first and the second silly thing.

The first 'It's now nine months and more
    Since I've drunk British beer' the second
'The last few years of this mad war
    Will be the cushiest, I've reckoned'

The third 'The silly business is
    I'll only die in the next war,
Suppose by luck I get thro' this,
    Just 'cause I wasn't killed before.'

Quietly laughs, and at that token
    The first thought should come round again
But crack!
        The weary circle's broken
And a bullet tears thro' the tired brain.

MACHINE GUN FIRE: CAMBRIN
(September 25 1915)

The torn line wavers, breaks, and falls.
'Get up, come on!' the captain calls
'Get up, the Welsh, and on we go!'
(Christ, that my lads should fail me so!)
A dying boy grinned up and said:
'The whole damned company, sir; it's dead.'
'Come on! Cowards!' bawled the captain, then
Fell killed, among his writhing men.

THE FUSILIER – (For Peter)

I left the heated mess-room, the drinkers and the cardplayers
My jolly brother officers all laughing and drinking
And giving them goodnight, I shut the door behind me
Stepped quickly past the corner and came upon the wind.
A strong wind a steady wind a cool wind was blowing
And flowed like a waterflood about the steamy windows
And washed against my face, and bore on me refreshfully:
Its good to step out into the beautiful wind!
But giving goodnight to that gallant hearty company
And walking all alone through the greyness of evening
The sparkle of wine and the quick fire went out of me
My gay whistle faded and left me heavy hearted
Remembering the last time I'd seen you and talked with you –
(Its seldom the Fusilier goes twice across the parapet
Twice across the parapet, returning safe again)
    Yet Life's the heated messroom and when I go under
That cool wind will blow away the Fusilier, the furious
The callous rough ribald-tongue the Fusilier captain
The gallant merry Fusilier that drank in the messroom
He'll drain his glass, nod good-night and out into the wind,
While the quiet one the poet the lover remaining
Will meet you little singer and go with you and keep you
And turn away bad women and spill the cup of poison
And fill your heart with beauty and teach you to love.
Forget, then, the Fusilier: you'll never understand him,
You'll never love a Regiment as he has learned to love one
Forget the Fusilier: there are others will remember him
In the jolly old mess-room, the pleasant idle messroom
But for you let the strong sea wind blow him away.

O

What is that colour on the sky
   Remotely hinting long-ago,
That splendid apricot-silver? Why,
   That was the colour of my 'O' –
It's strange I can't forget –
In my first alphabet.

TO MY UNBORN SON†

A Dream

Last night, my son, your pretty mother came
Bravely into the forest of my dreams:
I laughed, and sprang to her with feet of flame,
And kissed her on the lips: how queer it seems
That the first power of woman-love should leap
So sudden on a grown man in his sleep!

She smiled, and kissed me back, a lovely thing
Of slender limbs and yellow braided hair:
She set my slow heart madly fluttering,
Her silver beauty through the shadowed air.
But oh, I wish she'd told me at first sight,
Why she was breaking on my dreams last night!

For tears to kisses suddenly succeeded,
And she was pleading, pleading, son, for you:
'Oh, let me have my little child,' she pleaded,
'Give me my child, as you alone can do.'
And, oh, it hurt me, turning a deaf ear,
To say 'No, no!' and 'No, no, no!' to her.

I was most violent, I was much afraid
She'd buy my freedom with a kiss or curl,
And when she saw she'd die a sad old maid,
She wept most piteously, poor pretty girl –
But still, if Day, recalling Night's romance
Should write a sequel, child, you've got a chance.

RETURN

'Farewell,' the Corporal cried, 'La Bassée trenches!
No Cambrins for me now, no more Givenchies,
And no more bloody brickstacks – God Almighty,
I'm back again at last to dear old Blighty.'

But cushy wounds don't last a man too long,
And now, poor lad, he sings this bitter song:
'Back to La Bassée, to the same old hell,
Givenchy, Cuinchey, Cambrin, Loos, Vermelles.'

THE SAVAGE STORY OF CARDONETTE†

To Cardonette, to Cardonette,
    Back from the Marne the Bosches came
With hearts like lead, with feet that bled
    To Cardonette in the morning.

They hurry fast through Cardonette:
    No time to stop or ask the name,
No time to loot or rape or shoot
    In Cardonette this morning.

They hurry fast through Cardonette,
    But close behind with eyes of flame
The Turco steals upon their heels
    Through Cardonette in the morning.

And half a mile from Cardonette
    He caught those Bosches tired and lame,
He charged and broke their ranks like smoke
    By Cardonette in the morning.

At Cardonette, at Cardonette,
    He taught the Bosche a pretty game:
He cut off their ears for souvenirs
    At Cardonette in the morning.

DIED OF WOUNDS†

And so they marked me dead, the day
That I turned twenty-one?
They counted me as dead, did they,
The day my childhood slipped away
And manhood was begun?
Oh, that was fit and that was right!
Now, Daddy Time, with all your spite,
Buffet me how you can,
You'll never make a man of me
For I lie dead in Picardy,
Rather than grow to man.
Oh that was the right day to die
The twenty-fourth day of July!
God smiled
Beguiled
By a wish so wild,
And let me always stay a child.

SIX POEMS FROM 'THE PATCHWORK FLAG' (1918)

FOREWORD†

Here is a patchwork lately made
Of antique silk and flower-brocade
Old faded scraps in memory rich
Sewn each to each with featherstitch.
But when you stare aghast perhaps
At certain muddied khaki scraps
And trophy fragments of field-grey
Clotted and stained that shout dismay
At broidered birds and silken flowers;
Blame these black times: their fault, not ours.

LETTER TO S.S. FROM BRYN-Y-PIN

Poor Fusilier aggrieved with fate
That lets you lag in France so late,
When all our friends of two years past
Are free of trench and wire at last
Dear lads, one way or the other done
With grim-eyed War and homeward gone
Crippled with wounds or daft or blind,
Or leaving their dead clay behind,
Where still you linger, lone and drear,
Last of the flock, poor Fusilier.
Now your brief letters home pretend
Anger and scorn that this false friend
This fickle Robert whom you knew
To writhe once, tortured just like you,
By world-pain and bound impotence
Against all Europe's evil sense
Now snugly lurks at home to nurse
His wounds without complaint, and worse
Preaches 'The Bayonet' to Cadets
On a Welsh hill-side, grins, forgets.
That now he rhymes of trivial things
Children, true love and robins' wings
Using his tender nursery trick.
Though hourly yet confused and sick
From those foul shell-holes drenched in gas
The stumbling shades to Lethe pass –
'*Guilty*' I plead and by that token
Confess my haughty spirit broken
And my pride gone; now the least chance
Of backward thought begins a dance
Of marionettes that jerk cold fear
Against my sick mind: either ear
Rings with dark cries, my frightened nose
Smells gas in scent of hay or rose,
I quake dumb horror, till again
I view that dread La Bassée plain
Drifted with smoke and groaning under
The echoing strokes of rival thunder
That crush surrender from me now.
Twelve months ago, on an oak bough
I hung, absolved of further task,
My dinted helmet, my gas mask,

My torn trench tunic with grim scars
Of war; so tamed the wrath of Mars
With votive gifts and one short prayer.
'Spare me! Let me forget, O spare!'
'*Guilty*' I've no excuse to give
While in such cushioned ease I live
With Nancy and fresh flowers of June
And poetry and my young platoon,
Daring how seldom search behind
In those back cupboards of my mind
Where lurk the bogeys of old fear,
To think of you, to feel you near
By our old bond, poor Fusilier.

NIGHT MARCH†

Evening: beneath tall poplar trees
    We soldiers eat and smoke and sprawl,
Write letters home, enjoy our ease,
    When suddenly comes a ringing call.

'Fall in!' A stir, and up we jump,
    Fold the love letter, drain the cup,
We toss away the Woodbine stump,
    Snatch at the pack and jerk it up.

Soon with a roaring song we start,
    Clattering along a cobbled road,
The foot beats quickly like the heart,
    And shoulders laugh beneath their load.

Where are we marching? No one knows,
    Why are we marching? No one cares.
For every man follows his nose,
    Towards the gay West where sunset flares.

An hour's march: we halt: forward again,
    Wheeling down a small road through trees.
Curses and stumbling: puddled rain
    Shines dimly, splashes feet and knees.

Silence, disquiet: from those trees
    Far off a spirit of evil howls.
'Down to the Somme' wail the banshees
    With the long mournful voice of owls.

The trees are sleeping, their souls gone,
    But in this time of slumbrous trance
Old demons of the night take on
    Their windy foliage, shudder and dance.

Out now: the land is bare and wide,
    A grey sky presses overhead.
Down to the Somme! In fields beside
    Our tramping column march the dead.

Our comrades who at Festubert
    And Loos and Ypres lost their lives,
In dawn attacks, in noonday glare,
    On dark patrols from sudden knives.

Like us they carry packs, they march
    In fours, they sling their rifles too,
But long ago they've passed the arch
    Of death where we must yet pass through.

Seven miles: we halt awhile, then on!
    I curse beneath my burdening pack
Like Sinbad when with sigh and groan
    He bore the old man on his back.

A big moon shines across the road,
    Ten miles: we halt: now on again
Drowsily marching; the sharp goad
    Blunts to a dumb and sullen pain.

A man falls out: we others go
    Ungrudging on, but our quick pace
Full of hope once, grows dull, and slow:
    No talk: nowhere a smiling face.

Above us glares the unwinking moon,
    Beside us march the silent dead:
My train of thought runs mazy, soon
    Curious fragments crowd my head.

I puzzle old things learned at school,
　　Half riddles, answerless, yet intense,
A date, an algebraic rule,
　　A bar of music with no sense.

We win the fifteenth mile by strength
　　'Halt!' the men fall, and where they fall,
Sleep. 'On!' the road uncoils its length;
　　Hamlets and towns we pass them all.

False dawn declares night nearly gone:
　　We win the twentieth mile by theft.
We're charmed together, hounded on,
　　By the strong beat of left, right, left.

Pale skies and hunger: drizzled rain:
　　The men with stout hearts help the weak,
Add a new rifle to their pain
　　Of shoulder, stride on, never speak.

We win the twenty-third by pride:
　　My neighbour's face is chalky white.
Red dawn: a mocking voice inside
　　'New every morning', 'Fight the good fight'.

Now at the top of a rounded hill
　　We see brick buildings and church spires.
Nearer they loom and nearer, till
　　We know the billet of our desires.

Here the march ends, somehow we know.
　　The step quickens, the rifles rise
To attention: up the hill we go
　　Shamming new vigour for French eyes.

So now most cheerily we step down
　　The street, scarcely withholding tears
Of weariness: so stir the town
　　With all the triumph of Fusiliers.

Breakfast to cook, billets to find,
　　Scrub up and wash (down comes the rain),
And the dark thought in every mind
　　'To-night they'll march us on again.'

POETIC INJUSTICE†

A Scottish fighting man whose wife
    Turned false and tempted his best friend,
Finding no future need for life
    Resolved he'd win a famous end.

Bayonet and bomb this wild man took,
    And Death in every shell-hole sought,
Yet there Death only made him hook
    To dangle bait that others caught.

A hundred German wives soon owed
    Their widows' weeds to this one man
Who also guided down Death's road
    Scores of the Scots of his own clan.

Seventeen wounds he got in all
    And jingling medals four or five.
Often in trenches at night-fall
    He was the one man left alive.

But fickle wife and paramour
    Were strangely visited from above,
Were lightning-struck at their own door
    About the third week of their love.

'Well, well' you say, 'man wife and friend
    Ended as quits' but I say not:
While that false pair met a clean end
    Without remorse, how fares the Scot?

THE SURVIVOR COMES HOME†

Despair and doubt in the blood:
Autumn, a smell rotten-sweet:
What stirs in the drenching wood?
What drags at my heart, my feet?
What stirs in the wood?

Nothing stirs, nothing cries.
Run weasel, cry bird for me,
Comfort my ears, soothe my eyes!
Horror on ground, over tree!
Nothing calls, nothing flies.

Once in a blasted wood,
A shrieking fevered waste,
We jeered at Death where he stood:
I jeered, I too had a taste
Of Death in the wood.

Am I alive and the rest
Dead, all dead? sweet friends
With the sun they have journeyed west;
For me now night never ends,
A night without rest.

Death, your revenge is ripe.
Spare me! but can Death spare?
Must I leap, howl to your pipe
Because I denied you there?
Your vengeance is ripe.

Death, ay, terror of Death:
If I laughed at you, scorned you, now
You flash in my eyes, choke my breath ...
'Safe home.' Safe? Twig and bough
Drip, drip, drip with Death!

THE PUDDING

'Eat your pudding Alexander.'
''Tis too sour to eat.'
'Take it quickly, Alexander.'
'Now 'tis far too sweet.'
And now 'tis thin and slippy-sloppy
And now 'tis tough as leather,
Now too hot and now too cold,
And now 'tis all together.

MOTHER'S SONG IN WINTER

The cat is by the fire,
    The dog is on the mat:
The dog has his desire,
    So also has the cat.
The cat is white
    The dog is black,
The year's delight
    Will soon come back.
The kettle sings, the loud bell rings
And fast my baby clings.

TO JEAN AND JOHN

What shall we offer you, Jean and John?
The softest pillows to sleep upon,
The happiest house in the whole of Wales,
Poodle puppies with wingle tails,
Caldicott pictures, coloured toys
The best ever made for girls or boys
Plenty to drink, plenty to eat
A big green garden with flowers complete
A kind Scotch nurse, a Father and Mother
Doesn't this tempt you?
                            All right, don't bother.

1920s–1930s

FROM AN UPPER WINDOW

Dark knoll, where distant furrows end
In rocks beyond the river-bend,
    I make my visionary stand
    In your secure well-wooded land
Where idle paths of idle fancy tend.

The charts that threaten all things free
With bondage of geography
    That loop you with a road way round
    Or pin you to some parish bound
Cannot withdraw your loveliness from me.

Nor though I went with hound and stick
With compass and arithmetic
    To gain myself a closer view
    Could I in space come up with you
Your glades with moving shades and colours quick.

You are remote in space and time
As inenarrable in rhyme,
    Yet by this very rareness doubt
    That you are you is blotted out –
Hill of green hopes with slopes no foot may climb.

DRINK AND FEVER

In fever the mind leaps three paces forward;
In drink the mind draws back the same three paces.

It turns about and sees the face twitching;
Stares ahead and sees the back stiffening.

It hears the voice auguring monstrously;
Hears the voice arguing meticulously.

Man is located then as man sleep-walking
Midmost between delirious and drunken.

So drink and fever touch and are combined
In the clear space where should be man's mind.

VESTRY

My parents were debtors,
And flung out of doors,
My brothers were eunuchs,
My sisters were whores;
If I tell the whole story,
You'll laugh till you cry,
That I am what I am
None knows better than I.

My breath smelt of garlic,
My body was lean,
My lovelocks were lousy,
My garments not clean;
When I strolled in the desert
Or dozed by the sea,
There was no one gainsaid me
In all Galilee.

I was all things to all men
But death to the rich;
I coaxed the dung-fire
And made cakes in the ditch;
My proverbs came pat,
And my features were flame,
And I paid the tax-penny
When quarter-day came.

I drove my disciples
With daily advice
About rubies and talents
And pearls of great price,
About laying up treasure
And profit and loss.
It was what my mind ran on
From manger to cross.

When my hearers went hungry
I bade them sit down,
And I fed them with fables
Of white bread and brown,
Of old wine and new wine,
Of herrings and salt;
And what happened after
Was never my fault.

THE END

Who can pretend
To spy to the very end
The ultimate confusion
Of belief and reason,
Perfection of all progress?
But I say, nevertheless:
That when instead of chairs
The altars of the martyrs
Are taken by philosophers
As vessels of reality;
When Cardinals devoutly
Canonize *in curia*
Some discarded formula
Of mad arithmetician
Or mad geometrician
Now seated in a swivel-chair
Widowed of its philosopher,
In that General Post
Down will come Pepper's Ghost
And proclaim Utopia,
The final synthesis,
With a cornucopia
And halitosis.

The dogs will bark,
The cats will cry,
And the Angel of Death go drumming by.

THE SAND GLASS

The sand-glass stands in frame both ways the same,
Single   broad   based;   but   so   enclosed   the   glass
Alters   in   action,   most   revengeful,   trickling
      Minute by minute, minute-minus-moment,
              By broken minute, nervous time,
                      Narrowing time,
                        Nearly time,
                          No time,
                           Time!
                          Upend,
                        Equilibrize
                  Eyes near maddened,
              Sand-roped nonsensically:
          Now sense, sight, sand, no nonsense.
Turn, suicide, from the wasp-waist, while time runs
A new five minutes: then view once more with calm
The   base   root-firm,   each   base,   solid   in   time.

THIS WHAT-I-MEAN

A close deduction about close deduction.
Or, starting at an earlier point than that
With any pavement-rainbow after rain,
First, the experience of an easy pleasure,
Then the close observation 'filmed with oil',
Then qualification of that easy pleasure,
Then close deduction about doubtful pleasure,
Then close deduction about close deduction.

How to outgo this vistaed close deduction,
To find if anything is behind or not?
If not, no matter; no matter either way.
We are not collecting worms for the Museum.

And we are not taking Cat's Cradle, say,
Beyond the ninth, or is it the nineteenth, stage,
The last stage that the oldest experts know.
(That would be physical and scientific,
A progress further into the same close vista)

And we are not leaping the unknown gap;
Any poor fugitive does that with razor
Or lysol as the spring-board, and he knows
One brink of the gap at least before he jumps.

This what-I-mean is searching out the gap
Under all closeness and improving on it
And the new gaps above and every which way,
Gradually loosening everything up
So nothing sticks to anything but itself –
A world of rice cooked Indian fashion
To be eaten with whatever sauce we please.

THE FINGERHOLD

He himself
Narrowed the rock shelf
To only two shoes' width,
And later by
A willing poverty
To half that width and breadth.

He shrank it then
By angry discipline
To a mere fingerhold,
Which was the occasion
Of his last confusion:
He was not so bold
As to let go
At last and throw
Himself on air that would uphold.

He wept
Self-pityingly and kept
That finger crooked and strained
Until almost
His life was lost
And death not gained.

THEN WHAT?

If I rise now and put my straw hat on
  Against the strong sun lying in wait outside
Scorching the flowers and over the flat stone
  Making the air dance – what? The prospect's wide:
The sea swimming to nowhere, the near hills
  Incredible of ascent and horned with crags,
The blank sky darted through with the sun's quills,
  The pleasant poplar grove where the eye drags.
Then what? The path curves to the gate, from which
  A dusty road curves to my neighbour's gate:
Stroll past it, pausing at the boundary ditch
  Then turn, slowly, as granting leave to fate
To exploit this chance in grossness of event,
Then what? Then gladly home with nothing spent.

HISTORICAL PARTICULARS

And if at last the anecdotal world
Records my name among ten million more
In the long-drawn-out story of itself
(O tediousness) and far from the last page? –
'English poet and miscellaneous writer,
Eccentric of the Later Christian era,
Sometime a subject of King George the Fifth,
(While the ninth, eighth and seventh Popes of Rome
Before the last were reigning). It was the time
Of the World War – he served throughout – the time
Of airships and top-hats and communism,
Passports and gangsters, breach of promise cases,
When coal was burned in grates and gold coin minted,
When radio was a novelty and horses
Still ran with vans about the city streets … '
And if with such quaint temporal statistics
They date me in their books and bury me,
Could I protest an honest alibi
Who dreamed ill dreams one night and woke, staring,
In those too populous and wealthy streets
And wandered there, as it were dreaming still,
Out at heels and my heart heavy in me,
And drank with strangers in the bright saloons
And gossiped there of politics and futures?

My alibi's the future: there I went
And in the idle records found my record,
And left my spectre fast between the pages
As a memorial and a mockery
Where they shall find it when they come to be.
And as I am, I am, the visit over.
What name, what truth? Unbiographical.
The fixity of one who has no spectre.
I learn slowly, but I may not wander.

ADDRESS TO SELF

Our loves are cloaked, our times are variable,
We keep our rooms and meet only at table.

But come, dear self, agree that you and I
Shall henceforth court each other's company

And bed in peace together now and fall
In loving discourse, as were natural,

With open heart and mind, both alike bent
On a just verdict, not on argument,

And hide no private longings, each from each,
And wear one livery and employ one speech.

I worked against you with my intellect,
You against me with folly and neglect,

Making a pact with flesh, the alien one:
Which brought me into strange confusion

For as mere flesh I spurned you, slow to see
This was to acknowledge flesh as part of me.

PROSPERITY OF POETS

Several instances in time occur
When, numbers reckoned, there appears a quorum
Sufficient to explain the way of the world
To the world, in plural singularity.
The agenda, often, has been mass conversion
From sin, often mass resort to reason,
Rarely poems, and then what an array
Of unrelated beauties marshalled!
Mutual indulgence, each to each,
Among these poets being the arbiter
Of what shall stand. The world, noting
A harmless literary renascence,
Snatches up certain poems (as a sample)
Where the indulgence has been strained
To exclude poetry and include world,
And flutes them under academic escort
To that Glass Palace where the Great consort.

1940s–1950s

DIOTIMA DEAD

Diotima's dead – how could she die?
Or what says Socrates, now she is dead?
Diotima's wisdom he might credit
While still she looked at him with eyes of love:
He could his life commit to Diotima,
Clear vessel of the Word's divinity,
Until she cloaked herself in deathward pride
And ruin courted by equivocation –
Did he not swear then, she had always lied?

Scholars, the truth was larger than herself.
The truth it was she had told Socrates
(Though peevish in her immortality
And starving for what meats the God forbade)
Until her vision clouded, her voice altered,
And two lives must have ended, had he stayed.

THE HEARTH

The cat purrs out because it must,
    So does the cricket call;
The crackling fire in which they trust
    Cares not for them at all.

Though cat-and-cricket-like we cry
    Around a fatal fire,
And give 'because we must' for 'why',
    As children of desire,

Care is our reading of that glow
    Which to repay is wise:
Who will not yet his distance know
    For his own folly fries.

IN THE LION HOUSE

That chance what traveller would not bless
    In midday glare to see
Lion and tawny lioness
    At lust beneath a tree?

Here, superannuated bones
    Of leathery bull or horse,
An ailing panther's muffled moans
    And Monday's dismal course –

Who would not turn his head aside
    From this connubial show
Of *Felis Leo* and his bride,
    Half-hearted, smug and slow?

AN APPEAL

Though I may seem a fool with money, Lord,
To spend and lend more than I can afford,
Why should my creditors and debtors scoff
When tearfully I urge them to pair off,
Yet booze together at one bar; and why
Should all sport newer coats and hats than I?

A GHOST FROM ARAKAN

He was not killed. The dream surprise
Sets tears of joy pricking your eyes.
        So cheated, you awake:
A castigation to accept
After twelve years in which you've kept
        Dry-eyed, for honour's sake.

His ghost, be sure, is watching here
To count each liberated tear
        And smile a crooked smile:
Still proud, still only twenty-four,
Stranded in his green jungle-war
        That's lasted all this while.

1960s–1970s

ROBIN AND MARIAN

He has one bowstring, and from the quiver takes
        An only shaft. Should Robin miss his aim
He cannot care whether that bowstring breaks,
        Being then undone and Sherwood put to shame.
Smile, Marian, smile: resolve all doubt,
Speed Robin's goosequill to the clout.

NEVER YET

For History's disagreeable sake
I could review the year and make
A long list of your cruelties
As they appear in the world's eyes
(And even, maybe, in your own),
Until it shamed me to have grown,
By culling so much strength therefrom,
The sagest fool in Christendom.
But what would the world think if I
Declared your love for me a lie,
Courting renown in my old age
As Christendom's least foolish sage?
Or if in anger, close to hate,
Your truth you dared repudiate –
A truth long fastened with a fine
Unbreakable red thread of mine –
And called what seemed a final curse
Upon the tottering universe?
Nothing can change us; you know this.
The never-yet of our first kiss
Prognosticated such intense
Perfection of coincidence.

TANKA

Apricot petals on the dark pool fallen
Tassel both flanks of a broken cane:
Our Poet Emperor himself extols them
In five brief lines confounding
All foolish commentary.

HOUSE ON FIRE

The crowd's heart is in the right place:
Everyone secretly backs a fire
Against massed murderous jets of water
Trained on a burning house by the city's hoses –
While he still swears it cannot spread to his.

THE LILAC FROCK

How I saw her last, let me tell you. I heard screams
In a dream, four times repeated. It was Grimaut Castle.
She wore a lilac frock, her diamond ring,
Gold beads and the dove brooch.

                                        'Escape!' she whispered.
'Emilio's mad again.'
                        He came from behind her
Flourishing a sharp Mexican machete.

Nonchalantly, I turned my back on him
And asked her: 'Could a young witch, taking the veil,
Count on the Mother Superior's connivance
If she kept a toad-familiar in her cell?'

She faltered: 'Yesterday I tried to join you –
I had even bought my ticket and packed my bags
But seeing a mist of sorrow cloud his eyes
How could I desert him? He had a painful boil.
I decided to eat beans with Emilio
Rather than suffer happiness with you …
So keep my paint box and my paint brushes,
I shall never have occasion to use them now:
Women born under Cancer lead hard lives.'

Sun blotted out sun, dogs howled, and a silver coffin
Went sailing past over the woods and hedges
With a dead girl inside. The man who saw it
Pointed in which direction the coffin flew,
Should I ever be drawn to pilgrimage.

DEPARTURE

With a hatchet, a clasp-knife and a bag of nails
He walked out boldly to meet the rising sun.
His step was resolute and his hair white.

Granted, death was lurking under that roof
And his funeral planned, down to the last speech.
But why not face it honourably, in comfort?

Neighbours looked glum, grandchildren whimpered.
'He has no right to leave us,' everyone said,
'He belongs here, our most familiar landmark.'

Visitors had flocked from a great distance
To inspect the forge and watch him tirelessly
Beating red-hot iron on his anvil.

It was hoped to keep it up, when he had died,
As a museum, with a small entrance fee,
And the grave, of course, would be refreshed with flowers.

Why did he defy them? And yet his bearing
Suggested no defiance – on the contrary,
He wore an innocent and engaging smile.

'I have given your own town back to you,'
Said he, 'though I had not thought myself the thief,
And with no choice but to start work elsewhere.'

NORTH SIDE

On the north side of every tree
  Snow clings and moss thrives;
The Sun himself can never see
  So much of women's lives;
But we who in this knowledge steer
Through pathless woods find the way clear.

A-

va Gardner brought me á
One winged angel yesterday
To kneel beside me when I pray
And guide me through the U.S.A. –
With one wing she won't fly away
Thank you, dearest Ava!

SONG: JOHN TRUELOVE

The surnames from our parents had
    Are seldom a close fit:
There's Matthew Good who's truly bad,
    And Dicky Dull's a wit.

There's Colonel Staid who's far from staid,
    There's glum old Farmer Bright
And Parson Bold who's much afraid
    Of burglars in the night.

So though my name be John Truelove,
    Take warning, maidens all,
I shall keep true to none of you
    Unless the worst befall.

REQUIREMENTS FOR A POEM†

Terse, Magyar, proud, all on its own,
Competing with itself alone,
Guiltless of greed
And winged by its own need.

THE ATOM

Within each atom lurks a sun,
Which if its host releases,
Opening a foolish mouth for fun,
The world must fly in pieces.

THE CUPID

A cupid with a crooked face
Peered into Laura's jewel-case:
'Emerald, diamond, ruby, moonstone,
Jacinth, agate, pearl, cornelian,
Red and black garnet, sapphire, beryl,
Topaz, amethyst and opal,
Pure rock-crystal.'

'These are hers, Cupid, for instruction
In love's variety, to have and hold.
No common glass intrudes among them
And all are set in gold.'

'But if she fails you?' asks the mannerless cupid.
'Will she return them? Will she sell them?
Will they be mine when sold?'

Dear God, how stupid can a cupid be,
Asking such mercenary questions of me?

OLIVES OF MARCH

Olives of March are large and blue, but few,
Peering like sapphires from the thick grass,
Yet none has ever known them to take root.

Pallas Athene sent an owl to wrench
A grey-green sprig from the sole Nubian stock:
Grafting it on an ancient oleaster
At her Acropolis, for distribution
Of olive-grafts by the Archimorius
To every city of Greece. Who dares neglect
An olive harvest must incur despair,
Starvation, haplessness and rootlessness.

THE UNDYING WORM

'The damned in their long drop from Earth to Hell,
    Meaning no fewer than ten thousand miles
At headlong speed – Hell may be nowhere
Yet friction of the fall causes rope-burns –
    Take only a few hours,' our verger smiles.

Return by Act of Mercy takes far longer
And though an angel's kiss is often praised
    As balm for penitents, you may be sure
That those red scars will glow again in sullen
    Resentment of their cure.

The damned are rendered down eventually
To clinker or a fine white ash. Yet what
   Of throats from which no cry of guilt is wrenched?
Can it be there that the worm dieth not
   And the fire is not quenched?

SONG: THOUGH TIME CONCEALS MUCH

Though time conceals much,
Though distance alters much,
Neither will ever part me
From you, or you from me,
However far we be.

So let your dreaming body
Naked, proud and lovely –
There is no other such,
So wholesome or so holy –
Accept my dream touch.

One kiss from you will surely
Amend and restore me
To what I still can be –
Though distance alters much,
Though time conceals much.

ALWAYS AND FOR EVER

Come, share this love again
Without question or pain,
Not only for a while
With quick hug and sweet smile
But always and for ever
In unabated fever
Without guess, without guile.

ACROSS THE GULF (1992)

THE SNAPPED ROPE†

When the rope snaps, when the long story's done
Not for you only but for everyone,
These praises will continue fresh and true
As ever, cruelly though the Goddess tricked you,
And lovers (it may be) will bless you for
Your blindness, grieved that you could praise no more.

THE GOLDSMITHS†

And yet the incommunicable sea
Proves less mysterious to you and me
Than how, through dream, we run together nightly
And hammer out gold cups in a dancing fury
Patterned with birds of prey, with tangled trees,
Lions, acanthus, wild anemones;
And that these cups are master-works is proved
By the deep furrows on our foreheads grooved;
And to sip wine from them is to be drunk
With powers of destiny, this mad world shrunk
To bean or walnut size, its ages flown
To enlarge the love-hour that remains our own.

ADAM IN HELL†

From the pit of Hell a whisper of pure love
Rises through crooked smoking crannies
To the lawns of Paradise.

Adam lies fettered by his basalt pillar:
A lodestone of male honour,
A moral for the damned.

So proud a lover, suffering no woman
To endure the torments that are his:
It was not Eve who sinned but the bright Serpent
Conspiring against man –
Tomorrow she will bruise her enemy's head
And raise up Adam from the loveless dead.

THE CARDS ARE WILD†

Tell me, how do you see me? Ring the changes
On father, lover, brother, friend and child –
A hand is dealt you, but the cards are wild.

You spoil me with a doubled span of years;
Having already overspent my due
Should I, or should I not, be grateful to you?

This cruel world grows crueller day by day,
And you more silent, more withdrawn and wise.
I watch its torments mirrored in your eyes –
Sweetheart, what must I say?
With you still here I dare not move away.

UNLESS†

Ink, pen, a random sheet of writing paper,
A falling inescapably in love
With you who long since fell in love with me …
But where is the poem, where my moving hand?

And if I am flung full length on a bed of thorns
How can I hope to retrieve lost memory,
Lost pride and lost motion,
Unless, defying the curse long laid upon me,
You prove the unmatchable courage of your kind?

THE POISED PEN†

Love, to be sure, endures for ever,
   Scorning the hour
That ends untimely in a hurried kiss
   And a breach of power.

Must I then sit here still, my pen poised
   As though in disgrace,
Plotting to draw strength from the single grief
   That we still dare face?

Or must I set my song of gratitude
   In a minor key,
To confess that you and I compound a truth
   That is yet to be?

[FRAGMENT]†

A smoothly rolling distant sea,
A broad well-laden olive tree,
A summer sky, gulls wheeling by
With raucous noise, and here sit I
For seven years, not yet set free.

[HOW IS IT A MAN DIES?]†

How is it a man dies
   Before his natural death?
He dies from telling lies
   To those who trusted him.
He dies from telling lies –
   With closed ears and shut eyes.

Or what prolongs men's lives
   Beyond their natural death?
It is their truth survives
   Treading remembered streets
Rallying frightened hearts
   In hordes of fugitives.

GREEN FLASH†

Watch now for a green flash, for the last moment
When the Sun plunges into sea;
And breathe no wish (most wishes are of weakness)
When green, Love's own heraldic tincture,
Leads in the mystagogues of Mother Night:
Owls, planets, dark oracular dreams.
Nightfall is not mere failure of daylight.

PEISINOË†

So too the Siren
Under her newly rounded moon
Metamorphoses naked men
To narwhale or to dolphin:
Fodder for long Leviathan
Or for his children
Deep in the caves of Ocean.

ACROSS THE GULF†

Beggars had starved at Dives' door
    But Lazarus his friend
Watched him lose hope, belayed a rope
    And flung him the loose end,
Sighing: 'Poor sinner, born to be
Proud, loveless, rich and Sadducee!'

TO HIS TEMPERATE MISTRESS†

You could not hope to love me more,
    Nor could I hope to love you less,
Both having often found before
    That I was cursed with such excess,
Even the cuckold's tragic part
Would never satisfy my heart.

FOOT-HOLDER-ROYAL†

As Court foot-holder to the Queen of Fishes
I claim prescriptive right
To press the royal instep when she wishes
And count her toes all night.
Some find me too assiduous in my task.
That is for her to say; they need but ask.

THE PRESSURE GAUGE†

Quoth the King of Poland
To his gipsy Roland:
'Wretch, go fetch my idle pages –
Ask them where my pressure-gauge is!'
Hurrah, hurrah, hurrah!

'Sire,' replied the gipsy,
'Thou art wondrous tipsy,
In these Polish Middle Ages
No one's heard of pressure-gauges – '
Hurrah, hurrah, hurrah!

INDEX OF TITLES

£. s. d.   704
1805   412
1915   20
1999   793

A   829
Above the Edge of Doom   562
Absent Crusader   693
Accomplice, The   649
Acrobats   526
Across the Gulf   836
Act V, Scene 5   321
Adam in Hell   833
Address to Self   823
Advent of Summer   720
Adventure, The   16
Advice from a Mother   669
Advice on May Day   435
Advice to Colonel Valentine   769
Advice to Lovers   72
Advocates   377
After the Flood   554
After the Play [The Forbidden Play]   65
After the Rain   734
Against Clock and Compasses   148
Against Kind   300
Against Witchcraft   626
Age Gap   692
Age of Certainty, The, *see* New Legends
Ageless Reason   686
Ages of Oath, The   381
Alabaster Throne, The   524
Alcaics Addressed to My Study Fauna   730
Alexander and Queen Janet [A Ballad of Alexander and
    Queen Janet]   471
Alice   217
Alice Jean, The   80
All Except Hannibal   609
All I Tell You From My Heart   556
Allansford Pursuit, The   418
Allie   73
Alphabet Calendar of Amergin, The, *see* Amergin's Charm

Always   676
Always and For Ever   832
'Am and Advance: A Cockney Study   727
Ambience   566
Ambrosia of Dionysus and Semele, The   530
Amergin's Charm [The Alphabet Calendar of Amergin]   419
Ample Garden, The   537
Anagrammagic [The Tow-Path]   306
Ancestors   269
Anchises to Aphrodite   506
Angry Gardener   793
Angry Samson [A False Report]   125
Ann at Highwood Hall   559
Antigonus: An Eclogue   190
Antinomies   183
Antorcha y Corona, 1968; Torch and Crown, 1968   631
Any Honest Housewife [The Poets]   364
Ape God, The   731
Apollo of the Physiologists   408
Appeal, An   826
Apple Island   499
Apples and Water   76
Ark, The   608
Armistice Day, 1918   633
Around the Mountain   484
Arrears of Moonlight   581
Arrow on the Vane   661
Arrow Shots   613
As a Less Than Robber   708
As All Must End   698
As It Were Poems, i, ii, iii   334
As When the Mystic   686
Assault Heroic', 'The   54
Assumption Day   767
Astymelusa   611
At Best, Poets   534
At First Sight   358
At Seventy-Two   600
At the Games   242
At the Gate   709
At the Savoy Chapel   413
At the Well   647
Atom, The   830
Attercop: The All-Wise Spider   182

Augeias and I 780
Avengers, The 148
Awakening, The 659
Awkward Gardener, The, *see* Gardener

Babylon 25
Back Door 305
Bait, The 755
Ballad of Alexander and Queen Janet, A, *see* Alexander and
   Queen Janet
Ballad of the White Monster, The 728
Baloo Loo for Jenny 79
Bank Account 536
Barabbas's Summer List 782
Bards, The [Lust in Song] 337
Bargain, The 754
Basket of Blossom (*Song*) 622
Bathunts at Bathurst 777
Battle of the Trees, The 422
Batxóca 563
Bay of Naples 323
Bazentin, 1916 741
Beach in Spain, A (Song) 776
Beach, The 399
Beacon, The 82
Beast, The, *see* Saint
Beast, The, *see* The Glutton
Beatrice and Dante 687
Beauty in Trouble 463
Bedpost, The 120
Beds of Grainne and Diarmuid, The 549
Beggar Maid and King Cophetua, The 609
Being Tall 357
Between Dark and Dark, *see* Sick Love
Between Hyssop and Axe 565
Between Moon and Moon 525
Between Trains 552
Beware, Madam! 525
Beyond Giving (*Song*) 618
Big Words 17
Bird of Paradise 540
Birth of a Goddess 687
Birth of a Great Man 772
Birth of Angels 586

Bites and Kisses   592
Bitter Thoughts on Receiving a Slice of Cordelia's Wedding
    Cake, *see* A Slice of Wedding Cake
Black   565
Black Goddess, The   550
Black Horse Lane   114
Blackening Sky   594
Blanket Charge   628
Blessed Sun   594
Blind Arrow, A   543
Blonde or Dark?   277
Blotted Copy-Book, The   459
Blow, The   569
Blue-Fly, The   454
Bodies Entranced   799
Boots and Bed   278
Bough of Nonsense, The   22
Bouquet from a Fellow Roseman, A   478
Bower-Bird   588
Bowl and Rim, The   156
Boy in Church, A   52
Boy-Morality   802
Boy out of Church, The   64
Bracelet, A   594
Breakfast Table   678
Briar Burners, The   736
Brief Reunion   641
Brittle Bones   75
Broken Compact   691
Broken Girth, The   527
Broken Neck   551
Brother   323
Burn It!   510
Burrs and Brambles   218

Cabbage Patch [Green Cabbage-Wit]   302
Call It a Good Marriage   482
Callow Captain   349
Cards Are Wild, The   834
Careers   26
Carol of Patience   656
Caroline and Charles, *see* Mike and Mandy
Casse-Noisette   663
Castle, The   303

Caterpillar, The   34
Cat-Goddesses   454
Catherine Drury   56
Catkind   490
Cell, The, *see* The Philosopher
Certain Mercies   347
Challenge, The   378
Change   564
Charm for Sound Sleeping, A   713
Cherries or Lilies (*Song*)   602
Cherry-Time   11
Child with Veteran   643
Child's Nightmare, A   50
Children of Darkness   125
China Plate, The   368
Chink, The   428
Christmas Eve   130
Christmas Robin, The [Wanderings of Christmas]   347
Circus Ring   685
Civil Servant, A   416
Clearing, The   466
Cliff and Wave   668
Cliff Edge, The   526
Climate of Thought, The   382
Clipped Stater, The   237
Cloak, The   371
Clock Man, The [The Clock Men]   344
Clock Men, The, *see* The Clock Man
Clocks of Time, The (*Song*)   621
Clothed in Silence, *see* Strangeness
Cock in Pullet's Feathers   581
Cold Weather Proverb   405
College Debate, The   229
Colophon   694
Colours of Night, The   552
Come, Enjoy Your Sunday! (*Song*)   511
Commons of Sleep, The   344
Compact   620
Complaint and Reply   671
Confess, Marpessa   674
[Confess, sweetheart, confess]   797
Confiteor Ut Fas   788
Conjunction   576
Considine   771

Consortium of Stones 550
Conversation Piece 434
Cool Web, The 283
Coracle, The 803
Coral Pool, The 473
Corner Knot, The 270
Coronation Address 462
Coronation Murder, The 117
Coronet of Moonlight 680
Corporal Stare 53
Cottage, The 36
Counting the Beats 429
Country at War 94
Country Dance, The 267
Country Mansion, A 374
Court of Love, A 565
Co-Walker, The, *see* My Ghost
Crab-Tree, The 667
Cracking the Nut Against the Hammer, *see* Tap Room
Crane, The 598
Crown of Stars (*Song*) 602
Crucibles of Love 716
Cruel Moon, The 34
Crusader, A 152
Cry Faugh! 447
Crystal, The 713
Cuirassiers of the Frontier, The 348
Cupboard, The 82
Cupid, The 830
Cure, The 503
Cyclone, The 731
Cynics and Romantics 747

Damocles 441
Dance of Words 542
Dancing Flame 585
Dancing Green, The 743
Danegeld 341
Dangerous Gift, The 507
Dans un Seul Lit 605
Darien 438
Dawn Bombardment 390
Day in February, A 733
Dazzle of Darkness 538

De Arte Poetica	610
Dead Boche, A	27
Dead Cow Farm	32
Dead Fox Hunter, The	18
Dead Hand	581
Dead Ship, The, *see* The Furious Voyage	
Death by Drums	401
Death Grapple, The	501
Death of the Farmer [The Figure-Head]	221
Death Room, The	430
Dedication of Three Hats, A	268
Dedicatory	155
Dedicatory, *see* The Hoopoe Tells Us How	
Deed of Gift	534
Defeat of the Rebels	365
Defeat of Time	794
Deliverance	576
Departure	828
Depth of Love	678
Descent into Hell	579
Desert Fringe	677
Despite and Still	394
Destroyer, The	426
Destruction of Evidence	476
Dethronement	453
Devil at Berry Pomeroy, The	452
Devil's Advice to Story-Tellers, The	354
Devilishly Disturbed, *see* Devilishly Provoked	
Devilishly Provoked [Devilishly Disturbed]	331
Dew-drop and Diamond (*Song*)	603
Dewdrop, A	161
Dialecticians, The [The Philosophers]	127
Dialogue on the Headland	448
Dichetal do Chennaib	421
Dicky	62
Died of Wounds	809
Dilemma, The	442
Dilemma, The	687
Diotima Dead	824
Diplomatic Relations [George II and the Chinese Emperor]	174
Discarded Love Poem, The	703
Dismissal	298
Distant Smoke	106
Diversions	224

Door, The   400
Double Bass   579
Double Red Daisies   45
Down   112
Down, Wanton, Down!   338
Dragon-Fly, The   802
Dragons   325
Dream of a Climber   392
Dream of Frances Speedwell, A   692
Dream of Hell, A   591
Dream Recalled on Waking   694
Dream Warning (*Song*)   617
Dream, The, *see* What Did I Dream?
Dreaming Children   664
Drink and Fever   817
Druid Love   673
Dumplings' Address to Gourmets   279
Dying Knight and the Fauns, The   5
Dynamite Barbee   789

Eagre, The   584
Earlier Lovers   704
East Wind, An   542
Ecstasy of Chaos   583
Elsewhere   714
Encounter, The   457
Encounter, The   692
End of Play   382
End of the World   467
End, The   819
Endless Pavement   545
English Wood, An   137
Enlisted Man, The   480
Envoi   702
Envy   735
Epigrams   154
Epilogue, *see* I Am the Star of Morning
Epitaph on an Unfortunate Artist   139
Eremites, The   376
Esau and Judith   449
Escape   27
Essay on Continuity   197
Essay on Knowledge, *see* Vanity
Established Lovers   487

Eugenist, The 411
Eurydice 539
Everywhere Is Here 575
Exhaust-Pipe, The 738
Expect Nothing 532

Face in the Mirror, The 470
Face of the Heavens, The 6
Fact of the Act 612
Falcon Woman, The 499
Fallen Signpost, The 367
Fallen Tower of Siloam, The 383
False Report, A, *see* Angry Samson
Familiar Letter to Siegfried Sassoon [Letter to S.S. from Mametz
    Wood] 37
Far Side of Your Moon, The (*Song*) 575
Fast Bound Together 704
Faun 40
Feather Bed, The 163
Felloe'd Year, The 328
Fetter, The 570
Fever, A 779
Field-Postcard, The 717
Fiend, Dragon, Mermaid 352
Fiery Orchard 793
Fig Tree in Leaf (*Song*) 603
Fight to the Death, A 129
Figure-Head, The, *see* Death of the Farmer
Finding of Love, The 103
Fingerhold, The 821
Fingers in the Nesting Box 781
Finland 34
[Fir and Yew] 787
Fire Walker 533
First Funeral, The 15
First Love 649
First Poem, The 801
First Review, A 99
Five; *Quinque* 661
Five Rhymes 734
Flight Report 783
Florist Rose, The 357
Flowering Aloe, The 685
Flying Crooked 323

Food of the Dead   539
Foolish Senses, The   330
Fools   669
Foot-Holder-Royal   837
For Ever   610
For the Rain It Raineth Every Day   436
Forbidden Play, The, *see* After the Play
Forbidden Words   470
Forced Music, A   157
Foreboding, The   446
Foreword   809
Former Attachment, A [Quayside]   310
Fortunate Child   584
Four Children   753
Fox's Dingle   60
Fragment   499
[Fragment]   835
Fragment of a Lost Poem   353
Free Verse, *see* In Spite
Freehold   593
Friday Night   474
Friday Night   682
Frightened Men   395
Frog and the Golden Ball, The   567
From an Upper Window   816
From Otherwhere or Nowhere (*Song*)   710
From Our Ghostly Enemy   219
From the Embassy   460
Front Door, *see* Front Door Soliloquy
Front Door Soliloquy [Front Door]   306
Frosty Night, A   61
Full Moon   178
Furious Voyage, The [The Dead Ship; Ship Master]   288
Fusilier, The   806
Future, The   729

Galatea and Pygmalion   353
Garden, The   663
Gardener [The Awkward Gardener]   291
Gardens Close at Dusk (Song)   788
Gateway, The   669
General Bloodstock's Lament for England   443
General Eliott', 'The   128
Gentleman, The   671

George II and the Chinese Emperor, *see* Diplomatic Relations
Ghost and the Clock, The 434
Ghost from Arakan, A 826
Ghost Music 8
Ghost Raddled, *see* The Haunted House
Gift of Sight 563
Give Us Rain 73
Glorious Harshness of the Parrot's Voice, The 735
Glutton, The [The Beast] 387
Gnat, The 108
Goblet, The 351
God Called Poetry, The 69
Gold and Malachite 566
Gold Cloud 622
Golden Anchor 519
Goldsmiths, The 833
Goliath and David 23
Good Night to the Old Gods 578
Gooseflesh Abbey 606
Gorge, The 583
Gorgon Mask 661
Grace Notes 578
Grandfather's Complaint, The 775
Gratitude for a Nightmare 474
Great-Grandmother, The 384
Green Cabbage-Wit, *see* Cabbage Patch
Green Castle, The 546
Green Flash 836
Green Loving, *see* Variables of Green
Green Woods of Unrest, The 722
Green-Sailed Vessel, The 664
Grotesques, i, ii, iii, iv, v, vi 409
Growing Pains 682
Grudge, The 365
Guessing Black or White 299
Gulls and Men 417

H 658
Hag-Ridden 503
Half-Finished Letter, The 678
Halfpenny, The 366
Halls of Bedlam, The 372
Hate Not, Fear Not 97
Haunted 92

Haunted House, The [Ghost Raddled]   84
Hawk and Buckle   80
Hazel Grove, The   679
Hearth, The   548
Hearth, The   825
Heaven   681
Hector   300
Hedgepig, The   795
Hedges Freaked with Snow   529
Hell   287
Hemlock   176
Henry and Mary   136
Her Beauty   676
Her Brief Withdrawal   597
Hercules at Nemea   447
Here Live Your Life Out!   490
Here They Lie   93
Hero, The   456
Hero, The   599
Heroes in Their Prime   489
Hidden Garden, The   572
Hide and Seek   599
Hills of May, The   117
Hippopotamus's Address to the Freudians   770
Historical Particulars   822
History, A   752
History of Peace, A   139
History of the Fall   714
History of the Word   314
Homage to Texas   442
Home-Coming, The   606
Hooded Flame   597
Hoopoe Tells Us How, The [Dedicatory]   660
Horizon   519
Hotel Bed, *see* Hotel Bed at Lugano
Hotel Bed at Lugano [Hotel Bed]   355
House on Fire   827
Housing Project, The   768
How and Why, *see* Two Rhymes About Fate and Money
How Can I Care? (*Song*)   601
[How Is It a Man Dies?]   835
How It Started   640
Hung Wu Vase, The   553

I Am the Star of Morning [Epilogue]   173
I Hate the Moon   17
I Have a Little Cough, Sir   561
I Will Write   540
I Wonder What It Feels Like to be Drowned?   44
I'd Die for You [Postscript]   577
I'd Love to Be a Fairy's Child   46
I'm Through with You For Ever   457
Iago   626
Ibycus in Samos   520
Idle Hands   369
Idyll of Old Age, An   140
If and When   635
If Love Becomes a Game   791
If No Cuckoo Sings   718
Imminent Seventies, The   656
Impossible, The   570
Impossible Day, The   695
In Broken Images   296
In Committee   273
In Disguise   545
In Her Only Way   529
In Her Praise   524
In Jorrocks's Warehouse   778
In No Direction   295
In Perspective   588
In Procession   134
In Single Syllables [This Is Noon]   276
In Spite [Free Verse]   9
In the Beginning Was a Word   754
In the Lion House   825
In the Name of Virtue   619
In the Vestry   650
In the Wilderness   10
In Time   533
In Time of Absence   546
In Trance at a Distance   523
Incubus   116
Independent, An   755
Injuries   597
Inkidoo and the Queen of Babel   528
Instructions to the Orphic Adept   402
Intercession in Late October   425
Interlude: On Preserving a Poetical Formula   138

Interruption   315
Interview   469
Intruders, The   785
Intrusion, The   502
Invitation to Bristol   658
Iron Palace   571
Is It Peace?   780
Is Now the Time?   605
[Is there another man?]   797
It Was All Very Tidy   311
It's a Queer Time   19

Jackals' Address to Isis, The   430
Jane   87
Jealous Man, A   370
Joan and Darby   491
Jock o' Binnorie   495
John Skelton   43
John Truelove (*Song*)   830
Jolly Yellow Moon   7
Jonah   42
Joseph and Jesus   561
Joseph and Mary   542
Judgement of Paris   536
Judges, The   641
Juggler, The   771
Jugum Improbum   610
July 24th   513
June   414
Jus Primae Noctis   675
Just Friends (*Song*)   603

King's Highway, The   735
King's Son, The   724
Kingfisher's Return, The   227
Kiss, The   58
Kit Logan and Lady Helen   111
Knobs and Levers   672
Knowledge of God   200

La Mejicana   553
Lack   517
Lady Visitor in the Pauper Ward, The   26
Lament for Pasiphaë   404

Lament in December 732
Lamia In Love 553
Land of Whipperginny, The 127
Landscape, *see* Nature's Lineaments
Language of the Seasons 397
Largesse to the Poor 327
Last Day of Leave, The 414
Last Drop, The 804
Last Fistful, The 690
Last Poem, A 535
Last Post, The 27
Late Arrival, A 555
Late Daffodil for the Prince of Gwynedd, A 792
Laugh, The 501
Laureate, The 369
Leap, The 535
Learn That By Heart 791
Leave-Taking, *see* Superstition
Leaving the Rest Unsaid 386
Leda 356
Legion, The 30
Legs, The 331
Letter from Wales, A 232
Letter to a Friend, A 275
Letter to S.S. from Bryn-y-pin 810
Letter to S.S. from Mametz Wood, *see* Familiar Letter to
  Siegfried Sassoon
Leveller, The 96
Liadan and Curithir 451
Lift-Boy (*Song*) [Tail Piece: A Song to Make You and Me Laugh] 321
Like Owls 587
Like Snow 381
Lilac Frock, The 828
Limbo 14
Lion Lover 520
Lion-Gentle 595
Logic 648
Lollocks 393
Lord Chamberlain Tells of a Famous Meeting, The 142
Lost Acres 290
Lost Jewel, A 464
Lost Love 59
Lost World, A 506
Love and Black Magic 49

Love and Night   642
Love as Lovelessness   697
Love Charms   709
Love Gifts   638
Love in Barrenness [The Ridge-Top]   122
Love Letter, The   707
[Love makes poor sense in either speech or letters]   796
Love Story, A   387
Love Without Hope   227
Lover Since Childhood, A   121
Lovers in Winter   449
Loving Henry   74
Loving True, Flying Blind   585
Lunch-Hour Blues   354
Lure of Murder   582
Lust in Song, *see* The Bards
Lyceia   496

Machine Gun Fire: Cambrin   806
Magical Picture, The   104
Majorcan Letter, 1935   760
Man Does, Woman Is   536
Man of Evil   651
Manifestation in the Temple, The   158
Mankind and Ocean   639
Manticor in Arabia   77
Marginal Warning   456
Marigolds   48
Mark, The   450
Marmosite's Miscellany, The   252
Martyred Decadents, The: A Sympathetic Satire   153
Matador Gored   788
Max Beerbohm at Rapallo   774
Measure of Casualness, A   546
Meeting, The   516
Merlin and the Child   732
Mermaid, Dragon, Fiend [Old Wives' Tales]   129
Metaphor, The   541
Midsummer Duet   756
Midway   302
Mid-Winter Waking   398
Mike and Mandy [Caroline and Charles]   480
Miller's Man, The   513
Miracle, The   666

Mirror, Mirror! 60
Miser of Shenham Heath, The 725
Misgivings, on Reading a Popular 'Outline of Science' 750
Mist 589
Mock Beggar Hall: A Progression 201
Moment of Weakness, The 265
Moon Ends in Nightmare, The 768
Moon's Last Quarter, The 699
Moon's Tear, The 709
Moral Law, The 798
Morning Before the Battle, The 14
Morning Phoenix, *see Song:* A Phoenix Flame
Motes, The 634
Mother's Song in Winter 816
Motto to a Book of Emblems 156
Mountain Lovers 719
Mountain Side at Evening, The 723
Mr. Philosopher 33
Music at Night 342
My Ghost [The Co-Walker] 653
My Hazel-Twig 734
My Moral Forces 469
My Name and I 432
Myrrhina 179
Myrrhina 538

Naked and the Nude, The 475
Name 711
Name Day 516
Nape of the Neck, The 280
Narrow Sea, The 616
Nature's Lineaments [Landscape] 308
Near Eclipse, The 585
Nebuchadnezzar's Fall 72
Necklace, The 593
Neglectful Edward 84
Never Such Love 366
Never Yet 827
New Eternity, The 714
New Legends [The Age of Certainty] 316
New Moon Through Glass 789
New Portrait of Judith of Bethulia, A 152
New Year Kisses (*Song*) 621
Next Time, The 325

Next War, The   46
Night March   811
Nightfall at Twenty Thousand Feet   508
Nightmare   801
Nightmare of Senility   693
Nine o' Clock   89
No Letter   533
No More Ghosts   385
Nobody   340
Non Cogunt Astra   544
None the Wiser   615
Noose, The   798
North Side   829
North Window, The   181
Northward from Oxford   187
Not at Home   518
Not Dead   28
Not to Sleep   547
Note, The   794
Nothing   481
Nothing Now Astonishes   577
Nuns and Fish   426
Nursery Memories   16

O   551
O   807
O Jorrocks, I Have Promised   288
O Love in Me, *see* Sick Love
Oak, Poplar, Pine   320
Oath, The   396
Occasion, An   268
Of Course (*Song*)   604
Ogres and Pygmies   332
Oh, and Oh!   11
Old Lob-Lie-by-the-Fire   750
Old Wives' Tales, *see* Mermaid, Dragon, Fiend
Old World Dialogue   492
Oldest Soldier, The   408
Oleaster, The   543
Olive Tree (*Song*)   637
Olives of March   831
Olive-Yard, The   616
On Christopher Marlowe   154
On Dwelling   329

On Finding Myself a Soldier 12
On Giving 586
On Necessity 330
On Portents 336
On Rising Early 329
Once More (*Song*) 637
One Hard Look 67
One in Many (*Song*) 792
Or to Perish Before Day 373
Organ Grinder, The 739
Our Self 592
[Ours has no bearing on quotidian love] 796
Ours Is No Wedlock 703
Outlaws 78
Outsider, The 479
Ouzo Unclouded 527
Over the Brazier 20
Ovid in Defeat 222
Oxford English School, The 745

Pact, The 683
Palm Tree, The (*Song*) 595
Pandora 645
Pardon, The 580
Parent to Children 360
Patchwork Bonnet, The 110
Patience 502
Pavement, *see* Wm. Brazier
Peace 740
Pearl, The 535
Peeping Tom 727
Peisinoë 836
P'eng that was a K'un, The 587
Penny Fiddle, The 494
Penthesileia 461
Perfectionists 590
Persian Version, The 407
Person from Porlock, The 493
Personal Packaging, Inc. 608
Personal Touch, The 744
Philatelist-Royal, The 292
Philosopher, The [The Cell] 339
Philosophers, The, *see* The Dialecticians
Phoenix Flame, A (*Song*) [Morning Phoenix] 56

Picture Book, The   89
Picture Nail, The   492
Piebald's Tail, A   784
Pier-Glass, The   102
Pinch of Salt, A   24
Pity   679
Plea to Boys and Girls, A   478
Poem: A Reminder   630
Poet in the Nursery, The   3
Poet's Birth, The   149
Poet's Curse, The   696
Poetic Injustice   814
Poetic State, The   240
Poets, The *see* Any Honest Housewife
Poets' Corner   461
Point of No Return   580
Poised Pen, The   835
Poisoned Day   618
Poor Others   683
Portrait, The   437
Possessed   521
Possibly [The Question]   467
Postscript, *see* I'd Die for You
Pot and Kettle   83
Pot of White Heather, A   723
Powers Unconfessed   644
Prepared Statement, The   690
Presence, The   237
Pressure Gauge, The   837
Pride of Love   596
Pride of Progeny   700
Primrose Bed, The   658
Prison Walls   590
[Privacy]   788
Problems of Gender   674
Progress, The   287
Progressive Housing   356
Prohibition, The   665
Prologue, *see* The Witches' Cauldron
Prometheus   440
Promise, The (*Song*)   624
Promised Ballad, The   695
Promised Lullaby, The   91
Prosperity of Poets   824

Pudding, The 815
Pumpkin, The 774
Pure Death 282
Purification 643
Pygmalion to Galatea 272

Quayside, *see* A Former Attachment
Queen, A 790
Queen of Time, The (*Song*) 701
Queen Silver and King Gold 791
Queen-Mother to New Queen 440
Question, The, *see* Possibly
Questions in a Wood 436
Quiet Glades of Eden, The 488

Raft, The 652
Railway Carriage, *see* Welsh Incident
Rain of Brimstone 549
Rainbow and the Sceptic, The 214
Raising the Stone 108
Read Me, Please! 482
Reader Over My Shoulder, The 314
Reassurance to the Satyr 324
Recalling War 358
Recognition 515
Reconciliation (*Song*) 672
Records 685
Records for Wonder 748
Red Ribbon Dream, The 133
Red Shower, The 562
Reduced Sentence, A 670
Reiteration, The 651
Renascence, A 13
Repair Shop, *see* Vision in the Repair-Shop
Reproach 104
Reproach to Julia 453
Requirements for a Poem 830
Research and Development: Classified 655
Restless Ghost, A 525
Retrospect: The Jests of the Clock 92
Return 115
Return 808
Return Fare 310
Return of the Goddess 427

Reversal, A   153
Rhea   455
Rhyme of Friends, A   97
Richard Roe and John Doe   126
Ridge-Top, The, *see* Love in Barrenness
Ring and Chain, The (Song)   744
Risk, The   654
Robbers' Den   648
Robin and Marian   826
Robinson Crusoe   494
Rock at the Corner, The   398
Rock Below, The   139
Rocky Acres   71
Rondeau   726
Rose, The   666
Rose and the Lily, The   267
Ruby and Amethyst   512

Sacred Mission, The   459
Safe Receipt of a Censored Letter   514
Sail and Oar   606
Saint [The Beast]   317
St Antony of Padua   691
St Valentine's Day   560
Sand Glass, The   820
Sandhills, *see* Sea Side
Saul of Tarsus   113
Savage Story of Cardonette, The   808
Scared Child, The   697
School Hymn for St Trinian's   784
Sea Horse, The   452
Sea Side [Sandhills]   308
Secession of the Drone   441
Second-Fated, The   476
Secrecy   541
Secret Land, The   504
Secret Theatre   640
Seldom Yet Now   505
Self-Praise   377
Semi-Detached   625
Sentence, The   719
September Landscape   716
Septuagenarian, The   544
Sergeant-Major Money   232

Serpent's Tail   665
Seven Fresh Years (*Song*)   707
Seven Years [Where Is the Truth?]   696
Sewing Basket, The   145
Shadow of Death, The   13
Sharp Ridge, The   497
She Is No Liar   534
She Tells Her Love While Half Asleep   402
She to Him   614
Sheet of Paper, A   312
Shift of Scene, A   580
Ship Master, The, *see* The Furious Voyage
Shivering Beggar, The   41
Shot, The   392
Should I Care?   701
Sibyl, The   151
Sick Love [Between Dark and Dark; O Love in Me]   295
Sigil, The (*Song*)   636
Silent Visit   679
Simpleton, The   508
Sincèrement   605
Single Fare   311
Singleness in Love   708
Sirens' Welcome to Cronos, The   420
Sirocco at Deyá   460
Sit Mihi Terra Levis   610
Six Badgers, The   495
Six Blankets   794
Slice of Wedding Cake, A [Bitter Thoughts on Receiving a Slice
     of Cordelia's Wedding Cake]   477
Smile of Eve, The (Song)   787
Smoke-Rings   50
Smoky House, The   350
Snake and the Bull, The   131
Snap-Comb Wilderness   564
Snapped Rope, The   833
Snapped Thread, The [The Tangled Thread]   584
Solomon's Seal   645
Something to Say   654
Son Altesse   574
Song for New Year's Eve   471
Song for Two Children, A   62
Song in Winter   123
Song of Blodeuwedd, The   425

Song of Contrariety   122
Sorley's Weather   35
Sorrow   280
Sospan Fach   95
Spite of Mirrors   596
Spoils   465
Spoilsport, The   40
Spring 1974   720
Stable Door   782
Stake, The   101
Starred Coverlet, The   501
Star-Talk   4
Stepmother and the Princess, The   746
Stolen Jewel   583
Storm: At the Farm Window   113
Strangeness   598
Stranger at the Party, A   396
Stranger, The   350
Strangling in Merrion Square, The   659
Straw, The   445
Strayed Message, The   629
Strong Beer   47
Succubus, The   340
Suicide in the Copse, The   395
Sullen Moods (*Song*)   124
Sundial's Lament, The (*Song*)   629
Sun-Face and Moon-Face   593
Superman on the Riviera   492
Superstition [Leave-Taking]   618
Surgical Ward: Men   507
Survival of Love   316
Survivor, The   439
Survivor Comes Home, The   814
Sweet-Shop Round the Corner, The   579
Sword and Rose (*Song*)   545
Symptoms of Love   497
Synthetic Such   324

Tail Piece: A Song to Make You and Me Laugh, *see Song:* Lift-Boy
Taint, The   278
Tangled Thread, The, *see* The Snapped Thread
Tanka   827
Tap Room [Cracking the Nut Against the Hammer]   318
Technique of Perfection, The   150

Teiresias 785
Tenants, The 468
Terraced Valley, The 319
Testament 667
Tetragrammaton, The 426
That Other World 548
That Was the Night 700
Theme of Death, The 647
Then What? 822
Theseus and Ariadne 404
Thief [To the Galleys] 297
Thieves, The 388
This Holy Month 569
This Is Noon, *see* In Single Syllables
This Is the Season 800
This What-I-Mean 820
Those Blind from Birth 668
Those Who Came Short 568
Though Once True Lovers (*Song*) 601
Though Time Conceals Much (*Song*) 832
Three Drinkers, The 64
Three Locked Hoops 668
Three Pebbles, The 466
Three Rings for Her (*Song*) 604
Three Songs for the Lute 529
Three Times In Love 719
Three Words Only 705
Three Years Waiting 712
Three-Faced, The 538
Through a Dark Wood 650
Through Nightmare 400
Through the Periscope 805
Thunder at Night 86
Tilly Kettle 228
Tilth 689
Time 328
Time of Day, The 276
Time of Waiting, A 532
Timeless Meeting 701
Title of Poet, The 677
To a Caricaturist, Who Got Me Wrong 777
To a Charge of Didacticism 291
To a Pebble in My Shoe 468
To a Poet in Trouble 444

To a Rose (*Song*)   617

To an Editor   224

To an Ungentle Critic   29

To Any Saint   160

To Be Called a Bear [To Be Named a Bear]   416

To Be In Love   612

To Be Less Philosophical (*Song*)   293

To Be Named a Bear, *see* To Be Called a Bear

To Be Poets   662

To Become Each Other (*Song*)   681

To Beguile and Betray   540

To Bring the Dead to Life   363

To Calliope   445

To Challenge Delight   361

To Come of Age   716

To E.M. – A Ballad of Nursery Rhyme, *see* Wild Strawberries

To Evoke Posterity   363

To His Temperate Mistress   836

To Jean and John   816

To Juan at the Winter Solstice   405

To Lucasta on Going to the Wars – for the Fourth Time   30

To Lucia at Birth   401

To M. in India   251

To Magdalena Mulet, Margita Mora & Lucia Graves   773

To My Unborn Son   807

To Myrto About Herself   537

To Myrto of Myrtles   505

To Ogmian Hercules   613

To Poets Under Pisces   414

To Put It Simply   646

To R. Graves, Senior   155

To R.N. [To Robert Nichols]   32

To Robert Nichols, *see* To R.N.

To Sleep   389

To Tell and Be Told   646

To the Galleys, *see* Thief

To the Sovereign Muse   380

To the Teumessian Vixen   552

To Walk on Hills   361

To Whom Else?   333

Toads, The   751

Toast to Death, A   684

Tolling Bell   627

Tom Taylor   93

Tomorrow's Envy of Today 572
Touch My Shut Lips 698
Tousled Pillow 611
Tower of Love, The 706
Tow-Path, The, *see* Anagrammagic
Traditionalist, The 690
Traveller's Curse After Misdirection 228
Treasure Box, The 57
Trench Life 804
Trenches, The 15
Trial of Innocence 618
Troll's Nosegay, The 102
Troublesome Fame 626
Troughs of Sea 500
Trudge, Body! 342
True Evil 699
True Johnny 67
True Joy 571
True Magic 706
Truth Is Poor Physic 529
Turn of a Page, The 158
Turn of the Moon 503
Twelve Days of Christmas, The 405
Twice of the Same Fever 487
Twin of Sleep, The 483
Twin Souls 180
Twin to Twin 770
Twinned Heart (*Song*) 636
Twins 605
Two Brothers, The 739
Two Children [The Young Goddess] 490
Two Crucial Generations 715
Two Disciplines 711
Two Fusiliers 31
Two Moods 736
Two Rhymes About Fate and Money 509
Two Witches, The 509
Tyranny of Books, The 737

Ugly Secret, The 712
Ulysses 337
Uncalendared Love 516
Unco 800
Uncut Diamond, The 653

Undead, The   557
Under the Olives   498
Under the Pot   400
Undying Worm, The   831
Unicorn and the White Doe   123
Unless   834
Unnamed Spell, The   531
Unpenned Poem, The   721
Unposted Letter (1963)   686
[Untidy Man, The]   756
Until We Both   665
Utter Rim, The   588

Vain and Careless   88
Valentine, A   161
Vanity [Essay on Knowledge]   241
Variables of Green [Green Loving]   351
Vehicle, to Wit, A Bicycle', 'A   155
[Verse Composed over the Telephone]   787
Vestry   818
Victims of Calumny (*Song*)   638
Village Conflict, A, *see* A Village Feud
Village Feud, A [A Village Conflict]   154
Villagers and Death, The   399
Virgil the Sorcerer   270
Virgin Mirror   639
Virus, The   673
Vision in the Repair-Shop [Repair Shop]   307
Visit to Stratford, A   281
Visitation, The   498
Voice of Beauty Drowned, The   68
Vow, The   566

Wall, The   688
Wand, The   660
Wanderings of Christmas, *see* The Christmas Robin
Warning to Children   297
Wasp, The   733
Watch, The   515
Weather (Song)   793
Weather of Olympus, The   407
Wedding, The   573
Well-Dressed Children, The   85
'¡Wellcome, to the Caves of Artá!'   443

Welsh Incident [Railway Carriage] 303
Were-Man, The 493
What Can We Not Ask? 715
What Did I Dream? [The Dream] 137
What Did You Say? 582
What Is Love? 623
What Times Are These? 345
What We Did Next 620
What Will Be, Is 573
When a Necklace Breaks 790
When and Why 700
When He Sat Writing 795
When I'm Killed 37
When Love Is Not 650
Where Is the Truth? *see* Seven Years
Wherever We May Be (*Song*) 623
Whipperginny 119
White Goddess, The 428
Who Must It Be? 799
Whole Love 568
Why of the Weather, The 533
Wigs and Beards 607
Wild Cyclamen 562
Wild Strawberries [To E.M. – A Ballad of Nursery Rhyme] 86
Will o' the Wisp, The 724
Willaree 6
Window Pane, The 700
Window Sill, The 464
Winged Heart, The 522
Witches 188
Witches' Cauldron, The [Prologue] 162
With a Gift of Rings 662
With Her Lips Only 458
With No Return (*Song*) 556
With the Gift of a Lion's Claw 607
With the Gift of a Ring 450
Withering Herb, A 391
Within Reason 614
Without Pause 343
Wm. Brazier [Pavement] 309
Woman and Tree 476
Woman of Greece 551
Woman Poet and Man Poet 717
Women and Masks (translation) 688

Word, The   589
Work Drafts   675
Work Room   608
Worms of History, The   390
Wreath, The   523

X   359

Yes   479
Yesterday Only (*Song*)   624
Yet Unsayable, The   615
Young Cordwainer, The   431
Young Goddess, The, *see* Two Children
Young Sibyl, The   684
Young Witch, The   772
Your Private Way   432
Youth and Folly   7

INDEX OF FIRST LINES

A bitter year it was. What woman ever	523
A black wall from the east, toppling, arches the tall sky over	508
A bracelet invisible	594
A breeze fluttered the cape and you were caught	788
A charm for sound sleeping	713
A close deduction about close deduction	820
A cupid with a crooked face	830
A day which never could be yesterday	695
A difficult achievement for true lovers	501
A last poem, and a very last, and yet another	535
A Libyan pilgrim-ship tied up at Joppa	555
A lion in the path, a lion	617
A miser lived on Shenham Heath	725
A month of vigilance draws to its close	577
A page, a huntsman, and a priest of God	149
A perverse habit of cat-goddesses	454
A purple whale	42
A round moon suffocates the neighbouring stars	582
A Scottish fighting man whose wife	814
A shaft of moon from the cloud-hurried sky	108
A simple nosegay! was that much to ask?	102
A smoothly rolling distant sea	835
A sunbeam on the well-waxed oak	428
A towering wall divides your house from mine	688
A wild beast falling sick	529
About midnight my heart began	434
Above this bramble-overarched long lane	466
Accept these records of pure love	685
Across the room my silent love I throw	110
Across the strand of no seaside	768
After a week spent under raining skies	14
After close, unembittered meditation	534
After our death, when scholars try	671
After the hour of illumination, when the tottering mind	566
After three years of constant courtship	669
Against the far slow fields of white	345
Alas for obstinate doubt: the dread	525
Alas, England, my own generous mother	443
'Alice, dear, what ails you	61
Alienae civitates	788
All bodies have their yearnings for true evil	699
All ends as all must end	698

All saints revile her, and all sober men 428
All such proclivities are tabulated 488
All the wolves of the forest 496
Allie, call the birds in 73
Almost I could prefer 502
Almost I welcome the dirty subterfuges 545
Alone, alone and well alone at last 493
Alone, you are no more than many another 574
Although only a fool would mock 440
Ambergris from John Whale's moans 179
Ambition in the herb denied his root 391
An ancient rule prescribed for true knights 693
An ancient saga tells us how 32
Anagrammatising 306
And glad to find, on again looking at it 310
And have we done with War at last? 31
And if at last the anecdotal world 822
And if I suddenly die, will she have killed me 799
And if no cuckoo sings 718
And so they marked me dead, the day 809
And so to Ireland on an Easter Tuesday 310
And that inevitable accident 325
And the magic law long governing our lives 708
And though your hasty note be bare 794
And was he innocent as you protest 281
And what of home – how goes it, boys 94
And yet the incommunicable sea 833
Ann in chill moonlight unlocks 57
Ann ran away from home, where she had been 559
Ante mortem qui defletus 610
Any honest housewife could sort them out 364
Apricot petals on the dark pool fallen 827
Arabs complain – or so I have been told 436
Are they blind, the lords of Gaza 125
'Are you awake, Gemelli 4
Are you shaken, are you stirred 499
Are you shaken, are you stirred 58
Arguing over coffee at the station 552
As a scurrying snow-flake 663
As Court foot-holder to the Queen of Fishes 837
As I happened one day in a World Exhibition 252
As I lay quietly in the grass 753
As I stood by the stair-head in the upper hall 133
As I walked out that sultry night 178

As I was a-hoeing, a-hoeing my lands 495
As Jane walked out below the hill 87
As Jesus and his followers 64
As the committee musters 273
As the war lengthened, the mail shrank 514
As you are woman, so be lovely 272
Asleep on the raft and forced far out to sea 652
Asleep, amazed, with lolling head 116
'Astymelusa!' 611
At history's compulsion 356
At last we could keep quiet, each on his own 716
At seventy-two 600
At sunset, only to his true love 540
At the end of Tarriers' Lane, which was the street 309
At the tangled heart of a wood I fell asleep 606
At Viscount Nelson's lavish funeral 412

Back from the Line one night in June 53
Back from the Somme two Fusiliers 22
Back in '15, when life was harsh 717
Barabbas, once a publisher 782
Bat- 777
Bats at play taunt us with 'guess how many' 562
Be advised by me, darling 669
Be angry yourself, as well you may 533
Be assured, the Dragon is not dead 241
Be sure the crash was worse than ever 307
Bears gash the forest trees 416
Beasts of the field, fowls likewise of the air 608
'Beauty dwindles into shadow 148
Beauty in trouble flees to the good angel 463
Because of love's infallibility 667
Become invisible by elimination 300
Before God died, shot while running away 672
Beggars had starved at Dives' door 836
Being born of a dishonest mother 278
Believe me not a dolt: I would invent 318
Below the ridge a raven flew 122
Between insufferable monstrosities 302
Beware the giddy spell, ground fallen away 542
Beware, madam, of the witty devil 525
Beyond the Atlas roams a glutton 387
Black drinks the sun and draws all colours to it 565
Blacksmith Green had three strong sons 64

Blush as you stroke the curves – chin, lips and brow   539
Born from ignoble stock on a day of dearth   517
Boy: Most venerable and learned sir   50
Bravely from Fairyland he rode, on furlough   527
Breakfast peremptorily closes   678
Bullfight critics ranked in rows   787
But did not Adam, Eve's appointed playmate   714
But I *was* dead, an hour or more   27
But if that Cerberus, my mind, should be   588
But our escape: to what god did we owe it   645
But should I not pity that poor devil   651
'But that was nothing to what things came out   303
But what is love? Tell me, dear heart, I beg you   623
'But why so solemn when the bell tolled?'   627
By moonlight   434
By sloth on sorrow fathered   393
By this exchange of eyes, this encirclement   575
By way of Fishguard, all the lying devils   311
By your knees they rightly clasp you   551

Call down a blessing   637
Call it a good marriage   482
Camp-stool for chair once more and packing case for table   608
Can I find True-Love a gift   91
Capital letters prompting every line   630
Caria and Philistia considered   447
Caught by the lure of marriage   711
Challenged once more to reunite   636
Characteristic, nevertheless strange   629
Cherries of the night are riper   11
Children are dumb to say how hot the day is   283
Children born of fairy stock   46
Children, if you dare to think   297
Chill moonlight flooding from chill sky   471
Christ harrowed Hell in pity for all damned souls   579
Circling the circlings of their fish   426
Circling the Sun, at a respectful distance   674
City parks and gardens close   788
Clear knowledge having come   648
Close bound in a familiar bed   440
Cold wife and angry mistress   444
Come along, gents: I'll play you a tune   739
Come, ancient rival, royal weird   770
'Come as my doctor   658

Come close to me, dear Annie, while I tie a lover's knot   83
Come closer yet, my honeysuckle, my sweetheart Jinny   127
Come, human dogs, interfertilitate   411
Come, live in Now and occupy it well   544
Come, playmates, lift your girlish hands   784
Come, share this love again   832
'Come, surly fellow, come: a song!'   84
Comes a muttering from the earth   139
Concerned, against our wish, with a sick world   570
Confess, Marpessa, who is your new lover?   674
Confess, sweetheart, confess   797
Content in you   316
Courtesies of good-morning and good-evening   329
Courtship of beasts   785
Cronos the Ruddy, steer your boat   420
Crouched on wet shingle at the cove   641
Cry from the thicket my heart's bird!   68
Cunning and art he did not lack   418
Cunning indeed Tom Fool must be to-day   744

Daintily stepped the son of the king   724
Dame Jane the music mistress   114
Dark knoll, where distant furrows end   816
Darling, if ever on some night of fever   649
De minimis curat non Lex, utcumque poeta   610
Dear love, since the impossible proves   570
'Dear love, why should you weep   506
Death can have no alternative but Love   602
Death, eager always to pretend   152
Death is the twin of Sleep, they say   483
Death never troubled Damocles   441
Debating here one night we reckoned that   380
December's come and all is dead   732
'Decrees of God? Of One Prime Cause?   214
Deep in Nile mire   770
Desire, first, by a natural miracle   584
Despair and doubt in the blood   814
Despite this learned cult's official   408
Detective, criminal or corpse   359
Devilishly provoked   331
Didactic, I shall be didactic   291
Diffidently, when asked who might I be   644
Diotima's dead – how could she die?   824
Discourse, bruised heart, on trivial things   218

Do not mistake me: I was never a rival   552
'Do you delude yourself?' a neighbour asks   500
Do you know Beaumont Street in Oxford, city of ghosts and damps? 187
Do you still love, once having shared love's secret   686
Do you wear away time   751
Dolon, analyst of souls   155
Double red daisies, they're my flowers   45
Down in the mud I lay   54
Down, wanton, down! Have you no shame   338
Downstairs a clock had chimed, two o'clock only   112
Drowsing in my chair of disbelief   498
Dung-worms are necessary. And their certain need   330
Dust in a cloud, blinding weather   76
Dutifully I close this book....   694
Dying sun, shine warm a little longer!   404
Dynamite Barbee, no clo'es on   789

Each night for seven nights beyond the gulf   543
Each time it happened recklessly   709
'Eat your pudding Alexander.'   815
Eighth child of an eighth child, your wilful advent   772
Either we lodge diurnally here together   714
Enhanced in a tower, asleep, dreaming about him   663
Entrance and exit wounds are silvered clean   358
Entre deux belles femmes dans un seul lit   605
'Envy' I'm loth to call the blight   735
Equally innocent   638
Even in childhood   451
Even in hotel beds the hair tousles   355
Evening: beneath tall poplar trees   811
Every choice is always the wrong choice   568
Every gentleman knows   777
Every morning, every evening   621
Every woman of true royalty owns   504

Fairies of the leaves and rain   773
Fame is the tail of Pegasus   784
Far away is close at hand   122
'Farewell,' the Corporal cried, 'La Bassée trenches!   808
Fast bound together by the impossible   704
Fatedly alone with you once more   548
Father: Have you spent the money I gave you to-day?   65
Father is quite the greatest poet   26
Fear never dies, much as we laugh at fear   804

Fearless approach and puffed feather 405
Feet and faces tingle 34
Fetch your book here 510
Feverishly the eyes roll for what thorough 330
Fierce bodily control, constant routine 711
Fierce though your love of her may be 537
Finis, apparent on an earlier page 386
Fir, womb of silver pain 787
Fire and Deluge, rival pretenders 589
Firm-lipped, high-bosomed, slender Queen of Beanstalk Land 563
First came fine words softening our souls for magic 704
Five beringed fingers of Creation 661
Five summer days, five summer nights 454
Flowers remind of jewels 604
Folks, we have zero'd in to a big break-thru 608
For annoyance, not shame 396
For bringing it so far, thank you 305
For fear strangers might intrude upon us 584
For History's disagreeable sake 827
For me, the naked and the nude 475
Forewarned of madness 372
Forget the foolishness with which I vexed you 618
Forget the rest: my heart is true 535
'Forgive me, love, if I withdraw awhile 597
Four collier lads from Ebbw Vale 95
From a crowded barrow in a street-market 368
From the pit of Hell a whisper of pure love 833
From this heroic skull buried 351
From where do poems come? 716
Frowning over the riddle that Daniel told 72
Fugitive firs and larches for a moment 377

'Gabble-gabble, ... brethren, ... gabble-gabble!' 52
Galatea, whom his furious chisel 353
Gammon to Spinach 275
Gentle wild flowers, each with its own strange, twisting 793
Girl. What's that you're humming, gammer? 743
Give, ask for nothing, hope for nothing 532
'Give us Rain, Rain,' said the bean and the pea 73
Glandular change provokes a vague content 479
Glinting on the roadway 104
Gloomy and bare the organ-loft 8
Goddess of Midsummer, how late 505
Going confidently into the garden 502

Gone: and to an undisclosed region   519
Gone are the drab monosyllabic days   689
'Goodbye, but now forget all that we were   163
Good night, old gods, all this long year so faint   578
Goths, Vandals, Huns, Isaurian mountaineers   348
Grant Anup's children this   430
Grass-green and aspen-green   351
Green cabbage-wit, only by trying   302
Grey haunted eyes, absent-mindedly glaring   470
Grieve for the loveless, spiritless, faceless men   581
Grow angry, sweetheart, if you must, with me   712
Guessing black or white   299
Gulp down your wine, old friends of mine   92
Guns from the sea open against us   390

H may be N for those who speak   658
Hateful are studied harmonies   735
Have we now not spent three years waiting   712
Have you not read   394
He, a grave poet, fell in love with her   687
He broke school bounds, he dared defy   459
He coils so close about his double-bass   579
He fell in victory's fierce pursuit   128
He found a formula for drawing comic rabbits   139
He had done for her all that a man could   540
He had met hours of the clock he never guessed before   92
He has one bowstring, and from the quiver takes   826
He himself   821
He is quick, thinking in clear images   296
He noted from the hill top   350
'He numbed my heart, he stole away my truth   643
He, of his gentleness   10
'He suddenly,' the page read as it turned   158
He was not killed. The dream surprise   826
He woke to a smell of smoke   350
He won her Classic races, at the start   690
Heart, with what lonely fears you ached   356
Heather and holly   592
Henceforth old Lob shall sweat for no man's hire   750
Henry, Henry, do you love me?   74
Henry was a young king   136
Her beauty shall blind you   787
Her hand falls helpless: thought amazements fly   151
Her house loomed at the end of a Berkshire lane   518

Her inevitable complaint or accusation 625
Her young one dead, some mother of the grey 731
Here by a snow-bound river 32
Here down this very way 40
Here in this wavering body, now brisk, now dead 278
Here in turn succeed and rule 36
Here is a patchwork lately made 809
Here is Kit Logan with her love-child come 111
Here is ouzo (she said) to try you 527
Here it begins: the worm of love breeding 548
Here ranted Isaac's elder son 154
Here rest in peace the bones of Henry Reece 139
Here some sit restless asking the time of day 276
Here they lie who once learned here 93
Here's an end to my art! 13
Here's flowery taffeta for Mary's new gown 85
High on his figured couch beyond the waves 404
His appearances are incalculable 474
His ears discount the ragged noise 354
His eyes are quickened so with grief 59
His lucky halfpenny after years of solace 366
His name was Tilly Kettle 228
Historians may scorn the close engagement 572
Honest morning blesses the Sun's beauty 594
Hope, not Love, twangles her single string 683
How can I care whether you sigh for me 601
How closely these long years have bound us 709
How hard the year dies: no frost yet 425
How I saw her last, let me tell you. I heard screams 828
How is it a man dies 835
'How is it,' I was asked, 'to be a poet?' 240
How long is love, or how short is love 794
How many secret nooks in copse or glen 549
How may a lover draw two bows at once 685
How most unnatural-seeming, yet how proper 460
How often have I said before 585
However artfully you transformed yourself 537
Husks, rags and bones, waste-paper, excrement 287

I am a stag: *of seven tines* 419
'*I am oppressed, I am oppressed, I am oppressed*' 539
I am the Star of Morning poised between 173
I am working at a poem, pray excuse me 675
I, an ambassador of Otherwhere 460

I arose at dawn with this end in mind   733
I ask the young daughter   785
I awoke in profuse sweat, arms aching   503
I begged my love to wait a bit   556
I brought a Death of Nelson home, where I   492
I cannot pity you   468
I face impossible feats at your command   596
I fell in love at my first evening party   692
I had been God's own time on travel   327
I had long known the diverse tastes of the wood   563
I had once boasted my acquaintance   768
I hate the Moon, though it makes most people glad   17
'I have a little cough, sir   561
I have apples in a very pleasant orchard   802
I heard two poets   127
I held a poor opinion of myself   653
I knew an old man at a Fair   72
I left the heated mess-room, the drinkers and the cardplayers   806
I never dreamed we'd meet that day   37
I now delight   9
I remember, Ma'am, a frosty morning   462
I sat in my chamber yesternight   727
I shall wrap myself in a many-coloured cloak   789
I was a child and overwhelmed: Mozart   270
I was walking my garden   679
I'd die for you, or you for me   577
I've watched the Seasons passing slow, so slow   20
'I've whined of coming death, but now, no more!'   17
Iago learned from that old witch, his mother   626
If, as well may happen   482
If, doubtful of your fate   450
If ever against this easy blue and silver   315
If he asks, 'Is now the time?', it is not the time   605
'If I am Jesse's son,' said he   23
If I rise now and put my straw hat on   822
If I cried out in anger against music   401
If love becomes a game the sweet young fool   791
If one of thy two loves be wroth   450
If strange things happen where she is   336
If there's a poem in this book   791
If you keep your heart so true   556
If you want life, there's no life here   298
In a deep thought of you and concentration   319
In ancient days a glory swelled my thighs   378

In Chapel often when I bawl   7
In club and messroom let them sit   747
In fever the mind leaps three paces forward   817
In India you, cross-legged these long years waiting   251
In my heart a phoenix flame   56
In my childhood rumours ran   129
In Northern seas there roams a fish called K'un   587
In passage along an endless, eventless pavement   545
In sudden cloud that, blotting distance out   162
In the bad old days a bewigged country Squire   607
In the last sad watches of night   525
In the legend of Reynard the Fox   334
In the name of Virtue, girl   619
In time all undertakings are made good   533
Incalculably old   713
Injure yourself, you injure me   597
Ink, pen, a random sheet of writing paper   834
Interalienation of their hearts   590
Into a gentle wildness and confusion   308
Into exile with only a few shirts   371
Into your outstretched hands come pouring   511
Is red the ghost of green? and green, of red?   466
'Is that the Three-and-Twentieth, Strabo mine   30
Is there another man   797
Is this a sentence passed upon us both   719
'Is this,' she asked, 'what the lower orders call … ?'   492
It came at last, a letter of true love   707
It doesn't matter what's the cause   30
It is a poet's privilege and fate   438
It is easy, often, and natural even   523
It is hard to be a man   499
It is over now, with no more need   650
It is seven years now that we first loved   697
It started, unexpectedly of course   640
It was a hippocamp addressed her darling   473
It was always fiercer, brighter, gentler than could be told   615
It was John the Baptist, son to Zechariah   687
It was no costume jewellery I sent   662
It was not he who broke their compact   691
It was not the words, nor the melody   578
It wasn't our battalion, but we lay alongside it   232
It's hard to know if you're alive or dead   19
It's hardly wise to generalize   442
It's odd enough to be alive with others   323

J'étais confus à cet instant   605
James derided Walter   182
Janet. 'Where are those treasures that you promised me   744
Jewels here lie heaped for you   622
John Cole, Esquire   224
John. Why, James!   190
Johnny, sweetheart, can you be true   67
Judging the gift, his eye of greed   365
Julia: how Irishly you sacrifice   453
July the twenty-fourth, a day   513
June, the jolly season of most bloodshed   414
Just friend, you are my only friend   603
Just why should it invariably happen   659

Kill if you must, but never hate   97
King Alexander had been deified   237
King Duncan had a fool called Leery   495
King George who asked how was the dumpling packed   279
King George, still powder-grimed from Dettingen   174

Lady, lovely lady   88
Last night, my son, your pretty mother came   807
Laugh still, write always lovingly, for still   681
Lest men suspect your tale to be untrue   354
Let me put on record for posterity   676
Let me tell you the story of how I began   321
Let other women wrangle with their dooms   790
Let the weeks end as well they must   722
Let us at last be dull   265
Let us never name that royal certitude   531
Light was his first day of Creation   426
Lightning enclosed by a vast ring of mirrors   594
Like a lizard in the sun, though not scuttling   369
Lion-heart, you prowl alone   602
Listen now this time   97
Listen, you theologians   293
Little slender lad, toad-headed   530
Little winds in a hurry   6
Live sparks rain from the central anvil   562
Living among orchards, we are ruled   397
Living is delight   361
Long had our Kingfisher been   227
Long poems written by tall men   357
Look at my knees   44

Look forward, truant, to your second childhood 430
Looked tough, was tall and permanently bronzed 492
Looking by chance in at the open window 446
Lost manor where I walk continually 102
Louder than gulls the little children scream 399
'Love at first sight,' some say, misnaming 358
Love, Fear and Hate and Childish Toys 99
Love is a game for only two to play at 675
Love is a universal migraine 497
Love makes poor sense in either speech or letters 796
Love, never count your labour lost 124
Love, never disavow our vow 595
Love, the sole Goddess fit for swearing by 474
Love, there have necessarily been others 706
Love, this is not the way 590
Love, though I sorrow, I shall never grieve 597
Love, to be sure, endures for ever 835
Love, when you lost your keepsake 691
Love without hope, as when the young bird-catcher 227
Loveliest flowers, though crooked in their border 291
Lovers are happy 541
Lovers in the act dispense 388
Lovers in time of absence need not signal 546
Lying between your sheets, I challenge 501
Lying disembodied under the trees 576
Lying in long grass one hot afternoon 183

Magic is tangled in a woman's hair 564
'Make a song, father, make a new song 62
Man's life is threescore years and ten 656
Mandy: O, I'd like to be a Rug 480
Manifest reason glared at you and me 573
May they stumble, stage by stage 228
Mercury, god of larceny 649
Merlin went up the mountain side 732
Mine eye commends thee, Japanese elephant 730
Mirror, Mirror, tell me 60
More slowly the sun travels West 267
Mother: Edward will not taste his food 56
Mother: Oh, what a heavy sigh! 62
Mother: What's in that cupboard, Mary? 82
Muse, you have bitten through my fool's-finger 447
My bud was backward to unclose 12
My Chinese uncle, gouty, deaf, half-blinded 409

My earliest love, that stabbed and lacerated   682
My familiar ghost again   40
My friends are those who find agreement with me   491
'My front-lamp, constable? Why, man, the moon!   155
My grandfather, who blessed me as a child   692
My hazel-twig is frail and thin   734
My heart lies wrapped in red under your pillow   581
My heart would be faithless   781
My love for you, though true, wears the extravagance of centuries 620
My moral forces, always dissipated   469
My New Year's drink is mulled to-night   269
My parents were debtors   818
My stutter, my cough, my unfinished sentences   476
My wish, even my ambition   755

Nancy: 'Edward back from the Indian Sea   84
Naseboro' held him guilty   101
Near Clapham village, where fields began   41
Near Martinpuisch that night of hell   96
Need of this man was her ignoble secret   553
'Neighbour, neighbour, don't forget   509
Never again remind me of it   536
Never be disenchanted of   400
Never forget who brings the rain   503
Never sing the same song twice   435
Never was so profound a shadow thrown   586
Nine of the clock, oh!   89
No argument, no anger, no remorse   529
No Druid can control a woman's longing   673
No lover ever found a cure for love   503
No, not for me the lute or lyre!   801
No, of course we were never   604
No one can die twice of the same fever?   487
No one can understand our habit of love   666
No Pindar, I, but a poor gentleman   632
No, self-praise does not recommend   377
No smile so innocent or angelic   626
No vow once sworn may ever be annulled   566
Noah retrieves the dove again   554
Nobody, ancient mischief, nobody   340
None ever loved as Molly loved me then   659
None yet have been good jocund days   720
Nor can ambition make this garden theirs   572
Not of father nor of mother   425

Not to sleep all the night long, for pure joy 547
Not today, not tomorrow 624
NOTHING is circular 481
Now by a sudden shift of eye 616
Now Earth has drunk her fill of rain 734
Now even falls 723
Now I begin to know at last 69
Now like the cattle byre of Augeias 780
Now must all satisfaction 347
Nuns are allowed full liberty of conscience 606

O friend of Shenstone, do you frown 155
O Love, be fed with apples while you may 295
'O per se O, O per se O!' 551
O sixteen hundred and ninety-one 509
O the clear moment, when from the mouth 353
O think what joy that now 756
O what astonishment if you 596
O, why judge Myrrhina 538
Of Love he sang, full-hearted one 157
Of old this universe was born 736
Often, half-way to sleep 134
Oh, and oh! 11
Oh, now has faded from the West 7
Oh, some warlock's spell has bound me 801
Oh, what does the roseman answer 478
Old Becker crawling in the night 117
Old Mr. Philosopher 33
Olive-green, sky-blue, gravel-brown 716
Olives of March are large and blue, but few 831
On a clear day how thin the horizon 519
On Christmas Eve the brute Creation 130
On Friday night the wind came, fumbling at my window 731
On her shut lids the lightning flickers 455
On Janet come so late 471
On pay-day nights, neck-full with beer 93
On the brink of sleep, stretched in a wide bed 682
On the eighth day God died; his bearded mouth 390
On the High Feast Day in that reverent space 158
On the north side of every tree 829
On the other side of the world's narrow lane 612
On the rough mountain wind 6
Once there came a mighty, furious wind 748
Once two brothers, Joe and Will 739

One day in early Spring   603
One day when I am written off as dead   678
One hundred years ago, hard-riding Mr Jorrocks   778
One moonlit night a ship drove in   80
Only a madman could mistake   613
Our loves are cloaked, our times are variable   823
Our one foreboding was: we might forget   641
Ours has no bearing on quotidian love   796
Ours is no wedlock, nor could ever be   703
Out shines again the glorious round sun   585
Owls – they whinny down the night   78

Pale at first and cold   103
Palm-tree, single and apart   595
Pass now in metaphor beyond birds   585
Peace is at last confirmed for us   645
Peace, the wild valley streaked with torrents   445
Penthesileia, dead of profuse wounds   461
Perfect beneath an eight-rayed sun you lie   553
Perfect reliance on the impossible   646
Permit me here a simple brief aside   445
Pictures and books went off ahead this morning   468
Píndaro no soy, sino caballero   631
Poet. Last night I dreamed about a haunted house: it was hardly   201
Poets are guardians   677
Poised impossibly on the high tight-rope   526
Poor Fusilier aggrieved with fate   810
Possibly is not a monosyllable   467
Posturing one-legged on a slack wire   771
Prejudice, as the Latin shows   456
Presage and caveat not only seem   464
Privacy finds herself a nook   788
Pure melody, love without alteration   667
Pyrrha, jugo tandem vitulum junges-ne leoni?   610

Queen of Sharon in the valley   617
Queen of the Crabs, accept this claw   607
Queen Silver and King Gold for untold years   791
Quinque tibi luces vibrant in nomine: quinque   661
Quoth the King of Poland   837

R. That was a curious night, two years ago   741
Recklessly you offered me your all   660
Respect his obstinacy of undefeat   690

Restless and hot two children lay 86
Restore my truth, love, or have done for good 696
Richard Roe wished himself Solomon 126
Rising early and walking in the garden 329
Robbed of his birthright and his blessing 449
Robinson Crusoe cut his coats 494
Romantic love, though honourably human 769

Said hermit monk to hermit monk 150
Said Joseph unto Mary 561
Scratches in the dirt? 15
See a gleam in the gloaming – out yonder 724
Seldom yet now: the quality 505
Seth and the sons of Seth who followed him 106
Several instances in time occur 824
'Share and share alike 113
She appeared in Triad – Youth, Truth, Beauty 611
She hates an *if*, know that for sure 635
She is no liar, yet she will wash away 534
She let her golden ball fall down the well 567
She listened to his voice urgently pleading 582
She speaks always in her own voice 437
She tells her love while half asleep 402
She trod the grasses grey with dew 152
She, then, like snow in a dark night 381
She: Love, why have you led me here 431
She: You'll not forget these rocks and what I told you? 448
She's in the second row, see? No, not that one! 745
Shepherd. 'Little Lamb of the Spring, in your pale-hued mountainy
     meadow 729
Shepherds armed with staff and sling 656
'Should I care,' she asked, 'his heart being mine 701
Should I treat it as my own 703
Should I wander with no frown, these idle days 721
Should not the white lie and the unkept promise 580
Should the building totter, run for an archway! 383
Should unknown messengers appear 710
Siamese twins: one, maddened by 605
Sickness may seem a falling out of love 679
Silence, words into foolishness fading 550
Since depth of love is never gauged 678
Since first you drew my irresistible wave 668
Since I was with you last, at one with you 276
Since love is an astonished always 647

Since much at home on	629
Since no one knows the why of the weather	533
Since now I dare not ask	497
Since now in every public place	452
Since the night in which you stole	515
Sing baloo loo for Jenny	79
Sixty bound books, an entire bookcase full	469
Sleepy Betsy from her pillow	120
Slowly stroking your fingers where they lie	676
Slowly with bleeding nose and aching wrists	599
Small gnats that fly	67
Snake Bull, my namesake, man of wrath	131
Snow and fog unseasonable	452
So, as I say, the Dean of Saul Hall, shuffling	229
So daylight dies	699
So far from praising he blasphemes	200
So, overmasterful, to sea!	288
So soon as ever your mazed spirit descends	402
So too the Siren	836
Socrates on the seventh day	176
'Some forty years ago or maybe more,'	551
Some of you may know, others perhaps can guess	484
Something occurred after the operation	507
Soon after dawn in hottest June (it may	457
Souls in virginity joined together	639
Spring passes, summer's young	737
Sprung of no worthier parentage than sun	288
Stirring suddenly from long hibernation	398
Strawberries that in gardens grow	86
Studiously by lamp-light I appraised	536
Stumbling up an unfamiliar stairway	636
Such subtile filigranity and nobless of construccion	443
Such was the circumstance of our first love	680
Suddenly, at last, the bitter wind veers round	661
Suddenly the Eagre mounts upstream	584
Sulkily the sticks burn, and though they crackle	400
Sweetheart, I beg you to renew and seal	610
Swordsman of the narrow lips	426
T.C. 'Would you care to explain	654
Take now a country mood	60
Tangled in thought am I	121
Tears from our eyes	705
Tears of delight that on my name-day	516

Tell me truly, Valentine 560
Tell me, how do you see me? Ring the changes 834
Terse, Magyar, proud, all on its own 830
That aged woman with the bass voice 384
That ancient common-land of sleep 344
That chance what traveller would not bless 825
That he knows more of love than you, by far 671
That was the night you came to say goodnight 700
The act of love seemed a dead metaphor 541
The bards falter in shame, their running verse 337
The bearded rabbi, the meek friar 156
The Best of Both Worlds being Got 461
The blind are their own brothers; we 587
The blind man reading Dante upside-down 323
The Bower-bird improvised a cool retreat 588
The broken spray left hanging 123
The bugler sent a call of high romance 27
The butterfly, a cabbage-white 323
The cat is by the fire 816
The cat purrs out because it must 825
The century-plant has flowered, its golden blossom 685
The child alone a poet is 25
The child dreaming along a crowded street 579
The climate of thought has seldom been described 382
The clocks are ticking with good will 344
The clocks of time divide us 621
The clouds dripped poisonous dew to spite 618
The cottage damson, laden as could be 154
The Crane lounes loudly in his need 598
The crowd's heart is in the right place 827
The cruel Moon hangs out of reach 34
The curious heart plays with its fears 392
'The damned in their long drop from Earth to Hell 831
The death of love comes from reiteration 651
The demon who throughout our late estrangement 569
The dewdrop carries in its eye 161
The difference between you and her 603
The difficulty was, it was 754
The doubt and the passion 396
The enemy forces are in wild flight 365
The established lovers of an elder generation 487
The eunuch and the unicorn 658
The far side of your moon is black 575
The fire was already white ash 219

The fires are heated, watch Old Age   804
The first heaven is a flowery plain   546
The first name cut on a rock, a King's   516
The flame guttered, flared impossibly high   538
The full moon easterly rising, furious   387
The grammar of Love's Art   222
The great sun sinks behind the town   29
The hairs of my beard are red and black mingled   324
The happiest of exiles he, who shakes   774
The hermit on his pillar top   180
The hunter to the husbandman   161
The identity of opposites had linked us   683
The impartial Law enrolled a name   432
The impassioned child who stole the axe of power   405
The imperturbable miller's man   513
The King of Hearts a broadsword bears   545
The King's Highway is all too wide   735
The letter that you wrote me in your head   795
The mind's eye sees as the heart mirrors   389
The moment comes when my sound senses   532
The monstrous and three-headed cur   694
The moon is full   772
The Moon never makes use of the Sun's palette   552
The moral law, being male, need not apply   798
The naturalists of the Bass Rock   417
The nymph of the forest, only in whose honour   566
The oddest, surely, of odd tales   457
The old man in his fast car   153
The omens being less than sympathetic   794
The only Fiend, religious adversary   352
The parson to his pallid spouse   436
The patriarchal bed with four posts   385
The persons in the thought, like shapes, waver   300
The Philatelist-Royal   292
The pleasure of summer was its calm success   328
The posture of the tree   449
The Prepared Statement is a sure stand-by   690
The pupils of the eye expand   373
The quarrymen left ragged   398
The Rector's pallid neighbour at The Firs   399
The Romans had no word for YES   479
The Rose and the Lily   267
The round breasted hill above   736
The sand-glass stands in frame both ways the same   820

The selfish poet, falling sick 738
The seven years' curse is ended now 115
The shepherd Watkin heard an inner voice 108
The signpost of four arms is down 367
The silent shepherdess 82
The snows of February had buried Christmas 347
The stable door was open wide 754
The stones you have gathered, of diverse shapes 550
The storm is done, the sun shines out 672
The suicide, far from content 395
'The sum of all the parts of Such 324
The sun beams jovial from an ancient sky 349
The sun shines warm on seven old soldiers 408
The surnames from our parents had 830
The swing has its bold rhythm 684
The temple priests though using but one sign 320
The tops of the beech tree 422
The torn line wavers, breaks, and falls 806
The trees are tall, but the moon small 599
'The trenches are filled in, the houseless dead 268
The unco-guid and unco-ordinated 800
The ungainsayable, huge, cooing message 459
The unruly member (for relief 113
The vague sea thuds against the marble cliffs 328
The warring styles both claim him as their man 755
The whole field was so smelly 15
The women of Samos are lost in love for me 520
The Word is unspoken 589
The Word that in the beginning was the Word 314
The youngest poet down the shelves was fumbling 3
The youngest poet launched his boat 803
Then must I punish you with trustfulness 693
Then was blank expectation 312
There are some words carry a curse with them 470
There is a giving beyond giving 618
There is a travelling fury in his feet 287
There is a you, a you yourself, denies 280
There is no fool like an old fool 669
There is no now for us but always 702
There is one story and one story only 405
There was a man, a very untidy man 756
There was this road 331
'There's less and less cohesion 138
These acres, always again lost 290

These ancient dragons not committed yet   325
These are the good old days: appreciate them!   793
These churchyard witches in pursuit   188
These drones, seceding from the hive   441
These quiet months of watching for   637
These tears flooding my eyes, are they of pain   660
Theseus: was he an old, bald King of Athens   489
They have space enough, however cramped their quarters   664
They have taken Sun from Woman   648
They turned together with a shocked surprise   542
They were confused at first, being well warned   670
They would be none the wiser, even could they overhear   615
Thick and scented daisies spread   77
This ancient house so notable   374
This augurs well; both in their soft beds   695
This Blatant Beast was finally overcome   317
This fever doubtless comes in punishment   628
This foul February day   733
This honest wife, challenged at dusk   458
This is a question of identity   232
This is a wild land, country of my choice   71
This is, indeed, neither the time nor the place   684
This is my own clear voice   798
This is ours by natural, not by civil, right   653
This is the season   800
This prince's immortality was confirmed   456
This round hat I devote to Mars   268
This tall lithe Amazon armed herself   524
This they know well: the Goddess yet abides   524
This valley wood is pledged   137
This wax-mannequin nude, the florist rose   357
'This year she has changed greatly' – meaning you   564
This year we are all back again in time   760
Those blind from birth ignore the false perspective   668
Those famous men of old, the Ogres   332
Those who came short of love for me or you   568
Those who dare give nothing   586
Thou, a poor woman's fairing, white heather   723
Though cruel seas like mountains fill the bay   499
Though I am an old man   75
Though I may seem a fool with money, Lord   826
Though love be gained only by truth in love   638
Though love expels the ugly past   593
Though once true lovers   601

Though ready enough with beak and spurs 581
Though the moon beaming matronly and bland 401
Though there are always doctors who advise 654
Though time conceals much 832
Though you read these, but understand not, curse not! 156
Though your blind arrow, shot in time of need 543
Though your professions, ages and conditions 642
Three blank walls, a barred window with no view 339
Thrice fortunate is he who winneth 792
Through fogs and magic spells 746
Through long nursery nights he stood 50
Through the dreams of yesternight 5
Through the window 490
Thus will despair 340
To be adored by a proud Paladin 609
To be born famous, as your father's son 626
To be defrauded often of large sums 508
To be homeless is a pride 370
To be in so few hours translated from 783
To be lost for good to the gay self-esteem 686
To be loved by many and to love many 792
To be near her is to be near the furnace 533
To be possessed by her is to possess 521
To be the only woman alive in a vast hive of death 557
To be well loved 679
To bed, to bed: a storm is brewing 700
To beguile and betray, though pardonable in women 540
To bring the dead to life 363
To Cardonette, to Cardonette 808
To cards we have recourse 119
To die with a forlorn hope, but soon to be raised 439
To evoke posterity 363
To find a garden-tulip growing 381
To go in no direction 295
To have attained an endless, timeless meeting 701
To have it, sweetheart, is to know you have it 614
To know our destiny is to know the horror 565
To lie far off, in bed with a foul cough 580
To love one woman, or to sit 476
To love you truly 681
To make them move, you should start from lightning 542
To speak of the hollow nape where the close chaplet 280
To spring impetuously in air and remain 612
To the galleys, thief, and sweat your soul out 297

To the much-tossed Ulysses, never done   337
To the woods, to the woods is the wizard gone   49
To walk on hills is to employ legs   361
To whom else other than   333
To Winifred   145
To work it out even a thought better   647
To you who'd read my songs of War   27
To-day I killed a tiger near my shack   16
To-day, all day, for once he did nothing   369
To-day, the fight: my end is very soon   14
Together, trustfully, through a dark wood   650
Tom Noddy's body speaks, not so his mind   687
Too fierce the candlelight; your gentle voice   546
Touch my shut lips with your soft forefinger   698
Trapped in a dismal marsh, he told his troops   609
Tree powers, finger tips   421
Trench stinks of shallow-buried dead   805
Trudge, body, and climb, trudge and climb   342
Truth-loving Persians do not dwell upon   407
Trying to read the news, after your visit   522
Twined together and, as is customary   366
Two blind old men in a blind corridor   129
Two crucial generations parted them   715
Two full generations   707
Two generations bridge or part us   701
Two gods once visited a hermit couple   140
Two lovers sat together under a tree   790
Two quiet sportsmen, this an Englishman   242
Two women: one as good as bread   512

Under this loop of honeysuckle   34
Under your Milky Way   427
Unicorn with burning heart   123
Unkind fate sent the Porlock person   493
Unknown to each other in a hostile camp   142
Until the passing years establish   414
Until we both …   665
Up to the wedding, formal with heirloom lace   413
Urged by your needs and my desire   618

va Gardner brought mc á   829
Variegated flowers, nuts, cockle-shells   593
Violence threatens you no longer   526
Virgil, as the old Germans have related   270

Voices in gentle harmony 342
Von Masoch met the Count de Sade 692

Walking through trees to cool my heat and pain 28
Walking with a virgin heart 117
Walls, mounds, enclosing corrugations 303
Watch how my lank team-fellow strains 782
Watch how this climber raises his own ladder 392
Watch now for a green flash, for the last moment 836
We are like doves, well-paired 664
We are two lovers of no careless breed 662
We can do little for these living dead 673
We drave before a boisterous wind 728
We five looked out over the moor 414
We found the little captain at the head 18
We have reached the end of pastime, for always 382
We laugh, we frown, our fingers twitch 686
We looked, we loved, and therewith instantly 282
We love, and utterly 316
We may well wonder at those bearded hermits 376
We never would have loved had love not struck 498
We reckon Cooke our best chemist alive 655
We spurred our parents to the kiss 125
We still remain we 714
We stood together, side by side, rooted 571
We strain our strings thus tight 153
We twin cherubs above the Mercy Seat 593
We, two elementals, woman and man 516
We wandered diligently and widely 719
We were not ever of their feline race 395
Were I to cut my hand 507
Were you to break the vow we swore together 565
'What ails the Master, do I think? 221
'What can I do for you?' she asked gently 562
What can we not ask you? 715
What could be dafter 43
What demon lurked among those olive-trees 706
What did I dream? I do not know 137
'What do you think 47
What happens afterwards, none need enquire 576
What if Prince Paris, after taking thought 536
What is it I most want in all the world? 646
What is that colour on the sky 807
What, keep love in *perspective*? – that old lie 588

What life to lead and where to go   20
'What peace,' came Jehu's answering yell   780
What rules the weather for your lover   793
What shall we offer you, Jean and John?   816
What she refused him – in the name of love   697
What was wrong with the day, doubtless   767
What we did next, neither of us remembers....   620
What's all this hubbub and yelling   633
When a dream is born in you   24
When a live flower, a single name of names   677
When all is over and you march for home   465
When and why we two need never ask   700
When, at a sign, the Heavenly vault entire   467
When down I went to the rust-red quarry   573
When first we came together   592
When from your sleepy mind the day's burden   640
When her need for you dies   529
When I ceased to be a child   341
When I reached his place   311
When I was a callant, born far hence   528
When I was not quite five years old   89
When I was ten years old   775
When I'm killed, don't think of me   37
When in my first and loneliest love I saw   752
When *Libra, Solidus, Denarius*   704
When man forswears *God* and dispels *taboo*   750
When mountain rocks and leafy trees   308
When on the cliffs we met, by chance   515
When outside the icy rain   35
When she came suddenly in   400
When that glad day shall break to match   740
When that prime heroine of our nation, Alice   217
When the alcoholic passed the crucial point   580
When the chapel is lit and sonorous with ploughmen's praise   181
When the great ship ran madly towards the rocks   661
When the immense drugged universe explodes   583
When the rope snaps, when the long story's done   833
When Time, though granting scope enough   442
When was it that we swore to love for ever?   666
When we was wed my 'Erbert sed   727
When Will sat forging plays with busy friends   795
When, wounded by her anger at some trifle   535
When you are old as I now am   665
When you grow up, are no more children   360

Where are poems? Why do I now write none? 709
'Where is love when love is not?' 650
Where is the landlord of old Hawk and Buckle 80
Where is the truth to indulge my heart 696
Where poems, love also 799
Where the room may be, I do not know 779
Wherever we may be 623
Whether it was your way of walking 432
While deep in love with one another 700
While in this cavernous place employed 416
While you were promised to me 624
White flabbiness goes brown and lean 13
Who calls for women, drink and snuff 277
Who calls her two-faced? Faces, she has three 538
Who can pretend 819
Who grafted quince on Western may? 148
Who on your breast pillows his head now 464
Who'd drag the yet unopened lily-bud 802
Whoever has drowned and awhile entered 571
Why do you break upon this old, cool peace 26
Why have such scores of lovely, gifted girls 477
Why say 'death'? Death is neither harsh nor kind 237
'Why', they demand, 'with so much yet unknown 771
Will she ever need to fetch him home again 793
Window-gazing, at one time or another 490
With a fork drive Nature out 48
With a hatchet, a clasp-knife and a bag of nails 828
With pain pressing so close about your heart 453
With unvexed certainty 197
With women like Marie no holds are barred 553
With you for mast and sail and flag 616
Within each atom lurks a sun 830
Without cause and without 343
Woman poet and man poet 717
Woman sails, man must row 606
Woman with her forests, moons, flowers, waters 534
Women and masks: an old familiar story 688
Word comes of a pursuing robber-band 726

Yelled Corporal Punishment at Private Reasons 480
Yesterday I bought a penny fiddle 494
'Yet from the antique heights or deeps of what 306
Yet if they trust by lures or spells 549
Yonder beyond all hopes of access 583

You call the old nurse and the little page   321
You can scarcely grant me now   708
You celebrate with kisses the good fortune   639
You chose a lion to be your lover   520
You could not hope to love me more   836
You have lived long but over-lonely   720
You have now fallen three times in love   719
You have wandered widely through your own mind   614
You learned Lear's *Nonsense Rhymes* by heart, not rote   478
You like to joke about young love   634
You, love, and I   429
You love me strangely, and in strangeness   598
You may not believe it, for hardly could I   774
You neigh and flaunt your coat of sorrel-red   476
You, reading over my shoulder, peering beneath   314
You reject the rainbow   591
You struck me on the face and I, who strike   569
You turn the unsmitten other cheek   160
You weep whole-heartedly – your shining tears   583
You were a child and I your veteran   643
You were as venturesome as I was shy   490
You were by my side, though I could not see you   665
You young friskies who to-day   46
Young wives enjoy the statutory right   776
Your gold cloud, towering far above me   622
Your grieving moonlight face looks down   104
Your Labours are performed, your Bye-works too   613
Your sceptre awes me, Aphrodite   506
Your sudden laugh restored felicity   501
Yourself, myself and our togetherness   668
Youth is the ruggedest burden that can score   544

Zeus was once overheard to shout at Hera   407